A First Course in Computer Science
with Turbo Pascal
(Versions 4.0, 5.0, and 5.5)

PRINCIPLES OF COMPUTER SCIENCE SERIES

Series Editors
Alfred V. Aho, Bell Telephone Laboratories, Murray Hill, New Jersey
Jeffrey D. Ullman, Stanford University, Stanford, California

A First Course in Computer Science with Turbo Pascal

(Versions 4.0, 5.0, and 5.5)

LOWELL A. CARMONY
ROBERT L. HOLLIDAY
Lake Forest College

COMPUTER SCIENCE PRESS
An imprint of W. H. Freeman and Company • New York

Library of Congress Cataloging-in-Publication Data

Carmony, Lowell A., 1943–
    A first course in computer science with Turbo Pascal: versions
    4.0, 5.0, and 5.5 / Lowell A. Carmony, Robert L. Holliday.
        p.   cm.—(Principles of computer science series)
        ISBN 0-7167-8216-2
        1. Pascal (Computer program language)   2. Turbo Pascal (Computer
    program)   3. Computer science.   I. Holliday, Robert.   II. Title.
    III. Series.
    QA76.73.P2C365   1991   90-30084
    005.2′42—dc20   CIP

Printed in the United States of America

Computer Science Press

An imprint of W. H. Freeman and Company
41 Madison Avenue, New York, NY 10010
20 Beaumont Street, Oxford OX1 2NQ, England

1 2 3 4 5 6 7 8 9 0   RRD 9 9 8 7 6 5 4 3 2 1 0

Where the mind is without fear
   and the head is held high,
      Where knowledge is free;
   Where the world has not been broken
up into fragments by narrow domestic
         walls;
   Where words come out from the
         depth of truth;
   Where tireless striving
      stretches its arms towards
         perfection;
   Where the clear stream of reason
      has not lost its way into the
dreary desert sand of dead habit;
   Where the mind is led forward
by thee into ever-widening
         thought and action—
into that heaven of freedom,
      my Father,
         let my country awake.

Rabindranath Tagore

CONTENTS

PREFACE

TO THE READER

Pascal is a landmark language that provides users with an elegant vehicle for studying important concepts of computer science. Turbo Pascal is a landmark Pascal compiler that provides unparalleled user-friendliness and pedagogical features. We are excited and delighted to present the reader with this introduction to computer science with Turbo Pascal.

This book is designed as a text for readers new to Pascal as well as a reference for readers who already know some Pascal. The book begins at an elementary level and contains all the information the novice needs to get started. New constructs are carefully developed with many examples. The reader who works through the material presented here and writes the programs suggested in the exercises will have gained a thorough understanding of Pascal and problem solving.

This text contains a careful explanation of the Turbo Pascal environment (versions 4.0, 5.0, and 5.5) as well as of standard Pascal. Learning Pascal while learning to guide a program through the computer can be frustrating, particularly if you must flip back and forth between a Pascal text and various computer manuals. In this book, we guide the beginner step by step through the language and the operating system.

Turbo Pascal is an extension of standard Pascal. We have made every effort to indicate which features belong to standard Pascal and which are extensions, so that the reader can transfer the knowledge obtained here to other Pascal systems. The main nonstandard feature that we have included is the string type. We have done this because strings are such a useful problem-solving tool and problem solving—not standard Pascal syntax—is our real objective. We introduce strings early (Chapter 3) and use them throughout the book, because the beginner is not ready for the subtleties of arrays of characters, especially if he or she has never heard of arrays! We do, however, eventually tell the truth about strings (Chapter 14) and show the reader how to define a string as a record.

We include Turbo Pascal's built-in random-number generator early (Chapter 5) because it provides the opportunity for interesting examples and exercises. We also include a discussion of random-access files (Chapter 15) because they are so useful and so simple in Turbo Pascal. Separate compilation is included, but in an optional separate chapter (Chapter 20). Chapter 7 introduces the Turbo Pascal integrated debugger (available in versions 5.0 and 5.5). In general, special Turbo Pascal features such as clearing the screen and range checking are introduced as needed, but this text is certainly *not* a Turbo Pascal manual. For example, because it is not germane to the topics of a first course in computer science, there is no discussion of Turbo Pascal's graphics routines. Thus, although this text is meant to be used with Turbo Pascal on an IBM PC or compatible, it strives to present a balanced approach to Pascal and problem solving with a computer, so that the successful reader will have no trouble in moving to another machine (or language).

This text teaches **structured programming** through an extensive number of **problem-solving examples** that are worked out in the text. Algorithms are designed and expressed in pseudo-code before any Pascal code is developed. Functions and procedures are introduced (Chapter 6) as soon as meaningful bodies can be written for them; they are then used throughout the remainder of the text. Since problem solving and sound programming skills are only learned by actually solving problems and writing programs, we urge the reader to write programs for as many of the exercises as possible. Fortunately, the computer checks programs carefully and gives the reader feedback about the programs presented to it. For our part, we have tried to provide interesting and challenging exercises that we hope you will enjoy as have our many students over the years.

This text is reader-directed. Each chapter concludes with a list of keywords that the reader can use to check understanding. There are numerous problem-solving examples throughout the text that illustrate the problem-solving approach. Study these well. In addition, the text contains our favorite examples and exercises; we hope you find these interesting and, occasionally, humorous. May your journey through Pascal be as exciting as ours was.

Sample Disk of Programs

As a convenience for the reader, a disk is available to accompany this book. (Information on ordering this disk is provided following the index.) The disk contains all the sample programs from the book so that you can run or modify them. The disk also contains text files for the exercises as well as intentionally buggy programs. We have saved some of our students' best errors and provide them for you to hone your debugging skills. There is much to be learned in the debugging of programs. Indeed, you can't call yourself a programmer until you can debug your own programs.

REMARKS TO THE INSTRUCTOR

Organization of this Book

The first four chapters provide an elementary introduction to the science of computing. Chapter 1 provides a brief history of computers and serves to introduce some of the terminology common to the field.

Chapter 2 introduces the Turbo Pascal system and gives the reader enough information to create, edit, save, run, load, and print a Turbo Pascal program.

Chapter 3 begins the development of Pascal by introducing the integer, real, character, and string types. The write and assignment statements are introduced and the first simple programs are written. Programs with just these constructs are necessarily trivial, but we believe that the Sonny Tan example provides an excellent early introduction to problem solving. We stress program clarity through such techniques as meaningful identifiers and judicious use of comments.

Chapter 4 completes the elementary material by introducing the read statements. Both interactive input and reading from a text file are explained. When the amount of data is very small, the flexibility of interactive input provides an excellent data-entry modality. Text files are introduced for those situations when the amount of data is large, or when the instructor wants the students to use common data. There are many text files on the disk that accompanies this book. Some of these are used in the sample programs and many are used in the exercises.

Chapters 5 to 14 provide the core of the course and, with small exceptions, should be covered in order. Chapter 5 introduces the Boolean type and then the While and the If as the fundamental control structures. Suddenly, interesting programs can be written and challenging exercises can be assigned. Chapter 5 alone has 23 exercises, and we urge the reader to attempt as many of them as possible. Assertions and loop invariants are becoming a popular and valuable method of commenting. These topics are introduced and discussed in Chapter 5, but in a first course we prefer an informal style of commenting rather than a strictly formal style of assertions.

Chapter 6 introduces the critically important topic of procedures and functions. The use of variable and value parameters is discussed extensively and illustrated in correct and intentionally incorrect examples. The advantages of informal preconditions and postconditions for procedures and functions are explained. Informal preconditions and postconditions are used with procedures and functions throughout the remainder of the book. The dangers arising from the use of global variables in procedures and functions are also discussed. The chapter concludes with one of our favorite examples, the game of Bagels. Bagels, a listing of approximately 5 pages, provides an excellent example of the divide-and-conquer strategy with procedures and functions. Because of the importance of this chapter, 27 graded exercises are provided.

Chapter 7 discusses program design, implementation, and debugging. It describes an eight-step process outlining the typical development of a software project. We emphasize understanding the problem and developing an algorithm in pseudo-code before writing any Pascal code. As a problem-solving example, a simulation is developed for the most famous duel in American history, that between Alexander Hamilton and Aaron Burr. Chapter 7 also discusses the art of debugging, both with and without the Turbo Pascal integrated debugger. Chapter 7 also includes more detail on the Turbo Pascal environment, including such topics as blocking, searching, and replacing. Again, this text is not a Turbo Pascal manual, but it does strive to include information on the most useful features of the Turbo Pascal system.

Chapter 8 completes the discussion of basic control structures by introducing the Repeat/Until, the For, and the Case statements. These statements were not included in Chapter 5 to keep the discussion of the If and While as simple and short as possible. The instructor who prefers to cover all the control structures at once can proceed to Chapter 8 immediately after Chapter 5. Only the final problem-solving example of the chapter, concerning the simulation of a lottery, involves procedures and functions.

Chapter 9 covers Pascal's scope rules in considerably more detail than traditionally done at this level. We believe this study, illustrated with a large number of diagrams, is significant because the student who masters Pascal's scope rules understands local and global variables as well as value and variable parameters. These are difficult but critical concepts for the beginning computer science student.

Chapter 10 introduces user-defined types and also discusses the character type in more detail. Subranges are also introduced in this chapter. Because range checking is not performed automatically in Turbo Pascal, the compiler directive {$R+} is introduced and its importance is discussed. Every subsequent sample program of the text includes this directive.

Chapter 11 introduces one-dimensional arrays. The need for arrays is discussed and basic array operations are illustrated through a multitude of examples. As an illustration of problem solving with arrays, the chapter includes one of our favorite problem-solving examples: Soggies, the breakfast of programmers.

Chapter 12 discusses searching and sorting. Both the linear and binary searches are introduced. Bubble, modified bubble, and insertion sort are developed in the text and selection sort is left as an exercise. Two major programs, Searches and Sorts, allow readers to run the various algorithms against one another and time their executions (roughly) with various size arrays. This permits readers to discover graphically the nature of each of the algorithms. For example, readers can see the $O(N^2)$ nature of each of the sorts and, with random data, how much, if any, the modified bubble outperforms bubble. In Chapter 18, quick sort is introduced and the program Sorts can be modified to illustrate the power of this $O(NLogN)$ sort over any of the elementary sorts of Chapter 12.

Chapter 13 discusses multidimensional arrays. The emphasis is on two dimensions, since readers who can handle two dimensions well can handle 17 dimensions with ease. The problem-solving example is Conway's game of Life. This presents readers with an interesting, but moderately complex, situation in which to manipulate a two-dimensional array.

Chapter 14 introduces records and discusses the differences and similarities between records and arrays. An array of records (of records) is used to develop an example of a database on students. Finally strings—introduced in Chapter 3—are defined as records with an array and a length attribute. Several procedures and functions are discussed so that the development of a full string package can be undertaken if desired.

Chapters 15 to 20 are the advanced chapters of the text and the instructor can choose to cover them in any order.

Chapter 15 introduces files, both sequential and random-access. Random-access files are not included in standard Pascal, but they are included here because of their importance and because in Turbo Pascal random-access files are very easy to use.

Chapter 16 introduces sets, a topic often neglected in Pascal. Time permitting, we urge the instructor to reconsider the introduction of sets in a first course. Readers find them easy and, as a data structure, they simplify many situations. As problem-solving examples, we solve the Soggies problem from Chapter 11 again and we introduce our all-time favorite example: the game of Taxman. If you aren't convinced of the utility of sets in Pascal, we suggest you write Taxman without them!

Chapter 17 discusses string manipulation using the Turbo Pascal built-in procedures and functions. As such, the chapter is nonstandard, but it is elementary, useful, and fun.

Chapter 18 introduces the important concept of recursion. This introductory chapter is provided for the instructor that wants to introduce this topic in a first course, knowing that much more will be made of it in the second course. Quick sort is introduced and by adding quick sort to our Sorts program of Chapter 12 (an elementary exercise) readers can graphically see the difference between an NLogN sort and the N^2 sorts of Chapter 12.

Chapter 19 introduces pointers and linked lists. Again, this material is provided as an introduction to material to come in the second course, No attempt is made at a complete discussion of linked lists.

Chapter 20 introduces the important, but nonstandard topic of separate compilation. This powerful, but simple tool, allows readers to begin building their own library of routines which are then as easy to use as the routines in Turbo Pascal's libraries.

Supplements

An instructor's manual and a solutions disk are available, upon adoption, from the publisher. The instructor's manual contains brief suggestions for each chapter, solutions to all the exercises, and suggested examination questions. The solutions disk contains Turbo Pascal programs for all programming exercises in the text.

ACKNOWLEDGMENTS

We wish to thank the many students who have assisted us with the development of this book, especially Ben Bramwell, Brian Brown, Adam Campbell, Lynette Cook, Julie DeMuyt, Valerie Duncan, Jennifer Evans, Anthony Fagan, Qiang Feng, Erica Frohm, Don Gassmere, Thomas Graff, Kina Gray, Craig Hallier, Andrew Hill, Bob Hlavacek, Bill Howell, Brent Hudson, Shelly Keller, Joeal Lach, Diana Lee, Eileen Mallon, Joanna Mason, Patty Moran, Jill Morrison, Viren Murthy, Amy Olson, Jason Peterson, Sander Read, Glenn Rickard, Elizabeth Stanley, and Rob Wrather. Our special thanks go to David Haines and Rachel Hertel who provided many helpful suggestions and also assisted on the solutions manual.

Lowell A. Carmony
Robert L. Holliday
May 11, 1990
Lake Forest, Illinois

A First Course in Computer Science with Turbo Pascal

(Versions 4.0, 5.0, and 5.5)

1

COMPUTERS AND STRUCTURED PROGRAMMING

The invention of the computer has caused a revolution in today's society. One need not look very far to find seminars on computer literacy, special sections in nearly every bookstore of computer-related magazines and books, and segments on television news shows about the latest developments in computer technology. The amount of attention given to computers is unlike the attention focused on any other human invention. Microwave ovens, washers and dryers, and video recorders have also revolutionized modern life, but we seldom see a videocassette-recorder section in a bookstore or a washer-and-dryer literacy course.

The revolution brought about by the computer is best called an information-processing revolution. The magnitude of this revolution can be appreciated when it is likened in importance to such events as the discovery of fire, the invention of the wheel, the invention of the printing press, or the industrial revolution. Only the future will tell whether such comparisons are justified, but there is little doubt that computers will continue to have a major impact on the quality and style of life we experience. Whether these impacts are positive or negative is an important question, but is not one for us to address directly here. Instead, we will be concerned with learning enough about the computer that we can make it do what we want.

Why has the computer become the focus of such widespread media attention? There are several reasons. For a long time, science fiction authors have endowed computers with all-powerful, humanlike qualities. Although there are no thinking, reasoning HAL computers as in the film, *2001—A Space Odyssey,* many people think of computers in this way. On a more practical level, computers have proved their worth in many diverse areas: information storage and retrieval, scientific research, education, medicine, and recreation, to name just a few. It is this general-purpose nature that we believe contributes most to the appeal of computers. That is the reason this book is about programming—so that we can learn to take advantage of the general-purpose capabilities of the computer.

We mention one last reason that computers have become so prevalent—affordability. Unlike nearly every other phenomenon, as computer technology has increased, the cost of this technology has decreased. The amount of computing power that is found on many executives' desks today is thousands of times less expensive and hundreds of times more powerful than that of the computers of just 30 years ago. It has been said that if the automobile industry worked like the computer industry, everyone would be driving a Rolls Royce that costs $3.95, never needs any maintenance, and gets 250 miles to the gallon.

A HISTORICAL SKETCH OF COMPUTING

We think it is important that the reader see the development of the computer in its historical perspective. Moreover, this historical sketch will also provide a good opportunity to introduce some computer terminology. One does not have to read very many advertisements to get the impression that the computer field is loaded with buzzwords and technical jargon. This can be very discouraging to the beginner. We emphasize that one need not be technically inclined to deal with computers, just as one need not be mechanically inclined to drive an automobile. However, because of the widespread use of buzzwords, it becomes necessary to include some of them in any discussion of computers.

Humans have been computing for thousands of years. The earliest form of computing was simple counting—for example, a shepherd counting sheep to make sure all of them returned from grazing. Humans have used tools to assist with computing for thousands of years. The early shepherd likely used pebbles to help count sheep. A very common counting device that is as much as 4000 years old is the abacus. This device consists of beads and rods and was used by Chinese merchants to handle business transactions. It is still used by millions of people throughout Asia today to perform routine numerical calculations.

In the mid-1600s, a French philosopher and mathematician named **Blaise Pascal** developed a mechanical adding and subtracting machine, the Pascaline. Pascal's father worked for the French equivalent of the Internal Revenue Service and was continually adding long columns of numbers by hand. The young Pascal believed that this was the sort of work appropriate for a machine, so he constructed one using gear-driven counter wheels. The Pascaline is shown in Figure 1.1. Of course, the Pascaline did not run on batteries or solar power, but was powered by turning a crank. Although other such machines had been tried previously, Pascal's was one of the first such machines to be reliable. Because of this contribution to computing, the programming language that we will study in this book is named after Blaise Pascal.

Before we turn to other, more general computers, we mention two other names associated with calculating machines. In 1671, **Gottfried Leibniz** invented the first calculator that could multiply and divide as well as add and subtract. His machine also worked on a gear-driven principle and, in fact, this principle was used in nearly all mechanical calculators up through the 1950s. Of course, calculators are now electronic, but the staying power of Leibniz's idea is a feat seldom repeated today. In 1884, **William Burroughs** developed the first commercially successful adding machine. Today, the Burroughs name remains at the front of the computer industry.

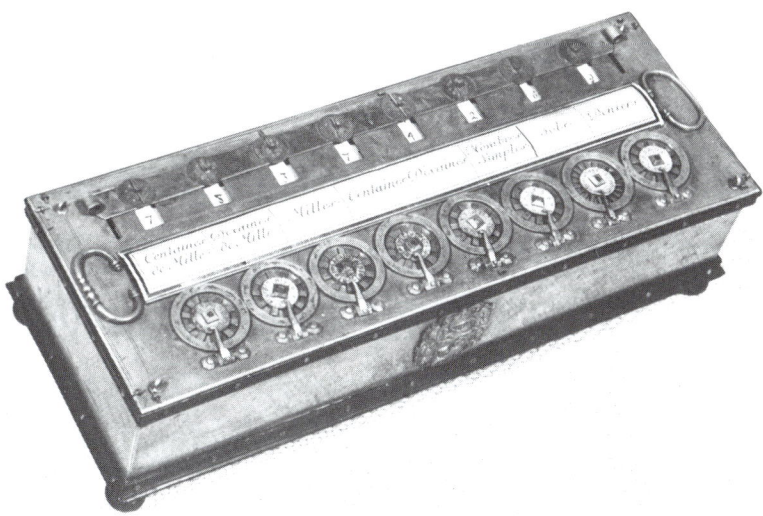

Figure 1.1 (**Courtesy of International Business Machines Corporation**)

The advent of more general computers—i.e. tools that can do more than just numerical calculations—is often traced to an unexpected place: the looms of France and **Emil Jacquard**. As Jacquard watched the weavers constantly resetting the looms for the various patterns, he came upon the idea of using punched cards to record the loom settings and, in 1801, designed a loom that could read these punched-card instructions. Note the punched cards controlling the loom in Figure 1.2.

Figure 1.2

Figure 1.3 (Courtesy of International Business Machines Corporation)

In the late 1800s, **Herman Hollerith** used Jacquard's idea to develop a punched-card system to handle the 1890 United States census. Hollerith's machine is shown in Figure 1.3. It is interesting to note that Hollerith's company was eventually bought out by a firm known as International Business Machines Corporation (IBM). While the 1880 census took nearly 10 years to count by hand, Hollerith counted the 62.5 million people residing in the U.S. in 1890 in just over a year. The punched card was also the way early programmers communicated their instructions to computers and, in fact, was widely used, particularly in learning environments, through the mid-1970s.

While the Jacquard/Hollerith punched-card idea is familiar to many people, a more fundamental, but less well-known, development occurred in the 1830s. In 1833, Englishman **Charles Babbage** conceived the first general-purpose computer; that is, a computer that could do more than just numerical calculations. Babbage's computer had the capability of accepting different sets of instructions to carry out different tasks. Babbage was truly a man ahead of his time. Because there were no transistorized circuits in his day, Babbage's computer, called the Analytical Engine, would have been driven by steam and been the size of a football field. Unfortunately, the technology of the 1830s was not advanced enough for Babbage to build a working model of his Analytical Engine. Babbage did build some calculating machines, called Difference Engines, but because of the steam technology, they turned out to be too slow and unreliable. These setbacks caused years of struggling to receive funding from the British government for his Analytical Engine project, and he eventually gave up his work and died a bitter man. Interestingly enough, when some of the 1950s pioneers of the first electronic computers became aware of Babbage's work, they were amazed at the similarity of Babbage's design of the Analytical Engine and the actual design of the early computers. Many people feel today that if anyone deserves the title Father of the Computer, it is indeed Charles Babbage.

In 1842, **Ada Augusta**, the Countess of Lovelace and the daughter of the poet, Lord Byron, read, carefully analyzed, and refined Babbage's theoretical work. Not only was she convinced that Babbage's ideas were sound, she actually wrote sets of instructions that the Analytical Engine could conceivably carry out. Thus, Ada Augusta was the first computer programmer, and it is in her honor that the latest Department of Defense language is named. This language, Ada, is considered by many to be the language of the future, or at least the language of the 1990s.

The Ada programming language is the result of a United States Department of Defense international design competition that lasted from 1975 to 1979 and involved those individuals who were considered to be the best language designers in the world. It is worth mentioning that all four finalist languages in the competition (including Ada) are considered to be derivatives or descendants of Pascal. That is, the overall design of Pascal was in some sense a starting point for these new languages. So, a good way to learn Ada, admittedly a difficult language to master, would be to learn Pascal now.

Let us now investigate the modern history of computing. The impetus for the birth of computer science was World War II. Both the United States and Great Britain were expending tremendous efforts to build computers to assist in the war effort. The first general-purpose computer was the MARK I, built at Harvard in 1944 under the guidance of **Howard Aiken**. This computer used electromagnetic relays and was very slow, requiring six seconds to perform a multiplication.

In 1946, the ENIAC, Electronic Numerical Integrator and Calculator, was developed at the University of Pennsylvania under the direction of **John Mauchly** and **J. Presper Eckert**. ENIAC is often considered the first electronic digital computer. It used vacuum tubes to store information (similar to the tubes found in older radios and television sets). The entire memory of the computer could store only twenty 10-digit numbers. Twelve vacuum tubes were needed to store each digit. The ENIAC could perform about 300 multiplication operations per second, weighed 60,000 pounds, occupied 1600 square feet of floor space, and required a roomful of air conditioners to offset the heat of the vacuum tubes.

Who actually invented the modern digital computer still remains in some doubt. In 1939, **John Atanasoff**, a professor at Iowa State University, and his graduate student, **Clifford Berry**, with a $650 grant, built a prototype of a digital computer. The machine was expanded with further grants and became known as the ABC (Atanasoff Berry Computer). Iowa State never sought a patent on the ABC even though this was urged by Atanasoff. This led to problems after Mauchly visited Atanasoff and studied the ABC for several days in June, 1941, and then later designed and built ENIAC. Atanasoff maintained that the design for Mauchly's ENIAC was taken from his design of the ABC. Mauchly maintained that the ABC was "just a crude little machine that wouldn't really do anything," while ENIAC was "a highly sophisticated and operational computer." The matter actually went to suit and, in 1973, the judge found, in a somewhat contradictory ruling, that Atanasoff invented the concept of the digital computer, while Eckert and Mauchly invented the actual ENIAC machine. Apparently the Atanasoff versus Mauchly controversy will not soon be laid to rest, but it is clear that Atanasoff, who for many years was not even mentioned in brief historical sketches, is now being regarded as one of the important computer pioneers.

During this time period, there were several other machines developed with equally strange-sounding names. One that deserves special mention is the EDVAC, Electron Discrete Variable Automatic Computer, developed in 1952. One of the individuals working on the EDVAC project was **John von Neumann**. While von Neumann made numerous important contributions to the field of computer science, we mention two that first appeared with EDVAC.

The first of these was the concept of a **stored program**. Without becoming too technical, the major components of a computer system include the input/output device, memory, and the processor/controller. The input/output device is necessary so that people can communicate with the computer. The memory is where information (for example, numbers) is kept during processing. The processor/controller is that part of the computer that reads the instructions of a computer program, determines what is to be done, and does it. It is in the manner in which the processor/controller finds the instructions that von Neumann had his impact. With early computers, each time a new program was to be executed, the actual circuits had to be set, either by rewiring or by positioning a number of switches. Von Neumann felt that the set of instructions should be loaded into memory, just like the data on which the instructions were to operate. It would then be up to the processor/controller to distinguish between instructions and data. Although this makes the processor/controller more complex, it greatly facilitates the entering and running of new programs. Thus, the flexibility of the general-purpose computer can be realized. Because of his idea, modern-day computers are often referred to as von Neumann machines and the general layout of a computer is called von Neumann architecture.

Von Neumann's second contribution to EDVAC was in the way computers do arithmetic. In general, computers operate based on the presence or absence of electrical current. The presence is usually indicated by a 1 and absence by a 0. Thus, inside a computer, all one really finds are strings of 0s and 1s. Humans, of course, use more than just 0s and 1s to communicate. When communicating numerically, we use the digits 0 through 9 and operate in the base 10 or decimal system. Although this is very natural for us, this is not the natural way for computers to do things. So, von Neumann proposed that computers do their arithmetic in base 2, or the **binary** system. This idea made the inner workings of computers much more efficient, and today all computers operate using a binary system.

We take this opportunity to mention some terminology. The numerals that we humans use are called digits. The 0s and 1s of a computer are called **b**inary dig**it**s, which you may have seen abbreviated as **bits**. So, a bit in a computer is simply a 0 or a 1. The memory of a computer is filled with millions of bits. Dealing with information bit by bit is very slow and tedious, so bits are generally grouped together. A group of 8 bits is called a **byte**. A byte is a convenient grouping because it is used to store one character of alphabetic information. A computer's memory is usually given by the number of bytes of information that it can store: 1024 bytes are called one **K** (kilobyte). Think of a K as approximately equaling 1000 bytes. So a computer with a memory of 640K can internally store approximately 640,000 characters of information. A megabyte is 1000K, or approximately one million bytes of storage. Large personal computers can have several megabytes of main memory and hundreds of megabytes of disk storage.

Small computers process information one byte at a time. Such machines are called 8-bit machines. The typical personal computer of the late 1970s and early 1980s was an 8-bit computer. Now, 16- and 32-bit microcomputers are quite commonplace and mainframe computers are usually 32- or 64-bit machines. In general, the more bits a computer can handle at a time, the faster the computer operates. The number of bits handled at a time is often referred to as the **word size** of the computer.

Computers of the Modern Era

In the 1960s, the vacuum tube was replaced by the transistor. Computers using tubes are often called **first generation** computers, while those employing transistors are **second generation** computers. What the bulky vacuum tube could do, the tiny transistor could accomplish at a much smaller cost. Because the transistor does not give off nearly as much heat, its reliability is also much greater than that of the vacuum tube. In the late 1960s, the integrated circuit, a cluster of very tiny transistors packed onto a chip of silicon, was introduced. In 1970, scientists were able to pack about 3000 transistors on a single chip of silicon about the size of a baby's fingernail. In 1975, the figure rose to 8000, in 1980 to 70,000, and to 400,000 by the mid-1980s. Packing thousands of transistors onto a chip is known as LSI (Large Scale Integration) technology, and computers using this technology are known as **third generation** computers. VLSI (V for Very) technology, like the latter figures above, constitutes **fourth generation** computers.

From a cost standpoint, one dollar bought 300 transistors in 1970, while one dollar in 1980 bought 5000 transistors. These statistics should make it clear to the reader why the computer industry can offer more for less as long as such progress continues. How much more? Well, how does a typical microcomputer compare with the ENIAC? It is 50 times faster, at least 1000 times more reliable, 1/30,000 of the volume, 1/100,000 the cost, and consumes the power of a light bulb instead of a jet plane.

At the end of 1984, the Japan Information Processing Development Center proposed a plan to develop an advanced computer by the early 1990s. Following this announcement, the race began to see who will build the first **fifth generation** computer. Such computers are expected to make use of advances in the field of artificial intelligence, that area of computer science concerned with computers that can perform functions normally associated with human behavior (e.g., learning and improving).

TERMINOLOGY

We now give a survey of some computer terms. With the mastery of these terms comes the ability to read sales pitches for various computer-related products. The order of the terms is not alphabetical, but rather designed for ease of discussion.

Computer—A device (usually electronic) that is capable of storing and retrieving data and of executing logical or mathematical operations without human intervention.

With the previous historical sketch, we hope this definition of a computer is understandable. Because many people tend to be frightened by computers (because of their seemingly mystical capabilities), we recommend that the reader keep in mind the following alternative definition (given with the companion definition of a human being):

A **computer** is a fast, accurate moron.
A **human being** is a slow, error-prone genius.

Note that the computer, moron that it is, has some good qualities that most people lack; namely, speed (we're talking speed of light, so don't be offended) and accuracy. But with all of its wonderful qualities, computers do not possess one bit of intelligence. That is where the human comes in. Although most of us possess less intelligence than we would really like, there is never any reason to be intimidated by a computer.

Memory—This is the area where the computer stores information. This information can of course be recalled, or **fetched,** any time it is needed. Think of memory as consisting of rows of cells, or mailboxes, each with its own address. There are several adjectives that pertain to memory that should be discussed.

RAM (Random Access Memory)—The memory that is available to the user of the computer. For our purposes, this is where programs and data are stored.
ROM (Read Only Memory)—These are memory cells in the computer that contain information necessary for the operation of the computer itself. When information is fetched from a memory location, we are **reading** from that location. When information is placed into a memory location, we are **writing** to that location. So random access memory is read and write memory; i.e., we can change the contents of RAM if we wish. ROM, on the other hand, has special information in it that the programmer can access but cannot change. Thus, it has the designation read only.
Volatile—This refers to the memory inside the computer and is also called internal memory. Volatile memory loses its contents when the power source is disconnected. So, a program stored in the computer's internal memory is lost if the computer is turned off, if there is a power failure, or if there is a blown fuse.
Nonvolatile—This refers to external sources of memory; for example, floppy disks, hard disks, magnetic tape, and punched cards. This memory retains its contents indefinitely, short of natural disasters like fires, floods, and spilled coffee. Any program that is used repeatedly is stored on an external source, usually a disk, and is simply loaded into the computer's memory when needed. The loading of information from a disk into a computer is performed by a mechanical device called a **disk drive**.

Hardware—Any component of a computer system that you can touch. The keyboard, which is the standard input device for most computers, the monitor (TV screen, sometimes called a CRT (Cathode Ray Tube)), the chips inside the computer, the disks, and disk drives are all hardware components.

Software—Computer programs. Without instructions, the computer hardware just sits there. Computers need software, called the **operating system**, to function properly. In addition, when you purchase a commercially developed program, such as an accounting program, an inventory-control program, or a word-processing program, you are paying for the software—the instructions that allow the computer to behave as an accountant, an inventory controller, or a word processor. In this book, we are going to learn how to develop our own software. Writing good software is not easy. The following ironic definition of software is often given: Software is the *hard* part of a computer system.

We mention that the suffix "ware" is one that has certainly made its impact on computer jargon. In fact, commercial software that has been announced but is not yet available is often called *vaporware*. We hope that with the *diskware* that accompanies this *bookware,* we have provided you with excellent *courseware* for learning Turbo Pascal.

Documentation—The comments or explanatory remarks that accompany software. Documentation comes in two types—internal and external. Internal documentation consists of comments included with a computer program. External documentation is like an automobile owner's manual and should be provided on any software project that is sold commercially or that is of a complex nature.

Printer—An output device that provides a paper copy (hard copy) of a computer program or its execution. Printers are divided into several categories. Dot matrix, letter quality, and laser printers are the most common kinds. Dot matrix printers draw the characters by using tiny dots (the same way the monitor displays characters on the screen). Letter quality printers strike a ribbon with some type of wheel that contains the raised imprint of the characters. Laser printers, capable of printing very high-quality pages in a short period of time, format an image of a page electronically and then produce a copy of that image much as a copying machine produces an image from an actual original.

ALGORITHMS

Algorithm is a very old English word, and algorithms are a fundamental concept in computer science, but the term is not commonly used in everyday English, so you should not be surprised if the word is new to you. Because of its importance to what follows, please do take a moment to add the word to your vocabulary.

An **algorithm** is a precise set of instructions that solves some problem in a finite number of steps. Standard examples that are usually given to express the idea of an algorithm are a recipe for a cake, instructions for changing a flat tire, or instructions on a bottle of shampoo. These are good first examples, but none is perfect because they do not have the precision necessary to be called algorithms. For example, cooking instructions often contain such instructions as add a pinch of salt, or season to taste. While the first could perhaps be defined precisely, the second seems really to call for an open-ended decision on the part of the cook. If you have a flat tire, the instruction, "Put the jack under the fender and jack up the car," is probably clear, but if your computer were doing the job, it would need to know which fender to put the jack under. It doesn't do much good to jack up the left front, if the flat is on the right rear! This may seem like a silly example, but when you start to write algorithms for computers, we predict that just this kind of thing will happen to you. You are almost certainly not accustomed to the precision needed to deal with computers, so we won't be surprised if you occasionally leave out important steps that were obvious to you. Unfortunately, nothing is obvious to the computer and, therefore, every step in an algorithm must be completely and unambiguously specified.

Consider the following instructions found on a typical bottle of shampoo:

Wet hair. Apply shampoo and work to a lather. Rinse and repeat.

These instructions must be fairly clear to humans, since most humans don't seem to have problems washing their hair. But imagine the problems a literal-minded robot (with hair) that understands all the terms might have:

1. Wet hair with what? Kerosene, paint, water, or beer?
2. How much shampoo do we apply? The whole bottle? If so, how do we repeat?
3. How long do we work to a lather?
4. When we repeat the process, do we begin at the beginning? If so, why do you wet hair that has just been rinsed?
5. How many times do we repeat the process? Forever?

It is easy to imagine that the literal-minded robot would get stuck in an infinite loop repeating the shampoo instructions. We predict that, as beginners, you may well write muddled instructions that stick the computer in an infinite loop. If so, your instructions are not an algorithm, because an algorithm must terminate in a finite number of steps. In summary, an algorithm is a *precise* set of instructions for solving some problem in a *finite* number of steps.

We have given three examples of near algorithms. How about an example of a real algorithm? Consider the following example from arithmetic. Suppose we want to know the sum of the squares of the first 100 positive integers. That is, we want to know the sum

$$1^2 + 2^2 + 3^2 + ... + 99^2 + 100^2$$

The following is an algorithm to compute this result for us:

Set a variable Sum to zero
Set a variable Number to one
Repeat
    Add the square of Number to Sum and store the new result in Sum
    Add 1 to Number
Until Number > 100

You should examine the above instructions carefully until convinced that they tell you precisely how, in a finite number of steps, to compute the sum in question. In fact, the reader should learn to play computer and trace the above instructions step by step to see how Sum and Number take on the following values during execution of the algorithm (with 100 replaced by 10 to make the problem more manageable for humans):

Sum	Number
0	1
1	2
5	3
14	4
30	5
55	6
91	7
140	8
204	9
285	10
385	11

The role of playing computer is a very valuable one to learn, especially when the computer executes your algorithm but does not produce the correct answer. By playing computer, hopefully you can determine what the computer is actually doing and correct the problem.

PROGRAMMING A COMPUTER

Since this book is really about programming, it is appropriate that we include some remarks about programming. The first and most important remark is that this book is really about *problem solving*. Beginners often lose sight of this fact, and it is for this reason that programming often becomes a difficult activity. Programmers must first be problem solvers, and solving a problem means finding (or designing) an algorithm that solves that problem, because a program is nothing more than the expression of the algorithm in some computer language. The computer executes the instructions, but it is the human who must design the algorithm and write the instructions. Of these two steps, designing the algorithm is the challenging and interesting step. The second, or programming step, which translates the algorithm into a language such as Pascal, should be very straightforward. Many beginners spend far too much time learning all the technical aspects of the programming language and far too little time sharpening their problem-solving skills. Such people never get much of a chance to use their programming knowledge because they get stuck at step 1—what to do after the problem is posed to them. Realize that you will have very little success at programming if you do not understand what you are trying to express in the programming language. As we get into actual problems in the pages to follow, we will be more precise about how one proceeds both with the design and the implementation (programming) phases of problem solving.

The preceding paragraph used the word Pascal. The computer language Pascal was developed by Niklaus Wirth of Switzerland in 1969. Wirth intended Pascal to be an educational language, so he kept the design small. Pascal will be the vehicle by which we learn this problem-solving process called programming. Earlier, we saw that the computer is a binary machine, storing everything as either a 0 or a 1. If we wanted to (we don't, take our word for it), we could communicate to the computer in its native language, its **machine language**, by using strings of 0s and 1s. Such a language is called a **low-level language**. This is the way the earliest programmers worked with computers. Not only was this process extremely tedious, it also was unnecessarily complicated, making programming a very specialized activity. The advent of **high-level languages** in the 1950s has proved to be as important a factor in making programming a common activity as has the technological progress outlined in this chapter, which made the computer affordable. High-level languages like Pascal make computers understandable. High-level languages are closer to English than they are to machine languages. People who have had no training at all in programming are sometimes able to look at high-level programs and figure out what they do.

It will be Chapter 7 before we cover the technical details of the following Pascal segment, but we think that you can determine (not in exact details, but in general terms) what this segment does. This points out that well-written Pascal programs are easy to read and understand.

```
Enter(Name, Weight, HeightFt, HeightIn, Sex);
FindBestWeight(HeightFt, HeightIn, Sex, IdealWeight);
ReportFindings(Name, Sex, HeightFt, HeightIn, Weight, IdealWeight);
```

Evidently, it is Enter's job to obtain the five listed items of information from the user. We can guess from its name that FindBestWeight's job is to take the user's height and sex information and determine, by some unspecified means, an IdealWeight for that individual. Notice that the user's Name and current Weight are not relevant to computing the individual's IdealWeight. Obviously, the job of ReportFindings is to print a report to the user. These reports could take the form

```
William Perry, as a 6 foot 4 inch male, your current weight of 375
pounds is 135 pounds over your ideal weight of 240 pounds.
```

or

```
Twiggy, as a 5 foot 3 inch female, your current weight of 75
pounds is 22 pounds under your ideal weight of 97 pounds.
```

or

```
Alf, as a 3 foot 2 inch male, your current weight of 57
pounds is exactly your ideal weight.
```

Note that ReportFindings printed all the information it was given, as well as computing how much (if any) the individual was overweight or underweight and printing an appropriate message to the user. We shall soon learn how to instruct the computer to make such decisions.

If we are to write programs in a high-level language and if the computer can only understand its native machine language, there must be someone, or something(!), that performs a translation process between the high-level language and the low-level language needed by the computer. This translation process is, in fact, performed by another computer program, called a **compiler** or an **interpreter**, depending on how it carries out its translation. An **interpreter**, like an interpreter at the United Nations, translates a line of the source and then executes that line before translating the next line. A **compiler** translates the entire source before beginning the execution of any of it. For this reason, the Pascal program that you write is often called the **source code**, while the compiled version that the machine actually executes is called the **object code**. Note that works of literature are usually compiled. That is, if you buy the poetry of Yevtushenko in translation, then you expect to get the compiled version (object code in a form you can directly read), rather than an interpreter who comes along with the original Russian (source code) to translate just for you. Also note that with interpretation, the translation is not preserved. Interpretation must take place during each execution of a line of a program. With compilation, on the other hand, the translation is preserved and, thus, the compilation of a program need be done but once. This means that compiled code is usually much faster than interpreted code, and much of the speed of Turbo Pascal is due to its efficient compiler.

A translator is an example of a **systems program**. The writing of a language translator is an extremely complicated task requiring several thousand person-years of work. This compiler (and the documentation accompanying it) is what you are paying for when you purchase your copy of Turbo Pascal. Such compilers have sold for thousands of dollars. Borland International, the publishers of Turbo Pascal, deserve credit for creating a "VolksPascal" for the PC. The combination of an easy-to-use system, an incredibly fast compiler, and a reasonable price has made Turbo Pascal the standard Pascal for the PC.

STRUCTURED PROGRAMMING

A common buzzword in computer programming these days is **structured**. Programs should be structured and languages should be structured. So that we can support our contention that Pascal is an excellent language for students who are serious about learning to program, we will explain what structured programming means to us.

Often, a program is a piece of work written by one group of people to be read by another group of people. A well-written composition is more than just a bunch of paragraphs thrown together. Likewise, a computer program is more than just a bunch of instructions thrown together. Each needs to be held together by some overall structure. It is this structure that is the primary focus of most beginning writing courses, although some time is spent discussing grammar, spelling, punctuation, and sentence construction. Similarly, in a beginning programming course, a certain amount of time must be spent learning the atomic constructs of a programming language, so that these may be combined to form complete programs. We must also learn how to operate a computer if we want to see the results of our programs. But like the writing course, the bulk of the emphasis should be on the ability to solve a problem and convey that solution in a complete, well-structured program.

Some synonyms of structured programming are **top-down programming** and **modular programming.** To us, all of these terms mean the following: When presented with a problem to solve, don't try to solve it all at once. Don't start worrying about the intricate details. Instead, break the problem up into major components and focus on each of these components in turn. Apply this same technique to each of these components until you have broken the problem down into subproblems that are easy to solve. Solve the subproblems and then combine these solutions into one overall solution for the original problem. While this strategy is worthwhile in almost any type of environment, it is especially appropriate in the programming environment. When dealing person-to-person, we can sometimes be a bit sketchy in our instructions, allowing the recipient to use his or her own intelligence to figure out our intent. But, because the computer is a moron, extremely detailed instructions must be given so that there is absolutely no doubt about what is to be done. Most major software projects are so complex that one soon becomes lost in a forest of details if the problem is not first cut down to size. The aim of this book is to teach you to write structured programs and to understand why this is so important. It is a little early to explain fully what we mean by this term, but in the pages to come we shall return to this topic and we intend to convince you, with many examples and discussions, of the value of structured programming. As a first example, we point out that `Enter`, `FindBestWeight`, and `ReportFindings` certainly subdivided the task of finding and reporting an individual's ideal weight into three logical and relatively simple subtasks.

Now we know what a structured program is. What makes a language structured? If we attack a problem as above, we should be able to write the solutions to the subproblems as their own separate subprograms. A language is structured if it provides the programmer with the features necessary to carry out this modular approach easily and to link these subprograms together into a complete program. It is our hope that the readers who work through the chapters in this book will possess the ability to write structured programs and provide their own arguments that Pascal is indeed a structured language.

EVOLUTION OF MODERN SOFTWARE ENGINEERING PRINCIPLES

Structured programming is not just an academic concern. The real world writes huge programs. Many programs are measured in tens of thousands of lines. Some number in the hundreds of thousands or millions of lines. Today's production programs are orders of magnitude bigger than programs written in the 1940s and 1950s. It is obvious that big programs are inherently more complex to work with than small ones. With a program of 50 lines, it is possible to remember the purpose of each line, even if it isn't self-evident. With a program of 50,000 lines, no human can recall what each line does, let alone what major sections of the program are supposed to do.

Also, real programs are written not by single individuals, but by teams of people. But people come and go. Imagine how difficult it would be to inherit someone else's messy 50,000-line program! Programs must also be maintained to reflect the new social-security withholding rate, or the new thrust of the rocket's engines. Programs have to be modified or extended to handle new cases. Too often, managers find that the only feasible way to modify a program is to throw it out and write it over, because huge programs are hard to debug, maintain, modify, or extend. Throwing out the original is very expensive and wasteful of the initial effort. There has to be a better way.

There are, of course, no 50,000-line programs included in this text. For one reason, such a listing would run about 1000 pages by itself! Nor will any of the exercises ask you to write such large programs. In education, we get to play mind games. Our example programs illustrate certain concepts and, hence, are quite brief. Your exercises are of the same nature. Yet, we will make a big deal of applying modern programming techniques to our examples and we ask that you do the same in the exercises. The mind game that we are asking you to play is to pretend that every program, no matter how small or silly, is a real program that others will have to understand, maintain, modify, and extend.

The first successful high-level language, FORTRAN, was released in April, 1957. In the last 30 years, hundreds of languages have been developed to deal with the complexity of large programs. Over these 30 years, through popular languages like BASIC, Algol, PL/I, C, and many others, an evolution has occurred. Pascal is a relatively new language and contains many techniques for managing complexity. We mention five of these: structure, subprograms, separately compiled units, data sharing, and local variables. Much more will be said of each of these in the chapters to follow. Indeed, these topics are the focus of the remainder of this text.

Structure

Structure has already been discussed. We remind you that a language is said to be structured if it contains powerful constructs that allow the programmer to express naturally algorithms in that language. Pascal is highly structured, and we will begin to see this when we introduce the fundamental control structures in Chapter 5 and when we extend the control structures in Chapter 8.

Subprograms

A feature that was first introduced in FORTRAN II, early in 1958, and has been accepted ever since by programmers, is the subprogram. This device allows a large program to be broken down into smaller, more manageable pieces. It is the programmer's way of applying the much revered problem-solving heuristic known as **divide and conquer**, which says that to solve a big problem, it is sufficient to break it into smaller problems and solve each of them in turn. From the programmer's point of view, it is not necessary to try to keep track of all the details involved in a large program; it is only necessary to understand the small piece you are now working on. If you understand how the problem was decomposed, then it is an easy task to build the solution to the original problem from the solutions to the smaller problems. In our earlier example the subtasks `Enter`, `FindBestWeight`, and `ReportFindings`, are all subprograms.

As another example, suppose that your boss wants a program that spits out all the prime numbers between two values supplied by the user. For example, if the user enters 100 and 1000, then the program would print all the three-digit primes. (Recall that a prime is a whole number, like 17, that has no divisors other than 1 and itself.) Of course, this is not a very complex problem and can easily be solved without a divide-and-conquer technique, but play along with us and pretend that it is very complex. How do we approach this complex problem? Can we divide it into smaller pieces? Clearly, the first thing that needs to be done is to get the user to enter the range for our search for primes. Thus, we could write a subprogram, `EnterData`, that would obtain from the user these `Low` and `High` values. Wouldn't it be nice if the computer already knew what a prime number was? Well, it doesn't, but we can still imagine a black box called `Prime` that will take a candidate number and tell us yea or nay whether the candidate is prime or not. This black box is exactly the notion of a subprogram. Indeed, if we imagine that designing an algorithm for the subprogram `Prime` is too mathematical for us, we could hire a mathematician to do it for us, and then we could implement his or her design as a subprogram in our program. Here is the structure of our *main* program that solves the original problem:

Call subprogram **EnterData** to get the Low and High range values
Loop a Candidate through all values from Low up to High
    Call **Prime** to see if the Candidate is prime or not
    If the Candidate is prime then print it out

Several points are worthy of explicit mention. First, the main program for this complex problem is easy to understand because it is short and makes clear, explicit calls to other slave subprograms. Second, each subprogram is short because it does one clearly defined task. Therefore, each subprogram is easy to understand. Third, different subprograms can be written by different people, allowing groups of people a reasonable way to work on large programs. Finally, the huge program is easy to debug, maintain, and extend. It is easy to debug, since each subprogram can be bench tested before being turned loose in the big program. Even if a bug appears in the final program, it is usually easy to determine which subprogram is in error, and once the error has been localized, it is usually easy to find and correct. The program is easy to maintain or extend, because only certain subprograms need to be changed, and again it is clear from the decomposition which these are. The result is a large program that does not have to be thrown out to be modified.

   Subprograms in Pascal are called procedures and functions. They are explained in detail in Chapter 6.

Separately Compiled Units

Suppose you have a 72,343-line payroll program, and you find that the federal government has just changed the social-security witholding rate from 7.15 percent to 7.35 percent. If your program is well written, only one line, where you define this important value, needs to be changed. In most Pascals, all 72,343 lines need to be recompiled before your program can be run again. Even on a fast system, this will require several minutes. It seems silly, since only one line has changed, that all need to be recompiled, even those subprograms that have nothing to do with this particular number. That is exactly the point of the separately compiled unit (a piece of your program that can be compiled by itself). In Turbo Pascal, a unit may consist of one or several related subprograms, or just of constant declarations of the type we are talking about. If our huge program is broken into 10 units, then only the unit that changes will have to be recompiled. Separately compiled units provide an additional way to make the debugging, maintenance, and extension of large programs more manageable.

   It is important to note that separate compilation is *not* a feature of Wirth's standard Pascal, but is an extension provided by Turbo Pascal. In general, Turbo Pascal provides several valuable extensions to standard Pascal. We will use many of these extensions, but also point them out to the reader so that the reader knows what is standard and what is special to Turbo Pascal. Separate compilation is discussed in Chapter 20.

Data Sharing

Once a program is broken into subprograms, it becomes clear that the subprograms need some way of communicating with each other and with the main program. Consider our simple example of the subprogram `Prime`. `Prime` needs to be given a `Candidate` number to consider. After `Prime` makes its decision, it needs to return via some means a yea or nay to the main program. The subprogram `EnterData` needs nothing from the main program, but it does pass back two values, `Low` and `High`, to the main program for its further use. Hence, we see that some means of data sharing between subprograms is necessary, and that this data sharing can go in either direction. Chapter 6 introduces data sharing between subprograms, and Chapter 9 discusses these concepts extensively. Chapter 20 introduces data sharing between separately compiled units.

Local Variables

Another important consequence of data sharing and data hiding is that different people should be able to write subprograms, without worrying about the variables they choose to use in the internal details of that subprogram. There should be a way for these details to be local to a subprogram and, therefore, not accessible outside of the subprogram. This means that two different subprograms should be able to have local variables with the same names, without the system confusing them. If you wonder why two subprograms would both want to use the same variable for different purposes, then look at it this way: You are writing a new subprogram for an existing 50,000-line program. How can you be sure that the variables you need locally have not been used elsewhere? Wouldn't it be nice if you could use the variable `Count`, if it seemed appropriate, without worrying about whether anyone had ever used it before? In a language that supports local variables, this can be done, and the variable `Count` can be used locally in as many different subprograms as you want without confusing the system. Without this feature, the power of the divide-and-conquer strategy would be greatly compromised. Divide and conquer gives us a way to focus our attention on one subprogram without worrying about the details of the whole problem. If we didn't have local variables, then we wouldn't be able to write a subprogram without knowing all the details of the entire program. Local variables, their declaration and use, are introduced in Chapter 6 and are also discussed extensively in Chapter 9.

WHY PASCAL?

No computer language is perfect, and the introduction in the last three decades of hundreds of computer languages only serves to underscore this point. FORTRAN II, introduced in 1958, was a surprisingly powerful language for its day and was the standard language of American universities in the 1960s and early 1970s. FORTRAN supported subprograms, separate compilation, and local variables and had decent data-sharing mechanisms, but was particularly weak in control structures. In the mid-1970s, Pascal began to replace FORTRAN as the standard language taught in most American universities. The main reason for this was that Pascal was very strong in control structures, while still providing subprograms with local variables and good data-sharing techniques. As we have mentioned, Turbo Pascal also supports separate compilation, making it a particularly attractive dialect of Pascal.

DOCUMENTATION

Another feature of well-written software, no matter what language is used, is documentation or comments. In a large project, this documentation will take two forms, external and internal. External documentation takes the form of a manual, or guide, to the software being developed. Good external documentation can ease the task of maintainance, but keeping external documentation current can be difficult. It is important to maintain the documentation as well as the software, since incorrect documentation is probably worse than none at all.

Internal documentation is documentation within the program itself, and this is the kind of documentation that we shall stress in this text. Again, the importance of documentation grows with the size of the program, but documentation should be used in all programs, large and small. The only reason to use documentation is to provide clarity to your programs, so the only firm rule is: **Use comments when they will help an intelligent human reader of your program**. Since this rule is found by most beginners to be too vague to be helpful, we will provide, as we develop Pascal constructs, discussions of the commenting system that will be used in this text. Since commenting programs is such an individualistic process, your instructor or boss may set additional guidelines for your computer center, but our guidelines are fairly well-accepted software engineering procedures.

One form of documentation is local documentation, which involves commenting actual lines of code. For example, use a comment to help break straight-line code into more easily understood segments. A comment such as

```
{ The next loop reads the input data and counts the students. }
```

makes the intent of the next section clear to anyone who can read. Note that comments in Pascal are enclosed within braces, { and }.

Another use of local documentation is to provide a hint to the reader for a particularly tricky portion of the program. If you use some programming trick that is not transparent, you should comment that line for the reader. If you suddenly pull some formula out of the air, you should comment that line so that the reader has some reference as to where the expression came from. Here is a simple example:

```
Sum := Principal * (1.0 + Rate) * Time;{Compound Interest Formula}
                    {Rate is expressed as a decimal, not a percent.}
```

Too many beginners think that their task is complete when their program runs. First, you should check that the output is correct (at least reasonable), and second, you should ensure that the program is as readable as you can make it. This final step may include adding white space (blank lines) or documentation to your program.

Do not, however, comment the obvious. For example, the comment

```
Total := Score1 + Score2; {Add up the total of the two scores.}
```

really only clutters up the program. Comments should be helpful to the intelligent reader, not insults to the intelligence of the reader. Also avoid a comment for every line of your program. While beginners usually err on the side of too few comments, it is possible to have too many comments. Again, we repeat the only firm rule: Use comments to provide clarity to your program. Don't use too many or too few; use just the right number of comments!

THE ART OF PROGRAMMING

It is not unusual for the beginning programmer to make the following statement: "There's something wrong with this computer." Such a statement usually follows a frustrating session, in which the computer won't follow even the simplest of instructions. There is even a chance that the statement might actually be true. Silicon chips do go bad, either by misuse or on their own (every hundred years or so). Disks do get damaged through misuse or normal wear and tear. Because of their tremendous complexity, compilers and interpreters actually get written and marketed with mistakes in them. This happens more often than it should, but it is the price we pay to avoid writing in machine language. Nonetheless, there is probably a 99.9 percent chance that the beginner's statement is false. The statement should read: "There's something wrong with the instructions I gave to the computer." If you take this approach and start analyzing your instructions, you may overcome your problem much more quickly. All too often, our human pride causes us to insist that the first statement is true and we repeatedly give the same instructions to the computer, with the same undesired results. Not only is the computer a moron, it is also infinitely patient. It is so stupid that it can't help us find and correct our mistakes and it doesn't mind when we keep asking it to do the same thing over and over.

The level of precision required in programming is typically much higher than has ever been required of the programmer in any other activity. For this reason, be suspicious and critical of the instructions you give to the computer. It is only through a critical look that you can convince yourself that your programs are correct. Never expect the computer to make any kind of distinction between what you type and what you mean. Make sure that you type *exactly* what you mean. Computer languages are often criticized for being overly picky, with every punctuation mark having a significant impact. This is just the nature of computers and we must learn to accept it. But, to show the importance of punctuation in natural languages, consider the following prize-winning paragraph from the May, 1984, issue of **GAMES** Magazine:

My wife. I think I'll keep her. In a spaceship, orbiting the globe until the end of time, I could never find another woman on earth like her. If I wanted to, I could go on and on about her face and figure. I'm reminded of Henry Kissinger when the subject of her intelligence comes up. I often think of the time the neighbor's Chihuahua gave birth to brain-damaged pups. My wife, my gracious Clara, was willing to sit up nights with the pups. In an effort to learn to speak more effectively, Clara began taking a night class at the local college. She's learning how to become a human relations counselor. Sam Wilkins, from the school, told me Clara is at the head of her class. When it comes to "stupidity"—golly, the word's not even in her vocabulary.

Note what happens when this paragraph is *only* repunctuated—none of the words, nor their order, is changed.

My wife. I think I'll keep her in a spaceship, orbiting the globe until the end of time. I could never find another woman on earth like her, if I wanted to. I could go on and on. About her face and figure—I'm reminded of Henry Kissinger. When the subject of her intelligence comes up, I often think of the time the neighbor's Chihuahua gave birth to brain-damaged pups. My wife—my gracious! Clara was willing to sit up nights with the pups in an effort to learn to speak more effectively. Clara began taking a night class at the local college. She's learning how to become a human. Relations counselor, Sam Wilkins, from the school, told me Clara is at the head of her class when it comes to stupidity. "Golly"—the word's not even in her vocabulary.

The above paragraphs were submitted to **GAMES** by Joyce Rogers in response to a contest (**GAMES**, Jan., 1984) asking readers to create double messages by changing punctuation. The magazine closed the challenge with the following information:

All entries will be considered. If they are clever, however, they will be eliminated. If sufficiently stupid, any entry stands a good chance of winning.

Of course, the intended message was:

All entries will be considered if they are clever. However, they will be eliminated if sufficiently stupid. Any entry stands a good chance of winning.

The reader who enjoys these examples will get an opportunity, in the exercises at the end of this chapter, to repunctuate some other paragraphs that were submitted to **GAMES** Magazine.*

SUMMARY

Although the concept of the present-day computer has been around since Babbage's Analytical Engine of the 1830s, it is the technological advances of integrated circuitry that have brought computers into the home and into the reach of the average person. Along with the technological advances have come advances in software design, most notably high-level languages, which have placed the power of computers into the hands of the average person. Because of these phenomena, the computer will have an

---

* Paragraphs reprinted from **GAMES** Magazine, 810 Seventh Avenue, New York, NY 10019. Copyright © 1984 PSC Games Limited Partnership.

impact on society like few other human inventions. Most people will benefit from computers and, in the near future, everyone will be a computer user. But, to really understand how a computer works and to harness and control the power of the computer, one needs to learn programming. While programming comes naturally for some people, it proves to be quite a challenge for many others because of the cold logic of the computer and the precision required of the programmer. The environment provided by the user-friendliness of the Turbo Pascal system, coupled with the features found in a small, modern, structured language like Pascal, can help make the beginning programmer's experience an enjoyable one instead of a frustrating one.

This brief chapter has tried to provide you with a rationale for the topics that will come and the reasons for our fussiness concerning the style of programs that you will write. The purpose was simply to provide you with the big picture, so that you will appreciate the details that are about to unfold. Too many beginners approach a language with their total attention on the syntax of that language. Their total obsession is to get a program that runs, and, with that narrow focus on detail, they can't understand where they are going or why. While you must use the language correctly to get programs to run, we implore you to keep one eye on the concepts being developed. Our objectives are to develop broad problem-solving tools and to learn to write clear, easily maintained programs. These are the valuable skills that the reader can take from this text. Pascal is simply our vehicle for this trip.

KEYWORDS AND KEY PEOPLE

Many terms have been introduced in this chapter. For each of the terms listed below, give a one- or two-sentence definition or description.

ABC	Nonvolatile
Ada	Object code
Analytical Engine	Pascal
Binary	Pascaline
Compiler	Program
Computer	RAM
Documentation	ROM
EDVAC	Software
ENIAC	Source code
FORTRAN	Stored program
Hardware	Structured program
High-level language	Subprogram
Low-level language	Tabulating machine
Memory	Volatile

Many people important to the development of computers and the language Pascal have been introduced in this chapter. Some of them are listed below. Identify each of these individuals and write for each a brief description of his or her accomplishments.

John Atanasoff	Gottfried Leibniz
Ada Augusta	John Mauchly
Charles Babbage	Blaise Pascal
Herman Hollerith	John von Neumann
Emil Jacquard	Niklaus Wirth

SELF-TEST QUESTIONS

These self-test questions are designed to show the logic required in programming.

1.1 A boy is sent to a stream with a 5-quart jug and a 3-quart jug and is asked to bring back 4 quarts of water. How can he do it? Can you come up with two different ways of obtaining 4 quarts of water?

1.2 A jeweler has in his possession 9 gold coins and a two-pan balance. One of the coins is counterfeit and is lighter than the authentic coins. How can the jeweler, with just two weighings, determine which coin is the counterfeit coin?

1.3 Consider a very strange universe where there are only two types of people—Computer Programmers, who always tell the truth except on Mondays, Tuesdays, and Wednesdays, when they always lie, and Computer Salespersons, who always tell the truth except on Thursdays, Fridays, and Saturdays, when they always lie. (We are being generous to the salespersons, at least according to the following old joke: *How can you tell when a computer salesperson is lying?* Answer: Whenever the salesperson's lips are moving.)

a)   You meet two people one day and they say the following:

First person: I'm a computer salesperson.
Second person: I'm a computer programmer.

What day is it and which person is which?

b)   Later that same month, you come across the same two people. Your digital wristwatch is broken, so you don't know what day of the week it is. However, the two acquaintances help you with the following statements:

Programmer: I lied yesterday.
Salesperson: I lied yesterday, too.

What day of the week is it?

1.4 A word processor is a device that assists in the writing of documents. Word processors have a variety of commands that can be used to correct mistakes. Suppose you own a very limited word processor that has only one correcting command; namely, a change command of the following format:

CHANGE*first word*second word*

The CHANGE command finds all occurrences of the word listed between the first two asterisks and changes each occurrence to the word listed between the last two asterisks. You are typing an important document and notice the following paragraph:

Morris is the dog on commercials who doesn't like to eat his food. Sylvester is a dog on cartoons. **Old Yeller** is a movie about a cat that makes almost everyone cry. Probably the most famous cat is Lassie. I wonder if a dog really does have nine lives. Elvis Presley sang a song about a hound cat.

Obviously, you have been careless and completely mixed up the uses of the words cat and dog. How could you use the CHANGE command (maybe more than once) to make the paragraph read normally? (Note: This isn't as easy as it first seems.)

EXERCISES

The next three exercises in this chapter are courtesy of **GAMES** Magazine.* Exercises 1.5 and 1.6 are from the May, 1984, issue, and were submitted by Ellen Jackson and Bob Schnitzer, respectively. Exercise 1.7 appeared in the January, 1984, issue. You are to repunctuate each of the passages to obtain a passage with a completely different meaning.

1.5 Dear President Reagan,
I would like to compliment you. I can't stop thinking that you are one of the best Presidents we have had. So many leaders go ahead and propose policies and then botch the job. We expect it. From you, in years to come, I know we will get better results.

1.6 Car for sale. A classic! Lemon yellow coupe. Exterior is completely rust-proof. Can be delivered upon request. No engine runs better. If the sun is out, you can remove the roof for the feel of wind in your hair. Go ahead and kick the tires. As soon as they see it your neighbors will hassle you for a ride. Call 222-4401.

1.7 Dear John,
I want a man who knows what love is all about. You are generous, kind, thoughtful. People who are not like you admit to being useless and inferior, John. You have ruined me for other men. I yearn for you. I have no feelings whatsoever when we're apart. I can be forever happy. Will you let me be yours?
Gloria

* Reprinted from **GAMES** Magazine, 810 Seventh Avenue, New York, NY 10019. Copyright © 1984 PSC Games Limited Partnership.

1.8 A large program written in an unstructured language is sometimes referred to as a plate of spaghetti. Explain this anology with respect to the task of maintaining a large program.

1.9 Use divide and conquer to explain what is meant by the divide-and-conquer problem-solving technique.

1.10 A positive integer is called **perfect** if it is the sum of its proper divisors. For example, 6 is perfect since 6 = 1 + 2 + 3, and 1, 2, and 3 are the only divisors of 6 (other than 6 itself). Twelve, on the other hand, is not perfect since $12 \neq 1 + 2 + 3 + 4 + 6$.

a) Verify by hand calculations that 28 is perfect.

b) Suppose that a mathematician has written a `SumDivs` procedure for you that will sum the proper divisors of whatever positive integer that you give it. Write an outline in English using a `LOOP` and an `IF` construct, and using `SumDivs`, for an algorithm to find all perfect numbers between 6 and 500. Do not attempt to execute your algorithm by hand! We shall return to this problem in Chapter 7.

1.11 Describe the operation of subprograms such as `GiveRules`, `CheckWin`, `CheckLegalPlay`, etc. for a game of tic-tac-toe. Using your subprograms, write an English main program that plays a game of tic-tac-toe with a human against the computer. Assume appropriately named subprograms that allow the human to enter a play and allow the computer to choose an intelligent reply. You do not have to describe how the subprograms actually work. Rather, your task is to write the global documentation that describes the black boxes that you could use to get the computer to play tic-tac-toe.

ANSWERS TO SELF-TEST QUESTIONS

1.1 Fill the 3-quart jug and pour its contents into the 5-quart jug. Again fill the 3-quart jug and fill the 5-quart jug from it. This will leave 1 quart in the 3-quart jug. Empty the 5-quart jug and pour the 1 quart into the 5-quart jug. Fill the 3-quart jug again and add the 3 quarts to the 1 quart giving 4 quarts in the 5-quart jug.
Here is another solution: Fill the 5-quart jug and pour 3 quarts into the 3-quart jug. Empty the 3-quart jug and pour the remaining 2 quarts into the 3-quart jug. Fill the 5-quart jug and then fill the 3-quart jug from the 5-quart jug. This takes 1 quart, leaving 4 quarts in the 5-quart jug.

1.2 The jeweler puts any 3 of the coins in the left pan and any 3 coins in the right pan (first weighing). If the pans balance, the bad coin is among the 3 not yet weighed. If the pans do not balance, then the bad coin is in the pan that goes up. At this point the jeweler knows which group of 3 contains the bad coin. The jeweler takes these 3 coins and arbitrarily puts 1 in the left pan and 1 in the right pan (second weighing).

If the coins balance then the third coin is the bad coin. If the coins do not balance, then the lighter coin is the counterfeit. Notice how important it was to know that there was just 1 counterfeit coin and that it was lighter than the others.

1.3 **a)** The people are not both programmers or salespersons, for, if so, they would have to make the same statement concerning their occupations. Therefore, one of the people is a programmer and the other is a salesperson. Suppose the first person is the programmer and the second is the salesperson. Then by looking at their statements, we see that both are lying. But programmers lie only on Mondays, Tuesdays, and Wednesdays, while salespersons lie only on Thursdays, Fridays, and Saturdays. Hence, there is no day that both can lie. We conclude that the first person must be the salesperson and the second person must be the programmer. Also, we see that both are telling the truth. Programmers tell the truth only on Thursdays, Fridays, Saturdays, and Sundays. Likewise, salespersons tell the truth only on Sundays, Mondays, Tuesdays, and Wednesdays. Hence, Sunday is the only day that both tell the truth and it must, therefore, be Sunday when you hear these two remarks.

b) First we investigate on which days the programmer could say, "I lied yesterday." Clearly, programmers can make such a statement on Thursday, since programmers lie on Wednesdays and tell the truth on Thursdays. But programmers can also make this statement on Mondays, when they lie about their activities on Sunday. By inspection, we see that Thursday and Monday are the only two possibilities for the programmer. Likewise, the salesperson can truthfully make this statement on Sunday and falsely on Thursday. Hence, it must be Thursday when you overheard these remarks.

1.4 CHANGE*dog*aardvark*
CHANGE*cat*dog*
CHANGE*aardvark*cat*

2

THE TURBO PASCAL ENVIRONMENT

In this chapter, we are going to enter, debug, and run our first Turbo Pascal program. For the beginner, there are two hurdles to overcome: One is to learn a little Pascal and the second is to learn to steer a program through the computer. That is, once we have written a program, we must learn how to enter it into the computer, how to edit it, how to run it, how to get a printed listing of it, and, finally, how to save it. These housekeeping tasks are performed by the operating system. With many systems, this is another foreign language that stands between the user and the computer. Fortunately, Turbo Pascal gives us easy-to-use pull-down menus and single-key shortcuts with which to communicate our wishes. Nonetheless, the full Turbo Pascal environment is very powerful and will require some study. This chapter introduces those features of this system that the beginner needs. Further information about advanced features of Turbo Pascal's environment is given in Chapter 7. This chapter is specific to the 4.0, 5.0, and 5.5 versions of Turbo Pascal. Minor differences between these versions are pointed out in the discussions below.

BACKING UP YOUR DISKETTES

Before you use your original Turbo Pascal disks, you should make backup copies of them. You should then put the originals away in a safe place and use the copies. If you are not familiar with the procedure for backing up a disk, see Appendix A: Formatting and Backing Up Disks.

INSTALLING TURBO PASCAL ON YOUR SYSTEM

Turbo Pascal must be installed before you can use it on your computer. Detailed instructions for various configurations of computers are given in Appendix B:

```
Program Simple;
{This simple program prompts the user for his or her name.}
Var Name : String[30];
Begin
  Writeln('Hello, what is your name?');
  Readln(Name);
  Writeln('Good to meet you, ', Name)
End.
```

Listing 2.1

Installing Turbo Pascal. Before you proceed, please make sure that you have backed up your original diskettes and installed Turbo Pascal for your computer.

A FIRST PROGRAM

Listing 2.1 shows a complete program called `Simple`. More will be said about the structure of Pascal programs in the chapters to come, so there is no need to worry about understanding the program now. In fact, you can probably guess what `Simple` will do. The first line just names the program. The second line is a comment telling us what the program does. The `Var` section declares that `Name` will be a string "var"iable; i.e., `Name` will be able to hold a string of up to 30 characters. The executable portion of the program begins and ends, reasonably enough, with `Begin` and `End`. (Note the period.) The `Writeln` statements write lines on the screen for us. The `Readln` (read line) pauses the execution of the program and allows the user to enter a response from the keyboard. Thus, `Simple` is very simple and is not a very useful task to give to a computer. Our objective here, however, is to place only one hurdle at a time before you. In this chapter, we will accept the program `Simple` and use it to illustrate how we create, edit, save, list, debug, and run a program with Turbo Pascal.

STARTING TURBO PASCAL

The procedure for starting Turbo Pascal depends on whether you have a hard drive, or only floppy drives, on your computer.

Two Floppy Drives

If you have two floppy drives, then follow these steps:

1. Place your TP System Disk in drive A: and your Turbo Pascal Work Disk (See Appendix B for a description of these disks) in drive B: and turn on the computer.

2. Depending on your system, you may need to enter the date and time, but eventually you will receive the system prompt:

```
A>
```

3. At this point, type

```
B:Turbo
```

and press the RETURN or ENTER key. This will load and launch Turbo Pascal.

One Floppy Drive

If you have only one floppy drive, then follow these instructions:

1. Place your TP System Disk in drive A: and turn on the computer.
2. Answer time and date questions if necessary until you reach the system prompt:

```
A>
```

3. Remove the TP System Disk from drive A: and put the Turbo Pascal Work Disk in drive A:. Type

```
Turbo
```

and press RETURN or ENTER. This will load and launch the Turbo Pascal system.

   As a one-drive user, you will, from time to time, need to swap the disks in drive A:. For example, you will want the TP System Disk (or another data disk) in drive A: when you save programs, and you will need the Turbo Pascal Work Disk in drive A: when you run programs that need the facilities of the Turbo Pascal Libraries or when you want to access the Turbo Pascal built-in help screens. With a little practice, you will learn to know which disk the system needs next.

A Hard Drive

If you have a hard drive, then the instructions are:

1. Turn on the computer.
2. Depending on your system, you may need to enter the date and time, but eventually you will receive the system prompt:

```
C>
```

3. If you followed the standard installation procedure, then the Turbo Pascal programs are in the \TP\ subdirectory, so you need to type

```
CD TP
```

and then press the RETURN or ENTER key to change to that subdirectory of the hard drive.

4. Type

```
Turbo
```

and press the RETURN or ENTER key. This will load and launch the Turbo Pascal system.

TURBO PASCAL'S MAIN SCREEN

Any of the above procedures should, in a few seconds, bring up a copyright message centered in Turbo Pascal's main screen. Press any key to clear the copyright message and display the main screen of Figure 2.1 or 2.2. Figure 2.1 shows the main screen for versions 5.0 and 5.5, while Figure 2.2 shows version 4.0's main screen. These screens are very similar, and the small differences between them are discussed below.

The screen of Figure 2.1 is divided into four areas: the top line, the Edit window, the Watch window (Output window in version 4.0), and the bottom line.

The top line is the main menu with a list of options. The first three of these, File, Edit, and Run, are discussed below. The other four, Compile, Options, Debug, and Break/Watch, are more advanced and will not be discussed until Chapter 7. Version 4.0 users will note that Debug and Break/Watch are features that are not available in their version.

The bottom line displays some of the function keys that are currently active. These function keys provide one-key shortcuts for actions that would otherwise require several keystrokes. Much more will be said about these function-key shortcuts soon. Unfortunately, the function keys perform slightly different operations in version 4.0 from what they do in versions 5.0 and 5.5. These differences are detailed below.

File	Edit	Run	Compile	Options	Debug	Break/Watch
				Edit		
Line 1	Col 1	Insert	Indent	Unindent		A:NONAME.PAS
				Watch		
F1-Help	F5-Zoom	F6-Switch	F7-Trace	F8-Step	F9-Make	F10-Menu

Figure 2.1

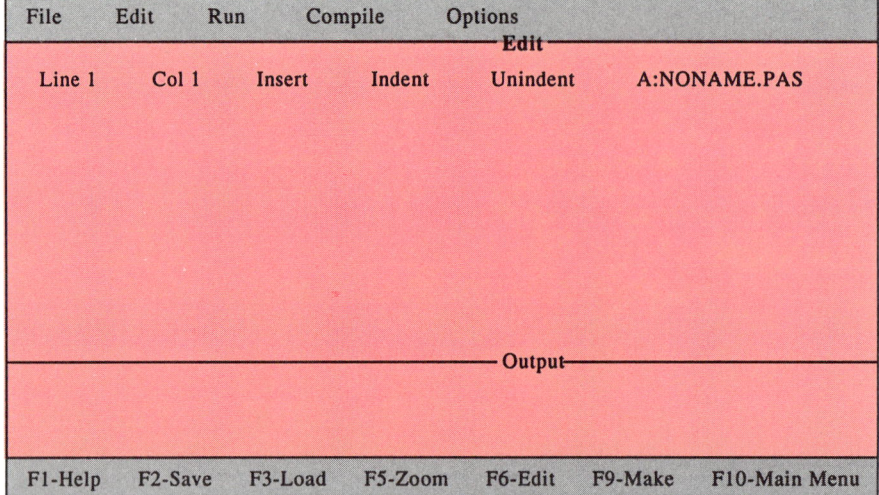

Figure 2.2

The Edit window is where you will edit (create, modify) your program. Turbo Pascal's editor is very powerful and has its own set of commands. A beginner's subset of these is discussed below. More details on the editor will be found in Chapter 7.

The Watch window allows you to observe the contents of the variables in your program as it executes. This is a very valuable tool for debugging programs, but we postpone any discussion of the Watch window until after we have learned more about Pascal. Version 4.0 does not support the Watch window and has the Output window (where the output of our programs appears) in its place. Version 5.0's output window is hidden, but we will soon learn how to make it visible.

CREATING A PROGRAM

Let's use the editor to enter that first Simple program of Listing 2.1. Press the E key to enter the editor. There is now a flashing underscore in the Edit window, indicating that that window is the active window of the system. This means that characters that we type will appear in the Edit window, at the position of the flashing cursor (underscore). Keep in mind that when you want to type a program, you must first enter the editor.

Now, enter the eight lines of the program of Listing 2.1. Please be especially careful about the punctuation details (which are presently mysterious, but will be discussed in the next chapter, where we begin our study of Pascal).

1. Note that exactly four of the lines end in semicolons.
2. Note that the last line ends with a period.
3. Note the use of single quotes in the two Writeln statements. All these are the leftward slanting single quote (`), not the rightward pointing character (').

4. Note the placement of the commas, with respect to the quotation marks, in the second `Writeln`.
5. Note the use of parentheses in the `Writeln` and `Readln` statements.
6. Note the use of indentation for the three statements between the `Begin` and the `End`. To indent the first `Writeln`, press the space bar twice. Observe that the editor remembers this indentation. That is, it automatically returns the cursor to the same indentation on the next line. This is one of the helpful features of the Turbo Pascal editor. To unindent the last line, use the left arrow key (←). Unfortunately, many keyboards have two left arrow keys. Either will work here and the difference between these keys is discussed below.

CORRECTING TYPING ERRORS

If you make any typographical errors, you can correct them as you go with the BACKSPACE key. Suppose you type `Progarm`. You can use the BACKSPACE key to erase characters back to `Prog` and then retype the `ram` to obtain `Program`. A word of caution is necessary to correctly identify the BACKSPACE key on your keyboard. Unfortunately, keyboards are not standard, but this key is usually in the upper right-hand corner of the *main* (or center) section of the keyboard and is usually denoted by a left arrow (←) and/ or some phrase such as BKSP. Be aware that the BACKSPACE key is *not* the left arrow (←) key in the far right-hand section of the keyboard. The use of this key, a cursor-moving key, is discussed below.

If you make a typographical error, and don't notice it right away, you can use the cursor-moving keys to move the cursor to the position of the error. These cursor-moving keys, in the far right section of the keyboard, with up, down, left, and right pointing arrows on them, move the cursor in the obvious manner, without modifying the text of the Edit window. For example, if you notice that you typed `Progrum` on line 1, but you are now on line 7, then you can use the up and left or right arrows to move the cursor to just behind the `u` in `Progrum`. Use BACKSPACE to erase the `u` and then retype the `a`. Now you can use the down arrow key to get back to line 7. Later, we will introduce other cursor-moving keys, but the arrow keys give you enough power to create and edit simple programs. Please note that to use the cursor-moving keys, you must not have the NUM-LOCK key on. If the NUM-LOCK key is on, then the up, down, left, and right arrow keys take on their numeric functions and enter 8s, 2s, 4s, and 6s into your program.

You should experiment with the BACKSPACE key and the cursor-moving keys until you feel comfortable with them. If you didn't make any typing errors while entering the program, then make a couple now, on purpose, just to see how these keys work. It is unfortunate that many keyboards have two left arrow keys that perform distinct operations, but it helps to understand the difference between them by seeing what the two keys actually do.

We want to run our great program, but first we should save it. The program is currently only in the volatile memory of the computer. If the power should fail, the program would be lost. Before that happens, we should put a copy of the program onto disk for safekeeping.

SAVING PROGRAMS

The easiest way to save the program is to press the F2 key. You will save programs frequently, and soon the F2 shortcut for saving will seem very natural to you. F2 is Save in all versions, and version 4.0 continually reminds you of this on the bottom line. Since your program has not been named yet, the system gives it the name NONAME.PAS, as shown in Figure 2.3. Hard-drive users will see NONAME.PAS specified with a different drive and subdirectory, such as C:\TP\. In the future, we will not continue to mention this small distinction. When you press F2, you see the box of Figure 2.3.

  You may, and should, change the name of your program. To do so, simply type the new name and NONAME.PAS will disappear. You can name this program whatever you like, but we think it will help to preserve your sanity to give it the same disk name that you gave it in the program statement. Therefore, we suggest you name this program Simple. The word Simple is sufficient. You do not need the .Pas **extension** (which signifies that Simple is a Pascal program), because Turbo Pascal is smart enough to add this extension by itself. You do not need the drive specification, as this will also be supplied. The name is confirmed, after you type the name Simple and press RETURN, by having the last part of the first line of the Edit window read

A:SIMPLE.PAS

instead of

A:NONAME.PAS

as it did before your save (see Figure 2.1 or 2.2). Note that the system has converted all the characters to uppercase. You can name this program simple, SIMple, or sIMPLE and the system will display it as A:SIMPLE.PAS. When you save your program with no drive specification, it will be saved on the disk or subdirectory from which Turbo Pascal was started. If you followed our instructions for starting Turbo Pascal, this will be A: for floppy-drive users and C:\TP\ for hard-drive users. These are appropriate for now, but later we will see how to save to other disks or subdirectories. Only if your program has not been named will the system give you the chance to name it. So, if you press F2 a second time, your program will be saved without any interaction from you. Try it!

  One last word about disk names is in order. Due to a limitation of PC DOS (the PC's Disk Operating System), names can be only eight characters long (plus the three-character extension PAS). Thus, it is sometimes necessary to abbreviate a program's name to keep it within eight characters.

──── **Rename NONAME** ────

A: \NONAME. PAS

Figure 2.3

RUNNING AND SIMPLE DEBUGGING OF PROGRAMS

Finally, it is time to run our first program. This can be done with one keystroke, but different versions use different keys.

Version 5.0 and 5.5 Users: To run your program, press CTRL–F9.

Version 4.0 Users: To run your program, press ALT-R.

CTRL-F9 means to hold down the control key, usually marked CTRL, like a SHIFT key and then press F9, while still depressing the CTRL key. Likewise, ALT-R means to hold down the ALT key and then press the R key once, while holding down the ALT key. CTRL–F9 (ALT-R) may seem hard to remember as a shortcut for *run*, but you will use this key so frequently that it will soon become second nature to you.

If all goes well, the computer should begin executing your program and prompt you with

```
Hello, what is your name?
```

Let's suppose you type

```
Fred
```

and then press RETURN. In version 4.0, you will see the ouput of your program, which should look like Figure 2.4, in the Output window. With versions 5.0 and 5.5, if your eyes are good, you will see the final line of the output

```
Good to meet you, Fred
```

flash on the screen, before you find yourself back in the editor. For some reason, the later versions of Turbo Pascal do not keep the User or Execution screen (where output appears) active after the program terminates, but automatically return to the editor. You can see the Execution screen in versions 5.0 and 5.5, at any time, by typing ALT-F5 (hold the ALT key down and then press F5). By pressing ALT-F5, you should see the complete execution of your program as in Figure 2.4. Another ALT-F5, or any key for that matter, will return you to the editor.

If you got an error message, instead of the output that we have shown, don't panic. Somehow your program is not exactly like ours. Read your error message carefully, then press the ESC (Escape) key to make the message disappear and return you to the editor. Carefully examine the line in question (and the line above) and the corresponding lines in our program. Use the cursor-moving keys and BACKSPACE to correct your

```
Hello, what is your name?
Fred
Good to meet you, Fred
```

Figure 2.4

program. Save your program again with F2 and run it again with CTRL–F9 or ALT-R. Repeat this process until there are no more error messages and your program runs.

A SECOND PROGRAM

You've gotten your first program to run and it's all downhill from here! Let's try a second program, Buggy, which is shown in Listing 2.2. Buggy has some intentional errors in it, so that you can get used to debugging programs.

   To keep things simple, Buggy is a variant of Simple. It's not fair, since we haven't discussed Pascal yet, to ask you what's wrong with Buggy, but by careful comparison of the two programs, you can see that they do differ in several ways. Let's enter Buggy and see what happens.

CLEARING THE EDIT WINDOW

How can we enter Buggy with Simple already in the Edit window? Actually, the two programs are so similar that it would be reasonable to edit Simple and change it into Buggy, but, for the practice, let's see how to clear the Edit window. There is no one-key shortcut for the clear command and, therefore, we will use the following three-keystroke sequence:

1. Press the F10 key to exit the editor and return to the main menu.
2. Press the F key to bring down the File menu. This gives you a new menu of nine items: Load, Pick, New, Save, Write to, Directory, Change dir, OS shell, and Quit. These will all be discussed in a later section; for now we want New because we are beginning a new program.
3. Press the N key to select New. If you have not saved the current version of the program in the editor, you will be asked if you want to save it before the editor is cleared.

   Note that the name of the program in the first status line of the editor is again NONAME.PAS. The system is back to the state it was in when you first loaded Turbo Pascal.


```
Program Buggy;
{Watch it, this program has some intentional bugs in it. }
Var Name : String[30];
Begin
  Print('Hello, what is your name?');
  Readln(Nane);
  Writeln'Good to meat you, ' , Name)
End.
```

Listing 2.2

DEBUGGING PROGRAMS

Now, enter the program `Buggy` exactly as it is shown in Listing 2.2. Save (F2) your program and run (CTRL–F9 or ALT-R) your program. If your program is just like ours, you will get the error message

`Error 3: Unknown identifier`

and the cursor will be flashing under the `P` in `Print`. As you may have guessed, Pascal uses a `Writeln`, not a `Print`, to do its output, and the system is simply saying that it does not know how to `Print`.

We introduce a new editing key to help us replace `Print` with `Writeln`. This key is the dclcte or DEL key and is very much like the BACKSPACE key. The difference is that the BACKSPACE key erases the character to the *left* of the cursor and the DEL key erases the character at the cursor's position, with the character to the *right* then filling in for the deleted character. Since the cursor is at the `P` of `Print`, pressing the DEL key five times deletes `Print`. We then type `Writeln` and the error is fixed!

Save and run the new version of the program. We get the same error message about an unknown identifier. Are we getting anywhere? Actually, we are, since the cursor is now flashing under the `N` in `Nane`. What's wrong with that? After all, we did declare `Name` in the `Var` section of our program. Careful inspection, however, shows that we declared `Name` and then, apparently by mistake, typed `Nane` with an `n` instead of an `m`. The computer is certainly fussy!

We could make this error go away by declaring `Nane` in the `Var` section. That's what we should do if we had intended to use `Nane`, but had forgotten to declare it. Here, however, we don't want a variable `Nane`. We want to edit `Nane` and make it `Name`. You should not let the computer tell you what to do, but should decide, based upon your intent, what needs to be done to correct the error. In this case, we simply use the right arrow to move over to the `n`, use DEL to delete it, and then type the `m` in its place. Again, save and run your program.

This time we get the error message

`Error 85: ";" expected`

and the cursor is flashing under the first quotation mark in the final `Writeln`. This is a good example of a poor error message. We say the example is good, because it is good for you to see that error messages are not always much help in diagnosing the actual problem. We say the message is poor, since the problem has nothing to do with a semicolon. Nevertheless, the beginner seems to think that the computer is ordering him or her to put a semicolon at this spot. If you do so, then you will just get another error (`Error in statement`) on the same line. To solve the problem, you must think about what you intended to do (a `Writeln` statement) and, if necessary, look up the syntax of that statement. As mentioned before, a `Writeln` statement encloses what is to be written within parentheses. In this case, the left parenthesis was omitted. Hence, all we need do is insert a `(`. Do this, then save and run again.

Amazing! This time the program ran (if you have no other errors in it). Maybe you were surprised that the program ran even though `meat` was misspelled. As we will see in the next chapter, Pascal will accept any string, even `'Paskal'`, if it is between quotation marks.

We hope you followed along with us in the debugging of `Buggy`. You will certainly make mistakes when writing programs, so you will probably get plenty of practice at it. Indeed, you can't call yourself a programmer unless you can also debug your programs. When you get an error message, remember that the computer doesn't know what you are trying to do, and often its error messages will not be very helpful. You are the only one who knows what your *intent* was, and that must be your guide in fixing the bug. If you do not quickly see your error, then examine the syntax of similar statements in the book, or look up the syntax of the given statement. The computer is almost certainly *not* broken and you almost certainly *have* violated the grammar of Pascal. If you can't find the problem yourself, then you will, of course, have to get help from someone. If you get help, make sure that afterwards you understand what the problem was, so that if it ever happens again you will be able to fix it yourself.

You now have the minimal skills you need to use the Turbo Pascal editor to create and modify programs. You can also save, run, and debug simple programs. The remainder of this chapter builds on this knowledge to make you a more sophisticated user of Turbo Pascal. Since there is so much to learn about the Turbo Pascal system, we will not reveal all of it now, but will return to this subject in Chapter 7. We suggest that you read and try to digest (but not memorize) the topics that follow in this chapter. You should try to understand *what* the system can do for you, perhaps without worrying about all the details at this time. Then, as we begin to introduce Pascal in the next chapters, you can return to the topics listed here and try them out.

WINDOWING

As shown in Figure 2.1, in the later versions of Turbo Pascal, there are two windows, the Edit window and the Watch window. The key, F6, labeled Switch on the bottom line, takes you back and forth between these windows. We will discuss the use of the Watch window in Chapter 7.

The key F5 zooms the currently active window (where the cursor is located). By zooming, we mean that it makes the window large, if it was small, and makes it small, if it was large. That is, F5 toggles the size of the given window. It is often convenient, with a large program, to make the Edit window the full size of the screen. This permits you to see as much of the surrounding program as possible.

You can use F5 (Zoom) in combination with F6 (Switch) to zoom either of the windows in or out. Recall that, in versions 5.0 and 5.5, you can see the User screen (Output window) with ALT-F5. Try out these keys, so that you see what the possibilities are.

In version 4.0, the two windows of the main screen are the Edit window and the Output window. F6 again switches between these windows. It is labeled Output when you are in the Edit window, and Edit when you are in the Output window. Likewise, F5 zooms either of these windows to full size.

LOADING PROGRAMS FROM DISK

Earlier, we saved a program Simple to the disk. Let's suppose that we want to do some more work on that program. By pressing F3 (the shortcut for load) and typing Simple (and RETURN), we can load Simple into the editor. Furthermore, if the contents of the editor have not been saved, you will be given the opportunity to save them before they are overwritten by the loading of Simple.

One word of caution is that Turbo Pascal will look only in one place for your program. If you started Turbo Pascal as we indicated, Turbo Pascal will look only on the A: drive or in C:\TP\ (and should, therefore, find Simple because that is where it was saved). To load a program, Diffcult (eight-letter maximum explains spelling), which is now on a disk in drive B:, you will have to type B:Diffcult after pressing F3. Later, we will see that you can instruct Turbo Pascal always to look on drive B: instead of on drive A:. Or, if you have a hard drive, you can instruct Turbo Pascal to look in another subdirectory of the hard drive. (See the Change dir command in the discussion of the File menu below.)

Suppose we want to load a program but we can't remember exactly what we called it. In this case, we can give the system a wild card and let it list all the programs on the disk for us. To do this, proceed as follows:

1. Press F3, type *.Pas, and then press RETURN. If the Load-File-Name box already contains *.Pas, you don't need to type it again. You will need to type a B:*.Pas if you want to load something from drive B:, or C:\TP\Samples*.Pas to load from the subdirectory Samples of the hard drive. The character * is the wild card that will match with any program name.
2. The system will display all the Pascal programs (in alphabetical order) on the given drive or subdirectory. The first will be highlighted (shown in inverse video), and the highlighting can be moved by using the arrow keys. Typing a letter, such as S, will also move the highlighting. In this case, the first program to begin with that letter is highlighted. When you have highlighted the program that you want to load, press RETURN and the program you have selected will be loaded.

In many ways, the above method is the easiest way to load any program, even one for which you remember the name. This new method requires almost no typing and allows you to select the program by *pointing* at it with the arrow keys.

THE FILE MENU

The File menu provides various housekeeping tasks that, from time to time, are necessary. Figure 2.5 shows the menu that is obtained by pressing F10, if necessary, to get to the main menu (top line of the screen) and then pressing the F (File) key.

All these menu items can be selected in either of two ways, and some can be selected in a third way (by using the one-keystroke shortcuts shown). First, you can type the first letter of the item (N for New, for example) or, second, you can use the up and down arrow keys to highlight the item that you want and then press RETURN to select it. Try both of these ways and decide which method seems simpler to you. Finally, for those choices such as Load, for which a shortcut is shown, you can type that single key to invoke the choice. Turbo Pascal is generally well designed, with the most commonly used commands having single-key shortcuts. By repeated use, these shortcuts will soon seem natural to you.

Load has already been discussed extensively through its shortcut, F3. Because it is more convenient, you will probably continue to use F3 to load programs, but you can use **Load** from the File menu to accomplish the same action.

Pick displays up to eight of the most recent programs that you have worked on and permits you to pick one of them for loading into the editor. Pick is a fairly specialized option that the beginner need not worry about. It can, however, be a very useful option when you are working on several programs at once.

New clears the edit window and gives you a blank page on which to create a new program. New will ask, if you haven't saved, if you want to save the current contents of the editor.

Save writes the current contents of the editor to the disk using the name supplied in the editor status line. If the name is NONAME.PAS, then the user is asked to supply a name. Save writes to the disk that Turbo Pascal was started from, unless you give directory information in the name or change the directory with the Change dir command (see below). Save has a single-key shortcut, F2, that you will probably find more convenient than bringing down the File menu.

Write to prompts the user for a new name for the current contents of the editor and then writes the program to disk using this new name. If a file with the new name already exists, the system asks the user if the old file should be overwritten. Write to also updates the name in the status line to reflect the new name of the program. Subsequent Saves will be made using this new name. Write to, in summary, is a save that allows the file to be renamed as it is saved.

Directory displays the files that are stored on a given disk or subdirectory. When you select Directory, you are prompted for a mask, which is computerese for a pattern to look for. The mask suggested by the system is *.*, which means to look for any file with any extension. If you press RETURN, you will see the directory of the disk that Turbo Pascal was started from. You can type B:*.* or C:\TP\Samples*.*, if you want

```
Load              F3
Pick          ALT-F3
New
Save              F2
Write to
Directory
Change dir
OS shell
Quit          ALT-X
```

Figure 2.5

the directory of another disk or subdirectory. The mask $*$.Pas will display just the Pascal programs (on the startup disk), while the mask Z$*$.$*$ will display all files that begin with the letter Z. As the bottom line shows, once you have a directory, you can get help (F1), enter a new mask (F4), choose a file with the arrow keys, load the selected file with RETURN, or abort (ESC). Abort, as harsh as it sounds, is the proper way to exit from the Directory command, if you don't want to load any program. Since Load permits the same use of wildcards, and displays the same directories, we think you will find Load (especially through its shortcut, F3) more convenient than the Directory command.

Change dir allows you to select the disk or subdirectory that you want programs saved to, or loaded from. As we have mentioned several times, Turbo Pascal always saves to, and loads from, the startup disk or subdirectory. To save or load programs on drive B:, choose Change dir and then type the new directory B:\ and RETURN.

OS shell permits the user to suspend the Turbo Pascal system, exit to the operating system (DOS), and then return to Turbo Pascal at the point where it was suspended. To return to Turbo Pascal from the operating system shell, you simply type EXIT. Later in the chapter, we see how to use the OS shell to print the execution from a program.

Quit exits Turbo Pascal and returns the user to the DOS (operating system) level. Quit will prompt the user, if the current contents of the editor have not been saved.

HOT KEYS

Turbo Pascal defines several hot keys that provide effective shortcuts in many situations. Most of the hot keys listed below have already been discussed, but we have collected them together, in Table 2.1, for your quick reference. Most of these keys apply in all versions, but the few differences between 4.0 and the later versions are noted in the table. The notation 5.X means version 5.0 or version 5.5.

Table 2.1

Versions	Key	Action
All	F1	Help
All	F2	Save
All	F3	Load
All	F5	Zoom
All	F6	Switch (switches Edit and Watch in 5.0 and 5.5) (switches Edit and Output in 4.0)
All	F10	Toggles between Main menu and active window
All	ALT-E	Go to Edit window
All	ALT-F	Go to File menu
All	ALT-X	Exit from Turbo Pascal
5.X	CTRL-F9	Run the program in the Edit window
4.0	ALT-R	Run the program in the Edit window
5.X	ALT-F5	Go to the User screen (Output window)

All the hot keys, except F1, ALT-E, ALT-F, and ALT-X, have already been discussed. **F1** provides you with context-sensitive help. That is, the help that the system provides depends on what you are doing when you ask for help. Try F1 in several situations to see the kind of on-line help that is available. ALT-**E** takes you directly to the editor from wherever you are. ALT-**F** brings down the File menu and is, therefore, short for F10 (Main menu) followed by F (File menu). ALT-**X** is the quick way to exit from Turbo Pascal. It is equivalent to the three-keystroke sequence: F10 (Main menu), F (File menu), and Q (Quit). ALT-**X** will ask, if you haven't saved your program, if you want to save it before you quit.

ADDITIONAL CURSOR-MOVING KEYS

We have already learned to use the four arrow keys, which are the principal cursor-moving keys. However, in larger programs, the use of these four keys can become quite tedious. For example, if we are at the right end of a line and want to go to the beginning of that line, we can get there with left arrow keys, but if the line is long, this is very tiresome. Likewise, if we are at the bottom of the file and want to go to the top, we can get there with up arrows, but it is tedious to do so. Therefore, we introduce 10 new cursor-control keys in Table 2.2 and invite you to try them out. Remember this section, for reference, when you find yourself involved in tiresome and tedious cursor movements.

The commands in Table 2.2 are fairly easy to remember, if you will notice that the CTRL key makes the action of a key bigger than it is by itself. For example, the Left

Table 2.2

Key	Action
Right Arrow	Right one character
Left Arrow	Left one character
Up Arrow	Up one line
Down Arrow	Down one line
HOME	To the beginning of the current line
END	To the end of the current line
PgUP	Scroll up one page on the screen
PgDN	Scroll down one page on the screen
CTRL-Left Arrow	Left one word
CTRL-Right Arrow	Right one word
CTRL-HOME	Top of the screen
CTRL-END	Bottom of the screen
CTRL-PgUP	Top of the file
CTRL-PgDN	Bottom of the file

Arrow key, by itself, moves left one character, while CTRL-Left Arrow moves left a word at a time. Remember that the CTRL key is used like a SHIFT key; you hold down the CTRL key while pressing the other key.

PRINTING A LISTING OF A PROGRAM

You will probably want to keep listings of all your programs for quick reference. During the installation procedure, we had you place the program Lister on your startup disk. It is this Turbo Pascal program that will produce listings for you. Use it as follows:

1. Be sure the contents of the editor have been saved (F2).
2. Load Lister from your startup disk (F3 ...).
3. Make sure the printer is turned on and ready to print.
4. Run Lister (CTRL-F9 or ALT-R).
5. You will be prompted for the name of the file to print. Type MyProg.Pas to print MyProg. The extension .Pas is required here. Also, you will need to type B:MyProg.Pas if you have MyProg on a disk in drive B:.

At this point, the printing of your program listing should begin. Lister is just a Pascal program that reads your program from the disk and prints it. Lister will paginate your program if it is longer than one page, so check that the printer head is at the top of the page before printing your program. If you want to see what a longer Pascal program looks like, use Lister to print out a listing of Lister.Pas.

PRINTING AN EXECUTION OF A PROGRAM

You can also get the execution of your program in a hard-copy (paper) form. The easiest way to do this is to send the output from the screen to the printer. To do this, follow these instructions:

1. Type ALT-F to bring down the File menu.
2. Type the letter O (not the digit zero) to invoke the OS shell command. This will temporarily exit you from Turbo Pascal and give you a system prompt such as A> or C:\TP>.
3. Make sure the printer is turned on and ready, and then type CTRL-P. You will not see anything in response to your typing. Make sure that you hold down the CTRL key, while pressing the P key once. CTRL-P toggles the printing of the screen on and off, so if you accidentally type two CTRL-P's you will not accomplish anything!
4. Type the word EXIT to return to Turbo Pascal. At this point, you should hear a brief noise from the printer. If you inspect the paper in the printer, you should see that the EXIT you typed has been printed.
5. Run your program with CTRL-F9 or ALT-R. You will see the output on the screen, and the printer will produce a copy of the execution for you.
6. You must now repeat steps 1 to 4 (ALT-F, O, CTRL-P, and EXIT) in order to break the

connection with the printer. If you forget to do this, everything that you do will continue to be sent to the printer.

The above procedure is the simplest way that we know of to obtain a hard copy of the execution of your program. However, this method does not work if your program contains `Uses CRT`. See the discussion below for the purpose of the `Uses CRT` statement, and our suggestion for printing the execution of programs that contain this statement.

CLEARING THE OUTPUT WINDOW OR USER EXECUTION SCREEN

You may have already noticed that, when you run a program, it doesn't clear the output from previous programs, but simply adds its output to the same window. This can make it difficult to tell where the output of the previous program ends and the current program begins. It would be nice if we could clear the Output window as the program begins its execution. Turbo Pascal has provided for this with a `ClrScr` (clear screen) routine, but, unfortunately, `ClrScr` is not built in. It is provided in a library called `CRT` (Cathode Ray Tube) and to use `ClrScr`, you need do only the following:

1. Place the statement

   `Uses CRT;`

   immediately after the `Program` statement (or after the comment after the `Program` statement).

2. Place the statement

   `ClrScr;`

   immediately after the `Begin` of your program.

The `Uses` statement lets your program access any of the routines from the `CRT` library. `ClrScr` is the only one we need now, but the interested reader is referred to the Turbo Pascal manuals to see the other kinds of things that are in the library. See Listing 2.3, which shows `Simple2`, a new version of `Simple`, illustrating the use of the statements `Uses CRT` and `ClrScr`. Run `Simple` and `Simple2` to see the differences in their execution.

We strongly recommend the use of `ClrScr` in all your programs. We have included `Uses Crt` and `ClrScr` in all the sample programs, from this program forward, on the disk that accompanies this book. However, to conserve space, `Uses Crt` and `ClrScr` *will not be shown in our listings.*

As alluded to above, there is a problem with our method for printing the execution of a program that contains the `ClrScr` statement. Namely, it doesn't work—`ClrScr` is not a command that a printer understands, and rather than just ignore that statement, our experience has been that none of the execution is printed. We have argued that

```
Program Simple2;
{This simple program prompts the user for his or her name and
illustrates the use of Uses CRT and ClrScr.                   }
Uses CRT;
Var Name : String[30];
Begin
  ClrScr;
  Writeln('Hello, what is your name?');
  Readln(Name);
  Writeln('Good to meet you, ', Name)
End.
```

Listing 2.3

ClrScr is very useful, and, in a class situation, printing the execution of a program is certainly necessary. Fortunately, there is a fairly simple solution to our problem, and the next paragraph shows us how we can have our cake and eat it, too.

Because ClrScr is helpful as you develop and debug your program at a video monitor, we suggest that you include Uses CRT and ClrScr as you write your program. Then, when you are ready to print the execution of your program, you must *cancel* these two commands. Instead of physically deleting them, we suggest that you make comments of them as follows:

1. Use the up and down arrows to bring the cursor to the Uses CRT line. Press HOME and then the opening brace, {. Press END and the closing brace, }. The line should now read

   {Uses CRT;}

2. Move down to the ClrScr line and make a comment of it in the same manner.

Now you can print the execution of your program as described above, because the offending statements are treated simply as comments. The advantage of commenting-out, rather than deleting, these two statements is that they can be restored to the program by deleting just four braces.

SAMPLE DISK OF PROGRAMS TO ACCOMPANY THIS BOOK

For your convenience, a disk is available to accompany this book. This disk contains over 100 programs and text files. Included are all sample programs from the book (such as Simple, Buggy, and Simple2 of this chapter), buggy programs for the exercises (see Bugs below), as well as text files that provide data for the sample programs and the exercises. The disk is offered so that you can spend your time examining, running, modifying, and debugging our sample programs instead of typing in the examples. To order this disk, see the coupon at the end of the book. Because of the number of programs on the sample disk, it is organized into subdirectories named \Ch2\ to \Ch20\. For example, to load Buggy from our sample disk (which we suppose is in drive A:), press F3, then type A:\Ch2\Buggy and press RETURN.

FINAL WORDS OF ENCOURAGEMENT

We hope this introduction to the Turbo Pascal system has been successful for you. You should work through the examples in the text until you feel reasonably comfortable about the system. The entire system has not been presented in this chapter, but the subset of the system that we have discussed should be enough to allow the beginner to create, debug, run, save, and load simple programs. Later, we will introduce cutting and pasting for quick editing of programs and we will introduce powerful debugging aids. First, however, you need to learn some Pascal, and that is the subject of the next chapter (indeed, of most of the rest of this book).

SELF-TEST QUESTIONS

2.1 Distinguish between the BACKSPACE key and the DEL key.

2.2 Describe 10 cursor-moving operations and give the keystroke for each.

2.3 How do you save your program? Why do you save your program?

2.4 How do you clear the Edit window?

2.5 How do you load a program into the editor?

2.6 How, in your version of Turbo Pascal, do you run the program in the Edit window?

2.7 What is the difference between the listing and the execution of your program?

EXERCISES

2.8 Enter, debug, and run the following program, Cubes. Cubes is a correct program, so you will not need to debug it, unless you add your own errors. Because of integer overflow, however, you will need to keep the input to the program at 31 or less.

```
Program Cubes;
{This program cubes your favorite number.}
Var   Number : Integer;
      Cube   : Integer;
```

```
Begin
  Writeln('Please enter a small whole number.');
  Readln(Number);
  Cube := Number * Number * Number;
  Writeln('The cube of your number is ', Cube)
End.
```

2.9 Make some intentional errors to your program `Cubes` to see how the system reacts. In particular, omit the declaration of the variable `Cube` in the `Var` section, and change the `:=` of the third line after the `Begin` to an `=` by itself. This last error is another common one for beginning programmers. Hence, it is a good idea to get used to the error message that it generates.

2.10 The program `Bugs`, given below, has five intentional errors in it. Although we haven't discussed Pascal yet, can you find the five errors? If you have any trouble doing so, let the Turbo Pascal compiler help you! That is, enter and try to run the program, then fix the errors as they are identified by the compiler. To save you typing time, this program is also available on the sample disk that accompanies the book as `\Ch2\Bugs`.

```
Program Bugs:
{This program converts your age from years to weeks (approxi-
mately). The program has five intentional bugs in it. Can you
find them?                                                       }

Variable Years : Integer;
         Weeks : Integer;
Begin
  Writeln('How old are you?');
  Readln(Years);
  Weeks = Years * 52;              {* denotes multiplication.}
  Writeln('You are ', Weeks, ' weeks old.')
End
```

ANSWERS TO SELF-TEST QUESTIONS

2.1 BACKSPACE deletes the character to the left of the cursor, while DEL deletes the character at the cursor.

2.2 See Table 2.2, which describes 14 cursor-moving operations.

2.3 To save your program, press F2 and name the program (if not done already). You save programs because otherwise they are in the volatile memory of the computer and will be lost when the computer is turned off.

2.4 Press ALT-F to get the File menu. Select N for New.

2.5 To load a program, press the F3 key. Enter the name of the program or * . Pas to see all the programs on the disk. Select a program by highlighting and press RETURN.

2.6 To run your program, press CTRL-F9 in versions 5.0 and 5.5; press ALT-R in version 4.0.

2.7 The listing is a list of the actual instructions that make up the program. See Listing 2.1 for an example of a program listing. The execution of your program is what it produces when it runs. The execution is the output of your program. See Figure 2.3 for an example.

3

BEGINNING PASCAL

In this chapter, we will learn how to write computer programs in Pascal. A program is nothing more than the expression of an algorithm in a language that the computer can understand. As such, a program is a set of instructions that the computer carries out (or executes). Programs can, in general, be executed without human intervention, and it is this property that makes computers so useful and so much more powerful than calculators, which can, of course, do many of the things that a computer can do. For example, averaging three bowling scores is a simple task on a calculator. We enter the three scores, adding each one to the previous total, and then divide by three. But a secretary of a bowling league might find this process a little tedious after handling dozens of bowlers. Since the process of averaging is the same regardless of the scores involved, it would be nice if we could teach our calculator how to average three numbers. Then, whenever we needed to prepare a league statistics sheet, we could provide the numbers to the calculator, but we wouldn't have to keep repeating the add and divide instructions. This is essentially what computers (and some programmable calculators) can do.

To teach the computer how to do something, all we need to do is figure out for ourselves how this something is to be accomplished and, then, communicate this to the machine in a language that it understands. Interestingly enough, while it is the second job that most people consider computer programming, it is the first task (designing the algorithm) that is the most important. So, we state here for emphasis a fundamental truth of programming:

The computer cannot solve any problem that the programmer, in principle, cannot solve first.

Throughout this book, we will try to introduce methods whereby both algorithm design and programming can be learned. While Turbo Pascal will be our vehicle for communicating with the computer, we will use what are considered to be sound, general programming techniques that can be applied to nearly any situation.

47

A PASCAL PROGRAM

Because computers are very literal-minded and always do exactly what you tell them (instead of what you meant to tell them), when we communicate with computers we have to be very precise about how we say things, and we must learn to obey exactly the rules of the language we are using. Pascal is no exception. This precise way of expressing a program is known as the **syntax** of the language—how programs are physically constructed or, even more specifically, what strings of letters, numbers, and punctuation marks constitute a legal Pascal program. We begin by looking at the overall structure of a Pascal program.

Listing 3.1 is an example of a complete, but very simple, Pascal program. There is a **heading**, which consists of the word Program followed by the name of the program. The name is selected by the programmer, should start with a letter and then be followed by letters or numbers, and can be pretty much whatever we want, except for some **reserved** words (or **keywords**) that mean special things in Pascal (like Begin, End, and Program). A list of Turbo Pascal reserved words is found in Appendix D. Note that the program name is followed by a semicolon.

Following the heading is the **body** of the program. The body begins with the keyword Begin and ends with the keyword End. The keyword End may occur several times in a Pascal program, but there is always an End to mark the end of the program and this End must be followed by a period. In fact, this is the only time that End. should occur in a program.

Between the Begin and End. of the body come the statements of the program. These statements are the instructions that the computer is supposed to carry out. The next several chapters of this book will introduce you to the kinds of statements that you can use in a Pascal program. There aren't many, so it really doesn't take long to master the Pascal syntax. This is the easy part of programming. There also aren't that many keywords to worry about. Most of the keywords do what they should; e.g., Begin marks the start of something, End marks the end.

The first Pascal statement we consider is the Writeln statement. Writeln is an example of an output statement that causes something to be printed to the screen. It is Pascal's way of allowing us to get information out of a computer. In a Writeln, if we place something in parentheses and between single quotes, the computer will print exactly what it sees. To emphasize how precise we need to be in programming languages, we point out that using regular quotation marks, "like this," instead of single

```
Program Example;
{This program illustrates the use of Writelns with strings.}
Begin
  Writeln('Here is a complete Pascal program.');
  Writeln('Even though I am just learning, I think');
  Writeln('I can figure out what it does.')
End.
```

Listing 3.1

quotation marks, 'like this,' will cause a syntax error, as will forgetting either parenthesis.

Every language has an output statement, but different languages say things differently. So, instead of `Writeln`, you might have to say `Print` or `Put`, but the effect is the same. Many beginners to programming ask why things have to be different. The answer is that different languages were designed by different people and there is no reason to expect that computer-language designers, as a group, should be able to get along and agree on things any better than any other group of people. There are several brands of microwave ovens on the market, and their keyboards look very different, with ENTER keys and START keys and COOK keys that perform the same function. As Steve Martin once pointed out in a comedy routine, "Those French have a different word for everything!" Actually, because computer languages are small and more uniform than most other forms of communication, the differences among them are easily overcome once we become programmers. Good Pascal programmers can learn BASIC in a few hours and FORTRAN in a few days. So the moral of the story is:

Learn the concepts. Mastering the language will then follow.

If we expect programming languages to be logically designed, it is certainly fair to wonder a little bit about the choice of `Writeln` for writing something. What's wrong with `Write`? The answer is, nothing! In fact, `Write` is the other type of output statement in Pascal. If all this is supposed to be logical, why a `Writeln` *and* a `Write`? Remember that a program is generally run without human intervention. Many times, the output of a computer program is an extensive written report, and the most important thing about the appearance of the report is its layout on the paper—for example, in five columns across the page. Since programs are run without human intervention, we don't have anyone to throw the typewriter carriage for us to get to the next line. The computer has to know when to advance the output to the next line. But the computer doesn't know unless we tell it. That is what the `ln` after the word `Write` does. It is simply a signal to the computer to move to a new line *after* it has written the `Writeln` message. Thus, the program in Listing 3.1 should print out the quoted message (the quotes are not printed) on three lines, while the program in Listing 3.2 will print its message on two lines.

```
Program Example2:

{This program illustrates the use of Writes and Writelns.}

Begin
  Write('Now I see the difference between "Write"');
  Writeln(' and "Writeln"');
  Writeln('and will never confuse the two.')
End.
```

Listing 3.2

Figures 3.1 and 3.2 show the output from the programs in Listings 3.1 and 3.2, respectively.

```
Here is a complete Pascal program.
Even though I am just learning, I think
I can figure out what it does.
```

Figure 3.1

```
Now I see the difference between "Write" and "Writeln"
and will never confuse the two.
```

Figure 3.2

We, of course, will not discuss every aspect of Pascal in such agonizing detail. As we become more comfortable with Pascal, a few remarks will usually suffice. But there are two points to the above discussion:

1. Pascal (for the most part) is a well-designed language, and there is usually a good reason for why things are done the way they are.
2. Even in these simple examples, you should be able to see that the power of these sample programs (i.e., when to start printing on a new line) is derived from the programmer *telling* the computer what to do and not vice versa.

THE SEMICOLON IN PASCAL

We make one final comment about the syntax of the above examples. The body of a Pascal program consists of a sequence of statements. To *separate* one statement from the next, Pascal uses the semicolon. Notice that the last statement in each program does not have a semicolon after it. This is because the semicolon does *not terminate* statements, but is used *between* statements. In this regard, the semicolon is used like the comma in English, rather than like the period. The period is a terminator in English, and every sentence ends with a period or another terminator such as the question mark or exclamation mark. The comma, on the other hand, is used in lists to separate the elements. Consider a list of four computer languages:

FORTRAN, COBOL, Pascal, Ada

This list of four items is separated by three commas. You would consider it odd to find another comma at the end of the list. Hopefully, this example helps to make the distinction between a separator and a terminator clear. Remember, the semicolon is a separator in Pascal. Although this seems like nitpicking, probably the most common syntax error made by beginning programmers is an error involving a semicolon. More will be said about this later, when we deal with conditional statements. For now, our programs will consist of a sequence of simple statements. Place a semicolon after each one except the last one. Actually, because we are honest, we point out that an extra semicolon after the last statement will not cause an error message. We are so fussy, because extra semicolons in other places will cause you errors, and we want you to learn to use semicolons correctly. If you understand the separator/terminator distinction, you will have no problems and will agree that a semicolon after the last statement is superfluous in this case.

VARIABLES AND MEMORY LOCATIONS

The concept of a variable is most important for a beginning programmer to understand. Edsgar Dijkstra, an important voice in the computer-science community, said, "Once a programmer learns the concept of a variable, he has learned the quintessence of programming." We strongly concur with this sentiment and, in fact, believe that it also applies to female programmers as well. Once you learn exactly how variables behave, you should have no trouble grasping the more complex features of programming.

We begin with the analogy of a simple calculator. Many hand-held calculators have a special button, usually called M or MEM or STORE, for storing a particular value. This is useful in the following type of situation:

Compute (123 + 456 + 789) / (987 + 654 + 321)

Note that we really have to compute several additions before we can even begin to think about performing the division. If we had a primitive calculator (with no Memory key), we might want to have a pencil and piece of paper handy to help perform this calculation. We first add 987, 654, and 321, obtaining 1962. Then we clear the calculator and add 123, 456, and 789 to obtain 1368. So all we do is divide 1368 by, uh, let's see, what was the result of that first calculation? I forgot, so I'll do it again. That's right, 1962. So I divide 1962 into, uh, now I forgot the result of the other calculation. With a pencil and paper, we could at least write down the 1962; then, when we do our second set of additions, we simply look at the paper to find our divisor. But how much simpler this becomes if our calculator has a Memory key. We do the first calculation and *store* the answer using the M key. The calculator will remember this result for us. For the time being, the M key can help us get this result back. That is, we can imagine that M equals 1962. Now after we add 123, 456, and 789, we simply instruct the calculator to divide this sum by M. No pencil, no paper, no repeating any calculation. Our memory is not so good, so we use the calculator's memory.

If you followed the above example, you should appreciate how convenient it is that the calculator had a memory, even though it could remember only one number for us. In fact, it doesn't take us very long to wish our calculator could remember two numbers. Consider the computation

(321 * 987 - 123 * 789) / (123 + 456 + 789)

If we had two memory keys, M1 and M2, we could add 123, 456, and 789 and store the result in M1. Then, we multiply 123 by 789 and store that result in M2. Finally, we multiply 321 by 987, subtract M2, and then divide that result by M1.

Of course, it is not long before our greed begins to show, and we think that the more memory locations we have, the more things we could do. Well, from a memory standpoint, computers are essentially like calculators. But computers have thousands (some even millions) of memory locations that we can use. In fact, when you hear people, mostly computer salespeople, talking about Ks, as in 640K-machine, they are telling you how many RAM memory locations you have to work with. All we have to do is learn how to use these memory locations. This is where variables come in.

Imagine a very large keyboard with keys M1, M2, M3, ... , M100, ... , M640000. Without the concept of variables, this is what we might be stuck with to handle the approximately 640,000 memory locations at our disposal. Like a calculator, the computer would keep track of the names of the locations for us. Not only would the keyboard be rather awkward, but we might also have a hard time remembering whether we put the calculation that we did five minutes ago in M3478 or in M3487. The power of variables is that the computer allows us to call the memory locations anything we want! In other words, **a variable is just a name for a memory location**. While this may seem like a small breakthrough, it is precisely this idea that makes programming so accessible. Now, when we want to save a piece of information, we think up a name for where this information should be stored. Then, when we want this information back, all we have to do is remember the name. The important point here is that *we, the programmers,* are allowed to select the name. So if we are computing how much money we spent last month on recreation, we could store our subtotals in memory locations called Movies, Restaurants, and Skiing, instead of locations like M1, M2, and M3.

IDENTIFIERS IN PASCAL

Variables in Pascal are often called **identifiers**. We will use the two terms identifier and variable interchangeably. In Pascal, identifiers must start with a letter and then be followed by letters or digits. Turbo Pascal also allows identifiers to contain underscores (but they still must start with a letter). The underscore serves the purpose of a blank space, which is not allowed in legal variables. So, `First Name` is an illegal identifier, but `First_Name` is legal in Turbo Pascal. Also, Pascal does not worry about the case of letters in identifiers, so `First_Name` and `first_name` refer to the same memory location. In this text, we will not use the underscore but will capitalize the first letter of each significant word in a variable. Thus, we will use `FirstName` instead of any of

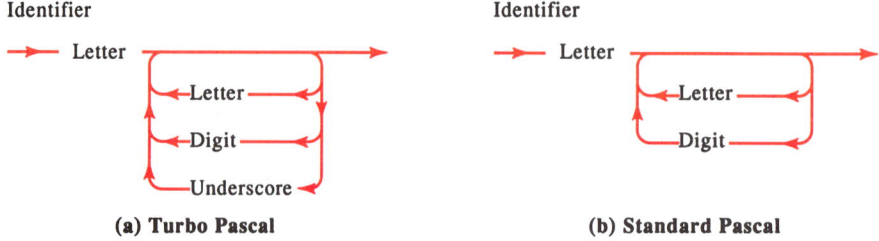

(a) Turbo Pascal   (b) Standard Pascal

Figure 3.3

the above. We adopt this uppercase and lowercase convention because we think it makes variables very readable. We urge you to do likewise in your programs.

The syntax (grammar) of Pascal constructs is often given using **railroad** or **syntax diagrams**. We illustrate these in Figure 3.3, which contrasts the railroad diagrams for identifiers in Turbo Pascal and in standard Pascal. These figures are called railroad diagrams because, by driving around and around the tracks in the given directions and choosing objects of the indicated types, you can produce any legal identifier. The identifier A3b_x is a legal Turbo Pascal identifier, as can be seen by choosing the letter A, then looping through the digit circuit selecting 3, and so on, finally exiting after selecting the x. Obviously there is no way to generate A3b_x using the standard Pascal diagram, so it is an illegal identifier in standard Pascal.

These diagrams provide a concise way to summarize the syntax of Pascal and provide a very quick reference for the programmer who needs to check out a certain detail of the language. For this reason, we have gathered all the railroad diagrams for Pascal in Appendix C: Syntax Diagrams. When you get a compiler error involving some violation of the language, turn to the proper syntax diagram to see if it will help you understand how you have violated Pascal's syntax. It is also instructive for the reader to draw his or her own diagrams, as a check on the understanding of a particular Pascal construct. We will, therefore, usually give English descriptions of new constructs and leave the syntax diagrams to the exercises.

In choosing identifiers, we must avoid using the reserved words of the language, such as Program, Begin, and End. See Appendix D for a list of Turbo Pascal's reserved words. Beyond that, our choices for identifiers are unlimited. Because of this freedom of choice, we state a very important principle for good programming. This principle is one of the easiest to obey and, yet, one of the most abused:

Use descriptive variable names!

While this may seem like an unimportant rule for some of our early, short programs, this principle is indispensable in dealing with long, complex programs over a long period of time. Computer programs are documents that are meant to be read by other people. So although the computer doesn't care whether we use identifiers like M1, M2, and M3 or Principal, Interest, and Payment, the human reader (maybe even a grader) will be most appreciative of the latter choices.

THE ASSIGNMENT STATEMENT

With a calculator, we store a value in memory by pushing the Memory key. In a programming language, we give values to variables by using an assignment statement. The syntax of the assignment statement in Pascal is

```
<variable> := <expression>
```

where the left-hand side is a legal variable name and the right-hand side is some expression resulting in a value. For the time being, think of <expression> as being any arithmetic expression.

While Pascal's syntax (grammar) is important because it must be used correctly, the **semantics**—that is, the meaning—of a Pascal construct must also be understood if the construct is to be used effectively. The assignment statement has the following semantics: The `<expression>` is evaluated and the resulting value is assigned to the memory location with the name `<variable>`. Let us consider some examples. Suppose that `Result` is the name of a variable that can be assigned integer values. Then

```
Result := 7
```

would assign the value 7 to `Result`, while

```
Result := 2 * (3 + 2)
```

would assign the value 10 to `Result`, since in Pascal (and most other languages), `*` is the multiplication symbol. If `Result` is currently equal to 10, then

```
Result := Result + 2
```

would assign the value 12 to `Result`. Finally, if `Number` is another variable, currently equal to 6, and if `Result` is currently equal to 12, then

```
Result := 3 * Result - 2 * Number
```

would assign the value 24 to `Result`, since the system, in the absence of parentheses, always multiplies before it adds or subtracts.

It is important to realize that the assignment operator in Pascal is `:=` and not just the equal sign, `=`. Think of `:=` as one symbol and do not put a space between the colon and the equal sign. The assignment statement simply assigns a value to a variable; it does *not* make any assertion about equality. Many other languages use the equal sign alone as the assignment operator, resulting in the following kind of assignment statement:

```
Result = Result + 1                              {ERROR in Pascal!}
```

This is often read "`Result` equals `Result` plus 1." Of course, `Result` does *not* equal `Result` plus 1. `Result` equals `Result`. Instead, you should read an assignment operator as *becomes* or *is assigned*. So in Pascal, read

```
Result := Result + 1                    {Correct Pascal assignment.}
```

as "`Result` is assigned the value `Result` plus 1." All an assignment statement does is give a new value to the variable on the left-hand side of the assignment operator.

ELEMENTARY TYPES

In the above examples, we assumed that `Result` and `Number` were variables that held integer values; that is, whole numbers. Such variables are said to be of type **Integer**.

There are other types available to the Pascal programmer. We will mention three of them here. In later chapters, we will examine other types, and eventually we will see how a programmer can define new types.

The other types we consider now are the **Real** type, the **Char** type, and the **String** type. Real variables, like integers, also hold numeric values, but these values do not have to be whole numbers. Computers, generally, have two ways of expressing real numbers. The first way is using standard decimal notation; e.g., 2.5, 3.14159, 1.414, and so on. The other way is called **scientific notation** (or E notation). This method is used to handle very large numbers (the number of inches to the sun) or very small numbers (the weight, in pounds, of a politician's brain). Rather than writing a number that requires many digits, scientific notation allows us to specify how many digits to the right or left the decimal point should be moved to give us the actual number.

Examples: The speed of light is 186,000 miles per second, or 5,865,700,000,000 miles per year. In scientific notation, these numbers are written as 1.86E5 miles per second, or 5.8657E12 miles per year, where E5 means move the decimal point five places to the right and E12 means move the decimal point 12 places to the right.

The mass of an electron is 0.00000000000000000000000000911 gram. This is much easier to write as 9.11E-28, where E-28 means move the decimal point 28 places to the left.

A few general comments are in order. Because computers can represent only a finite number of objects, there is a limit to how many numbers can be represented on a computer. The limitations concerning real numbers are discussed briefly in Chapter 10. Integer variables in Turbo Pascal are limited to values from -32768 to +32767. While this range may be different for other computers, all versions of Pascal have a built-in constant, called Maxint, that represents the largest possible integer value. So, in Turbo Pascal, Maxint is an integer constant that equals 32767. Turbo Pascal does have a long integer type that allows larger integers, but long integers are not standard in Pascal, so we will generally avoid use of them in this book. Long integers are briefly discussed in Chapter 10, where types are discussed in more detail.

When writing numbers on a computer, *do not* use commas. Commas serve a purpose in Pascal, but it is not to make numbers easier to read. Also, when using scientific notation, it is standard practice to express the number between 1 and 10 and then indicate the number of places to move the decimal point. However, this is not required. So we could also say that the mass of an electron is 91.1E-29 or 0.911E-27 gram. Furthermore, not all real numbers must have a decimal point. 1E34 is an example of a real number with no decimal point. But, in Pascal, all real numbers with decimal points must have at least one digit on each side of the decimal point. Thus, .5 and 3. are examples of illegal real numbers. These numbers should be written as 0.5 and 3.0, respectively.

Because modern computers deal as much with character information as with numbers, it is also convenient to have variables that hold alphabetic information as opposed to numeric information. The Char (short for character) type is the simplest example of this. A Char value is any single character such as 'X'. Character constants in Pascal are enclosed in single quotes. Thus, 'Q', 'q', '+', '?', and '7' are also examples of character constants. Later, we will see why we need 7, 7.0, and '7', as well as the distinctions between these integer, real, and character constants.

Assignment and writing are simple examples of operations that can be performed with Char values. For example, if we assume that Answer is a Char variable, then the following segment assigns a value to Answer and then prints that value:

```
Answer := 'Y';
Writeln(Answer);
```

Later, we will see many other operations that can be performed on characters.

We emphasize that Char values can hold only a *single* character. Thus 'Yes' is not a character constant. It is an example of a **string**. A string is a sequence of zero or more characters. The given string is the sequence of the three characters 'Y', 'e', and 's'. Note that strings in Pascal are also delimited by single quotes. The main use of string constants, also called literal strings, is in labeling output. For example,

```
Writeln('The winning lotto number is ', WinNum);
```

produces, assuming that WinNum has the value 382, the clear output:

```
The winning lotto number is 382
```

In standard Pascal, the string is not a first-class citizen. Standard Pascal allows string literals, but does not allow string variables. Because string variables are so useful (for storing names, addresses, and all kinds of alphabetic information about people and objects), most versions of Pascal, including Turbo Pascal, provide for string variables. Because our interest is to make problem solving as natural as possible, we will introduce and use strings in this book. This is the one major way in which we digress from standard Pascal. We will return to the topic of strings in Chapter 14 and show the reader how we can define, in standard Pascal, the string type using arrays and records. Apparently, Niklaus Wirth, the author of Pascal, omitted strings to keep the language small and simple. He provided the user with the tools to build his or her own string package, but, unfortunately, those tools are beyond the beginner. Therefore, we will use the string type freely, and then come clean in Chapter 14, when the reader has developed enough sophistication to see how strings can be defined within Pascal.

To make the above discussion concrete, let us assume that Str is a string variable in Turbo Pascal. Then the following two segments have the same output :

```
Writeln('This is a string example.');        {OK in any Pascal.}

Str := 'This is a string example.';          {OK in Turbo Pascal,}
Writeln(Str);                        {but not legal in standard Pascal.}
```

In Turbo Pascal, each of the above segments will cause the quoted sentence to be

```
Num1 := 40;
Num2 := 20;
Num3 := 30;
Ch1 := 'P';
Ch2 := '?';
Str1 := 'The value of Num1 is';
Str2 := 'If you want to insert spaces, do it between quotes.';
Str3 := 'The value of Num3 is ';
Writeln(7, Num1, Num2 + Num3, Ch1, Ch2);
Writeln;
Writeln(Str1, Num1);
Writeln;
Writeln(Str2);
Writeln;
Writeln('The value of Num2 is ', Num2);
Writeln(Str3, Num3);
```

Listing 3.3

```
74050P?

The value of Num1 is40

If you want to insert spaces, do it between quotes.

The value of Num2 is 20
The value of Num3 is 30
```

Figure 3.4

printed. Note that the object of an output statement can be a variable. In this case, the *value* of the variable is printed. In general, the object of a write statement can be a variable, a constant (i.e., a number constant like 7 or a string constant like 'Seven'), an expression (for now, think of an arithmetic computation), or any sequence of these separated by commas (now we see a use for the comma in Pascal). The program segment in Listing 3.3 illustrates various output statements, where we suppose Num1, Num2, and Num3 are integer variables, Ch1 and Ch2 are character variables, and Str1, Str2, and Str3 are string variables.

The statements in Listing 3.3 will produce the output shown in Figure 3.4. Observe that the numbers and characters from the first output statement are not easy to read, as they are printed next to each other. Later, we will see how to format the output into a more legible form. Notice how Writeln; by itself is used to force a blank line to appear in the output. Finally, make sure you see how the blanks in the last two lines of output (before the 20 and 30) are obtained.

To see that you really understand variables and output statements, stop and figure out what the output of the following segment is (assume that Num is an integer variable and that Ch is a character variable):

```
Num := 5;
Ch := '5';
Writeln(5);
Writeln(Ch);
Writeln('Ch');
Writeln(Num);
Writeln('Num is ', Num);
```

The answer is

```
5
5
Ch
5
Num is 5
```

If you do not understand exactly how the above five lines of output were produced, you should go back and reread the preceding discussion.

THE VAR SECTION

Now that we know about variables and types, it is time to add to our Pascal programs. Pascal is a **strongly typed** language. To the beginning programmer, this means several things:

1. Each variable must have a single type throughout the program.
2. The values that are assigned to variables must be compatible in type. For example, an integer variable cannot be assigned the real value 2.54.
3. The programmer must explicitly declare, at the beginning of each program, the variables that will be used and their types.

   The explicit declaration of variables comes after the program heading and before the program body. The declaration section begins with the reserved word Var. Following this come all the variable declarations. A variable declaration consists of a list of variable names (separated by commas), followed by a colon and the name of the type (either Integer, Real, Char, or String for now). The variables can be declared in any order. Every variable that is used in the program must be declared, and none can be declared more than once. A semicolon follows every declaration, even the last one.

   Suppose we are writing a program with Integer variables Num1, Num2, and Num3, Char variables Ch1 and Ch2, Real variables Score1 and Score2, and String variables Word1 and Word2. Then, each of the Var sections shown below is a proper way to declare these variables. There can be more than one integer, real, or string declaration, and these can be in any order.

```
Var    Num1, Num2 : Integer;
       Ch1, Ch2 : Char;
       Score1, Score2 : Real;
       Word1, Word2 : String;
       Num3 : Integer;
```

or

```
Var     Num3      : Integer;
        Word1     : String;
        Ch1       : Char;
        Score2    : Real;
        Score1    : Real;
        Num2      : Integer;
        Ch2       : Char;
        Word2     : String;
        Num1      : Integer;
```

The second declaration is clearly easier to read. We will, therefore, try to show our variable declarations in our sample programs in this aligned format, and we urge the reader to do likewise in his or her programs.

When string variables are declared as shown, the computer reserves space for 255 characters. Usually, we don't need that much space, and we can specify how much we need by placing a number in square brackets after the word `String`. For example,

```
Word1 : String[20];
```

reserves space for a string of at most 20 characters. We will study strings in detail in Chapters 14 and 17, but we caution the reader to conserve memory by specifying a size for strings. Henceforth, in our sample programs, we will not use the type `String` alone but will always use `String[N]` with some suitable value for `N`.

While strong typing places a responsibility on the programmer to inform the computer what variables will be used, any inconvenience the programmer experiences is offset by the capability of the Pascal system to detect spelling errors in the names of variables. For example, BASIC is not a strongly typed language. Can you guess the output of the following BASIC program (which uses only BASIC assignment and output statements)?

```
10 LET N1 = 7
20 LET N2 = 3
30 LET N3 = N1 + N2
40 PRINT N3
```

This program produces the output

```
3
```

Do you agree with the output? If this were a 1000-line program, with hundreds of computations, would you agree with the output? If the value for `N1` were 0.03768 and the value for `N2` were 34.78654, how would you know to be suspicious of the output? If you were suspicious, would you perform all the calculations by hand? If so, why write a program in the first place? Actually, the intended output is 10, so you were right to disagree. The program above has an error in that `N1` (N ONE) is given a value in line

10, but in the calculation in line 30, we accidentally use N1 (N lowercase L). Languages like BASIC, which are not strongly typed, usually assign a value of 0 to a new variable like N1 and proceed merrily on their way. While this may seem like a contrived situation, this error actually occurs fairly often, particularly with programmers who learned to type many years ago. Earlier typewriters did not have a 1 key and, in fact, it was proper to use the lowercase L to represent a 1. In general, any spelling error that you make with variable names in BASIC is undetected, and erroneous results are sure to follow.

The same mistake in Turbo Pascal would produce the following message:

Error 3: Unknown identifier

and the cursor would be flashing under the N of the offending identifier N1 (N lowercase L). So, instead of a program that runs, produces erroneous output, and lets us hunt for the error, we get a message from the system that allows us the chance to correct our program and obtain reliable results. Note that the cursor is under the N, not the 1. It is too much to expect the computer to know what we *intended*. All it can do is point out that an identifier was used that was not declared.

The fact that some languages automatically assign a value of zero to numeric variables (and blanks to string variables) is worthy of comment, because such a policy can lead to some sloppy programming habits. Standard Pascal requires the programmer to explicitly **initialize** variables in the program before using them. Many beginners believe this means setting all variables equal to zero. This is not the case unless a zero is the desired initial value. Initialization of variables simply means the following: The first time a variable is used in a program, it should appear *only* on the left-hand side of an assignment statement or as the object of a Read or a Readln statement (see Chapter 4). If you follow the above practice, no matter which language you use for programming, you are taking matters into your own hands and making sure that variables have the desired initial values. Some Pascal compilers do initialize numeric variables to zero. Turbo Pascal, however, does not initialize and uses leftover values from previous calculations as the initial value of an uninitialized variable. Thus, for example, the segment

```
Var Num : Integer;
Begin
  Writeln(Num);                                    {Uninitialized variable.}
```

will produce unpredictable results, depending on the contents of whatever cell is assigned to the identifier Num. Be aware of this and suspect the use of an uninitialized variable if your results are totally off the wall.

CLARITY IN PROGRAMS

As an example of a poorly written program, consider the following example of Listing 3.4:

```
program sloppy;
{This is an example of a poorly written program.}
var x1,x2,x3:
real;x4:real;begin
x1:=67.5;x2:=57.8;x3
:=78.2;x4:=(x1+x2+x3)/3;
writeln(x4) end.
```

Listing 3.4

While the above program is legal in Pascal, it is certainly difficult to read and understand. Was it clear to you that Sloppy computed the average of three quiz scores?

   What is it that makes Sloppy such a poor program? One thing Sloppy points out is that Pascal is not very fussy about lines. In some instances, Sloppy has several statements per line and, in other instances, Sloppy breaks up a statement and puts it on two lines. While this is all legal Pascal (you can't split an identifier or a keyword on two lines, however), it is a general rule that each statement should stand by itself on a line. Later, we'll see that there can be exceptions to this rule, but it is a good idea, if you want your program to be readable, to put exactly one statement per line. If Sloppy is in fact a program to average three quiz scores, the choice of identifiers is also very poor. It is entirely up to the programmer to choose meaningful variable names. The version in Listing 3.5 is an equivalent program with each statement on a line, good identifiers, and the output clearly labeled. Notice how much clearer Neat is.

   The output from Neat is

```
The quiz average for Joe College is 6.7833333333E+01
```

The output from Neat is correct, but it is certainly an awkward way to write 67.83

```
Program Neat;
{This is an understandable version of the program Sloppy.}

Var    Quiz1   : Real;
       Quiz2   : Real;
       Quiz3   : Real;
       Average : Real;

Begin
  Quiz1 := 67.5;
  Quiz2 := 57.8;
  Quiz3 := 78.2;
  Average := (Quiz1 + Quiz2 + Quiz3) / 3;
  Writeln('The quiz average for Joe College is ', Average)
End.
```

Listing 3.5

(which Joe would understand better). The next section discusses how to format such output.

ARRANGING OUTPUT

In an earlier example, we saw that when we printed the three integer values 7, 40, and 50, and two characters 'P' and '?', they appeared in an unreadable, continuous stream, 74050P?, with no spaces between the items. It is very easy to ask for integers or characters to be printed in a readable format, and this is an important step in making the results of computer programs understandable.

Special formatting instructions may be placed in either Write or Writeln statements. These formatting directions are specified immediately after the items that we want to format. For example, suppose we wanted each item printed in a column of width 6. Then, consider

```
Writeln(7:6, Num1:6, (Num2 + Num3):6, Ch1:6, Ch2:6);
```

which produces the output

```
     7    40    50     P     ?
```

With integer or character values, we simply follow the identifier to be printed with a colon and then the width of the printing field. If the number of digits to be printed is less than the field width, then the value is right-justified, which means that blanks are inserted to the left of the value, so that the total number of characters (blanks and characters) equals the field width. For example, if Num is an integer variable with current value 4926, then the following statements:

```
Writeln(Num:4);
Writeln(Num:6);
Writeln(Num:8);
```

will produce the following output:

```
4926
  4926
    4926
```

If the formatting width is less than the number of digits, Turbo Pascal will elbow more room and print the value in as narrow a field as possible. For example, if Num still has the value 4926, then Writeln(Num:2) prints 4926 in *four* columns.

When real numbers are formatted like integers—that is, with a specified field width—they are printed in scientific notation. They are also right-justified, if the number of digits is less than the field width.

If we want real numbers to appear in ordinary decimal notation, we specify two values, in the form :W:D. These signify

1. A total width, W, which includes a place for the decimal point and the sign (if any)
2. The number of digits, D, to the right of the decimal point

For example, suppose Pi is a real variable with value 3.1415926. Then

```
Writeln(Pi, ' using no format');
Writeln(-Pi, ' using no format');
Writeln;
Writeln(Pi:15, ' using a :15 format');
Writeln(-Pi:15, ' using a :15 format');
Writeln;
Writeln(Pi:10, ' using a :10 format');
Writeln(-Pi:10, ' using a :10 format');
Writeln;
Writeln(Pi:7:5, ' using a :7:5 format');
Writeln(-Pi:7:5, ' using a :7:5 format');
Writeln;
Writeln(Pi:8:3, ' using an :8:3 format');
Writeln(-Pi:8:3, ' using an :8:3 format')
```

will produce the following output:

```
 3.1415926000E+00 using no format
-3.1415926000E+00 using no format

 3.14159260E+00 using a :15 format
-3.14159260E+00 using a :15 format

 3.142E+00 using a :10 format
-3.142E+00 using a :10 format

3.14159 using a :7:5 format
-3.14159 using a :7:5 format

   3.142 using an :8:3 format
  -3.142 using an :8:3 format
```

From this, we can deduce that Turbo Pascal, given no formatting instructions, prints real numbers in 17 columns. It displays 10 digits to the right of the decimal point, an E, a sign, a 2-digit exponent, the decimal point itself, 1 digit to the left of the decimal, and 1 column for the sign of the number. This leftmost column is left blank if the number is positive, but a - is printed if the number is negative. Hence, there are 7 characters (3 at the front, 4 at the end of the number) besides the decimal digits. Thus, with the :15 and :10 formats, we get 8 (15 - 7) and 3 (10 - 7) digits to the right of the decimal point. With the :W:D formats, we get much more familiar output. Observe that, since our number is between 1.0 and 10.0, W should be at least 3 larger than D (since we have a sign, a leftmost digit, and a decimal point to print *before* the digits to the right of the decimal point). The :7:5 example shows what happens when we ignore this rule. Turbo Pascal does its best and prints Pi:7:5 in 7 columns by suppressing the column for the sign. However, -Pi:7:5 requires 8 columns, since the sign cannot be dropped and, as with integers, Turbo Pascal elbows enough room to print the value. This is why these two lines of output do not align on the decimal. The :8:3 format shows that, if given more space than needed, Turbo Pascal will also right-justify real numbers and pad from the left with blanks. Also, note how the printed value of Pi is rounded in each case to the given specifications. Of course, the value of Pi stored within the computer is not rounded by these output statements.

Turbo Pascal also permits formatting of strings. As with integers and characters, one simply gives the number of columns in which to print the string. Strings are also right-justified when shorter than the given field width and will elbow more room when longer than the field width. Thus, for example,

```
Writeln('Short String');
Writeln('Short String':20);
Writeln('Short String':10);
Writeln('ShortString:20'); { Error??? }
```

produces

```
Short String
        Short String
Short String
ShortString:20
```

Notice that the last line, while not an error to the computer, is probably not what the programmer intended. Be careful about the placement of your format specifications with respect to the string quotation marks.

SIMPLE ARITHMETIC

Just as with inexpensive calculators, we expect more powerful computers to be able to perform numeric calculations. In fact, we have included such calculations in some of the previous examples. Because of the different types of numbers that Pascal allows, we need to be specific about some of the arithmetic operators. We first consider real numbers.

The standard operations of addition, subtraction, multiplication, and division are denoted by +, -, *, and /, respectively. For those readers who are familiar with an exponentiation operator (raising a number to a power), we remark that standard Pascal has no built-in exponentiation. Later, we'll learn how to construct one ourselves.

As in standard mathematical practice, there is a **precedence** of operations. Therefore, * and / have precedence over + and -. This means that multiplications and divisions are performed *before* additions and subtractions. If we want to change this order, we must group quantities in parentheses. Since * and / have equal precedence, those operations are performed left-to-right unless altered by parentheses. The same holds true for + and -. For example,

```
3 + 4 * 5 is 23
(3 + 4) * 5 is 35
12 / 6 - 4 / 2 is 2 - 2 or 0
12 / (6 - 4) / 2 is 12 / 2 / 2, which is 6 / 2 or 3
12 / ((6 - 4) / 2) is 12 / (2 / 2), which is 12 / 1 or 12
```

There are no restrictions on calculating with real numbers, except, of course, *do not* try to divide by 0 and do avoid overflow, which is caused by results larger than 1.7E38. We will postpone a more complete discussion of reals until Chapter 10. However, someone new to computers should realize that the machine will occasionally introduce errors into real calculations. There is a good explanation as to why this happens. There is an infinite number of real numbers, but even the largest computers can still represent only a finite number of these. Therefore, the computer has to approximate many numbers. Consider, for example, the number 1/3. Although the computer doesn't use a decimal representation, we may think of 1/3 as being stored in the computer's memory as a decimal number. From elementary mathematics, we know that 1/3 is *exactly* equal to 0.3333333..... where we have an *infinite* number of threes. However, the computer can only approximate 1/3 to a certain finite number of terms. Although this may be a very close approximation, there is still a slight error. As programs get more complex, and thousands and thousands of computations are performed, these errors sometimes get magnified and results can become worthless. Although this is a real problem, especially to numerical analysts, we shouldn't have to worry much about this while we are in a first course. However, if we know that the solution to an equation is 6.0, we should not be surprised if the computer finds 5.9999999999 or 6.0000000001.

Now we turn to integers. The arithmetic operations are sometimes called **binary** operations because they take two inputs (for example, the numbers to be added) to produce an output (the sum). In a strongly typed language like Pascal, the binary arithmetic operations produce an output that is of the same type as the inputs. Note that this causes no problem with addition, subtraction, and multiplication; and, in fact, the same three symbols, +, -, and *, as used with reals, are also used with integers. But when we divide the integer 7 by the integer 2, what is the quotient? Another way of phrasing the question is, "How many times will 2 go into 7?" If we insist on an integer answer, then the only logical answer is 3.

When performing integer division, the / operator is replaced with Div and the quotient is computed as an integer. In other words, we disregard any remainder in the division. So 10 Div 3 is 3, 10 Div 4 is 2, and 10 Div 5 is 2. This can cause some unusual results, because in dealing with integers, the order of division and multiplication can be significant. For example, (14 * 6) Div 4 is 84 Div 4 or 21, while 14 * (6 Div 4) is 14 * 1 or 14.

The rules for integer division involving negative numbers are demonstrated with the following examples:

```
 7  Div  -3 is  -2
-7  Div   3 is  -2
-7  Div  -3 is   2
```

Although it appears that we lose something (namely, the remainder) when we perform integer division, there is a way to retrieve the remainder when dealing with positive integers—the Mod operation. This operation is a standard mathematical operation, and A Mod B is defined to be the remainder upon dividing A by B. So 17 Mod 5 is 2. In Turbo Pascal, A or B is allowed to be negative. If A is negative, the result is also negative. So -17 Mod 5 is -2, and -17 Mod -5 is also -2, but 17 Mod -5 is 2. Fortunately, one seldom uses the Mod operator with negative operands, so the reader who understands that Mod gives the remainder in an integer division involving positive integers is in good shape.

CONVERSIONS BETWEEN INTEGERS AND REALS

For beginning programmers, there is often a great deal of confusion about how the two numeric types can be mixed. Technically, there shouldn't be any mixing if Pascal is truly a strongly typed language. But, for convenience, there are a few times when types can be mixed. It seems proper to consider the set of integers as a subset of the set of real numbers. An integer can be viewed as a real number whose fractional part just happens to be zero. However, it doesn't really make any sense to try to consider a real number, like 3.14159, as an integer. With this in mind, it should be easy to remember the following basic rules:

1. Integer values can be used where reals are expected, but not vice versa.
2. In performing a computation, real values and integer values can be mixed as long as the overall result will be real. However, when mixing, do not apply Div or Mod to real numbers.

To see why we might want to mix integers and reals, consider converting a Fahrenheit temperature to a Celsius temperature. The formula for doing this is

```
Cels = 5/9 * (Fahr - 32);
```

So, if we start with a Fahrenheit temperature of 66, its Celsius equivalent will not be a whole number, but rather a decimal number. As a second example, suppose we wanted to compute the area of a circle with a radius of 2 inches. We need to multiply Pi (which is approximately equal to 3.14159265) by 4 (the square of the radius). Again, we start with an integer, but expect a real result.

Now, we give some examples that demonstrate the above type-mixing rules. Because there is no context for the following statements, other than to demonstrate the type-mixing rules, we will temporarily allow ourselves to use short, nondescriptive variable names (since there is nothing to describe). So suppose I, J, and K are integer variables and A, B, and C are real variables. Then each of the next seven statements is legal:

```
I := 1;
J := 2;
K := 3;
A := 1;
```

```
B := 2.0;
C := I;
A := (A*I+(J Mod K)/B);
```

Each of the following three statements is illegal:

```
I := 2.0;                          { Illegal statement.}
J := B;                            { Illegal statement.}
K := (A*I+(J Mod K)/B);            { Illegal statement.}
```

What we have seen so far is that the computer will automatically convert integers to reals. There is no automatic conversion in the other direction, but sometimes we want to convert reals to integers. In this situation, we have to do the conversion explicitly. We do this with either of two built-in functions. The first of these is Round and, as its name implies, it rounds a real number to the nearest integer. So, Round(3.4) is 3 and Round(3.7) is 4. Turbo Pascal rounds 3.5 up to 4 and -3.5 down to -4. In general, Turbo Pascal rounds the halfway numbers away from zero (that is, to the number of greater absolute magnitude). Other versions of Pascal might always round the halfway numbers toward zero. Be sure to check this on other versions of Pascal.

The second operation is Trunc, which always chops off the fractional part of a real number (i.e., Trunc chops toward zero). So Trunc(3.7) is 3, Trunc(3.0) is 3, and Trunc(-3.7) is -3. Thus, if I and J are integer variables and X is a real variable, then the following two statements are legal:

```
I := Round(X);
J := Trunc(X);
```

We close this section by pointing out that there is more to the numeric types than we have explained in this chapter. We are just trying to get started, so we don't want to get lost in a forest of details. We will see, in Chapter 10, that there are different varieties of integers and reals. We will learn of the limits on how big or small numbers can be and how precise the computer is when dealing with the various kinds of numbers.

COMMENTING PROGRAMS

One of the programmer's most important jobs is to make his or her computer programs readable. This is not a difficult thing to do, and we believe it is largely a matter of cultivating good programming habits. For example, one of the most important things that beginning programmers should learn is the value of choosing good variable names. Another good habit that has already been mentioned is producing clear output. This can be accomplished with ample labeling (using string constants to tell what results mean) and by using the formatting capabilities of Pascal. Just as important, and often neglected, is the use of **comments** in programs. Comments are ignored by the computer—they are exclusively for humans. Comments in Pascal are enclosed in braces, { and }, and can occur at the end of any program line, or as a line by themselves. All programs should contain a heading comment stating such information as the author, date, and purpose of the program. For beginning programs, this may be all that is necessary. But as programs get longer and more complex, comments can also explain what is really going on in complicated parts of the program. We feel that it is extremely beneficial to get in the habit of using comments in every program.

To emphasize the importance of readability, we quote some findings reported by Elshoff and Marcotty in the August, 1982, issue of **Communications of the ACM** (Association for Computing Machinery). Much of the information came from a survey of programmers for General Motors.

About 75 percent of all programmers' time in a commercial data processing installation is spent on program modification.

It was found that most programs were poorly written. They were very large, extremely difficult to read, and more complex than necessary.

A readable program always seems to exhibit a common set of properties. The program is well commented. . . .Variable names are mnemonic.

Comments can be the most important contribution that a programmer makes.

A COMPLETE EXAMPLE: THE AREA OF A CIRCLE

Since all we currently have at our disposal are the assignment statement and the output statement, we conclude this introductory chapter with a couple of examples that require only these constructs. The first example is a series of three attempts to solve a simple problem. All three attempts do solve the given problem, but not all three are of equal quality. We hope the reader can recognize the better efforts and from them learn to write better programs. Also, the third solution introduces the important concept of a **constant**. We will make some remarks about constants after the example. The final example of the chapter is a bit more complicated and again demonstrates that it is the programmer, not the computer, who must solve the problem.

We will write a program to print out the area and circumference of a circle whose radius is 6.72 inches. For this simple problem, designing the algorithm simply entails recalling the appropriate circle formulas:

Area = Pi * R * R

and

Circumference = 2 * Pi * R

where Pi is approximately equal to 3.14159265 and R is the radius of the circle. Hence, in this simple problem, we proceed directly to the implementation phase. As mentioned, we give three solutions of improving quality.

Solution A: The first solution to this problem is found in Listing 3.6 and produces the output of Figure 3.5.

```
Program A;
{This is a mysterious program.}
Begin
  Writeln(2*3.14159265*6.72:12:6, 3.14159*6.72*6.72:12:6)
End.
```

Listing 3.6

```
  42.222970  141.869178
```

Figure 3.5

A second solution, Circle, is given in Listing 3.7. Its output is found in Figure 3.6. The third solution, Circle2, to this example is found in Listing 3.8. Its output is the same as that from Circle.

```
Program Circle;
{This program computes the area and circumference of a circle.}

Var   R : Real;
      X : Real;
      Y : Real;
Begin
  R := 6.72;
  X := 3.14159 * R * R;
  Y := 2 * 3.14159265 * R;
  Writeln('The area of a circle whose radius is 6.72 inches');
  Writeln('is ', X:6:2, ' square inches, while');
  Writeln('the circumference is ', Y:6:2, ' inches.')
End.
```

Listing 3.7

```
The area of a circle whose radius is 6.72 inches
is 141.87 square inches, while
the circumference is  42.22 inches.
```

Figure 3.6

```
Program Circle2;
{This program computes the area and circumference of a circle. It
also demonstrates the use of CONSTANTS. Constants look like
variables, but they are not allowed to change their values during
the program's execution.                                         }

Const   Pi = 3.14159;
        R  = 6.72;


Var   Area   : Real;
      Circum : Real;

Begin
  Area := Pi * R * R;
  Circum := 2 * Pi * R;
  Writeln('The area of a circle whose radius is ', R:4:2,
                                              ' inches');
  Writeln('is ', Area:6:2, ' square inches, while');
  Writeln('the circumference is ', Circum:6:2, ' inches.')
End.
```

Listing 3.8

Discussion: Although solution A produces the correct answers, one needs to look at the program to see what the answers mean. Even then, it may not be easy for someone other than the author to decipher things. In particular, someone who knows very little about the mathematical formulas for a circle would likely be lost. Another comment worth making is that output statements are for printing and assignment statements are for computing. Try to keep computations within output statements to a minimum.

The program Circle produces good, clear output, but the program itself is not particularly nice to read. Again, someone who is unfamiliar with circle formulas can't really tell what is being computed without looking at the output statements. Clearly, better identifiers could have been chosen than the all-too-popular X and Y.

The program Circle2 is a well-written program that produces clear output. The use of constants is something new, so we discuss them now. As stated in the program's comment, constants look like variables, but are not allowed to change in the program. Notice that constants are defined in a constant section, which precedes the Var section and begins with the reserved word Const. We point out two significant differences between constant definitions and variable declarations. First, there is no mention of a type in a constant definition. This is because the type is implicit in the value that we give the constant. For example, the constants Pi and R are both real because we have given them real values. Second, the constant definitions use the equal symbol and *not* the assignment operator. This is because the constant name really is *equal* to the indicated value throughout the program.

There are two general advantages to using constants. First, constants provide some security against a programmer accidentally changing a value that should not be changed, since Pascal will not allow constants to change their values. This can be very important in long, involved programs. Second, constants can help us rid our programs of magic numbers, which are numbers that occur throughout a program, but often the quantities they represent are not readily apparent. For example, instead of cluttering up a program with lots of 3.14159265s, we should use `Pi` instead. Moreover, we can save ourselves some work if we have to use a better approximation for `Pi`, such as 3.1415926536, in a later version of the program. We can simply change the constant definition for `Pi` without having to change any of the other statements in the program.

The careful reader might object to our use of the variable `R` as a meaningful variable. In fact, one-letter variables are usually poor choices. However, in this case, such a choice may well be justified, because anyone who is familiar with the circle formulas would probably recite them using `R`s (Pie are square!). Of course, any other one-letter variable would be a poor choice, and we would certainly not argue against the choice of `Rad` or `Radius` as a variable name.

Finally, note that although both `Circle` and `Circle2` produce the same output, the first `Writeln` statement in program `Circle2` is more flexible because it doesn't contain the magic number 6.72. To compute the area and circumference for a different circle, program `Circle` would need to have its first `Writeln` statement altered, as well as the `R` assignment statement. `Circle2`, on the other hand, would need only to have the `R` constant definition changed. Computer programs should be as flexible as possible, so that modifications to them can be kept to a minimum. Since variable names and constant names add to that flexibility, use them.

PROBLEM-SOLVING EXAMPLE: SONNY TAN

We conclude this chapter with a more complex example. Sonny Tan has just completed another trip from the windy city of Chicago to the sunny beaches of Miami, a distance of 1397 miles. As an almost law-abiding citizen, Sonny averaged a driving speed of 67 miles per hour. While lying on the sand soaking up the sun, Sonny decided to experiment with his new digital wristwatch. After timing everything in sight, Sonny began timing the blinking of his eyes. He noticed that he blinks about 17 times each minute and even determined that each blink lasts about 0.12 second. With all this information, determine how long it took Sonny to drive from Chicago to Miami, how many times he blinked during his trip, and how many miles he drove with his eyes closed.

We are given lots of information. Our first task is to develop some means of ordering this information and planning what to multiply (or divide) by what in order to obtain the solution. In other words, we need an algorithm, or plan, for the solution of the problem.

Since Sonny's problem sounds like a distance-rate-time story problem, we begin with the well-known formula:

Distance = Rate * Time

Instead of looking for one huge calculation that gives us the final answer, let's take it step by step and determine a sequence of intermediate results. We suggest a possible sequence of intermediate results, but we leave most of the details to the reader. We urge you to fill in the missing details, so that you understand where our final solution really comes from. Here is the outline of the algorithm we propose to use to solve Sonny's problem:

1. Since we know the total distance in miles, and the speed in miles per hour, we can find the time (in hours) of the trip. The formula is

   Time in Hours = Distance ÷ Speed

2. Since the frequency of blinking is given in blinks per minute, we convert the Time in Hours to Time in Minutes. The appropriate formula, of course, is

   Time in Minutes = Time in Hours * 60

3. Now it is an easy matter to find the Total Number of Blinks. We leave the formula to the reader.
4. Since we know the duration in seconds of each blink, it is also straightforward to find the Total Seconds with Eyes Closed. Again we leave the explicit formula to the reader.
5. Since the speed is given in miles per hour, we need to convert Total Seconds with Eyes Closed to Total Hours with Eyes Closed. We leave the details to the reader with the suggestion that, if useful, an intermediate step finding the Total Minutes with Eyes Closed be inserted.
6. Now we use our distance-rate-time formula, again, to find the number of miles Sonny drove with his eyes closed:

   Miles Blind = Speed * Total Hours with Eyes Closed

The reader should notice that we have written a general algorithm, not one that is specific to the particular numbers given in Sonny's case. Usually, it is easier (because you can ignore the details of one particular case) to develop a general algorithm for a problem. The general algorithm is certainly more useful, as it allows us to solve other instances of the same problem (Frosty Toes drove 2345 miles to the North Pole ...).

As soon as the reader supplies the missing details in our outline, the implementation of the program in Pascal should be a piece of cake. Our solution to this problem is given in Listing 3.9. Notice how it follows the development of the algorithm. As we have said (and will repeat, until you believe it), it is the development of the algorithm that is the interesting (and sometimes difficult) task. The actual program simply implements the design. It should be obvious, therefore, that the design is crucial. If your design is incorrect or incomplete, you have no chance of writing a correct program. Learn to spend the time to design well. It saves time in the long run.

The output from the program Sonny is shown in Figure 3.7.

Note the built-in flexibility of the Sonny program. If we change a quantity like the duration of each blink, the number of blinks per minute, or the driving speed or distance, we need modify only a single line of the program. Although we used constants for several quantities, we did not use a constant for converting times from one unit to

```
Program Sonny;
{This program uses the assignment statement and the write statement
to determine how far Sonny Tan drove with his eyes closed on his
trip from Chicago to Miami. We know the distance of the trip, his
driving speed, and the frequency and duration of his blinks.   }

Const   Distance   = 1397;    {miles}
        Speed      = 67;      {m.p.h.}
        Frequency  = 17;      {blinks per minute}
        Duration   = 0.12;    {seconds}

Var Hours              : Real;
    Minutes            : Real;
    Blinks             : Real;         {Too big to be an integer.}
    Miles              : Real;
    MilesBlind         : Real;
    HoursEyesClosed    : Real;
    MinutesEyesClosed  : Real;
    SecondsEyesClosed  : Real;

Begin
  {Determine how long the trip took in minutes.}
  Hours := Distance / Speed;
  Minutes := Hours * 60;

  {Now determine the total number of blinks.}
  Blinks := Minutes * Frequency;

  {Next, determine how long Sonny's eyes were closed.}
  SecondsEyesClosed := Blinks * Duration;
  MinutesEyesClosed := SecondsEyesClosed / 60;
  HoursEyesClosed := MinutesEyesClosed / 60;

  {Compute distance traveled with eyes closed.}
  MilesBlind := HoursEyesClosed * Speed;

  {Finally, output the results of the program.}
  Writeln('Sonny Tan''s trip to Miami took ', Hours:5:1,
                                          ' hours.');
  Writeln('During his trip, Sonny blinked ', Blinks:5:1,
                                          ' times.');
  Writeln;
  Writeln('At a speed of ', Speed:2, ' mph, Sonny drove');
  Writeln(MilesBlind:5:1, ' miles with his eyes closed.')
End.
```

Listing 3.9

```
Sonny Tan's trip to Miami took 20.9 hours.
During his trip Sonny blinked 21267.8 times.

At a speed of 67 mph, Sonny drove
 47.5 miles with his eyes closed.
```

Figure 3.7

another. In this case, the 60 is not really a magic number. Most people will know what purpose the 60 is serving, particularly in the context of the statements, and we feel it would make the program unnecessarily wordy to introduce a constant like MinutesPerHour that is set equal to 60.

We point out that we printed the apostrophe (single quote) in the first line of output (see Figure 3.7) by entering it *twice* in the Writeln statement. That is, we used the following Writeln statement in our program:

```
Writeln('Sonny Tan''s trip to Miami took ',Hours:5:2);
```

There are *two* single quotes between the n and the s, not one double quote. If we had used a double quote, the computer would have printed a double quote. If we had used just one single quote, the computer would have interpreted this as the matching, closing quote for the first quote before the word Sonny. Remember, to print out an apostrophe in a string, enter it twice.

SUMMARY

In this chapter, we have learned the fundamentals that apply to all Pascal programs. We have learned to declare identifiers and to write assignment and output statements. These constructs will be used in all Pascal programs to follow. Finally, note that it is the programmer who *solves* problems. If we don't know which operations to perform when, the computer will not be of much help to us. Computers do not solve problems. People do.

KEYWORDS

Many important concepts have been introduced in this chapter. As a study guide, make sure that you can describe each of the following terms:

Variable	Identifier
Integers	Reals
Characters	Strings
Div	Mod
Round	Trunc
Constants	Assignment statements
Write	Writeln

SELF-TEST QUESTIONS

3.1 What is the role of the semicolon in Pascal?

3.2 What is the distinction in Pascal between a `Write` and a `Writeln` statement?

3.3 Which of the following are legal Pascal identifiers? For those that are illegal, indicate why they are illegal. (Note that if you have any doubts about an answer, you can always write a short program testing the given identifier.)

a) `Turkey`   b) `Why Not`

c) `Cost$`   d) `Program`

e) `XYZ32`   f) `Legal?`

g) `1Student`   h) `Var`

i) `BeginEnd`   j) `Hot-Dog`

3.4 What are the three primitive data types of standard Pascal that have been introduced in this chapter? What is the additional data type from Turbo Pascal that has also been introduced? Describe the kinds of values that variables of each of these four types can have.

3.5 You are writing a Pascal program and have identified the need to store the following information on a student:

a) Name
b) Age in years
c) Sex (M or F)
d) Grade Point Average
e) Social Security Number (XXX-XX-XXXX)

Write a `Var` section declaring appropriate variables. Justify your choice of a type for each variable. Avoid the use of the string type whenever you can find a more appropriate type.

3.6 Suppose X is a real identifier with the value 123.456789. Write the value that would be printed in each of the following cases. Indicate spaces with a beta, β, for blank.

a) `Writeln(X:10:5);`   b) `Writeln(X:10);`

c) `Writeln(X:10:1);`   d) `Writeln(X:15);`

e) `Writeln(X:8:5);`   f) `Writeln(X:5:5);`

3.7 Suppose Y and Z are real variables with the values 98765.4321 and 13579.8642, respectively. Supply `Writeln` statements that produce exactly the output shown.

a) Y has the value 98765.43 and Z is 13579.9

b) 98765.43210is Y and13579.86420is Z.

c) 98765.43210 is Y and 13579.86420 is Z.

3.8 Write valid Pascal assignments expressing each of the following formulas. Where the meaning of the formula is apparent, use meaningful identifiers.

a) $F = 9/5C + 32$ b) $e = mc^2$

c) $A = \dfrac{bh}{2}$ d) $V = \dfrac{4}{3}\pi r^3$

3.9 Suppose Num is an Integer identifier with value 874. Determine the values assigned to the Integer identifiers H, T, and U by each of the following assignment statements:

a) H := Num Div 100;

b) T := (Num Mod 100) Div 10;

c) U := Num Mod 10;

3.10 Suppose that N is an Integer identifier with value 4 and that X is a Real identifier with value 8.75, before each of the following assignment statements. Which of the following are legal/illegal assignments? For those that are legal, what is the value that is assigned?

a) N := X;

b) X := N;

c) N := Trunc(X);

d) X := Round(N);

e) N := Trunc(X + 0.5);

f) N := Trunc(X) + Trunc(0.5);

EXERCISES

3.11 Using categories such as Identifier and Integer, draw standard Pascal and Turbo Pascal syntax diagrams for variable declarations as we now know them.

3.12 What is the output of the following Pascal program? In particular, how many lines of output are there and what is on each line?

```
Program Rhyme;
{How many lines of output does this simple program produce?}
Begin
  Writeln('Mary had a little lamb ');
  Write('Little lamb ');
  Writeln('Little lamb ');
  Write('Mary had a little lamb ');
  Writeln('Its fleece was white ');
  Write('As snow.')
End.
```

Rhyme is available on the sample disk available for this book as Ch3\Rhyme.Pas so that you can check your answer.

3.13 What is the output of the following program?

```
Program Mystery;
{What is the output of this program?}
Var X, Y, Z : Integer;
Begin
  X := 80;
  Y := X Div 12;
  Z := X Mod 12;
  Writeln(X, '" = ', Y, ''' and ', Z, '"')     {Here '" is }
                {a single quote followed by a double quote,}
                  {''' is three single quotes in a row, and}
                {'"' is a single quote followed by a double}
                    {quote followed by another single quote.}
End.
```

For your convenience, Mystery is available on the disk of sample programs as Ch3\Mystery.Pas.

3.14 Suppose Sonny Tan was in a much bigger hurry than in the example problem and averaged 85 m.p.h. instead of 67 m.p.h. Modify the program Sonny to determine, in this case, how far he drove with his eyes closed. Guess whether the distance will increase, decrease, or stay the same. Explain any relationship you notice between this answer and the answer in the example in the text. Use Ch3\Sonny.Pas from the sample disk to avoid retyping Sonny.

Write well-commented, readable, and correct Pascal programs to solve problems 3.15 through 3.21.

3.15 Write a program to convert a temperature of 75 degrees Fahrenheit to Celsius. Convert a temperature of 17 degrees Celsius to Fahrenheit. The conversion formulas are as follows:

$F = 9/5 * C + 32$
$C = 5/9 * (F - 32)$

3.16 The amount of beer brewed in the United States in 1975 was 4,894,000,000 gallons. If all this beer were placed in 12-ounce cans and if all of these cans were stacked one on top of the other, how high would the stack be in inches? How high in feet? How high in miles? How many times would the stack reach the moon? The following conversion factors will be helpful:

1 gallon = 128 ounces   1 mile = 5280 feet
1 beer can = 4.75 inches   1 moon trip = 239,000 miles

Note: You should use reals for all variables in this problem because the numbers will become too large for integers. In particular, 4894000000 is an illegal integer, so be sure to write it as the real 4894000000.0 or, better, as the real 4.894E9.

Problems 3.17 through 3.21 were taken from the article "Second Guessing," by Monny Sklov and Bob Spitzer, which appeared in the September, 1983, issue of **GAMES** Magazine.* The article was a quiz to see how well people could quickly judge the proper unit of time (i.e., seconds, minutes, hours, days, weeks, months, years, decades, centuries) that a task would take. Take the quiz yourself on the following problems. Check the answers below and then write Pascal programs that compute the time for each task in the correct unit. Again, you should use real variables because of the large quantities involved.

3.17 Suppose you can swim 3.8 miles per hour with flippers on. How long would it take you to swim around the world at the equator? (Assume a distance of 25,000 miles.)

3.18 Suppose you can write an average person's name in 6 seconds. How long would it take you to write all the names of the people living in New York City (approximately 7 million people)?

3.19 A cement company has just built a sidewalk from your front door to the sun (93 million miles away). After you've put on your hiking boots, how long will it take you to walk to the sun (assuming a hiking speed of 3 miles per hour)?

3.20 Every day for 18 years, your father takes 1 foot of 8-mm film of you in action. On your 18th birthday, your father shows you the film in its entirety. How long will the film last? (It takes approximately 3.18 seconds for 1 foot of film to pass through the projector.)

3.21 You own a square mile of land. If one-tenth inch of rain falls on your land and you catch all the water before it hits the ground, how long will it take you to drink

* Reprinted from **GAMES** Magazine, 810 Seventh Avenue, New York, NY 10019. Copyright © 1983 PSC Games Limited Partnership.

all the water, assuming a drinking rate of 3 gallons of water per day? There are 231 cubic inches in one gallon.

(Answers: The proper units of time for problems 3.17 through 3.21 are: months, years, centuries, hours, and centuries, respectively.)

3.22 The following buggy program is supposed to convert your height from feet and inches into centimeters, but the program contains five errors that have been discussed in this chapter. Can you find them? Use the Turbo Pascal compiler to check your work. This program is on the sample disk as Ch3\BuggyCms.Pas.

```
Program BuggyCms;
{Warning, this program contains five intentional bugs. It tries
to convert a 5 foot 10 inch height into centimeters. Can you
find and fix the bugs?                                        }

Const CmsPerInch := 2.54;    {One inch is 2.54 centimeters.}

Var    HtCms   : Integer;
       Feet    : Integer;
       Inches  : Integer;

Begin
  Feet := 5;
  Inches := 10
  Ht Cms := CmsPerInch * (12 * Feet + Inches);
  Writeln('At ', Feet, ' ', Inches, ', you are ',
                                  HtCms, ' cms tall.')
Stop.
```

3.23 The following brief program generates an unknown identifier error for the variable A, even though A is clearly declared in the program. Can you find and explain the problem? This one is tricky, but we have seen it happen in student programs many times. To save typing, and to get exactly the intended program, load Ch3\Declare.Pas from the sample disk.

```
Program Declare;
{This buggy program declares that the variable A is undeclared.
Do you see why?                       .

Var A : Integer;
{Please note that it certainly seems as if A was declared!}

Begin
  A := 5;
  Writeln(A)
End.
```

ANSWERS TO SELF-TEST QUESTIONS

3.1 The semicolon in Pascal is used as a separator, not a terminator.

3.2 A `Write` writes to the screen but does not execute a carriage return. A `Writeln` writes and then executes a carriage return, causing the next line of output to begin on a new line.

3.3 a) Legal. b) Illegal, blank not allowed. c) Illegal, $ not allowed. d) Illegal, a reserved word. e) Legal, but bad choice. f) Illegal, ? not allowed. g) Illegal, must begin with a letter. h) Illegal, a reserved word. i) Legal, but strange. j) Illegal, - not allowed. `Hot_Dog` is legal in Turbo Pascal.

3.4 The three primitive data types of standard Pascal that have been introduced are Integer, Real, and Char. The Turbo Pascal extra type is String. Integers are whole numbers like -17 and 345. Reals have a decimal point or an exponent like 3.5 or 9.2E7. Chars are single characters like `'Q'` or `'&'`. Strings are sequences of zero or more characters, such as `'This is a string'`.

3.5
```
Var  Name      : String[30];
     Age       : Integer;
     Sex       : Char;
     GPA       : Real;
     SocSecNo  : String[11];
```

3.6 a) ß123.45679   b) ß1.235E+02
c) ßßßßß123.5   d) ß1.23456789E+02
e) 123.45679   f) 123.45679

3.7 a) `Writeln('Y has the value ', Y:8:2, ' and Z is ', Z:7:1);`
b) `Writeln(Y:11:5, 'is Y and', Z:11:5, 'is Z.');`
c) `Writeln(Y:11:5, ' is Y and ', Z:11:5, ' is Z.');`

3.8 a) `Fahr := 9/5 * Cels + 32;`
b) `e := m * c * c;`
c) `Area := (Base * Height)/2;     {Parentheses not required.}`
d) `Vol := 4/3 * Pi * R * R * R;`

3.9 H is 8, T is 7, and U is 4, the hundreds, tens, and units digits of Num.

3.10 a) Illegal. b) Legal. X is 4.0. c) Legal. N is 8. d) Legal (but silly). X is 4.0.
e) Legal. N is 9.   f) Legal (but silly). N is 8.

4

INTERACTIVE INPUT AND TEXT FILES

One of the computer's features that has caused its greatest impact is that people can use and execute complex programs without having the slightest idea of how the programs are put together or what makes them work. From businesspeople who use spreadsheet programs, to secretaries using word-processing programs, to airline-ticket agents who book seats on an airplane, thousands of computer users have little idea about how things work. Of course, someone must eventually know what is going on. This is the programmer's job. It is also apparent that another job of the programmer is to write programs that are easily used by others. One fundamental way to do this is through **interactive input**, which is the primary emphasis of the first part of this chapter.

All the programs in the previous chapter ran from start to finish without any interruptions from the user. This is sometimes a good thing, because we may not want to be around while a long program is executing. We want to be able to start the program and walk away. Such behavior was common in the early days of computers when programmers presented a deck of punched cards (the program and the data) to a computer operator. The computer operator would read the cards into the computer at some later time and the computer would execute the program. If the program generated some output, the operator would return the printout to the programmer. Such a system is referred to as a **batch** system, since programs are run in batches.

With the advent of terminals, programmers began writing programs on a screen instead of using a keypunch, and programmers had the capability of executing their programs from their own terminals. With this environment, it became feasible for programs to request additional information while they were running. This type of environment is called an **interactive** environment, because there is a continuous interaction between the user and the computer. This interaction can make programs extremely flexible, and this flexibility makes programs easy for nonprogrammers to use. The PC is, of course, such an interactive computer.

For example, consider the situation of the airline-ticket agent. There is usually a computer terminal hooked into an extremely complicated reservation program. When you approach the agent, the program is already executing. But, in this case, the program halts several times to obtain information, such as your name, destination, date of travel, etc. It is precisely this interaction that allows you the flexibility to book a seat on any flight, on any day, with any agent at the counter. Of course, the agent probably has no idea of how the program works, but can respond to such questions as "Destination? First class? Nonsmoking?" We are not ready to write airline reservations programs, but we will see how to add these interactive features to our simple Pascal programs.

Exercise 3.15 had you write a program to convert 75 degrees Celsius to Fahrenheit. Now, suppose we want to convert a different temperature, such as 29 degrees. If you have a solution to Exercise 3.15 available, this new problem is easy. Simply change the 75 to 29 and run the program again. Although this is easy, notice that this simple task requires that you know how to list the program (i.e., look at it on the screen), be familiar enough with Pascal to realize which statement needs to be changed, and be familiar with the editing mechanisms of the computer to generate a new program. Finally, you need to know how to run the program. Of all these tasks, running the program is the simplest. Wouldn't it be nice if, when the program is run, you would be asked to enter from the keyboard the temperature you wanted to convert? Then you would need only one program to handle any Celsius temperature.

READ AND READLN

In Chapter 3, we learned how to assign values to variables using the assignment statement. Of course, when we use the assignment statement, we have to know the values ahead of time, because these values are typed into the program while we are creating it. In many cases, as the above example indicates, we need more flexibility. We may not always know, at the time the program is written, what values we will be working with.

To give us the flexibility we need, Pascal contains two statements that provide a facility for interactive input. These statements are

```
Read (List of variables);
Readln(List of variables);
```

We will explain how these statements execute and then detail the differences between the two.

In essence, the Read and Readln statements behave like assignment statements in that they assign values to variables. The variables that receive the values are those in the list after the word Read (or Readln). The values themselves are entered through the keyboard. We will give several examples, and again we take this opportunity to mention that, since there is no context for these examples, we will use one-letter variables.

Example: Suppose A, B, and C are integer variables, and we execute the statement

```
Readln (A,B,C);
```

If the person at the keyboard types in

2 4 6

and then presses the RETURN key, A would contain the value 2, B the value 4, and C the value 6.

As with assignment statements, Pascal requires that types be compatible. If the data entered from the keyboard were

2 4.2 6

Turbo Pascal would report a **run-time** type-incompatibility error (**Error 106: Invalid numeric format**) for trying to assign the real value 4.2 to the integer variable B. A run-time error is an error that occurs while the program is running. The previous errors that we have discussed have been **compile-time** errors, which are, of course, errors that were caught by the compiler. Obviously, the compiler cannot know what values we intend to enter from the keyboard, so while an assignment can be checked for compatibility at compile time, a read can be checked only at run time.

When the computer reaches a read statement in a program, it pauses until it receives, through the keyboard, all the values that it is expecting. In the above example, if only the two values

2 4

were entered, and then the RETURN key was pressed, the computer would wait (forever if necessary) until a third value for C was entered. Once the expected number of values has been entered, and a final RETURN key has been pressed, the execution of the program proceeds normally.

One might ask what happens if we type in too many values. With the Read statement, any extra value that is entered will be assigned to the next variable appearing in the next Read statement.

Example: Consider the following segment:

```
Read(A, B);
Writeln(A:5, B:5);
Read(C);
Writeln(C:5)
```

When this segment is run, the computer pauses at the first Read statement and waits for you to enter values. Suppose you type

45 67 89 143 (RETURN)

The 45 and the 67 are assigned to A and B, respectively, but the rest of your input is not lost. It is saved in a **buffer**, or holding area, in the computer. The first Read statement is satisfied and, thus, execution resumes with the first Writeln statement. This causes the values of A and B to be printed. Since the input buffer is not empty, the computer does not pause for you to enter a value for C, but takes the 89 from the buffer. This value is then printed in the final Writeln. The computer is so fast that the last three statements execute instantly, producing the output

```
45    67
89
```

as soon as you enter the line of data and press the RETURN key. If there are no more reads in the program, then the value 143, still in the input buffer, will be lost.

Now it is time to explain the difference between Read and Readln. Although the difference is similar to the difference between Write and Writeln, the input statements tend to cause more confusion among beginning programmers. Stated simply, Read statements take their data values as a continuous stream of values, with no regard to how many lines they are on. On the other hand, once a Readln statement has obtained all its values, any data values for the *next* input statement (whether a Read or a Readln) must begin on a new line. The following examples illustrate the difference between Read and Readln. In all cases, we assume that X, Y, and Z are integer variables.

Examples: The statements

```
Readln(X,Y);
Readln(Z)
```

with keyboard input

2 4 6 (RETURN)

would assign 2 to X and 4 to Y. The computer would continue waiting for a third data value, because after the first Readln statement is completed, the input buffer is flushed (emptied), and the next input statement needs data from a new line. Thus, the 6 is lost. The statements

```
Readln(X);
Readln(Y);
Readln(Z);
```

with the keyboard input

2   4   (RETURN)
6   8   (RETURN)
10   12   (RETURN)

would assign 2 to X, 6 to Y, and 10 to Z, with the other three values lost forever.

Suppose that the Readln(Y) statement above were changed to Read(Y) and that we tried to type in the same input. Then the 2 would be assigned to X, the 4 would be lost, the 6 would be assigned to Y, and the 8 to Z (since the Readln does not require that the current input start on a new line, but rather that the next input, if any, begin on a new line). Execution would then resume before we could even begin the typing of the 10 and 12.

When reading strings, some words of caution are in order. Suppose Name has been declared as a String[30] and Age is an integer. Then the data line

Mickey Mouse 50 (RETURN)

will not be read, as you might expect, by the statement

Readln(Name, Age)

Since only 15 characters (counting the blanks) were entered, Name will get them all and have the value 'Mickey Mouse 50'. The computer will continue to wait for a value of Age to be entered.

On the other hand, if the data line is

Ruthane Richardson Van Newenhizen 21

then the same Readln will produce a run-time error message. The message, **Error 106: Invalid numeric format**, is a bit of a surprise, since the problem is clearly that the string that was entered is too long for the string variable. What happens is that the first 30 characters of input, 'Ruthane Richardson Van Newenhi', are assigned to Name and then the system chokes when trying to assign 'zen 21' to the integer variable Age.

Note that the data line

Neal Wells   21 (RETURN)

will work properly with our Readln, if 20 extra blanks are typed, so that the value 21 begins in column 31. This is, however, a very poor solution to the problem, because humans have a difficult time including exactly the correct number of spaces in the input. In Chapter 5, we will learn how to read such input (a name followed immediately by an age) character by character, place all the characters up to a digit into Name, and then assign Age the appropriate value. For the present, we suggest that you put each string value by itself on a line of data and that you always read strings with Readln. That is, if you wanted to read an individual's Name, Age, Weight, HeightFeet, and HeightInches then the lines of data

Mickey Mouse
50 134 4 2

would be read correctly with

Readln(Name);
Readln(Age, Weight, HeightFeet, HeightInches);

Suppose `First` and `Last` are string variables. The following short example shows why you should use `Readln`, not `Read`, with strings:

```
Read(First);
Read(Last);
Write(Last, ', ', First);
```

We know that if the user enters

Wendell Willkie

and then RETURN, `First` will be `'Wendell Willkie'`. What if the user tries to enter

Wendell
Willkie

on separate lines, with RETURNS after each line? The answer is that you never get a chance to type `Willkie`. As soon as you press RETURN, after typing `Wendell`, that value is assigned to `First` and the RETURN is saved in the buffer for the next `Read`. A `Read` only reads new data when the buffer is empty. Since the buffer is *not* empty, all the characters up to but not including the RETURN are assigned to `Last`. Hence, `Last` is assigned the null or empty string. That is why the output of this little segment is

, Wendell

In this case, the `Read` never processes the RETURN at the end of the line, and all strings that are read after the first will be empty. If the `Read`s are changed to `Readln`s, the RETURNS are processed and the output from the two lines of data is

Willkie, Wendell

as expected. In the next chapter, we'll discover that `Read` is handy for reading characters, but for now remember that `Readln` must always be used with strings.

As programs get more complex, there may be several items of data that need to be entered. How does the airline agent know whether the computer wants a name, a destination, a date, or a seating class? To avoid type-compatibility errors and to make sure that the right values get assigned to the right variables, it is important for the person at the keyboard to know what is expected. Thus, we arrive at the fundamental rule for interactive input:

Always precede interactive `Read` or `Readln` statements with a prompting message explaining what type of information is expected.

The purpose of the prompt is to tell the *user, not the programmer,* how to interact with the running program. For example, if we want to convert someone's height from inches to meters, the following sequence would be appropriate:

```
Writeln('Enter your height in inches.');
Readln(Height)
```

Note the importance of the phrase "in inches," to coax the proper response. Moreover, if a program might be executed by a total beginner, the following sequence would be better:

```
Writeln('Enter your height in inches.');
Writeln('Then press the "Return" key.');
Readln(Height)
```

The programmer probably will not be around when the program is executed and should think of as many problems and plan for as many contingencies as possible. Programs with interactive input statements should be written in such a way that the person at the keyboard has no question as to what information is being requested.

PROBLEM-SOLVING EXAMPLE: MAKING CHANGE

We now consider an extended example of an interactive program. This example is motivated by the deplorable arithmetic skills we observe in retail clerks throughout America. Have you ever been in a fast-food restaurant when the computer was down and the clerks couldn't just push the pictures of the hamburger, large fries, and a medium coke? It's not a pretty sight to see them write down $1.45, $.85, and $.65, try to add them up, look up the sales tax in a table, and finally make change for a $5 bill. It certainly removes the adjective "fast" from the food!

For a long time, cash registers have been smart enough to compute the amount of change to give the customer. After pushing the pictures of the objects ordered, the clerk pushes a total button and announces the total (say, $18.04) to the customer. The clerk then enters the amount tendered by the customer (say, $20) and the machine responds with the change due ($1.96). But we have now seen cash registers that tell the clerk how to give the correct change to the customer. That is, in the above case, the cash register displays information telling the clerk to give the customer 1 dollar bill, 3 quarters, 2 dimes, and 1 penny. Let us write such a program as an example of interactive input.

We need to decide what the input to our program will be. To keep things simple (and to focus on the main problem of making change), we will assume that the customer is buying just one object. Obviously, we will need to enter the purchase price of this object. Of course, we will also need to know the amount tendered by the customer, so this will be an input to our program also. We will have to charge sales tax, but since the sales-tax rate does not change from purchase to purchase, we will use a constant for the sales-tax rate. Hence, we have already identified two variables that our program will need (`Purchase` and `AmtTendered`) and one constant (`SalesTax`).

The output from our program should be a clearly labeled, detailed report of the transaction. It should specify the total due, but should itemize this by showing the purchase price and the amount of tax due. It should show the amount tendered by the customer and the total change due the customer. It must show the number of dollars, quarters, dimes, nickels, and pennies to give the customer. Thus, we see that the program will also need identifiers such as `AmtTax`, `Total`, `Change`, `NumDollars`, `NumQuarters`, `NumDimes`, `NumNickels`, and `NumPennies`.

Now we get to the interesting (hard) part of the problem. How do we compute all of these outputs from the inputs? The worst way is to sit at the computer and (randomly) type assignment statements until the program works. Murphy has a law about this:

The sooner you start programming, the longer the whole process takes.

What Murphy's law means is that time spent in planning is time well spent. If you do not understand what *you* want to do, you will never get the computer to do it for you. Although the problem at hand is relatively simple, we believe that the learner should get into the habit of writing the algorithm in **pseudo-code**, before sitting down at the computer. Pseudo-code is not a new language to learn; rather, it is a mixture of English and Pascal-like constructs with which we express our algorithm. Once we know what we want to do and have expressed it roughly, it will be relatively easy to implement the ideas in Pascal. If you find that you are spending too much time debugging programs because they don't run correctly, then that is a sure sign that you haven't spent enough time in planning. Again, if you are not quite sure what you want to do, how can you expect the moronic computer to do the correct thing? You have to have an algorithm in mind before you can write a program.

We present two possible pseudo-codes for our change-making program. Study them carefully and learn the important skill of pseudo-coding. Learn to use pseudo-coding as a means of expressing your algorithm for solving the problem. Do this before you have to worry about the details of Pascal, for with well-written pseudo-code, the actual implementation in Pascal will be a piece of cake. Pseudo-coding will save you time and make you a more successful programmer!

Our first pseudo-code algorithm for the change-making problem is just an outline, in English, of what we want to do:

Set a constant equal to the sales tax rate
Obtain from the user the purchase price and the amount tendered
Compute the amount of tax as the purchase price times the sales tax rate
Compute the total as the purchase plus the amount of tax
Compute the change due as the amount tendered minus the total
Set the number of dollar bills equal to the whole part of the change
Find the total amount of Change due in coins
Find the number of quarters to return to the customer
Find the amount of change still due the customer (after quarters)
Find the number of dimes to return to the customer
Find amount still due customer (after quarters and dimes)
Find the number of nickels to return to the customer
Amount left is number of pennies due customer
Output the results

We suggest that you trace the above outline, supposing that the sales tax is 6.25 percent, the purchase is $16.98, and the amount tendered is $20.00. You should discover that the amount of tax is $1.06, the total due is $18.04, the change due is $1.96

and, therefore, the customer gets 1 dollar bill and 96 cents in coins (3 quarters, 2 dimes, 0 nickels, and 1 penny). Tracing the outline is a very important step, because you will often find details that you have omitted. It is better to discover this early, when you can easily modify the algorithm, rather than later, when you have a program that doesn't work properly.

Our second pseudo-code for this problem is much more Pascal-like. In it we have used identifiers and expressed our ideas in notation that is easily translated into Pascal.

Set SalesTax = 0.0625 (a constant)
Prompt for and read Purchase and AmtTendered
AmtTax ← Purchase * SalesTax
Total ← Purchase + AmtTax
Change ← AmtTendered - Total
NumDollars ← whole part of the Change
Change100 ← the total amount of Change due in coins
NumQuarters ← Change100 divided by 25 (an integer division)
Change100 ← remainder of last division (amount still due customer)
NumDimes ← Change100 divided by 10
Change100 ← remainder of last division
NumNickels ← Change100 divided by 5
NumPennies ← remainder of last division
Output the results

There is no one right way to express an algorithm. Pseudo-coding is not a new language to learn, but just your shorthand outline of the solution. The advantage of pseudo-code is that it frees you from the strict syntax of Pascal and lets you concentrate on the problem. The first pseudo-code version shown above is probably easier to read (but harder to write). The second version is easier to transform to Pascal. As you learn to pseudo-code, you will develop your own style.

Notice that neither pseudo-code describes the complete details of our method. In both versions of pseudo-code, we have the simple line

Output the results

which will obviously translate to a large number of `Writelns`. While tedious, yet important to the overall quality of the program, these `Writelns` probably do not need to be specified in further detail at the pseudo-code level.

In the more detailed version, the lines that deal with integer divisions and remainders are not very Pascal-like. These statements will, of course, become `Div` and `Mod` operations, but the programmer needs to realize this before the translation to Pascal can be accomplished smoothly.

The two lines

NumDollars ← whole part of the Change
Change100 ← the total amount of Change due in coins

are quite vague about how they are to be accomplished. This is all right because the object of our pseudo-code is to get down the idea of what we want to do. We can then refine the pseudo-code, as necessary, until we have a completely specified algorithm. The first of these two statements calls for a conversion of a real (such as 1.96) to an integer (1). Therefore, we might annotate the first line to make it read

NumDollars ← whole part of the Change (Truncate real to integer)

For the second statement, we have to find a way to get 96 cents (an integer) from a real value of Change (such as 1.96). The 96 cents is the remainder when we take away the whole dollars. But our remainder operator works only with integers, so we can't use Mod directly. But notice that 196 Mod 100 is 96, so we can write the following refinement for the second statement:

Change100 ← (Change * 100) Mod 100 (amount of change due in coins)

Actually, this pseudo-code statement, when translated to Pascal,

```
Change100 := (Change * 100) Mod 100;        {Amount due in coins.}
```

will result in an error message (**Operand types do not match operator**) when compiled. The problem, of course, is that Change is real and so the left operand to Mod is real. We should not be too concerned that this kind of detail was missed at the pseudo-code level. The pseudo-code should be detailed enough that the translation to Pascal proceeds smoothly, but occasional unforseen problems will arise. The solution, in this case, is to realize that we must convert Mod's left operand to the integer type, and the proper way to do this is with

```
Change100 := Round(Change * 100) Mod 100;{Amount due in coins.}
```

Of course, Trunc could have been used in place of Round, but Round is probably a better choice in this instance, since the tax rate, being a fraction of a percent, may make Total, and therefore Change, into amounts representing fractions of pennies. On the other hand, perhaps the hard-nosed retailer would prefer to truncate 195.75 to 195, since this figure represents the change *due* the customer.

Finally, the Pascal version of the program is shown in Listing 4.1. Notice how much it resembles either of the pseudo-code versions. This demonstrates that our pseudo-coding was done to sufficient detail that the translation to Pascal was accomplished without trauma!

Typical output from Coins is shown in Figure 4.1. Notice how Writes, not Writelns, are used to get the prompt and the user's response on a single line on the Execution screen.

We remark that Coins is not bulletproof (protected from bad input). For instance, in the above example, if the customer gives the clerk a $50 bill, then the clerk will be on his or her own to figure out how to give the customer 31 dollars in bills as change. Furthermore, if the customer gives the clerk only a $10 bill, then the program will obediently tell the clerk to give the customer a *negative* number of dollars and coins as change. Also, the program will die, with a run-time error, if the user enters the dollar

```
Program Coins;
{This program computes the change due on a purchase and figures out
for the clerk the number of dollar bills, quarters, dimes, nickels,
and pennies to give the customer to make the correct change. The
program assumes that a 6.25 percent sales tax is also applied to
the purchase.                                                        }

Const  SalesTax = 0.0625;          {6.25% expressed as a decimal.}

Var    AmtTendered  : Real;            {Amount paid by customer.}
       Purchase     : Real;             {Amount of the purchase.}
       AmtTax       : Real;     {Amount of sales tax on purchase.}
       Total        : Real;             {Total of purchase and tax.}
       Change       : Real;           {Change due to the customer.}
       Change100    : Integer;        {Amount of change in coins.}
       NumDollars   : Integer;       {Number of dollars in change.}
       NumQuarters  : Integer;                          {quarters}
       NumDimes     : Integer;                             {dimes}
       NumNickels   : Integer;                           {nickels}
       NumPennies   : Integer;                           {pennies}

Begin
  {First obtain the input from the user.}
  Writeln('Enter the amount of the purchase.);
  Write('Do not use commas or a "$" in the price:  ');
  Readln(Purchase);
  Write('Enter the amount tendered by the customer:  ');
  Readln(AmtTendered);

  {Now compute the total amount due, the change for the customer,
  and specific bills and coins to give the customer.             }
  AmtTax := SalesTax * Purchase;
  Total := Purchase + AmtTax;
  Change := AmtTendered - Total;
  NumDollars := Trunc(Change);
  Change100 := Round(Change*100) Mod 100;{Amount due in coins.}
  NumQuarters := Change100 Div 25;    {Find number of quarters.}
  Change100 := Change100 Mod 25;   {Amount left after quarters.}
  NumDimes := Change100 Div 10;
  Change100 := Change100 Mod 10;
  NumNickels := Change100 Div 5;
  NumPennies := Change100 Mod 5;

  {Print the results to the waiting world.}
  Writeln; Writeln; Writeln;
```

Listing 4.1

```
  Writeln('Amount of purchase':30, Purchase:6:2);
  Writeln('Sales Tax':30, AmtTax:6:2);
  Writeln('***Total***':30, Total:6:2);
  Writeln;
  Writeln('Amount tendered':30, AmtTendered:6:2);
  Writeln;
  Writeln('Change due customer':30, Change:6:2);
  Writeln;
  Writeln;
  Writeln('Give the customer the following amounts:');
  Writeln('Dollar bills':15, NumDollars:3);
  Writeln('Quarters':15, NumQuarters:3);
  Writeln('Dimes':15, NumDimes:3);
  Writeln('Nickels':15, NumNickels:3);
  Writeln('Pennies':15, NumPennies:3)
End.
```

Listing 4.1 (continued)

sign or a comma in the price. We can take care of all these problems when we learn a little more Pascal. For now, we accept that Coins will be given correct input.

REDIRECTING INPUT

An alternative to interactive input is to prepare and save data to disk before a program is run. Of course, the program can no longer be interactive, but if there is a large amount of data, and the data are fixed, a disk file can be handy. With interactive input, you must enter all of the data each time you run a program. Since you may make several runs

```
Enter the amount of the purchase.
Do not use commas or a "$" in the price: 16.98
Enter the amount tendered by the customer: 20.00

            Amount of purchase   16.98
                    Sales Tax    1.06
                ***Total***     18.04

              Amount tendered    20.00

          Change due customer    1.96

Give the customer the following amounts:
   Dollar bills    1
       Quarters    3
          Dimes    2
         Nickels   0
        Pennies    1
```

Figure 4.1

before you completely debug the program, interactive input, while providing great flexibility, can become very tedious. By saving the data once to a **text file** on disk, execution becomes faster, more automatic, more reliable, and easier for the user.

A text file on disk also provides an easy way for us—or your instructor—to provide data for programming examples and exercises. The disk available for this book contains many such data files that are referenced throughout the sample programs and exercises.

Our intent, at this point, is to show you how to write programs that can *read* such text files. Also, we briefly discuss how to use the Turbo Pascal editor to create your own text files. In Chapter 15, we present file processing in a much more general setting. There we will learn to read and write general files.

As an example of the use of a text file, let us suppose that a two-line text file, `Sales.Txt`, has been created for a salesperson. Suppose line one of that file contains the salesperson's name and line two contains sales amounts for that salesperson for each day of the week (Monday through Friday). For example, the file might contain

```
Blaise Pascal
53.27 48.64 22.38 79.46 58.38
```

Let us write a program that will read the file `Sales.Txt` and total the sales for the given salesperson. Admittedly, this is not a very useful program, but, in the next chapter, we will learn how to modify the program so that it will process the weekly sales for 100 or 1000 salespersons. If you learn the simple skill of reading from text files, then, when combined with the conditional and iterative methods of the next chapter, you will be able to write powerful programs.

To redirect input in Turbo Pascal, so that it comes from the text file, `Sales.Txt`, on our disk in drive `A:`, in a subdirectory `Ch4`, we need add only two statements to our program. These are

```
Assign(Input, 'A:\Ch4\Sales.Txt')
Reset(Input);
```

While `Assign` and `Reset` are discussed in more detail in a later chapter, their effect can quickly be described as follows: `Assign(Input, 'A:\Ch4\Sales.Txt')` breaks the connection between input to the computer and the keyboard and establishes that input will come from the external file `Sales.Txt`. `Reset(Input)` locates and opens the text file in preparation for reading. Don't forget the single quotes around the filename in the `Assign` statement. Of course, the name `Sales.Txt` is arbitrary and you can use the name of any text file, but be sure to specify it completely or you may get a file-not-found error on the `Reset`. For example, if you had a text file `MyData.Txt`, in a `TextFile` subdirectory, of a `Samples` subdirectory, of the `TP` subdirectory of your hard drive, then you would need to specify the file with the complete path name

```
C:\TP\Samples\TextFile\MyData.Txt
```

Warning: Do *not* type any blanks, anywhere, in the description of the file name. These blanks can be significant and make the system look for a nonexistent file name.

After input has been redirected to come from a text file, rather than the keyboard, every Read or Readln in your program will get values from the file. This means that the programmer must know the structure of the data file. That is, the programmer must know that Sales.Txt consists of a name followed by five real numbers on the next line. Note that the programmer does not need to know the name or the actual values involved. Whenever, in an exercise, we ask you to read such-and-such a text file, we will always explicitly give you the structure of that file. This is your starting point for the analysis of the given problem.

Listing 4.2 shows the program Sales (Sales.Pas) that reads the file Sales.Txt and totals the sales figures. Figure 4.2 shows the execution of the program. Of course, the program and the text file both do not have to be named Sales. The program has to have the extension .Pas, but the text file does not have to have the extension .Txt. The program Sales.Pas could read the text file Anything.Xyz, if that is how you had named your text file. The extension .Txt is customary, however, for text files and we will follow that convention in this book.

```
Program Sales;
{This program illustrates the reading of a text file. The text file
Sales.Txt contains a name on one line, then 5 real sales figures
on the next line. The program totals these sales figures.        }

Var    Mon, Tues, Wed, Thurs, Fri : Real;
       Total                       : Real;
       Name                        : String[30];

Begin
  Assign(Input, 'A:\Ch4\Sales.Txt');        {Redirect Input to be}
  Reset(Input);                       {from the text file 'Sales.Txt'.}
  Readln(Name);
  Readln(Mon, Tues, Wed, Thurs, Fri);
  Total := Mon + Tues + Wed + Thurs + Fri;
  Writeln(Name, ', your sales figures are:');{Echo input file.}
  Writeln(Mon:10:2, Tues:10:2, Wed:10:2, Thurs:10:2, Fri:10:2);
  Writeln;
  Writeln('The weekly total for ', Name, ' is $', Total:5:2)
End.
```

Listing 4.2

```
Blaise Pascal, your sales figures are:
     53.27     48.64     22.38     79.46     58.38

The weekly total for Blaise Pascal is $262.13
```

Figure 4.2

Note that the `Readln`s of program `Sales` have no prompts before them. Is this a violation of our earlier programming rule of always preceding `Read`s with `Write`s? No. *Interactive* input from the keyboard should *always* be prompted, so that the human will know what to do. But it is silly and unnecessary to prompt a computer that is reading data from a text file. The moronic computer will not understand the prompts; rather, it is the responsibility of the programmer to understand the structure of the data and sequence the `Read`s and `Readln`s so that the computer finds appropriate values for each input statement it executes.

CREATING A TEXT FILE

You may not have the disk that accompanies this book, or you may wish to create your own text files. Fortunately, Turbo Pascal makes this a very easy thing to do. You simply clear the editor and type your data, remembering our warning to put strings on lines by themselves. The only other word of caution is that when you save your file, be sure to give it the `.Txt` extension, for if you provide no extension, Turbo Pascal will automatically save your file with a `.Pas` extension. That is, when you save your file, replace `NONAME.PAS` with `MyData.Txt`, or whatever you choose to name your file. We remind you that the `.Txt` extension is simply a convention, so that you can easily distinguish your Pascal programs from your text files. Your text file, if it accidentally gets named `MyData.Pas`, will still work as a text file, but you, at a later date, may think that it is a Pascal program and try (not with much success) to run it!

SUMMARY

This chapter has introduced two new concepts: interactive input and text files. Even though these are opposites, we have extolled the virtues of each. How could we be so vacillating? The answer is that each has its place. If the amount of input is small and unknown before the program is run, as in the case of the intelligent cash register, then interactive input is exactly what is needed. On the other hand, if the amount of data is large and known in advance—say, 100 students' names and their scores on 10 homework assignments and 3 quizzes—then it is a real pain to enter these data interactively, over and over, while we debug our program. In this case, a text file is the answer to our prayers. Our text file example in this chapter was not very long or complex, because we do not yet have iterative (repetitive) or conditional statements at our disposal. All of that is about to change, as these are introduced in the next chapter. There we will learn to write a short program to process the 100 students and their homework and quiz scores. However, we caution the reader to understand carefully the fundamentals introduced in this chapter before continuing with the next chapter.

KEYWORDS

Several important concepts have been introduced in this brief chapter. As a study guide, make sure that you can describe each of the following terms:

Interactive input   Text file
Read   Readln
Assign   Reset

SELF-TEST QUESTIONS

4.1 Indicate the output (including any error messages) of each of the following segments. Indicate any leading blanks with a β. In each case, assume that the user types the following data:

```
Fahrenheit451
299 W. Birch
X Y Z
```

Also assume the following declarations for each segment:

```
Var   A, B : String[100];
      C, D : Char;
      M, N : Integer;
      X    : String[10];
      Y    : String[5];
```

a)   Readln(A);
      Readln(M, B);
      Readln(C, D);
      Writeln(A);
      Writeln(B);
      Writeln(D, C);
      Writeln(M);

b)   Read(A);
      Read(B);
      Readln(X);
      Readln(Y);
      Writeln(A);
      Writeln(B);
      Writeln(X);
      Writeln(Y);

c)   Readln(Y, M);
      Read(C, D);
      Writeln(Y, M, C, D);

d)   Readln(X, M);
      Readln(N, C, D);
      Readln(Y);
      Writeln(X);
      Writeln(C, D, M, N);
      Writeln(Y);

EXERCISES

4.2   Write a program that interactively requests three real numbers from the keyboard and prints out the average of the numbers.

4.3   Write a program that interactively requests a person's name and his or her weight in pounds and converts the weight to kilograms. One kilogram equals 2.2 pounds.

4.4   Write a program that interactively requests a mileage figure before the last fill-up, a mileage figure before the current fill-up, and an amount (in gallons) of gasoline purchased. Then print out the miles per gallon obtained on the last tankful of gas.

4.5   Write an interactive version of Exercise 3.22 that prompts the user to enter his or her name and height in feet and inches and converts the user's height to centimeters.

4.6   Write an interactive program for Pepi Roni's Pizza Parlor that fills pizza orders as follows: Request both the customer's name and phone number. Then obtain the number of small, medium, and large pizzas requested by the customer. Prices are $5.80, $7.20, and $8.60, respectively, for small, medium, and large pizzas. Then add a 6 percent sales tax and print out a total bill that is clearly labeled with the customer's name, phone number, and a breakdown of the pizzas purchased. (Note that since the phone number is not really an arithmetic quantity and since it contains a hyphen, it should be read as a string.)

4.7   Write a program to read the information in the text file `Ch4\Sales.Txt` and print out the average daily sales for the salesperson involved. You should pretend that you don't know what data are in the file. All you know is the structure of the file. (Two lines, a name on the first line, and five real numbers on the second line.) In other words, if your Pascal program has the name Blaise Pascal in it, you have missed the point.

4.8   Three friends are starting a software company. They have agreed to name the business **X, Y, and Z Software**, where X, Y, and Z are to be replaced by their actual names. They want you to write a program that will output all six possible orderings of their names so they can determine which ordering sounds best. Read the three names from the three-line text file `Ch4\Friends.Txt`.

4.9   Write a program for Ferty Lizer's Lawn and Garden Shoppe. The user will enter the width and depth of a lawn in feet. The program will compute the area of the lawn, subtract 2500 square feet for an average house and driveway, and then tell the user how many bags of fertilizer are needed to fertilize the lawn. One bag of fertilizer covers 5000 square feet. Since Ferty wants to sell products, if the customer needs 3.2 bags, the computer should indicate that 4 bags are needed. See if you can devise a `Trunc` or `Round` trick to *round* 3.2 up to 4. Do not worry if your trick also rounds 3.0 up to 4, for Ferty will cheerfully accept an unopened bag for a refund. **Warning**: Integer overflow occurs at 32767. This means that to avoid overflow in this problem, you will have to use the Real type or enter only small city lots (approximate dimensions 100' x 300'). In Chapter 10, we will learn that Turbo Pascal also has long integers that can help alleviate this problem.

4.10 The program `BuggyTax`, shown below, contains several bugs. Debug it. The program should compute the total amount due on a given purchase assuming an

8.125 percent sales tax. Just because a program runs with no errors, does that mean that it is correct?

```
Program BuggyTax;
{This buggy program is supposed to compute the total due on
a purchase using an 8.125% sales tax.                        }

Const    TaxRate = 8.125%

Var    Price : Real;
       Total : Real;

Begin
  Write('Please enter the price of the object ');
  Readln(Price);
  Total := TaxRate * Price;
  Writeln;
  Writeln('The total purchase price is $', Total:4:2)
End.
```

For your convenience, this program is on the sample disk as Ch4\BuggyTax.

ANSWERS TO SELF-TEST QUESTIONS

4.1 a) Fahrenheit451   b) Fahrenheit451
            ßW. Birch
            ßX
            299   299 W

     c) Error: Invalid Numeric Format when   d) Fahrenheit
         'nheit451' is read as an Integer.   ßW451299
                                                     X Y Z

5

FUNDAMENTAL CONTROL STRUCTURES

In this chapter, the real power of the computer is finally introduced. The programs that we have written in previous chapters have not been worthy of an expensive computer. Each program has asked the computer to perform some fairly trivial computation and output its results. The form of each program has been nearly the same: Execution begins at the first statement and continues directly to the bottom of the program. Each statement is executed exactly once. Hence, it has been more bother than it was worth to write a program to solve one of our problems! Now, all of that changes. We will learn in this chapter how to alter the flow of control, so that programs can make decisions and choose between executing one group of statements and another group of statements. We will also see how the computer can perform a series of statements over and over, without getting caught in an infinite loop. These fundamental control structures allow us to write short, powerful programs that produce interesting output. The material of this chapter is key to the understanding of Pascal. No program in the remainder of the book fails to contain one of the features learned here. Time spent studying and understanding these concepts will pay you hefty dividends.

In the previous paragraph, we stated that the computer is able to make decisions. This sometimes makes people nervous. They think that making decisions implies intelligence and, therefore, that moronic computers should not be capable of such acts. We simply point out that many mechanical devices make simple decisions. My toaster decides when my toast is burned and then presents it to me. My smoke alarm decides that when my toaster has completed its task, the fire department should be called. My clock radio decides when I have finally gotten back to sleep and keeps reminding me every five minutes that I have dozed off again. My car speaks to me when it decides that I don't have enough gas to reach the next station. Therefore, it should really be no surprise that the computer can make simple decisions. It is the blinding speed of the computer that allows it to make what seem like complex decisions. For example, landing a space shuttle, as complex as it seems, can be broken down into simple, discrete steps where each decision is as simple as deciding if the toast is burned. We repeat our caveat from Chapter 3:

You won't get the computer to solve any problem that you cannot, in principle, solve yourself.

Computers can land space shuttles because the mathematics and physics involved in such procedures is well understood. We will not consider examples of such complexity in this text. But always begin by trying to understand the problem and then proceed to divide and conquer the problem until, eventually, it is in pieces small enough to give to the computer. As we get to more complex problems, we will have more to say about the process of problem solving on a computer.

BOOLEAN VARIABLES

Before we can actually discuss the main content of this chapter, we must take care of a couple of preliminaries. The first of these is the notion of a **logical** or **Boolean** variable. The term Boolean is taken in honor of George Boole (1815-1864), a British logician who discovered many of the fundamental laws of logic. Boolean variables are among the simplest concepts in Pascal, because they are variables that may take on only one of the two values, True or False. In this regard, True and False should be regarded as constants known by the system, just as 0 and 3.14159 are numeric constants of the system. Do not misquote us as saying that "Pascal knows the meaning of truth." It is simply that Pascal has decided upon some internal representations for True and False and allows us to use these terms as an aid in writing programs. Also, as we'll see, Pascal already knows some fundamental logical operations (And, Or, and Not, for example), and these can be used to simplify the expression of our algorithms.

A Boolean variable, then, is simply a variable whose only possible values are True and False. We declare Boolean variables just as we do integers, reals, characters, and strings:

```
Var    Count : Integer;
       Rate  : Real;
       Maybe : Boolean;
       Sex   : Char;
       Name  : String[30];
       Done  : Boolean;
```

Notice that variables can be declared in any order. Of course, Count is now allowed to take any integer value. Likewise, Maybe can take any Boolean value—Maybe can be True or False. Boolean variables can also be used in assignment statements:

```
Done := False;
```

or

```
Maybe := True;
```

or even the more interesting example:

```
Done := (Count > 10);
```

Here, `Count > 10` is an expression, but it is a *Boolean* expression, not an arithmetic expression, since it evaluates to `True` or `False`. If the current value of `Count` is greater than 10, then `Done` is assigned the value `True`; otherwise, `Done` is assigned the value `False`. We will soon see how such Boolean expressions are used to alter the flow of control within a program.

Simple Boolean expressions can be created from the following **relational operators**:

Algebraic Symbol	Pascal Symbol	English Meaning
<	<	less than
>	>	greater than
=	=	equals
≤	<=	less than or equals
≥	>=	greater than or equals
≠	<>	not equals

Here are some more examples of simple Boolean expressions. Note that these are expressions, as $2 + 3$ is an expression. They are *not* complete Pascal statements. Also, the value of each expression, `True` or `False`, depends upon the current value of the variables in the expression:

```
Rate <> 0.135
Name = 'Mickey Mouse'
Sum <= 100.0
```

Boolean expressions can be combined into compound expressions using the logical operators `Not`, `And`, and `Or`. While not as familiar as the arithmetic operations, the logical operations are surely as simple to understand. The **conjunction** operator is `And`. We use it when we wish to make two assertions and assert that both are, in fact, true. That last sentence is a conjunction, for example. In Pascal, the keyword `And` stands between the two expressions that you wish to conjoin. Of course, the value of a conjunction is `True` only if both parts are `True`. Otherwise, the conjunction is `False`. Thus,

```
(Count < 10) And (Name = 'Mickey Mouse')
```

is `True` if and only if `Count` contains some value less than 10 and `Name` contains exactly the value `'Mickey Mouse'`.

The **disjunction** of two expressions is formed by using the `Or` operator. Reasonably enough, a disjunction is `True` if either or both of the expressions are `True`. The disjunction is `False` only if both parts are `False`. For example,

```
(Rate > 1.12) Or (Sum <> 50.0)
```

is `True` if `Rate` exceeds 1.12 or if `Sum` has any value other than 50.0.

Finally, the **negation** of an expression is formed by applying the `Not` operator. This gives the expression exactly the opposite truth value. So,

```
Not (Count <= 25)
```

is `True` if and only if `Count` exceeds 25. The results of these operators are often summarized in so-called truth tables:

X	Y	X And Y	X Or Y
True	True	True	True
True	False	False	True
False	True	False	True
False	False	False	False

X	Not X
True	False
False	True

You should check that these are consistent with our interpretations above. For example, the conjunction is `True` only if both conjuncts are `True`. Often, the beginner tries to memorize tables such as these. That is the wrong approach. If one really understands the discussion that precedes these tables, there is nothing to memorize. Once they have been understood, these operations are so simple that one cannot forget them!

One very important word of caution, when forming complex Boolean expressions, is the following: Always use parentheses around the operands of the expressions unless they are simple Boolean variables. That is, we must write

```
(Count = 10) And (Rate > 1.0)
```

rather than

```
Count = 10 And Rate > 1.0
```

As additional examples,

```
Maybe Or Done
```

and

```
Maybe Or (Name = 'Donald Duck')
```

are both okay. The reason the parentheses are necessary in the first example is the order in which the relational and logical operators are applied. In Chapter 3, we discussed the precedence of the arithmetic operations. Here is the order of precedence of the arithmetic, relational, and logical operations:

Highest Precedence: Not
Second Precedence: `*, /, Div, Mod, And`
Third Precedence: `+, -, Or`
Lowest Precedence: `=, <>, <, >, <=, >=`

This means that, in the absence of parentheses, Not will be applied first, then the multiplying and dividing operators, then the adding and subtracting operators, and then, finally, the relational operators. Within any level, evaluations will be from the left. Thus,

```
X + Y * Z
```

means

```
X + (Y * Z)
```

since the * operator has higher precedence than the + operator. Likewise,

```
X + Y - Z
```

means

```
(X + Y) - Z
```

since the operators are of equal precedence and, hence, evaluation proceeds from the left. To return to our logical example, we see that

```
Count = 10 And Rate > 1.0
```

is evaluated as

```
(Count = (10 And Rate)) > 1.0
```

which is, unfortunately, nonsense. Remember, parentheses are needed to force the meaning we want:

```
(Count = 10) And (Rate > 1.0)
```

Rather than memorize all the technical details of precedence, we suggest you remember that the multiplicative operators (`*`, `/`, Div, and Mod) have higher precedence than the additive operators (+ and -); otherwise, simply use parentheses to guarantee that your expression has the meaning you desire. For example, although

```
This And That Or Whatever
```

and

```
((This And That) Or (Whatever))
```

and

```
(This And That) Or Whatever
```

are all equivalent, the last expression is the clearest. Don't use every parenthesis possible, or omit every parenthesis possible. Strive for clarity.

COMPOUND STATEMENTS

We need one more syntactical ingredient before we begin the main event. A compound statement is simply a mechanism whereby we can combine many statements into one statement. Its format is

```
Begin
   Statement;
   Statement;
   .  .  .
   .  .  .
   .  .  .
   Statement;
   Statement
End;
```

where each Statement is replaced by any legal Pascal statement. Note that, since semicolons are used to separate Pascal statements, no semicolon is needed after the last statement *before* the End. We have shown a semicolon *after* the End, but this semicolon is needed only if there is another Pascal statement following the compound statement. We should point out that placing a semicolon after the last statement before the End does not give an error—it is simply unnecessary. In this book, we will not include extra semicolons, except that in segments that are not complete programs, we will place a semicolon after the last statement shown, because we expect other statements (not shown) to follow our segment.

A common error that beginners make is to write

```
Statement-1 And Statement-2
```

when they want the computer to do Statement-1 and then Statement-2. The intent may be clear to the programmer, but Pascal does not understand such nonsense. Since And is a logical operator, it is allowed to stand only between two Boolean expressions. To combine two statements into one, the programmer needs the compound statement:

```
Begin
  Statement-1;
  Statement-2
End;
```

The Begin and End should be thought of as big grouping symbols. In this regard, they are like the Begin and End. that delimit the actual executable portion of the program. Note that the End in the compound statement does not include a period. The necessity for the compound statement and for Boolean variables will now be made clear.

THE CONDITIONAL: IF...THEN

The conditional statement is used to decide, based upon the value of some Boolean expression, which of several courses of action the computer should take. The conditional in Pascal takes two forms, the first of which is known as the If...Then. Its format is

```
If Boolean expression Then
   Statement;
```

When this statement is executed, the computer evaluates the Boolean expression. If the expression is False, the action of the If is complete and execution continues with the next statement (if any) in the program. If the Boolean expression is True, the statement following the Then is executed and control passes to the next statement. It is important to realize that, in either case, the flow of the program continues with the next statement in the program. If the condition happens to be True, an extra step is added; otherwise, it is skipped. The flow diagram of Figure 5.1 may help to make this situation clearer. If the Boolean expression is True, program control, as shown in Figure 5.1, flows to the right and then on to the next statement in the program. On the other hand, if the expression is False, then flow *falls through* directly to the next statement.

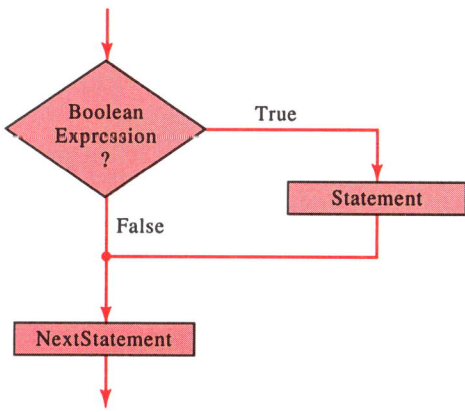

Figure 5.1

For example, suppose we would like to print the value of the variable Count only if Count is a multiple of 100 (Count = 100, 200, 300, etc.). We can do this with

```
If Count Mod 100 = 0 Then
   Writeln('The value of Count is ', Count);
```

The statement following the Then may be, as you have probably guessed, a compound statement. Suppose that each time Count is a multiple of 100, we would like to print Count and assign to the variable Century the value of Count divided by 100. To do so, we can write

```
If Count Mod 100 = 0 Then
   Begin
     Century := Count Div 100;
     Writeln('The value of Count is ', Count)
   End;
```

Any time you want to perform more than one action in the Then clause, remember that you need to use a compound statement to bind all of your actions together into one statement. What happens if you forget? Suppose you type

```
If Count Mod 100 = 0 Then
   Century := Count Div 100;
   Writeln('The value of Count is ', Count);      {Logical error!}
```

The system finds no syntax error and your program runs, but it does not execute as you expect. Every value of Count is printed, whether Count is a multiple of 100 or not. This helps us see how the computer interprets the above segment. Since there is no Begin, the Then clause has only one statement in it. If Count is a multiple of 100, then the assignment is performed and execution continues with the Writeln statement (which is what we wanted). However, if Count is not a multiple of 100, the assignment is skipped and control proceeds to the next statement, which is the Writeln. Thus, the flow of control is as shown in Figure 5.2a, rather than what we had intended (Figure 5.2b).

   This example shows that the indentation, which we have used to indicate the statements that we want to be within the If, is ignored by the computer. Although we indented both statements under the If, the computer ended the If with the first statement found in its Then clause. The fact that the computer ignores indentation does not mean that we should abandon the use of it. Indentation is a great aid to the human, because it clearly and instantly shows the extent of a construct. Almost nothing makes a program more unreadable than typing the code straight down the left margin. Use indentation, but, in debugging your programs, remember that Turbo Pascal pays no attention to the indentation.

   For completeness, we provide the following example of *poor* programming technique:

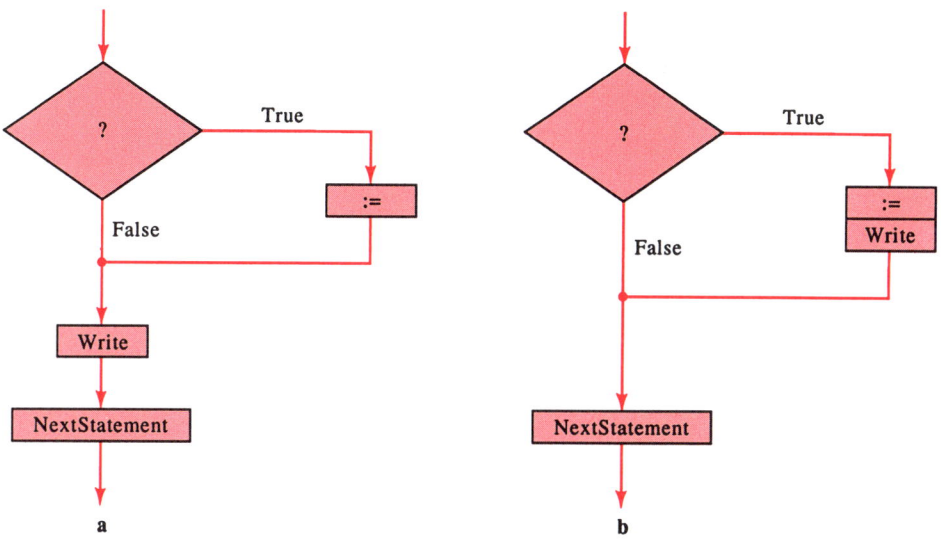

Figure 5.2

```
If Count Mod 100 = 0 Then
  Begin
    Writeln('The value of Count is ', Count)        {Poor style.}
  End;
```

The problem is that no Begin/End block is needed here. When you have only one statement in the Then clause, there is no need to make it a compound statement. The Begin/End pair is overused as it is in Pascal. Don't use extra pairs. They only make your program more difficult to read.

ANOTHER CONDITIONAL: IF...THEN...ELSE

The other form of the conditional in Pascal is very handy for choosing between two alternative courses of action. Its format is

```
If Boolean expression Then
  Statement
Else
  Statement;
```

When execution reaches this If...Then...Else statement, the Boolean expression is tested. If True, the Then clause is executed, and control skips the Else clause and proceeds to the next statement. However, if the Boolean expression evaluates to False, then the Else clause is executed and execution continues with the next

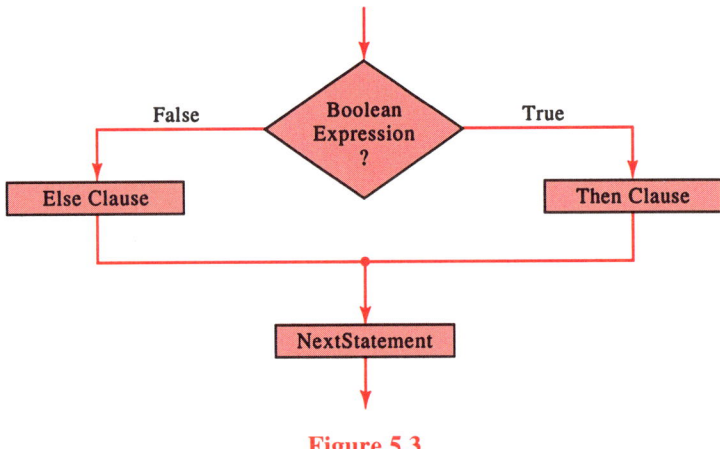

Figure 5.3

statement. Thus, the flow diagram for this situation is as shown in Figure 5.3.

The easiest Pascal error to make is to insert a semicolon after the statement in the Then clause:

```
If Boolean expression Then
   Statement;                              {This ; is a syntax error!}
Else
   Statement;     {This ; is needed if another statement follows.}
```

The semicolon before the Else ends the If (making it an If of the first form). The system is then unable to match the Else to an If, and the compiler issues the not extremely informative error message, **Error in statement**, with the cursor flashing under the Else. Please keep in mind that an extra semicolon on the line above can cause this particular error message.

EXAMPLES OF CONDITIONALS

Let us begin our examples with the standard case of regular pay versus overtime pay. Let us suppose that the variables Rate and Hours already have values. We are to write a segment that computes the appropriate value of the variable Pay. Naturally, if the value of Hours is 40 or less, we use the simple formula

Pay ← Rate * Hours

If the employee has worked more than 40 hours, we must compute time-and-a-half for the overtime hours. So we use the formulas

Regular ← Rate * 40.0
Overtime ← 1.5 * Rate * (Hours - 40.0)
Pay ← Regular + Overtime

All of these, except perhaps the middle one, should be clear. The middle one computes the overtime pay by multiplying the overtime rate (1.5 * Rate) times the number of hours that were overtime (Hours - 40.0). In Pascal, our segment becomes

```
If Hours <= 40.0 Then                              {Regular case}
  Pay := Rate * Hours
Else                                               {Overtime case}
  Begin
    Regular := Rate * 40.0;
    Overtime := 1.5 * Rate * (Hours - 40.0);
    Pay := Regular + Overtime
  End;
Writeln('The pay is $', Pay:6:2);
```

You should trace the above segment to see that if Rate has the value 5.00 and Hours is 30, then the output is

```
The pay is $150.00
```

while, if Rate is 5.00 and Hours is 50, then the output is

```
The pay is $275.00
```

This example also points out that the Else clause may be compound while the Then clause is simple. In this case, it would be possible to make both clauses simple by combining the overtime formulas into one long formula:

```
If Hours <= 40.0 Then                              {Regular case}
  Pay := Rate * Hours
Else                                               {Overtime case}
  Pay := (Rate * 40.0) + 1.5 * Rate * (Hours - 40.0);
Writeln('The pay is $', Pay:6:2);
```

The advantage of this method is that the program is shorter and, therefore, a little clearer. The disadvantage of this method is that the overtime formula is more complex and, hence, the Else clause is, perhaps, less clear. In other words, it is a trade-off and a personal decision as to which method is better. Remember to strive to make your programs as clear as possible. Sometimes, too many variables will muddle the situation, while too few variables are sure to make the program hard to read. In this situation, either of the above is acceptable, but watch for this trade-off. Here is a poorer version of the segment. Can you spot the problem?

```
If Hours <= 40.0 Then
  Begin                                            {Regular case}
    Pay := Rate * Hours;
    Writeln('The pay is $', Pay:6:2)
  End
```

```
Else
  Begin                                                   {Overtime case}
    Pay := (Rate * 40.0) + 1.5 * Rate * (Hours - 40.0);
    Writeln('The pay is $', Pay:6:2)
  End;
```

This time there is no syntax error, and even the correct results are produced. Our objection is that the `Writeln` statement is repeated in both the `Then` and the `Else` clause. A good programming rule of thumb is:

If something is repeated in the `Then` clause *and* the `Else` clause of an `If` statement, it doesn't belong inside the `If`.

In our case, the `Writeln` belongs after the `If`. Note that when the `Writeln` is moved, neither the `Then` nor the `Else` clause needs to be compound.

Here is another poor method on the same example. Can you spot the problem?

```
If Hours <= 40.0 Then
  Pay := Rate * Hours;
If Hours > 40.0 Then
  Pay := (Rate * 40.0) + 1.5 * Rate * (Hours - 40.0);
Writeln('The pay is $', Pay:6:2);
```

Once again, the sytem finds nothing wrong with this segment, and it produces correct results. How picky can we get? Well, this time we object because of the use of two `If` statements where only one is needed. The computer must check to see if `Hours` is less than or equal to 40.0, then turn around microseconds later and check to see if `Hours` is greater than 40.0. `Hours` either is, or it isn't, larger than 40.0, and we shouldn't make the computer check it twice. An `If...Then...Else` is far more appropriate in this case.

An `If...Then...Else` is a natural two-way decision-maker. How would we make a three-way decision? No, there is no `If...Then...Else...Otherwise` to learn. We simply use two `If...Then...Else` statements nested inside one another. Figure 5.4 shows a flow diagram for this situation.

Suppose that `Age` is an integer variable and that we would like to print `Child` if `Age` is less than 13, `Adult` if `Age` is greater than 19, and `Teenager` otherwise. The following segment accomplishes this. (The line numbers are for the discussion that follows.)

```
1.      If Age < 13 Then
2.         Writeln('Child')
3.      Else If Age > 19 Then
4.         Writeln('Adult')
5.      Else
6.         Writeln('Teenager');
7.      Writeln('Done');
```

Lines 1-6 are all one statement! It is an `If...Then...Else` that just happens to have

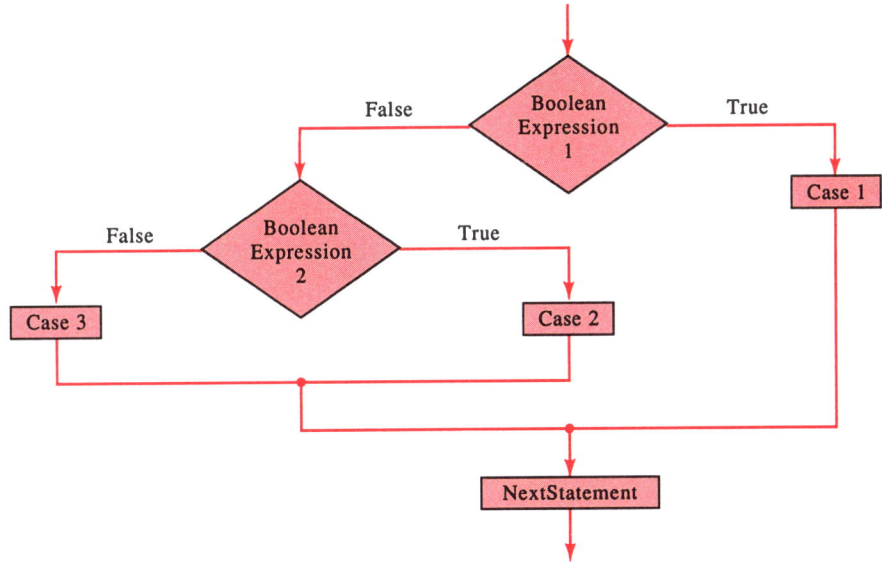

Figure 5.4

an If...Then...Else in its Else clause. Of course, if Age has the value 7, the Boolean expression in line 1 is True and the output is the two lines Child and Done. That is, since the Then clause was taken, the Else clause (lines 3-6) is skipped, and execution continues with the statement following line 6. If Age has the value 98, the condition on line 1 is False and, therefore, the flow of control skips to the Else clause, which begins on line 3. Here, another Boolean expression is found and this one evaluates to True. Hence, Adult and Done are output. To follow the flow of control, note that since we have executed the Then clause of the If beginning at line 3, we have finished that If. Moreover, that completes the Else clause of the outer If and, hence, control again passes to the statement following line 6. Finally, if Age is 17, then both the Boolean expressions are False and so control passes in each case to the Else clause, and Teenager and Done is the output. Therefore, for every value of Age, exactly one of the three clauses is executed and control then passes, in each case, to the writing of the Done message.

There is an alternative, acceptable way to indent our nested If example. Consider the segment:

```
1.    If Age < 13 Then
2.       Writeln('Child')
3.    Else
4.       If Age > 19 Then
5.          Writeln('Adult')
6.       Else
7.          Writeln('Teenager');
8.    Writeln('Done');
```

You should trace this segment until you are convinced that it is completely equivalent to the previous segment. The first method of indentation has the advantage that the three cases are aligned and immediately obvious to the human eye. The second method of indentation follows the rule that each If is aligned with its own Else, making it easy to see which If and Else go with one another.

When Ifs are used within one another, they are said to be **nested**. That is, the second If is nested inside the first If. Remember, one If...Then...Else gives a two-way decision procedure. Two nested If...Then...Else statements give a three-way decision procedure. Likewise, 17 nested Ifs will provide an 18-way decision procedure, but, in Chapter 8, we will learn a better way to handle large numbers of cases.

The next example shows that compound statements are quite possible with nested Ifs. In addition to writing Child, Adult, or Teenager, let us suppose that we also want to increment the appropriate variable NumKids, NumAdults, or NumTeens. If NumKids, NumAdults, and NumTeens have the values 23, 9, and 56, respectively, and Age has the value 13, then we want our segment to output Teenager and also to count the teenager by incrementing NumTeens to 57. Identifiers like NumTeens, which *count* something, are called **counters**. Incrementing a counter is a very common operation in computer programs. Be sure you understand how this works. The structure of this segment is just like the previous one, except each clause is now compound:

```
If Age < 13 Then                              {Kid case}
  Begin
    Writeln('Child');
    NumKids := NumKids + 1
  End
Else If Age > 19 Then                         {Adult case}
  Begin
    Writeln('Adult');
    NumAdults := NumAdults + 1
  End
Else                                          {Beware of teenager!}
  Begin
    Writeln('Teenager');
    NumTeens := NumTeens + 1
  End;
```

The reader should trace the above segment for at least three carefully chosen values of Age.

Sometimes, beginners fall in love with nested Ifs and get a bit carried away. See if you can spot any excesses in the following segment, which assumes that Score has a value and uses this value to assign and print a letter Grade. (Grade is a character and Score is an integer.)

```
1.     If Score >= 90 Then
2.        Begin
3.          Grade := 'A';
4.          Writeln(Grade)
5.        End
```

```
6.      Else If (Score < 90) And (Score >= 80) Then
7.        Begin
8.          Grade := 'B';
9.          Writeln(Grade)
10.       End
11.     Else If (Score < 80) And (Score >= 70) Then
12.       Begin
13.         Grade := 'C';
14.         Writeln(Grade)
15.       End
16.     Else If (Score < 70) And (Score >= 60) Then
17.       Begin
18.         Grade := 'D';
19.         Writeln(Grade)
20.       End
21.     Else If Score < 60 Then
22.       Begin
23.         Grade := 'F';
24.         Writeln(Grade)
25.       End;
```

There are many ways to improve this solution. First of all, each clause contains a `Writeln` and, hence, the `Writeln` should be brought out of the `If`. The beginner is often so intent on printing the `'A'`, `'B'`, `'C'`, `'D'`, or `'F'` that the commonality of the `Writeln` is often overlooked. More importantly, the Boolean expressions are far more complex than they need to be. We, as programmers, are doing unnecessary work and we are making the computer do unnecessary work as well. For example, the only way to get to line 6 or beyond is to fail the test at line 1. That is, the flow of control does not come to any line after line 6 unless `Score` is less than 90. Hence, it is unnecessary to check if `Score` is less than 90 at line 6. Likewise, the only way to get to the test at line 11 is to fail the tests at lines 1 and 6. Thus, if flow reaches line 11, we already know that `Score` is less than 80. Hence, the above can be greatly simplified to

```
1.      If Score >= 90 Then
2.        Grade := 'A'
3.      Else If Score >= 80 Then
4.        Grade := 'B'
5.      Else If Score >= 70 Then
6.        Grade := 'C'
7.      Else If Score >= 60 Then
8.        Grade := 'D'
9.      Else
10.       Grade := 'F';
11.     Writeln(Grade);
```

Note that the condition at line 21, in the original version, is completely unnecessary. In the new version, the only way to get to line 10 is to enter the `Else` clause at each opportunity by failing the tests at lines 1, 3, 5, and 7. That is, we reach line 10 only if Score is less than 60.

Sometimes, compound Boolean expressions can avoid the need for complex nested Ifs. For example, suppose we need to count all male, senior, computer science majors at Granola State University. If we assume that Sex, Class, and Major are string variables with the appropriate values, the following set of Ifs does the trick:

```
If Sex = 'Male' Then
  If Class = 'Senior' Then
    If Major = 'CS' Then
      Count := Count + 1;
```

However, the following single If statement is certainly clearer:

```
If (Sex = 'Male') And (Class = 'Senior') And (Major = 'CS') Then
  Count := Count + 1;
```

The moral of this example is that some thought is required in writing clear programs. Even in a limited language like Pascal, there is usually more than one way to express your intentions. Strive for clarity!

As a final example of nested Ifs, let us consider the following simple problem. We would like to provide an appropriate message for students with exceptional performance on an examination. Any student who scored over 90 on the exam should be given an encouraging message. A student who scored less than 50 on the exam should be given a warning. Those who scored between 50 and 90 do not receive any message. See if you can figure out why the following segment does *not* work:

```
If Score > 50 Then                                        {Logical Error}
  If Score > 90 Then
    Writeln('Way to go!! Keep it up.')
Else
  Writeln('Have you considered another major???');
```

The problem is that we have two If statements fighting for one Else. In this case, we want a simple If...Then nested in an If...Then...Else. Unfortunately, even though we aligned the Else with the outer If, Pascal always attaches an Else to the nearest If. Thus, Pascal interprets the segment as if we had an If...Then...Else nested within a simple If...Then:

```
If Score > 50 Then
  If Score > 90 Then
    Writeln('Way to go!!! Keep it up.')
  Else
    Writeln('Have you considered another major???');
```

This is certainly not equivalent to what we had intended, for even Neal Lee Perfect, who has a Score of 90, gets our nasty message, while Noe Hope, with a Score of 4, escapes our wrath! Use indentation to make your intent clear to humans, but remember that indentation is ignored by the computer.

How can we correct the problem? One method is to rewrite the Boolean expressions so that an If...Then...Else inside an If...Then will solve the problem. We leave that solution to the reader because it dodges the main problem, which is to nest a simple If...Then inside an If...Then...Else. Since an Else is always attached to the nearest If, one way to fix the problem is to provide a do-nothing-else for the inner If. The proper terminology for a do-nothing-else is a **null** Else:

```
If Score > 50 Then
  If Score > 90 Then
    Writeln('Way to go!!!  Keep it up.')
  Else {do nothing}
Else
  Writeln('Have you considered another major???');
```

What we have done is change the inner If..Then to an If...Then...Else, so that the nesting is as we expect. Remember, if you are nesting Ifs and some of them are If...Then...Else statements, you would be wise to make them all If...Then...Else statements by providing null Else clauses as needed.

REPETITION: THE WHILE

We now begin our discussion of control structures that allow for the repetition of groups of statements. The If allows us to choose between two courses of action, while the repetitive statements allow our programs to loop repeatedly through a given set of statements. For example, a payroll program loops through the employees, creating the individual paychecks. It would really not be worth the effort if we had to write a separate program for each employee! The use of the conditional If allows us to plan for all contingencies, and then the loop structure allows one program to process all the employees. This allows a program of 10 lines, if it loops 100 times, to be the equivalent of a 1000-line program. We begin to see the power and convenience of repetitive control structures.

It will be common for us to want to loop through some group of statements while some property remains true. For example, for the payroll problem above, we want to loop through the process of computing and printing checks while we haven't come to the end of the list of employees. Because this is often a useful way to view a problem, Pascal provides a While statement. Its syntax is

```
While Boolean expression Do
  Statement;
```

Fortunately, of course, the Statement may be compound. When execution reaches the While, the Boolean expression is tested. If it is False, the statement following the Do is skipped and the flow of control passes to the next statement in your program. On the other hand, if the Boolean expression is True, the statement following the Do is executed once. Then the expression is tested again, and the statement is repeatedly executed *while* the expression remains True.

It is possible to write an infinite loop—one that never terminates. But it is the responsibility of the programmer to make sure that there is some mechanism within the body of the loop to make the Boolean expression eventually False, thus terminating the loop. Some examples will help to make these points clear. Let us try to write a program that prints the integers from 1 to 20. That seems simple enough. Of course, we could use 20 separate Writelns, but that would get pretty tedious if we wanted to modify the program to print the integers from 1 to 1000! Here is a basic outline of our approach:

Initialize Num to 1
While Num < 20
    Output Num
    Increment Num by 1

You should trace the above outline to see that it does, indeed, produce a 1, then a 2, then a 3, etc. In fact, if you trace it very carefully, you should be able to spot a small problem (which we will discuss later). Our outline is another example of what computer scientists call pseudo-code. The outline is not yet Pascal. Rather, it is very English-like and easy to read. Writing good pseudo-code is an art that you will need to practice, but the advantage of good pseudo-code is that it makes the writing of Pascal programs a much simpler task. With pseudo-code, one breaks a problem down into its constituent parts and repeats this process until the task is broken into manageable pieces. The use of pseudo-code is an important step in top-down, structured programming. We do not believe you should be forced to use a specific pseudo-code, and we will not attempt to create a new pseudo-code language for you to memorize. Rather, we illustrate, throughout this text, our pseudo-code for the example programs in the text. We think it is as worth your while to understand and practice writing pseudo-code outlines as it is to study the listings of our programs.

Now back to the problem at hand. Listing 5.1 shows a Pascal program Count that implements our simple pseudo-code.

```
Program Count;
{This amazing program is supposed to count from 1 to 20 with a While.}

Var    Num : Integer;

Begin
  Num := 1;
  While Num < 20 Do
    Begin
      Writeln(Num);
      Num := Num + 1
    End {While}
End.
```

Listing 5.1

The reader should compare the pseudo-code with the program to see how each statement in the pseudo-code was translated into Pascal. The advantage of the pseudo-code is that it is an intermediate step between raw English and the precise syntax needed in Pascal. Notice that, in Pascal, whenever the body of a `While` is more than one statement, a `Begin` and `End` pair is necessary to make the statement following the `Do` a compound statement. Also, notice that this detail was not displayed in the pseudo-code. The pseudo-code is not Pascal, and the purpose of pseudo-code is to get down our ideas without worrying about these fussy details. Then, when we have the idea expressed in pseudo-code, we can do the rather straightforward translation to Pascal.

If you haven't guessed what is wrong with the above program, load `Count` from the sample disk (or type it in) and run it. What happened to that final value? Remember, `Count` was supposed to print the integers from 1 to 20, but it stopped at 19. The explanation is, of course, quite simple. `Num` is incremented at the *bottom* of the loop. After the incrementation, the expression `Num < 20` is tested and the loop is repeated until the condition becomes `False`. Now, when `Num` is finally incremented to 20, control exits from the loop before the value of `Num` can be printed. We could fix the problem by putting another `Writeln(Num)` statement after the `While`, but it would be better simply to change the Boolean expression to read `Num <= 20`.

The moral of this story is that you should learn to check the special boundary values and make sure your loop ends when you want it to. A common error is to have a `While` that loops one too many, or one too few, times. In Chapter 8, we'll see that there is, in fact, a better way to do a counted loop than the method we have used here.

As another simple, but important, example, let us write a program to add together the 10 numbers 1, 2, 3, . . . , 10. The reason that this example is important is that it teaches us how the computer can sum a large group of numbers, and we will use this fact over and over in the pages to come. Of course, the simplest way to add the integers from 1 to 10 is to use the assignment statement

```
Sum := 1 + 2 + 3 + 4 + 5 + 6 + 7 + 8 + 9 + 10;
```

However, that is not a very general solution and is certainly very tedious if we want to sum all the integers from 1 to 1000. Therefore, we will devise a better, more general solution. Not surprisingly, we'll use a `While`. But what is it that is going to be repeated? The answer is that we are going to loop 10 times and, on each execution of the loop, add the next number to a **running summation**. At the end of the loop, the running summation will have accumulated the proper value. Trace the following pseudo-code carefully to see that `Sum` takes on the successive values 0, 1, 3, 6, 10, 15,..., 55.

Initialize Sum to 0
Initialize Num to 1
While Num ≤ 10
   Add Num to Sum
   Increment Num to the next number
Output the results to a waiting world

This pseudo-code is easily translated to Pascal. The Pascal equivalent is called `Add` and is shown in Listing 5.2.

```
Program Add;
{This program adds the first 10 integers. It introduces the
important notion of a Running Summation.                    }

Var   Num : Integer;
      Sum : Integer;

Begin
  Sum := 0;
  Num := 1;
  While Num <= 10 Do
    Begin
      Sum := Sum + Num;
      Num := Num + 1
    End; {While}
  Writeln('The sum of the first ten integers is ', Sum)
End.
```

Listing 5.2

Again, notice how the pseudo-code has made the final step, the writing of an actual Pascal program, an easy task. Another point to be made about using a running summation is that one must always initialize Sum to zero before beginning. Here is the way we look at it: Each time through the loop, we drop another Num into the Sum bucket. At the end of the loop, the bucket contains the Sum of all the Nums. But, to get the correct answer, we must make sure that we began with an empty bucket! That is the purpose and need for the statement Sum := 0.

Sometimes, students initialize every variable in sight. Consider the following nonsense example, which adds 5 and 7 to some number Z, read in from the keyboard, and stores the answer in Sum. Do you see any initializations that are unnecessary?

```
X := 5;
Y := 7;
Z := 0;
Sum := 0;
Read(Z);
Sum := X + Y + Z;
```

Since Z is given a value in the Read, it is pointless to initialize Z to zero two lines before. Z does not need a value to obtain a value from the Read. Hence, initializing Z is poor programming style. Likewise, Sum does not participate in the final line, but only receives a value. Hence, Sum does not need to be initialized in this example. However, if the last line were Sum := Sum + X + Y + Z, then, since Sum does participate in the addition, it would have to have an initial value. Finally, initializing a variable does not always mean setting it to zero. For example, in the program of Listing 5.2, the variable Num is initialized to 1. The key to understanding when a variable needs to be initialized is to understand the notion of a variable (Chapter 3) and how that variable is used:

Any time a variable participates on the right-hand side of an assignment or in the evaluation of any expression, it must already have been given a value.

THE STRUCTURE OF A LOOP

Loops are very important for what follows, so we consider the notion in more detail. A loop consists of four parts. There is an **initialization** portion that is needed before we enter the loop. Any variables that are referenced on the right-hand side of assignments must have values, even on the first loop execution. In the previous examples, this initialization is handled by the statements Num := 1 and Sum := 0. The **body** of the loop is the group of statements that is repeated. In a While, the body is usually compound and, therefore, caught between a Begin and an End. A loop also contains a **test**, or Boolean condition, that is used to decide when to terminate the loop. In our two examples, the conditions have been Num <= 20 and Num <= 10, respectively. Finally, to avoid an infinite loop, there must be some means for the loop to eventually terminate. This is called the **modification** portion of the loop, which is a part of the body. In our examples, the statement Num := Num + 1 guarantees that the loop eventually terminates. Often, the modification is at the bottom of the body. In summary, the four parts of any loop are:

1. Initialization before the loop
2. The body of the loop
3. The test to end the loop
4. Modification to avoid an infinite loop

Look for these parts in our examples. We'll also see how they can be rearranged, when we discuss additional Pascal control structures in Chapter 8.

COMPARING THE WHILE AND THE IF

Since the While and the simple If have similar formats,

```
While Boolean expression Do
   Statement;

If Boolean expression Then
   Statement;
```

let us compare and contrast them, so that you clearly understand the difference. Both check the Boolean expression and skip the given statement if the expression is False. Likewise, both execute the given statement if the expression is True. However, the If executes the given statement *at most once* and then continues on to the next statement in your program. The While, on the other hand, continues to execute the given statement as long as the expression remains True. The If is used to choose between two courses of action; the While is used to create a loop.

EXAMPLE: PROFESSOR PEDANTICS—FIRST TWO VERSIONS

Professor Pedantics likes to give quizzes and, therefore, she needs a program to compute averages for her students. Suppose that each of her students has taken three quizzes and that names and quiz scores for her students are stored in a text file, `Scores.Txt`. Each student has two lines in the text file. The first line consists of the name (up to 30 characters), while the second line contains the three scores. Thus, the beginning of the text file might look like

```
Ruta Baga
67 56 72
Ben Bramwell
98 97 99
Brian Brown
95 92 99
Lowell Carmony
38 47 59
. . .
```

Clearly, we want to loop, reading students' names and quiz scores, and output averages as we go. How will we terminate the loop? Probably, the most obvious suggestion would be to count Professor Pedantics' students and to loop that many times. But Professor Pedantics teaches at large Granola State University and even she doesn't know how many students she has. She could count them, but that seems unnecessary with a computer around and, besides, humans are error-prone. Also, students, from our experience, are a pretty shifty lot. They add classes late; they drop like flies after the first exam. In short, you can never count on them anyway! Therefore, a better and more general solution to our problem is to make up a final, fictitious student whose sole purpose will be to signify the end of the data. This final value is often called a **trailer**, or **sentinel**, value. It is chosen as some ridiculous value that could not possibly be in the real data. For example, if we were entering student ID numbers, a value of 0 or -1 would make a nice trailer value. Another term for a trailer value is a Mickey-Mouse value. For this example, we choose to end the loop when we encounter the string `'Mickey Mouse'`. Hence, the line `'Mickey Mouse'` has been added as the last line of the text file `Scores.Txt`. Observe that adding Mickey as a trailer to the file is far easier than counting the number of people in the file.

Stated in `While` language, we want our algorithm to loop, processing people while we haven't found `'Mickey Mouse'`. Here, then, is our outline for Professor Pedantics:

Read a line of data containing the Name of the first individual
While the Name is not 'Mickey Mouse' do
    Read a line of data with the three scores
    Total the three scores
    Average the three scores
    Output the Name and the Average
    Read the next line of data with the next Name

Note that since this is pseudo-code, we have omitted the `Begins`, `Ends`, and semicolons that are necessary in the final, Pascal version. Also note that, as always, we must be sure that the condition in the While makes sense the first time. Since this condition involves a comparison of Name with the string 'Mickey Mouse', we must make sure that Name has an initial value. Thus, it is necessary to read the first name from the file before the While. Likewise, we know that there must be some mechanism for the condition eventually to become False. Hence, at the bottom of the body, we modify the value of Name by obtaining the next name. Now, of course, the expression comparing Name and 'Mickey Mouse' is tested again, and if the name is a legitimate one, the body is executed again. Then Name is again updated. Eventually, at the bottom of the loop, Name becomes 'Mickey Mouse' and the loop terminates. Note that the loop terminates without trying to process three scores for our fictitious Mickey. The Pascal equivalent is shown in Listing 5.3.

In all our examples using text files, we assume that our sample disk is in drive A:. If you don't use our disk, or drive A:, be sure to change the file name in the Assign appropriately.

Several changes between the pseudo-code and the Pascal version of Pedant1 are worthy of discussion. Note that in the program, the average was computed on one line, combining two lines from the pseudo-code. The pseudo-code is still the outline for the program, but it shouldn't be considered a straitjacket for the writing of the program. In the program, we included a Writeln to announce the purpose of the program. This

```
Program Pedant1; {Pedantics, Version 1.}
{This program averages 3 quizzes for a class of students using the
text file Ch5\Scores.Txt which has a trailer name of Mickey Mouse.
For each person, except Mickey, there are two lines in the file.
The first contains the name, the second contains 3 integer quiz
scores.                                                           }

Var    Name                 : String[30];
       Quiz1, Quiz2, Quiz3  : Integer;
       Average              : Real;

Begin
  Assign(Input,'A:\Ch5\Scores.Txt');{Get input from text file.}
  Reset(Input);
  Writeln('Professor Pedantics'' program - first version.');
  Writeln;
  Readln(Name);                       {Read first Name before loop.}
  While Name <> 'Mickey Mouse' Do     {Has sentinel been found?}
    Begin
      Readln(Quiz1, Quiz2, Quiz3);
      Average := (Quiz1 + Quiz2 + Quiz3) / 3.0;
      Writeln('The average for ', Name, ' is ', Average:5:2);
      Readln(Name)                    {Read the next Name here.}
    End {While}
End.
```

Listing 5.3

```
The average for Ruta Baga is 65.00
The average for Ben Bramwell is 98.00
The average for Brian Brown is 95.33
The average for Lowell Carmony is 48.00
...
```

Figure 5.5

is not really part of the solution, but it is a good programming practice. We also remark that if this program had used interactive input from the keyboard, we would also want to use a `Writeln` to remind the user of the trailer value needed to terminate the `While` loop. Finally, Figure 5.5 shows the first part of the output from `Pedant1`.

THE END-OF-FILE FUNCTION

If you are interactively entering data from the keyboard, a trailer value is an effective way to control the processing loop. If you are reading data from a text file, there is another alternative supplied by Pascal. This is the built-in `Eof` or End-of-file function. `Eof` is a Boolean function that is `True` only if the system has detected the end of the data file. Thus, unless the file is empty, `Eof` is initialized by a `Reset` command to `False`. When the last item is read from the file, `Eof` becomes `True`. Thus,

```
While Not Eof Do
  ...
```

is a natural construct to use with text files. Listing 5.4 shows `Pedant2`, which uses `Eof` to control the processing of a text file, `Scores2.Txt`.

The only difference between `Scores.Txt` and `Scores2.Txt` is that `Scores2.Txt` does *not* contain any trailer value. Rather than terminate the loop when `'Mickey Mouse'` is found, `Pedant2` terminates when the system sets `Eof` to `True`.

SENTINEL VALUES VERSUS END OF FILE

We would like to emphasize that `Eof` is particularly useful with disk files, but not of much use with interactive input from the keyboard. The reason for this is simple: With a file on disk, the system has the complete file and, hence, can easily tell when the end of the file has been reached. On the other hand, with interactive input, the system is unable to read the mind of the user and is, therefore, unable to decide when all the data have been entered. Thus, in what follows, we will often use `Eof` with text files and use trailer or sentinel values to terminate interactive input.

The output from `Pedant2` is, of course, exactly the same as that from `Pedant1` (except for the version number). There is, however, a subtle difference between Listings 5.3 and 5.4 that is quite important. This difference is illustrated in Figures 5.6

```
Program Pedant2;
{This program averages 3 quiz scores for a class of students. The
program reads the text file Scores2.Txt until the End of File. For
each person, there are two lines in the file. The first contains
the name, the second contains the 3 quiz scores. This time there
is no Mickey Mouse or trailer value in the text file.          }

Var    Name                 : String[30];
       Quiz1, Quiz2, Quiz3  : Integer;
       Average              : Real;

Begin
  Assign(Input,'A:\Ch5\Scores2.Txt');{Get input from text file.}
  Reset(Input);
  Writeln('Professor Pedantics'' program - Second Version.');
  Writeln;
  While Not Eof Do                         {While not end of the}
    Begin                                  {file do process the data.}
      Readln(Name);
      Readln(Quiz1, Quiz2, Quiz3);
      Average := (Quiz1 + Quiz2 + Quiz3) / 3.0;
      Writeln('The average for ', Name, ' is ', Average:5:2)
    End {While}
End.
```

Listing 5.4

and 5.7. Consider Figure 5.6 first. As we have said, the condition in the While must be initialized *before* the While. Hence, we must obtain the first item *before* the loop, so that the test of the item with the sentinel value will make sense. If the item is not the sentinel, it is processed and the next item is obtained at the foot of the While. Eventually, after the last actual data value is processed, the sentinel is read and the flow of execution exits the While. Note that the sentinel value is not processed as an actual data value. Figure 5.6 illustrates the standard processing loop for a situation controlled by a sentinel value.

On the other hand, Figure 5.7 illustrates the standard processing loop for a situation controlled by Eof. Note that all the data values (including the first one) are read *inside* the loop, at the top of the While. The reason for this placement of the Reads (or Readlns) is clear, if you understand how Eof works. Eof is initialized by the Reset statement and, unless the file is empty, Eof is set to False (because we are not at the end of the file). Hence, as always, we have ensured that the condition in the While makes sense when execution reaches the While. It is also important to note that the last data value is not lost. When the last data item is read, Eof becomes True, but execution does not exit the While until the body of the While is completed. Thus, the last item is processed before the condition is tested again and before control exits the While.

```
Read first item
While the item is not the sentinel do          --Processing loop with sentinel
   Begin
      ...
      ...
      Process the item
      ...
      ...
      Read the next item
   End
```

Figure 5.6

```
Reset the text file
While not Eof do                               --Processing loop with Eof
   Begin
      Read item
      ...
      ...
      Process the item
      ...
      ...
   End
```

Figure 5.7

The differences between Figures 5.6 and 5.7 may seem slight, but they are not unimportant. Using the wrong processing method can lead to errors that are difficult to debug. Make sure you understand how to write a correct processing loop controlled by a sentinel and a correct processing loop controlled by Eof. Pause to understand why the first method (using a sentinel) requires two Readln(Name) statements, one before the loop and one at the foot of the loop. Notice that the second method (using Eof) is much more natural and doesn't require adding anything to the text file.

As another example of Eof, we present in Listing 5.5 a very short program called UTFR. UTFR stands for Universal Text File Reader. The program UTFR reads *any* text file of normal 80 column lines. It works by prompting the user to enter the name of a file and then resetting Input as that file. This shows that Assign can be used with a string variable as well as with a string literal, as we have done in past examples. The program UTFR simply reads and writes lines of the file until the end of the file is encountered. Remember that you must, of course, include the drive name and any subdirectory names to access files. For example, if our sample disk is in drive A:, you would type A:\Ch5\Scores.Txt to see the contents of the file Scores.Txt. If you type A:\Ch5\UTFR.Pas at the prompt, then UTFR would view itself!

```
Program UTFR; {Universal Text File Reader}
{This program reads any text file, while watching for Eof. }

Var    FileName : String[30];{30 characters for a file name.}
       Line     : String[80];    {80 characters for a line.}

Begin
  Writeln('What is the name of the text file you wish to view?');
  Writeln('Don''t forget to add the ".Txt" and the "A:" etc.');
  Readln(FileName);
  Assign(Input, FileName)
  Reset(Input);
  While Not Eof Do          {While not the end of the file,}
    Begin                        {do read and write lines.}
      Readln(Line);          {Read a line from the file.}
      Writeln(Line)          {Write a line to the screen.}
    End {While}
End.
```

Listing 5.5

EXAMPLE: PROFESSOR PEDANTICS—A THIRD VERSION

One of the first things you learn about writing programs for people is that they are always thinking of changes to make to the programs. For example, Professor Pedantics would like to have class averages for each of the three quizzes. This seems like a reasonable request, so let's consider what modifications will be needed to the program. To compute an average for the first quiz, we simply need to total all the scores for that quiz and then divide the total by the number of students. Likewise, for the second and third quizzes. Hence, our program needs three new variables, Total1, Total2, and Total3. Also, we need to have the program count the students, since Professor Pedantics refuses to do such work. Hence, we also add a variable Count to the program. All of our new variables, being running sums and counters, must be initialized to zero. Figure 5.8 shows the pseudo-code for our new algorithm. Trace the pseudo-code with this small amount of data:

```
Ruld Bayd
67 56 72
Ben Bramwell
98 97 99
Brian Brown
95 92 99
Lowell Carmony
38 47 59
```

to see how it computes the average for each of the four students, as well as the class average on each of the three quizzes.

Redirect input to come from the text file Scores2.Txt
Set Total1, Total2, Total3, and Count to zero
While the end of the file has not been found do
   Increment Count
   Read a line of data with a Name
   Read a line of data with three scores
   Total and average the three scores
   Output the Name and the student's average
   Total1 ← Total1 + Quiz1 (Likewise for Total2 and Total3)
Output the Count of the students
Output class averages (Total1/Count. Likewise for Total2 and Total3.)

Figure 5.8

Listing 5.6 shows Pedant3, which reads the text file Scores2.Txt again and implements our pseudo-code design.

Beginners often have trouble deciding which statements go in the loop, which go before the loop, and which go after the loop. Consider the Writelns. Obviously, those Writelns that are to be repeated should go in the loop. Any headings that are to be printed only once, at the beginning, should be placed before the loop. Any summaries printed at the end should be placed after the loop. Likewise, we can use the same strategy to place assignment statements. Those done once do not go in the loop; those done many times belong in the loop. This seems simple enough, but for some reason, in the above example, beginners are inclined to include the class-average calculations in the loop. Of course, class averages don't make much sense until after all the quizzes have been read in and the totals found. Remember this simple rule: How many times should a given statement be executed? If the answer is once, then the statement does not belong in a processing loop.

LOOP INVARIANTS

As computer programs become more and more complex, there is concern about how one might ever really know that programs are in fact correct; that is, that they do what they are supposed to do. The notion of a **loop invariant** is gaining favor in the computer-science world as a method for proving the correctness of programs. While this topic is appropriately discussed at a more advanced level, the idea is important enough to hear about in a first course. Essentially, a loop invariant is an assertion, in a loop, about the state of the program environment each time the flow of control reaches the assertion. In fact, as its name implies, the invariant assertion should remain true, on each iteration, during the execution of the body of the loop, and should still be true upon loop termination. In Pedant3, an invariant involving the variable Count is

Count = the number of students processed

The loop invariant is often used as a comment for the loop:

```
Program Pedant3;
{This program computes student averages and class averages on three
quizzes. It also reads the file Scores2.Txt to the end of file.}


Var    Name    : String[30];
       Quiz1   : Integer;
       Quiz2   : Integer;
       Quiz3   : Integer;
       Total1  : Integer;
       Total2  : Integer;
       Total3  : Integer;
       Count   : Integer;
       StudAve : Real;


Begin
  Assign(Input,'A:\Ch5\Scores2.Txt');{Get input from text file.}
  Reset(Input);
  Writeln('Professor Pedantics'' program - Third Version.');
  Writeln;
  Total1 := 0;
  Total2 := 0;
  Total3 := 0;
  Count := 0;
  While Not Eof Do
    Begin
      Count := Count + 1;
      Readln(Name);
      Readln(Quiz1, Quiz2, Quiz3);
      StudAve := (Quiz1 + Quiz2 + Quiz3) / 3.0;
      Writeln('The average for ', Name, ' is ', StudAve:5:2);
      Total1 := Total1 + Quiz1;
      Total2 := Total2 + Quiz2;
      Total3 := Total3 + Quiz3
    End; {While}
  Writeln;
  Writeln('The class contains ', Count, ' students.');
  Writeln;
  Writeln('The class average on quiz #1 is ',
                                   Total1 / Count:5:2);
  Writeln('The class average on quiz #2 is ',
                                   Total2 / Count:5:2);
  Writeln('The class average on quiz #3 is ',
                                   Total3 / Count:5:2)
End.
```

Listing 5.6

```
Count := 0;
While Not Eof Do      {Count = the number of students processed.}
  Begin
    Count := Count + 1;
    ...
  End;
Writeln('The class contains ', Count, ' students.');
```

Our loop invariant is clearly true before the loop, since Count is 0 and we have not yet read any student data. In the body of the loop, Count is incremented. If the end of the file hasn't been found yet, then Count , in fact, is equal to the number of students processed by the loop. If the end of the file has been found, we exit the loop without any further incrementing of Count, so the assertion is still true. The fact that the assertion is true prior to the loop, remains true throughout execution of the loop body, and is true upon exit from the loop proves that the module does in fact count the students correctly. The real value of assertions and loop invariants is seen in proving correctness of complex algorithms, but we hope the reader can see how assertions and loop invariants can be useful even in simple programs. We encourage you to attempt to formulate loop invariants as you practice your programming skills.

FINDING MAXIMA AND MINIMA

A frequent problem is to find the biggest or smallest value from among a set of values. For example, let us suppose we are to find the highest and lowest temperatures reported from among a group of cities. We might have a list as follows:

```
Lake Forest
77
Carbondale
92
Oblong
88
...
```

Think, for a moment, how the human processor would find the answer.

Figure 5.9

To find the maximum, we can imagine the human in Figure 5.9 scanning down through the data, remembering the largest number encountered so far. Likewise for the minimum. If we give our human a little larger memory, he can find both the minimum and the maximum on one scan. Our program attempts to simulate this behavior. However, both `Max` and `Min` need to be initialized before the loop. One method (we will see more general methods later) is to initialize `Max` and `Min` to ridiculous values so that any real temperature will be bigger than `Max`'s initial value and smaller than `Min`'s initial value. For example, letting `Min` start at `Maxint` (i.e., 32767) and `Max` at `-Maxint` (i.e., –32767) should do the trick. That is, since `Max` is getting bigger and bigger, we initialize `Max` to the smallest integer in the computer. Actually, -32768 is the smallest integer, but `-Maxint` is easier to remember. Likewise, `Min` is getting smaller and smaller, so it begins as the largest integer in the computer. Here is the outline of the algorithm to find the maximum and minimum:

Redirect the input to come from the text file
Initialize Max to -Maxint
Initialize Min to Maxint
While there are more Cities do
    Obtain a City
    Obtain a Temp for the city
    Echo the input to the screen
    Compare Temp and Max, and change Max if necessary
    Compare Temp and Min, and change Min if necessary
Output the Max and Min

Again, some of the details of this design are not completely specified. For example, the line

Compare Temp and Max, and change Max if necessary

means that if the `Temperature` just read is bigger than the `Maximum` seen so far, then we should reassign this value of `Temp` to `Max`. That is,

If Temp is bigger than Max ,hen
    Max ← Temp

is the refinement of the original. As you learn to pseudo-code, also learn to refine your pseudo-code, so that it finally specifies your algorithm completely. In fact, if we trace our algorithm with the indicated fragment of data, we see that it finds a maximum of 92 and a minimum of 77. One would certainly be interested in knowing *where* these extrema occurred, which suggests a further refinement of our pseudo-code. Namely, whenever we find a bigger temperature, we need to remember not only that temperature, but also where it occurred:

Redirect the input to come from the text file
Initialize Max to -Maxint

Initialize Min to Maxint
While there are more Cities do
   Obtain a City
   Obtain a Temp for the city
   Echo the input to the screen
   If Temp is bigger than Max then
      Max ← Temp
      MaxCity ← City
   If Temp is smaller than Min then
      Min ← Temp
      MinCity ← City
Output the Max and Min as well as MaxCity and MinCity

The program corresponding to our pseudo-code is shown in Listing 5.7. It reads a text file, `Temps.Txt`, such as the list of cities and temperatures shown above.

When you run `TempCity` with the text file from our sample disk, the end of the output is

```
...
The maximum temperature was 102 in Eutaw
The minimum temperature was 72 in International Falls
```

We point out that the two `If`s in the above program cannot be replaced, in this case, by a single `If...Then...Else`. We leave it to the reader to explain why.

NESTED LOOPS

Since the statements in the body of a loop can be any legal Pascal statements, it is possible for one loop to be nested within another. That is, a `While` can be inside another `While`. As an example of the complexities involved in nested loops, try to determine the output of the program `Nested` shown in Listing 5.8 (page 132).

In anticipating the output of this program, realize that the first and last `Writeln`s are outside all loops and, hence, execute exactly once, providing a header and a footer to our output. On the other hand, the `Multiples of` statement is in the outer loop, which clearly executes 15 times. This, of course, gives us 15 slightly different lines of output. The `Write(Outer * Inner:4)` is caught inside both loops. It clearly executes 10 times (`Inner` runs from 1 to 10) for each value of `Outer`. Hence, this inner `Write` executes 150 times. However, since it is a `Write`, it does not produce 150 lines of output. Nor, however, do all these `Write`s produce one very long line of output. Because of the `Writeln` near the bottom of the outer loop, each of the 15 executions of the inner loop produces one line of output. Therefore, each execution of the outer loop produces two lines, and the program produces 32 lines of output in all. We leave it to the reader to trace, and then run, the program `Nested` to see the output as it is produced.

It is sometimes difficult for beginners to decide which statements go inside both loops, which outside both loops, and which in the outer, but not in the inner, loop. Considering how many times the statement should execute usually solves this

```
Program TempCity;
{This program finds the highest and lowest temperatures from among
a group of reporting cities. It reads the text file Ch5\Temps.Txt
until the end of file is found. For each city, there are two lines
in the file: the name of the city followed by the temperature in
that city.                                                         }

Var   Max     : Integer;
      Min     : Integer;
      Temp    : Integer;
      City    : String[30];
      MaxCity : String[30];
      MinCity : String[30];
Begin
  Assign(Input, 'A:\Ch5\Temps.Txt');
  Reset(Input);
  Max := -Maxint;            {Give Max a ridiculously small value.}
  Min := Maxint;             {Give Min a ridiculously large value.}
  While Not Eof Do
    Begin
      Readln(City);
      Readln(Temp);
      Writeln(City:30, Temp:5);
      If Temp > Max Then                {Remember new Temp and City}
                                            {as biggest seen so far.}

        Begin
          Max := Temp;
          MaxCity := City
        End;
      If Temp < Min Then                {Remember new Temp and City}
                                           {as smallest seen so far.}

        Begin
          Min := Temp;
          MinCity := City
        End
    End; {While}
  Writeln;
  Writeln('The maximum temperature was', Max,'in', MaxCity);
  Writeln('The minimum temperature was', Min,'in', MinCity)
End.
```

Listing 5.7

problem. If the answer is one, then the statement belongs outside all loops. If the answer is 15 times or 150 times, then the placement of the statement should be clear.

The value of the index in the inner loop changes most quickly. Hence, the successive values of `Outer` and `Inner` in the above program are 1,1, 1,2, 1,3, 1,4, . . . , 1,10, 2,1, 2,2, 2,3, . . . , 2,10, 3,1, 3,2, . . . , 15,10. To see that the order of the inside and outside

```
Program Nested;
{This program illustrates nested loops. Can you determine the
output of this program?                                          }
Var   Outer : Integer;
      Inner : Integer;
Begin
  Writeln('This is the output from program Nested.');
  Outer := 1;
  While Outer < = 15 Do
    Begin
      Writeln('Multiples of ', Outer);
      Inner := 1;
      While Inner <= 10 Do
        Begin
          Write(Outer * Inner:4);
          Inner := Inner + 1
        End; {Inner While}
      Writeln;        {Complete line from Writes of inner loop.}
      Outer := Outer + 1
    End; {Outer While}
  Writeln('That''s all folks!')
End.
```

Listing 5.8

loops is critical, consider Nested2 in Listing 5.9. Nested2 is similar to Nested, except that the loop from 1 to 10 is now on the outside. Predict the output from Nested2 and run it to see if you were correct.

EXAMPLE: PROFESSOR PEDANTICS—A FOURTH VERSION

As a more useful example of nested loops, let's consider another program for Professor Pedantics. Because different students have taken different numbers of quizzes, she would like a program that would read a student's name, the number of quizzes that student has taken, and then the actual quiz scores for that student. The program should properly compute the average for each student. For example, the data might look like this:

```
Otto Mobile
4 87 45 77 86
Dyna Sore
3 97 95 76
Neal Lee Perfect
5 100 99 100 100 99
```

```
Program Nested2;
{This program illustrates nested loops. It is a modification of
Nested. Can you determine the output of this program?          }

Var   Outer : Integer;
      Inner : Integer;
Begin
  Writeln('This is the output from program Nested2.');
  Outer := 1;
  While Outer <= 10 Do
    Begin
      Writeln('Multiples of ', Outer:2);
      Inner := 1;
      While Inner <= 15 Do
        Begin
          Write(Outer * Inner:4);
          Inner := Inner + 1
        End; {Inner While}
      Writeln;
      Outer := Outer + 1
    End; {Outer While}
  Writeln('That''s all folks!')
End.
```

Listing 5.9

```
Noe Hope
2 43 7
. . .
```

Thus, Otto has taken four quizzes, with the scores indicated, Dyna only three quizzes, and so on. Obviously, we loop on the students and, since different students have taken different numbers of exams, we need an inner summing loop for each student. Here is a pseudo-code outline for our algorithm:

Redirect the input to come from the text file Scores4.Txt
While there is more data do
   Read a line of data with a Name
   Read the Number of Quizzes taken by this student
   Initialize Sum to zero
     Initialize a counter, Count, to zero
     While Count < Number of Quizzes do
     Read the next score on the line
     Add the Score to Sum
     Increment the counter

Compute the average for the student
Output the average for the given student
Move to the next line of the file (Readln)

Notice how the indentation makes the extent of each loop clear. Once again, the translation into Pascal is straightforward. Run `Pedant4`, which is shown in Listing 5.10.

This time, `Pedant4` reads the scores from the text file `Ch5\Scores4.Txt`. The purpose of the `Readln`, after the inner `While`, is to advance to the next line (if there is one) in the file, since the inner `While` contains only `Read` statements (and not `Readln` statements). That is, after the first execution of the inner `While`, the file has been processed up to the end of the second line:

```
Otto Mobile
4   87   45   77   86
```

In order that the next execution of `Readln(Name)` finds Dyna's name (and not the End-of-Line), the file pointer needs to be positioned at the start of the third line:

```
Otto Mobile
4   87   45   77   86
Dyna Sore
```

The `Readln` accomplishes this for us.

PROBLEM-SOLVING EXAMPLE: PRIME NUMBERS

An example that illustrates many of the topics covered up to this point is a program that determines prime numbers. This example requires no higher mathematics, only arithmetic. Recall that a prime number is a positive integer larger than 1 whose only divisors are 1 and itself. For example, 17 is prime, but 15 is not, since 3 * 5 = 15. Let us write a program to find all primes between 10,000 and 11,000. Obviously, we have found our outer loop. However, since there are no even primes between 10,000 and 11,000, we need consider only the odd numbers between 10,001 and 10,999. Hence, we may initialize a variable to 10,001 and increment it by 2 each time. Of course, to permit easy modification of the program, the numbers 10,000 and 11,000 should be expressed as constants. Here is a preliminary outline of the program:

Set LowerLimit to 10,000 and UpperLimit to 11,000 (Constants)
Initialize Number to LowerLimit + 1 (First odd number)
While Number < UpperLimit
   Determine whether Number is prime and print it if so
   Increment Number by 2 (skip to next odd number)

```
Program Pedant4;
{This program computes averages for students and allows for
different students having taken different numbers of quizzes. The
program reads the text file Scores4.Txt, which contains two lines
for each student. The first line contains the name and the second
contains the number of quizzes followed by that many scores.  }

Var    Name     : String[30];
       NumQuiz  : Integer;
       Score    : Integer;
       Sum      : Integer;
       Ave      : Real;
       Count    : Integer;

Begin
  Assign(Input, 'A:\Ch5\Scores4.Txt');          {Get input from}
  Reset(Input);                                  {the text file.}
  Writeln('Professor Pedantics'' program - Fourth Version.');
  Writeln;
  While Not Eof Do
    Begin
      Sum := 0;
      Readln(Name);
      Read(NumQuiz);                             {Note Read, not Readln.}
      Count := 0;
      While Count < NumQuiz Do
        Begin
          Read(Score);
          Sum := Sum + Score;
          Count := Count + 1
        End; {Inner While}
      Ave := Sum / NumQuiz;
      Writeln('The average for ', Name, ' is ', Ave:5:2)
      Readln            {Advance to next line of the text file.}
    End {Outer While}
End.
```

Listing 5.10

What is involved in determining if a given number is prime? We must try all possible divisors. Another loop! But where does this inner loop begin and end? Since the number is odd, it has only odd divisors (why?). Hence, we may begin our testing with the possible factor 3, and we increment the factor by 2 each time. What is the largest factor we need to try? If a number has a factor, then it has a cofactor too. For example, 2 and 12 are cofactors of 24, since 2 * 12 = 24. Likewise, 6 and 9 are cofactors of 54.

Notice that 7 is its own cofactor with respect to 49. We claim that if a number has a factor, then it has a factor less than or equal to its own square root. For if both cofactors are bigger than the square root, then the product of the two cofactors would be bigger than the given number. Hence, to determine if a given odd number is prime, we need try only odd divisors between 3 and the square root of the number. For example, to decide if 391 is prime, we need try only the factors 3, 5, 7, 9, 11, 13, 15, 17, and 19, since $\sqrt{391} = 19.7737$. In this case, we would find that 391 is not prime, since $391 = 17 * 23$.

Of course, as we try the factors, if we find one that divides evenly into the given number, we may reject that number and continue with the next. However, just because 3 doesn't divide evenly into the number, we are not permitted to declare the number to be prime. We can safely certify a number as prime only when no factor at all is found for it. Here is the refined pseudo-code for our plan:

Set LowerLimit to 10,000 and UpperLimit to 11,000 (Constants)
Initialize Number to LowerLimit + 1 (First odd number)
While Number < UpperLimit
    Initialize a Boolean Prime to True (Give Number a chance)
    Initialize Factor to 3
    Initialize Limit to $\sqrt{\text{Number}}$
    While (Factor <= Limit) and Prime
        If Factor divides Number evenly then
            Set Prime to False
        Else
            Increment Factor by 2
    If still Prime then
        Output the Number as a prime
    Increment Number by 2

Several points about the outline still need to be discussed. Notice that the inner `While` loops either until we find a `Factor` or until `Factor` exceeds the `Limit`. Since there are two ways to exit from the `While`, an `If` is needed after the `While` to determine how the `While` ended. If it ended because all `Factor`s were tried and none were found that would divide the `Number`, then the `Number` is prime. Of course, using such operations as `Mod`, we can express in Pascal the question of whether `Factor` divides `Number` evenly. Namely, `Factor` divides `Number` evenly if the remainder upon division of `Number` by `Factor` is zero. Since the `Mod` function computes the remainder upon an integer division, we have that `Factor` divides `Number` evenly if `Number Mod Factor` equals zero. The complete Pascal program `Primes` is shown in Listing 5.11.

Notice in Listing 5.11 that the Boolean expression `Factor <= Limit` cannot be changed to `Factor < Limit`, because to prove that numbers like 49 are not prime, we must include $\sqrt{49}$ in our list of factors. Also, conserving on variables and writing `Factor <= Sqrt(Number)` is not wise, because this forces the system to recompute the square root each time it makes the comparison. Using the variable `Limit`, the system needs to take the square root of each number only once. See the exercises for further details on this matter, an efficiency question.

```
Program Primes;
{This program finds primes between 10,000 and 11,000.

Const LowerLimit = 10000;
      UpperLimit = 11000;

Var    Number : Integer;
       Factor : Integer;
       Prime  : Boolean;
       Limit  : Integer;

Begin
  Writeln('Here are the primes between ', LowerLimit, ' and ',
                                           UpperLimit:');
  Writeln;
  Number := LowerLimit + 1;
  While Number < UpperLimit Do
    Begin
      Prime := True;                    {Give Number every chance.}
      Factor := 3;
      Limit := Trunc(Sqrt(Number));       {Sqrt is the built-in}
                  {square-root function which returns a Real.}
      While (Factor <= Limit) And Prime Do
        If Number Mod Factor = 0 Then
          Prime := False              {A factor has been found.}
        Else
          Factor := Factor + 2;           {Try next odd factor.}
      If Prime Then {Time to announce the Primehood of Number.}
        Writeln(Number);
      Number := Number + 2       {Increment to next odd Number.}
  End {Outer While}
End.
```

Listing 5.11

AVOIDING STRINGS—A FIRST ATTEMPT

As we have indicated previously, standard Pascal does not include a built-in string type. In this section, we discover that we can solve many of the problems of this chapter without the string type. However, we also will see that some of our problems are very awkward to solve, at this point, in standard Pascal, with no strings.

We have introduced the string type because it is such a natural problem-solving tool.

However, it is instructive for the reader to understand that strings are not always available in other Pascal compilers and are not always the best way to solve a given problem. Reading information character by character, as we will do in this section, provides the user with the greatest possible flexibility over the data.

Let us return to a previous version of one of the Pedantics problems and rewrite the program so that it does not need strings. For example, recall that `Pedant2`, of Listing 5.4, reads data of the form

```
Ruta Baga
67 56 72
Ben Bramwell
98 97 99
Brian Brown
95 92 99
Lowell Carmony
38 47 59
...
```

and produces output of the form

```
The average for Ruta Baga is 65.00
The average for Ben Bramwell is 98.00
The average for Brian Brown is 95.33
The average for Lowell Carmony is 48.00
...
```

Instead of a string variable `Name`, we will use a Char variable `Ch`. The obvious problem is that `Ch` can hold only one character, not an entire name. Therefore, we will have to read and print characters, one by one, as we find them. The pseudo-code for reading and printing a line of data might be written:

```
While there are still characters on the line
    Read a character
    Write the character
```

Fortunately, Pascal has a built-in `Eoln` (End of line) Boolean function that tells us when we have reached the end of a line of data. Thus, `Eoln` is a cousin of `Eof`, which indicates when we have reached the end of a file. To see how `Eoln` works, consider carefully how the data are processed by the following Pascal segment that expresses our pseudo-code:

```
While Not Eoln Do
  Begin
    Read(Ch);
    Write(Ch)
  End;
```

The `Reset`, which found the text file, positioned a pointer at the beginning of the first line of data, as indicated in Figure 5.10a.

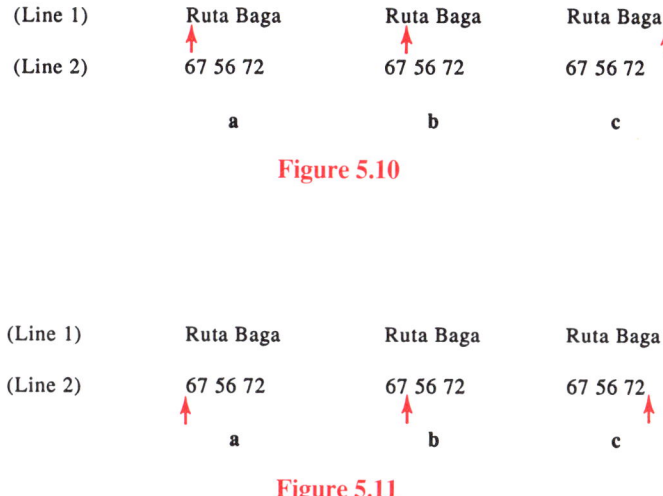

Figure 5.10

Figure 5.11

As each character is read, the pointer moves over that character. Figure 5.10b shows the situation after the first `Read(Ch)` has been executed and `Ch` has the value `'R'`. Notice that the `'R'` is written, then the `'u'` is read and written, until eventually the final `'a'` has been processed and the file pointer is as shown in Figure 5.10c. At this point, we have reached the end of the line. The system is able to recognize this because an end-of-line marker is inserted into a text file whenever you press the RETURN key during creation of that file. The built-in `Eoln` function simply checks to see if the next character is this end-of-line marker. If so, `Eoln` reports `True`; otherwise, `Eoln` reports `False`. Therefore, `Eoln` was initialized to `False` by the `Reset`(see Figure 5.10a), is `False` during the reading of characters on the line (Figure 5.10b), but eventually becomes `True` (Figure 5.10c), when all of the characters on the line have been processed.

There is one more detail that must be understood before the discussion is complete. Note that the file pointer in Figure 5.10c is still at the end of line 1. In order to process the second line of data, we need to move the file pointer down to the beginning of line 2. To do this, we use a `Readln` by itself that reads no values, but simply moves the file pointer to the next line. This is indicated in Figure 5.11a.

At this point, we have three integers on line 2. They can be read by any of the following equivalent methods:

```
Readln(Quiz1, Quiz2, Quiz3);
```

or

```
Read(Quiz1);
Read(Quiz2);
Read(Quiz3);
Readln;
```

or

```
Read(Quiz1, Quiz2, Quiz3);
Readln;
```

or

```
Read(Quiz1, Quiz2);
Readln(Quiz3);
```

The reader should check that all these are, indeed, equivalent and eventually advance the file pointer to the beginning of the third line of data. Since the first method is the shortest, it is the normal way to read the three integers. As a further check of your understanding, note that Figures 5.11b and 5.11c show the situation after `Read(Quiz1)` and `Read(Quiz2, Quiz3)`, respectively.

Thus, finally, we see that the following segment reads and writes one line of data:

```
While Not Eoln Do{While there are more characters on the line.}
  Begin
    Read(Ch);                              {Read 'em and write 'em.}
    Write(Ch)
  End;
Readln;                          {Advance file pointer to next line.}
```

Another problem we have, in converting `Pedant2` to run without strings, is that `Pedant2` contains the line

```
Writeln('The average for ', Name, ' is ', Average:5:2)
```

which labels and displays all the information about the given individual. Since we are printing characters from the name as we read them, we must make some modifications to the printing of the output. Namely, we see that we must print the message `The average for`, before we read and write the name, then we can print the word `is`, and the `Average` in its formatted form. That is, we compose the line of output piece by piece:

```
Write the message 'The average for '
Read and write the name
Compute the average
Finish the line with the phrase ' is ' and the formatted Average
```

We invite the reader to study carefully the final Pascal version shown in Listing 5.12. The output of `Pedant5` is, except for the version number, exactly the same as the output of `Pedant2`. We leave it to the reader to verify this.

`Pedant5` has shown that it is possible to solve the given problem without the use of strings. Will the indicated method always work? No. For example, the program `TempCity` would be very awkward to rewrite, at present, without string variables. This is because `TempCity` must remember the city with the highest temperature and, with a single character variable, we can remember only one character. To remember 30 characters, we would need, with what we now know, to declare 30 character variables! Compare the situation with that of `Pedant5`. In `Pedant5`, it is sufficient to read and immediately write each student's name. Suppose we wanted to modify the program so that it printed out the name of the student with the best average. That would be an easy exercise with strings, but very awkward with only character variables. There are many situations where strings provide the beginner with a simple and powerful tool for solving problems. Therefore, we have introduced this nonstandard feature of Turbo Pascal. In later chapters (14 and 17), we will return to this subject and eventually see how, in standard Pascal, to solve such problems.

```pascal
Program Pedant5;
{This program is a version of Pedant2 that avoids the string
type. It reads the names character by character and watches for
Eoln. The program averages 3 quiz scores for a class of students
and reads the text file Scores2.Txt until End of file. For each
person, there are 2 lines in the file. The first contains the
name; the second contains the 3 quiz scores.              }

Var    Quiz1, Quiz2, Quiz3  :  Integer;
       Average              : Real;
       Ch                   : Char;

Begin
  Assign(Input, 'A:\Ch5\Scores2.Txt');
  Reset(Input);
  Writeln('Professor Pedantics'' program - Fifth Version.');
  Writeln;
  While Not Eof Do{While there are more data, keep looping.}
    Begin
      Write('The average for ');
      While Not Eoln Do   {While more characters on the line}
        Begin
          Read(Ch);                    {Read 'em and write 'em.}
          Write(Ch)
        End; {Inner While}
      Readln;                    {Prepare to read the next line.}
      Readln(Quiz1, Quiz2, Quiz3);
      Average := (Quiz1 + Quiz2 + Quiz3) / 3.0;
      Writeln(' is ', Average:5:2)
    End {Outer While}
End.
```

Listing 5.12

KEYWORDS

Many key concepts have been introduced in this chapter. As a study guide, make sure
that you can describe each of the following terms and Pascal constructs:

Boolean variable   And operator
Or operator   Not operator
Compound statement   If...Then
If...Then...Else   Running summation
Counter   While statement
Loop structure   Sentinel value
Eof   Eoln
Nested loops

SELF-TEST QUESTIONS

5.1 Assume that L and M are integer identifiers and determine the output of each of the
following segments:

```
a) L := 7;                          b) L := -6;
   M := 5;                             M := 6;
   While L > 0 do                      While L * M < 0 do
     Begin                               Begin
       L := L - 2;                         Writeln(L:5, M:5);
       M := M + 2;                         L := L + M Div 2;
       Writeln(L:5, M:5)                   M := M - 2
     End;                                End;
   Writeln(L:5, M:5);                  Writeln(L:5, M:5);
```

5.2 Assume that J and K are integer identifiers. What is the output of the following
segment?

```
J := 12;
While J > 0 do
  Begin
    K := 2 * J;
    While K > 0 do
      K := K - 5;
    J := J + K;
    Writeln(J:5, K:5)
  End;
```

5.3 Suppose Count is an integer identifier with value 10, Salary is a real identifier
with value 2398.52, Sex is a character identifier with value 'F', and Name is a
string identifier with value 'Donald Duck'. Indicate the value of each of the
following Boolean expressions.

a) `Count < 100`   b) `Name = 'Donald'`

c) `(Sex = 'M') Or (Salary > 1000.0)`   d) `Name < 'Mickey'`

e) `(Sex = 'f') And (Count = 10)`   f) `Not (Count > 12)`

EXERCISES

5.4 Using the syntactic categories `Boolean-Expression` and `Statement`, draw the syntax (railroad) diagram for the `While` statement. Here the category `Statement` means any legal statement. Hence, it includes either simple or compound statements.

5.5 Using the syntactic categories `Boolean-Expression` and `Statement`, draw the syntax (railroad) diagram for the `If...Then...Else statement`.

5.6 Write a program that creates a table of Celsius-to-Fahrenheit temperature conversions from 20 degrees to 40 degrees Celsius. Of course, the magic formula is

$$F = 9/5 * C + 32$$

5.7 Modify the program of Exercise 5.6 so that the user may choose the starting and ending temperatures for the table.

5.8 Modify the program of Exercise 5.7 so that the user may also choose the interval (in degrees Celsius) between entries of the table. Use the program to request a table from -40 degrees Celsius to 50 degrees Celsius, in steps of 5 degrees Celsius.

5.9 A colony of 700 Wallalumps increases by 8 percent each year. Write a program to predict the population of the colony for each of the next 25 years.

5.10 Write a program that plays the following word game: Player 1 chooses a word and enters it into the computer as the secret word for the game. Use `ClrScr` after the entry of the secret word, so that Player 2 cannot see it. Player 2 then enters words, trying to guess the secret word. Suppose the secret word is PASCAL and the user guesses FORTRAN. Then the computer gives the hint:

`My word comes after FORTRAN in the dictionary.`

Likewise, if the user guesses ZEBRA, the computer responds with

`My word comes before ZEBRA in the dictionary.`

Finally (we hope), Player 2 guesses the secret word and the game ends with the message

```
You guessed my word in XX guesses.
```

where XX is, of course, replaced by the appropriate value.
Hint: If Guess and SecretWord are string variables, then

```
Guess < SecretWord
```

is True if the value of Guess is alphabetically before the value of SecretWord.
Actually, the computer orders the letters from 'A' to 'Z' and then from 'a' to
'z'. Hence, 'A' < 'M' and 'M' < 'a' are both True. To avoid this confusion,
play the game with the CAPS-LOCK key depressed.

5.11 A piece of paper is 0.005 inch thick. How thick would the paper be if we folded
it in half 35 times? Note that each time we fold the paper over on itself, it becomes
twice as thick.

5.12 The programs Ex5_12a, Ex5_12b, and Ex5_12c shown below (and stored on the
disk of sample programs) are all buggy versions of program TempCity. Execute
each of these versions and, from the erroneous output, determine the error in each
program. Ex5_12a and Ex5_12b are so buggy that they will misbehave with any
data, including our Temps.Txt. The error in program Ex5_12c is more subtle,
however. When run with most text files (including our Temps.Txt), Ex5_12c
runs perfectly. However, if it reads the following text file (Temps2.Txt):

```
Annapolis
32
Birmingham
100
Chicago
72
```

then Ex5_12c will produce an error. This illustrates that debugging can be a very
difficult task. Just because a program runs with one set of data does not mean that
it will run correctly with other legal data. Big commercial programs sometimes
crash after running correctly for years, when finally the right set of data has
appeared to spring the hidden bug.
In each case, the declarations in the following three programs are identical to
those in TempCity. Therefore, only the body of each program is shown.

```
Begin                          {Body of buggy program Ex5_12a.}
  Assign(Input, 'A:\Ch5\Temps.Txt');
  Reset(Input);
  Max := Maxint;
  Min := -Maxint;
  While Not Eof Do
```

```
     Begin
       Readln(City);
       Readln(Temp);
       Writeln(City:30, Temp:5);
       If Temp > Max Then
         Begin
           Max := Temp;
           MaxCity := City
         End;
       If Temp < Min Then
         Begin
           Min := Temp;
           MinCity := City
         End
     End; {While}
   Writeln;
   Writeln('The maximum temperature was ', Max,' in ', MaxCity);
   Writeln('The minimum temperature was ', Min,' in ', MinCity)
 End.

 Begin                              {Body of buggy program Ex5_12b.}
   Assign(Input, 'A:\Ch5\Temps.Txt');
   Reset(Input);
   Max := -Maxint;
   Min := Maxint;
   While Not Eof Do
     Begin
       Readln(City);
       Readln(Temp);
       Writeln(City:30, Temp:5);
       If Temp > Max Then
         Begin
           Temp := Max;
           City := MaxCity
         End;
       If Temp < Min Then
         Begin
           Temp := Min;
           MinCity := City
         End
     End; {While}
   Writeln;
   Writeln('The maximum temperature was ', Max,' in ', MaxCity);
   Writeln('The minimum temperature was ', Min,' in ', MinCity)
 End.
```

```
Begin                               {Body of buggy program Ex5_12c.}
  Assign(Input, 'A:\Ch5\Temps2.Txt');               {Note use}
  Reset(Input)                                     {of new file.}
  Max := -Maxint;
  Min := Maxint;
  While Not Eof Do
    Begin
      Readln(City);
      Readln(Temp);
      Writeln(City:30, Temp:5);
      If Temp > Max Then
        Begin
          Max := Temp;
          MaxCity := City
        End
      Else If Temp < Min Then
        Begin
          Min := Temp;
          MinCity := City
        End
    End; {While}
  Writeln;
  Writeln('The maximum temperature was ', Max,' in ', MaxCity);
  Writeln('The minimum temperature was ', Min,' in ', MinCity)
End.
```

5.13 In the text file Porridge.Txt, each line contains the temperature of a bowl of porridge. Write a program for Goldilocks that prints the temperature of each bowl of porridge, and Too Hot, Too Cold, or Just Right. Print Too Hot if the temperature exceeds 140 degrees, Too Cold if the temperature is less than 90 degrees, and Just Right otherwise. At the end of the program, you should also print a count of how many bowls of each kind were found.

5.14 FICA (Social Security) tax is withheld at the rate of 7.65 percent on the first $48,000 of your total salary. If you work for two or more employers and each withholds 7.65 percent of your first $48,000, you may end up paying too much FICA tax. Write a program that inputs the number of employers and the salary from each and then computes the overpayment, if any, of your FICA tax.

5.15 Write a program that tabulates the totals of the Granola State University Cow-Chip Throwing Contest. The information concerning the contest is found in the text file Chips.Txt. There are four lines of information for each entrant in the contest. The first line contains the name of the contestant, the second line contains a sex designation, the third line contains a status (Student or Faculty), and the fourth line contains the length of the throw in feet. A sample entry might look like this:

Polly Tishun
Female
Student
203.75

Your program should read the Chips.Txt file and print out a table of all contestants, listing the name, sex, status, and throw. At the end of the table, you should announce, with suitable fanfare, the winners in each of four categories (Male-Faculty, Male-Student, Female-Faculty, Female-Student) and the overall winner of the contest.

5.16 Write a program to help the Lemon Motor Company decide whether to keep its V–16 economy car, the Belchfire, in production. Data for the car are available in the text file Lemons.Txt and consist of two lines of data for each dealer. For example, the first four lines of the file are

Tricky Dicks
10 5 8 3 0 7 2
Ottos Autos
100 7 56 24 0 89 120 99 34

The first entry of the second line means that Tricky Dick is expected to sell 10 Belchfires per month. The second value on that line indicates that 5 months of data are available for Tricky. The remaining data indicate that he has, in fact, sold 20 cars ($8 + 3 + 0 + 7 + 2$) in the last 5 months. Likewise, Otto, a big city dealer, is expected to sell 100 Belchfires a month; 7 months of data are available for Otto, and he has sold $56 + 24 + 0 + 89 + 120 + 99 + 34 = 422$ cars in the last 7 months. Your program for LMC should read the text file Lemons.Txt and output the following for each dealer: Dealer's name, expected monthly sales, average monthly sales, and an appropriate comment. If the dealer's average is less than half the expected average, then the dealer should be warned severely that his or her business (or family) is in danger. On the other hand, dealers who have sold more Lemons than expected should be heartily congratulated. Those who deserve neither censure nor praise should receive a noncommital comment. Arrange the above output in four columns with appropriate headings. Finally, output the average monthly sales, the average expected sales, and an appropriate recommendation for the Lemon Motor Company itself.

5.17 Run the sample program Primes from the text and time its execution. Also run Ex5_17, shown below, and time its execution. Compare the two programs. Notice that they produce the same output. Why is Ex5_17 so much slower? (Depending on the speed of your processor, it may be necessary to make Upperlimit larger to see the difference between the execution times of these two programs.)

```
Program Ex5_17;
{This program finds primes between 10,000 and 11,000. Why is
it much slower than the sample program Primes of the text?}

Const  LowerLimit  = 10000;
       UpperLimit  = 11000;

Var      Number  :  Integer;
         Factor  :  Integer;
         Prime   :  Boolean;

Begin
  Writeln('Here are the primes between ', LowerLimit,
                              ' and ', UpperLimit:');
  Writeln;
  Number := LowerLimit + 1;
  While Number < UpperLimit Do
    Begin
      Prime := True;                 {Give Number every chance.}
      Factor := 2;
      While (Factor < Number) And Prime Do
        If Number Mod Factor = 0 Then
          Prime := False             {A factor has been found.}
        Else
          Factor := Factor + 1;            {Try next factor.}
      If Prime Then      {Announce the Primehood of Number.}
        Writeln(Number);
      Number := Number + 1       {Increment to next Number.}
    End {While}
End.
```

5.18 Write a program to generate a sequence of numbers according to the following scheme:

Begin with any positive integer greater than 1. If the current term is odd, then the next term is obtained by tripling the current term and adding 1, but if the current term is even, then the next term is obtained by halving the current term. Repeat this process until you obtain a term equal to 1.

For example, suppose we begin with 7. Then, the sequence of terms is

7 22 11 34 17 52 26 13 40 20 10 5 16 8 4 2 1

Of course, your program should prompt the user for the starting term. Run your program, with 7 as the input, to verify your program. Also, use 97 for an interesting sequence.

The claim that you will always come down to 1 has never been proven, but it has already been verified by computer for all small numbers. In our system, however, overflow occurs quickly. For example, why won't the program work properly if you begin the sequence with 30001? In Chapter 10, we will see that Turbo Pascal has a long integer type that is useful if you wish to test the conjecture on larger integers.

Hint: Use Mod with a divisor of 2 to test the current term to see if it is even or odd.

5.19 (Armstrong Numbers) The number 153 has the odd property that

$$1^3 + 5^3 + 3^3 = 1 + 125 + 27 = 153$$

Namely, 153 is equal to the sum of the cubes of its own digits. Are there other three-digit numbers that have this property? Write a program that tests all three-digit numbers and prints out those that have the above property. There are four such numbers and they are known as the Armstrong Numbers of order three. Hint: If you want to break a three-digit number into its separate digits, use Div and Mod tricks with divisors like 100 or 10.

5.20 (Perfect Numbers) A number is said to be **perfect** if it is the sum of its own divisors (excluding itself). For example, 6 is perfect since 1, 2, and 3 divide evenly into 6 and $1 + 2 + 3 = 6$. Verify, by hand, that 28 is also perfect. Write a program to find the next perfect number.

5.21 (Abundant Numbers) A number is **abundant** if it is less than the sum of its divisors (excluding itself). For example, 12 is abundant since 1, 2, 3, 4, and 6 are the divisors of 12 and their sum is 16. The term abundant comes from the fact that such a number has an abundance of divisors. Write a program to find all abundant numbers less than 500. Since 1 is a special case, you may begin your search at 2. After your program runs, what do you notice about all abundant numbers less than 500?

5.22 (Odd Abundant Numbers) Write a program to find the first odd abundant number. Try to make your program as efficient as possible and use the results of Exercise 5.21.

5.23 (Mad Dog) A man is in the center of a square garden, 200 meters on a side, as depicted in Figure 5.12. A well-trained, but vicious, dog is standing on the wall at the southwest corner of the garden. The dog can run pi (3.14159) times faster than the man, but the dog is trained to stay on the wall and not enter the garden at all.

Show, by hand calculation, that the ratio of distances for dog and man to point N is less than Pi, and, hence, the dog would be the winner to that point. Show, by another hand calculation, that the ratio of distances to corner C is even less favorable for the man. Thus, if the man can escape, he can do so only between points N and C (or by symmetry at similar points on the east wall).

Write a program that outputs the ratio for each point at 2 meter intervals from N to C. At each point, print its distance from N, the ratio, and a message (OUCH or SAFE), depending on the ratio at that point. Can the man escape unscathed from the dog?

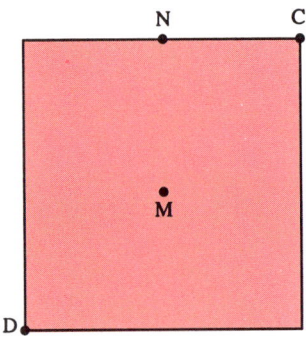

Figure 5.12

ANSWERS TO SELF-TEST QUESTIONS

5.1 a) 5   7   b) -6   6
        3   9   -3   4
        1   11   -1   2
       -1   13   0   0
       -1   13

5.2   11   -1
        8   -3
        4   -4
        2   -2
        1   -1
       -2   -3

5.3 a) True   b) False   c) True

    d) True   e) False   f) True

6

PROCEDURES AND FUNCTIONS

In this chapter, we develop the tools with which we can truly implement the **divide-and-conquer** problem-solving strategy. The divide-and-conquer paradigm requires that we decompose a large problem into smaller pieces and repeat this process until we have small, manageable subunits that can be implemented as small, separate subprograms. Procedures and functions serve the role of subprograms in Pascal. For now, think of procedures and functions as **black boxes** that do small, distinct tasks for us. At this point, we do not want to cloud the issue by distinguishing between procedures and functions. Think of both of them as slave subprograms that will do tasks at our bidding.

The main program calls, or invokes, these procedures and functions to do its work. We will give many examples in the pages to follow, but, for now, consider a simple generic example without worrying about actual Pascal syntax. Many simple problems can be solved with the following three subunits:

1. Obtain the input data
2. Calculate some simple results
3. Output the results in an understandable form

A program using this design, with a black box for each subunit, would be structured as in Figure 6.1. Note that the body of the main program is short and, therefore, easy to read and understand. If the reader needs further details about the operation of any of the black boxes, that information can be obtained by looking at their definitions. But these specifics are separated from the main program, which, therefore, is not crowded with all the details of the entire program.

In a specific problem, one can choose appropriate names for the procedures and functions, as well as the identifiers. This makes the program nearly self-documenting. For example, we leave it to the reader to guess what the following Pascal segment is designed to do (note that Pascal does not use an explicit Call statement):

151

```
Begin
  AskUser(Name, HtFeet, HtInches, Weight, Sex);
  FindPerfectWt(HtFeet, HtInches, Weight, Sex, IdealWeight);
  Display(Name, HtFeet, HtInches, Weight, Sex, IdealWeight)
End.
```

Our black boxes can have inputs to them and outputs from them. Hopefully, it is obvious that AskUser's job is to prompt the user for various personal information and **output** these data back to the main program for further use. Likewise, from the context it is, hopefully, clear that FindPerfectWt takes as *input* the data about the user's height, weight, and sex and *outputs,* in return, an IdealWeight for that user. Notice that FindPerfectWt does not care whether the user's name is Dave or Sue, as this is clearly not relevant to its task. Display takes as *input* all the data and prints it to the screen in a readable format. As such, Display is very simple, but, as we know, all the Writelns for Display can be very lengthy and tedious. The advantage of using Display is that these statements, which tend to clutter the main program, are removed and kept in the definition for Display, where they can be inspected or modified, if necessary.

Procedures and functions make Pascal an **extensible** language. This means that it is possible, using procedures and functions, to extend the language. Imagine how simple it would be to determine an individual's ideal weight if Pascal had a built-in black box named FindPerfectWt that did all the work for you! Of course, Pascal doesn't

Program Main;

Constant and variable declarations for Main

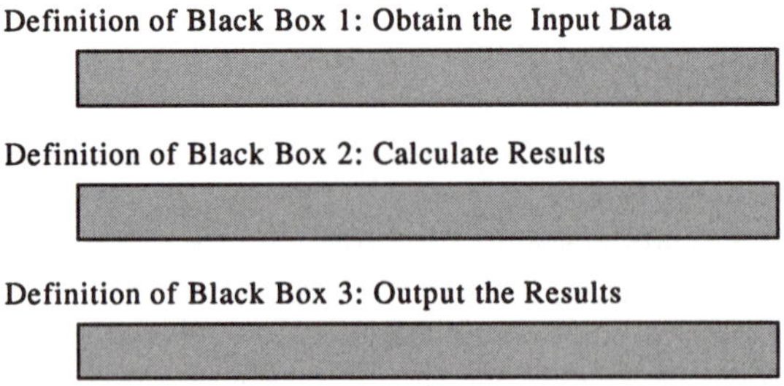

Definition of Black Box 1: Obtain the Input Data

Definition of Black Box 2: Calculate Results

Definition of Black Box 3: Output the Results

Begin   { Body of Main program in pseudo-code, not Pascal.}
  Call the Obtain-the-Input-Data subprogram
  Call the Calculate-Results subprogram
  Call the Output-the-Results subprogram
End.

Figure 6.1

contain such a built-in, but it is easy to define your own `FindPerfectWt` black box and then use it to solve the given problem. This is the great problem-solving tool that procedures and functions provide: When presented with a problem, we should not ask ourselves, "What Pascal construct can we use to model this problem?" Rather, we should ask, "What black boxes do we need to design to enable us to divide and conquer this problem?" This strategy, also called top-down design, further subdivides those black boxes, if necessary, until manageable units are obtained. The implementation of these subunits as Pascal procedures and functions should then be straightforward. Once again, our discussion has been primarily concerned with *design,* not *coding,* in Pascal. If you are spending too much time in debugging code, or are not being successful in getting programs to run (as is often the case with beginners), then that is a sure sign that you are not spending enough time in the design phase before going to the implementation phase. It should be clear that you won't have much success implementing a design that you don't really understand.

THE DISTINCTION BETWEEN PROCEDURES AND FUNCTIONS

It is time to indicate what procedures and functions are and to indicate the small, but important, ways in which they differ from one another. Let us begin with functions. **A function is a black box that returns, through its name, exactly one value back to the calling environment**. You have already used many functions in Pascal. `Trunc` is an example of a built-in function that converts reals to integers. For example, if `X` is the real `3.7`, then `Trunc(X)` is the integer value `3`. Note that

```
Trunc(X);                         {ERROR, Incomplete Statement.}
```

is not a complete statement in Pascal, since it names just a value, not a complete action. To make it into a complete statement, some action needs to be done with the value returned by the function. For example, if `K` is an integer, then both of the following are valid Pascal statements:

```
Writeln(Trunc(X));
K := Trunc(X);
```

In contrast to functions, **procedures are black boxes that name complete actions**. They return no value through their names, but as we'll see, they can return results. In this respect, procedures are a generalization of functions. A very simple example of a Turbo Pascal built-in procedure is `Halt`, which simply halts program execution. `Halt` is an example of a procedure that returns no result. Since procedures, in contrast to functions, name complete actions, each stands alone as a single statement. For example, the following are valid examples of procedure invocations:

```
ExplainPurposeOfProgram;
AskUser(Name, HtFeet, HtInches, Weight, Sex);
Halt;
```

ExplainPurposeOfProgram is a procedure, like Halt, with no inputs and no outputs. Apparently, it is composed of a large number of Writelns that explain to the user what the present program is all about. AskUser is a procedure with five outputs, or results, since its job appears to be to obtain values for the five arguments listed and to return these five values to the main program for further processing.

The single most troublesome distinction for beginners is that functions never stand alone as complete statements, while procedures always do. This is simply a consequence of the fact that the function name is simply holding a value, while the procedure is naming a complete action. This difference will also explain the subtle ways in which function definitions differ from procedure definitions. However, let us first look at some of the standard functions and procedures supplied with Turbo Pascal.

SOME USEFUL BUILT-IN FUNCTIONS AND PROCEDURES

The most commonly used procedures and functions, such as taking square roots or absolute values, are provided in the language so that the user does not need to re-create them. Turbo Pascal provides more functions and procedures than called for in Wirth's standard Pascal. Table 6.1 lists the standard built-ins (all of which are supplied in Turbo Pascal), and Table 6.2 lists some of the most useful of the additional procedures and functions provided by Turbo Pascal. Some of these procedures and functions will not be discussed until later chapters. They are listed in the tables for completeness and easy reference.

Table 6.1: Built-in Functions and Procedures of Pascal

Mathematical Functions

Abs(X)	Absolute value function
ArcTan(X)	Arctangent function
Cos(X)	Cosine function
Exp(X)	Exponential function (e^X)
Ln(X)	Natural logarithm function
Odd(X)	Odd function (returns true if X is an odd integer)
Round(X)	Round function (converts real to integer)
Sqr(X)	Squaring function (X^2)
Sqrt(X)	Square root function ($\sqrt{X}$)
Trunc(X)	Truncation function (converts real to integer)

Type Functions (See Chapter 10)

Chr(I)	The character function
Ord(T)	The ordinal function
Pred(T)	The predecessor function
Succ(T)	The successor function

A Dynamic Allocation Procedure (See Chapter 19)

New(P)	Allocate memory procedure

Abs is the absolute value function. It accepts either integer or real input and returns the same type. Therefore, Abs(-3) is the integer 3 and Abs(-3.45) is the real 3.45.

ArcTan, Cos, and Sin are the standard trigonometric functions. Likewise, Exp and Ln are the standard exponential and natural logarithm functions of elementary mathematics. We assume that the user who has need for these functions understands them. They are *not* critical for the development that follows.

Odd is a function that expects an integer input and returns a Boolean result. Thus, Odd(4) is False, while Odd(5) is True and Odd(3.5) is an error.

Round and Trunc convert reals to integers. They were discussed in Chapter 3, but we remind you that Trunc(8.9) is 8, while Round(8.9) is 9.

Sqr and Sqrt are inverses of each other. Sqr squares its input, accepts either an integer or a real, and returns that same type. That is, Sqr(3) is the integer 9, while Sqr(3.5) is the real 12.25. Sqrt returns the real square root of its argument, no matter whether that argument is integer or real. Sqrt(2) is the real 1.414 and

Table 6.2: Some Special Turbo Pascal Functions and Procedures

Mathematical Functions and Procedures

Frac(X)	The Fraction function (the fractional part of real X)
Int(X)	The Integer function (the whole part of X as a real)
Pi	The Pi function (returns 3.1415926535897932385)
Randomize	The Randomize procedure (randomly initializes the built-in random-number generator)
Random	The Random function (returns the next random number)

Character and String Functions and Procedures (See Chapter 17)

Concat	The Concatenation function
Copy	The Copy function
Delete	The Delete procedure
Insert	The Insert procedure
Length	The Length function
Pos	The Position function
Str	The String function (en-strings a numeric value)
UpCase	The UpCase function (converts a letter to uppercase)
Val	The Value function (e"val"uates a string to a numeric value)

Increment and Decrement Procedures (See below)

Dec(t)	The Decrement procedure
Inc(t)	The Increment procedure

A Dynamic Allocation Procedure (See Chapter 19)

Dispose	The Dispose function (to free allocated memory)

`Sqrt(4.0)` is the real `2.0`. Please note that `Sqr` and `Sqrt` are easily confused with each other, and using `Sqr` when you mean `Sqrt`, or vice-versa, can lead to errors that are hard to find.

Niklaus Wirth's goal in designing Pascal was to keep the language small, so that it would be easy to learn. In general, he did an admirable job in designing Pascal. However, we do wonder why he bothered to include the two functions `Odd` and `Sqr` in the language. Each is quite specialized and easily defined with other constructs of the language. For example,

```
Odd(X)
```

is equivalent to the Boolean expression

```
X Mod 2 = 1
```

and

```
Sqr(X)
```

is equivalent to the expression

```
X * X
```

We conjecture that `Sqr` was included as a bone to throw to those who objected because Pascal had no built-in powering function (X^n). `Sqr`, of course, provides the most commonly used case of powering, but, since it is so easy to square something yourself, and, since `Sqr` is easily confused with `Sqrt`, we will tend to avoid further use of `Sqr`.

The other standard functions of Pascal—`Ord`, `Chr`, `Succ`, and `Pred`—as well as the standard procedure `New`, will be introduced in later chapters of this book.

None of the objects in Table 6.2 are contained in standard Pascal, as originally defined by Niklaus Wirth. They are often very convenient, but the reader must be aware that they are not available in all Pascals.

The function `Frac(X)` returns the fractional part of its real input. For example, `Frac(-3.7825)` is `-0.7825`. `Int(X)` returns, as a real, the whole part of its real input. For example, `Int(5.842)` is `5.0`, while `Trunc(5.842)` is the integer `5`.

`Pi` is the function, of no arguments, that returns the value of the mathematical constant π. `Pi` can therefore be used without being declared either as a constant or as a variable (it is built in) as in

```
Area := Pi * Rad * Rad;
```

where we are assuming that `Area` and `Rad` are real identifiers and that `Rad` already has a value.

`Randomize` and `Random` control the built-in random-number generator supplied by Turbo Pascal, and their use is explained later in this chapter.

The string-manipulation functions and procedures will be discussed extensively in Chapter 17. Briefly, these functions and procedures let us operate on strings, making, for example, 'Mozart, Wolfgang A.' from 'Wolfgang Amadeus Mozart'. In passing, we do mention the character function, UpCase, which turns its input into its uppercase equivalent. For example, if Ch is the character 'q', then UpCase(Ch) returns 'Q'. If Ch is 'W', or even '+', UpCase(Ch) does nothing and returns 'W' or '+', respectively. UpCase is useful when you are trying to obtain some specific input from the user, but can't be sure whether the user will type uppercase or lowercase. For example, consider the loop

```
Ch := 'X';                 {Initialize Ch for the test in the While.}
While (Ch <> 'Y') And (Ch <> 'N') Do
  Begin
    Writeln('Do you want to play a game? (Y/N)');
    Readln(Ch);
    Ch := UpCase(Ch)            {Make sure response is uppercase.}
End;
```

This loop traps the user until an appropriate answer to the question is given. In this case, an appropriate response is 'Y', 'N', 'y', or 'n'. The use of UpCase simply reduces the cases to be tested and makes the code easier to read. In Chapter 10, we'll learn how to define our own UpCase, as well as its missing companion, DownCase.

Most of the built-ins are functions, but Inc and Dec are procedures. Dec is the decrement procedure. Dec(X) reduces its input by one step. For example, if Ch is a character identifier with the value 'Q', then

```
Dec(Ch);
```

reassigns Ch the value 'P'. If Index is an integer identifier with the value 7, then

```
Dec(Index);
```

reduces Index to 6. As such, it is shorthand for the longer statement:

```
Index := Index - 1;
```

Dec will not work with the real type, but only with types like integer and char, where each value, except the first, has a logical previous value. Dec can also be used with the user-defined types that are introduced in Chapter 10.

The procedure Dec also has a second form for decrementing by more than one. For example, if we again assume that Ch has the value 'Q' and Index the value 7, then

```
Dec(Ch, 3);
Dec(Index, 2);
```

reduces Ch by 3 letters to 'N' and Index by 2 to 5.

Inc is the increment procedure. If Ch and Index are character and integer identifiers with the values 'Q' and 7, respectively, then

```
Inc(Ch);
Inc(Index);
```

makes them 'R' and 8, respectively. Inc is not allowed with the real type.

The procedure Inc also has a second form. For example, if Ch and Index are again 'Q' and 7, then

```
Inc(Ch, 5);
Inc(Index, 2);
```

makes them 'V' and 9, respectively.

The procedure Dispose is the companion to the standard procedure New, and the use of both of these, to allocate and reclaim memory dynamically, is discussed in Chapter 19.

RANDOM-NUMBER GENERATION

To illustrate the use of built-in functions, let us consider some simulation problems. Computer simulation is an important applications area and, in many simulations, the computer needs to exhibit random behavior. Examples of randomness include the tossing of a coin, the rolling of dice, and the presence of a genetic defect in an organism. Because the computer is a deterministic machine (meaning that it always does the same thing given the same instructions and the same circumstances), it might seem that a computer can't really exhibit random behavior. In fact, computers don't exhibit truly random behavior, but they can follow a pseudorandom pattern (meaning almost truly random), which in many applications is good enough. To generate a random number, the computer does some numeric computations on a starting number, called the random-number **seed**. This seed, in some sense, needs to be random, if random output is to be generated. How does the computer get this random seed? There are various methods for doing this. In computers with a built-in clock, part of the seed may come from the precise time of day when we ask the computer to generate a random number for us. For now, we just accept the fact that Randomize randomly sets the seed for the random-number generator, so that the function Random can generate random numbers for us. You should be aware that Randomize and Random are not part of standard Pascal, but are provided in Turbo Pascal because they are very useful. Later, we'll see how to write our own versions of these tools.

Realize that the Randomize procedure needs to be executed only once to seed the process of generating random numbers. Therefore, the procedure Randomize should not be contained in any processing loop, but should be listed with any other initializations at the top of the body of your program. The function Random, on the other hand, will probably be in the processing loop and, each time it is called, it will produce another random value. Random is unusual in that it can be used with or without an argument. Random, with no argument, will return a real value between 0.0 and 1.0. Random, with a positive integer argument, will return a nonnegative integer less than the argument. For example, Random(6) will randomly return one of the six values 0, 1, 2, 3, 4, or 5. Thus, the following expression assigns to Die (the singular of dice) an integer for a die-rolling experiment:

```
Die := Random(6) + 1
```

In a moment, we'll use this expression to simulate the tossing of a die, but first let us write a program that simulates the tossing of a coin 1000 times, counting the number of heads and the number of tails. All we need to do is generate 1000 random reals between 0.0 and 1.0 and agree that each number less than or equal to 0.5 is a tail and each number greater than 0.5 is a head. We point out that it doesn't matter which way 0.5 is counted, since there are so many real numbers between 0.0 and 1.0 that we don't expect to ever actually get 0.5. Of course, we could also use the expression Random(2) to generate the integers 0 (for tails) or 1 (for heads), but, in this example, we want to illustrate the real random-number generator Random (with no arguments). The program, Coin, is shown in Listing 6.1. Run Coin several times and observe its random behavior.

```pascal
Program Coin;

{This program simulates the tossing of a fair coin.}

Const NumFlips = 1000;

Var
  Toss      :  Integer;
  NumHeads  :  Integer;
  NumTails  :  Integer;

Begin
  Randomize;                     {Stir up the random-number generator.}
  Writeln('Please wait while I toss the coin ', NumFlips,
                                                ' times.');
  Writeln;
  NumHeads := 0;
  Toss := 1;
  While Toss <= NumFlips Do
    Begin
      If Random > 0.5 Then
        NumHeads := NumHeads + 1;
      Toss := Toss + 1
    End; {While}
  NumTails := NumFlips - NumHeads;
  Writeln('After ',NumFlips,' tosses,the number of heads is ',
                                                NumHeads);
  Writeln('and the number of tails is ', NumTails)
End.
```

Listing 6.1

When we ran `Coin`, we obtained the following results:

```
Please wait while I toss the coin 1000 times.

After 1000 tosses, the number of heads is 512
and the number of tails is 488
```

Observe that we did not keep track of `NumTails` in the loop in program `Coin`. Instead, we compute `NumTails` after the loop, by a simple subtraction. If we know the number of heads and the total number of coin flips, we can easily compute the number of tails.

In our next example, `Die`, we roll a fair die 600 times, printing the number of times each of the possible outcomes, 1 through 6, occurs. In a random situation, each should occur about 100 times. You should run this program, shown in Listing 6.2, several times to see how close the results are to what is expected. In Chapter 8, we'll learn that there is a simpler way than nested `If`s to handle so many cases.

The output, from one execution of `Die`, is shown below. Note that the frequencies are nearly equal, but, of course, one cannot expect exactly 100 of each outcome.

```
Please wait while I roll the die 600 times.
Summary of 600 rolls of a die

        Outcomes      Occurrences
           1               96
           2              102
           3              112
           4               87
           5               95
           6              108
```

```
Program Die;
{This program simulates the rolling of a fair die.}

Const  NumRolls = 600;

Var    Ones     : Integer;
       Twos     : Integer;
       Threes   : Integer;
       Fours    : Integer;
       Fives    : Integer;
       Sixes    : Integer;
       Roll     : Integer;
       Outcome  : Integer;
```

Listing 6.2

```
Begin
  Randomize;
  Ones := 0; Twos := 0;
  Threes := 0; Fours := 0;
  Fives := 0; Sixes := 0;
  Writeln('Please wait while I roll the die ', NumRolls,
                                            ' times.');
Roll := 1;
  While Roll <= NumRolls Do
    Begin
      Outcome := Random(6) + 1;    {Roll the die--note outcome.}
      If Outcome = 1 Then
        Ones := Ones + 1
      Else If Outcome = 2 Then
        Twos := Twos + 1
      Else If Outcome = 3 Then
        Threes := Threes + 1
      Else If Outcome = 4 Then
        Fours := Fours + 1
      Else If Outcome = 5 Then
        Fives := Fives + 1
      Else
        Sixes := Sixes + 1;
      Roll := Roll + 1
    End; {While}
  Writeln('Summary of ', NumRolls, ' rolls of a die');
  Writeln('Outcomes':12, 'Occurrences':14);
  Writeln(1:8, Ones:12);
  Writeln(2:8, Twos:12);
  Writeln(3:8, Threes:12);
  Writeln(4:8, Fours:12);
  Writeln(5:8, Fives:12);
  Writeln(6:8, Sixes:12)
End.
```

Listing 6.2 (continued)

Notice that although this program is quite simple, it is somewhat bothersome and repetitive. Think how bothersome it would have been had we been rolling two dice instead of just one, or if we were performing an experiment that had 50 different outcomes. Remember, computers are supposed to make such repetition and drudgery easier to handle. This is exactly what arrays will do for us in Chapter 11.

There are many other applications for random numbers. Many of the most popular arcade games have their main characters move in a random fashion, so that the game does not play exactly the same every time. See the exercises at the end of this chapter for several applications of random numbers.

USER-DEFINED FUNCTIONS

Built-in functions are very useful because they allow us to do complex things, like taking a square root, by just using the name of the square root function. But the real power of functions in Pascal comes not from the built-in functions of the language, but from the programmer's ability to define any *new* function that is needed.

As our first example of a user-defined function, let us write the missing power function, so that we can easily compute expressions such as X^5. For this simple example, we will assume that the base (X) is real while the exponent is an integer. Let us agree to call our function Power and note that we expect Power(X,K) to return a real value. For example, Power(1.5,3) should be the real value $(1.5)^3 = 3.375$.

Every function definition begins with a header that tells

1. The name of the function
2. The name and type of each argument to the function
3. The type of the output of the function

For Power, this header will be

```
Function Power(X : Real; K : Integer) : Real;
```

From this, it is obvious that the name of the function being defined is Power and that Power expects two arguments; the first must be a real and the second must be an integer. It is the final Real, on the end, that indicates that Power is returning a real value through its name, as its output.

As we'll see, the only differences in procedure headings are that they begin with the keyword Procedure instead of the keyword Function and that they fail to have a final value stated (as the procedure carries no value back through its name). In this book, we will follow the practice of beginning each function or procedure with a comment

```
{ This function (or procedure)...
Pre:  ...
Post: ... }
```

that describes the purpose of the function (or procedure) being defined, so that the reader of the program can gather, from reading the comment, what it is that the procedure or function does. We will also state what **preconditions** must be true before a call to a procedure or function is valid. Likewise, we state what **postconditions** will hold after the procedure or function has executed a valid call. These preconditions and postconditions make programs easier to understand, debug, maintain, and verify. Much more will be said about preconditions and postconditions in the next chapter.

With two other exceptions, the body of the definition of a function looks exactly like the body of any program definition. The first exception is that a function definition *should* contain an assignment statement that assigns some value to the function name. This tells the system what value to return through that name. Finally, End, at the end of the definition, is followed by a semicolon rather than a period. With these

```
Function Power(X : Real; K : Integer) : Real;
{This function raises X to the power K by successive multipli-
cations. Note that if K is zero, Power returns the value 1.0.
Pre:   X and K have appropriate values, so that X to the Kth power
       does not cause overflow or underflow.
Post: Power returns X to the Kth power.                              }

Var  LoopIndex : Integer;
     Product   : Real;

Begin
  Product := 1.0;
  LoopIndex := 1;
  While LoopIndex <= K Do
    Begin
      Product := Product * X;
      LoopIndex := LoopIndex + 1
    End {While}
  Power := Product
End;
```

Listing 6.3

distinctions carefully in mind, study Listing 6.3, which contains the complete definition of function `Power`.

  Listing 6.3 shows why subprogram is a good name for a function. Except for very
minor differences, the function `Power` looks like a small program. We see that
functions can have their own variable declarations. They can also have constant
declarations and can use `If`s and `While`s. They can use any construct that we have
introduced for programs. As long as you can remember the syntax for the function
heading, can remember to assign a value to the function, and can remember not to use
a period at the end of the function definition, functions are easy to write.

  The observant reader might question our need for the variable `Product` in the body
of `Power`. Can't we simplify the body of `Power` to the following?

```
Power := 1.0;
LoopIndcx :- 1;
While LoopIndex <= K Do
  Begin
    Power := Power * X;
    LoopIndex := LoopIndex + 1
  End {While}
```

The answer is no, but the reason is fairly subtle. If you try the above, you will receive
an error message at the statement

```
Power := Power * X;
```

with the cursor after the second `Power`. The error message will be something mysterious about insufficient arguments. The problem is that it is legal in Pascal for a procedure or function to call itself, and that is what the compiler thinks you are trying to do. Of course, whenever you call a procedure or function, you must supply the correct number of arguments. (Hence, the error message.) Procedures and functions that call themselves are said to be **recursive**. Recursion is very important in Pascal, but is not an elementary topic. In fact, it will be Chapter 18 before we take up recursion. Thus, for the time being, we make the rule that, in a function definition, the function name appears only on the left-hand side in an assignment. We should be able to remember this rule, since it is the job of the body to assign a value to the function name.

This assignment to the function's name does not need to be the last statement in the body of the function, but it often is. There can be several conditional assignments. An example of these possibilities is given by the following fragment of a function body for `FareRate`, which determines a percentage to be applied to the full fare to determine the fare to be charged for a given individual, depending on that individual's age:

```
If (Age < 13) Or (Age > 64) Then
   FareRate := 0.50     {Kids and Senior Citizens at 50 percent.}
Else
   FareRate := 1.00;        {Adults pay full fare of 100 percent.}
```

Notice that every identifier used in the body of the function `Power`, in Listing 6.3, is listed in one of two places. It is either in the function heading or in the `Var` list inside the function.

For the present, we make the rule that every identifier used in a function should be found in one of these two places.

Later, after more examples and after we introduce procedures, we'll have much more to say about this subject and we will see that our rule, while still a good one, can be relaxed a little.

The identifiers listed in the `Var` section within the function are called the **local** variables of the function. They are created when the function is invoked and are destroyed when the function has completed its task. Thus, they cannot be accessed from outside the function—that is why they are called local to the function. They can be thought of as scratch variables, or work variables, that the function needs to complete its task. For example, our algorithm to compute X^5 needs a `LoopIndex` to count from 1 to 5. This `LoopIndex` is neither input to, nor output from, the function, but is needed for the function to do its work properly. These local variables can even have the same names as variables in the outer program and the system will keep them separate, because memory isn't allocated for local variables such as `LoopIndex` and `Product` until `Power` is invoked. If such variables exist in the outer environment, then these new ones **mask** the old ones and `Power` will be able to see only the local `LoopIndex` and `Product`. When `Power` has completed its execution, memory for the local variables is reclaimed and the other `LoopIndex` and/or `Product` are unmasked. We will have much more to say about this subject, the scope of an identifier, in Chapter 9.

The identifiers listed in the function heading, within the parentheses, are called the **dummy** or **formal parameters** to the function. We'll simply call them the parameters to the function. For the function `Power`, these parameters serve to provide it with the necessary inputs. After all, how can `Power` raise X to the Kth power if it doesn't know what the values of X and K are?

However, it is important to realize that we can invoke `Power` with any pair of real and integer values. If we have a program in which `Principal, Rate,` and `BalanceDue` are real and `Term` is an integer, then the total amount due at the end of a loan with simple interest is

BalanceDue $\leftarrow$ Principal $* (1.0 + \text{Rate})^{\text{Term}}$

and it is legal to write this in Pascal, assuming that `Principal, Rate,` and `Term` already have values, as:

```
BalanceDue := Principal * Power(1.0 + Rate, Term);
```

The identifiers, or expressions, that we actually use when we invoke a function are called the **arguments** or **actual parameters**. We will simply call them arguments, in contrast to the parameters used to define the function. The actual arguments do not have to be the same as the dummy parameters, but they can be. This means that we do not have to remember what the dummy parameters were. We can use new arguments, or we can accidentally use the same names—either way, no harm comes to us!

It is time to see how our function `Power` fits into a complete program that uses it to do something practical. For this purpose, consider the program `Table` of Listing 6.4, which produces a table of the squares, cubes, and fourth powers of the first 13 whole numbers. For this purpose, the type of the first parameter to `Power` has been changed to integer, and its output type is, therefore, also changed to integer. To make this clear, the function has been renamed `IntPower`. Notice that the definition of the function comes after the `Var` section of the main program and before the `Begin` of the main program. It is important to realize that the system reads and accepts the function definition, but does not execute the function until it is invoked in the main program. As always, execution begins with the first statement after the `Begin` of the main program.

The output from program `Table` is

```
A table of squares, cubes, and fourth powers:
```

Number	Square	Cube	Fourth Power
1	1	1	1
2	4	8	16
3	9	27	81
4	16	64	256
. . .	. . .	. . .	. . .
13	169	2197	28561

The reason that the table stops at 13 is that 14^4 already causes integer overflow on many systems, including Turbo Pascal.

```
Program Table;
{This program illustrates a user-defined function, IntPower, to
calculate a table of some numbers and their small powers.      }

Var    Index : Integer;
       Expon : Integer;

Function IntPower(J, K : Integer) : Integer;
{This function raises J to the Kth power by successive multi-
plications. Note that if K is 0, IntPower returns the value 1.
Pre:   J and K are integers such that J to the Kth power does not
       cause overflow.
Post:  IntPower returns the value of J to the Kth power.       }

   Var    LoopIndex : Integer;
          Product   : Integer;

   Begin
     Product := 1;
     LoopIndex := 1;
     While LoopIndex <= K Do
       Begin
         Product := Product * J;
         LoopIndex := LoopIndex + 1
       End; {While}
     IntPower := Product
   End ;                               {Definition of function IntPower.}

Begin                                  {Body of main program Table.}
  Writeln('A table of squares, cubes, and fourth powers:');
  Writeln;
  Writeln(' Number    Square    Cube    Fourth Power');
  Writeln;
  Index := 1;
  While Index <= 13 Do    {14 to the 4th power causes overflow.}
    Begin
      Expon := 1;
      While Expon <= 4 Do
        Begin
          Write(IntPower(Index, Expon):10);
          Expon := Expon + 1
        End; {Inner While}
      Writeln;
      Index := Index + 1
    End {Outer While}
End.
```

Listing 6.4

Note that in the heading for `IntPower`, we have written

```
Function IntPower(J, K : Integer) : Integer;
```

This is shorthand for

```
Function IntPower(J : Integer; K : Integer) : Integer;
```

When several consecutive parameters have the same type, they may be listed together (separated by commas) to conserve on space and typing. Notice that there is a semicolon separating parameter declarations. For example, to declare an integer function, `StrangeAndWeird`, with two real, one char, and two Boolean parameters, we could write

```
Procedure StrangeAndWeird(This, That : Real; Ch : Char; S, T :
                          Boolean) : Integer;
```

which also points out that, if a function declaration is too long to fit on one line, we can break the heading at any reasonable point and simply continue it, indented, on the next line. At any reasonable point means at any place where a blank could appear. You cannot break a line in the middle of an identifier or type name.

Notice in Listing 6.4 that we have indented the declarations and body of function `IntPower`. This is done so that the reader's eye can quickly see that these are not the declarations and main body of the program. The main body begins, as always, at the leftmost `Begin` in the entire listing. We'll soon see that procedures and functions can have other procedures and functions nested within them. At that point, proper use of indentation becomes very important to preserve the readability of programs.

PROBLEM-SOLVING EXAMPLE: PERFECT NUMBERS

Let us consider a more interesting problem from arithmetic, so that we can illustrate the divide-and-conquer strategy. Pythagoras, the famous Greek mathematician, was reportedly fascinated with perfect numbers. A whole number is **perfect** if it is exactly the sum of its own proper divisors. By divisors, we simply mean numbers that divide another number evenly. For example, 1, 2, 3, 4, 6, and 12 are the divisors of 12. By proper, we exclude the number itself, so the proper divisors of 12 are 1, 2, 3, 4, and 6. Therefore, 12 is not perfect, since

$$12 \neq 1 + 2 + 3 + 4 + 6 = 16.$$

Again, 6 is a perfect number, since

$$6 = 1 + 2 + 3$$

The next perfect number is 28, since

$28 = 1 + 2 + 4 + 7 + 14$

The next perfect number is much larger and you are not likely to find it by hand (but Pythagoras did). Let's write a program to find the next perfect number.

To approach this problem with a top-down design, we should ask ourselves what black box(es) would make the problem easy to solve. Obviously, if Pascal had a built-in SumDivs(Num) function that returned the sum of the proper divisors of Num, we would be in the clear—for a number is perfect only if it satisfies the equality test Num = SumDivs(Num). If we had SumDivs, we could start at 29 and just keep trying whole numbers until we found the next perfect number.

We know that there is a next perfect number, but you don't—and, anyway, due to a bug, our program might miss perfect numbers and keep on and on in its search. Therefore, it is a good idea to always put a limit to such a search. If we are wrong about there being a next perfect number, or if the program is buggy and keeps searching on and on, we will eventually be told that we have reached the limit of our search. Of course, if we find a perfect number, we should stop the search and not continue on to the limit. To help us decide when to stop, we can use a Boolean variable, Found. We can summarize our ideas in the following pseudo-code:

> Initialize the Limit of the Search to some arbitrary value, say, 5000
> Set Found to False to indicate we haven't found a perfect number yet
> Set Candidate to 28 to begin the search
> While a perfect number is Not Found and Candidate ≤ Limit of the Search
>   Increment the Candidate
>   If Candidate = SumDivs(Candidate) then
>   Set Found to True   --Perfect number has been found
> If Found then
>   Write out Candidate as the next perfect number
> Else
>   Write out a message that the search failed up to the given limit

This pseudo-code certainly isn't Pascal, but it won't be difficult to implement it in Pascal, assuming the existence of the function SumDivs. Before we write SumDivs, notice that Candidate was initialized to 28, not 29, because we incremented the Candidate before we tested to see if it was perfect. If anything about the above pseudo-code is not clear, you should initialize Candidate to some small value, such as 25, and trace the algorithm, step by step, to see how it finds 28 and stops.

Our divide-and-conquer process has left us with a function SumDivs to design. If this were a difficult function to write, we could continue to break it down into more manageable pieces. As it turns out, however, SumDivs is very easy to write, if we make the following observations: All the possible proper divisors of a given number are between 1 and half of the number. To decide if one number divides another evenly, we simply use Mod, since Mod gives us the remainder. That is,

TrialDivisor divides Num evenly

if and only if

The remainder upon division of Num by TrialDivisor is zero

Expressed in Pascal, this can be written as the assertion (not statement)

```
(Num Mod TrialDivisor) = 0
```

Finally, of course, we need to keep a running summation of those TrialDivisors that do divide the given number evenly. Hence, we have the following pseudo-code for our algorithm for the function SumDivs:

Function SumDivs(Num)   --Finds the sum of the proper divisors of Num
    Initialize local variable Sum to zero
    Initialize local variable TrialDivisor to 1
    While TrialDivisor is $\leq$ half of Num
       If Num Mod TrialDivisor is zero then
          Sum $\leftarrow$ Sum + TrialDivisor
       TrialDivisor $\leftarrow$ TrialDivisor + 1
    SumDivs $\leftarrow$ Sum

Again, the reader should trace this algorithm with a value of Num of 6, or 12, to see how SumDivs returns its result (6, or 16, respectively). Notice that every identifier used in SumDivs is either a dummy parameter (Num) or a local variable (Sum, TrialDivisor) of the function SumDivs.

Listing 6.5 shows the complete program Perfect with the function SumDivs. Observe how closely the structure of the program follows the outline given by the pseudo-code. This indicates that our design was complete and that the implementation phase proceeded without trauma!

Program Perfect does find another perfect number, and its output is

```
496 is the next perfect number.
```

We leave it to the reader to verify that this is correct.

```
Program Perfect;
{This program searches for the next perfect number after 6 and 28.
A number is perfect if it is the sum of its own proper divisors.
For example,

        6 = 1 + 2 + 3

and

        28 = 1 + 2 + 4 + 7 + 14

To find perfect numbers, the main program calls the user-defined
function SumDivs(Num), which simply returns the sum of the proper
divisors of its input. The program reports failure if it finds no
perfect number before a predetermined limit for the search.   }
```

Listing 6.5

```
Const  LimitOfSearch = 5000;


Var   Candidate  : Integer;
       Found      : Boolean;


Function SumDivs(Num : Integer) : Integer;

{This function computes the sum of the proper divisors of Num. To
do so, it loops through all integers from 1 to Num Div 2, using Mod
to see if they divide Num evenly.

Pre:   Num is a positive integer.
Post: SumDivs returns the sum of the proper divisors of Num.   }

  Var TrialDivisor : Integer;
      Sum          : Integer;

  Begin
    Sum := 0;
    TrialDivisor := 1;
    While TrialDivisor <= (Num Div 2) Do
      Begin
        If (Num Mod TrialDivisor) = 0 Then      {Divide evenly?}
          Sum := Sum + TrialDivisor;
        TrialDivisor := TrialDivisor + 1
      End; {While}
    SumDivs := Sum
  End;                                {Definition of function SumDivs.}

Begin                                   {Body of main program Perfect.}
  Found := False;                       {Perfect number not found yet.}
  Candidate := 28;        {Begin search at the perfect number 28.}
  While (Candidate <= LimitOfSearch) And Not Found Do
    Begin
      Candidate := Candidate + 1;
      If Candidate = SumDivs(Candidate) Then
        Found := True                   {EUREKA! We have found it.}
    End; {While}
  If Found Then
    Writeln(Candidate, ' is the next perfect number.')
  Else
    Writeln('No perfect number was found less than ',
                                            LimitOfSearch)
End.
```

Listing 6.5 (continued)

```
Function UserKeepsPlaying : Boolean;
{This parameterless function returns True if the user wants to keep
playing and False otherwise. Note that there are no parameters.

Pre:   None
Post:  UserKeepsPlaying is True if and only if the user responds
       with 'y' or 'Y'.                                          }

  Var Answer : Char;         {Local variable for user's response.}

  Begin
    Write('Do you want to play (Y/N): ');
    Readln(Answer);
    Answer := UpCase(Answer);     {Make sure we have uppercase.}
    If Answer = 'Y' Then
      UserKeepsPlaying := True          {Player wants to keep on.}
    Else
      UserKeepsPlaying := False            {Player is a quitter.}
  End;
```

Listing 6.6

PARAMETERLESS FUNCTIONS ARE POSSIBLE

Occasionally, we have the need for a function with no parameters. For example, suppose you are writing the next successful computer game and you want to give the user the option, at the end of the game, of playing again. In pseudo-code, we could write

While the user wants to keep playing do
  Play the game

The unit the-user-wants-to-keep-playing can be implemented as a Boolean function that prompts the user and returns his or her response. As such, it has no input from the main program and, hence, no parameters. Our pseudo-code can be translated into

```
While UserKeepsPlaying Do
  Play Game(NumDragonsSlayed, NumDamselsSaved);
```

where `PlayGame` is the procedure that plays the game and `UserKeepsPlaying` is our simple Boolean function. Listing 6.6 shows the function `UserKeepsPlaying`.

  Notice that, for our convenience, we have used the Turbo Pascal built-in `UpCase` function to make sure that the response of the user is in uppercase. We do this since many people do not follow instructions well and will enter `'y'` instead of `'Y'` in response to our prompt. We could eliminate the `UpCase` function and write the `If` as

```
If (Answer = 'Y') Or (Answer = 'y') Then ...
```

but this is clearly not as simple as our `If`.

SIMPLE USER-DEFINED PROCEDURES

Let us now turn to the subject of procedures. As we know, a procedure does not return a value through its name. A procedure heading looks like a function heading, except that the keyword Procedure is used instead of the keyword Function. Also, because it returns no value through its name, a procedure has no final type listed in the heading and no assignment is made to the procedure name within the body of the procedure. These are the three minor differences between the syntax of procedure and function definitions.

Let us consider two simple procedure examples. Suppose you are writing a program that produces a large report. In order to impress the boss, you decide you will put strings of *s across the page at various points:

```
********************************************************************
```

to help divide the report into sections. Of course, it isn't difficult to write such code, but it's tedious to keep repeating it. If we define a procedure, Stars, to do this task for us, then we can invoke Stars with the simple and clear statement

```
Stars;
```

as many times as we wish in our program. Listing 6.7 shows the definition of Stars. Note that Stars has no parameters and no type, and, of course, no assignment of a value is made to Stars. Stars is a very simple procedure—with only one local variable to Count the 80 columns of the screen.

```
Procedure Stars;
{This parameterless procedure provides a line of '*'s.
Pre:  None
Post: A line of 80 stars is produced, but no result is computed.}

  Var Count : Integer;

  Begin
    Writeln;
    Count := 1;
    While Count <= 80 Do
      Begin
        Write('*');
        Count := Count + 1
      End; {While}
    Writeln
  End;
```

Listing 6.7

```
Procedure Break(Symbol : Char; Length : Integer);
{This procedure provides a line of Symbols of the given Length.

Pre:  Symbol is any Char and Length does not exceed line length.
Post: The symbol is written Length times followed by a Writeln.}

  Var Count : Integer;

  Begin
    Writeln;
    Count := 1;
    While Count <= Length Do
      Begin
        Write(Symbol);
        Count := Count + 1
      End; {While}
    Writeln
  End;
```

Listing 6.8

The simple procedure Stars is not very flexible. It prints 80 *s, whether that is what you want or not. Let's define a new procedure Break(Symbol, Length) that will print whatever symbol you want and as many of that symbol as you want. For example,

```
Break('$', 40);
```

will print 40 dollar signs, while

```
Break('+', 60);
```

will print 60 plus signs. Listing 6.8 shows the procedure Break(Symbol, Length). Notice that the extra flexibility, over the simple procedure Stars, is obtained from the two input parameters Symbol and Length. Observe that these replace the constants ('*' and 80) from the listing of Stars.

Again, note that all of the identifiers used in procedure Break are listed in one of two places. They are either parameters, listed in the procedure heading, or local variables, declared in the procedure. Again, it is our temporary rule that every identifier used in a procedure or function be found in one of these two places.

VALUE AND VARIABLE PARAMETERS

For simplicity, we have concealed one relevant fact about parameters. This fact is that there are two kinds of parameters in Pascal: value and variable parameters. Value parameters are the kind that we have illustrated in our examples to this point. Variable parameters, as we will soon see, are indicated by the keyword Var.

With a value parameter, it is the value of the actual argument that is passed to the procedure or function.

If a parameter is a value parameter, the procedure or function makes a *copy* of the actual argument. This means that the procedure or function *cannot* change the value of an argument passed by a value parameter, since it is only the copy, not the original, that can be modified by the procedure or function.

How then can a procedure, which has no assignment of a value to its name, pass any results back to the caller? The answer is provided by variable parameters.

A variable parameter is an *alias* for the actual argument, and, hence, any changes to a variable parameter are immediately reflected in the actual argument.

Let us consider a specific example. The procedure FindPerfectWt takes the height of the user in Feet and Inches, takes the Sex of the user, and determines the IdealWeight for the user. Feet, Inches, and Sex should be value parameters in FindPerfectWt, since the procedure must have these values, but it should not change them. (It shouldn't do a Sex change operation, for example.) On the other hand, FindPerfectWt computes (by some unspecified means) a new value for the parameter IdealWeight. Thus, IdealWeight must be a variable parameter. This means that the heading for FindPerfectWt is

```
Procedure FindPerfectWt(Feet, Inches : Integer; Sex : Char;
                                        Var IdealWeight : Real);
```

You indicate value parameters by not doing anything special with them. That is, a value parameter is what you get if you don't specify a variable parameter by using Var.

The value and variable parameters can come in any order, so

```
Procedure FindPerfectWt(Var IdealWeight : Real;
                          Feet, Inches : Integer; Sex : Char);
```

is also an acceptable heading for the procedure. If the procedure Strange has two real variable parameters, and two char value parameters, the heading for Strange can be written

```
Procedure Strange(Var X, Y : Real; A, B : Char);
```

Note, in particular, that the Var applies only to X and Y. The effect of the Var ends at the semicolon following Real.

RIGHT AND WRONG: THE NEED FOR VARIABLE PARAMETERS

Experience teaching many students over many years has shown us that a very common programming error that beginners make is to forget the Var in a parameter that needs to be a variable parameter. So that you understand the severity of this error, we'll write incorrect and correct versions of a very simple, but useful, procedure. Our procedure is Swap(J, K) and its objective is to swap, or exchange, the values of J and K, which we assume are integer identifiers. The first thing to realize is that

```
J := K;              {Incorrect first attempt at the body of Swap.}
K := J;
```

does *not* properly swap the values of J and K. To see this, suppose J is 3 and K is 7 before the above statements. After the first assignment, we see that both J and K have the value 7. Hence, the second assignment has no effect and surely does not assign K the value 3. The easiest way to rectify this problem is to add a temporary variable, Temp, where the value 3 can be placed before it is lost. Trace the following segment to see that it does correctly exchange the values of J and K:

```
Temp := J;                  {Store the old value of J in Temp.}
J := K;                         {Put K's old value into J.}
K := Temp;                      {Put J's old value into K.}
```

Listing 6.9 shows a program, Wrong, that uses this segment in a procedure Swap.

```
Program Wrong;
{This program illustrates a common beginner's error involving the
failure to use Var parameters.                                    }
Var    J : Integer;
       K : Integer;
Procedure Swap(J, K : Integer);
{This procedure is supposed to swap the values of J and K.
Pre:   None
Post: Supposedly, the values of J and K are exchanged.           }
  Var Temp : Integer;                    {A temporary for the swap.}
  Begin
    Temp := J;
    J := K;
    K := Temp
  End;                                  {Definition of procedure Swap.}
Begin                                    {Body of main program Wrong.}
  J := 38;
  K := 695;
  Writeln('Before the swap the values of J and K are ', J, ' and ', K);
  Writeln;
  Swap(J, K);
  Writeln('After the swap the values of J and K are ', J, ' and ', K);
End.
```

Listing 6.9

Here is the output of `Wrong`:

```
Before the swap the values of J and K are 38 and 695

After the swap the values of J and K are 38 and 695
```

Wait a minute! Something is wrong with `Wrong`. The values of `J` and `K` were not exchanged. The problem, as we have already indicated, is that both of `Swap`'s parameters must be variable parameters, if the actual arguments, `J` and `K`, of the program are to be changed by the procedure `Swap` (even though it uses the same dummy parameters `J` and `K`). It is important to see why `Wrong` does not work. When `Wrong` is invoked, the values of the program's `J` and `K` (38 and 695) are passed to `Swap`, which stores these values in its own *copies* of `J` and `K`. `Swap` then exchanges the values of the copies, but no changes are made to the originals! This is shown in Figure 6.2, which shows a snapshot of memory just before the end of the execution of procedure `Swap`.

When `Swap` is finished executing, the memory for `Swap`'s copies of `J` and `K` and `Swap`'s local variable `Temp` is reclaimed by the system. Hence, `Swap` fails to exchange the values of the original `J` and `K`. It is worth noting that if we put a `Writeln(J:5,K:5)` (Try it!) inside of `Swap`, just before its `End`, we would see that `Swap` has swapped the values of *its* `J` and `K`.

What is needed is something like Figure 6.3, where the `J` and `K` of `Swap` are really the original `J` and `K`. This is exactly what variable parameters do for us.

Listing 6.10 shows the program `Right`, which is exactly like program `Wrong`, except for its name, the comment, and the *critical* fact that the parameters to `Swap` are now variable.

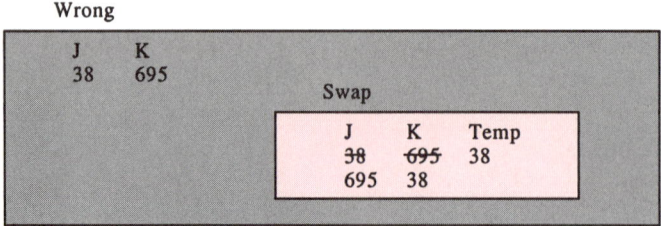

Figure 6.2

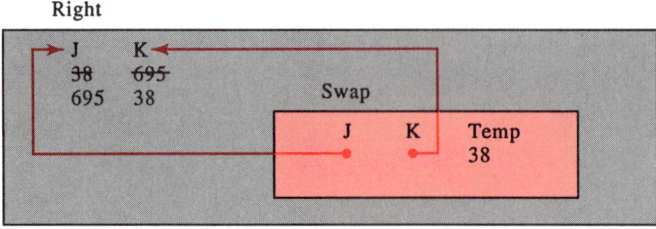

Figure 6.3

```
Program Right;

{This program illustrates correct usage of Var parameters.     }

Var    J : Integer;
       K : Integer;

Procedure Swap( Var J, K : Integer);              {Note the Var!}
{This procedure swaps the values of J and K.
Pre:   None
Post:  The values of J and K have been exchanged.            }

  Var Temp : Integer;                  {A temporary for the swap.}

  Begin
    Temp := J;
    J := K;
    K := Temp
  End;                                  {Definition of procedure Swap.}

Begin                                  {Body of main program Right.}
  J := 38;
  K := 695;
  Writeln('Before the swap the values of J and K are ', J, 'and', K);
  Writeln;

  Swap(J, K);

  Writeln('After the swap the values of J and K are ', J, 'and', K);
End.
```

Listing 6.10

 Finally, the output of Right is right:

```
Before the swap the values of J and K are 38 and 695

After the swap the values of J and K are 695 and 38
```

PROBLEM-SOLVING EXAMPLE: 3025

Somebody once noticed that the number 3025 has the odd property that

$$3025 = (30 + 25)^2$$

Let us write a program to find all four-digit numbers with the property that they are equal to the square of the sum of their left and right parts. It is our claim that this would be easy if Pascal had a built-in `Parts(Num, Left, Right)` procedure that would separate `Num` into its 2 two-digit parts. If Pascal also had a `SqrSum(J, K)` function that would return the square of the sum of its inputs, we could solve the problem with the following pseudo-code:

```
Initialize Num to 1000
While Num ≤ 9999                                  --Try all four-digit numbers
    Call Parts to separate Num into Left and Right
    If Num = the square of the sum of Left and Right then
        Write out Num as one of the numbers we seek
    Increment Num by 1
```

We have solved the problem with a main program that will use the two subunits, `Parts` and `SqrSum`. `Parts(Num, Left, Right)` will be a procedure because it computes two results, `Left` and `Right`, and a function should return only one value through its name. Thus, we see that `Left` and `Right` will be `Var` parameters to `Parts`. After all, it is `Parts`' job to assign values to these parameters. `Num`, on the other hand, can be a value parameter to `Parts`. It is easy to separate `Num` by using `Div` and `Mod` tricks. Here is the pseudo-code for `Parts`:

```
Procedure Parts(Num, Var Left, Var Right)    --This separates Num into its Left
                                               and Right halves. Since it is easy to forget,
                                               we have shown Left and Right as Var parameters.

    Left ← Num Div 100
    Right ← Num Mod 100
```

Since `SqrSum` returns a single value, it can be written as a function. Here is its pseudo-code:

```
Function SqrSum(J, K)                          --Returns the square of the sum of J and K
    SqrSum ← (J + K)²
```

Listing 6.11 shows the entire program `OddProp` that finds all four-digit numbers with the given odd property. Note how the function `SqrSum` is invoked from within the condition of the `If` statement, while the procedure `Parts`, as a complete statement, stands on a line by itself. Also notice that the dummy parameters used to define `Parts` are the same as the actual arguments in the program, but that the dummy parameters used to define `SqrSum` are different from the actual parameters. Both ways are valid and, in our final example of the chapter, we offer some advice about our preferences for the dummy parameter names.

```
Program OddProp;
{This program finds all four-digit numbers, like 3025, that have
the odd property that they are equal to the square of the sum
of their left and right halves:

      3025 = (30 + 25) * (30 + 25)                          }

Var    Num    : Integer;
       Left   : Integer;
       Right  : Integer;

Procedure Parts(Num : Integer; Var Left, Right : Integer);
{This procedure separates Num, which is assumed to be a four-
digit number, into its Left and Right halves.
Pre:  Num is a four-digit integer.
Post: Left contains the left 2 digits of Num. Likewise, Right
      contains the right 2 digits of Num.                   }

  Begin
    Left := Num Div 100;
    Right := Num Mod 100
  End;                            {Definition of procedure Parts.}

Function SqrSum(J, K : Integer) : Integer;
{This function returns the square of the sum of its inputs.
Pre:  J and K are integers such that (J+K) squared will not cause
      overflow.
Post: SqrSum returns the square of the sum of its inputs.  }

  Begin
    SqrSum := (J + K) * (J + K)
  End;                            {Definition of function SqrSum.}

Begin                            {Body of main program OddProp.}
  Writeln('Here are the 4-digit numbers equal to the');
  Writeln('square of the sum of their left and right parts:');
  Writeln;
  Num := 1000;
  While Num <= 9999 Do           {Try all four-digit numbers.}
    Begin
      Parts(Num, Left, Right);
      If Num = SqrSum(Left, Right) Then
        Writeln(Num);
      Num := Num + 1
    End {While}
End.
```

Listing 6.11

The output from `OddProp` finds the three numbers 2025, 3025, and 9801, which have the given property. We invite the reader to check by calculator that these do have the stated property.

PROCEDURES AND FUNCTIONS: WHY DOES THE LANGUAGE HAVE BOTH/EITHER?

Since procedures and functions are so similar, students often ask the reasonable question as to why the language bothers to have both concepts. Couldn't we just have one or the other? Sometimes beginners even get frustrated enough to ask why the language bothers to have functions or procedures at all. Couldn't we just put the code in-line and do away with the need for procedures and functions (and, therefore, parameters) altogether? We now proceed to try to answer these questions, starting with the last question first.

Theoretically, it is true that any program, written with procedures and functions, can also be written without any procedures or functions. As suggested above, one simply replaces the function or procedure call with specific code that does the same task. Therefore, procedures and functions do not add any new power to the language. However, we use procedures and functions because they provide clarity to our programs, support a structured approach to problem solving, and help us avoid repetitive code. We now discuss these three important points in more detail.

1. Procedures and functions add clarity to our programs

Without procedures and functions, a program quickly becomes too long for the human to grasp quickly and understand. If we don't use procedures and functions to hide some of the details, all of the specifics of the program must be handled at once. In even moderately complex situations, this can be overwhelming. A good rule of thumb is that no subunit of the whole program should be more than one page in length. Each subunit should do one clearly specified task that is reflected in its name. The main program should be a short sequence of statements, involving calls to various subprograms. As such, the main program is easy to read and very closely resembles its pseudo-code.

2. Procedures and functions support a structured approach to problem solving

This is one of the most important reasons that the reader needs to learn to use procedures and functions. They make the language extensible and allow us to think with a top-down or divide-and-conquer approach to problem solving. Rather than solve the whole problem at once, we decompose the problem into smaller subproblems. Each of these in turn is subdivided, if necessary, into smaller pieces. When we have decomposed the problem into manageable pieces, we need some way to reassemble the pieces to provide the solution to the original problem. It is procedures and functions, and the easy way that we can invoke them from one another, that allow us to implement our design in a straightforward manner. Of course, as problems becomes more complex, this justification for procedures and functions becomes even more valid. Our examples have been fairly simple, since we have just begun to study these concepts. We invite the reader to consider the final example of this chapter, a program listing of approximately four pages, and consider how complex and difficult it would be to understand if it were written without procedures and functions.

3. Procedures and functions help us avoid repetitive code

Suppose you are writing a Lotto simulation in which you need to compare a user's three-digit number, `UserNum`, digit by digit against another three-digit number, `DailyWinNum`, because the payoff, if any, depends on the number of digits the user has correct. It might be convenient to have a procedure `Split(Num, Huns, Tens, Ones)` that would split a three-digit number into its digits. That is, `Split` would separate 384 into the 3, the 8, and the 4. The point is that we need `Split` twice, once to `Split` the `UserNum` into its digits, and once to `Split` the `DailyWinNum` into its three digits. If we didn't use a procedure, we would have to write very similar code twice. With a procedure, we can define the procedure `Split(Num, Huns, Tens, Ones)` *once* and invoke it *twice*:

```
Split(UserNum, UserHuns, UserTens, UserOnes);
...
Split(DailyWinNum, WinHuns, WinTens, WinOnes);
```

Realize that `Split` is capable of splitting any three-digit number into its parts and, therefore, the same `Split` can be applied to both the `UserNum` and the `DailyWinNum`. It is not necessary, as beginners often think, to write two separate `Split` procedures. `Split` is completely general and can be invoked in many different ways. Observe the flexibility that is permitted by being able to use arguments that are distinct from the dummy parameters. This is the power of procedures and functions. Learn to use it well.

Now, hopefully, having convinced you that procedures and functions are useful, we turn to the question of why we have both in the language. After all, it is fairly easy to see that any function can be rewritten as a procedure. We leave this as an exercise, with the hint that you will need to change the number of parameters.

To see that we could also eliminate procedures and replace them by functions, we consider a specific example. Note that `Split(Num, Huns, Tens, Ones)`, as a procedure, is returning three results through the variable parameters `Huns`, `Tens`, and `Ones`. Hence, we could replace `Split(Num, Huns, Tens, Ones)` with three functions, `SplitHuns(Num)`, `SplitTens(Num)`, and `SplitOnes(Num)`, each of which would return one result. While possible, three functions are less convenient and less clear than one procedure. They are also less efficient, since the three functions may each have to repeat some of the computations that the procedure does once.

We also point out that we could write a function that would be equivalent to a parameterless procedure, such as `PurposeOfProgram`, that uses `Writelns` to print many lines of description, but computes no result. We could replace this procedure with the function `ProgramPurpose`, which `Writelns` the descriptions and then returns some value such as zero, which is then discarded by the calling unit.

Notice that the invocations will need to be modified, because we are using functions instead of procedures. Thus, in our first example, we could replace

```
Split(UserNum, UserHuns, UserTens, UserOnes);
```

with

```
UserHuns := SplitHuns(UserNum);
UserTens := SplitTens(UserNum);
UserOnes := SplitOnes(UserNum);
```

and in the second case, we could replace

```
PurposeOfProgram;
```

with

```
DiscardValue := ProgramPurpose;
```

where `DiscardValue` is an otherwise unused integer identifier.

This long argument, which has shown that it is possible to replace procedure calls with function calls, has, hopefully, also shown why we don't want to do so in practice: It is not convenient! It is awkward to write three functions for the one procedure `Split` or to use the dodge of returning a garbage value. Although we have shown the concepts to be equivalent, it is the convenience of a procedure that can return zero or more results that makes it a concept worth keeping.

In the exercises, we have asked you to show how functions can be rewritten as procedures. This argument is simpler and less awkward than the one we gave, but still, the reasons that we keep functions in the language are convenience and custom. We are all familiar with many functions like `Round` and `Sqrt` from previous studies. It would be awkward if we couldn't use these functions in the natural way. Furthermore, functions, since they return a value and do not name a complete statement, can be nested within one another and used within other Pascal statements. For example, the fragment

```
If Round(Sqrt(X) - Sqrt(Y)) < Cube(Z) Then ...
```

would be many lines longer, with the need for several additional identifiers, if we had to replace the functions `Round`, `Sqrt`, and `Cube` (assumed to be user-defined) with procedures. We leave the details to the reader in the exercises.

In summary, we have both procedures and functions in the language for the convenience of the programmer. There are many instances in which exactly one result is computed and where functions are the natural construct to use. There are also many instances where we need a black box that returns zero, or two, or more, results. In such an instance, a procedure is the natural construct to use.

While legal in Pascal, it is considered poor programming style to use `Var` parameters with functions. The reason for this is that we expect a function to take a number of inputs, make no changes to their values, but, somehow, compute and return a *single* result through the function's name. `Var` parameters allow functions to return other results by modifying the parameters. This leads to unexpected **side effects** and confusing code. For example, it is possible, but not good style, to replace the procedure `Split(Num, Huns, Tens, Ones)` with `HunsSplit(Num, Tens, Ones)` a function that returns the value of the hundreds digit through its name and the new values of the tens and ones digits through the Var parameters Tens and Ones. The header for this function would then look like

```
Function HunsSplit(Num : Integer; Var Tens, Ones : Integer) :
                                                       Integer;
```

and then we could replace

```
Split(Num, Huns, Tens, Ones);
```

with

```
Huns := HunsSplit(Num, Tens, Ones);
```

It is the asymmetry of the statement that makes it an example of poor programming style. It is obvious that the statement is changing the value of Huns. At the same time, the obvious nature of this assignment conceals the fact that Tens and Ones are also receiving values. We believe that clarity is enhanced by insisting that functions *not* be allowed to have such side effects. Hence, in this text, functions will always have (with one exception discussed in Chapter 11) value, not variable, parameters; thus, functions will return exactly one result. We urge you to adopt this convention in your programming and to reserve the use of Var parameters to procedures, which must, of necessity, use them to return their results.

GLOBAL VARIABLES

Earlier we stated the rule that every identifier that appeared in a procedure or function should be listed as a parameter or declared as a local variable in that procedure or function. We indicated that this rule would be discussed, explained, and extended at a later time. To begin that discussion, let us consider the program GlobSwap of Listing 6.12.

Observe that none of the identifiers used in this version of Swap are declared as parameters or as local variables. Swap is using the variables of the outer program GlobSwap and, hence, these variables are **global** to Swap. Pascal requires that each identifier used in the body of a procedure or function be one of three kinds. Each identifier must be a parameter (value or variable), a local variable, or global, by which we mean that the identifier is declared in some program, procedure, or function in which the current procedure or function is nested. Any identifier found by the compiler that is not of one of these three types will be flagged as an undeclared identifier.

We are going to argue that global identifiers, although legal and often popular with beginners, are generally to be avoided. What makes globals popular with the beginner? We believe that it is the perceived simplicity of globals and a lack of understanding of the correct use of parameters that make globals the choice of beginners. After all, look at the invocation of Swap in Listing 6.12. It is simply

```
Swap;
```

```
Program GlobSwap;   {Global Swap}
{This program illustrates the use of global variables. WARNING:
While legal, the use of global variables is not recommended as good
style.                                                              }

Var    J    : Integer;
       K    : Integer;
       Temp : Integer;

Procedure Swap;
{This procedure swaps the values of global J and K.
Pre:   None
Post:  The values of the global J and K are exchanged.              }
  Begin
    Temp := J;
    J := K;
    K := Temp                          {Definition of procedure Swap.}
  End;
Begin                                  {Body of main program GlobSwap.}
  J := 38;
  K := 695;
  Writeln('Before the swap the values of J and K are ', J, ' and ', K);

  Swap;

  Writeln('After the swap the values of J and K are ', J, ' and ', K);
End.
```

Listing 6.12

with no parameters to worry about. Further, the definition of Swap in Listing 6.12 is simple, as there are no local variables to be concerned with.

However, there are reasons, in our opinion, that make the perceived simplicity of global variables shortsighted. These include:

1. The use of global variables hinders the clarity of programs

Imagine that our procedure Swap is part of a large program. Then, as we know, each time we invoke the global version of Swap, we simply write

```
Swap;
```

But how can we remember what gets swapped with what? On the other hand, with our version of Swap with parameters, we have to write

```
Swap(Profit, Loss);
```

from which it is immediately clear to any reader (and the IRS) what Swap is up to. We have given just one simple example, but the principle is clear. The use of globals will make the action of procedures and functions more difficult for the reader to fathom. In a simple program, the use of globals can perhaps be defended. But in complex programs, they will hinder program clarity.

2. The use of global variables limits the flexibility of programs

The version of Swap using global variables always swaps the same two things (what they are we can't remember, though). Swap written with parameters, as in program Right, is a fully general procedure that will swap any two variables (of the proper type). Thus, with such a general Swap(X, Y) procedure, we can invoke it at different times with

```
Swap(Profit, Loss);
...
Swap(MySalary, YourSalary);
...
Swap(This, That);
```

as long as all of the arguments shown are identifiers of the same type as the dummy parameters X and Y. With global variables, we would have to write three separate but similar procedures, SwapProfitForLoss, SwapMySalaryForYourSalary, and, finally, SwapThisForThat to perform all of the indicated swaps. A procedure with parameters is a *general* black box that will perform operations on the arguments that you supply to it. A procedure that uses global variables is a *specific* black box that does only one particular task. Avoid global variables to keep your procedures and functions general.

3. The use of global variables makes programs difficult to debug, maintain, and modify

The programmer who makes extensive use of global variables writes programs that are difficult to debug, because identifiers are not restricted to certain sections of the program. For example, if the identifier X is printing as garbage, it can be that the main program, or any function or procedure that is accessing X globally, is causing the problem. This means that the programmer does not know where to look for the problem. With the proper use of parameters, the locus of the problem can be ascertained much more readily. Once we know where the error is, we can usually figure out what the problem is. The same remarks apply to maintaining and modifying programs. If the author used global variables, then your task of locating and changing a given set of identifiers, in all the appropriate spots, can be very difficult.

In summary, we have many valid reasons to avoid the use of global variables. Do not fall into the trap of using global variables. They may seem simpler than learning to use parameters correctly, but this is only an illusion. In complex programs, the extensive use of globals is unacceptable.

Is there ever an instance when global variables should be allowed? On this point, authors and instructors differ. Many say categorically, "Never, never use globals!" We back away from a complete denial of global variables, but think their use, for the reasons listed above, should be very much restricted.

Where would we permit the use of globals? Suppose that in a large program you have an `Initialize` procedure and a `DisplayResults` procedure. The `Initialize` procedure needs to initialize 17 various counters, Booleans, etc. It is rather tedious to define or invoke `Initialize` with all those parameters and arguments. Likewise, `DisplayResults`, with parameters, needs to have 29 different things passed to it. We believe that in such cases it is permissible to use global variables with these procedures whose task is clear to everyone. Still, we think globals, when used, should always be commented, so we would write

```
Initialize;              {Initialize everything in sight, globally.}
...
DisplayResults;{Globals used to avoid long list of parameters.}
```

However, our advice to the beginner is to avoid the use of global variables. Our original rule that every identifier used in a procedure or function should be a parameter or a local variable, while not strictly required by Pascal, is still a good idea and is a generally accepted rule of good programming style.

STRINGS AS PARAMETERS

Since the string is not a full-fledged type in Pascal, a circumlocution is required to use a string as an argument or parameter in a procedure or function. The full details of the problem will not be discussed until Chapters 10 and 11, but suffice it to say that Pascal will not accept the heading

```
Procedure AskUser(Var Name : String[30]); {ERROR: Invalid type}
                                           {for the string parameter.}
```

The problem is that Pascal does not accept the type specification as valid for a parameter. The way around the problem is to use the `Type` statement (much more on `Type`s in Chapter 10) to define a new string type. This is done by placing the following `Type` declaration in the main program, just after the `Program` or `Const` section:

```
Type String30 = String[30];
```

Then the heading of the procedure can be written as

```
Procedure AskUser(Var Name : String30);
```

In other words, the `Type` statement allows us to give a short name to the complex type that we want to use. To the reader, the difference between `String30` and `String[30]` may appear fairly small, but those brackets make a big difference to the compiler. All this will be explained in the next chapters. For now, we simply state the rule that you must use a `Type` statement to define a type name without brackets, if you want to use a string as a parameter in a procedure or function.

That is all there is to using strings as parameters in procedures and functions. The use of strings as parameters is illustrated in our final example of the chapter. (See the procedure `GiveMessage` in the program `Bagels`.)

PROBLEM-SOLVING EXAMPLE: THE GAME OF BAGELS

We conclude this chapter with a lengthy example. This allows us to illustrate not only how procedures and functions can make a long program easy to understand, but also how our divide-and-conquer strategy applies in a more realistic situation.

We are going to write a program that will play the game of Bagels with the user. Assuming that most readers are not familiar with the game, we now explain how to play. First, the computer generates a secret three-digit number. To make it easier for the player, this secret number will be composed of three different digits, and the hundreds digit will not be zero. For example, the secret number might be 482. The player guesses three-digit numbers (with the same stipulations about distinct digits and no leading zeros) until the secret number is guessed. The computer gives hints after each guess as follows:

The computer says `Fermi` for each digit in the guess that is in the same place in the secret number. For example, for a guess of 382, the computer will respond with `Fermi Fermi`.

The computer says `Pico` for each digit in the guess that is in the secret number, but in another place. For example, the guess of 328 receives a `Pico Pico`.

To give the user minimal information about the number, all `Fermi`s are printed before any `Pico`s. Thus, the guesses 284, 842, and 428 all generate the hint `Fermi Pico Pico`.

Finally, to a guess with no correct digits at all, the computer responds with `Bagels!` When we play this game with students, they often groan when they get `Bagels`, but the reader should realize that this gives a lot of information about the number.

The object of the game, of course, is to guess the computer's secret number in as few guesses as possible.

Students often ask why Bagels uses the terms `Fermi`, `Pico`, and `Bagels`. We respond that these are the international Bagels' conventions. Why does baseball use terms like foul ball? Why does football call a backward pass a lateral? Note that if a lateral is thrown laterally, it isn't a lateral, after all! There is no explaining terms in sports and you will simply have to accept Bagels as it is.

Our explanation of the game can be summarized by the following pseudo-code:

Give the user the instructions and some examples
Have the computer generate its secret number
Initialize a counter of the number of turns to zero
While the game is not over
    Obtain a guess from the user
    Increment the number of turns
    If the guess = the secret number then

> The game is over--congratulate the user
> Print the number of turns taken
> Else
>   Analyze the digits of the guess and the secret number and give the user hints

We may have no idea how, for example, to write a procedure that will generate a secret number, but that is the power of the divide-and-conquer approach. We separate the large problem into smaller pieces, with which it would be easy to design a solution to the original problem. Later, of course, we will have to consider each subunit in turn. Let's imagine a black box that will generate a three-digit number. That black box might generate 333 or 747, a number with repeated digits. Therefore, we should also have a procedure `Split` that will obtain the three separate digits for us, and a function `Valid` that will tell us whether the digits are distinct or not. That way, we can have the computer keep repeating the generation of three-digit numbers until it finally gets it right! Furthermore, note that the user is supposed to enter a guess containing three different digits. We can use our procedure `Split` and our function `Valid` to test the user's guess and make the user repeat until she or he enters a valid guess. Here, then, is a slightly more detailed pseudo-code outline of our program:

> Give the user the instructions and some examples
> While the digits in the secret number are not distinct (valid)
>   Have the computer generate its secret number
>   Split the secret number into its three digits
> Initialize a counter of the number of turns to zero
> While the game is not over
>   While the digits in the user's guess are not distinct (valid)
>   Obtain a guess from the user
>   Split the guess into its three digits
>   Increment the number of turns
>   If the guess = the secret number then
>   The game is over--congratulate the user
>   Print the number of turns taken
>   Else
>   Analyze the digits of the guess and the secret number and give the user hints

Since the listing for `Bagels` is lengthy, we will show it to you in pieces, displaying each piece as we develop the pseudo-code for it. This again illustrates the power of the top-down approach. You can read and understand the main program without being concerned about all the details of the program. The body of the main program is shown in Listing 6.13a. This is the end of the listing and there are many missing details yet to be supplied. But also note how readable the body of the program is and how closely it follows the outline of the pseudo-code. Notice that we have tossed into the pseudo-code one more `While` loop, which keeps playing the game until the user doesn't want to play again. We have also added a Boolean, `GameOver`, to make it easy to recognize when the game is over. Little modifications are possible between the pseudo-code and the final version, but the pseudo-code should be designed to a sufficient level of detail that the implementation remains a straightforward task.

```
Begin                                    {Body of main program Bagels.}
  Randomize;
  Instructions;
  KeepPlaying := True;            {Initialize condition for While.}
  While KeepPlaying Do     {Loop until the player wants to quit.}
    Begin
      Done := False      {Secret number has not been generated.}
      While Not Done Do{Keep trying to generate a valid number.}
        Begin
          Generate(SecretNum);
          Split(SecretNum, SecretHuns, SecretTens, SecretOnes);
          Done := Valid(SecretHuns, SecretTens, SecretOnes)
        End; {While}
      NumTurns := 0;   {User begins to guess the secret number.}
      GameOver := False;
      While Not GameOver Do          {Loop until guess is correct.}
        Begin
          Done := False              {User must enter a valid guess.}
          While Not Done Do              {Loop until guess is valid .}
            Begin
              Obtain(Guess);
              Split(Guess, GuessHuns, GuessTens, GuessOnes);
              Done := Valid(GuessHuns, GuessTens, GuessOnes)
            End; {While}
          NumTurns := NumTurns + 1;             {Count the guess.}
          GameOver := (SecretNum = Guess);        {Lucky guess?}
          If GameOver Then
            Summarize(NumTurns)
          Else
            Analyze(SecretHuns, SecretTens, SecretOnes,
                            GuessHuns, GuessTens, GuessOnes)
        End; {While}
      KeepPlaying := AskUserContinue
    End {While}
End.
```

Listing 6.13a

We now consider each of our procedures and functions in turn, first to design them and then to implement them. Instructions, being a long list of Writelns, is so simple, however, that we do not display it in pseudo-code, but show it complete in Listing 6.13b. Notice that Instructions does ask if you want to see the rules, thus letting the user who knows how to play skip them.

Next, we tackle the Generate procedure that determines the SecretNum of the computer. One simple way to generate such a number is to invoke Random with the argument 1000, since this will generate a number in the range 0 to 999. However, since

```
Procedure Instructions;
{This procedure Writelns the rules if requested by the user.

Pre:   None
Post:  The rules for Bagels are given, if requested by the user.}

Var  Ch : Char;                    {Local variable for user response.}

Begin
  Write('Do you want the rules (Y/N)? ');
  Readln(Ch);
  Ch := UpCase(Ch);               {Make sure response is uppercase.}
  If Ch = 'Y' Then
    Begin
      Writeln('The computer will generate a secret');
      Writeln('three-digit number with no digit repeated');
      Writeln('and the first digit nonzero. You are to guess');
      Writeln('the computer''s number in as few guesses');
      Writeln('as possible. Your guess must also be a');
      Writeln('three-digit number with no digits');
      Writeln('repeated and the first digit nonzero.');
      Writeln('You will be given hints as follows:');
      Writeln;
      Writeln('"Fermi" for a correct digit, correctly placed.');
      Writeln;
      Writeln('"Pico" for a correct digit, wrongly placed.');
      Writeln;
      Writeln('"Bagels" if no digit is guessed correctly.');
      Writeln; Writeln;
      Writeln('For example, if the secret number is 482, then');
      Writeln;
      Writeln('    A guess of 127 receives a Pico.');
      Writeln;
      Writeln('    A guess of 842 receives a Fermi Pico Pico.');
      Writeln;
      Writeln('    A guess of 375 receives a Bagels.')
    End; {If}
  Writeln; Writeln
End;
```

Listing 6.13b

the computer's SecretNum is supposed to have a nonzero hundreds digit, we use the
formula

```
SecretNum := Random(900) + 100;
```

```
Procedure Generate(Var SecretNum : Integer);

{This procedure generates the computer's SecretNum.
Pre:  None
Post: SecretNum will be assigned a random value between 100 and
      999.                                                      }

Begin
  SecretNum := Random(900) + 100{A value between 100 and 999.}
End;
```

Listing 6.13c

to generate numbers in the range from 100 (0 + 100) to 999 (899 + 100). You should examine this statement to see how the random numbers have been shifted to the interval desired. Of course, `Generate` could still generate 777, or some other number with repeated digits, but that will be the concern of `Split` and `Valid`.

The Pascal code for `Generate` is shown in Listing 6.13c. A call to procedure `Randomize` is not included in `Generate` because there is no need to call `Randomize` before each call to the `Random` function. The procedure `Randomize` was invoked once, in the beginning of the main program, as shown in Listing 6.13a.

Our next procedure is `Split`, which separates its input, `Num`, into its three digits `Huns`, `Tens`, and `Ones`. As we know from several examples, we can use `Div` and `Mod` tricks to do this. Hence, we omit the pseudo-code for `Split` and go directly to the Pascal version in Listing 6.13d. Notice that we have defined `Split` using the generic parameters `Num`, `Huns`, `Tens`, and `Ones`, which are meaningful, but distinct from any of the actual identifiers of the program. We do this because we intend to invoke `Split` twice. After the computer generates its `SecretNum`, we will invoke `Split` with

```
Split(SecretNum, SecretHuns, SecretTens, SecretOnes);
```

to separate the computer's number into its digits. Later, when the user enters a `Guess`, we will again invoke `Split`, in the form

```
Split(Guess, GuessHuns, GuessTens, GuessOnes);
```

to separate the user's `Guess` into its digits. We know that we can define `Split` with any four parameters, but since we intend to invoke `Split` in two distinct ways, it seems best to define `Split` with generic parameters. Also, note that these two slightly different invocations of `Split` would not be possible if `Split` used global variables!

On the other hand, note that we defined `Generate(SecretNum)` with the dummy parameter `SecretNum`, which is the same as the actual identifier of the main program. We did this because we intend only one invocation of `Generate`:

```
Generate(SecretNum);
```

```
Procedure Split(Num : Integer; Var Huns, Tens, Ones : Integer);
{This procedure splits its input, Num, a three-digit number, into
its 3 separate digits.
Pre:  Num is a three-digit integer.
Post: Huns, Tens, and Ones are assigned the respective digits of
      Num.                                                        }

Begin
  Huns := Num Div 100;
  Tens := (Num Mod 100) Div 10;
  Ones := Num Mod 10
End;
```

Listing 6.13d

There is no confusion if the dummy parameter SecretNum is bound to the actual argument SecretNum. Of course, it is legal to define Generate with some generic parameter such as Numb, but we see no advantage to doing so. In summary, here are our suggestions for selecting parameter names:

If the procedure or function is to be invoked exactly once, or always in exactly the same form, it makes sense to choose the dummy parameters to be exactly the same identifiers as the actual arguments. If the procedure or function is to be invoked in more than one way, it makes sense to select generic parameters that are distinct from the actual arguments. Finally, realize that these are just suggestions to help programmers preserve their sanity and that Pascal doesn't care what you choose for dummy parameter names.

The function Valid simply checks its three inputs, Huns, Tens, and Ones, to make sure they are all different. This is easy and is shown implemented in Listing 6.13e.

```
Function Valid(Huns, Tens, Ones : Integer) : Boolean;
{This function returns True if its 3 arguments are all different
from one another.
Pre:  Huns, Tens, and Ones are single-digit integers (0 to 9).
Post: Valid returns True only if all three digits are distinct.
      Otherwise, it returns False.                                }
Begin
  If (Huns = Tens) Or (Huns = Ones) Or (Tens = Ones) Then
    Valid := False
  Else
    Valid := True
End;
```

Listing 6.13e

```
Procedure Obtain(Var Guess : Integer);
{This procedure simply obtains a three-digit number from the user.

Pre:  None
Post: Guess is assigned the three-digit number chosen by the user.}

Begin
  Guess := 0;              {Initialize Guess for the While loop.}
  While (Guess < 100) Or (Guess > 999) Do        {Keep trying}
    Begin                        {until the user gets it right.}
      Write('Please enter your three-digit guess: ');
      Readln(Guess)
    End {While}
End;
```

Listing 6.13f

With the observation that a three-digit number must be between 100 and 999, procedure Obtain, which gets the user's Guess, is very simple to write. Obtain does not have to check for distinct digits, since we can reuse Split and Valid to do that for us. Obtain is shown in Listing 6.13f.

Summarize is a very simple procedure that is shown in Listing 6.13g.

Procedure Analyze takes the digits of the secret number and the digits of the guess, compares them, and gives appropriate hints. This is all rather straightforward except for one detail. For example,

If SecretHuns equals GuessHuns then
    Give the user a Fermi message

and similar tests for the tens and ones digits will print the Fermis, if any.

Likewise,

```
Procedure Summarize(NumTurns : Integer);
{This procedure congratulates the user and tells the user the number
of guesses needed to find the secret number.
Pre:  NumTurns contains the appropriate value.
Post: No result is computed. The value of NumTurns is displayed.}

Begin
  Writeln('C O N G R A T U L A T I O N S ! ! !');
  Writeln('You guessed my secret number in only ', NumTurns,
                                              ' turns');
  Writeln
End;
```

Listing 6.13g

If SecretHuns equals GuessTens or GuessOnes then
    Give the user a Pico message

along with two other similar tests will print the Picos, if any.

The difficulty is deciding when to print Bagels. We could write a series of complex tests, but it is easy, if we note that we say Bagels only if we didn't say Fermi or Pico. We can record whether we gave any hints by using a Boolean, GaveHint, which we initialize to False and change to True whenever we give a Fermi or Pico. If GaveHint is still False after all the Fermi and Pico tests, then we know it's time to say Bagels. This gives us the following pseudo-code for Analyze:

Procedure Analyze(SecretHuns, SecretTens, SecretOnes,
                                        GuessHuns, GuessTens, GuessOnes)

GaveHint ← False

If SecretHuns equals GuessHuns then
    Give the user a Fermi message
    GaveHint ← True   --Include two more such Ifs to test for other Fermis

If SecretHuns equals GuessTens or GuessOnes then
    Give the user a Pico message
    GaveHint ← True   --Include two more such Ifs to test for other Picos

If GaveHint is still False then
    Give the user a Bagels message

Since we are continually giving messages and resetting GaveHint, we create a simple procedure GiveMessage(Hint, GaveHint) to do this for us. Note that we have nested GiveMessage within Analyze, because no other procedure or function has any need for GiveMessage and, thus, it can be local to Analyze. Also, note that GiveMessage has a string parameter, so we will have to use a Type statement to declare a string type for this parameter. Since GiveMessage prints up to six characters in the string 'Fermi ' (don't forget to count the blank), we declare a new String6 type. All of these details are shown in Listing 6.13h, which includes Analyze and its subprocedure, GiveMessage.

```
Procedure Analyze(SecretHuns, SecretTens, SecretOnes,
                  GuessHuns, GuessTens, GuessOnes : Integer);
{This procedure analyzes the digits of the guess and the secret
number and calls the nested procedure GiveMessage to give
appropriate hints to the user. A Boolean, GaveHint, is used to
record if hints are given. If no hint is given, then Bagels is
printed.
Pre:  All six parameters have single-digit values between 0 and
      9.
Post: Fermis, Picos, and Bagels are printed as appropriate.   }
```

Listing 6.13h

```
Type    String6 = String[6];

Var     GaveHint : Boolean;

Procedure GiveMessage(Hint : String6; Var GaveHint : Boolean);
{This nested procedure actually prints the Fermis and Picos, if any.
It also uses the Var parameter, GaveHint, to record that a hint was
given.

Pre:   Hint contains the message to be printed.
Post:  GaveHint is set to True to record that a message was printed.}

  Begin
    Write(Hint);
    GaveHint := True
  End;                           {Definition of procedure GiveMessage.}

Begin                                    {Body of procedure Analyze.}
  GaveHint := False;                      {No hints have yet been given.}

{Check for a Fermi, which is a correct digit in the correct place.}
  If SecretHuns = GuessHuns Then
    GiveMessage('Fermi ', GaveHint);
  If SecretTens = GuessTens Then
    GiveMessage('Fermi ', GaveHint);
  If SecretOnes = GuessOnes Then
    GiveMessage('Fermi ', GaveHint);

{Check for a Pico, which is a correct digit, but in the wrong place.}
  If (SecretHuns = GuessTens) Or (SecretHuns = GuessOnes) Then
    GiveMessage('Pico ', GaveHint);
  If (SecretTens = GuessHuns) Or (SecretTens = GuessOnes) Then
    GiveMessage('Pico ', GaveHint);
  If (SecretOnes = GuessHuns) Or (SecretOnes = GuessTens) Then
    GiveMessage('Pico ', GaveHint);

{Finally, if no hints have yet been given, supply a Bagels.   }
  If Not GaveHint Then
    Writeln('Bagels');
  Writeln; Writeln
End;
```

Listing 6.13h (continued)

Next is the function AskUserContinue, with no parameters, which returns True if the user wants to continue and False otherwise. This simple function is shown in Listing 6.13i.

```
Function AskUserContinue : Boolean;
{This function asks the user if she or he would like to continue
and returns True if so and False otherwise.
Pre:   None
Post:  AskUserContinue returns True only if the user responds with
       a 'y' or 'Y'.                                              }

Var Ch : Char;                    {Local variable for user response.}

Begin
  Write('Would you like to continue playing? (Y/N) ');
  Readln(Ch);
  Ch := UpCase(Ch);
  If Ch = 'Y' Then
    AskUserContinue:= True
  Else
    Begin
      Writeln('Thanks for playing Bagels with me.');
      AskUserContinue := False
    End
End;
```

Listing 6.13i

Finally, Listing 6.13j shows the first portion of the program, the general comments, and the Var declarations for the identifiers used in the main program. Since the program is of some length, a procedure and function dictionary is also provided. Recall that the main body of the program Bagels was previously displayed in Listing 6.13a.

```
Program Bagels;

{This program plays the game of Bagels with the user. See the
Instructions procedure for the rules of the game. The program is
an example of procedures and functions and of the divide-and-
conquer problem-solving strategy.

The procedures and functions used to solve the problem are:

Instructions
  A parameterless procedure that states the rules.

Generate(SecretNum)
  A procedure that returns the SecretNum, a three-digit number.

Split(Num, Huns, Tens, Ones)
  A procedure that splits the three-digit number Num into its
  hundreds, tens, and ones digits.
```

```
Valid(Huns, Tens, Ones)
  A Boolean function that indicates whether the digits
  are distinct.

Obtain(Guess)
  A procedure that obtains a guess from the user.

Analyze(SecretHuns, SecretTens, SecretOnes, GuessHuns, GuessTens,
                                                         GuessOnes)
  A procedure that analyzes the digits of the secret number and
  the guess of the user and calls a nested procedure GiveMessage
  to give the appropriate hints.

Summarize(NumTurns)
  A procedure that congratulates the user when he or she
  finally guesses the secret number and tells the user the
  number of guesses needed.

AskUserContinue
  A Boolean function that asks if the user wants to continue
  playing the game.

  * * * * * * * * * * * * * * * * * * * * * * * * * * * * *   }

Var   SecretNum                           : Integer;
      SecretHuns, SecretTens, SecretOnes  : Integer;
      Guess                               : Integer;
      GuessHuns, GuessTens, GuessOnes     : Integer;
      NumTurns                            : Integer;
      GameOver                            : Boolean;
      KeepPlaying                         : Boolean;
      Done                                : Boolean;
```

Listing 6.13j

SUMMARY

We cannot overestimate the importance of this chapter in the development of problem-solving skills. Most real-world problems are too difficult to be attacked with a single program. The top-down, divide-and-conquer strategy, with its use of procedures and functions, provides an organized method for making difficult programs manageable. Often, very large programs of thousands of lines have a main program consisting of just a few dozen lines. These few lines are procedure and function invocations.

   The concepts of local and global variables, arguments and parameters, and value and variable parameters are all critical to understanding the programming process and are relevant regardless of the language one is using.

KEYWORDS

Many very important concepts have been introduced in this chapter. As a check of your understanding, you should be able to define or describe each term on the following lists. Please notice that the items have been arranged in pairs of similar terms. You should be able to compare the similarities and contrast the differences within each pair.

Procedure	Function
Argument	Parameter
Value parameter	Variable parameter
Global variable	Local variable
Randomize	Random

SELF-TEST QUESTIONS

6.1   What is meant by the divide-and-conquer problem-solving technique? How do procedures and functions support this technique?

6.2   What is meant by saying that Pascal is an extensible language?

6.3   What are the three syntactic differences between a procedure definition and a function definition?

6.4   From the following descriptions, decide whether the object should be implemented as a procedure or as a function. Then, write the heading for each procedure or function, including an indication of the value and variable parameters. Assume that each parameter is an integer.

a) `ExplainRules`, with no parameters, states the rules of the game.

b) `FtInToCms` converts a given height in feet and inches into an equivalent height in centimeters. For example, `FtInToCms` converts 5 feet and 10 inches into 178 centimeters.

c) `CmsToFtIn` converts a given height in centimeters into an equivalent height in feet and inches. For example, `CmsToFtIn` converts 178 centimeters into 5 feet and 10 inches.

d) `Squares` returns the squares of its two inputs. For example, given 4 and 12, `Squares` returns 16 and 144.

e) `SquareSum` returns the sum of the squares of its two inputs. For example, given 4 and 12, `SquareSum` returns 160.

6.5   Assume that A and B are procedures with the headings

```
Procedure A(Var M : Integer);
Procedure B(J, K : Integer; Var L : Integer);
```

and that X and Y are functions with the headings

```
Function X(P : Integer) : Integer;
Function Y(R, S : Integer) : Integer;
```

Indicate which of the following are legal Pascal statements. Assume that each identifier has been declared an integer. For each erroneous statement, explain the error.

a) `A(This);`

b) `X(That);`

c) `A(This, That);`

d) `Writeln(Y(3,5));`

e) `B(P, Q, R) := 0;`

f) `If X(7) = Y(10, 12) Then Writeln('Equal');`

g) `If A(This) = B(One, Two, Three) Then Writeln('Equal');`

h) `Writeln(X(Y(1, 2)));`

i) `A(B(One, Two, Three));`

j) `B(X(1), Y(2, 3), Result);`

EXERCISES

6.6 Distinguish between the following pairs of concepts:

a) Local and global identifiers

b) Arguments and parameters

c) Value parameters and variable parameters

6.7   Write guidelines to determine when a given subprogram should be written as a procedure and when it should be written as a function.

6.8   You are the Computer Science I instructor. You have just fought your way through a long program, turned in by Ima Hacker, that contains no procedures or functions. Write an essay explaining to Ima the need for procedures and functions.

6.9   You are still the Computer Science I instructor. You made Ima Hacker redo her work and now it contains procedures and functions, but without parameters, as Ima has used global variables exclusively. Write an essay explaining to Ima the dangers and poor style caused by globals.

6.10   The text argues that any procedure could be replaced by an equivalent function. Give the converse of this argument and show how any function could be replaced by an equivalent procedure. As an example, include the procedure heading and the procedure invocation that would replace the function heading

```
Function SomeFunc(X : Integer; Ch : Char) : Integer;
```

and the function invocation

```
Writeln(SomeFunc(10, 'C'));
```

6.11   All functions are broken today! Instead of the functions `Round(X)`, `Sqrt(X)`, and `Cube(X)`, you must use the procedures `RoundProc(X,Y)`, `SqrtProc(X,Y)`, and `CubeProc(X,Y)`, which set `Y` to the indicated function of `X`. Use the procedures to rewrite the following line of code:

```
If Round(Sqrt(X) - Sqrt(Y)) < Cube(Z) Then Writeln('OK')
```

Hint: The one line will become at least five lines long and will need additional variables (which you may assume have been declared).

6.12   What is the output of each of the following programs? You should draw pictures, as in done in the book for `Right` and `Wrong`. For your convenience, each of the following programs is available as `Ex6_12a`, `Ex6_12b`, `Ex6_12c`, and `Ex6_12d`, respectively, on the sample disk available for this book.

a)
```
Program Ex6_12a;

Var A, B : Integer;
Procedure Silly(Var A: Integer; B : Integer);
  Begin
    A := A - 5;
    B := B + 3
  End;
```

```
Begin
  A := 12;
  B := 10;
  Writeln('The original values of A and B are: ', A,
                                        ' and ', B);
  Silly(A, B);
  Writeln('The final values of A and B are: ', A,
                                        ' and ', B)
End.
```

b) The same program as in part a), except the procedure heading is

```
Procedure Silly(A: Integer; B : Integer);
```

c) The same program as in part a), except the procedure is

```
Procedure Silly(Var X: Integer; Var Y : Integer);
  Begin
    X := X - 5;
    Y := Y + 3
  End;
```

d) (Tricky.) The same program as in part a), except the procedure is

```
Procedure Silly(X: Integer; Y : Integer);
  Begin
    X := X - 5;
    B := B + 3
  End;
```

6.13 The following function, BuggySum, is supposed to sum all the integers between its two inputs. For example, BuggySum(5, 10) is supposed to return 45 (5 + 6 + 7 + 8 + 9 + 10). However, BuggySum contains several bugs and needs to be debugged. For your convenience, this function is included in the complete program, Ex6_13, on the sample disk for this book.

```
Function BuggySum(Start, Stop : Integer);
{Pre: Start and Stop have values with Start <= Stop.
Post: BuggySum is supposed to be the sum of all integers
between Start and Stop, including both Start and Stop.   }

  Var Index : Integer;

  Begin
    BuggySum := 0;
    Index := Start;
    While Index < Stop Do
```

```
        Begin
          Index := Index + 1;
          BuggySum := BuggySum + Index
        End
  End;
```

6.14 Consider the following procedure Strange, whose heading is

```
Procedure Strange(A : Integer; C : Char; X : Real);
```

Assuming the given declarations, which of the following invocations of Strange are legal? Indicate what is wrong with each incorrect invocation.

```
Var    One   : Integer;
       Two   : Char;
       Three : Real;
```

a) Strange(One: Integer; Two: Char; Three : Real);

b) Strange(One, Two, Three);

c) Strange(Three, Two, One);

d) Strange(One, Two);

e) Strange(10, 'X', 5.0);

6.15 Write a program that prints out 10 pseudorandom numbers generated by the built-in function Random. Do not include Randomize in your program. Save your program, turn off the computer, and then load and run your program. Turn off the system a second time and load and run your program again. What do you notice about the output from these two runs?

6.16 Redo problem 6.15 with the Randomize procedure in your program. How do the results compare?

6.17 Write a program that uses the Random function to simulate 50 rolls of two dice, a red die and a green die. The output should be a table consisting of three columns showing red's value, green's value, and the total value.

6.18 Why do none of the following statements properly simulate the rolling of two dice?

a) Dice := Random(12);

b) Dice := Random(11) + 1;

c) `Dice := Random(12) + 2;`

d) `Dice := Random(11) + 2;`

6.19 (Computer Roulette) Write a structured program that simulates the following perverse version of Russian Roulette. In a six-cylinder gun, place one silver bullet and two blanks. Three of the cylinders are left empty. Spin the cylinder and pull the trigger. If an empty chamber is beneath the firing pin, the gun goes CLICK. If either a blank or the silver bullet is under the firing pin, the gun goes BANG. After a brief pause, you find out whether you are still alive and still playing or the game is over. Hint: Use a `Readln` to halt execution and allow the user to pull the trigger by typing the RETURN key. Simulate the pause after the BANG by giving the computer a big do-nothing loop, such as

```
Index := 1;
While Index <= 30000 Do              {Count to 30000.}
   Index := Index + 1;
```

or, if you have a fast processor,

```
Delay := 1;
While Delay < = 10 Do           {Do the counting 10 times.}
   Begin
     Index := 1;
     While Index <= 30000 Do              {Count to 30000.}
       Index := Index + 1;
     Delay := Delay + 1
End;
```

This problem shows the value of simulations, which are often safer and less messy than the real event. Absolutely no extra credit will be given for anything other than a simulation of this event!

6.20 A dog, Cookie, has buried three bones randomly in her backyard, which is 50 feet by 50 feet. Naturally, she has forgotten where the bones are buried, so she randomly begins digging holes. Her nose is so good (and her holes so big!) that she will find a bone if she digs within one foot of it. Suppose a bone is buried at point (X,Y). Cookie finds the bone if she digs at (X,Y), $(X-1,Y)$, $(X+1,Y)$, $(X,Y-1)$, or $(X,Y+1)$. For simplicity, we assume X and Y are integers. That is, Cookie digs only at points with integer coordinates.

Write a program to bury, randomly, three bones and then randomly dig holes (and count them) until a bone is found. Have the program repeat the experiment 20 times so that Cookie gets a feeling for the average number of holes needed to find a bone. Make sure the program is structured by using functions and procedures. Also, notice that Cookie is so dumb that she may dig the same hole more than once.

6.21 A man leaves a pub in a slightly tipsy state. His home is eight blocks west of the pub, while the jail is eight blocks east of the pub. The man is as likely to go east as west and after each block, he falls down. When he gets up, he goes east or west with equal probability. In his journey, if he passes the pub, he goes in for one last drink before continuing his journey. Write a structured program to simulate the man's walk, which ends when he reaches home or jail. The output should include the man's current position (three blocks east, etc.) and, at the end, the program should output the length (in blocks) the man walked and the total number of times he returned to the pub.

6.22 Write a procedure Time that converts a number N of seconds into hours, minutes, and seconds. For example, 3724 seconds is 1 hour, 2 minutes, and 4 seconds.

6.23 (Abundant Numbers Revisited, see Exercise 5.21) Use the function SumDivs of the text to find all abundant numbers between 2 and 500.

6.24 (Odd Abundant Numbers Revisited, see Exercise 5.22) Use the function Sum-Divs to find the first odd abundant number.

6.25 (Primes Revisited) Even though it is not very efficient, use the function SumDivs to find all primes between 2 and 500.

6.26 Two integers M and N are said to be **amicable** if each is the sum of the divisors of the other. Use SumDivs to write a program that finds the first pair of amicable numbers.
Historical note: This pair was known to Pythagoras, 2500 years before computers were invented, and had great mystical significance into the middle ages, where the pair was used in witchcraft and astrology. In 1636, Pierre de Fermat found the next amicable pair, 17,296 and 18,416. You can use SumDivs to verify that this is not a misprint. Computers have aided in the search for amicable numbers, and now more than 600 pairs are known.

6.27 Surprisingly, the date of Easter in any given year can easily be determined. For any Year between 1900 and 2099, the following algorithm determines the Month and Day of Easter in that year:

```
A  ←  Year minus 1900
B  ←  The remainder when A is divided by 19
C  ←  The integer quotient when 7 * B + 1 is divided by 19
D  ←  The remainder when 11 * B + 4 - C is divided by 29
E  ←  The integer quotient when A is divided by 4
F  ←  The remainder when A + E + 31 - D is divided by 7
G  ←  25 minus the sum of D and F
If G <= 0 then
    Month ← March
    Day ← 31 + G            --Remember G is negative, so 31 + G makes sense
Else
    Month ← April
    Day ← G
```

a) Use the algorithm, by hand, to verify that in the year 2000 Easter will be on April 9.

b) Write a procedure Easter(Year,Month,Day) that takes a Year and returns the date of Easter in that year.

c) Write a program to print out the date of Easter for each year from 1901 to 2000. When, during the 20th century, did Easter fall on April Fools' Day (April 1)?

d) Write a program to determine the next time that Easter will fall on April Fools' Day.

ANSWERS TO SELF-TEST QUESTIONS

6.1 The divide-and-conquer problem-solving technique breaks a large problem into smaller problems. It continues to break the small problems into even smaller problems until the decomposition results in simple problems. Procedures and functions are the solutions to these small subtasks, and the modularity of procedures and functions allows us to put them together easily to get a solution to the original large, complex problem.

6.2 Pascal is extensible because it is easily *extended* to include new terms. These new terms are implemented as procedures and functions and they are used exactly like built-in procedures and functions.

6.3 i) A procedure definition begins with the keyword Procedure, while a function definition begins with the keyword Function.

ii) A function heading ends with a final type that describes the type of the result returned by the function. A procedure, because it returns no value through its name, has no such final type.

iii) Somewhere in the function body, a value is assigned to the function name. This is not done with procedures.

6.4 a) ExplainRules should be implemented as a procedure:
Procedure ExplainRules;

b) FtInToCms should be implemented as a function with two value parameters:
Function FtInToCms(Ft, In : Integer) : Integer;

c) CmsToFtIn should be implemented as a procedure with one value and two variable parameters (because it returns two results):
Procedure CmsToFtIn(Cms : Integer; Var Ft, In : Integer);

  d) `Squares` should be implemented as a procedure with two value and two variable parameters (because it returns two results):
  `Procedure Squares (Num1, Num2: Integer; Var Sq1, Sq2: Integer);`

  e) `SquareSum` should be implemented as a function with two value parameters:
  `Function SquareSum (Num1, Num2 : Integer) : Integer;`

6.5 a) Legal.
  b) Illegal, a function never stands alone as a complete statement.
  c) Illegal, procedure A has only one parameter so it must have only one argument.
  d) Legal.
  e) Illegal, a procedure cannot be assigned a value.
  f) Legal.
  g) Illegal, procedures always stand alone as complete statements.
  h) Legal.
  i) Illegal, procedures always stand alone as complete statements.
  j) Legal.

7

PROGRAM DESIGN AND IMPLEMENTATION

Now that we have seen a little of what programming in Pascal is like, it is time to pause and consider our real objective: problem solving. As an introductory text in computer science, it is the objective of this book to instruct you in some of the concepts of fundamental importance in the application of computers to the solutions of problems. The language Pascal is the means we have chosen to implement our solutions, but Pascal, with its fussy syntax, is not our main objective. If you spend the time to learn the concepts discussed here, you will take something valuable and permanent away from this study.

By now, it is clear that a program will not run if you don't pay careful attention to semicolons and other syntax issues, but it should also be clear that the placement of semicolons and the exact syntax of Pascal's `While` are hardly issues of such significance as to be studied at the college level. This chapter discusses and illustrates our real objective: a disciplined, structured approach to problem solving through stepwise refinement. This careful and reasoned approach to problem solving is the true benefit that you can take from this study. To see the importance of developing good problem-solving skills, as opposed to just a knowledge of Pascal syntax, consider the following two hypothetical students:

Student A knows Pascal forward and backward, but is weak in problem-solving skills. Student A likes to show off his (yes, these types are often male) knowledge by writing a 10-line program to illustrate any feature of Pascal. But student A's problem-solving skills are so weak that he cannot use his knowledge to solve the simplest of problems. Even though he is an expert in the language of the computer, he cannot form any meaningful utterances.

Student B is a good problem solver, but is weak in Pascal syntax. Student B writes good pseudo-code, but has to refer frequently to the syntax diagrams of Appendix

C to translate the pseudo-code into Pascal. However, other than being a bit slow, student B is very successful.

Unfortunately, we have seen many students like student A. Student B is much rarer, because practice in programming quickly teaches Pascal syntax. We hope that you can learn to be a good problem solver, who also recalls Pascal syntax, but the point of the example is that the syntax is easy to look up, while the problem-solving skills are not so easily obtained.

LEARNING PROBLEM-SOLVING SKILLS

How does one learn problem-solving skills? We believe that the only way to learn such skills is through disciplined practice. That is why this book has so many complete sample programs in the text and the large number of exercises. We urge you to read the book in an active mode, which means that you study, run, modify, and rerun the sample programs of the book as well as solve a significant number of the exercises. The passive learner who only attends lectures, or just reads programs written by others, will not learn problem solving on the computer.

One method of teaching swimming is to toss people into the deep end of the pool. Those who learn, swim out, while the rest drown. Often, problem solving has been presented to students in much the same manner. Class discussions (often about Pascal syntax) take place in the wading pool, then the students find themselves in the deep end with no idea how to begin a solution to the assigned problem. Realize that the responsibility for teaching and learning problem-solving skills is shared by the instructor, the text, and the student. The text and the instructor must present methods and examples. The student must study these materials carefully and practice the methods extensively. Unfortunately, there are no royal shortcuts to learning problem-solving skills.

In this chapter, we gather together in one place a discussion of problem-solving and disciplined-programming strategies that have gained wide acceptance in computer science. Many of these topics have already been introduced, but in a somewhat abstract fashion. Now that we have discussed procedures and functions in the previous chapter, we are in a position to discuss these concepts in much more concrete terms. In this chapter, we also provide a complete, annotated example of the problem-solving process. We urge the reader to study it carefully and to model his or her approaches to those given here. This is what we mean by the phrase "disciplined practice of problem-solving strategies." As this text continues to introduce new concepts and new Pascal syntax, we will continually return to the problem-solving methods discussed in this chapter. Study these examples carefully and return to this chapter, as necessary, when you find yourself in over your head with a particular problem.

THE PROGRAM DESIGN PROCESS

We now describe an eight-step process that outlines the typical development of software projects.

1. Problem Specification

In the real world, problems often come poorly specified. The person who wants the computer to do some task is often unaware of exactly what it is that he or she wants the computer to do. Often, several meetings are necessary between potential users and program design specialists before problem specifications can be written. It is important that both sides (user and programmer) agree on the specifications. The user must be satisfied that the specifications will properly solve the original problem, and the programmer must be satisfied that the specifications do fully and completely specify a problem that can be solved with the given resources in the given time.

In a text, we are constrained *to strive* to give you complete program specifications. Since you cannot easily query us about our intentions, we try to think of every possible question in advance. Your instructor, however, may wish to give you vague specifications for an assignment and let you define the problem in further discussion. In any case, it should be clear that proper specification of the problem is an important first step. Nothing is so frustrating (to the programmer) as users who keep changing their minds about what they want the computer to do.

2. Understanding the Problem

An essential step and, in our experience, one that is often shortchanged by students is the simple task of taking the time to understand the given problem. This means several things to us. One is carefully reading (and rereading) the problem statement. One quick reading is almost certainly insufficient for understanding.

A second, very important part of understanding the problem is to devise a small amount of data and work out by hand the output from the given data. In so doing, the emphasis should be on "*How* am I getting these results?" not just on "*What* are the results?" The data that one prepares for these hand tracings need not be extensive, but should be diverse—they should be chosen to help you think about all of the possible cases that could occur in real data.

We believe that this data-driven approach to understanding the problem is probably the single most important component often omitted by students. We feel that these hand tracings should be written and should be kept by the student. They are extremely helpful for the next step, and many instructors demand to see such hand executions before they will give students help on a problem. In any case, it should be clear to the learner that failure to understand the problem will mean certain failure in the steps to follow. How can we expect to design, let alone implement, a plan to solve a problem that we don't even understand?

3. Designing an Algorithm

Now that we understand the problem, we can focus on designing a plan for its solution. This plan should be specified in pseudo-code so that our attention is on algorithm design rather than the syntax of our programming language. In this stage, our hand executions from step 2 become very important in guiding our design. In this regard, it is important to be able to step outside ourselves and observe ourselves as we work. We need to do this because we are not interested in the actual results, but in the method used to obtain those results. This point of view is often foreign to beginners and requires some practice. Careful attention to the pseudo-code examples in the text and imitation of their styles are suggested. It is also at this stage that comments begin to take form as we outline the main points of the solution.

Of course, the design of the algorithm should proceed in a disciplined or structured manner. **Top-down** design is the suggested method. Top-down design has been discussed previously, but for completeness we describe the process again. Now that we have introduced procedures and functions, we have a concrete means of implementing top-down design.

Top-down design simply means that we use the divide-and-conquer strategy to break our problem into manageable pieces. These pieces are then further subdivided, as necessary, to reduce the problem, eventually, to modules that are easy to understand. This continued subdivision of parts of the program is called **stepwise refinement**. The point is that we continue to refine our descriptions until we are left with simple actions that will be relatively easy to implement.

Another important part of the design phase is to repeat the hand executions done in step 2. This means to take the data developed above and carefully trace the pseudo-code as if you were a literal-minded computer. The point of this step is to subject your algorithm to as many tests as you can. You may discover parts of your pseudo-code that are incomplete or incorrect. If so, you must modify your design to correct it. Again, this data-driven test of the algorithm is extremely important and a step that you should not omit, because it provides the best test possible of your design at this stage.

This third step in the problem-solving process is of extreme importance. You can't, of course, design an algorithm until you understand the problem, nor can additional steps proceed without a well-understood algorithm. Too often, we find students mired down in the implementation phase without a real understanding of the design they are trying to implement. It should be clear that the implementation will not succeed unless you know what it is that you wish to implement! Remember Murphy's Law: **"The sooner you begin coding (implementing) the longer the whole process takes"** and spend time designing and testing your algorithm.

4. Implementation

This step should be a straightforward translation of the pseudo-code into Pascal. If the pseudo-code has been refined sufficiently, this step proceeds quickly. Of course, it is via procedures and functions that a complex pseudo-code is implemented. In this way, the main program greatly resembles the pseudo-code solution.

Documentation in the form of comments should be included as the translation occurs. Elsewhere in this chapter, we discuss commenting conventions that have helped programmers with their coding.

An important point (mentioned several times) is that students too often try to start at the implementation phase. The danger in doing so is that you have to combine and juggle all of the previous phases, while considering the fussy syntax of a particular computer language. That is, you may be worrying about the placement of semicolons when you should be worrying about *what* you are trying to express. Worse yet, if you do not really understand the problem, you are wasting your time deciding whether or not you need a semicolon. Even if you eventually succeed with the syntax, your program has no chance of running correctly. This is the road to ultimate frustration. If you find that your efforts can be described like this, then you must go back to the understanding and designing steps.

Another point worthy of mention is that the implementation phase is also not the end of the problem-solving process. Too often, students who do succeed at the implementation phase think that their work is complete. Just because a program runs without errors does not mean that it produces correct output. It only means that the program is free of syntax errors.

5. Testing and Debugging

Of course, if your implementation produces error messages, it needs to be debugged. As mentioned, just because it runs does not imply that it also isn't buggy. The very minimum you need to do is to inspect the output and gauge the results for reasonableness. Is it reasonable that someone with quiz scores all between 60 and 90 has an average of 7482.39? Evidently not! Another use of your hand tracings is to check the computer's results on those cases where you know the correct answers. The amount of data may be so extensive that you cannot check all the results, but you should spot check your program by verifying some of its results. You can never be sure that your program is completely correct, and big commercial programs do occasionally blow up after many years in service. But you can at least check that your results are not garbage.

What do we do if we do have errors? This phase of finding and removing errors is called **debugging**. Debugging is another skill that is best learned with practice. You will probably generate several bugs of your own, but to ensure that you get plenty of practice, we have included intentionally buggy programs in the exercises. In another section of this chapter, we'll take up general methods of debugging. We'll also illustrate the special debugging techniques of Turbo Pascal (versions 5.0 and 5.5).

6. Final Documentation and Proofreading

Your program is a form of communication. It is a communication not just with a computer, but also with other humans. In a classroom situation, the other human is often a grader who will be more kindly disposed to your program if he or she can easily read and understand it. In the real world, your program will be read by colleagues and supervisors—or maybe you, six months later. Thus, it is important that your program be as clear as you can make it.

Methods for providing program clarity have been discussed and illustrated throughout this book. Some of the most important are:

Comments. Well-chosen comments that help the intelligent reader should be included with the program. A suggested form for commenting is discussed in a separate section below. Large projects may even have external documentation in the form of user manuals.

White Space. The well-chosen use of blank lines helps to divide your program into sections that make it easy to read and understand. Long programs should use white space to ensure that program listings are placed properly across page breaks.

Indentation. Make sure that you have observed standards of proper indentation for the bodies of procedures and functions as well as `Whiles` and `Ifs`. Indentation is ignored by the compiler, but is one of the most important tools you have to make your program understandable.

Meaningful Identifiers. Check that your identifiers add to the clarity of your program. Avoid identifiers that are too short to convey meaning.

Procedures and Functions. Avoid long sections of code. Use the divide-and-conquer approach to break your solution into easily understood units.

Clear Output. Check that the output from your program is not only correct, but also will make sense and be clear to the user. For example, is the output labeled properly?

7. Production

Real-world programs enter a production phase where they are used in real situations. Often, at this point, the user decides that some additional feature should be added, and the whole process begins again. In education, the production phase probably simply means running the program once or twice and turning in the results. If you are in charge of selecting the data, make sure that you select the data so as to show off your program. That is, make sure that the data let the program demonstrate that it handles all the different kinds of data that you can think of. You should have done this in the testing phase, because it's embarrassing when the user (or grader) discovers an error in your program at this late stage.

8. Maintenance

This, again, is a critical concern in commercial programming. Constants, such as the social-security withholding rate, change or new cases arise that must be accounted for. It is, therefore, necessary to modify the program. One test of how well the program was written is how easy (or difficult) it is to modify. Often, managers find it easier to throw a program out and start all over than to modify the program. This is extremely costly and wasteful of the initial effort. That is why the structured and disciplined programming techniques that we have been emphazing were developed. In education, we seldom have the time to let (make) students modify their own programs, but it would certainly make the need for a disciplined approach to programming very clear to everyone.

Other Problem-Solving Strategies

There are other problem-solving strategies that are often applicable to programming situations. One of the most famous is the suggestion to **solve a simpler problem**. That is, your first effort does not need to be a program that solves the entire problem. If you plan your approach, you can often create for yourself a sequence of problems, each encompassing the others, that leads to the solution of the final problem. For example, suppose that you are to read a data file that contains many lines of the form

M3.998Jacque Strappe

consisting of a character ('M' or 'F') representing sex, a real number representing a time in minutes to run a mile, and a name. Suppose that you are to print out the male and female winners of the race as well as the average male and female times. Here, we could, for example, successively solve the following sequence of problems:

1. Write a program to read and simply print out the data.
2. Modify the program so that it finds the male and female averages.
3. Modify the program so that it also finds the male and female winners.

This is an effective problem-solving strategy, and we recommend it highly when you have no idea how to begin. Begin with a simple problem and later add the complications one at a time.

Another related problem-solving strategy is to **modify a solution to a previous problem**. This is essentially what we were doing in the above example, but this method can also be applied to programs that you have previously written or to sample programs from the book. Modeling your solution after a successful one is a very good way to get started. That is why it is very valuable to study all the sample programs with great care.

COMMENTING CONVENTIONS

Documentation is a very important, and very individualistic, part of the programming process. There is no magic rule that says every fourth line should be a comment. The trick is to comment programs well in the absence of such rigid rules. The basic rule, as mentioned in Chapter 3, is that comments should benefit the intelligent user. This means that you should not comment the obvious:

Count := 0;   {Initialize Count to zero}   {POOR COMMENT!}

Nor should you comment every line. It is possible to overcomment just as it is possible to overindulge in any thing. To give the beginner some aid to proper documentation, we suggest the following guidelines that have been widely accepted as good principles of software design. Most of these principles have already been mentioned, but we gather them here for emphasis and easy reference. We divide comments into three broad kinds: local, procedural, and global.

Local Documentation

We will now discuss four kinds of local comments.

Tricky or Difficult Statements. Any statement that will perhaps not be immediately clear to an intelligent reader should be commented. For example, when a "magimatical" formula is pulled out of the air, a comment should document this:

```
Distance := Length * Height * Cos(Theta);                    {Theta in}
                                                          {radian measure.}
```

Another example is

```
...
Index := 1;
While Index <= NumQuiz Do
  Begin
    Read(Quiz);
    Sum := Sum + Quiz;
    Index := Index + 1
  End; {While}
Readln;    {Advance file pointer to next line in the text file.}
...
```

Here, the purpose of the very simple Readln statement has been made abundantly clear. Since this Readln is easily forgotten, it is a good idea to document its need.

Section Documentation. A well-chosen comment before a major section of code can make the intent of that section instantly clear. For example,

```
{Now find the maximum points scored and by whom.}
...
```

makes the next section's intended purpose obvious. Employed with judicious use of white space (blank lines and indentation), these kinds of comments make a program a joy to read.

Assertions. A special form of a comment, called an **assertion**, is becoming a standard means to comment programs. An assertion is simply a comment that is true at the point where it is placed in the program. An example of assertions about a While loop that is looking for a sentinel, 'Mickey Mouse', might be:

```
Readln(Name); {Name has the value of the 1st name in the file.}
While Name <> 'Mickey Mouse' Do
  Begin            {The value of Name is not the sentinel value.}
    ...
    process the data for this person
    ...
    Readln(Name)
  End; {While}
                              {Name is now the sentinel value.}
...
```

The first assertion states what is true before we test for the While loop the first time. The second assertion states what is true every time we execute the body of the While and, therefore, this special assertion is called a **loop invariant**. The third assertion indicates what is true when we exit from the While. Assertions are very important in an advanced subject, known as program correctness, where we attempt to prove that a program is correct. Since this is a first course, we will continue to use informal assertions, but the reader should be aware that assertions and invariants do provide a means for commenting programs.

Begin and End Documentation. The keywords Begin and End are overused in Pascal. It is often very helpful, especially with Ends that pile up together, to comment what each is actually the end of. For example,

```
      . . .
      End {If}
    End {Inner While}
End {Outer While}
. . .
```

Of course, the indentation also makes it possible to see what each End terminates, but the comment makes it obvious without the need to draw the eye up the page in a straight line.

A Begin can also benefit from a comment. For instance, the Begin of the main body of a program can be misplaced, if several functions and procedures are defined. For example,

```
Procedure Split(...);
  Begin
  . . .
  End;                          {Definition of procedure Split.}

Begin                  {Finally! The body of the main program.}
  . . .
```

Procedural Documentation

By the generic term **procedural**, we mean both procedures and functions. These should always begin with a comment so that the reader can quickly grasp what it is that the procedure or function does.

Preconditions and **Postconditions**, introduced in Chapter 6, are a special form of procedural comments that has gained wide acceptance. They state in contractual form what the procedure or function promises to do. The preconditions are conditions that must be true before you call the procedure or function. The postconditions are the promises which the procedure or function says will hold after its execution (if the preconditions were met). Preconditions and postconditions are helpful in many ways. First, they help us decide which parameters should be value and which should be variable. For example, any parameter mentioned in the postconditions as receiving a new value must be a variable parameter. Preconditions and postconditions also help in debugging a program by helping us locate the problem. If we have met the preconditions of a procedure, but it fails to uphold its postcondition, then we know that that procedure is not doing its stated job.

To write preconditions and postconditions, we suggest that you first write an English description of what the procedure or function does, and then decide what must be true *before* the procedure acts and what will be true *after* the procedure acts. For example, suppose the procedure Split is to take a three-digit Number and return its Huns, Tens, and Ones digits. Pay attention to the little words like "takes" and "returns," as they tell us that for Split to do its work, Number must already have a three-digit value and that Huns, Tens, and Ones will be variable parameters receiving single-digit values. Thus, we can write

```
Procedure Split(Number : Integer; Var Huns, Tens, Ones : Integer);
{Pre:  Number is a three-digit integer.
 Post:  Huns, Tens, and Ones are assigned the proper digits from Num.}
```

Procedure and function bodies can, of course, have local documentation as discussed above, so the preconditions and postconditions are not the only comments in a procedure or function, but they are important comments and you should learn to use them well.

Global Documentation

Global documentation is documentation for the entire program. This should include, as a minimum, a comment at the beginning of the program telling what it is that the program does. In a class situation, it is a good idea to include your name and your instructor's name, so that if your program is misplaced, it can be returned to you. Global documentation for a larger program should also indicate what procedures and functions will be employed in the solution of the problem and what the main variables are, as well as what they are for. The lengthy program Bagels at the end of Chapter 6 provides a good example of global documentation.

THE ART OF DEBUGGING

We think there is much to be learned from debugging, and that is why we have included intentionally buggy programs in the exercises. Debugging is another skill that is best learned with practice. However, there are certain general guidelines to aid the beginner in developing this skill. These are gathered here for easy reference. Also see the complete debugging example later in this chapter, as well as the Turbo Pascal integrated debugger (for versions 5.0 and 5.5) described at the end of this chapter.

Debugging Strategies

Locate the problem. This simple suggestion is probably the most important aid to debugging. When you have a large program that produces garbage, you have no idea what the problem is. If you can locate the procedure, function, or section of code that is causing the problem, you are well on your way to finding the problem. In this regard, debugging is like lawn-mower repair. A lawn-mower repairperson must first decide whether the problem is in the electrical system or the fuel system. If the problem is electrical, is it in the spark plug or the points? The repairperson continues in this manner until he or she has determined the exact location of the problem.

In a program, how does one locate the bug? Several suggestions for finding the location of a bug are now discussed.

Obtain additional output. Suppose that you have a program that reads the data and then produces nonsense. If you can identify several key intermediate steps and print out the values of these key variables, you can help to identify the step at which the calculation went off the track. Additional output is obtained, of course, by inserting `Writeln` statements into a program. These `Writeln`s will then be deleted when the problem is found and fixed. We often use this technique as an aid in debugging student programs brought to us. We find it convenient to include a small identifying message in the `Writeln` as well as to type the `WRITELN` in uppercase for easy identification and deletion later. For example,

```
WRITELN('READING DATA:', NAME:30, SEX:2, TOSS:5:2, ...);
```

placed in the main loop that (supposedly) reads the data will print the data as read. If all the data appears, the program is working up to that point. If only some or none of the data are printed, we have come a long way toward locating the problem.

Play computer. Playing computer means tracing the execution of the program step by step. At every stage, you should compare your results with those produced by the program. When you add additional output to the program, you can get frequent checks on its work. When you find that your work agrees with the computer's up to a certain stage, you have come close to isolating the problem.

Playing computer takes much patience and critical thinking. You must be careful to do exactly what you told the computer to do, not what you want the computer to do. Try to execute each instruction exactly as the computer would. In this manner, you can often catch a misstatement in your program.

Simplify the data. Sometimes, printing additional output results in a flood of output that is difficult to understand. Often, it is wise to reduce the amount of data given to the program until the bug is located. This may be as simple as creating a new, small data file for the program. If a short data file exhibits the bug, the human will be able to play computer far more easily and understand the modest amount of output produced by the smaller amount of data.

Bench-test procedures and functions. Suppose you have a procedure or function that you suspect is not doing its job. By bench-testing it, we mean to give it input and carefully monitor its output. In so doing, we isolate it from the other components and observe its behavior. Bench-testing is very simple. The preconditions tell us what we must do to be able to call the procedure or function. The postconditions tell us what is supposed to be true after the call. Thus, we simply create the preconditions, make the call, and test the postconditions. For example, to bench-test `Split`, whose heading and pre/postconditions are

```
Procedure Split(Num : Integer; Var Huns, Tens, Ones : Integer);
{Pre:  Num is a three-digit integer.
Post:  Huns, Tens, and Ones are assigned the proper digits from Num.}
```

we merely place the following lines just inside our main Begin:

```
Num := 123;
Split(Num, Huns, Tens, Ones);
Writeln('Split Test', Num:5, Huns:5, Tens:5, Ones:5);
Halt;
```

The value 123 is arbitrary, but it is important that Num have some three-digit value when called. A good choice would be a data value for which the program has shown that it does not work properly. If the output from this segment is *not*

```
Split Test   123     1     2     3
```

then we know that there is a problem within Split. Unfortunately, if we get the correct output, we cannot completely exonerate Split, but if we make several such tests to Split, we gain more and more confidence in Split and begin to look elsewhere for the problem. For example, before moving on, we might bench-test Split with a number that has repeated digits, like 122 or even 111.

   Bench-testing is a powerful technique for gaining confidence in your procedures and functions. It can and should be used as you write your procedures and functions to validate them as much as you possibly can.

A COMPLETE EXAMPLE: THE DUEL OF HAMILTON AND BURR

The most famous duel in American history occurred in 1804 when Alexander Hamilton (of 10-dollar bill fame), the nation's first secretary of the treasury, dueled with and was killed by Aaron Burr, vice president under Thomas Jefferson.

   We are going to make some historically inaccurate, simplifying assumptions about the duel and then simulate the duel many times to decide whether it was fair or not. Although Hamilton lost, we will assume that he was the better shot. In fact, we will arbitrarily say that Hamilton hits his target once in two tries, on the average, and that Burr hits his target only once in three tries, on the average. We will also assume that, 19th century medical care being what it was, any hit means death. Knowing that he is the better shot, and being a gentleman (and, apparently, a fool), Hamilton agrees to let Burr have the first shot. Hamilton will not shoot unless Burr misses, and then Burr will not get a second shot unless Hamilton misses, etc. Thus, the duel may go on for many shots with Burr getting the first (and every odd-numbered shot) and Hamilton getting the second (and every even-numbered shot) until death does them part.

   Because dueling is no longer considered a gentlemanly sport, we wish to simulate the duel. Burr goes first, but Hamilton is the better shot. Therefore, it is not obvious who has the advantage. Which position would you choose? To determine who has the advantage, we will simulate a large number of duels and count how many times Burr wins and how many times Hamilton wins. Because it is of interest, let us also determine the average length (in shots) of a duel.

Let us now consider in detail how our eight-step problem-solving process could be applied to this problem.

1. The first step was getting the **problem specified completely**. Again, normally, in a text, we have to try to do this step for you. We didn't say how far apart Hamilton and Burr were standing, but that clearly isn't relevant, since we know that at this distance Hamilton hits 50 percent of the time and Burr hits 33-1/3 percent of the time. A relevant detail that has been intentionally omitted is the number of duels to simulate to get a feeling for who will be the winner. Let's now agree that we will simulate 100 duels. Otherwise, we hope we have included all relevant details in the problem description.

2. The next step, **understanding the problem**, is a major one. You should not proceed until you feel that you have assimilated the problem completely. Reread the problem description a couple of times and ask yourself questions about the situation. Be sure that you realize that this duel is not like high noon in Tombstone, where both players draw and shoot at the same time. Also, realize that the phrase "Hamilton hits his target once in two tries" does not mean that he always hits, then misses, then hits, then misses, etc., on every other shot. Rather, the phrase means that, like a fair coin that comes up heads, on the average, once in two flips, Hamilton hits Burr, on the average, once in two tries. It is possible, but not likely, for Hamilton to hit (miss) Burr 10 straight times.

Another suggestion given for understanding a problem was to create a small amount of data and determine the output for those data. For this problem, unlike most, there is no input data, but we do strongly suggest that you use a die (singular of dice) and simulate by hand a few duels. We suggest a die because it is easy to get both the fractions 1/2 and 1/3 from a die. Explicitly, let us agree that if Hamilton rolls a 4, 5, or 6, then he hits Burr, while Burr hits Hamilton only if he rolls a 5 or a 6. Supposing the following 12 rolls of the die, verify that Hamilton wins three of the first five duels in an average of 2.4 shots:

4
3
6
2
5
1
1
4
6
5
2
4

3. The next step, **designing an algorithm**, is also critical to what follows. We invite the reader, before reading further, to stop and design by stepwise refinement his or her own pseudo-code version of an algorithm for this problem. You will obviously not design exactly the algorithm that we do, but that is to be expected, since this step is the most creative and individualistic part of the whole process. That also explains why this step is so important in our whole problem-solving stratagem.

Our approach to this problem proceeds as follows: Wouldn't it be nice if there were a built-in `Duel` procedure that would simulate *one* duel for us and tell us who won and how many shots it took? Of course, there is no such built-in procedure, but that is the advantage of the divide-and-conquer strategy and the stepwise-refinement technique. For now, we can pretend that there is such a procedure and use it to solve the given problem. Later, we will have to focus our attention on `Duel` and see how it can be designed. We do see from our description of `Duel` that it needs two parameters, one to indicate who won and one to indicate how many shots were needed. Since we can indicate the winner with a `'B'` or `'H'`, we can suppose that `Duel`'s parameters are a character and an integer, respectively.

Given `Duel`, the main program becomes quite easy. It simply needs to invoke `Duel` 100 times and keep track of the number of wins by Hamilton and Burr, as well as the total number of shots. Here is the pseudo-code:

Set a constant, NumDuels, to 100
Initialize HamWins and BurrWins both to zero
Initialize TotalShots to zero
Loop NumDuels times doing
   Duel(Winner, NumShots)   --Simulate one duel
   If Winner is 'H' then
     Increment HamWins
   Else
     Increment BurrWins
   Add NumShots to TotalShots
Output HamWins, BurrWins, and TotalShots/NumDuels (the average)

This, when implemented, will become our main program. It will be short and easy to understand. The loop will become a standard `While`, but that is a detail that can be left to the implementation. Assuming that `Duel(Winner, NumShots)` does its job, the reader should trace the above pseudo-code to make sure that it performs as desired.

The cautious reader will point out that we still have a big procedure to write. In fact, it may seem that all we have done is to strip the trivial part away from the difficult part, leaving the difficult part yet unsolved. That may be, but let us now apply the same divide-and-conquer approach to procedure `Duel`. We now get to ignore the rest of the details and focus our efforts on simulating one complete duel. This procedure must let Burr shoot first and must continue while both are still living. Eventually, it must report the winner and the number of shots needed through its parameters. Hence, we already see that this procedure has no preconditions, but the following important postconditions:

Winner will be 'H' if Hamilton wins and 'B' if Burr wins.
NumShots will count the number of shots needed in the duel.

The hard part of procedure Duel seems to be knowing how long the duel should continue. Sometimes it ends in one shot, sometimes two, sometimes more. It continues *while* they are both living. There it is! We can make the body of Duel a While loop with a Boolean BothLiving! Here is the broad pseudo-code outline as developed so far:

Initialize NumShots to zero
Initialize BothLiving to True   --We begin with both Hamilton and Burr healthy
While BothLiving
  Let them duel at one another

Now, we further refine the statement "Let them duel at one another." This involves Burr taking the first shot (don't forget to count the shot). If he hits, he wins and *both are no longer living*. If Burr misses, then Hamilton shoots (count it). If Hamilton hits, then he wins and *both are no longer living*. Otherwise, we keep looping. Putting this together with what we already had gives us the following outline:

Initialize NumShots to zero
Initialize BothLiving to True   --We begin with both Hamilton and Burr healthy
While BothLiving
  Increment NumShots   --Count Burr's shot at Hamilton
  If Burr hit Hamilton then
    Set BothLiving to False
    Set Winner to 'B'   --Burr won
  Else   --Burr missed, so give Hamilton a chance
    Increment NumShots   --Count Hamilton's return shot at Burr
    If Hamilton hit Burr then
      Set BothLiving to False
      Set Winner to 'H'   --Hamilton won

Here, everything but the phrases "Burr hit Hamilton" and "Hamilton hit Burr" will be easy to implement. Assuming that these phrases operate as planned (they can be True or False), the reader should verify, by hand, that Burr could win in three shots, or Hamilton could win in two or six shots, for example.

Thus, all we are left with is designing some way of telling when someone shoots his opponent. Since the two opponents shoot in similar ways, we propose a Boolean function Shoots with one input parameter. If this input parameter is 2, then one in two times, on the average, Shoots will return True; but, if the parameter is 3, only one in three times will Shoots return True. Thus, the Boolean condition "Burr hit Hamilton" can be replaced by the invocation Shoots(3), while the condition "Hamilton hit Burr" can be replaced by Shoots(2). Here, then, is our final pseudo-code for Duel:

Initialize NumShots to zero
Initialize BothLiving to True   --We begin with both Hamilton and Burr healthy
While BothLiving
   Increment NumShots   --Count Burr's shot at Hamilton
   If Shoots(3) then   --Did Burr hit Hamilton?
     Set BothLiving to False
     Set Winner to 'B'   --Burr won
   Else   --Burr missed, so give Hamilton a chance
     Increment NumShots   --Count Hamilton's return shot at Burr
     If Shoots(2) then   --Did Hamilton hit Burr?
       Set BothLiving to False
       Set Winner to 'H'   --Hamilton won

Finally, we need to design only $Shoots(N)$ that returns $True$ once in N times. The precondition for $Shoots$ is that N has some positive value, and the postcondition is that $Shoots$ returns $True$ about 1 of N times (on the average). Our strategy is to generate randomly a number between 1 and N and arbitrarily let 1 represent $True$. The pseudo-code for $Shoots(N)$ follows:

Let Randy (a local variable) be a random value between 1 and N
If Randy is 1 then
   Set Shoots to True
Else
   Set Shoots to False

Using stepwise refinement, we have developed a main program that calls a procedure $Duel$. This procedure then invokes the function $Shoots$ to actually simulate the duels. In this manner, we have broken a seemingly complex problem into several short modules. We have divided and conquered!

4. Now comes the easy part. Our final pseudo-code is so complete that the **implementation** shown in Listing 7.1 is a nearly direct translation of the pseudo-code. There are a few details worthy of discussion. Since the procedure calls the function, we need to define the function first. Since the function is only called by the procedure, it could have been declared within the procedure. More of this topic, called the scope rules, will be presented in Chapter 9. Also, since $Shoots$ uses the $Random$ function, the procedure $Randomize$ was added to the main program. Of course, numerous $Begins$ and $Ends$ were added during the translation. Otherwise, the bodies of $Shoots$, $Duel$, and the main program $HamBurr$ are exactly like their pseudo-code.

5. Now, we need to ***test*** and, if necessary, ***debug*** our program. In this case, other than simple typing mistakes that led to easily located syntax errors, we had no bugs in the program. This is the perfect case of everything going as planned. If your pseudo-code is well designed, this will begin to happen to you, too! Later in this chapter, we'll discuss several buggy programs so that we see what to do if the implementation does not proceed as planned.

```
Program HamBurr;
{This program simulates the famous duel between Alexander Hamilton
and Aaron Burr to decide who had the best chance. It also determines
the average number of shots fired in each duel.                    }

Const  NumDuels = 100;

Var    HamWins    : Integer;
       BurrWins   : Integer;
       TotalShots : Integer;
       Count      : Integer;
       Winner     : Char;
       NumShots   : Integer;

Function Shoots(N : Integer) : Boolean;
{Pre:  N has a positive value.
Post:  Shoots, on the average, will be True 1 in N times.         }

  Var Randy : Integer;            {Local variable for random value.}

  Begin
    Randy := Random(N) + 1;    {A random value between 1 and N.}
    If Randy = 1 Then
      Shoots := True
    Else
      Shoots := False
  End;                                {Definition of function Shoots.}

Procedure Duel(Var Winner : Char; Var NumShots : Integer);
{This procedure simulates one duel between Hamilton and Burr.
Pre:   None
Post:  Winner will be 'H' if Hamilton wins and 'B' if Burr wins.
       NumShots will count of the number of shots needed.         }

  Var  BothLiving : Boolean;

  Begin
    NumShots := 0;
    BothLiving := True;   {Begin with both contestants healthy.}
    While BothLiving Do
      Begin
        NumShots := NumShots + 1;              {Count Burr's shot.}
        If Shoots(3) Then                 {Did Burr hit Hamilton?}
          Begin
            BothLiving := False;
            Winner := 'B'                                {Burr won!}
          End {Then}
```

Listing 7.1

```
      Else
        Begin
          NumShots := NumShots + 1;    {Count Hamilton's shot.}
          If Shoots(2) Then            {Did Hamilton hit Burr?}
            Begin
              BothLiving := False;
              Winner := 'H'                          {Hamilton won!}
            End {Inner If}
        End {Else}
    End {While}
  End;                                 {Definition of procedure Duel.}
Begin                                  {The main body of the program HamBurr.}
  Randomize;
  HamWins := 0;
  BurrWins := 0;
  TotalShots := 0;
  Count := 1;
  While Count <= NumDuels Do
    Begin
      Duel(Winner, NumShots);                    {Simulate one duel.}
      If Winner = 'H' Then
        HamWins := HamWins + 1
      Else
        BurrWins := BurrWins + 1;
      TotalShots := TotalShots + NumShots;
      Count := Count + 1
    End; {While}
  Writeln('After ', NumDuels, ' duels the results are:')
  Writeln('Hamilton won ', HamWins, ' times.');
  Writeln('Burr won ', BurrWins, ' times.');
  Writeln('The average duel was ', TotalShots/NumDuels:4:2,
                                                ' shots.')
End.
```

Listing 7.1 (continued)

This program is more difficult to verify, because we are not sure what kind of results to expect. We can bench-test Shoots to verify it by changing the main program to something as simple as

```
Begin                              {Bench test Shoots' 1-in-3 accuracy.}
  NumHits := 0;
  Count := 1;
  While Count <= 300 Do
    Begin
      If Shoots(3) Then
        NumHits := NumHits + 1;
```

```
      Count := Count + 1
   End; {While}
 Writeln('In target practice Burr hit the target ', NumHits,
                                    ' out of 300 tries.')
End.
```

If the output from this segment is nowhere close to 100 hits, we know that Shoots is buggy. In this case, we can also use our die to simulate 10 to 20 duels and verify that the computer's findings are in line with ours. In our run of HamBurr, we obtained the following output:

```
After 100 duels the results are:
Hamilton won 52 times.
Burr won 48 times.
The average duel was 2.42 shots.
```

6. **Editing and documenting** of the program has been done throughout. Note how the comments began in the design phase and were preserved through to the final copy. Blank space and indentation have been used to make the presentation as pleasant as possible.

7. Now our program is ready for the **production** phase. In the real world, we deliver the program to the user (and pray that the user likes it). In education, we turn the program in (and pray that the instructor likes it).

8. **Maintenance** is our final step. In response to the user's comments, we may need to make some changes to the program. For example, based upon our output above, the duel appears to be pretty fair. Maybe we should run the simulation 1000 or 10,000 times to see what the results are. Since our program is well designed, this is a trivial modification. A more serious modification would be to determine the length of the longest duel during the simulation, or to introduce the possibility of a wound without death in, say, two-fifths of all hits. We might also suppose that a hit reduces the wounded shooter's accuracy by half. We leave such modifications to you in the exercises.

DEBUGGING EXAMPLES

We now present several examples of buggy student work. These buggy programs are on the sample disk that accompanies this book, and it would be most instructive for the reader to attempt to debug the programs before reading our explanations.

An Infinite Loop

The following simple program attempts to read and average five quiz scores. Assume that there is a text file Quizzes.Txt with the following contents:

87
76
92
82
56

Our objective is to loop five times, reading and summing the scores. Then we simply divide by 5 to get the average. What could be simpler? Do you see anything wrong with BuggyAve in Listing 7.2 that purports to solve this problem?

When BuggyAve runs, it runs (and runs), producing no output. It shouldn't take the computer long to read, sum, and average five integers. Clearly, something has gone wrong. To interrupt the program, type CTRL-BREAK. This will return you to the editor. In versions 5.0 and 5.5, because of the built-in debugger that we'll discuss soon, you will also need to type CTRL-F2 to reset the program. If you neglect to do this, when you rerun the program with CTRL-F9, it will resume its infinite loop at the point that you interrupted it. CTRL-F2 will reset the program so that the next CTRL-F9 begins execution all over from the beginning. In version 4.0, ALT-R always runs the program from the beginning, so no reset is necessary.

We do not understand why the program seems to loop forever, but let's add an output statement to the loop to see what is going on. Suppose, therefore, that we add

```
WRITELN('IN LOOP', SCORE:5, SUM:5)
```

```
Program BuggyAve;
{This program tries to average the five scores in Quizzes.Txt.}

Var   Sum   : Integer;
      Count : Integer;
      Score : Integer;

Begin
  Assign(Input, 'A:\Ch7\Quizzes.Txt');
  Reset(Input);
  Count := 1;
  Sum := 0;
  While Count <= 5 Do
    Begin
      Readln(Score);
      Sum := Sum + Score
    End; {While}
  Writeln('The average of the five scores is ', (Sum/5):5:2)
End.
```

Listing 7.2

to the end of the body of the While loop. Note that this will also require that a semicolon be added to the previous line of the program. This time, when we run the program, we get lots of output! It begins as follows:

```
IN LOOP    87    87
IN LOOP    76   163
IN LOOP    92   255
IN LOOP    82   337
IN LOOP    56   393
IN LOOP     0   393
IN LOOP     0   393
IN LOOP     0   393
. . .
```

and repeats that last line over and over. Again, we need a CTRL-BREAK to exit the infinite loop, then a CTRL-F2 (in versions 5.0 and 5.5) to reset the program. We can (and should) trace the first five lines of output to see that they are correct. It is apparent that the computer can't even count to five. The key to debugging this program is to investigate why the computer doesn't count to five. Therefore, we expand our WRITELN to include the value of Count. With the statement

```
WRITELN('IN LOOP', SCORE:5, SUM:5, COUNT:5)
```

at the bottom of our While, we obtain the output

```
IN LOOP    87    87    1
IN LOOP    76   163    1
IN LOOP    92   255    1
IN LOOP    82   337    1
IN LOOP    56   393    1
IN LOOP     0   393    1
IN LOOP     0   393    1
IN LOOP     0   393    1
. . .
```

from which it is clear that Count is stuck at 1. Oh my gosh, we forgot to increment Count in the body of the While. No wonder Count never reaches five and no wonder the loop is infinite. That is, we are missing

```
Count := Count + 1
```

at the bottom of our While and, as soon as we add it, the program runs correctly. The point is that the extra output finally made this omission clear. In the beginning, we had no idea what we were doing wrong. As soon as we printed the value of Count, our omission was obvious.

All Except the Last Are Lost

Let's forget that we know there are five lines in the file `Quizzes.Txt` and simply read it until end of file. If we count the lines as we go, we should then have a general solution to finding the average that would work for any number of lines. This is what `BuggyAv2` in Listing 7.3 tries to do. Do you see why it doesn't work?

When we run `BuggyAv2`, we get the output:

```
The average was 56.00
```

This is clearly incorrect. In fact, 56 is the last score in the file and all the other scores are larger. How can the computer have possibly gotten to the last line of the text file without having processed the first four lines? To find out, let's put the same

```
WRITELN('IN LOOP', SCORE:5, SUM:5, COUNT:5)
```

just after the incrementation of `Count`. This time, we get the output

```
IN LOOP    56    56     1
The average was 56.00
```

That certainly seems to confirm our suspicions. Somehow, the computer is jumping to the last line of the data.

However, the key to successful debugging is not to jump to conclusions. Consider the evidence carefully: We expected five `IN LOOP` messages and we got only one of them.

```
Program BuggyAv2;
{This program reads the text file Quizzes.Txt until end of file and
 purports to compute the average of all the quizzes.               }

Var    Score : Integer;
       Count : Integer;
       Sum   : Integer;

Begin
  Assign(Input, 'A:\Ch7\Quizzes.Txt');
  Reset(Input);
  Count := 0;
  Sum := 0;
  While Not Eof Do
    Readln(Score);
    Sum := Sum + Score;
    Count := Count + 1;
  Writeln('The average was ', (Sum/Count):5:2)
End.
```

Listing 7.3

```
Begin
  Assign(Input, 'A:\Ch7\Quizzes.Txt');
  Reset(Input);
  Count := 0;
  Sum := 0;
  While Not Eof Do
    Readln(Score);
  Sum := Sum + Score;
  Count := Count + 1;
  WRITELN('IN LOOP', SCORE:5, SUM:5, COUNT:5);
  Writeln('The average was ', (Sum/Count):5:2)
End.
```

Listing 7.4

What can we deduce from that fact? A statement that is not in any loop will execute only once. Could it be that the WRITELN is not in the body of the While? We can clearly see that it is in the body. But, in this case, things are not as they seem. In debugging, you must learn to stalk the mind of the literal computer. Do not be misled (as we hope you have been until now) by the indentation. It is a great help (normally) to the human, but is ignored by the computer. The body of a While is the *first* statement after the keyword Do and, therefore, the compiler sees our program as in Listing 7.4.

The problem, of course, is that we forgot the Begin and End that are necessary whenever we want the body of a While to be compound. As soon as we supply them, the program runs correctly. Remember this common error and check your programs for necessary Begins and Ends.

Where Have All the Females Gone?

Suppose the data have been modified to indicate the sex of the person involved. For example, the text file Quizzes2.Txt contains the lines:

```
F87
M76
F92
M82
M56
M79
F83
M72
```

which indicates that a female scored 87, a male scored 76, etc. Also notice that several extra lines of data have been added.

Suppose our simple objective is to write a program that finds the highest male and the highest female scores. We have discussed this kind of problem several times, so,

```
Program BuggyMax;
{This program tries to find the highest male and female scores from
the text file Quizzes2.Txt. Each line of Quizzes2 contains a
character ('M' or 'F') followed by an integer quiz score.      }

Var    Sex    : Char;
       Score  : Integer;
       MaleMax : Integer;
       FemMax  : Integer;

Begin
  Assign(Input, 'A:\Ch7\Quizzes2.Txt');
  Reset(Input);
  MaleMax := -1;                    {Initialize MaleMax and FemMax}
  FemMax := -1;                              {to ridiculous values.}
  While Not Eof Do
    Begin
      Readln(Sex, Score);
      If Sex = 'M' Then                              {Male case.}
        If Score > MaleMax Then
          MaleMax := Score
      Else                                        {Female case.}
        .If Score > FemMax Then
          FemMax := Score
    End; {While}
  Writeln('The male maximum was   ', MaleMax);
  Writeln('The female maximum was ', FemMax)
End.
```

Listing 7.5

without further ado, we invite you to study Listing 7.5. Doesn't it seem that it should solve the problem?

The output from BuggyMax is

```
The male maximum was   82
The female maximum was 79
```

Wait a minute. That 79 was obtained by a male. This simple program is really buggy. Let's add an output statement to the female case to determine what is going on. This will make that section compound, so we must not forget to add a BEGIN and END (uppercase to help find and delete them later). The body of our program is now as shown in Listing 7.6.

This time, the output from Listing 7.6 is

```
FEMALE CASE M    56
FEMALE CASE M    79
FEMALE CASE M    72
The male maximum was   82
The female maximum was 79
```

```
Begin
  Assign(Input, 'A:\Ch7\Quizzes2.Txt');
  Reset(Input);
  MaleMax := -1;                     {Initialize MaleMax and FemMax}
  FemMax := -1;                               {to ridiculous values.}
  While Not Eof Do
    Begin
      Readln(Sex, Score);
      If Sex = 'M' Then                                {Male case.}
        If Score > MaleMax Then
          MaleMax := Score
        Else                                         {Female case.}
          BEGIN
            WRITELN('FEMALE CASE', SEX:2, SCORE:5);
            If Score > FemMax Then
              FemMax := Score
          END
    End; {While}
  Writeln('The male maximum was   ', MaleMax);
  Writeln('The female maximum was ', FemMax)
End.
```

Listing 7.6

By tracing the program, we see that the male score of 76, and then 82, became the values of `MaleMax`. But we still don't see how the male scores of 56, 79, and 72 got into the female section. Also, where have all the females gone? To try to answer these questions, we add some `WRITELN`s to the bottom of the loop. These will indicate the current data being processed as well as the current values of the critical variables `MaleMax` and `FemMax`. The body of our program now appears in Listing 7.7. Notice the printing of a blank line to block the output into easy-to-understand paragraphs.

  This time, the output from Listing 7.7 is more extensive:

```
CURRENT DATA F   87
MALEMAX =   -1
FEMMAX =    -1

CURRENT DATA M   76
MALEMAX =    76
FEMMAX =    -1

CURRENT DATA F   92
MALEMAX =    76
FEMMAX =    -1
```

```pascal
Begin
  Assign(Input, 'A:\Ch7\Quizzes2.Txt');
  Reset(Input);
  MaleMax := -1;                          {Initialize MaleMax and FemMax}
  FemMax := -1;                                   {to ridiculous values.}
    While Not Eof Do
    Begin
      Readln(Sex, Score);
      If Sex = 'M' Then                               {Male case.}
        If Score > MaleMax Then
          MaleMax := Score
      Else                                            {Female case.}
        BEGIN
          WRITELN('FEMALE CASE', SEX:2, SCORE:5);
          If Score > FemMax Then
            FemMax := Score
        END;
      WRITELN('CURRENT DATA', SEX:2, SCORE:5);
      WRITELN('MALEMAX = ', MALEMAX:5);
      WRITELN('FEMMAX = ', FEMMAX:5);
      WRITELN
    End; {While}
  Writeln('The male maximum was  ', MaleMax);
  Writeln('The female maximum was ', FemMax)
End.
```

Listing 7.7

```
CURRENT DATA M    82
MALEMAX =    82
FEMMAX =    -1

FEMALE CASE M    56
CURRENT DATA M    56
MALEMAX =    82
FEMMAX =    56

FEMALE CASE M    79
CURRENT DATA M    79
MALEMAX =    82
FEMMAX =    79

CURRENT DATA F    83
MALEMAX =    82
FEMMAX =    79
```

```
FEMALE CASE M    72
CURRENT DATA M    72
MALEMAX =    82
FEMMAX =    79


The male maximum was    82
The female maximum was 79
```

Now it is clear that the females are being read, but for some reason being ignored. Notice an important clue: Exactly the males who are not generating a new `MaleMax` value are falling into the female case. It is as if the female case is the male-reject case. That's it! Again, the indentation is normally a great help in understanding a program, but as this and the previous example have shown, indentation can also hide bugs that are difficult to find. Pascal always matches an `Else` with the nearest `If`, so it is as if our original program were typed as in Listing 7.8.

The problem, of course, in Listing 7.8 is that we have an `If...Then...Else` nested inside an `If...Then`. Instead, what we want is a simple `If...Then` nested inside an `If...Then...Else`. Hopefully, you recall from Chapter 5 that a null `Else` can solve this problem. Thus, finally, a correct body for the program is shown in Listing 7.9.

```
Begin
  Assign(Input, 'A:\Ch7\Quizzes2.Txt');
  Reset(Input);
  MaleMax := -1;                        {Initialize MaleMax and FemMax}
  FemMax := -1;                             {to ridiculous values.}

  While Not Eof Do
    Begin
      Readln(Sex, Score);
      If Sex = 'M' Then                              {Male case.}
        If Score > MaleMax Then
          MaleMax := Score
        Else                               {Male reject case.}
          If Score > FemMax Then
            FemMax := Score
    End; {While}

  Writeln('The male maximum was   ', MaleMax);
  Writeln('The female maximum was ', FemMax)
End.
```

Listing 7.8

```
Begin
  Assign(Input, 'A:\Ch7\Quizzes2.Txt');
  Reset(Input);
  MaleMax := -1;                      {Initialize MaleMax and FemMax}
  FemMax := -1;                               {to ridiculous values.}
  While Not Eof Do
    Begin
      Readln(Sex, Score);
      If Sex = 'M' Then                               {Male case.}
        If Score > MaleMax Then
          MaleMax := Score
        Else                          {Do nothing with male rejects.}
      Else                                          {Female case.}
        If Score > FemMax Then
          FemMax := Score
    End; {While}
  Writeln('The male maximum was   ', MaleMax);
  Writeln('The female maximum was ', FemMax)
End.
```

Listing 7.9

Our debugging examples have been illustrated with very simple and short programs to keep the discussions as brief and focused as possible. How does one debug a large program? In the same manner, but first analyze the behavior of the program to try to determine which section, procedure, or function is buggy. That is, by selective use of WRITELNs, you determine where the program goes off the track. Then you apply all of your Sherlock Holmes skills to that section of code. Take nothing for granted. Be suspicious of every statement and follow the literal logic of the computer.

THE TURBO PASCAL ENVIRONMENT

In Chapter 2, we presented a beginners' subset of the commands available to the user of Turbo Pascal. Since your programming skills are becoming more sophisticated, it is time for you to learn more about the complete Turbo Pascal system. This environment provides powerful tools to ease program development, and we recommend that you learn to use them well. Rather than try to memorize all the information presented here, we recommend that you read the following material to see the kinds of things that are possible and then refer to this section for reference as needed.

Because we are discussing Turbo Pascal versions 4.0, 5.0, and 5.5, we will at times have to give slightly different explanations. Fortunately, these three versions agree far more than they disagree. In fact, 5.0 and 5.5 are so similar that we can usually refer to them together, and we will use the notation 5.X to refer to either version 5.0 or 5.5.

In all versions, there are four parts to the screen: the top line, the Edit window, the Output window (4.0) or Watch window (5.X), and the bottom line. These are shown in Figures 7.1 (versions 5.X) and 7.2 (version 4.0) and each is detailed in the following discussion.

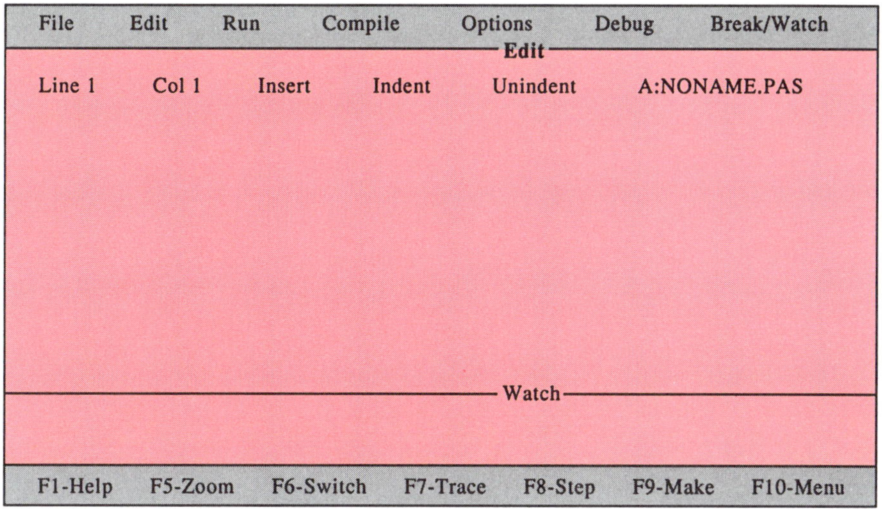

File	Edit	Run	Compile	Options	Debug	Break/Watch

──────────────── **Edit** ────────────────

Line 1	Col 1	Insert	Indent	Unindent	A:NONAME.PAS

──────────────── Watch ────────────────

F1-Help	F5-Zoom	F6-Switch	F7-Trace	F8-Step	F9-Make	F10-Menu

Figure 7.1

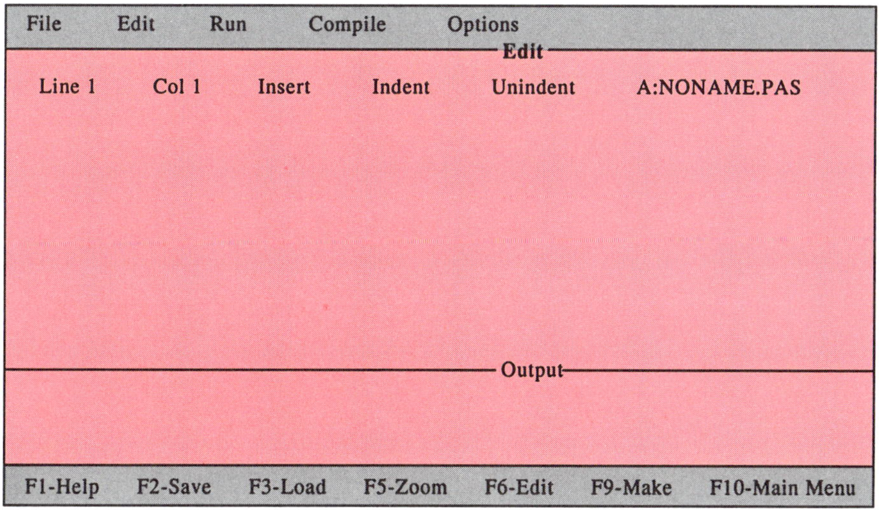

File	Edit	Run	Compile	Options

──────────────── **Edit** ────────────────

Line 1	Col 1	Insert	Indent	Unindent	A:NONAME.PAS

──────────────── Output ────────────────

F1-Help	F2-Save	F3-Load	F5-Zoom	F6-Edit	F9-Make	F10-Main Menu

Figure 7.2

THE TOP LINE

The top line displays the main menu of the system. In version 4.0, there are five main menu commands: File, Edit, Run, Compiler, and Options. Turbo Pascal 5.X has two more: Debug and Break/Watch. Generally, the common commands are the same in all versions or are extended in the later versions. The details of these seven commands are given below, after we complete our discussion of the four portions of the screen.

THE BOTTOM LINE

The bottom line reminds you of function keystrokes that execute common commands. Unfortunately, the bottom line is different in versions 4.0 and 5.X. Fortunately, the bottom lines of Figures 7.1 and 7.2 are not as different as they seem. In every case, F1 calls up context-sensitive help. This means that the information provided by the system depends upon the current situation. Learn to use the Help menus to see if they can provide you with assistance when needed. F2 and F3 save and load in all versions. They are just not listed on the bottom line in the later versions. The rationale for this seems to be that we use these keys so much that they become second nature to us; hence, version 5.X does not waste space listing them. In all versions, F5 zooms the active window in and out. That is, F5 makes the active window full screen size or reduces it back from full screen size to its original size. Don't forget that it is often very helpful to zoom the Edit window to full size during program development, since this allows you to see more of the surrounding program. F6 has been renamed in the newer versions, but its function remains the same in all versions. In 4.0, F6 reads Edit or Output and *switches* between the Edit and Output windows. In version 5.X, F6 is called Switch and it switches between the Edit and the Watch windows. F7 and F8 are different in versions 4.0 and 5.X. In version 5.X, they perform step and trace functions of the built-in debugger, which is detailed later in this chapter. This debugger is not implemented in version 4.0 and, in that version, F7 and F8 provide blocking functions that are also detailed below. F9 is Make in all versions, but this is an advanced feature of the Turbo environment that is beyond the scope of this book. The interested reader is referred to the Turbo Pascal manuals. Finally, F10, although named slightly differently, takes you, in all versions, back to the main menu on the top line of the screen.

THE OUTPUT WINDOW

The Output window is where output generated by programs appears. In version 4.0, this is a part of the main screen. You may wish to make it active with F6 and then zoom it with F5 to full size. In version 5.X, the Watch window replaces the Output window on the main screen, and the Output window (or User Screen, as it is called) is a separate window that is obtained by pressing ALT-F5.

THE WATCH WINDOW

This window, provided only in version 5.X, is a part of the Turbo Pascal integrated debugger described below. Basically, it allows you to watch your program as it executes and provides a powerful debugging tool. If you are fortunate enough to be using version 5.0 or 5.5, you will want to learn to use this window. (See the details below.)

THE EDIT WINDOW

The Edit window is where programs are created and modified. There are many useful commands that apply to this window that were not introduced in Chapter 2 (to keep the discussion there as simple as possible). For reference, we list the complete set of commands and urge the reader to try them out now and return to this section for reference as needed. The commands are divided into five groups: basic movement, extended movement, insert and delete, block, and miscellaneous commands. Each group is displayed and discussed below.

Basic Movement Commands. The basic movement commands are given in Table 7.1. Most of the commands of Table 7.1 should already be familiar to the user. Try any that you have not already learned. Scrolling the screen can sometimes be very useful to keep the cursor fixed while displaying more of the program above or below the cursor. Most of the commands can be obtained in two distinct ways. We believe that most users will prefer the arrow keys, but those who are used to the WordStar editor will recognize that the CTRL key sequences are from that word processor. Therefore, WordStar users may find those sequences more natural.

Extended Movement Commands. Table 7.2 displays another set of cursor-moving commands.

Table 7.1: Basic Movement Commands

Command	Key	Alternate
Character Left	CTRL-S	Left Arrow
Character Right	CTRL-D	Right Arrow
Word Left	CTRL-A	CTRL-Left Arrow
Word Right	CTRL-F	CTRL-Right Arrow
Line Up	CTRL-E	Up Arrow
Line Down	CTRL-X	Down Arrow
Scroll Screen Up	CTRL-W	
Scroll Screen Down	CTRL-Z	
Page Up	CTRL-R	PgUp
Page Down	CTRL-C	PgDn

Table 7.2: Extended Movement Commands

Command	Key	Alternate
Beginning of Line	CTRL-Q, S	HOME
End of Line	CTRL-Q, D	END
Top of Window	CTRL-Q, E	CTRL-HOME
Bottom of Window	CTRL-Q, X	CTRL-END
Top of File	CTRL-Q, R	CTRL-pgup
Bottom of File	CTRL-Q, C	CTRL-pgdn
Beginning of Block	CTRL-Q, B	
End of Block	CTRL-Q, K	
Last Cursor Position	CTRL-Q, P	
Last Error Position	CTRL-Q, W	

The first six commands from Table 7.2 are the most useful. The distinction between top of window and top of file is that the first goes to the top of the currently visible window, while the second goes to the top of the file, even if that means shifting the window. Blocks are discussed below, and it will become clear what CTRL-Q, B and CTRL-Q, K do. Note that these key sequences are obtained by typing CTRL and holding it down while pressing and releasing Q, and then pressing and releasing the second letter. The second letter may be pressed, but does not have to be, while CTRL is held down.

Insert and Delete Commands. Table 7.3 displays the commands for inserting and deleting text. The three commands with alternate keys (INS, BACKSPACE, and DEL) are the most useful of these, but we invite the reader to try the others to see their effect. We remind the reader that INS toggles the Insert/Typeover mode. In Insert mode, old text moves right to make room for new text, while in Typeover mode, old characters are deleted as new characters are entered. Insert mode is the default of the system and is displayed in the Edit window when Turbo Pascal is started. (See Figures 7.1 and 7.2.) Note that Typeover mode is in effect when Insert is not displayed in the Edit window.

Table 7.3: Insert and Delete Commands

Command	Key	Alternate
Insert Mode On/Off	CTRL-V	INS
Insert New Line	CTRL-N	
Delete Line	CTRL-Y	
Delete to End of Line	CTRL-Q, Y	
Delete Character to Left of Cursor	CTRL-H	BACKSPACE
Delete Character Under Cursor	CTRL-G	DEL
Delete Word to Right of Cursor	CTRL-T	

Table 7.4: Block Commands

Command	Key
Mark Block - Begin	CTRL-K, B
Mark Block - End	CTRL-K, K
Mark Single Word	CTRL-K, T
Print Block	CTRL-K, P
Copy Block	CTRL-K, C
Delete Block	CTRL-K, Y
Hide/Display Block	CTRL-K, H
Move Block	CTRL-K, V
Read Block From Disk	CTRL-K, R
Write Block to Disk	CTRL-K, W

Block Commands. None of the block commands shown in Table 7.4 were discussed in Chapter 2, but you should take the time to learn them now, as they provide elegant cut-and-paste functions that allow you to rearrange your program. For example, if you find that you have a procedure or function in the wrong place (or find a segment of code that should be made into a procedure or function), it is very easy, using the block commands, to move the code to another location in your program.

Before anything can be done to a block, it must be marked. Pretend we have seven lines out of place in our program. Move to the top of these lines and type CTRL-K followed by B to mark the beginning of the block. Use cursor-moving keys (seven down arrows in our case) to get to the other end of the block. Press CTRL-K and another K to mark the end of the block. The block will be highlighted on your screen. Now move the cursor to the position where you want to move these lines and press CTRL-K followed by a V. Presto, the lines have been moved for you! However, the lines are still highlighted, but this can be turned off with CTRL-K followed by H.

The difference between copy and move is that after a move you have one copy of the text (in a new place), while after a copy you have two copies of the same text. Use copy if you need a section of code similar to a previous section. After you have two copies, edit the new version to modify it as needed.

Printing, reading, and writing a block all do what they should and we invite the reader to try them. However, in our opinion, **C**opying, mo**V**ing, and **H**iding, along with block **B**egin and bloc**K** end, are the most useful of these commands.

In version 4.0, you can use F7 as a shortcut for CTRL-K, B and F8 as a shortcut for CTRL-K, K. However, in version 5.X, F7 and F8 perform debugging functions discussed below and cannot be used for blocking.

Miscellaneous Commands. The important miscellaneous commands are listed in Table 7.5. We refer the interested reader to the Turbo Pascal manuals for other, more advanced commands.

Table 7.5: Miscellaneous Commands

Command	Key
Find	CTRL-Q, F
Find and Replace	CTRL-Q, A
Language Help	CTRL-F1
Repeat Last Find	CTRL-L

Since it is the simplest, we discuss the Language-Help command first. This command provides information on the Pascal structure that the cursor is currently on. For example, if you forget the exact structure of a While, position the cursor in the While and press CTRL-F1. Remember that this valuable tool is available and use it when you get an error message indicating that you have violated Pascal's syntax rules.

The Find command lets you search for any string of up to 30 characters. When you press CTRL–Q followed by F (for **F**ind), you are prompted by

Find:

to enter the search string. After you do so and press ENTER, you are then prompted by

Options:

The options are:

B   Search **B**ackward from current cursor position
G   Search **G**lobally, stopping at the last occurrence of the string
L   Search **L**ocally, only in the marked block
n   Search for the **n**th occurrence, where **n** is some number
U   Ignore **U**ppercase and lowercase distinctions
W   Search for whole **W**ords only

These options can be combined. For example, B3UW searches backward for the third occurrence of the target string, as a separate word, but without regard to case. If you forget to indicate a word search and you search for "dog," you will stop at "dogma" and "boondoggle." If you give no options, the search will proceed forward for the first occurrence of the target string in the text.

The Repeat-Last-Find and Find-and-Replace commands from Table 7.5 are also useful. If the Find command did not find the correct occurrence of your target string, then Ctrl-L (Repeat Last Find) will repeat the find using the same target string and the same options. Find and Replace is useful for replacing all occurrences of one string by another. This can be used to replace an identifier such as NK by a more meaningful identifier such as NumKids. It can also be used to replace a specific number such as 2.54 with a constant such as CmsPerInch. Find and Replace is used much as Find, except that you are also prompted for a string to replace the target string with. The options as detailed above for the Find command apply, with the addition of one more:

N   Replaces without asking

Without the N option, the system will pause at each occurrence of the target string and ask you if you want to replace it with the second string. With the N option, the system makes all changes without asking. You need to think carefully before you Find and Replace with the N option. For example, if you change all NKs to NumKids with the N option, then words like think and BankBook unexpectedly become thiNumKids and BaNumKidsBook.

As an example of Find and Replace, consider the sequence of commands necessary to change all occurrences of NK into NumKids:

1. Press Ctrl-Q, A to begin the Find and Replace command.
2. To the prompt Find:, type NK and press the ENTER key.
3. To the prompt Replace With:, type NumKids and the ENTER key.
4. To the prompt Options:, type W for a word search and then ENTER.
5. At each occurrence of NK, decide whether you want to replace or not.

The point of the word search in step 4 is to make the system search for the word NK and to avoid finding the string nk in words such as think and bankbook. We invite the reader to use the two options WN and replace all NumKids back to NKs automatically to see the effect that the N option has.

THE FILE MENU

The File menu was discussed extensively in Chapter 2, but for completeness and reference, we review this menu here. Figure 7.3 shows the File menu that is obtained by pressing ALT-F.

Load is used to load a new program into the editor. Normally, it is more convenient to use the F3 shortcut than it is to select this option from the File menu.

Pick displays up to eight of the most recent programs that you have worked on and permits you to pick one of them for loading. **Pick** can be useful when you are working on several programs at once and copying from one to another.

New clears the edit window and gives you a blank page on which to create a new program. **New** will ask, if you haven't saved, if you want to save the current contents of the editor.

```
Load           F3
Pick           ALT-F3
New
Save           F2
Write to
Directory
Change dir
OS shell
Quit           ALT-X
```

Figure 7.3

Save writes the current contents of the editor to the disk using the name supplied in the editor status line. If the name is NONAME.PAS, the user is asked to supply a name. **Save** writes to the disk that Turbo Pascal was started from unless you give directory information in the name or change the directory with the **Change dir** command (see below). You will probably find **Save**'s single-key shortcut (F2) more convenient than bringing down the File menu.

Write to prompts the user for a new name for the current contents of the editor and then writes the program to disk using this new name. If a file with the new name already exists, then the system asks the user if the old file should be overwritten. **Write to** also updates the name in the status line to reflect the new name of the program. Subsequent **Saves** will be made using this new name. **Write to**, in summary, is a save that allows the file to be renamed as it is saved.

Directory displays the files that are stored on a given disk or subdirectory. When you select **Directory**, you are prompted for a mask, which is computerese for a pattern to look for. The mask suggested by the system is *.*, which means to look for any file with any extension. If you press RETURN, you will see the directory of the disk that Turbo Pascal was started from. You can type B:*.* or C:\TP\Samples*.* if you want the directory of another disk or subdirectory. The mask *.Pas will display just the Pascal programs (on the start-up disk), while the mask Z*.* will display all files that begin with the letter Z. As the bottom line shows, once you have a directory, you can get help (F1), enter a new mask (F4), choose a file with the arrow keys, load the selected file with RETURN, or abort (ESC). Abort, as harsh as it sounds, is the proper way to exit from the **Directory** command if you don't want to load any program. Since **Load** permits the same use of wildcards, and displays the same directories, we think you will find **Load** (especially through its shortcut, F3) more convenient than the **Directory** command.

Change dir allows you to select the disk or subdirectory that you want programs saved to or loaded from. As we have mentioned several times, Turbo Pascal always saves to and loads from the start-up disk or subdirectory. To save and load programs that you write on drive B:, choose **Change dir** and then type the new directory B:\ and RETURN.

OS shell permits the user to suspend the Turbo Pascal system, exit to the operating system (DOS), and then return to Turbo Pascal at the point where it was suspended. To return to Turbo Pascal from the operating-system shell, you simply type EXIT.

Quit exits Turbo Pascal and returns the user to the DOS (operating-system) level. **Quit** will prompt the user if the current contents of the editor have not been saved.

THE EDIT MENU

This is the simplest of the menus, as it really isn't a menu at all. All that happens when you type E from the main menu is that you are dropped into the editor. By this we mean that the cursor moves to the edit window, and all of the editing commands apply. (These were discussed in the section entitled The Edit Window.) Don't forget the hot key ALT-E that always take you to the editor from anywhere in Turbo Pascal.

THE RUN MENU

The Run menu is one place where version 4.0 differs from versions 5.0 and 5.5. In version 4.0, when you type R from the main menu, the program in the Edit window is first compiled, if it hasn't already been compiled, and is then run. In version 4.0, the hot key ALT-R will run the program in the editor from anywhere in Turbo Pascal.

In versions 5.0 and 5.5, there is more to the Run menu. Do remember, however, that CTRL–F9 is the hot key that will run your program. When you type R from the main menu, or ALT-R from anywhere, you will see the following list of six options:

```
Run                CTRL-F9
Program reset      CTRL-F2
Go to cursor       F4
Trace into         F7
Step over          F8
User screen        ALT-F5
```

Run is the most important option, but we usually invoke it via its hot-key sequence (CTRL–F9), rather than by taking the time to bring down this menu. As in version 4.0, **R**un includes a compile of the program in the editor, if necessary.

In versions 5.0 and 5.5, **P**rogram reset is necessary if you have interrupted a program during its execution and you want the program to start again from the beginning. If you forget the **P**rogram reset command, the program will simply continue executing from where it was interrupted. A program can be interrupted either by the user typing CTRL-BREAK or by commands of the debugger, which are discussed below. Remember that if you interrupt a program that is in an infinite loop, and forget to reset it, it will resume its infinite loop the next time you try to run it.

User screen displays the execution window for your program. The most convenient way to display this window is via the hot key ALT-F5, introduced in Chapter 2.

Go to cursor, **T**race into, and **S**tep over are all debugging commands. **T**race into and **S**tep over are very similar, and each executes one instruction in your program. This allows you to trace (or step) through your program at human instead of computer speeds. Each displays the statement that is about to be executed in inverse video. The difference between **T**race into and **S**tep over is the way in which they handle user-defined procedures and functions. **T**race into, when it reaches a procedure or function, *traces into* the procedure or function and continues to execute its code line by line. On the other hand, **S**tep over, when it encounters a procedure or function, *steps over* the procedure or function and treats it as a single statement. That is, it executes the procedure or function in full and then halts at the next statement after the procedure or function call. **G**o to cursor resumes execution of your program at computer speed, but only to the point of the cursor. Execution pauses when it reaches the instruction where the cursor is located.

Let us illustrate these various run commands by using them to debug, again, the simple program BuggyAv2 of Listing 7.3, the body of which, for convenience, is repeated as Listing 7.10.

```
Begin
  Assign(Input, 'A:\Ch7\Quizzes.Txt');
  Reset(Input);
  Count := 0;
  Sum := 0;
  While Not Eof Do
    Readln(Score);
    Sum := Sum + Score;
    Count := Count + 1;
  Writeln('The average was ', (Sum/Count):5:2)
End.
```

Listing 7.10

Press the F7 (**T**race into) key six times and watch as the `Begin` and subsequent lines up to the `While` are highlighted. Remember that it is the line that is highlighted that is *about* to be executed. Now, press the F7 key another half dozen times. Notice that the highlighting flashes back and forth between the `While` and the `Readln`, showing us beyond a shadow of a doubt that only the `Readln` is in the body of the `While`. Thus, just by using **T**race into, we have seen that the flow of the program is not what we had intended. Students can stare at Listing 7.10 forever without seeing that the problem is that the body of the `While` is not correct. We humans quickly grasp what was intended, but often fail to see what is actually stated. With the capability of tracing, the student is able to see the problem graphically. Even in this very simple situation, the trace capability is impressive.

Let us pretend that this is a large program and that, because of the program's behavior, we suspect the `While` loop is the problem. However, we do not want to single step through the long program until we get down to the `While`. This is a situation where **G**o to cursor is very useful. First, reset the program with a CTRL-F2. This is necessary to restart the program from the top. Before we run the program, place the cursor anywhere inside the word `While`. Then press F4 (**G**o to cursor). This causes your program to execute from the top down to the position of the cursor. That is, all the initializations (all four of them in this trivial case) are done without the need of your single stepping through the execution. The program is suspended at the point where we want to take a look at it. By pressing F7, we single step through the `While`, and it is again obvious that the `Readln` is the only statement in the body of the `While`.

Finally, reset the program again (CTRL-F2) and then add the `Begin` and `End` that are needed to enclose the three statements in the body of the `While`. Now trace through the program so that you can graphically see how the flow has changed.

We add many other capabilities for debugging below, but remember that tracing the flow of execution at critical points in your programs can be very useful when a program does not behave as intended.

THE COMPILE MENU

In any of the versions, typing C from the main menu or ALT-C from anywhere will bring down the following menu of seven options:

```
Compile          ALT-F9
Make             F9
Build
Destination      Memory
Find error
Primary file:
Get info
```

   Many of these options are advanced features that the beginner need not be concerned with. We will briefly discuss the two most useful options, Compile and **D**estination, and leave the rest of the details to the Turbo Pascal reference manuals.

   Compile, as you might guess, compiles your program but does not run it. Since **R**un includes Compile, we seldom need Compile by itself. One situation in which we do need to compile without running is described in Chapter 20 (separate compilation in Turbo Pascal). Basically, separate compilation allows us to break a large program into several pieces and then compile each of the pieces by itself. The advantages of separate compilation and an explicit example are given in Chapter 20.

   Destination determines where the compiled form of your program will be stored. The two possibilities are Memory and Disk. Memory is the default of the system, and this means that the executable form of your program is stored in the memory of the computer. Hence, it is lost when the computer is turned off or another program is compiled. Since the Turbo Pascal compiler is so fast, this is not usually a problem, as we still have our .Pas file and can easily recompile it. If you change the **D**estination setting to Disk, then the executable form of your program will be saved to your disk with the .Exe extension. That is, if you compile HamBurr.Pas with the disk as the destination, then afterward you will see both HamBurr.Pas and HamBurr.Exe listed on your disk. The advantage of having the .Exe version is that it can be executed from DOS without the Turbo Pascal system disks. For example, to execute HamBurr.Exe, you just type HamBurr at the DOS prompt. Also realize that the .Exe file is the compiled version of your program and the user cannot list it or modify it. Therefore, the user cannot pry into the details of your program to mess with it or see how it works.

   To change the destination for a compile, simply bring down the Compile menu with ALT-C and then press D until the menu displays your choice. That is, each successive D toggles the setting back and forth between Memory and Disk. Press ESC to get the Compile menu to disappear.

THE OPTIONS MENU

The Options menu contains many advanced features that allow you to control the way the compiler performs as well as the total environment in which Turbo Pascal operates. Most of these features are not needed by the beginner, so we omit a discussion of this menu. The interested reader is referred to the Turbo Pascal manuals for the details.

THE DEBUG MENU

The Debug menu is available only in versions 5.0 and 5.5 and its options apply only if you currently have a program in suspended execution. That is, they apply only if you are debugging a program. Here, we briefly describe the options and then, in the final section of this chapter, we illustrate the most useful of the options with another debugging example.

Choosing D from the main menu or an ALT-D from anywhere displays the options of the Debug menu:

```
Evaluate                CTRL-F4
Call stack              CTRL-F3
Find procedure
Integrated debugging    On
Stand-alone debugging   Off
Display swapping        Smart
Refresh display
```

Evaluate allows you to evaluate any identifier or expression. For example, you can evaluate Count or Sum/100 in the middle of your program. **E**valuate even lets you change the value assigned to an identifier. This can be useful if you wish to test your program with a special set of values. Note that the hot key for **E**valuate is CTRL-F4.

Call stack, when a program has been suspended, will show the current stack of procedure and function calls. That is, it shows the sequence of currently unfinished procedures and functions and who has called whom.

Find procedure, in debug mode, prompts you to enter the name of a procedure or function and then moves the cursor to the first executable line of the body of that procedure or function. This is useful in conjunction with the **G**o-to-cursor command of the Run menu. By first using **F**ind procedure and then **G**o to cursor, you can execute your program to the first line of any procedure or function that you want to investigate further.

Integrated debugging, which enables the features we are discussing, comes turned on and should normally stay that way. If you have a very large program and not enough memory in your computer to compile it, you could possibly save enough memory to compile your program by turning the debugging features off.

Stand-alone debugging, **D**isplay swapping, and **R**efresh display are advanced features that the beginner need not be concerned about. The interested reader should consult the Turbo Pascal reference manuals.

THE BREAK/WATCH MENU

The Break/Watch menu is also available only in versions 5.0 and 5.5 and, again, these commands apply only to a program whose execution has been suspended by a debugging command.

Pressing B from the main menu, or ALT-B from anywhere, provides you with the following menu of options:

```
Add watch                CTRL-F7
Delete watch
Edit watch
Remove all watches
Toggle breakpoint        CTRL-F8
Clear all breakpoints
View next breakpoint
```

Add watch allows you to add an identifier or an expression to the Watch window, which permits you to view the current value of that variable or expression. Furthermore, every time your program's execution is suspended, the updated value of the identifier or expression is displayed. Suppose you have an identifier Result that is printing an incorrect value. Then, by adding Result to the Watch window and by suspending the execution of your program at various points, you can observe intermediate values of Result in hope of determining where the calculation goes astray. Note that CTRL-F7 is the hot key for **A**dd watch. Furthermore, if the cursor is in the identifier that you want added to the Watch window when you press CTRL-F7, you will not even have to type the identifier, as it will be supplied by the system. We give an example of the use of watches in the final section of the chapter.

Delete watch deletes the expression in the Watch window at the current position of the cursor. **E**dit watch allows you to change an expression in the Watch window, while **R**emove all watches deletes all current watch expressions.

A breakpoint is simply a line in your program at which the program always stops, allowing you to watch or evaluate the execution of your program. When you run your program with CTRL-F9, it runs until a breakpoint is reached or until the program's execution is completed. A breakpoint in a While, for example, is a very good way to debug a loop that is not executing properly. Each time the line with the breakpoint is reached, execution is suspended, allowing you to inspect the progress of the program. Breakpoints are set and deleted with the **T**oggle-breakpoint command. That is, **T**oggle breakpoint sets a breakpoint on a line if none is present and deletes a breakpoint if one had already been set for that line. A line that contains a breakpoint is displayed in a different color (or brightness) on the monitor. **T**oggle breakpoint is a very important debugging command, and its usefulness is described in the final example of the chapter.

Clear all breakpoints removes all the breakpoints. Removing all the breakpoints is necessary after your program has been debugged to allow it to execute normally. **V**iew next breakpoint displays the next breakpoint in the program, but does not execute the program to that point.

AN EXAMPLE ILLUSTRATING THE INTEGRATED DEBUGGER

As an example of the debugging techiniques that we have been discussing, consider the buggy program, BuggyMx2, of Listing 7.11.

Recall that the data in the text file Quizzes2.Txt are

F87
M76

F92
M82
M56
M79
F83
M72

When BuggyMx2 runs, it produces the following output:

```
The male maximum was    -1
The female maximum was 92
```

Since all the scores in the text file Quizzes2.Txt are positive, there is clearly a problem with BuggyMx2. We will use the debugging feautes of Turbo Pascal to debug the program. We urge the reader to turn on his or her computer and follow our discussion, step by step, on the computer.

To monitor the program more closely, we will insert some breakpoints and watches into the program. A good strategy for placing breakpoints in a loop is to put one near

```pascal
Program BuggyMx2;
{This program tries to find the highest male and female scores from
the text file Quizzes2.Txt. Each line of Quizzes2 contains a
character ('M' or 'F') followed by an integer quiz score.      }

Var    Sex     : Char;
       Score   : Integer;
       MaleMax : Integer;
       FemMax  : Integer;

Begin
  Assign(Input, 'A:\Ch7\Quizzes2.Txt');
  Reset(Input);
  MaleMax := -1;      {Initialize MaleMax to a ridiculous value.}
  FemMax := -1;                            {Likewise for FemMax.}
  While Not Eof Do
    Begin
      Readln(Sex, Score);
      If (Sex = 'm' ) And (Score > MaleMax) Then    {Male case.}
        MaleMax := Score
      Else                                        {Female case.}
        If Score > FemMax Then
          FemMax := Score
    End; {While}
  Writeln('The male maximum was    ', MaleMax);
  Writeln('The female maximum was ', FemMax)
End.
```

Listing 7.11

the top and one near the bottom of the loop. This permits us to examine critical values before and after each execution of the loop's body. Remember that a breakpoint on a line stops execution just before the execution of that line. Thus, we often put a breakpoint on the instruction just after a critical instruction in our program. For example, if we put a breakpoint on the If in the body of the While, then our program will halt after each execution of the Readln. This will allow us to examine the values of Sex and Score just after they have been read from the text file. If we also put a breakpoint on the End of the While, then our program will suspend its execution after completing the body of the While. These two breakpoints permit us to see what the While has done on one execution of its body to whatever data we are viewing.

Therefore, we set two breakpoints as follows:

Step 1. With the cursor anywhere on the line containing the If, press CTRL-F8 to set a breakpoint on that line.

Step 2. Move the cursor to the End statement at the bottom of the While and press CTRL-F8 again to set the second breakpoint at the bottom of the While.

The program, when run, will suspend its execution at each breakpoint. We now use the Watch window to see the values of the program's key identifiers as the program executes. Let us agree that we would like to watch the values of Sex, Score, MaleMax, and FemMax. These can be added to the Watch window as follows:

Step 3. With the cursor anywhere inside the identifier Sex, press CTRL-F7 followed by RETURN to add Sex to the Watch window.

Step 4. Likewise, place the cursor anywhere in Score, MaleMax, and FemMax and then press CTRL-F7 followed by RETURN to add each to the Watch window.

It is not necessary that the cursor be on the identifier when you press CTRL-F7, but if it is, then the system will display the identifier for you and you do not have to type it yourself.

At this point, the Watch window will have grown a little so that your four identifiers are displayed in it, each with their final value from your run of the program. We are now ready to run the program again and view it as it executes:

Step 5. Press CTRL-F9 to run your program to the first breakpoint. Observe that the If statement is shown in inverse video to indicate that it is the line where the breakpoint occurred. Observe that the values in the Watch window are as follows:

```
FemMax: -1
MaleMax: -1
Score: 87
Sex: 'F'
```

Realize that these are the correct values for the program, since it has just initialized the two maxima and read the first line of the text file.

Step 6. Press CTRL-F9 to run your program to the next breakpoint. The program suspends execution at the bottom of the While and the Watch window shows

```
FemMax: 87
MaleMax: -1
Score: 87
Sex: 'F'
```

Again, check that these results are as expected, since the first data item is for a female, and her score is the biggest seen so far.

Step 7. Press CTRL-F9 again to run the program to the next breakpoint. Observe that the Watch window correctly shows the situation after the second individual's data item has been read and before it has been processed:

```
FemMax: 87
MaleMax: -1
Score: 76
Sex: 'M'
```

Step 8. Press CTRL-F9 yet again to let the program proceed to the bottom of the loop. This time, the Watch window shows the same values as in the step above. Wait a minute—the male's 76 should have been processed and should be the new value of MaleMax. How can MaleMax still be -1?

To answer that question, we will repeat the execution of the program to the point where it starts to go sour. Then we will trace the program, step by step, from that point.

Step 9. Press CTRL-F2 to reset the program, so that it begins all over, and then press CTRL-F9 three times to get to the point where the female's 87 has been read and processed and the male's score of 76 has just been read in. (Step 7 above.)

Step 10. At this point, if we trace the code ourselves, it seems that the male, since his Score is bigger than the current value of MaleMax, should have his Score replace the old value of MaleMax. That is, we expect the Then part of the If to be executed. To find out what really happens, press F7 to trace one step in the program. To our surprise, the program jumps down to the Else clause and prepares to do the inner If comparing the male's score with the FemMax.

For some reason, the condition (Sex = 'm') And (Score > MaleMax) must have evaluated as False. Let's use the Evaluate feature to check this out.

Step 11. Press CTRL-F4 and you will see a box with three parts, labeled Evaluate, Result, and New value. In the Evaluate box, very carefully type exactly the first part of the condition:

```
Sex = 'm'
```

When you press RETURN, the system evaluates this expression and FALSE is displayed in the Result box. How can that be? After all, the Watch window shows that the current value of Sex is 'M'. Why isn't it TRUE that Sex is equal to 'm'?

Hopefully, you now see that, by mistake, we are comparing an uppercase 'M', which is the way the data are supplied on the text file, with a lowercase 'm' in the program. Since these are different, the condition is always FALSE, and MaleMax never changes from its initial value of -1.

Step 12. Press ESC to make the Evaluate box disappear and then change the 'm' to an 'M'. Now reset the program (CTRL-F2) and then watch the execution with repeated CTRL–F9s. This time, the male case is handled properly and our program has been debugged. (We think!)

Step 13. As the final step, you should try your program without the debugging features. To do this, it is necessary to clear all breakpoints (ALT-B, C) and remove all watches (ALT-B, R). These steps are also necessary before you try to run another program in the editor. Finally, reset the program (CTRL-F2) one last time to make sure it executes from the beginning, and run the program at full speed with CTRL-F9.

Actually, BuggyMx2 still contains a subtle bug that shows up only when certain data are in a certain order. We leave the final debugging of BuggyMx2 to the reader in the exercises.

Our example has been a simple one, but we hope that it has shown you the power of the built-in debugging tools. Learn to use them to your advantage. Since these tools are scattered throughout the Run, Debug, and Break/Watch menus, we have gathered the most useful of them in Table 7. 6, for your reference. Don't memorize this table, but familiarize yourself with the possibilities and return to the table when you have a program that needs debugging.

SUMMARY

This focus of this chapter is different from the focus of most of the chapters in this book. New Pascal constructs are introduced in most of the chapters, and then the kind of problems that one can solve with those constructs is illustrated. This chapter introduces no new Pascal constructs, but we would argue that this is one of the most important chapters in the book. That is because this chapter is about the problem-solving process. Knowing the syntax of a While is critical to writing a program, but such knowledge does you absolutely no good if you have no idea what you want to write. The interesting (and challenging) part of problem solving is in designing the algorithm that solves the problem. With a well-designed algorithm, the final implementation in Pascal ought to proceed quickly. Hence, we urge the reader to study the step-by-step process outlined in this chapter for approaching a problem. We also urge the reader to study carefully the lengthy Hamilton and Burr example that is worked out in considerable detail.

Since we are only human, bugs will appear in our programs. Carefully study our examples and learn to debug your programs. Debugging skills must be practiced just

Table 7.6: Useful Turbo Pascal Debugging Commands

Key(s)	Name	Action
CTRL-F9	Run	Executes the program from its current position to the next breakpoint or to the end of the program.
CTRL-F2	Program reset	Resets the program so that its next execution begins from the beginning of the program.
F4	Go to cursor	Executes the program from its current position to the location of the cursor.
F7	Trace into	Executes one instruction and continues into procedures and functions in the same manner.
F8	Step over	Executes one instruction and treats a procedure or function call as a single instruction.
CTRL-F4	Evaluate	Brings down a box where you can evaluate any identifier or expression in your program. Identifiers can even be assigned new values.
CTRL-F7	Add watch	Inserts a new identifier or expression in the Watch window.
CTRL-F8	Toggle breakpoint	Sets or clears a breakpoint on the line the cursor is currently on.
ALT-B, C	Clear all breakpoints	Removes all breakpoints. This must be done at the end of the debugging session.
ALT-B, R	Remove watches	Removes all identifiers and expressions from the Watch window. This must be done at the end of the debugging session.

like other skills. That is one reason that this text has many intentionally buggy programs in the exercises. If you have one of the newer versions of Turbo Pascal, learn to use the built-in debugging techniques. They are very powerful and useful, but realize that people have been debugging programs for nearly 50 years without these built-in tools. If you are using Turbo Pascal 4.0, you are *not* excused from debugging your programs.

KEYWORDS

As a check of your understanding, be sure that you can define or describe each of the following terms:

Problem specification	Algorithm
Debugging	Bench testing
Documentation	Local documentation
Global documentation	Procedural documentation
Preconditions	Postconditions

SELF-TEST QUESTIONS

7.1 What is an example of a Pascal syntax question? Why are we concerned with syntax at all?

7.2 What is our course objective, if not to learn Pascal syntax?

7.3 How do preconditions and postconditions aid in debugging procedures and functions?

EXERCISES

7.4 Describe in your own words the student's responsibility at each stage of the problem-solving process.

7.5 Why does executing data by hand help you to understand a problem and design an algorithm for it?

7.6 What are the advantages of using pseudo-code instead of just writing Pascal to begin with?

7.7 Describe the top-down design process. What are stepwise refinements?

7.8 Describe three debugging techniques.

7.9 Distinguish between local, global, and procedural comments. Give an example or two of each kind.

7.10 Modify the program `HamBurr` of the text as follows:

a) Simulate 1000 duels. (Does the duel seem to be fair to Hamilton and Burr?)

b) Assume that two-fifths of the time, on the average, when a person is hit he is only slightly wounded and is able to continue, but at only at 50 percent of his previous accuracy. Assume that on the second hit the individual is killed.

Simulate 100 duels with these new rules. Is the duel still fair? What happens to the average length of a duel?

c) Modify part b) to simulate 1000 duels and, in addition, print out how many times each was wounded but then went ahead to win the duel.

7.11 (This problem requires some mathematical knowledge.)

a) In the original duel, find the probability that Burr wins after one and three shots, respectively. Find the probability that Hamilton wins in two and four shots, respectively. Argue that the duel is fair.

b) Argue that the expected length of a duel is given by the following (incomplete) summation:

$$1 * 1/3 + 2 * 1/3 + 3 * 1/9 + 4 *...$$

Add three or four more terms to this series and show that the expected length of a duel is 2.45 shots.

7.12 The following program, BuggyMx3, appears to be the final solution to the BuggyMax program of the text. Yet its behavior is exactly like that of BuggyMax. Can you find the rather subtle bug?

```
Program BuggyMx3;
{This program, like BuggyMax, tries to find the highest male
and female scores from the text file Quizzes2.Txt. Each line
of Quizzes2 contains a character ('M' or 'F') followed by an
integer quiz score.                                           }
Var    Sex     : Char;
       Score   : Integer;
       MaleMax : Integer;
       FemMax  : Integer;

Begin
  Assign(Input, 'A:\Ch7\Quizzes2.Txt');
  Reset(Input);
  MaleMax := -1;
  FemMax := -1;
  While Not Eof Do
    Begin
      Readln(Sex, Score);
      If Sex = 'M' Then                        {Male case.}
        If Score > MaleMax Then
          MaleMax := Score
        Else                                   {Do nothing.)
      Else                                     {Female case.}
```

```
      If Score > FemMax Then
         FemMax := Score
    End; {While}
  Writeln('The male maximum was   ', MaleMax);
  Writeln('The female maximum was ', FemMax)
End.
```

7.13 The following program contains several bugs. Its objective is to read the following simple text file until it finds the trailer value 'BULLMOOSE', determining student averages on two quizzes as it goes. It should also print class averages for both quizzes. Play computer and debug the program.

Here are the contents of the text file People.Txt:

```
David Haines
98 65
Rachel Hertel
97 72
Tek Nology
88 45
BULLMOOSE
```

Here is the program BugQuiz:

```
Program BugQuiz;
{This program tries to read People.Txt and print averages for
each student as well as determine class averages on each quiz.}

Var    Name          : String[30];
       Quiz1, Quiz2  : Integer;
       Total1, Total2 : Integer;
       Count         : Integer;

Begin
  Assign(Input, 'A:\Ch7\People.Txt');
  Reset(Input);
  Count := 1;
  Readln(Name);
  While Name <> 'Bullmoose' Do
    Count := Count + 1;
    Writeln(Name, ' your average is ',
                              ((Quiz1 + Quiz2)/2):5:2);
    Total1 := Total1 + Quiz1;
    Total2 := Total1 + Quiz2;
  Writeln;
  Writeln('The class average on quiz 1 was ',
                                  (Total1/Count):5:2);
  Writeln('The class average on quiz 2 was ',
                                  (Total2/Count):5:2)
End.
```

7.14 As mentioned, BuggyMx2 from the text still contains a subtle bug. In particular, for some reorderings of the following three-line data file, the program will produce incorrect results.

```
F 80
M 90
M 100
```

Verify that the program works for the data shown above. Try the same data in different orders until the program misbehaves. Complete the debugging of BuggyMx2.

ANSWERS TO SELF-TEST QUESTIONS

7.1 Are characters enclosed in single quotes ('X') or in double quotes ("X")? We are interested in syntax questions because if we don't get Pascal's syntax correct, our programs will not run.

7.2 Pascal syntax, by itself, is not very interesting or of much real importance. Our objective is to learn to use the computer to solve problems. We must be concerned with Pascal syntax in order to get our programs to run, but the more interesting (and difficult) question is how do we, in principle, solve our given problem. Only when we have devised an algorithm that solves our problem do we enter the implementation phase where Pascal's syntax becomes an issue.

7.3 The preconditions state what must hold before the procedure or function can be held responsible for the results. By checking the preconditions at the time of the call, we can help to locate the problem. If the preconditions hold and the postconditions don't, then the procedure or function is not performing up to its contract and must be debugged. In addition, postconditions remind us that certain parameters should be variable parameters. As this is easily forgotten by beginners, postconditions can help in debugging by reminding us to check for the appropriate variable parameters.

8

MORE CONTROL STRUCTURES

In Chapter 5, the `While` and the `If` were introduced for repetitions and selections, respectively. Here, we introduce two new repetitive statements and an additional statement for selections. These statements add no new power to the language, but they often do allow a more natural expression of algorithms.

THE REPEAT...UNTIL

It is common to want to *repeat* some group of statements *until* some property becomes true. Because this is often a useful way to view a problem, Pascal provides a `Repeat...Until` statement. Its syntax is

```
Repeat
   Statement;
   Statement;
   . . .
   . . .
   . . .
   Statement
Until Boolean expression;
```

The `Repeat...Until` is one statement. Those statements caught between the `Repeat` and the `Until` are called the **body** of the `Repeat...Until`. Note that a `Repeat...Until` never needs a `Begin` or an `End` to enclose its body. Also, observe that no semicolon is needed after the last statement in the body. There is a semicolon after the Boolean expression if another statement follows the `Repeat...Until`. When execution reaches the `Repeat`, the statements in the body are executed once, and then the Boolean expression is evaluated. If it is `False`, then the body is executed again. After each execution of the body, the Boolean expression is evaluated. If it is ever found to be `True`, the flow of control passes to the statement following the `Repeat...Until`.

To provide an example where the `Repeat...Until` is the appropriate control structure, we need the following fact: The series $1 + 1/2 + 1/3 + 1/4 + 1/5 + \ldots$ eventually exceeds any given value. That is, if you add enough terms of this series, you will eventually get a sum greater than one million. Our next program answers the burning question, "How many terms are needed to exceed 6.0?" This is a nice example for the `Repeat...Until`, for this time we have no idea how many times we should repeat the loop. Indeed, that is our question. But we can provide the answer by counting terms *until* our sum exceeds 6.0. Here, then, is the pseudo-code for this simple problem:

> Initialize Sum to 0
> Initialize a counter, Count, to 0
> Initialize Term to 1
> Repeat
>   Increment Count
>   Add the Term to the Sum
>   Compute the next Term
> Until the Sum exceeds 6.0
> Output the value of Count

While the above pseudo-code could be implemented, we do not do so. Rather, we make some changes to it that make the program much easier to write. The point of this exercise is that time spent in planning a program is often time well spent. As we have discussed extensively in the previous chapter, you should not dive into the writing of the program without having carefully considered the problem. Doing so only leads to a very complex program that is very difficult to get to run correctly. The observation that we would like to make about the current problem is that there is a very definite relationship between the value of `Count`, the counter of the terms, and `Term`, the current term. For example, the third term is 1/3, the eighth term is 1/8, etc. Hence, we do not need two different variables for `Term` and `Count`. `Term`, for example, can be obtained from `Count`. Here is a second, simpler, and more specific pseudo-code from which the program `Series` can easily be written:

> Initialize Sum and Count to 0
> Repeat
>   Increment Count
>   Add the reciprocal of Count to Sum
> Until the Sum exceeds 6.0
> Output the value of Count

The reader should play computer and trace the above to see how `Sum` takes the values 1.0, 1.5, 1.83333, 2.08333, etc., as `Count` takes on the values 1, 2, 3, 4, etc. In Listing 8.1, we have moved the `Writeln` into the body of the loop. This does not change the result, but gives us output to watch as the program runs.

```
Program Series;
{This program sums the series 1 + 1/2 + 1/3 + 1/4 + 1/5 ... until
the sum exceeds 6.0. It counts the number of terms needed to reach
6.0.                                                                  }

Var    Sum   : Real;
       Count : Integer;

Begin
  Sum := 0.0;
  Count := 0;
  Repeat
    Count := Count + 1;
    Sum := Sum + 1/Count;
    Writeln('The sum after ', Count:3, ' terms is ', Sum:8:6)
  Until Sum > 6.0     {Sum is the sum of the first Count terms.}
End.
```

Listing 8.1

Note the loop invariant shown as a comment. Clearly, this assertion is true before the loop, as no terms of the series have been summed. It is also clear on each loop iteration, because we add one to Count and one more term to Sum on each iteration. Since we exit the loop as soon as the Sum exceeds 6.0, we see that the program does indeed answer our original question. The reader is invited to make a guess as to how many terms are needed before the series exceeds 6.0, then run Series to see how far off the guess was.

REPEAT VS. WHILE

There are many instances where either a While or a Repeat...Until can be used. It is often a matter of programming convenience where you choose whichever fits the given situation better. Actually, the While is slightly more general than the Repeat...Until. Make sure that you understand the slight differences between them. Both are tools that are very important to your understanding of Pascal.

How do the While and Repeat...Until differ? The While tests the Boolean expression at the top of the loop, and the Repeat...Until tests the Boolean expression at the bottom of the loop. As a consequence, the Repeat...Until always executes the body of the loop at least once—even if the condition is initially True. The While, on the other hand, if the condition is initially False, will execute the body of the loop zero times and then continue with the next statement in your program. Fortunately, from the syntax of the Repeat...Until and the While, it is easy to remember which tests the Boolean expression where. Soon, we'll give an example of a situation where we might wish to execute some loop zero times. Hence, it is the While that is slightly more flexible than the Repeat...Until.

Another difference between these two statements is that the While loops *while* the expression is True and the Repeat...Until loops *until* the expression is True. Or, if you like to view things perversely: The While loops *until* the expression becomes False and the Repeat...Until loops *while* the expression is False.

Our next example illustrates a situation in which a While loop is more appropriate than a Repeat...Until loop. Suppose the Div instruction is broken on your computer. How could you live without it? Well, remember that X Div Y answers the question: How many Ys are there in X? A method (admittedly slow) of finding the answer is to use repeated subtraction. That is, 19 Div 5 is 3, since 19 - 5 = 14, 14 - 5 = 9, and 9 – 5 = 4. That is, we subtracted 5 from 19 *three* times before we obtained a remainder less than 5. This seems like an ideal situation for a Repeat...Until. We simply subtract Ys from X and remember how many Ys we subtract, until we get a remainder less than Y. The program Division of Listing 8.2 implements this algorithm to compute X Div Y. Note the use of a temporary variable, Temp, to avoid changing the value of the variable Dividend. Recall from fourth grade that the dividend is the number on the inside of the box that you divide into, and the divisor is the number on the outside that you divide the dividend by. However, the program Division of Listing 8.2 contains a subtle logical error. Can you spot it?

```
Program Division;
{This program illustrates that a Repeat...Until is not always as
appropriate as a While. The program does division by repeated
subtraction, but has a small bug in it. Can you find it?        }

Var    Divisor   : Integer;
       Dividend  : Integer;
       Quotient  : Integer;
       Temp      : Integer;
Begin
  Writeln('I will do division by repeated subtraction.');
  Write('Enter the divisor (the number on the outside): ');
  Readln(Divisor);
  Write('Enter the dividend (the number on the inside): ');
  Readln(Dividend);
  Temp := Dividend;                      {Make a copy of the Dividend.}
  Quotient := 0;
  Repeat
    Temp := Temp - Divisor;
    Quotient := Quotient + 1
  Until Temp < Divisor;
  Writeln(Dividend, ' Div ', Divisor , ' is ', Quotient)
End.
```

Listing 8.2

Consider output from various runs of the program `Division`:

```
19 Div 5 is 3
4 Div 9 is 1
10 Div 7 is 1
3 Div 11 is 1
```

Wait a minute! 4 `Div` 9 is 0, not 1. Likewise, 3 `Div` 11 is 0. The program produces correct output for X `Div` Y if X ≥ Y, but it produces the answer 1, not 0, if X < Y. The reason for this, of course, is that the body of any `Repeat...Until` is executed at least once, even if the condition (in this case, `Temp < Divisor`) is already true. What is needed is a `While` loop that executes *zero* times if the dividend is less than the divisor. The details of the conversion to a `While` loop are left to the reader as an exercise.

THE FOR STATEMENT

The final repetitive statement in Pascal is the `For`, which is useful if you know in advance how many times you would like a loop to be executed. The `For` is often referred to as a definite loop, as opposed to indefinite loops like the `While` and the `Repeat...Until`. The first format of the `For` loop is

```
For IndexVariable := Initial To Final Do
  Statement;
```

where, for now, the `IndexVariable` must be an integer or character identifier and `Initial` and `Final` are variables, constants, or expressions of the same type. For example, a counted loop that is to execute 10 times can be generated by

```
For Count := 1 To 10 Do
  Statement;
```

where, of course, `Count` is an integer identifier and `Statement` may be compound. A loop that is to print the letters of the alphabet can be generated by

```
For Letter := 'A' To 'Z' Do
  Writeln(Letter);
```

where `Letter` is a Char identifier.

Listing 8.3 shows a simple program, `TableFor`, that produces a table of the squares and cubes of the first 20 integers.

```
Program TableFor;
{This program prints squares and cubes of the integers from 1 to
20.                                                                   }

Var    Number : Integer;
       Square : Integer;
       Cube   : Integer;

Begin
  Writeln('Handy dandy table of squares and cubes.');
  Writeln;
  Writeln('Number':10, 'Square':10, 'Cube':10);
  Writeln;
  For Number := 1 To 20 Do
    Begin
      Square := Number * Number;
      Cube := Number * Square;
      Writeln(Number:10, Square:10, Cube:10)
    End {For}
End.
```

Listing 8.3

Notice that several of the parts of the loop are performed automatically by the For. For example, in the above program, when execution reaches the For, Number is automatically initialized to the beginning value 1. Also, before each execution of the body of the loop, the system tests to see if Number has exceeded the final value of 20. Moreover, after each execution of the body, the system automatically increments the index variable Number by 1. Hence, all four parts of a loop are present, but no longer is each the responsibility of the programmer. Notice that since the test is made before the loop is executed, it is possible for a For loop to execute zero times. Thus, although fairly dumb, the statement

```
For I := 5 To 1 Do
  Statement;
```

is not an error. In this case, the statement following the Do is not executed and control passes to the next statement in your program.

Very often, the final value of the index is given as a variable. For example, if we know that a student has taken NumQuiz quizzes, then we can read and sum those quizzes from a line of data with

```
. . .
For Count := 1 To NumQuiz Do
  Begin
    Read(Score);
    Sum := Sum + Score
  End; {For}
Readln;                        {Advance pointer to next line of data.}
```

As another example of the `For` statement, consider a program that prints a table of U.S. dollar-to-German mark conversions, with the user selecting the initial and final dollar values. Here is a pseudo-code outline:

Obtain starting dollar value, Start, and final dollar value, Stop
Output a heading for the Table
For Dollar from starting value to stopping value do
    Convert Dollar to German Marks
    Output Dollar and Mark values

Of course, to convert dollars to DM (Deutsche Mark), we need to know the conversion rate. Let us assume that it is 1.8389; i.e., each dollar is worth 1.8389 DM. The program given in Listing 8.4 is again a direct translation of the pseudo-code.

```
Program DollarDM;
{This program uses a For to create a table of Dollar-to-DM
conversions where the user inputs the starting and ending values.}

Const Rate = 1.8389; {One dollar is worth 1.8389 German Marks.}

Var    Dollar : Integer;
       DM     : Real;
       Start  : Integer;
       Stop   : Integer;

Begin
  Writeln('This program converts US Dollars to German DM.');
  Writeln;
  Write('Enter starting dollar value for the table -> ');
  Readln(Start);
  Write('Enter ending dollar value for the table -> ');
  Readln(Stop);
  Writeln;
  Writeln('Table of Conversions');
  Writeln;
  Writeln('Dollar':10, 'DM':10);
  Writeln;
  For Dollar := Start To Stop Do
    Begin
      DM := Dollar * Rate;
      Writeln(Dollar:8, DM:14:2)
    End {For}
End.
```

Listing 8.4

You should run `DollarDM` several times, including once where you enter a smaller final value than initial value.

There is an alternative form of the `For` that is useful if you need to run a loop backward. Its format is

```
For IndexVariable := Initial DownTo Final Do
  Statement
```

This time, the `IndexVariable` is initialized to the `Initial` value and the body is executed if the index variable is not *smaller* than the `Final` value. Also, after each execution of the body, the index variable is *decremented* by 1. Here is a segment that sings a famous college song:

```
...
For Verse := 100 DownTo 1 Do
  Begin
    Writeln(Verse, ' bottles of beer on the wall.');
    Writeln(Verse, 'bottles of beer.');
    Writeln('Take one down, pass it around');
    Writeln(Verse - 1, ' bottles of beer on the wall.');
    Writeln
  End; {For}
```

Remember, for now, that the `IndexVariable` in a `For` can be either integer or character, but not string or real. The reason for this restriction should, upon reflection, be clear. The `For` automatically increments (or decrements in a `DownTo` loop) the `IndexVariable` after each repetition and, hence, it must be obvious what the next value of the `IndexVariable` is. For integers and characters, there is always a unique next value. For example, the computer knows that 17 follows 16 and that `'Q'` follows `'P'`. But it doesn't make sense to speak of the next real number after 3.14159 or the next string after `'Pascal'`. Types like integer and character, where there is always a next and a previous value (except for the last and first values, respectively), are called **ordinal** types. Much more will be said about ordinal types in Chapter 10.

THE CASE STATEMENT

Pascal provides a `Case` statement that is useful when you have to choose one of many possibilities. For example, to make a six-way decision, one can use five nested `If...Then...Else` statements, but a `Case` statement is probably easier. For example, suppose we have given scores between 0 and 5 on a programming assignment and would like to make an appropriate comment to each student. Suppose for this segment that `Name` already has a string value and `Score` already has an integer value between 0 and 5. The following segment prints the appropriate messages:

```
...
Write(Name, ', your work is ');
Case Score Of
  5: Writeln('outstanding! !');
  4: Writeln('good.');
  3: Writeln('OK.');
  2: Writeln('barely passing.');
  1: Writeln('failing.');
  0: Writeln('hopeless.')
End; {Case}
```

When execution reaches the Case, the value of Score is matched with one of the labels, and the Writeln corresponding to that label is executed. For example, if Name is 'Neal Lee Perfect' and Score is 4, then the output is

```
Neal Lee Perfect, your work is good.
```

On the other hand, if the Name is 'Prokras Tonater' and the Score is 0, then the output is

```
Prokras Tonater, your work is hopeless.
```

Notice how the Write (and not Writeln) is used to write the first part of the line. As with Ifs, the Write should not be repeated in each case.

The syntax of the simple Case statement is

```
Case Index Of
  Value1  :  Statement1;
  Value2  :  Statement2;
  .  .  .
  .  .  .
  ValueN  :  StatementN
End; {Case}
```

Of course, if any of the cases are compound, then Begins and Ends are necessary. For the present, Index must be an integer or character identifier and Value1 to ValueN must be distinct *constants* of the same type, called the **case labels**. At execution, the value of the **case index**, Index, is compared with the labels and, if a match is found, the corresponding statement is executed. Flow of control then proceeds to the statement following the Case statement. Standard Pascal says that it is an error if the Index does not match any of the labels. Turbo Pascal provides an Else clause for such situations. The format of this extended Case is

```
Case Index Of
  Value1  :  Statement1;
  Value2  :  Statement2;
  .  .  .
```

```
   .  .  .
  ValueN   :   StatementN
  Else         StatementN+1
End; {Case}
```

If none of the values are matched, then the statement following the Else is executed. Note that in Turbo Pascal, it is *not* an error if none of the labels match and no Else clause is present. In that case, Turbo Pascal just falls through the Case to the next statement. Since this can cause errors that are difficult to debug, it is wise always to include an Else in a Case. While not included in the standard definition of Pascal, the Else clause is surely a convenient way to handle all the special cases.

The Case statement, we see, is useful when one of many possibilities is to be chosen. The Case is clearer than a long sequence of nested Ifs. But note that like the Repeat...Until or For that could be replaced with a While, the Case adds nothing but convenience to the language. Also, note that the Case has an End but no Begin. Sorry, there is no good reason for such inconsistency—that's just the way it is. Also, notice that the labels should be distinct. Violation of this should be an error, but Turbo Pascal does not report such an error and simply executes the first case that is matched.

A Case used with procedure calls provides a convenient way to present the user with a menu of choices. For example, getting a little ahead of ourselves, suppose that we have a database of information that the user can update, print, or sort. We can use a Repeat...Until and a Case to trap the user, allowing just these possibilities:

```
Repeat
  Writeln('You may');
  Writeln;
  Writeln('1. Update the database');
  Writeln;
  Writeln('2. Print the database');
  Writeln;
  Writeln('3. Sort the database');
  Writeln;
  Writeln('4. Quit this program');
  Writeln;
  Write('Please enter your choice (U/P/S/Q):  ');
  Readln(Choice);
  Choice := UpCase(Choice);
  Case Choice of
    'U':  Update(Database);
    'P':  Print(Database);
    'S':  Sort(Database);
    'Q':  {Do nothing here, but exit below.}
    Else  Writeln('Pay attention to the instructions!')
  End {Case}
Until Choice = 'Q';
...
```

Here, of course, Choice is a character identifier and Update, Print, and Sort are procedures that operate on the given Database. The user is repeatedly shown the menu until a 'Q' or 'q' is entered. If the user enters a 'U', 'P', or 'S' (or 'u', 'p', or 's'), then the appropriate procedure is invoked *before* the menu is displayed again. If the user enters any other character (such as a '1', '2', '3', or '4'), the pay-attention message is displayed and the entire menu is repeated. Thus, as promised, the user is trapped in the menu with the prescribed choices.

As another example, consider a program to compute a simple, progressive tax. A progressive tax is designed to take more from the wealthy and less, percentage-wise, from the poor. Let us suppose that our progressive tax is designed in $5000.00 blocks and is given by Table 8.1. Our first problem is to reduce the situation to a small number of cases, because we do not want to write a Case with 25,000 different cases! As we can see from the table, there are only six brackets in our progressive tax structure. We can almost compute each person's tax bracket by using

```
Bracket := (Income Div 5000) + 1;
```

Check that if Income has the value 12,500, Bracket is properly assigned the value 3. Unfortunately, Lotta Bucks, with an Income of $85,000, is assigned to a nonexistent bracket number 18. This is easily corrected with an If, and the program is as shown in Listing 8.5.

Finally, let us point out that a Case may have multiple labels. As an example, suppose we grade a project on a 20-point basis and then decide to give letter grades as follows:

18-20   A

15-17   B

13-14   C

10-12   D

0-9   F

Table 8.1: Tax Table

Income Range	Tax Rate
Up to $4,999.99	3%
Up to $9,999.99	8%
Up to $14,999.99	15%
Up to $19,999.99	24%
Up to $24,999.99	35%
$25,000 or more	50%

```
Program Taxes;
{This program computes taxes based upon a progressive scale. See
the Tax Table in Table 8.1 of the text.                              }

Var    Income  : Integer;
       Tax     : Real;
       Bracket : Integer;

Begin
  Writeln('Please enter your income--without the $ sign.');
  Writeln('To avoid overflow, keep your income below 32767.');
  Readln(Income);
  Bracket := (Income Div 5000) + 1;
: If Bracket > 6 Then    {Reduce any bracket that is too large.}
    Bracket := 6;
  Case Bracket Of
    1: Tax := Income * 0.03;
    2: Tax := Income * 0.08;
    3: Tax := Income * 0.15;
    4: Tax := Income * 0.24;
    5: Tax := Income * 0.35;
    6: Tax := Income * 0.50
  End; {Case}
  Writeln('The tax on your income of $', Income,
                                        ' is $', Tax:5:2)
End.
```

Listing 8.5

Since there are really only five outcomes, it doesn't seem that we should need 20 cases. The following segment illustrates the use of multiple labels on one statement, as well as an Else clause. In this segment, we assume that Mark and Name already have values:

```
...
Case Mark Of
  18, 19, 20   :  Grade := 'A';
  15, 16, 17   :  Grade := 'B';
  13, 14       :  Grade := 'C';
  10, 11, 12   :  Grade := 'D'
  Else            Grade := 'F'
End; {Case}
Writeln(Name, ', your grade is: ', Grade)
```

Here, naturally, if Mark matches any of the labels of a statement, then that statement is executed, while if Mark matches none of the labels, then the Else clause is executed. Note that the Else has no colon after it, nor does it need a semicolon before it. In this regard, it is more like an Else in an If than like a regular case label.

Case Labels as Ranges

Turbo Pascal, but not standard Pascal, permits a range for a case label. That is, we may write

```
Case Index of
  1..10  : ...
  11..20 : ...
  ...
End;
```

In standard Pascal, we would have to write

```
Case Index of
  1, 2, 3, 4, 5, 6, 7, 8, 9, 10         : ...
  11, 12, 13, 14, 15, 16, 17, 18, 19, 20 : ...
  ...
End;
```

Clearly, this extension does not change the expressive power of the language, but it certainly is convenient.

PROBLEM-SOLVING EXAMPLE: WINNING THE LOTTERY

Every day, Eddie Haskell bets his lucky number, 2786, in the Mayfield Lottery. The lottery works as follows: Each day, a four-digit number between 0000 and 9999 is randomly chosen as the daily winning number. If Eddie's number is chosen, he wins $5000. If Eddie gets three digits correct, he wins $100. If he gets two digits correct, he wins $3. It costs $1 to play the lottery.

For this lottery, a digit is correct only if it is in the correct place. Eddie, with his 2786, wins $100, for example, if the winning number is 4786, 2986, 2776, or 2780. But Eddie does not win anything if the daily number is 8627, even though his number is made up of the same four digits. Eddie begins with $100 and plays his single number every day. He will play until he goes broke or increases his stake to at least $5000. Eddie wants us to simulate the lottery (until he goes bust or wins big) 500 times to give him some idea of his chances.

Let us begin our top-down analysis of this problem. Eddie begins with a stake of $100 and plays until he loses his entire stake or increases his stake to at least $5000. If we had a procedure `Lottery(Stake)` that would take the original `Stake` and simulate the lottery until one or the other outcome was reached, we could solve the problem very simply. In fact, appropriate pseudo-code for our problem would be

Set a constant EdNum to Eddie's favorite number, 2786
Set a constant NumTrials to 500
Set a counter of Eddie's BigWins to zero
For Trial from 1 to NumTrials do

Set Stake equal to his original $100
Lottery(Stake)   --Run one simulation
If Stake is ≥ $5000 then
    Increment BigWins
Output the number of BigWins in all the simulations

Now, we must further refine our pseudo-code by developing the procedure Lottery. We know that the precondition is that Stake has the value $100. The postcondition is that Stake has been reduced to zero or Stake has increased to at least $5000. Lottery's job is to repeat the simulation until one or the other of those outcomes is reached. Therefore, we very naturally write the pseudo-code for Lottery using a Repeat...Until:

Repeat
    Decrement Stake by 1 (cost of playing the lottery)
    Generate a four-digit Daily Winning Number
    Set NumCorrect to # digits the same in EdNum and the DailyWinningNumber
    Case NumCorrect of
        4: Increment stake by $5000   --Grand Prize
        3: Increment Stake by $100
        2: Increment Stake by $3
        1,0: Do nothing
Until Stake = 0 Or Stake ≥ 5000

Note, also, that we used a pseudo-Case statement in the outline for Lottery, since there are several cases to consider.

There are still one or two lines of the description of Lottery that need further refinement. The line "Generate a four-digit DailyWinningNumber" will become a simple call to Random, and so we should add a call to Randomize to our main program. The line

Set NumCorrect to # digits the same in EdNum and the DailyWinningNumber

can be refined as a function call

Set NumCorrect to CountDigits(DailyWinNum)

where the function CountDigits tests the thousands, hundreds, tens, and ones digits of the DailyWinNum with the same digits in EdNum. Here is the pseudo-code for the function CountDigits with a dummy parameter Num:

Pre: Num is a four-digit number
Post: CountDigits is 0-4, depending on the number of correct digits in EdNum

Set a local, TempCount, to zero
If the thousands digits in Num = the thousands digit in EdNum then
    Increment TempCount

If the hundreds digits in Num = the hundreds digit in EdNum then
   Increment TempCount
If the tens digits in Num = the tens digit in EdNum then
   Increment TempCount
If the ones digits in Num = the ones digit in EdNum then
   Increment TempCount
Set CountDigits to TempCount

Finally, Div and Mod tricks can be used to pick off the indicated digits of the numbers. For example, we leave it to the reader to verify that the expression

```
(Num Div 100) Mod 10
```

evaluates to the hundreds digit of Num. The complete listing for program Eddie is shown in Listing 8.6. Note that since the procedure calls the function, the function is defined first. Also a please-be-patient message has been added to the main program, since it does take several seconds (on a slow processor) to run 500 simulations.

```
Program Eddie;
{This program simulates a lottery with a four-digit winning number.
Eddie always bets $1 on 2786. He wins $5000 if his number comes up.
He wins $100 if he gets three digits correct (correct digits in the
correct places). He wins $3 if he gets two digits correct. Eddie
starts with $100 and will play until he goes broke or increases his
stake to $5000. This program simulates 500 runs until bust or boom,
so that Eddie gets some idea of what his chances of success are.}

Const  EdNum     = 2786;              {Eddie's favorite number.}
       NumTrials = 500;

Var    Trial   : Integer;
       BigWins : Integer;
       Stake   : Integer;

Function CountDigits(Num : Integer) : Integer;
{Pre:  Num is a four-digit number.
Post:  CountDigits returns a value between 0 and 4, counting the
digits that are the same (same digit and same place) in EdNum and
Num.                                                              }

  Var  TempCount : Integer;

  Begin
    TempCount := 0;
    If (Num Div 1000) = (EdNum Div 1000) Then
      TempCount := TempCount + 1;       {Thousands digits same?}
```

Listing 8.6

```
    If ((Num Div 100) Mod 10) = ((EdNum Div 100) Mod 10)Then
      TempCount := TempCount + 1;           {Hundreds digits same?}
    If ((Num Div 10) Mod 10) = ((EdNum Div 10) Mod 10)Then
      TempCount := TempCount + 1;              {Tens digits same?}
    If (Num Mod 10) = (EdNum Mod 10)Then
      TempCount := TempCount + 1;              {Ones digits same?}
    CountDigits := TempCount
  End;                          {Definition of function CountDigits.}
Procedure Lottery(Var Stake : Integer);
{This procedure simulates the lottery until Eddie loses his Stake
or increases it to at least $5000.

Pre:   Stake contains the value 100, Eddie's original stake.
Post:  Stake is 0 if Eddie has lost it all, and at least 5000
       otherwise.                                                  }

  Var    DailyWinNum : Integer;
         NumCorrect  : Integer;

  Begin
    Repeat
      Stake := Stake - 1;                   {Eddie pays $1 to play.}
      DailyWinNum := Random(10000);
      NumCorrect := CountDigits(DailyWinNum);
      Case NumCorrect of
        4: Stake := Stake + 5000;           {Eddie struck it rich!}
        3: Stake := Stake + 100;
        2: Stake := Stake + 3;
        1, 0: {Do Nothing}
      End {Case}
    Until (Stake = 0) Or (Stake >= 5000)
  End;                          {Definition of procedure Lottery.}
Begin                                 {Body of main program Eddie.}
  Randomize;
  BigWins := 0;
  Writeln('Please wait while I run the simulation for you.');
  Writeln;
  For Trial := 1 To NumTrials Do
    Begin
      Stake := 100;    {Eddie begins each simulation with $100.}
      Lottery(Stake);     {Simulate lottery until bust or boom.}
      If Stake >= 5000 Then
        BigWins := BigWins + 1
    End; {For}
  Writeln('Out of ', NumTrials, ' trials, Eddie won it big ',
                                          BigWins, ' times.')
End.
```

Listing 8.6 (continued)

We invite you to run Eddie for yourself. On our first run, Eddie won on 11 of the 500 trials. In the exercises, we suggest some modifications that you can make to the program. The most obvious one is to find out how many days, on the average, each simulation lasts. That is, how long does it take Eddie, on the average, to blow his stake or strike it rich? The answer is not 100, because he probably wins a few minor prizes before he goes bust or makes it big. Maybe he even gets to $5000 by winning $100 lots of times.

SUMMARY

The Repeat...Until, the For, and the Case are in the language for your convenience. Learn to use them when they are more convenient than the While and the If. Look back at Eddie where a For, a Repeat...Until, and a Case (imagine that!) were the natural constructs. Also, remember for problems of any complexity to use a divide-and-conquer strategy with procedures and functions. For all these reasons, Eddie is a nice example to study and understand.

KEYWORDS

As a check of your understanding of this chapter, be sure that you can explain the purpose for each of the following Pascal constructs, as well as contrast the differences between them:

```
Repeat...Until          While
For
If...Then...Else        Case
```

SELF-TEST QUESTIONS

8.1 Rewrite the following For as an equivalent While.

```
For Index := Start to Stop Do
  Begin
    Statement1;
    Statement2;
    Statement3
  End; {For}
```

8.2 Rewrite the following Repeat...Until as an equivalent While.

```
Repeat
  Statement1;
  Statement2;
  Statement3
Until BooleanExp;
```

8.3 Rewrite the following `While` as an equivalent `For`. Keep your `For` as simple as possible.

```
Index := 1943;
While Index <= 2005 Do
  Begin
    If (Index Mod 4) = 0 Then
      Writeln(Index, ' is a leap year.');
    Index := Index + 1
  End; {While}
```

8.4 Rewrite the following series of nested `If`s as a `Case` statement.

```
If Code = 'I' Then
  Fare := 0.0                              {Infants fly free.}
Else If Code = 'K' Then
  Fare := RegFare/3          {Kids go at 1/3 the regular fare.}
Else If Code = 'S' Then
  Fare := RegFare/2            {Senior citizens go at 1/2 off.}
Else If Code = 'T' Then
  Fare := 1.5 * RegFare          {Teens must pay a surcharge!}
Else If Code = 'A' Then
  Fare := RegFare                     {Adults pay full fare.}
Else
  Writeln('Error in code: ', Code);
```

EXERCISES

8.5 What are the differences between the `While` and the `Repeat...Until`?

8.6 Give an example of a series of nested `If...Then...Else`s that cannot easily be converted to a `Case` statement. Hint: What kinds of things can be used as `Case` labels?

8.7 Is the variable `Temp` necessary in program `Division`? What happens if we just use `Dividend` in place of `Temp`?

8.8 Convert program `Division` to a correct program with a `While` loop.

Many of the exercises from Chapter 5 can be solved more naturally now that we have additional control structures as well as procedures and functions. Solve, or re-solve, some of the following problems from Chapter 5. In each case, use procedures or functions to divide-and-conquer the problem and use the control structures of this chapter if they make the statement of the algorithm more natural.

8.9 Problem 5.9.

8.10 Problem 5.11.

8.11 Problem 5.16.

8.12 Problem 5.18.

8.13 Problem 5.19.

8.14 Problem 5.21.

8.15 Program `Eddie` of the text is grossly inefficient in that `EdNum` is repeatedly broken into its four digits. Since `EdNum` is a constant, it need be decomposed only once. Modify `Eddie` to add this improvement and time the performance of the original `Eddie` and your new version. Is the improvement noticeable?

8.16 Modify `Eddie` (or your improved version of Exercise 8.15) as follows:

a) Determine the average length in days of a simulation until bust or boom.

b) Determine the percentage of $5000, $100, and $3 prizes won by Eddie during the 500 simulations.

8.17 Debug the following program that is supposed to print the integers from 1 to 20 along with their squares.

```
Program BugFor;
{This buggy program tries to print the integers from 1 to 20
and their squares.                                          }

Var Index : Integer;

Begin
  Writeln('Number':10, 'Square':10);
  For Index := 1 To 20 Do
    Begin
      Writeln(Index:10, Index * Index:10);
      Index := Index + 1
    End {For}
End.
```

ANSWERS TO SELF-TEST QUESTIONS

8.1 ```
Index := Start;
While Index <= Stop Do
  Begin
    Statement1;
    Statement2;
    Statement3;
    Index := Index + 1   {Don't forget to increment Index!}
  End;
```

**8.2** ```
Statement1;
Statement2;{These are always done once in the Repeat...Until.}
Statement3;
While Not BooleanExp Do              {Note insertion of Not.}
  Begin
    Statement1;
    Statement2;
    Statement3
  End; {While}
```

8.3 ```
For Index := 1943 To 2005 Do
  If (Index Mod 4) = 0 Then
    Writeln(Index, ' is a leap year.');   {No Begin/End or}
                                        {increment of Index!}
```

**8.4** ```
Case Code of
  'I' :  Fare := 0.0;
  'K' :  Fare := RegFare/3;
  'S' :  Fare := RegFare/2;
  'T' :  Fare := RegFare * 1.5;
  'A' :  Fare := RegFare
  Else   Writeln('Error in Code: ', Code)
End; {Case}
```

9

SCOPE IN PROCEDURES AND FUNCTIONS

The **scope** of an identifier is that part of the program in which it is known and can be used. Every identifier used in a procedure or function must be either a parameter, locally declared, or a global variable from some unit in which the current procedure or function is nested. Understanding how parameters, local variables, and global variables are managed in Pascal is essential for being able to write procedures and functions.

First, let us consider what happens if an identifier is declared more than once in any procedure or function. If an identifier is listed as a parameter and declared as a local variable, this will be flagged by the compiler as a **multiply-declared-identifier** error. That is, the parameters should not (indeed, cannot) be redeclared as local variables. The parameters represent those values that are carried in and out of the procedure or function, while the local identifiers represent the incidental scratch-work variables used by the procedure or function. No identifier can be both a parameter and a local variable at the same time.

On the other hand, if a parameter or local identifier has the same name as an identifier from an enclosing unit, then the parameter or local variable masks the global identifier and the global identifier cannot be seen from the procedure or function. If there is no masking identifier, the global identifier can be seen and referenced from within the function or procedure. As a simple example of some of these possibilities, consider Figure 9.1, which shows a main program, Global, with one procedure, Silly, and a snapshot of memory just before the execution of the Writelns in Silly.

In particular, in Figure 9.1, note that the program Global has three identifiers of its own, X, Y, and Z. Silly has one parameter, X, and two local variables, Z and B. This means that the parameter X, which is of type real, masks the integer X of the program. Therefore, X within Silly is the real X, while X within the body of the program is an integer. Likewise, the local variable Z of Silly masks the global Z of the program. Y,

```
Program Global;
{Snapshot of execution taken at point labeled below.}

Var  X : Integer;
     Y : Char;
     Z : Real;

Procedure Silly(X : Real);

          Var Z : Integer;
              B : Integer;

          Begin
              Z := 100;
              B := 17;

SNAPSHOT ⇒   Writeln(X:5:1, Y:5, Z:5);
          End;

Begin
   X := 3;
   Y := 'S';
   Z := 5.0;
   Silly(0.8);
   Writeln(X:5, Y:5, Z:5:1)
End.
```

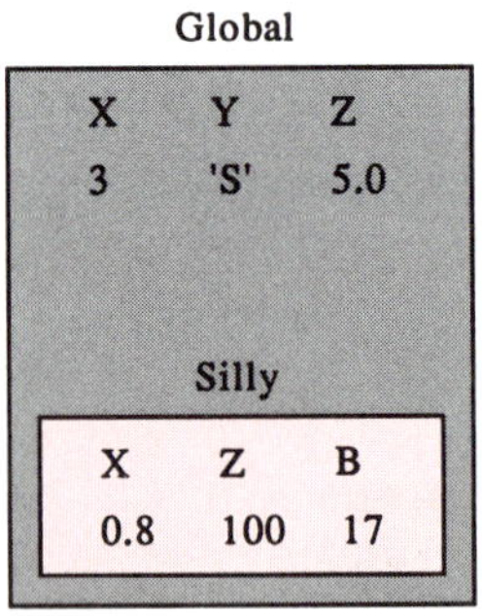

Global

X	Y	Z
3	'S'	5.0

Silly

X	Z	B
0.8	100	17

Figure 9.1

however, is not masked and can be accessed globally by Silly. When Silly writes X, Y, and Z, it writes its own X and Z, but the Y of the main program. This produces the values, 0.8, 'S', and 100. When we return from Silly to the main program, the memory allocated for Silly is reclaimed and all the identifiers of the program are unmasked. Thus, when the main program Global writes X, Y, and Z, the values produced are 3, 'S', and 5.0.

The program Global doesn't do anything useful, so you might think that the example is silly as well. Since there is no context for the program, we have even used junk identifiers like X, Y, and Z. However, the example is an important one, as it shows us how, in a real example, we can use a parameter Cost or a local variable Index without worrying about whether we used that identifier somewhere else in the program. Even if we did, the system will keep all the instances separated for us. This is the reason that we need to learn the scope rules of Pascal.

ENVIRONMENTS

Before we look at two complex, pathological examples of scoping, we need to explain in more detail how local variables and both value and variable parameters are handled by functions and procedures.

Each program, procedure, or function in Pascal has its own **environment** where the values of its identifiers are stored. These environments are nested within one another according to the way the procedures and functions were defined. For example, the box of Figure 9.1 shows the environment of procedure Silly nested within the main program's environment. These environments, as previously mentioned, are dynamically created and destroyed. They are created upon procedure or function call and are destroyed upon exit from the procedure or function. Figure 9.1, therefore, shows a snapshot of the environments during the execution of procedure Silly. Before or after the call to Silly, a snapshot would show only the main environment for Global.

Upon procedure or function call, the local variables and parameters are handled in the newly created environment as follows:

1. Local variables are given memory space, but no value.
2. Value parameters are given memory space and are given the **value** of the corresponding argument at the time of the call.
3. Variable parameters are handled as pointers to the actual argument in the calling unit. Thus, a variable parameter is really an *alias* for the actual argument. That is, **the variable parameter and the argument share the same memory location**.

If an identifier is not found within a given environment, the system looks out into environments in which the current environment is nested until the identifier is found (or an undeclared-identifier error is issued).

To illustrate these rules, consider the sample program, Environs, of Listing 9.1. Line numbers are supplied with the listing so that we can easily discuss the program.

Observe in Listing 9.1 that procedure P3 at line 13 is defined within procedure P2. We have exaggerated the indentation to help the eye more readily see the nesting of procedures in this program. Indeed, this nesting is illustrated in Figure 9.2.

Figure 9.2 helps us see why the assignment at line 18 in procedure P3 is an undeclared-identifier error. P3 has no identifier V, so we look out into P2 because P3 was defined within P2, and is, therefore, nested within P2. P2 also has no identifier V, so we continue to look out, this time into the main program. Since V is also not found there, the use of V at line 18 is illegal. In this regard, the boxes of Figure 9.2 are often described as one-way glass, since you can look out, but you can never look into a box. The only V declared in this program is in P1. None of P3, P2, or even the main program can look into P1 and see this V. Only P1 can use V; it is *local* and therefore private to P1.

The notion of local/global is somewhat relative. P2 has a local X that masks—within P2—the global X of the program. This local X of P2 is global, however, to P3, since P3 is nested inside P2 and P3 has no X of its own. When an environment does not have an identifier, it is always the nearest *nesting* environment that contains the identifier that supplies the identifier globally.

One important remark we need to make about the one-way glass analogy is that, while P3 cannot use the V of P1, P3 can call P1 if it wishes. The point is that P3 can look out through its walls and through P2's walls and see P1. Therefore, it can invoke P1 (an

```
1   Program Environs;
    {This program illustrates the scope rules of Pascal. Can you
    determine the output of this program?                        }

2   Var  X : Integer;
3        Y : Integer;

4   Procedure P1;
5     Var  V : Integer;
6     Begin
7       V := 1;
8       Y := 2;
9       Writeln(V:5, Y:5)
10    End;

11  Procedure P2;
12    Var  X : Integer;

13    Procedure P3;
14      Var  Y : Integer;
15      Begin
16        X := 5;
17        Y := 6;
18        V := 7                      {ERROR. P3 is nested inside P2,}
                                      {which is nested in Environs.}
19      End;                   {None of these has a declaration of V.}

20    Begin                                   {Body of procedure P2.}
21      X := 25;
22      Y := 35;
23      Writeln(X:5, Y:5);
24      P3;
25      Writeln(X:5, Y:5)
26    End;

27  Begin                           {Body of main program Environs.}
28    X := 100;
29    Y := 200;
30    Writeln(X:5, Y:5);
31    P1;
32    P2;
33    Writeln(X:5, Y:5)
34  End.
```

Listing 9.1

Program Environs

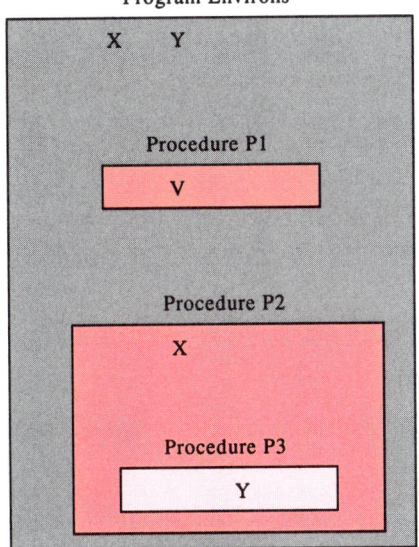

Figure 9.2

example like this will be given soon). However, P3 cannot look into P1's walls and cannot, therefore, access P1's V.

Let us trace the execution of program Environs and watch the environments dynamically grow and shrink as procedures are invoked and completed. Our trace will assume that line 18 has been deleted from the program.

It is important to realize that execution begins at line 28, the first executable statement in the main body of the program. Statements 28 to 30 are clear and produce our first line of output, the values 100 and 200. The situation, after execution of line 30, is shown in the snapshot of Figure 9.3a, since the main program is the only currently active unit.

At line 31, procedure P1 is invoked. Hence, a new environment is created and P1's local variable V is given space. At line 7, that V is set to 1 and, at line 8, the (global) Y of the main program is changed to 2. Thus, the Writeln, at line 9, produces the line containing the values 1 and 2. The environments, just before the termination of P1, at line 10, are as depicted in Figure 9.3b.

After execution of the call to P1, the memory used by P1's environment is reclaimed by the system. Thus, after execution of line 31, the snaphot is as depicted in Figure 9.3c. V is gone, but the change made to Y lingers on (showing one of the dangers of global variables).

Program Environs

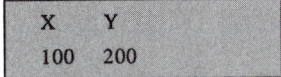

Figure 9.3a

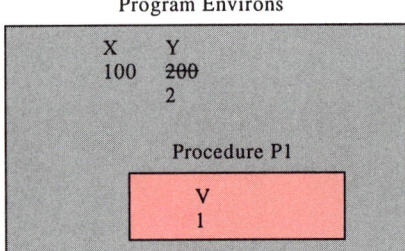

Figure 9.3b

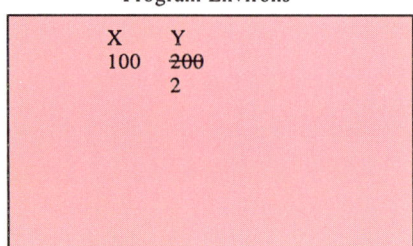

Figure 9.3c

When P2 is called, at line 32, an environment for P2 is created, including space for a local X. Execution then continues in the body of P2, skipping the definition of P3. Hence, our trace continues at line 21, which sets the local X to 25. Notice that the global X is masked from P2 and its value is not destroyed by P2. At line 22, it is the global Y that is changed to 35. It can't be P3's Y, declared at line 14, that is referenced at line 22, since that Y doesn't even exist yet. The situation at the Writeln, at line 23, is reflected in the snapshot of Figure 9.3d. Of course, this produces a line of output containing the values 25 and 35.

At line 24, P2 calls P3. Since P3 was defined inside P2, the new environment for P3 is nested inside P2. This innermost environment has its own local Y and, at lines 16 and 17, the (global) X of P2 and P3's local Y are given the values 5 and 6, respectively. This is shown in the snapshot of Figure 9.3e. There are two Xs and two Ys in the snapshot of Figure 9.3e. But, from P3's point of view, Y means its own Y and X means the closest surrounding X, which is P2's X. The X and Y of the main program are not visible from P3.

When P3 ends (remember that line 18 has been removed from the program), its environment is reclaimed and execution returns to the caller, P2, which resumes execution with the output statement at line 25. A snapshot of the program, at this point, is shown in Figure 9.3f. Clearly, the values output are 5 and 35.

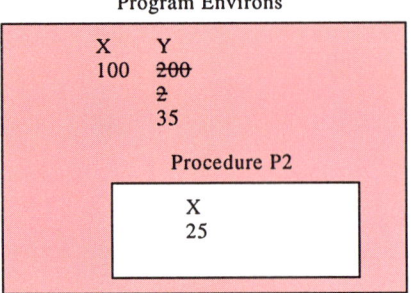

Figure 9.3d

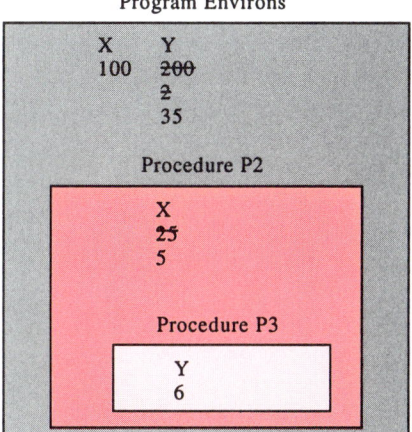

Figure 9.3e

P2 is now finished and its environment is deleted. Execution of the program is returned to the main program, which originally called P2. Thus, the X and Y of the main program are printed, at line 33, and then execution of the entire program is complete. Just before the main program completes execution, we have the final snapshot shown in Figure 9.3g. To summarize, the output of the program Environs is

```
100    200
  1      2
 25     35
  5     35
100     35
```

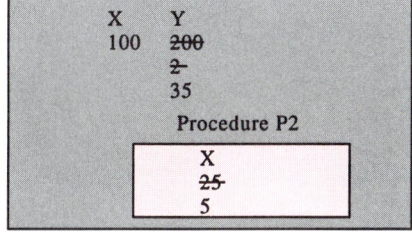

Figure 9.3f

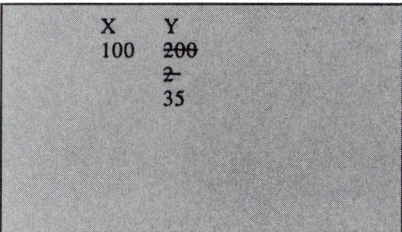

Figure 9.3g

ANOTHER SCOPING EXAMPLE

Our final, convoluted scope example is shown in Listing 9.2. The point is not that you will be writing such programs, but rather, if you understand how this perverse example works, we believe that you really understand scoping in Pascal and will be able to use this knowledge to your advantage in the writing of large programs. Again, line numbers are supplied to the listing for ease in the discussion that follows. Observe that the output from program Scope is not obvious. It is not even easy to say how many lines of output are produced by Scope. We believe it is worth your time to study carefully and understand how the trace of Scope proceeds, but this lengthy example can be omitted on a first reading.

```
1   Program Scope;
    {This program illustrates the scoping rules of Pascal. Note that
    there are two procedures P1 in this example, showing that even
    procedures and functions have scope and, in fact, scope for them
    is the same as scope for identifiers.

    Can you trace the execution of this program and determine its
    output?                                                          }

2   Var A, B, C : Integer;

3   Procedure P1(A : Integer; Var B : Integer);
4     Begin
5       A := 5;
6       B := 6;
7       C := A + B;
8       Writeln(A:5, B:5, C:5)
9     End;

10  Procedure P2(Var A : Integer; B : Integer);
11    Var C : Integer;
12      Begin
13        A := 10;
14        B := 20;
15        P1(50, C);
16        Writeln(A:5, B:5, C:5)
17      End;

18  Procedure P3;
19    Var C : Integer;

20    Procedure P1(Var X : Integer);
21      Begin
22        X := 0
23      End;
```

Listing 9.2

```
24    Begin                              {Body of procedure P3.}
25      C := 100;
26      P1(C);
27      Writeln(A:5, B:5, C:5);
28      P2(B, A);
29      Writeln(A:5, B:5, C:5)
30    End;
31  Begin                              {Body of main program Scope.}
32    A := 1000;
33    B := 2000;
34    C := 0;
35    Writeln(A:5, B:5, C:5);
36    P1(A, B);
37    P2(A, B);
38    P3
39  End.
```

Listing 9.2 (continued)

Figure 9.4 depicts the static nesting of the procedures as defined in the program Scope. When P3 calls P1, it will be its own local P1, since we always look locally before we look outside. In this case, inside P3, the local P1 masks the global P1 of the program. But, if P2 or the main program calls P1, they have to call the P1 of the main program, because they cannot look through P3's walls to see its P1. As we will emphasize in the trace of this program, it is the *static* nesting of the procedures in Figure 9.4 that determines how the environments, as they are *dynamically* created, are nested inside one another.

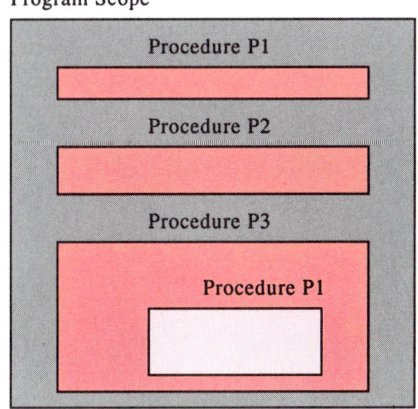

Figure 9.4

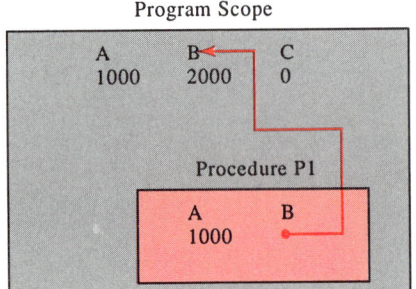

Figure 9.5a

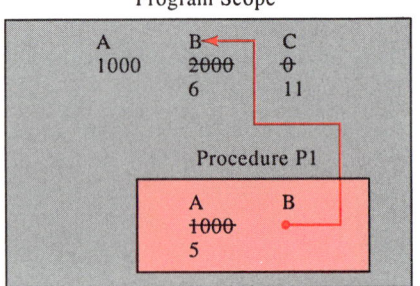

Figure 9.5b

Execution of program Scope begins at line 32. Clearly, lines 32 to 35 produce a line of output containing the values 1000, 2000, and 0. At line 36, the procedure P1 is invoked with the arguments A and B. Procedure P1 has a value parameter A, which is passed the value 1000, and a variable parameter B. This means that P1 has its own copy, also called A, of the A of the main program, while P1's B is really the B of the program. This is depicted, as P1 begins to execute, in the snapshot of Figure 9.5a.

P1 executes three assignments, at lines 5, 6, and 7. These change P1's copy of A, the outside B through its alias B, and, globally, the C of the program. This is depicted in the snapshot of Figure 9.5b. Therefore, the Writeln, at line 8, produces the values 5, 6, and 11, as expected.

Upon completion of P1, its environment is discarded and execution returns to the calling program. P1 was called at line 36, so now P2 is called with the arguments A and B, at line 37. In P2, the first parameter, A, is a variable parameter, and the second parameter, B, is a value parameter. P2 also has a local variable C. Thus, as P2 begins to execute, the snapshot is as shown in Figure 9.5c. We have denoted the value of C with a / to designate that space has been reserved for C, but no value has been assigned to it yet.

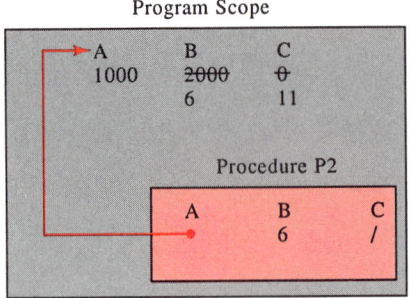

Figure 9.5c

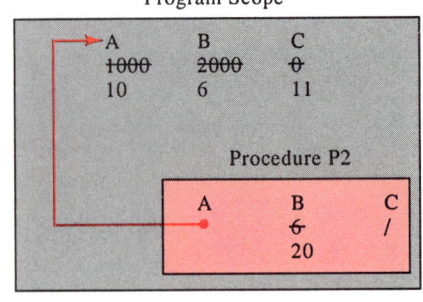

Figure 9.5d

Because A was a Var parameter, the assignment, at line 13, changes the actual argument A of the program. But, since B was a value parameter, only the copy is modified at line 14. These changes are shown in Figure 9.5d.

At line 15, P1 is invoked with the arguments 50 and C. This means that a new environment for P1 must be created. The standard error is to draw this environment inside P2, since P1 was called from within P2. Some languages do this, but not Pascal. When a new environment is created, it is always created at the nesting level shown in Figure 9.4. In other words, environments are **dynamically** created and destroyed in Pascal, but the nesting of these environments is **statically** determined by the nesting of the program at the time of its definition. The situation is, therefore, correctly depicted in Figure 9.5e. Note that the value parameter A has the value 50 and that the variable parameter B of P1 is an alias for the C of P2, since P1 was called from within P2. It makes no difference whether P1's environment is drawn above (Figure 9.4), below (Figure 9.5e), or to the side of P2's. The point is that P1 and P2 are at the same level in the program, so neither environment is ever nested inside the other.

P1 now executes its three assignments at lines 5, 6, and 7. Let us carefully trace these. The copy of A is changed to 5. C of P2, through its alias B, is changed to 6. C, which has to be the global C of the program, since P1 can't look inside P2, is reset to 11. Note that if P1's environment were erroneously nested within P2, then P1 would look out and see P2's C. This is why it is necessary to make such a big deal about the static nesting level of procedures in Pascal. The changes are reflected in the snapshot of Figure 9.5f. Of course, the Writeln, at line 8, of P1 accesses these same three variables and causes the values 5, 6, and 11 to be printed.

When P1 finishes executing, its environment disappears and control is returned to the caller. Remember that P2 called P1 this time, so execution resumes at the Writeln of line 16. From P2's point of view, A, B, and C are the values 10, 20, and 6, and these are

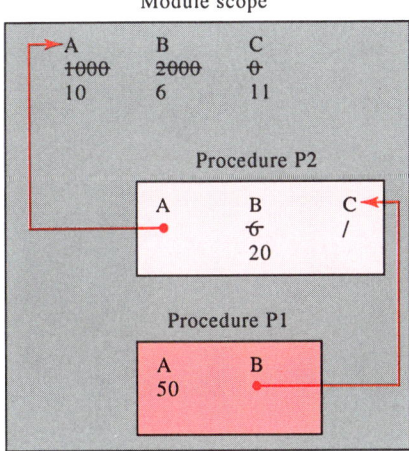

Figure 9.5e

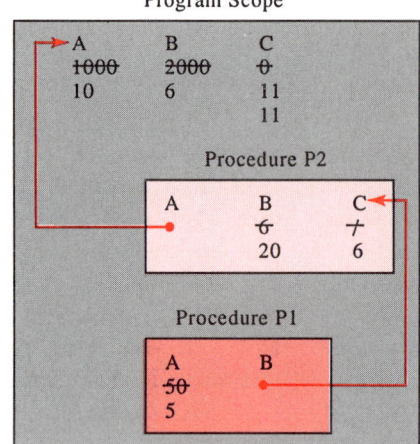

Figure 9.5f

printed. P2 now completes its execution and, thus, its environment is reclaimed and control passes back to the caller. P2 was called by the main program, at line 37, so the last thing that the program does is call the parameterless procedure P3.

The call to P3 creates a new environment with one local variable, C. Execution of the body of P3 begins, at line 25, with this C receiving the value 100. This is depicted in the snapshot of Figure 9.5g.

At line 26, P3 calls P1. This is, of course, its own local P1. Hence, a new environment is created *and* it is nested within P3. The variable parameter X of P1 is an alias for the C of P3. P1's only action is to set this parameter to zero. This is depicted in the snapshot of Figure 9.5h.

P1, its short life completed, is destroyed and control returns to the caller, P3, where, at line 28, P3 accesses A and B globally, and its own C, to print the values 10, 6, and 0.

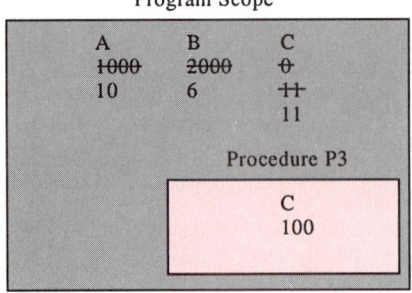

Figure 9.5g

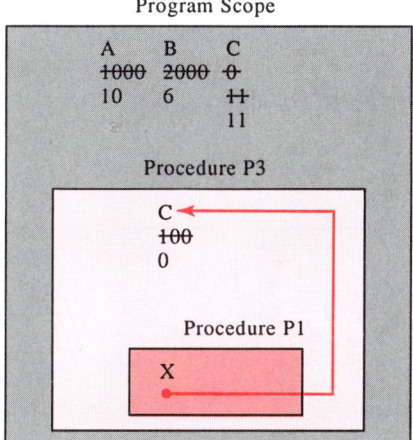

Figure 9.5h

P3, at line 28, now makes a perverse call to P2, with the actual arguments B and A, which correspond to the dummy parameters A and B, respectively. That is, what P2 calls A is actually an alias for the global B, and what P2 calls B is passed the value (10) of A of the program. P2 also has a local variable, C. This is shown, at the time P2 begins to execute, in Figure 9.5i. Note that P2's environment is not nested within P3's. Figure 9.4 explains why P1 was nested in P3, but P2 is not so nested.

As P2 begins to execute, it changes its variable parameter A to 10 (line 13), which results in the global B becoming 10. At line 14, the value parameter B is changed to

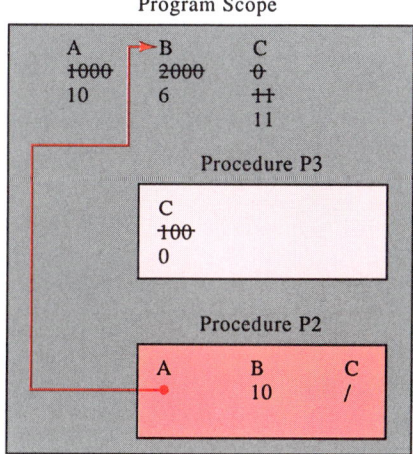

Figure 9.5i

20. Next, P2 invokes P1 with the arguments 50 and C. This causes a new environment to be created, as shown in the snapshot of Figure 9.5j.

P1 is now in control again. It assigns its own A, the C of P2 (through the alias B), and the global C the values 5, 6, and 11, respectively. It writes these values out, then goes away, leaving us with Figure 9.5k.

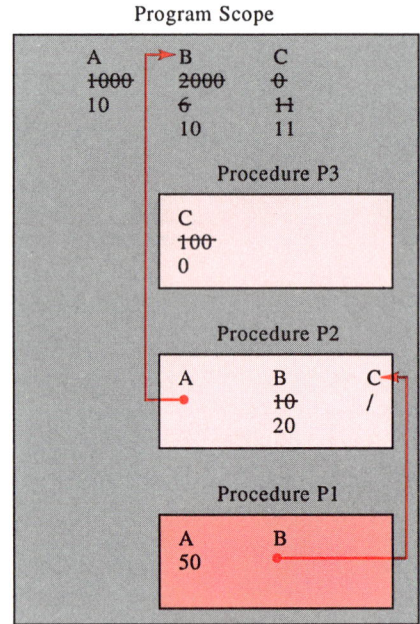

Figure 9.5j

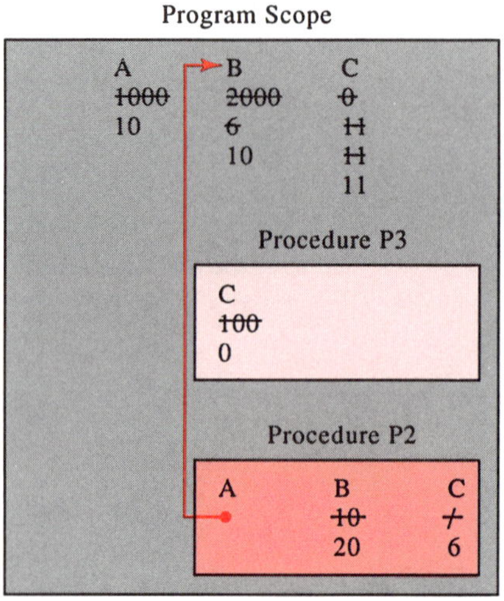

Figure 9.5k

Control is now returned to P2, at line 16, which writes out the values 10, 20, and 6. P2 now disappears and returns control to the Writeln, at line 29, where the values 10, 10, and 0 are written. P3 disappears and returns control to the main program. Execution is complete, and the environment of the main program is also reclaimed.

To summarize, the output of program Scope is

```
1000 2000    0
   5    6   11
   5    6   11
  10   20    6
  10    6    0
   5    6   11
  10   20    6
  10   10    0
```

SUMMARY

We believe that the reader who takes the time to understand these complicated scope examples will reap large benefits. Such an individual surely understands scoping in Pascal and should be able to trace and debug any program. That individual clearly understands the distinction between local and global variables, as well as the distinction between value and variable parameters. These are extremely important concepts, and that is why we have made such a fuss over these matters.

KEYWORDS

This brief chapter has introduced several important concepts. Be sure you can describe the meaning of each of the following:

Scope   Mask
Local variable   Global variable
Value parameter   Variable parameter

SELF-TEST QUESTIONS

9.1 What is meant by the scope of an identifier?

9.2 Why is it important to know the scope of identifiers in Pascal?

9.3 What is the difference in the implementation of a value and a variable parameter?

EXERCISES

9.4 Using diagrams, as in the text, carefully trace the execution of the following program and determine its output. Run the program to check your answers. Step through the program and watch its behavior with the built-in debugger (if available) to reconcile your answers with the computer's.

```
Program Ex9_4;
{Determine the output of the following program. Then run the
program to check your answer.                                }

Var A, B : Integer;

Procedure P(Var A : Integer);
  Begin
    A := A + 2
  End;

Begin
  A := 6;
  B := 11;
  Writeln(A:5, B:5);
  P(A);
  Writeln(A:5, B:5);
  P(B);
  Writeln(A:5, B:5)
End.
```

9.5 What is the output of the above program if the parameter A of procedure P is *not* a variable parameter?

9.6 Carefully trace the execution of the following program and determine its output.

```
Program Ex9_6;
{Trace this program and determine its output. Then run the
program to check your answers. Run the program in step mode (F7),
if available.                                                  }

Var   K, L, M : Integer;
      B       : Boolean;
      X       : Real;

Procedure P(X : Integer; Y : Boolean; Var Z : Real);
  Var   K : Char;
        L : Integer;
```

```
Begin
  If Y Then
    Z := X/2
  Else
    Z := X/3;
  K := 'A';
  L := 0;
  M := M * 2
End;

Begin
  K := 3;
  L := 7;
  M := 5;
  B := True;
  X := 3.14;
  Writeln(K:5, L:5, M:5, X:5:2);
  P(K, B, X);
  Writeln(K:5, L:5, M:5, X:5:2);
  B := False;
  P(M, B, X);
  Writeln(K:5, L:5, M:5, X:5:2);
  P(11, True, X);
  Writeln(K:5, L:5, M:5, X:5:2)
End.
```

9.7 Carefully trace the execution of the following program and determine its output.

```
Program Ex9_7;
{Carefully trace the execution of this program and determine
its output.                                                  }

Var  X, Y, Z : Integer;

Procedure P(X : Integer; Var Y : Integer);
  Var Z : Integer;
  Begin
    Z := 5;
    X := 2 * X;
    Y := X + Z;
    Writeln(X:5, Y:5, Z:5)
  End;
```

```
Procedure Q(Var Y : Integer);
  Var X : Integer;
  Begin
    X := 3;
    Z := Z - 2;
    Y := X + Z;
    Writeln(X:5, Y:5, Z:5);
    P(X, Y);
    Writeln(X:5, Y:5, Z:5);
    P(Y, Z);
    Writeln(X:5, Y:5, Z:5)
  End;

Begin
  X := 6;
  Y := 8;
  Z := 10;
  Writeln(X:5, Y:5, Z:5);
  P(Y, Z);
  Writeln(X:5, Y:5, Z:5);
  Q(Z);
  Writeln(X:5, Y:5, Z:5)
End.
```

9.8 Carefully trace the execution of the following program and determine its output.

```
Program Ex9_8;
{Determine the output of this pathological program.        }

Var  A, B, C : Integer;

Procedure P(Var A, B : Integer);
  Var C : Integer;
  Begin
    A := A + 1;
    B := B + 2;
    C := A + B;
    Writeln(A:5, B:5, C:5)
  End;

Procedure Q(Var A : Integer);
  Var B : Integer;
```

```
   Procedure P(D : Integer);
     Var C : Integer;
     Begin
       C := 3;
       D := C + 2;
       A := A - 2;
       B := B + 1;
       Writeln(A:5, B:5, C:5)
     End;

   Begin
     B := A + 5;
     C := A - 3;
     Writeln(A:5, B:5, C:5);
     P(A);
     Writeln(A:5, B:5, C:5)
   End;

 Begin
   A := 4;
   B := 7;
   C := 11;
   Writeln(A:5, B:5, C:5);
   P(A, B);
   Writeln(A:5, B:5, C:5);
   Q(C);
   Writeln(A:5, B:5, C:5)
 End.
```

9.9 Debug the following buggy program that tries to average two quiz scores.

```
Program Ex9_9;
{This program tries to average two scores. Debug the program,
but AVOID any use of global variables.                        }

Var    Score1 : Integer;
       Score2 : Integer;
       Ave    : Real;

Procedure Average(X, Y : Integer);
{Pre:  X and Y have values.
Post:  Ave is the average of X and Y.                          }

  Var Ave : Real;
```

```
  Begin
    Ave := (X + Y)/2
  End;                           {Definition of procedure Average.}

  Begin                          {Body of main program Ex9_9.}
    Score1 := 80;
    Score2 := 88;
    Average(Score1, Score2);
    Writeln('The average of ', Score1, ' and ', Score2,
                                     ' is ', Ave:5:2)
  End.
```

ANSWERS TO SELF-TEST QUESTIONS

9.1 The scope of an identifier is the area of the program where that identifier is known and can be used.

9.2 It is important to know the scope of identifiers so that you can understand how a local identifier in, or a parameter to, a procedure or function is separated from other occurrences of the same identifier in other parts of the program. This is important so that you can use the identifier Count without worrying about other uses of Count elsewhere in the program.

9.3 Value parameters are given storage space and the value of the actual argument that corresponds to the parameter. Variable parameters are implemented as pointers to the actual argument. A variable parameter and the actual argument share the same memory location.

10

THE PASCAL TYPE SYSTEM AND USER-DEFINED TYPES

Standard Pascal has four built-in types: Integer, Real, Char, and Boolean. These are for representing numbers, whole and decimal, characters, and conditions that are either `True` or `False`. Since variables of the standard type Char can only hold values that are *one* character long, it is usually more convenient for beginners to use the Turbo Pascal String type. However, because Char, and not String, is the standard Pascal type, we consider some examples of the Char type in this chapter. We also discuss, in Chapters 14 and 17, how one can write, in standard Pascal, a string package, so that one could survive in a Pascal that didn't have built-in strings.

Turbo Pascal has some additional types that are concerned with the precision of numeric data. These types will be discussed at the end of this chapter. Most older languages also have this same concept of different types. FORTRAN distinguishes between integers, real numbers, and characters, as do most versions of BASIC. Neither language has a corresponding Boolean type, although anyone who has programmed in either language should realize that a Boolean type is not required. In other languages, for example, a `True` condition can be represented as the number 1 and a `False` condition as the number 0. Since computer languages, by their nature, need to be as precise as possible, critics of such a representation say that Boolean conditions are not numbers and should not be represented as numbers. It makes sense to divide one number by another or take a square root of a number, but corresponding operations on Boolean conditions make no sense at all, and the language should prohibit such nonsense. While the reader may think that such criticism is unnecessarily picky, consider the following expression in BASIC, where X is 7, Y is 5, and Z is 2:

```
IF X < Y < Z THEN ...
```

Such an expression is usually written by a beginning programmer and is intended to test the compound Boolean conditions

```
IF (X < Y) AND (Y < Z) THEN...
```

This second version is the correct way to write the compound test; i.e., compound conditions in BASIC are built as they are in Pascal, by separating simple conditions with the words And and Or. However, many implementations of BASIC allow the syntactically incorrect versions and, even worse, assign the *wrong* truth value to them! The problem stems from the fact that Boolean conditions are actually treated as numbers. Thus, X < Y < Z is evaluated from left to right as follows: A test is made to see if 7 < 5. It isn't, of course, and so this part of the expression is replaced by the BASIC equivalent of False, which is 0. So now the computer tests to see if 0 < Z. But 0 < 2 is True, and so the entire expression is True. It is small wonder that beginners, who have been led to believe that computers don't make mistakes, find such occurrences to be very frustrating. This is also a frustrating problem for teachers who try to explain the correct way to form compound conditions, because the system seems to accept as syntactically correct almost any string of comparisons.

What would Pascal do with an expression like X < Y < Z? Regardless of the values of X, Y, and Z, the expression X < Y is of the type Boolean. Therefore, the compiler would issue a type-mismatch error, because this Boolean value cannot be compared to the integer Z. Thus, we see that one advantage of types is that the system can protect us from ourselves. In other words, languages with strict type rules tend to be more secure than languages with more permissive type mixing.

When we say that a variable (or a data object) has a particular type, we are actually specifying two properties of the data object:

1. The set of values that may be assigned to the object
2. The set of operations that may be performed on the object

For example, a variable of type Integer may take on any of the values from -32768 to +32767 and may have any of the standard numeric operations performed on it. Real variables, of course, take on a different set of values. In Turbo Pascal, Reals have about 11 digits of precision and range from approximately 10^{-38} to 10^{38} in absolute value. Also, there are certain operations allowed on integers that are illegal for reals (Mod and Div, for example). Boolean values may be operated on by And, Or, and Not, may be compared with other Boolean values and may be assigned to Boolean variables. Character values may be compared with other character values and assigned to character variables.

The Turbo Pascal string package is flexible and powerful, making character manipulation easy and convenient. As we mentioned earlier, strings were unfortunately omitted from standard Pascal. This omission makes character manipulation tedious and difficult. But, because the Char type is the standard Pascal type, it is worthwhile to consider an example.

A CHARACTER EXAMPLE: INITIALS

Write a Pascal program that inputs a name from the keyboard in the form

`Last, First Middle`

and prints the initials in the form

`F. M. L.`

For example, the input

`Bear, Smokey The`

should produce the output

`S. T. B.`

We will process the input character by character. All we need to remember from each individual name is the initial letter. So, we should scan these parts and save the initials. Then we print the initials, each followed by a period. Of course, we find our way through the name by looking for the blanks between the various parts of the name. Here is the pseudo-code, assuming that `Letter`, `Last`, `First`, and `Middle` are all character identifiers:

Prompt user for a name in the form Last, First Middle
Read the first Letter
Save Letter in Last
Read and ignore all Letters up to the next blank
Read the next Letter
Save Letter in First
Read and ignore all Letters up to the next blank
Read the next Letter
Save Letter in Middle
Ignore the rest of the letters on the line
Output the initials with appropriate punctuation and spacing

The statement "Read and ignore all Letters up to the next blank" will be refined to a `While` loop that will stop when the next blank is found:

While Letter is not a blank
   Read the next Letter

The program `Initials` is given in Listing 10.1. The main pseudo-code has been placed in a `Repeat...Until`, so that the program executes until the `UserQuits`.

```
Program Initials;
{This program is an example of character manipulation and converts
names of the form Bear, Smokey The into its initials: S. T. B.}

Const Period  = '.';
      Blank   = ' ';

Var   Letter, Last, First, Middle : Char;

Function UserQuits : Boolean;
{Pre: None
Post: This function returns True if the user wants to quit.    }

  Var Response : Char;

  Begin
    Writeln;
    Write('Do you want to enter another name? (Y/N) ');
    Readln(Response);
    Response := UpCase(Response);
    UserQuits := (Response = 'N')
  End;                           {Definition of function UserQuits.}

Begin                               {Body of main program Initials.}
  Repeat
    Writeln('Enter your name in the form Last, First Middle.');
    Read(Letter);
    Last := Letter;                 {Last initial is easy to get!}
    While Letter <> Blank Do              {Look for first blank.}
      Read(Letter);
    Read(Letter);
    First := Letter;             {First initial has been found.}
    While Letter <> Blank Do           {Look for the next blank.}
      Read(Letter);
    Read(Letter);
    Middle := Letter;           {Middle initial has been found.}
    While Not Eoln Do             {Look for end of input line.}
      Read(Letter);
    Readln;                           {Clear the Eoln marker.}
    Writeln;
    Write('Your initials are: ');
    Writeln(First, Period, Blank, Middle, Period, Blank, Last,
                                                          Period)
  Until UserQuits
End.
```

Listing 10.1

The main part of Initials consists of three While loops. The first two read over letters until they find the blanks separating the names. The third loops until it finds the end of the line. Actually, after Middle has been found, we could use Readln by itself to ignore the rest of the characters on the line. We have shown the While Not Eoln construct in case the reader wants to modify the example and needs to process all the characters on a line. In general,

```
While Not Eoln Do
  Begin
    Read a character
    Process a character
  End;
Readln;   {Reset Eoln}
```

is the proper way to process a line of characters, one character at a time.

USER-DEFINED TYPES

Now, we introduce the reader to a concept that first appeared in Pascal and has since been widely adopted in many recent programming languages. The topic is **user-defined types** and, as its name implies, this feature allows the programmer to invent types other than the standard data types (such as Integer, Real, Char, and Boolean) to aid in solving problems. This feature in a language is very important for two reasons:

1. Computer programs are tools to help people solve problems. The more closely the program can reflect the real-world situation, the better the solution is likely to be.

2. Computer programs should be written with the human reader, not the computer, in mind. In general, the more readable a program is, the easier it is to understand, debug, and modify.

We start by giving a simple example. Let us input from the keyboard an hourly pay rate and seven hourly figures representing the number of hours worked on the days Monday through Sunday, and let us compute the amount of pay for the week. We assume that the pay rate is standard for Monday through Friday, with time and a half for Saturday and double time for Sunday. Listings 10.2, 10.3, and 10.4 show three versions of this program, with each successive version striving for more readability.

The first and second versions are somewhat standard in that we use a loop controlled by an integer to get us through the weekdays. The second version makes some attempt at improving readability by using constants for Monday and Friday. In the third version, we see something truly different. Before the body of the program, up in the Const and Var section of the program, we now see a Type section. It is in this section that we can define new types. Note the For and the Case that are controlled by these types. Before we discuss these new types, let us review the purposes of types.

```
Program Pay1;
{This program computes a weekly pay, given the hours worked each
day. Saturday gets time and a half, Sunday gets double time. For
improved versions of this program, see Pay2 and Pay3.            }

Var    Rate  : Real;
       Hours : Real;
       Pay   : Real;
       Day   : Integer;

Begin
  Pay := 0;
  Write('Enter the pay rate per hour: ');
  Readln(Rate);

  For Day := 1 To 5 Do
    Begin
      Write('Enter the hours for day', Day:2, ': ');
      Readln(Hours);
      Pay := Pay + Hours * Rate
    End; {For}

  Write('Enter the hours for day 6: ');
  Readln(Hours);
  Pay := Pay + Hours * Rate * 1.5;
  Write('Enter the hours for day 7: ');
  Readln(Hours);
  Pay := Pay + Hours * Rate * 2.0;
  Writeln;
  Writeln('The total pay for the week is $', Pay:5:2)
End.
```

Listing 10.2

```
Program Pay2;

{This program computes a weekly pay, given the hours worked each
day. Saturday gets time and a half, Sunday gets double time. This
is an improved version of Pay1, but Pay3 is the best version.  }

Const   Monday = 1;
        Friday = 5;

Var    Rate  : Real;
       Hours : Real;
       Pay   : Real;
       Day   : Integer;
```

```
Begin
  Pay := 0;
  Write('Enter the pay rate per hour: ');
  Readln(Rate);

  For Day := Monday To Friday Do
    Begin
      Write('Enter the hours for day', Day:2, ': ');
      Readln(Hours);
      Pay := Pay + Hours * Rate
    End; {For}

  Write('Enter the hours for day 6: ');
  Readln(Hours);
  Pay := Pay + Hours * Rate * 1.5;
  Write('Enter the hours for day 7: ');
  Readln(Hours);
  Pay := Pay + Hours * Rate * 2.0;
  Writeln;
  Writeln('The total pay for the week is $', Pay:5:2)
End.
```

Listing 10.3

When we declare a variable to be of type Integer, we have implicitly accomplished two things:

1. We have specified the *values* that the variable is allowed to take; i.e., 5 and -234 are legal values, while 2.7, True, and 'X' are illegal values.

2. We have specified the *operations* that may be performed on the variable; e.g., assignment or addition.

So, in general, types define allowable values and operations. Also, types provide some security—again, the system tries to protect us from ourselves. If we try to assign a real value to an integer variable, or to divide one character value by another, the system alerts us that we are trying to do something illegal.

In the third version of the payroll program, a new type, Days, is defined. This type exists throughout the program and, as with other types, we can declare any variables we wish to be of this new type. Such a type is called an **ordinal** type, or an **enumerated** type, because we list in order (or enumerate) its possible values when we define the type. Thus, variables of type Days may take on any one of the values Monday, Tuesday, Wednesday, . . . , Sunday, but no other values. These are the so-called

```pascal
Program Pay3;
{This program illustrates user-defined types to provide program
clarity. As such, it is a vastly improved version of Pay1 and Pay2.}

   Type Days = (Monday, Tuesday, Wednesday, Thursday, Friday,
                                            Saturday, Sunday);

   Var  Rate : Real;
        Hours : Real;
        Pay  : Real;
        Day  : Days;

Procedure WriteDay(Day : Days);
{Pre: Day has a value of type Days.
Post: The string equivalent of Day is written.                       }
   Begin
     Case Day of
       Monday    : Write('Monday');
       Tuesday   : Write('Tuesday');
       Wednesday : Write('Wednesday');
       Thursday  : Write('Thursday');
       Friday    : Write('Friday');
       Saturday  : Write('Saturday');
       Sunday    : Write('Sunday')
     End {Case}
   End;                              {Definition of procedure WriteDay.}

Begin                               {Body of main program Pay3.}
   Pay := 0;
   Write('Enter the pay rate per hour: ');
   Readln(Rate);
   For Day := Monday To Sunday Do
     Begin
       Write('Enter the hours for ');
       WriteDay(Day);
       Write(' ');
       Readln(Hours);
       Case Day Of
         Monday..Friday : Pay := Pay + Hours * Rate;
         Saturday       : Pay := Pay + Hours * Rate * 1.5;
         Sunday         : Pay := Pay + Hours * Rate * 2
       End {Case}
     End; {For}
   Writeln;
   Writeln('The total pay for the week is $', Pay:5:2)
End.
```

Listing 10.4

constant values of the type `Days`, just as `True` and `False` are the constant values of the Boolean type, and integers such as 1, 2, and 3 are constant values of type Integer. We emphasize this point because many beginners confuse a constant value like `Monday` with the String constant `'Monday'`. In other words, the assignment statement

```
Day := 'Monday';                              {ERROR: Type Conflict.}
```

is illegal because the types are not compatible. Also, if `Str` is a String variable, then the statement

```
Str := Monday;                                {ERROR: Type Conflict.}
```

is also illegal because `Monday` is not a String. This distinction between the String and `Days` types is also seen in the procedure `WriteDay`, which is needed to print the days, since Pascal does not allow user-defined types to be written in a `Write` or `Writeln`. All `WriteDay` does is use a `Case` statement on the parameter `Day` of type `Days` to write the corresponding string value. It is unfortunate that you can't `Write` user-defined types, but as `WriteDay` shows, it is not difficult to write your own such procedure. As you might guess, you cannot `Read` user-defined types either. In the exercises, we suggest an ad hoc way to define your own `ReadDay` procedure and, in the next chapter, we will see how to write a more general read procedure for a user-defined type.

ORDINAL TYPES

A user-defined type is an example of an **ordinal** type. The adjective ordinal is important. An ordinal type has a *first* (or smallest) value, a *last* (or largest) value, and a well-defined ordering among the values, so that each value has a unique successor (except the last) and a unique predecessor (except the first). The standard Pascal built-in types of Integer, Boolean, and Char are all ordinal types. The type Real is not. The String type, when provided, is also not an ordinal type.

The reason the Real type is not an ordinal type should be clear after considering the following question: What real number comes *immediately* after 1.0376? Is it 1.0377, or 1.03761, or 1.0376000000000001? In a general mathematical setting, there is in fact no next number! Suppose there were. If X represents 1.0376 and Y represents the very next real number after 1.0376, then it is easy to see that $(X+Y)/2$ is smaller than Y and bigger than X. In fact, $(X+Y)/2$ is just halfway between X and Y. The reason there is no next number is related to the density of the set of all real numbers. Now, on a computer, we can represent only a finite number of real numbers, so why aren't the reals considered to be an ordinal type? One reason is that there would be too much confusion when programming on different machines. Suppose one computer stores real numbers to 10 decimal places of accuracy, while a larger computer stores real numbers to 30 decimal places of accuracy. Then the answer to "What comes after 1.0376?" has different answers on different machines. Consequently, programs that try to treat the real numbers as an ordinal type would give different results as they are moved from machine to machine. Therefore, the Reals are not considered an ordinal type on any machine.

Strings are not an ordinal type because, again, there is no succession that will take you from the first string to the last string. For example, you should be able to argue that there are an infinite number of strings between 'real' and 'ream'. To get you started, three of them are 'realaaa', 'realxyzv', and 'realamzpqr'.

Why are ordinal types important? There are many places in Pascal where we *must* use an ordinal type. For example, the variable that controls a Case statement (that is, the variable following the keyword Case) must be of an ordinal type, so we can list, or enumerate, the alternatives. Likewise, the control variable of a For loop must be ordinal. This restriction makes perfectly good sense, because when an iteration of a For loop is finished, the loop is executed again with the *next* value, and the loop is terminated after we have used the *last* value.

With the user-defined types that we are discussing, it is easy to see how we specify the ordering of the type. We list the values, *in order*, within parentheses, when the type is being defined. The next thing that we must know are the operations allowed on these types. These are not specified by the programmer, but are defined by Pascal. The most basic operations that are available with all user-defined types are **equality** and **assignment**. We can always assign values to variables as long as the types involved are the same, and we can always test two values of the same type for equality. For example, if Workday and Dayoff are both of type Days, then all of the following are legal:

```
Workday := Thursday;
Dayoff := Monday;
Dayoff := Workday;
If Dayoff = Workday Then...
If Dayoff <> Wednesday Then...
```

With ordinal types, there are some important features that are built in. The ordering of a user-defined type is given when we list the values in the type definition. So, in the program of Listing 10.4, Monday is the smallest value and Sunday is the largest. Thus, we can compare ordinal values using the relational operators <, <=, >, and >=. It is this ordering that also allows us to write For loops with ordinal types as control variables.

SUCC, PRED, AND ORD

A common operation performed on integers is that of incrementing a value, as in Index := Index + 1. With a type like Days, addition doesn't really make any sense. But getting to the next value does. For example, we may be keeping track of a company's records and the first thing we need to do each day is update the day of the week. So if we need to change the value of Day from Tuesday to Wednesday, we do it with the built-in function Succ (for successor), which applies to all ordinal types:

```
Day := Succ(Day);
```

To get to the previous value, Pascal employs the function Pred (for predecessor). Thus, if Day is Tuesday, then

```
Day := Pred(Day);
```

assigns `Day` the value `Monday`. Often, we may want to know where in the list a particular value is. For this, Pascal uses the function `Ord` (for ordinal position). One bothersome detail is that Pascal starts counting with zero. So `Ord(Monday)` equals 0 and `Ord(Thursday)` equals 3.

We point out that it is illegal to attempt to apply the `Succ` function to the last value of an ordinal type or to attempt to apply the `Pred` function to the first value of an ordinal type. So, to write a segment that updates the day of the week, we would need to employ some sort of test as follows:

```
If Day = Sunday Then
  Day := Monday
Else
  Day := Succ(Day);
```

REPRESENTATION OF CHARACTERS

The observant reader may have noticed that the functions `Succ` and `Pred` are inverses of each other. This means that each function undoes the effect of the other. Another way of looking at inverses is to notice that if we apply the functions in succession, we end up where we started. It might seem natural to expect an inverse function for `Ord`; that is, a function that takes a nonnegative integer as input and gives us the element of the ordinal list corresponding to the position denoted by the input. So, since `Ord` associates `Wednesday` with 2, there should be a function that associates 2 with `Wednesday`. The problem with such a general inverse is that we may define several different types in a single program. Then, how are we to know which type we are talking about? For example, if we have the following delarations in a program:

```
Type   Days   = (Monday, Tuesday, Wednesday, Thursday, Friday,
                                          Saturday, Sunday);
       Colors = (Red, Violet, Blue, Green, Yellow, Orange);
```

should the inverse function of `Ord` associate `Wednesday` with 2 or `Blue` with 2? Because of this problem, standard Pascal has only one special inverse of `Ord`, called `Chr`. `Chr` applies to only one specific ordinal type, the character type Char. `Chr` associates with the integer N the Nth character in the computer's set of characters. This does not necessarily mean the Nth letter of the alphabet, because the character set contains all the possible characters that can be typed from the keyboard, including special characters, some of which are invisible on the screen, but which, nevertheless, have meaning to the computer. This representation of the character set is known as the American Standard Code for Information Interchange, or ASCII (pronounced "as-key") for short. It is one of the two most common representations of characters in computers. The other representation is the EBCDIC ("ebsidik") representation, which is found primarily in IBM mainframe systems. Turbo Pascal uses an ASCII representation, but we caution the reader that one should always check the particular representation that a machine uses and try to write general programs that are independent of the character representation. If this is not possible, then such programs should be carefully documented in case problems arise when executing these programs on different machines.

The Chr function is useful when we want to embed instructions into output statements. For example, Chr(9) has the same effect as the TAB key (since the TAB key is the ninth character in the ASCII character set). Table 10.1 shows the ASCII values for standard characters of the Pascal character set. The ordinal value of each of the standard characters in the table is determined by adding its row and column labels. For example, Ord('A') is 65. Empty positions in the table correspond to unprintable control characters. In addition to the TAB key, Chr(9), there is the well-known (among junior-high-school boys, at least) BELL character, Chr(7), that rings the bell. Other useful invisible characters are the carriage return, Chr(13), which returns the carriage to the beginning of the current line, and the line feed, Chr(10), which causes printing to occur on the next line (but without returning the carriage to the left margin). Thus, the statement

```
Writeln(Chr(9), 'FirstValue', Chr(13), 'LastValue')
```

produces the peculiar line of output:

```
LastValueirstValue
```

That is, FirstValue is written after one tab stop (eight spaces), then the cursor is returned to the start of the line and LastValue is printed. Since nine characters are printed in the second case, the final 'e' overwrites the original 'F'.

The Chr(10) and Chr(13) combination, the line feed and a carriage return, is what a Writeln does after writing its message. As a beginner, you are not likely to have need for these control characters, but the curious reader may find them very interesting.

A good type system makes a language more secure by separating objects that are of differing types. But now, the truth must come out. Because the computer really only stores 0s and 1s in its memory (for the absence or presence of electrical current),

Table 10.1: ASCII Values for Standard Character Set

	0	1	2	3	4	5	6	7	8	9	10	11	12	13	14	15
0																
16																
32		!	"	#	$	%	&	'	(	)	*	+	,	-	.	/
48	0	1	2	3	4	5	6	7	8	9	:	;	<	=	>	?
64	@	A	B	C	D	E	F	G	H	I	J	K	L	M	N	O
80	P	Q	R	S	T	U	V	W	X	Y	Z	[	\	]	^	_
96	`	a	b	c	d	e	f	g	h	i	j	k	l	m	n	o
112	p	q	r	s	t	u	v	w	x	y	z	{	|	}	~	

everything, regardless of its type, is represented internally in the computer as a number! How, then, are we able to separate Boolean values from numeric values and numeric values from characters? The answer is that we don't have to worry about this problem—this is a problem for the writers of systems programs. As programmers, we are, in general, not concerned about the internal representation of data. The purpose of high-level languages (like Pascal) is to free the programmer from worrying about such details. If the systems writer does a good job of implementing a high-level language, we as programmers should be able to picture the data in our minds in any way that is convenient for us. However, there are occasional instances where we do need to know how data are represented. Most of these instances involve character data and require an understanding of the ASCII representation.

For example, the ASCII code for the uppercase `'A'` is 65. Suppose that `Ch` is a variable of type Char with current value `'A'` and that `Num` is a variable of type Integer with current value 65. Then, if it were possible for us to look into the computer's memory, at the cells corresponding to `Ch` and to `Num`, we would not be able to tell any difference between the two. To reinforce the discussion of the previous paragraph, it is the magic (through types) of high-level languages that causes the computer to convert the 65 to the letter `'A'` when we access `Ch` but leaves the 65 alone when we access `Num`. It is the compiler writer's job to make sure the magic works, and it is precisely this feature that makes high-level languages the powerful tool that they are to the programmer. Programmers do not have to be experts on machine architecture and internal representation. Their minds can be freed from such details so that they can focus on the problems they are trying to solve.

But what if we actually wanted to do some numeric calculations with some characters? This is where a knowledge of the ASCII code comes in handy, as we see in the next two examples.

A CHARACTER EXAMPLE: GRADE POINT AVERAGES

We will enter some grades from the keyboard, each of the form A, B, C, D, or F, and calculate a grade point average, where an A is worth 4 points, a B is worth 3 points, ... , an F is worth 0 points.

We will prompt the user for the number of grades to be entered and then loop that many times getting a grade from the user. We will need to add the appropriate point value for each of the grades to a running sum. One possibility would be to use a `Case` statement or nested `If...Then...Else` statements to assign the correct value. To illustrate the `Ord` function, we take a different approach in the program in Listing 10.5.

The statement involving the `Ord` function,

```
Value := Ord('A') - Ord(Grade) + 4;
```

assigns the correct number to `Value`, a 4 for an `'A'`, a 3 for a `'B'`, a 2 for a `'C'`, and a 1 for a `'D'`. Also note that it does this without the programmer needing to know the exact ASCII values involved. All the programmer needs to remember is that the ASCII of the character `'B'` is one more than the ASCII of an `'A'`, etc.

```
Program GPA;

{This program illustrates an Ord trick to average letter grades and
compute the user's GPA (Grade Point Average).                        }

Var    Grade       : Char;
       Count       : Integer;
       Value       : Integer;
       Total       : Integer;
       Ave         : Real;
       NumGrades   : Integer;

Begin
  Total := 0;
  Write('How many grades would you like to average? ');
  Readln(NumGrades);

  For Count := 1 To NumGrades Do
    Begin
      Write('Enter the next grade (A, B, C, D, or F): --> ');
      Readln(Grade);
      If Grade = 'F' Then
        Value := 0
      Else                                              {See discussion}
        Value := Ord('A') - Ord(Grade) + 4;                  {in text.}
      Total := Total + Value
    End; {For}

  Ave := Total / NumGrades;
  Writeln('The GPA is ', Ave:4:2,'.')
End.
```

Listing 10.5

A CHARACTER EXAMPLE: BASE CONVERSION

To follow this example, the reader needs some understanding of number bases. Ordinary numbers are written in base 10. Base 10 numbers have two basic properties:

1. These numbers are formed using any of 10 different digits, 0 through 9.
2. Each of the places represents a power of 10.

For example, 372 is $3 * 10^2 + 7 * 10 + 2 * 1 = 300 + 70 + 2$.

There is nothing special about 10, except for its standard use, and it is possible to write numbers in any base. So 243 (base 7) is equal to 129 (base 10), since 243 (base 7) is $2 * 7^2 + 4 * 7 + 3 * 1 = 98 + 28 + 3 = 129$ (base 10).

The reader may be wondering why bases other than 10 are ever used. It turns out that nondecimal bases are not used much outside of computer applications, but are extensively used in the computer field. We have mentioned several times that computers essentially store their information as strings of 0s and 1s. Since computers have only these two *fingers*, the most natural base for numeric operations in a computer is base 2, or the binary number system. The binary system is easy to understand, since the only digits (bits) used are 0 and 1, and the only number fact one needs to learn is that $1 + 1 = 10$ (base 2). However, for humans, base 2 is cumbersome because it takes so many digits to express even moderately sized numbers. For example, the decimal number 183 is written in binary as 10110111 (the reader should check that this is correct). Note that $183 = 128 + 32 + 16 + 4 + 2 + 1$.

Because of the clumsiness of the binary system, many computer systems also use base 8 (octal), or base 16 (hexadecimal). These systems are chosen because their bases are powers of 2 and, hence, conversions to and from the binary system are very easy. We will discuss a program, shortly, that converts base 8 numbers into decimal numbers. But first, we briefly explain the hexadecimal notation. Since in base 16 we need 16 different digits with which to form numbers, after using 0 through 9, we still need six more symbols. The symbols that are used are the uppercase letters A through F, where A stands for 10, . . . , F stands for 15. So in base 16, the decimal number 183 is written as B7 (which is $11 * 16 + 7$). The hexadecimal system is explored a bit further in the exercises.

Now we present an algorithm that reads, from the keyboard, a number in octal and prints out its decimal equivalent. If we read the input in as an integer, it is treated as a decimal number. Thus, we must read the input as a sequence of characters. Moreover, observe that we do not know how many characters we are reading (because we do not know how long the number is). While this may seem like a difficult problem at first glance, it becomes easy when one key observation is made:

Each time we scan a new digit, the previous number is multiplied by the base and the new digit is added.

To illustrate this, consider the *decimal* number 372. Now, pretend that you can't see all of the number and that you must scan it a digit at a time, from the left. So, you start with zero, see the 3, and add it to your total. After scanning the first digit, you think the number is 3. If there are, in fact, no more digits to be scanned, you are correct. However, when you scan the 7, you multiply the old number (3) by 10 and add in the new digit. This gives you 37, and, again, you are correct if the number stops there. Finally, upon scanning the 2, you multiply the previous number (37) by 10 and add in the 2, giving 372. We use the `Eoln` function to determine when we have read the last digit of the number. This method works for any base and is the idea behind the program in Listing 10.6.

Although the ordinal value of a digit is not equal to the value of the digit itself, the digits do in fact occur consecutively in the ASCII character set. That is, whatever the ASCII for a character `'7'` is, it is seven more than the ASCII for the character `'0'`. Thus, the expression

```
Ord(Digit) - Ord('0')
```

```
Program BaseConv; {Base Conversion}
{This program converts base 8 numbers into their base 10
equivalents.                                                        }

Var    Digit   : Char;
       Decimal : Integer;

Begin
  Repeat
    Decimal := 0;
    Writeln('Enter a number in OCTAL (base 8) notation: ');
    Write('Enter 0 to terminate the program: ');
    While Not Eoln Do
      Begin
        Read(Digit);
        Decimal := 8 * Decimal + (Ord(Digit) - Ord('0'))
                                    {See text for an explanation}
                                    {of the Ord function.}

      End; {While}
    Readln;                                 {Reset the Eoln marker.}
    Writeln;
    Writeln('The decimal equivalent is ', Decimal);
    Writeln
  Until Decimal = 0
End.
```

Listing 10.6

converts a character digit to its numeric value, by subtracting the ordinal value of zero
from the ordinal value of the digit in question.

SUBRANGES

There are occasions when we need use only a portion of the values of an ordinal type.
If the values that we need are consecutive values, we can define a **subrange** of an
ordinal type. Subranges are defined by listing the first and last values of the subrange,
separated by two periods. Subranges can be defined for any of the built-in ordinal types
or for any user-defined types. The following examples show the syntax of subrange
definitions:

```
Type   ExamScore = 0..100;
       LowerCase = 'a'..'z';
       Days      = (Mon, Tue, Wed, Thu, Fri, Sat, Sun);
       Workdays  = Mon..Fri;
       Weekend   = Sat..Sun;
```

The overall type from which the subrange is taken is referred to as the **parent** type. Subranges can be mixed freely with their parent type and with other subranges derived from the same parent type, but, of course, the values involved must lie within the allowable ranges. Subranges provide two benefits:

1. Again, the system can protect us from ourselves. Using the above Type definitions, suppose we declare a variable Grade to be of type ExamScore. Then, if we try to assign a value to Grade that is not in the range from 0 to 100, the system should report an error. However, if we just declare Grade to be of type Integer, such a mistake would go undetected.

2. Subranges, like user-defined types themselves, can make programs more readable. The declaration

```
Grade : ExamScore;
```

carries more meaning than the declaration

```
Grade : Integer;
```

   We point out that subranges can be used in the Var section of a Pascal program instead of the Type section, if desired. This is sometimes helpful if there is no real reason to have a separate type name for a subrange. For example, the following two alternatives are equivalent:

```
Type   ExamScore = 0..100;

Var   Grade : ExamScore;
```

and

```
Var   Grade : 0..100;
```

We caution the reader that type names are required for parameters of procedures and functions, so there may be occasions when it is necessary to define a type name. We point out some examples of this later in this book.

RANGE CHECKING IN TURBO PASCAL

Range checking means testing to see if values are in the proper range for a given identifier. For example, if Grade is an ExamScore, as defined above, then

```
Grade := 101;
```

and

```
Grade := -1;
```

are both examples of range-check errors. Unfortunately, in Turbo Pascal, range checking comes turned off and must be turned on by the user. The easiest way to do this is with the compiler directive

{$R+}

which *directs* the *compiler* to turn on range checking. This directive should be included in your program immediately after the program statement. It looks like a comment, but, because the comment begins with a dollar sign, it is interpreted as a special command by the compiler. The R, of course, signifies range checking and the + means turn it on.

As beginners, we want the system to find our errors for us, so all our programs should have range checking turned on. Turbo Pascal sets the feature to off to increase the speed of programs. We do not think you will notice the degradation in your programs by using range checking, and we think that any range-check errors that are found will be most beneficial to you. Therefore, we strongly urge you to include {$R+} in every program you write. To remind you, we will include it in all our sample programs, from this point on. We also point out that you must type the five characters {$R+} exactly as shown with no blanks. Unfortunately, { $R+ } is treated as a comment *with no effect at all*. In the exercises, we explore the effect that range checking (or forgetting it) has in a program.

SPECIAL TURBO PASCAL TYPES

Turbo Pascal has some additional built-in numeric types that give the user increased arithmetic capabilities. The simplest enhancement deals with integers. In addition to the standard Integer type, whose set of values ranges from −32768 to +32767, there is the long integer type, Longint. With Longint, the set of values ranges from −2147483648 to +2147483647. These strange values come from the way integers are stored in a computer. The upper range of the Integer type is $2^{15} - 1$, while the upper range of the Longint type is $2^{31} - 1$. Long integers require 32 bits of storage, as opposed to 16 bits for regular integers, so programmers should use variables of type Integer unless the expanded range is needed. In a computation in which the result is supposed to be of type Integer, Longint values can be mixed with regular Integer values as long as all numbers fall in the range from −32768 to +32767.

The situation with real numbers is not quite so simple. Computers are able to represent integers exactly and to perform exact integer arithmetic. Such is not the case with real numbers. Real numbers can only be approximated in a computer and, therefore, real arithmetic is approximate as well. For most beginners, real arithmetic can be assumed to be meaningful, although it should be pointed out that correct calculations involving real arithmetic can, because of roundoff errors, lead to nonsensical results. Without going into detail about how the computer stores real numbers, we simply list the type names in Table 10.2, giving their range of values and their precision.

Table 10.2: Turbo Pascal Real Types

Real Type	Range	Digits of Precision
Real	$2.9 * 10^{-39}$ to $1.7 * 10^{38}$	11-12
Double	$5.0 * 10^{-324}$ to $1.7 * 10^{308}$	15-16
Extended	$1.9 * 10^{-4951}$ to $1.1 * 10^{4932}$	19-20
Comp	$-2^{63} + 1$ to $2^{63} - 1$ or approximately $\pm 9.2 * 10^{18}$	19-20 (exact)

Remarks:

1. The **precision** is given in decimal digits and measures how many digits of accuracy are maintained. For example, suppose `Pi` is a Real variable with the value 3.14159265358979264846. It would be stored, as a Real, as 3.141592653589. But as a Double variable, it would be stored as 3.1415926535897926. If we needed the extra accuracy, we would declare `Pi` as follows:

```
Var Pi : Double;
```

2. The Real type is sufficient for most of our purposes. The computational type, whose type name in actual programs is Comp, is a special-purpose real type that provides exact arithmetic. If decimal numbers are desired, it is up to the programmer to keep track of where the decimal point belongs.

THE DANGERS OF REAL EQUALITY

We conclude this chapter with a simple example of the kind of problem that can occur with the approximations involved in real arithmetic. We ask the reader to run the program `RealEq` of Listing 10.7.

If you were surprised by the output of `RealEq`, just remember never to test real numbers for exact equality. Instead, decide on a margin of error (like nine decimal places for normal Real numbers). That is, if two numbers are equal to nine decimal places, then they are considered the same. Then test as follows:

```
Const  Margin = 0.000000001;

...
If ABS(X - 1.0) < Margin Then
  Writeln('Equal!')
Else
  Writeln('Not Equal.');
```

Although such problems are not of serious concern to us as beginners, it is important to be aware of the problems that can occur when doing real arithmetic on a computer.

```
Program RealEq; {Real Equality}

{$R+}                                    {Turn range checking on.}
{This program demonstrates why you shouldn't test two reals for
equality.                                                       }
Var    X      : Real;
       Count  : Integer;
Begin
  X := 0.0;
  For Count := 1 To 10 Do          {Add one-tenth to X 10 times.}
    X := X + 0.1;
  If X = 1.0 Then
    Writeln('Of course 0.1 added to itself 10 times is 1.0!')
  Else
    Writeln('What is going on here?')
End.
```

Listing 10.7

KEYWORDS

User-defined types	Ordinal types
Succ	Pred
Ord	Chr
ASCII	Subranges
Range checking	Longint
Double	Extended
Comp	

SELF-TEST QUESTIONS

10.1 Declare a user-defined type for the Months of the year.

10.2 Declare a new subrange type for the SummerMonths of June, July, and August.

10.3 If Day is an identifier of type Days and Day has the value Wednesday, what is the value of each of the following expressions?

a) Succ(Succ(Day))   b) Pred(Succ(Day))

c) Ord(Day)   d) Ord(Pred(Day)

e) Ord(Day) + 1   f) Ord(Succ(Day))

g) Day <= Friday   h) Day = Tuesday

EXERCISES

10.4   What is the value of user-defined types in Pascal? Do they allow you to solve problems that you could not otherwise solve? If not, what good are they to the Pascal programmer?

10.5   What is the value of subranges in Pascal?

10.6   Write a `ReadDay(Day)` procedure that will read a string such as `'Monday'` from the keyboard and assign the appropriate value to the identifier `Day` of user-defined type `Days`. Hint: Use nested `If`s to test for the various possibilities. Why isn't a `Case` appropriate?

10.7   Write a program that picks a card at random from a standard, 52-card bridge deck. Define a type `Suit` with values `Clubs`, `Diamonds`, `Hearts`, and `Spades`, and a type `Rank` with values `Ace`, `Two`, `Three`, `...`, `Jack`, `Queen`, `King`. Then generate two random integers, the first in the range 1 to 4 and the second in the range 1 to 13. Use these numbers to print out the card that was selected. Use a `Case` statement to assign the value of the `Suit` and use a loop to assign the appropriate `Rank`. For example, if the `Rank` value is 7, then loop through the values of the type `Rank` until you get to the seventh one. Extend your program to print out a five-card poker hand. (Note that your program may possibly deal you two of the same card.)

10.8   Roxy wants to write "Dear John" letters to her five steady boyfriends: Arnold, Bubba, Clarence, Drew, and Egbert, whose nicknames are Hunk, Moose, Cat, Bull, and Hulk, respectively. To make the letters as personal as possible, she will use the real names, the nicknames, and the cities (San Francisco, Chicago, New York, Monte Carlo, Carbondale) in which they met. Write a program that writes Roxy's five letters for her.

10.9   FEMALES (The Fair Employment to Men and Ladies Equally Society) needs a program to report on alleged salary discrimination at The Widget Works. A text file `Employee.Txt` contains, for each employee, a line with three items: Sex (`'M'` or `'F'`), Category (`'B'` or `'W'`), and monthly salary. For example, the line

```
FW2617.18
```

means some female, white-collar employee earns $2617.18 per month. Note that there are no spaces in the input, so you will have to read the `Sex` and `Category` codes as characters.

Your program should output three comparisons: Total male average vs. total female average, male blue-collar average vs. female blue-collar average, and male white-collar average vs. female white-collar average. Also, in each case, if any average exceeds the other by more than 10 percent, issue a comment indicating possible salary discrimination based upon sex.

Note: The data in the file Employee.Txt are arranged to give an unexpected result. What is the irony or paradox of the result?

10.10 The text file Payroll.Txt contains weekly payroll data on employees of The Widget Works. There are two lines of information for each employee in the following format:

```
C6.5 7.5 4.5 5.0 8.0 4.0 3.0
John Smith
```

The significance of each item in the data lines is:

First item: A, B, C, or D is the category of the worker. The hourly pay for these categories is $14.75, $16.25, $17.02, and $18.43, respectively.

Next seven items: These are the numbers of hours worked each day from Monday to Sunday. On Monday through Friday, the regular hourly rate is paid, while on Saturday, the worker is paid time and a half, and on Sunday, the worker is paid double time.

Last item: Worker's name.

Write a program that figures the payroll for The Widget Works. Your program should print a table with two columns—the first column should contain the name of the employee and the second column the weekly pay. Incorporate the following features into your program:

1. Define a type Days and use a variable of that type to control the loop for computing the pay.

2. Use a Case statement to determine the appropriate rate.

10.11 Write a program that reads in a number in hexadecimal and prints out its decimal equivalent. You should read in the number as a string of individual characters. To find the decimal equivalent of a particular hexadecimal digit, you need to consider only two basic cases: the hex digits 0 to 9, and the hex digits A to F.

10.12 Write a program that prints out a handy base-conversion table of the numbers from 1 to 31 as shown below:

```
                    Base Conversion Table

       Decimal        Binary      Octal       Hexadecimal
          1            00001        01              01
          2            00010        02              02
         ...           ...         ...             ...
         ...           ...         ...             ...
          31           11111        37              1F
```

Write three separate procedures ConvertToBinary, ConvertToOctal, and ConvertToHex. These procedures should write out the converted numbers character by character. For simplicity in aligning the columns of the table, print leading zeros as shown above. Note that we can convert 27 to Octal, for example, by computing 27 Div 8 and 27 Mod 8.

10.13 In the following program, which of the assignments to C are in error? For each error, state whether the error will be caught at compile time or at run time. We suppose that each line that is found to be in error is deleted from the program so that the next line that is in error is found.

```
Program BugRange;
{This program illustrates some range errors.              }
{$R+}                            {Turn range checking on.}

Type Small = 0..100;

Var A, B, C : Small;

Begin
  A := 50;
  B := 75;
  C := (A + B) Div 2;
  C := 107;
  C := 38 + 82;
  C := A + B;
  C := B - A;
  C := A - B;
  Writeln(A:5, B:5, C:5)
End.
```

10.14 Run the above program without the {$R+} compiler directive. What are the results? Run the program with a { $R+ } directive with blanks in it. What are the results? Delete each line that contains a compile-time error and rerun the program.

10.15 Study Table 10.1 to see if you can discover any relationship between the ASCII values of the lowercase letters and the corresponding uppercase letters. Use this fixed difference between the two cases to write your own version of Turbo Pascal's UpCase function. Also, write the missing DownCase function. Be careful that your functions do nothing to characters that are not letters. That is, UpCase('+') and DownCase('+') should both return '+'. Also, of course, UpCase('Q') should return 'Q' while DownCase('z') returns 'z'.

ANSWERS TO SELF-TEST QUESTIONS

10.1 Type Months = (January, February, March, April, May, June,
                                              July, August, September,
                                          October, November, December);

10.2 Type SummerMonths = June..August;

10.3 a) Friday   b) Wednesday
          c) 2   d) 1
          e) 3   f) 3
          g) True   h) False

11

ARRAYS: LISTS

Each of our identifiers has been capable of holding just one value. `Name`, a String identifier, can remember one name for us, while `Number`, an Integer, can remember one integer at a time. With each variable, we have associated one memory cell in the computer, and each cell is large enough to store one string, one integer, one real, etc. We now learn how to make the computer remember an entire **list** of values. For example, the tonnage of marshmallows produced in the United States in the years 1975 to 1984 is an example of such a list. This information is shown in Table 11.1. In Pascal, such a list is called an **array**.

Since this is not a history of marshmallow production in the United States, we will not go into detail on the reasons for the decline in U.S. production. Suffice it to say that, beginning in about 1980, the importation of foreign marshmallows began to have a serious effect on U.S. suppliers. This can be seen from Table 11.2, which shows the growing importance of marshmallow imports from the Grand Duchy of Fenwick.

Table 11.1: Tonnage of U.S. Marshmallows

1975	44,573.5
1976	46,734.9
1977	46,934.6
1978	48,324.3
1979	48,056.2
1980	47,298.4
1981	45,238.4
1982	44,573.2
1983	42,745.1
1984	39,298.0

Table 11.2: Tonnage of U.S. and GDF Marshmallows

	U.S. Tonnage	GDF Tonnage
1975	44,573.5	583.4
1976	46,734.9	692.5
1977	46,934.6	1,745.2
1978	48,324.3	2,482.4
1979	48,056.2	3,264.1
1980	47,298.4	6,392.5
1981	45,238.4	9,883.4
1982	44,573.2	12,389.0
1983	42,745.1	15,399.3
1984	39,298.0	19,343.2

In each of the tables, the year is called the **index** to the table. It is called an index since, if someone asks what the U.S. production in 1979 was, the answer can be found by looking in the row labeled 1979. Arrays, or lists, or tables, come in many sizes and shapes. Table 11.1 is an example of a one-dimensional array. That is, it is simply a **list** of 10 values, with a single index (the years from 1975 to 1984). Table 11.2, on the other hand, is an example of a two-dimensional array, since each row contains more than one value. Such two-dimensional arrays (with two indices needed to locate an item) are called **tables**. The subject of this chapter is simple lists, while higher dimensional tables are the subject of Chapter 13. Pascal allows arrays with any number of indices, but we will not consider the general case until later. For now, the terms **array** and **list** are synonymous with one-dimensional arrays.

Suppose that we wish to use the Pascal identifier USTonnage to denote the array of Table 11.1. We have two problems: How do we declare our intention to store many values under one name, and how do we access the individual values? Let us consider the declaration first.

Because integers, reals, strings, etc., all have different storage requirements, we must inform the system of the type of the components of the list. In our example, obviously, the tonnages are real numbers. Hence, the **component type** is real. Of course, we must also inform the system of the possible indices to be used with the array. The component type must be carefully distinguished from the **index type**. In our example, the indices are a subrange of integers (1975 to 1984), while the values being stored in the array are real. Here, finally, is the declaration for USTonnage:

```
Var USTonnage : Array [1975..1984] Of Real;
```

When the system sees this declaration, it realizes that USTonnage is an array, not a simple variable, that the indices are integers in the given subrange, and that the values being stored in this array are all real. With this information, the system can determine how many elements there are in the array (10 in this case) and can provide proper storage for the list.

To refer to a particular item in the array USTonnage, we simply supply the appropriate index between square brackets. This index is also called a **subscript**. In our example, USTonnage[1979] is the fifth value in the list. Note that USTonnage[1979] is a real value and, as such, can be read, written, or assigned a value as in

```
USTonnage[1979] := 48056.2;
```

The real power of arrays comes in the next section, where we learn how to manipulate arrays with *variable* indices. If Year is an integer variable in the range 1975 to 1984, USTonnage[Year] is a legal expression and, if the variable Year currently has the value 1983, then USTonnage[Year] names the ninth element of the array.

The general form of the declaration of a one-dimensional array is

```
Identifier : Array [LowIndex..HighIndex ] Of ComponentType;
```

where Identifier is the variable being declared, ComponentType is any Pascal type, and LowIndex and HighIndex are the limits of permissible indices for the array. The type of the indices is given implicitly by these limits and may be any *ordinal* type, such as Integer, Char, or a user-defined type. The index type may not be Real or String. Also, in Pascal, the limits of the indices must be *constants*, not variables with values supplied at execution time.

Consider the following declarations:

```
Const NumStudents = 30;

Type   Months      = (Jan,Feb,Mar,Apr,May,Jun,
                                    Jul,Aug,Sep,Oct,Nov,Dec);
       Children = (John, Kathryn, Sarah, Anne, Natalie);
       Grades   = (A, B, C, D, F);

Var    Rainfall   : Array [Jan..Dec] Of Real;
       BirthMonth : Array [John..Natalie] Of Months;
       SemGrade   : Array [1..NumStudents] Of Grades;
       FeeStatus  : Array [1..NumStudents] Of Boolean;
       Names      : Array [1..NumStudents] Of String[30];
       Month      : Months;
       Child      : Children;
       ID         : 1..NumStudents;
```

Rainfall is declared as an array of 12 reals, since the rainfall each month is measured to the nearest hundredth of an inch. Rainfall[Month] is used to denote the amount of rain received during the given Month. To initialize that amount to zero, we would write

```
Rainfall[Month] := 0.0;
```

BirthMonth has component type Months and index type Children. It has five elements, and BirthMonth[Child] is, of course, used to denote the month of birth of the given Child. To assign John's month of birth, we write

```
BirthMonth[John] := Oct;
```

SemGrade is an array of 30 Grades, and to assign the student with identification number ID, in the range from 1 to 30, the grade of C, we would use

```
SemGrade[ID] := C;
```

FeeStatus is an array of Boolean values. That is, the component type is Boolean. The interpretation is that FeeStatus[ID] is True only if the student with identification number ID has paid all the appropriate fees. Assuming that FeeStatus and Names already have values, we could check for negligent students with

```
If Not FeeStatus[ID] Then
  Writeln(Names[ID], ', you have not paid your fees.');
```

where Names[ID] is the name of the student with the given ID number. Of course, this If needs to be in a loop on ID numbers in order to check all students.

There is an alternative form of the array declaration whereby the index type is given explicitly and the limits of the index are given implicitly. For example, Rainfall or BirthMonth could be declared by

```
Var    Rainfall   : Array [Months] Of Real;
       BirthMonth : Array [Children] Of Months;
```

While this method is more consistent in that both the index and component types are named, it is often slightly less convenient than the previous method. To declare SummerRain to be an array of three real numbers to keep track of summer rainfall, we could use

```
Var    SummerRain : Array [Jun..Aug] Of Real;
```

whereas, to declare SummerRain using the second method, we must first declare explicitly a subrange type:

```
Type SummerTime = Jun..Aug;

Var SummerRain : Array [SummerTime] Of Real;
```

The reader should realize that the two methods are equivalent and that the system obtains the same information from each. For purposes of clarity, we think the first method is usually preferable and will use it throughout this book.

THE NEED FOR ARRAYS

Consider the following two problems:

1. Snidely Whiplash, sales manager at The Widget Works, has at most a 100-member sales staff. The name and dollar amount of sales for each person are kept on a text file, Widgets.Txt. Snidely wants a program to print the names of all salespersons who have sales of at least $5000.00 worth of widgets.

2. Snidely Whiplash, sales manager at The Widget Works, has at most a 100-member sales staff. The name and dollar amount of sales for each person are kept on a text file, Widgets.Txt. Snidely wants a program to print the names of all salespersons who have sales of at least the average sales of all salespersons.

Obviously, these two problems appear to be very similar. However, as we will see, the second is considerably more complex than the first. In the first problem, no arrays are needed. We read a name and a sales amount. If the amount is at least $5000.00, we print the name. We simply loop until the end of the file, making the above simple decision. Listing 11.1 contains such a program, called Snidely1. The data are shown in Figure 11.1 and are available on the sample disk. Note that the data actually contain considerably less than 100 salespersons. For each salesperson, there are two lines in the file. The first line consists of a name (30 characters), while the second line contains a sales amount.

```
Robert Holliday
4999.98
Lowell Carmony
5000.01
Jill Van Newenhizen
6930.35
Bill Butterworth
4509.34
Robert Troyer
7502.56
Ruthane Bopp
5124.52
James Fryxell
6202.33
Ed Packel
4572.39
DeJuran Richardson
7659.23
```

Figure 11.1

```
Program Snidely1;

{$R+}                                    {Turn range checking on.}
{This program reads the text file Widgets.Txt and commends persons
with sales of $5000.00 or more. This program needs NO arrays.
Contrast this program with Snidely2.

The program could be improved to print a get-on-the-stick message
to those with sales of less than $5000, as well as count the number
of each kind of salesperson.                                      }

Const  SalesQuota = 5000.0;

Var    Name   : String[30];
       Sales  : Real;
       Count  : Integer;

Begin
  Assign(Input, 'A:\Ch11\Widgets.Txt');
  Reset(Input);
  Writeln('Snidely Whiplash Program 1 - NO ARRAYS!');
  Writeln;

  Count := 0;
  While Not Eof Do
    Begin
      Readln(Name);
      Readln(Sales);
      Count := Count + 1;
      If Sales >= SalesQuota Then
        Begin
          Write(Name, ' has met Snidely''s quota ');
          Writeln('with sales of $', Sales:7:2)
        End {If}
    End; {While}

  Writeln;
  Writeln(Count, ' people were processed in all.')
End.
```

Listing 11.1

Figure 11.2 shows the output from Snidely1. We leave it to the reader to improve upon Snidely1 so that it also prints a get-on-the-stick message for those who have not met Snidely's quota, as well as counts of each kind of salesperson.

```
Lowell Carmony has met Snidely's quota with sales of $5000.01
Jill Van Newenhizen has met Snidely's quota with sales of $6930.55
Robert Troyer has met Snidely's quota with sales of $7502.56
Ruthane Bopp has met Snidely's quota with sales of $5124.52
James Fryxell has met Snidely's quota with sales of $6202.33
DeJuran Richardson has met Snidely's quota with sales of $7659.23

9 people were processed in all.
```

Figure 11.2

To solve the second problem, why can't we simply change the condition of the If to

```
If Sales >= Average Then ...
```

The answer, of course, is that the Average of the sales amounts is not known until all sales figures have been seen. That is, suppose the first person's name is 'Robert Holliday' and that Robert's sales are $4999.98. It is easy to see that Robert's sales do not exceed $5000.00, but it is impossible to say whether Robert's sales exceed the Average or not. We cannot compute the Average until all the sales amounts are known. In this case, we need the computer to remember all the sales figures. The basic difference between the above two problems is that there is no interaction among the data for the different salespersons in the first case. We can decide whether to commend a given salesperson, in the first case, simply by looking at the data for that salesperson. There is no need to save each of the names and sales figures; arrays should not be used in the first case. In the second case, however, arrays provide the elegant solution. We simply read the Names and Sales amounts into two arrays, compute the Average, then look through the Sales array to see whose sales have exceeded the Average.

Consider the alternatives to using arrays: We could have the computer read the data twice: Once for the computer to find the average and once to determine whose sales are above the average. But reading from the text file is slow (because it involves a mechanical disk drive)—and there is no need for the computer to do a second read, unless the text file is so large that it can't be read into arrays in memory. Another alternative would be to use 100 different name and sales variables: Name1, Name2, ..., Name100, Sales1, Sales2, ..., Sales100. But then, we would need distinct reads and writes for the different salespersons. We couldn't use a loop to read the data, and the program would be more bother than it would be worth!

The array solution is given in Listing 11.2. An improved version of Snidely2 is left for the exercises. Note that the program contains two loops, a While loop and a For loop. The first loop reads in the names and sales figures *while* there are more data. Note that the expressions Names[Count] and Sales[Count] run through the arrays Names and Sales as Count increases from 1. That is, when Count is 1, we read and store Names[1] and Sales[1]. Then Count becomes 2 and we read and store Names[2] and Sales[2], etc. Also, notice that the first loop sums the sales figures. Since this can be done as the sales amounts are read in, it should be done in the same loop as the reads. Furthermore, almost as a freebie, the While counts the actual number of salespersons. This Count is needed to compute the Average and to control the

```
Program Snidely2;
{$R+}
{This program reads the text file Widgets.Txt and commends persons
with average sales or better. This program USES arrays. Contrast
with Snidely1.                                                        }

Const NumWorkers = 100;

Var     Names     : Array[1..NumWorkers] Of String[30];
        Sales     : Array[1..NumWorkers] Of Real;
        Loop      : Integer;
        Sum       : Real;
        Average   : Real;
        Count     : Integer;

Begin
  Assign(Input, 'A:\Ch11\Widgets.Txt');
  Reset(Input);
  Writeln('Snidely Whiplash Program 2 - USES ARRAYS!');
  Writeln;
  Sum := 0.0;
  Count := 0;
  While Not Eof Do
    Begin
      Count := Count + 1;
      Readln(Names[Count]);
      Readln(Sales[Count]);
      Sum := Sum + Sales[Count]
    End; {While}
  Average := Sum / Count;
  Writeln('The average sales figure was $', Average:7:2);
  Writeln;
  Writeln('Snidely''s best salespersons include:');
  For Loop := 1 To Count Do
    If Sales[Loop] >= Average Then
      Writeln(Names[Loop], ' with sales of $', Sales[Loop]:7:2,
                                    ' beat the average.');
  Writeln;      {Note that no End was needed for the If or For.}
  Writeln(Count, ' people were processed in all.')
End.
```

Listing 11.2

second loop. Note that the calculation of the Average comes after the first loop and before the second loop. Beginners often place the Average calculation within the first loop. This is inefficient, as the system then computes a running average. All we need is one final average, so the Average calculation belongs outside all loops. Once we know the Average, it is a simple matter for the second For loop to output salespersons

```
The average sales figure was $5833.41

Snidely's best salespersons include:
Jill Van Newenhizen with sales of $6930.35 beat the average.
Robert Troyer with sales of $7502.56 beat the average.
James Fryxell with sales of $6202.33 beat the average.
DeJuran Richardson with sales of $7569.23 beat the average.

9 people were processed in all.
```

Figure 11.3

with better-than-average sales. Since the values were stored during the first loop, they are now referenced—*without rereading them*—in the second loop. The second loop is a For loop since we now know how many salespersons Snidely has. Also observe that the program does not need to be changed to handle a larger sales force (up to 100 salespersons).

Figure 11.3 shows the output of Snidely2 using the text file of Figure 11.1 as the input. Run Snidely1 and Snidely2 and study their listings until the small but important differences between these programs are clear to you. Notice that range checking has been turned on with {$R+} in both Snidely programs. You should do this in all of your programs, especially those dealing with arrays, because then the system watches for out-of-bounds subscripts for you. An **out-of-bounds** subscript is, of course, a subscript that is not in the range declared for the indices of the array. In the Snidely2 example, a subscript greater than 100 or less than 1 would be out of bounds. While we don't expect such a subscript to arise, it is certainly better to discover it sooner rather than later. With the {$R+} directive in your program, you will get an error message at the point where the subscript goes out of bounds. Without the directive, you may get erroneous results and no error message, making the program very difficult to debug. Therefore, get in the habit of using {$R+} in all your programs, especially those that deal with arrays.

SIMPLE OPERATIONS ON ARRAYS

This section presents many elementary array operations. The reader who takes the time to understand the segments that follow will be well prepared when it comes time to solve problems. For each of the examples, we assume the following declarations:

```
Var   List  : Array [1..50] Of Integer;
      Index : 1..50;
```

Example 1: Assign the value 37 to the 17th element of List. The solution is straightforward.

```
List[17] := 37;
```

Example 2: Assign the value 0 to each element of the array List. In this case, we use a For loop, since we know how many times we want to do the operation.

```
For Index := 1 To 50 Do
  List[Index] := 0;
```

Notice the power of the For loop. The same statement with 5000, in place of 50, would initialize a list of 5000 elements to all zeros.

Example 3: Assign 1 to List[1], 2 to List[2], . . . , 50 to List[50]. Again, a For loop provides the most elegant solution:

```
For Index := 1 To 50 Do
  List[Index] := Index;
```

Example 4: Assign List[1], List[3], List[5], . . . , List[49] the value 87. This time, since we want Index to take on only odd values (increment by two each time), we use a Repeat...Until.

```
Index := 1;
Repeat
  List[Index] := 87;
  Index := Index + 2
Until Index > 50;
```

Example 5: Input 50 values, obtained from the user, into List. Again, a For loop is called for.

```
For Index := 1 To 50 Do
  Begin
    Write('Enter the next number: ');
    Readln(List[Index])
  End;
```

Example 6: Assuming that List has values in it already, compute the sum of the elements of List. Assume that Sum is an Integer variable. This is another For loop with a running Sum.

```
Sum := 0;
For Index := 1 To 50 Do
  Sum := Sum + List[Index];
Writeln('The sum of your numbers is ', Sum);
```

Example 7: Let the user decide how many numbers are to be in the List. (The maximum is 50, of course.) Then, let the user enter that many numbers and compute the sum of them. This example is a generalization and combination of Examples 5 and 6. It shows that we should not always use small, separate loops, but should try to combine activities where possible into one loop. For this example, we assume that LenList is also a declared Integer variable.

```
Repeat
  Writeln('How many numbers do you want in your list?');
  Readln(LenList)
Until (LenList > 0) And (LenList <= 50);
Sum := 0;
For Index := 1 To LenList Do
  Begin
    Write('Enter the next number: ');
    Readln(List[Index]);
    Sum := Sum + List[Index]
  End;
Writeln('The sum of your numbers is ', Sum);
```

Example 8: Assuming that List already has values and that the length of the list is LenList, count the number of negative elements in the List. We assume that NegCount is an Integer variable and use a simple If.

```
NegCount := 0;
For Index := 1 To LenList Do
  If List[Index] < 0 Then
    NegCount := NegCount + 1;
Writeln(NegCount, ' negative elements were found.');
```

AN EXTENDED EXAMPLE

Let us return to The Widget Works and consider how we might use an array Sales to keep track of the number of widgets sold by each individual salesperson. Since The Widget Works has nearly 100 salespersons, who are identified by the ID numbers 1, 2, 3, ... , 100, we declare Sales as follows:

```
Var   Sales : Array [1..100] Of Integer;
```

Notice that The Widget Works may not have exactly 100 salespersons. We know there are at most 100, but salesperson 49 may have quit last week. Certain cells of the array Sales may not be used. The extra space provides for expansion by The Widget Works and, as long as the true number of employees is not drastically less than 100, we are not wasting much memory. Here is our plan: If ID is the valid identification number of a salesperson, then Sales[ID] will contain—eventually—the number of widgets sold by that salesperson.

We begin by initializing each entry of Sales to zero.

```
For ID := 1 To 100 Do
  Sales[ID] := 0;
```

Each time widgets are sold, the salesperson fills out a sales transaction containing the salesperson's ID and the Quantity of widgets sold. For example, the transaction 7 12 signifies that salesperson 7 has sold 12 more widgets. Suppose these transactions are saved (batched) for a two-week period and then entered into the computer to be analyzed. Since we do not want to enter the transactions by hand, we will create a text file, WidSales.Txt, with one transaction per line, as shown in Figure 11.4.

Since each salesperson is expected to turn in many transactions during the two-week period, Sales is really an array of running sums. Hence, we see the need for initializing each entry of Sales to zero before beginning the processing of the transactions. Here is the segment that processes the transactions:

```
Assign(Input, 'A:\Ch11\WidSales.Txt');
Reset(Input);
While Not Eof Do
  Begin
    Readln(ID, Quantity);
    Sales[ID] := Sales[ID] + Quantity
  End; {While}
```

The key statement in the above segment is the assignment

```
Sales[ID] := Sales[ID] + Quantity;
```

which, of course, adds the Quantity from the current transaction to the total of the salesperson whose ID is on the transaction.

```
7 12
3 18
7 8
2 9
9 11
5 6
7 6
2 8
8 15
7 10
2 9
5 19
8 14
5 17
9 3
3 7
5 15
8 8
```

Figure 11.4

Snidely Whiplash wants a program that determines the maximum quantity of widgets sold by anyone during the two-week period. We discussed finding a maximum in Chapter 5, and we can use that same method on arrays. Recall that, in Chapter 5, we initialized Max to some ridiculous value and then looped through the actual values, adjusting Max whenever a larger value was found. Since all the entries in Sales must be nonnegative, we can initialize Max to -1, if we wish. Here is a segment that determines Max:

```
Max := -1;                   {Initialize Max to a ridiculous value.}
For ID := 1 To 100 Do
  If Sales[ID] > Max Then              {New Max has been found.}
    Max := Sales[ID];
Writeln('The greatest number of widgets sold by anyone was ', Max);
```

When dealing with arrays, there is an alternative, more general, method of finding a maximum. We can initialize Max to the first value in the array and then compare all the other elements as before. This method has the advantage that it finds the maximum in an array even if all the numbers are negative (which the first strategy does not do). Of course, in our example, we know that the entries of Sales are nonnegative, so either method works. But if we are dealing with an array of low temperatures in International Falls, Minnesota, in January, it would be dangerous to begin by initializing Max to -1. At the end, Max might still be -1 and we would not know if that were correct or not. Here is the Sales segment using this alternative method:

```
Max := Sales[1];  {Initialize Max to 1st element in the array.}
For ID := 2 To 100 Do          {Start loop with second element.}
  If Sales[ID] > Max Then                 {New Max has been found.}
    Max := Sales[ID];
Writeln('The greatest number of widgets sold by anyone was ', Max);
```

The output from either of the above segments is

```
The greatest number of widgets sold by anyone was 57
```

When you take this information to Snidely, he is, of course, not pleased. Even though it answers his original question, it isn't what he wants to know. "Who," he wants to know, "is the salesperson who has sold 57 widgets?"

Let's see if we can modify the program that finds the maximum, so that it also finds the associated ID of the salesperson. This time, when we find a new Max, we will also have to remember the associated ID. Here is the segment:

```
Max := Sales[1];
WinnerID := 1;    {Initialize Max and WinnerID to first person.}
For ID := 2 To 100 Do
  If Sales[ID] > Max Then              {New Max has been found.}
    Begin
      Max := Sales[ID];                     {Remember new Max.}
      WinnerID := ID                        {Remember new ID.}
    End; {If and For}
Writeln('Salesperson #', WinnerID,' has sold ', Max, ' widgets.');
```

This time, the output is

```
Salesperson #5 has sold 57 widgets.
```

Snidely still isn't happy. "Who is salesperson #5? Why can't computers speak English?" The answer, of course, is that the computer can tell us the name of the winner of the sales contest *if* we give it the names of all the salespersons. From the personnel office we should be able to get the ID and name of each salesperson. Suppose that text file is called WidNames.Txt and is as shown in Figure 11.5.

```
7 Vic Trola
9 Daffy Dill
2 Mark Down
5 Polly Ester
3 Barry Beri
8 June Bug
```

Figure 11.5

Notice that the ID numbers are not in order. Also, we cannot use a For loop to read in the Names and ID numbers, because we are not sure of the exact number of salespersons on the current payroll. It's another great opportunity for a While that is looking for the Eof of the text file. We assume Names has been declared by

```
Names : Array [1..100] Of String[30];
```

Limiting the string's length is absolutely necessary to avoid wasting immense amounts of memory. Declaring an Array [1..100] Of String sets aside space for 100 strings of 255 characters each. This array would use 25,500 bytes of memory, compared to the 3000 bytes needed for our array.

Here is the segment that reads the text file WidNames.Txt and fills the array Names:

```
Assign(Input, 'A:\Ch11\WidNames.Txt');
Reset(Input);
While Not Eof Do
  Readln(ID, Ch, Names[ID]);
```

We assume that Ch is a Char variable. The purpose of the Ch is to absorb the blank in the data between the ID and the name. (See Figure 11.5.)

Notice how the IDs are accepted in any order. If the data begin as above, then 'Vic Trola' is the first name read in and it is stored in the seventh cell of the Names array. If we hadn't read the blank into Ch, the name would have been ' Vic Trola'. Likewise, 'Daffy Dill' goes into the ninth cell, etc. When all the names have been read in, they are in the correct places in the Names array. If there is no salesperson #59, Names[59] is undefined. This is not a problem, unless we try to print out, by order of ID number, the names of the salespersons. If we ever wanted to do this, we could, of course, initialize each entry of names to ' ', the **null string**, before reading the text file. The null string contains no characters and should not be confused with the string that consists of a single blank. The null string is written using two single quotes, a beginning quote and an ending quote, with nothing in between. More will be said about the null string in Chapter 17. After reading in all the names, we would know that those cells that are still equal to the null string correspond to ID numbers that are not currently being used.

Names and Sales are examples of parallel arrays. That is, the information in Names[ID] is related to the information in Sales[ID]. In this case, Names[ID] is the name of the person who has sold Sales[ID] widgets. This is illustrated in Figure 11.6.

Now that the system knows the names of the salespersons, we can modify the loop that determines the winner of the sales contest to provide Snidely, finally, with the desired information:

```
Max := Sales[1];
WinnerID := 1;        {Initialize Max and WinnerID to 1st person.}
For ID := 2 To 100 Do
  If Sales[ID] > Max Then              {New Max has been found.}
    Begin
      Max := Sales[ID];                    {Remember new Max.}
      WinnerID := ID                       {Remember new ID.}
    End; {If and For}
Writeln('The winner of The Widget Works sales contest is ...');
Writeln(Names[WinnerID], ' who sold ', Max, ' widgets.');
Writeln('That''s incredible!');
```

With the text files as shown in figures 11.4 and 11.5, the output of the above segment is

```
The winner of the Widget Works sales contest is ...
Polly Ester who sold 57 widgets.
That's incredible!
```

Snidely has one more request. He often needs to check up on a particular salesperson. Of course, if he knew the salesperson's ID number, then we could simply print out Sales[ID] to answer his question. But Snidely can't be expected to learn nearly 100 ID numbers. Hence, we need to write a segment that accepts a name of a salesperson and looks the person up in the arrays. To be more precise, since the name is the only

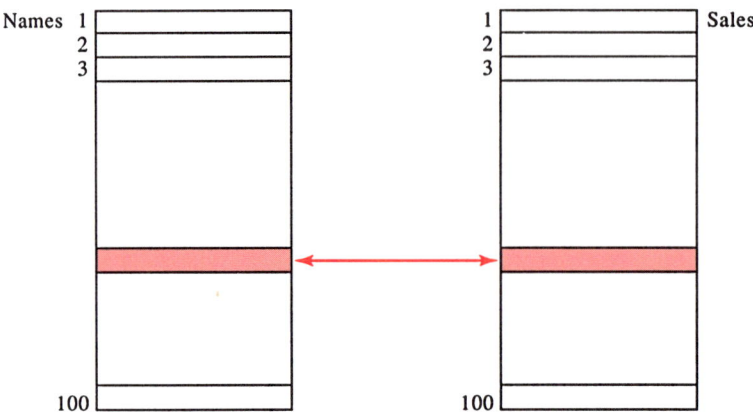

Figure 11.6

information that we have, we will need to look the person up in the Names array and note the ID number. Then, using that ID number, we can find the sales amount from the corresponding position in the parallel array Sales. Since human input is involved, we will also have to be careful to watch for bad input. As the result of a typing error or due to a recent dismissal, the name may no longer be in the Names array. In such a case, all we can do is report failure.

```
Writeln('Enter the name of the salesperson');
Readln(TargetName);
ID := 1;
Found := False;
While (ID <= 100) And (Not Found) Do
  If Names[ID] = TargetName Then
    Found := True
  Else
    ID := ID + 1;
If Found Then
  Writeln(TargetName, ' has sold ', Sales[ID], ' widgets.')
Else
  Writeln('Sorry, ', TargetName, ' is not in our records.');
```

Since there are two ways to exit from the While loop, either with the TargetName found or with ID having exhausted the possibilities, we need an If after the loop to determine which condition caused the exit .

The following While to search for the TargetName seems simpler:

```
ID := 1;
While (ID <= 100) And (Names[ID] <> TargetName) Do
  ID := ID + 1;
```

However, this can lead to a subtle error. Suppose the `TargetName` is not in the array of `Names`. Then, `ID` eventually becomes 101 and, we hope, the `While` terminates. Certainly, the condition

```
ID <= 100
```

is now `False`. Unfortunately, most Pascal compilers are not smart enough to realize that, since the first part of the `And` is `False`, the whole condition must be `False`. They go ahead and try to evaluate the condition

```
Names[ID] <> TargetName
```

But, since `ID` is 101, `Names[ID]` is not a valid expression. In common language, our subscript is out of bounds. Turbo Pascal's language is a bit more stilted. If the compiler option for Boolean evaluation is set to Complete, your program **abends** (abnormally ends), the cursor points to the `While`, and you receive the error message:

Range Check Error

Remember that the above message can mean subscript out of bounds.

On the other hand, if the compiler option for Boolean evaluation is set to Short Circuit, no error message will be generated, since the compiler is smart enough to stop evaluation of an `And` when `False` is found. Short Circuit is the default setting of this option in Turbo Pascal, meaning Short Circuit is what you will get unless you set the option otherwise. The setting Complete is provided so that Turbo Pascal can be made to imitate standard Pascal. We recommend that you leave the Boolean evaluation setting on Short Circuit, but if you wish to change it, this can be done with the Compiler submenu under the Options (ALT-O) menu. See the Turbo Pascal reference manuals for more information on this and other compiler settings. In summary, short circuiting is nice to have, but, since it is nonstandard, we will try, in this book, to write standard code that will work in any Pascal.

Listing 11.3 shows a complete program `Widgets` illustrating the ideas that we have been developing. In different parts of the program, data come from the text file `WidNames.Txt`, and the text file `WidSales.Txt`, as well as from the keyboard. To switch between these, it is necessary to `Close(Input)`, before we reopen it in a different way. Turbo Pascal's name for the keyboard is the console, which it abbreviates to `CON`, and, therefore, `Assign(Input,'CON');` followed by `Reset(Input);` is the correct way to restore input to come from the keyboard. Study the listing carefully to see how each detail has been implemented.

```
Program Widgets;
{$R+}
{This program illustrates the use of one-dimensional arrays to
solve several problems for the management at The Widget Works. The
program reads a text file WidSales.Txt, with transactions of the
form

 7 12
```

Listing 11.3

indicating that salesperson #7 sold 12 more widgets, and fills an array Sales with the sales totals of the salespersons. The program also reads a text file WidNames.Txt, which contains the ID numbers and names of the salespersons, into an array Names. The program then gives the user a menu of three options:

1. Find the winner of the sales contest.
2. List the sales of all the salespersons.
3. Check up on a particular salesperson.   }

Uses CRT;

Const NumPeople = 100;

```
Type   String30  =  String[30];
       NameList  =  Array[1..NumPeople] of String30;
       SalesList =  Array[1..NumPeople] of Integer;

Var    Names : NameList;
       Sales : SalesList;

Procedure Initialize (Var Sales : SalesList; Var Names : NameList);
{This procedure initializes Sales to all zeros and Names to all null
strings. The null string is the string of no characters, denoted
by the opening and closing quote with nothing in between: ''.

Pre:   None
Post:  Every entry of Sales is zero and every entry of Names is null.}

  Var Index : 1..NumPeople;

  Begin
    For Index := 1 To NumPeople Do
      Begin
        Sales[Index] := 0;
        Names[Index] := ''
      End {For}
  End;                             {Definition of procedure Initialize.}

Procedure ReadSalesData(Var Sales : SalesList);
{This procedure reads the text file WidSales.Txt and fills the array
Sales. Note that Sales is an array of running summations, since each
salesperson is expected to have many transactions in the file.

Pre:   None
Post   For each valid ID, Sales[ID] contains the total sold by that
salesperson.                                                         }
```

Listing 11.3 (continued)

```
Var    Quantity : Integer;
       ID       : Integer;

Begin
  Assign(Input, 'A:\Ch11\WidSales.Txt');        {Connect Input}
  Reset(Input);                                 {to WidSales.}
  While Not Eof Do
    Begin
      Readln(ID, Quantity);
      Sales[ID] := Sales[ID] + Quantity
    End; {While}
  Close(Input)        {Break connection of Input to Sales file.}
End;                      {Definition of procedure ReadSalesData.}
Procedure ReadPersonalData(Var Names : NameList)
{This procedure reads the text file WidNames.Txt and fills the array
Names. Note that the names in the file are not in order by ID number.

Pre:  None
Post: For each valid ID, a name is read and stored in Names[ID].}

  Var    ID : Integer;
         Ch : Char;

  Begin
    Assign(Input, 'A:\Ch11\WidNames.Txt');      {Connect Input}
    Reset(Input);                               {to WidNames.}
    While Not Eof Do
      Readln(ID, Ch, Names[ID]);        {Read the blank into Ch.}
    Close(Input)        {Break connection of Input to Names file.}
  End;                   {Definition of procedure ReadPersonalData.}

Procedure Menu(Var Sales : SalesList; Var Names : NameList);
{This procedure presents a menu of options for the user.

Pre:  The arrays Sales and Names already have values stored in them.
Post: Depending on the user's choice: 1) the winner of the sales
      contest is printed, 2) all the salespersons and their sales
      are printed, 3) a search is conducted for a user-specified
      name, or 4) the user quits this procedure.               }

  Var Response : Char;

  Procedure FindMax(Var Sales : SalesList; Var Names : NameList);
  {This nested procedure finds and prints the maximum number of
  widgets sold by any individual, as well as the name of that
  individual.
```

Listing 11.3 (continued)

```
      Pre:  The arrays Sales and Names already have values stored in them.
      Post: The maximum Sales amount and the Name of that individual are
             printed.                                                        }
         Var  Max       : Integer;
              WinnerID  : 1..NumPeople;
              ID        : 1..NumPeople;

         Begin
           Max := Sales[1];                    {Initialize Max and WinnerID}
           WinnerID := 1;                              {to first person.}
           For ID := 2 to NumPeople Do
             If Sales[ID] > Max Then
               Begin
                 Max := Sales[ID];            {Remember new sales amount.}
                 WinnerID := ID                       {Remember new ID.}
               End; {If and For}
           Writeln; Writeln;
           Writeln('The winner of The Widget Works sales
                                              contest is...');
           Writeln(Names[WinnerID], ' who sold ', Max, ' widgets.');
           Writeln('That''s incredible!');
           Writeln;
           Writeln('Please press the RETURN key to continue.');
           Readln
         End;                               {Definition of procedure FindMax.}

     Procedure Display(Var Sales : SalesList; Var Names : NameList);
     {This nested procedure displays all of the names and sales
     figures.

     Pre:  The arrays Names and Sales already have values stored in
            them.
     Post: The values from Names and Sales are printed.               }

         Var Index : 1..NumPeople;

         Begin
           Writeln;
           Writeln('Here are The Widget Works sales figures:');
           Writeln;
           For Index := 1 to NumPeople Do
             If Names[Index] <> '' Then
               Writeln(Names[Index]:25, Sales[Index]:10);
           Writeln;
           Writeln('Please press the RETURN key to continue');
           Readln
         End;                               {Definition of procedure Display.}
```

Listing 11.3 (continued)

```
Procedure FindName(Var Sales : SalesList; Var Names : NameList);
{This nested procedure looks for a given name in the Names array
and then looks up the sales figures for that individual.

Pre:  The arrays Sales and Names already have values stored in
      them.
Post: A TargetName is accepted from the user and, if found in the
      Names array, then that individual's Sales are printed.
      Otherwise, a not-found message is printed.              }
  Var  Who   : String30;
       ID    : Integer;
       Found : Boolean;
  Begin
    Writeln;
    Writeln('Enter the name of the salesperson');
    Readln(Who);
    ID := 1;
    Found := False;
    While (ID <= NumPeople) And (Not Found) Do
      If Names[ID] = Who Then
        Found := True
      Else
        ID := ID + 1;
    If Found Then
      Writeln(Who, ' has sold ', Sales[ID], ' widgets.')
    Else
      Writeln('Sorry, ', Who, ' is not in our records.');
    Writeln;
    Writeln('Please press the RETURN key to continue.');
    Readln
  End;                         {Definition of procedure FindName.}
Begin                                    {Body of procedure Menu.}
  Assign(Input, 'CON');{Restore Input to come from the CONsole.}
  Reset(Input);
  Repeat
    ClrScr;                 {Clear screen before presenting menu.}
    Writeln;
    Writeln('M E N U');
    Writeln; Writeln;
    Writeln('1. Find the winner of the Sales Contest.');
    Writeln;
    Writeln('2. List the sales of all the salespersons.');
    Writeln;
    Writeln('3. Check up on a particular salesperson.');
```

Listing 11.3 (continued)

```
      Writeln;
      Writeln('4. Quit the program.');
      Writeln; Writeln;
      Write('Please enter your choice (1, 2, 3, or 4:)  ');
      Readln(Response);
      Case Response Of
        '1' : FindMax(Sales, Names);
        '2' : Display(Sales, Names);
        '3' : FindName(Sales, Names);
        '4' : {Do Nothing}
        Else Writeln('Pay Attention!')
      End {Case}
    Until Response = '4'
  End;                                  {Definition of procedure Menu.}

Begin                                   {Body of main program Widgets.}
  Initialize(Sales, Names);
  ReadSalesData(Sales);
  ReadPersonalData(Names);
  Menu(Sales, Names)
End.
```

Listing 11.3 (continued)

ARRAYS AS PARAMETERS

The alert reader will have noticed that every array parameter in the program Widgets is a variable parameter, even in procedures such as FindNames where, clearly, there are not supposed to be any changes made to the array. Arrays are the one exception to the rule that parameters that are not to receive values should be protected by being sent as value parameters. The reason for this is that, as we know, value parameters are copied in the environment of the new procedure. Making a copy of a large array slows the execution of your program and wastes memory. Therefore, arrays, especially large arrays, should always be variable parameters in procedures and functions. Simple variables, containing a single value that is not to change in a procedure or function, should continue to be sent as value parameters, since these values are protected and it does not take long to make a copy of a single value.

PROBLEM-SOLVING EXAMPLE:
SOGGIES, THE BREAKFAST OF PROGRAMMERS

Each box of Soggies, the breakfast of programmers, has a prize in it. There are 10 different posters of famous persons from the history of computer science and you would, of course, like to be the first programmer in your class to collect all 10 premiums. We assume that the 10 different posters are randomly distributed in the boxes and, also, we assume that there are so many boxes of Soggies that the chances of getting any one prize always remains 1 in 10. Just because you already have 17 autographed pictures of Robert Holliday, and none of Lowell Carmony, doesn't mean that either is more likely than the other in the next box of Soggies. The problem (finally!) is: How many boxes of Soggies, on the average, would you expect to buy to obtain all 10 premiums? At first glance, that seems like a very vague question. You could, of course, obtain all 10 posters in your first 10 boxes, but we've never seen it happen in many years of discussing this problem. You could, of course, still not have all 10 posters after buying 1000 boxes of Soggies, but that is not likely either. Our question is this: If you repeated this experiment many times, what would the average of all your trials be? An experiment, of course, means buying boxes of Soggies until you have collected a full set of prizes.

There are two obvious ways to solve the Soggies problem. The first is to run to your neighborhood grocery and begin ripping open (buy them first, please) boxes of Soggies. Before we begin to feel that our answer is at all reliable, we need to make many trials. This solution is messy and expensive. The second solution, of course, involves a computer simulation. That is, using Random, the random-number generator from Chapter 6, we can easily instruct the computer to imagine that we are opening boxes of Soggies in order to note the prize within. We can put the simulation in a loop and quickly generate an average based upon many trials. We hope this simple simulation demonstrates the power and ease of computer simulations.

Here is our pseudo-code outline for the Soggies problem with 20 trials:

Set a constant NumTrials to 20
Initialize TotalBoxes to zero
For Trial from 1 to NumTrials do
    Run one experiment and remember NumBoxes used to collect all 10 prizes
    Increment TotalBoxes by NumBoxes needed on this trial
Compute and print the Average of the NumTrials trials

where, of course, "Run one experiment " is a procedure that we will have to refine further. We need some means of keeping track of which of the 10 prizes we already have. An array comes to mind! But an array of what? We could declare Prizes to be an array of Integers and then Prizes[7] would be 17 if we currently had 17 of prize 7. But we really don't need to know how many of each prize we have. We only need to know if we have, or still need, a prize. This suggests that Prizes could be an array of Boolean values, where Prizes[7] would be True if we have any of prize number 7. However, the most elegant way is to define a new type consisting of GotIt and NeedIt and use an array of GotIts and NeedIts.

The advantage of the user-defined type is that no one can fail to understand the meaning of the fact that Prizes[7] is GotIt. Although GotIt and NeedIt are equivalent to the Boolean values True and False, it is possible to become confused about whether Prizes[7] being True means it is true that we have it or it is true that we need it. To make our program as clear as possible, we will use GotIt and NeedIt. Here is the outline of the procedure "Run one experiment ":

Initialize NumBoxes to zero
Initialize the array Prizes to all NeedIts
Repeat
    Generate randomly a Premium number between 1 and 10
    Set Prizes[Premium] to GotIt
    Increment NumBoxes by one
Until no more premiums are needed

Of the above statements, each except "no more premiums are needed" is easily expressed in Pascal. The latter can be expressed as a function that looks through the array `Prizes` and returns `True` only if some premium is still marked as `NeedIt`. Here is the pseudo-code for a function `MoreNeeded`:

Initialize MoreNeeded to False
For each of the 10 entries of Prizes
    If any entry equals NeedIt Then
        Set MoreNeeded to True

Listing 11.4 shows the complete program `Soggies`. Please study it carefully. Make a "guesstimate" of the number of boxes that are needed on the average, and then run `Soggies` to see how it turns out.

The way to read Listing 11.4 is to begin with the body of the main program at the *end* of the listing. The main program calls a procedure `OneExperiment(NumBoxes)` that performs the experiment once and uses `NumBoxes` of Soggies in so doing. Then look at the details of the definition of the procedure `OneExperiment`, beginning with its

```
Program Soggies;
{$R+}
{This program simulates the purchase of boxes of Soggies until all
10 premiums have been collected. It performs the experiment 20 times
and provides an average of the 20 trials.                         }

Const  NumTrials  =  20;
       NumPrizes  =  10;

Var    TotalBoxes : Integer;
       NumBoxes   : Integer;
       Trial      : Integer;
       Average    : Real;

Procedure OneExperiment (Var NumBoxes : Integer);
{This procedure performs the experiment once and reports the number
of boxes of Soggies needed to collect all 10 premiums.

Pre:   None
Post:  NumBoxes contains the number of boxes needed to get all 10
       premiums.                                                  }
```

Listing 11.4

```
Type   PrizeStatus  =  (NeedIt, GotIt);
       PrizeArray   =  Array[1..NumPrizes] of PrizeStatus;
       PrizeType    =  1..NumPrizes;


Var    Index   : PrizeType;
       Premium : PrizeType;
       Prizes  : PrizeArray;


Function GenPremium : PrizeType;
{This function generates a premium between 1 and NumPrizes.


Pre:  None
Post: GenPremium randomly returns an integer between 1 and
      NumPrizes.                                                }

   Begin
     GenPremium := Random(NumPrizes) + 1
   End;                       {Definition of function GenPremium.}


Function MoreNeeded(Prizes : PrizeArray) : Boolean;
{This function tells if you need more premiums or have them all.


Pre:  Prizes records the prizes that we presently have.
Post: MoreNeeded is True if some entry of Prizes is NeedIt.  }

   Var  Index : PrizeType;
   Begin
     MoreNeeded := False;
     For Index := 1 To NumPrizes Do
       If Prizes[Index] = NeedIt Then
         MoreNeeded := True
   End;                       {Definition of function MoreNeeded.}

 Begin                          {Body of procedure OneExperiment.}
   NumBoxes := 0;
   For Index := 1 To NumPrizes Do            {In the beginning,}
     Prizes[Index] := NeedIt;                {we need them all.}
   Repeat
     Premium := GenPremium;    {Open box and find its premium.}
     Prizes[Premium] := GotIt;              {Record the premium.}
     NumBoxes := NumBoxes + 1                    {Count the box.}
   Until Not MoreNeeded(Prizes)
 End;                        {Definition of procedure OneExperiment.}
```

Listing 11.4 (continued)

```
Begin                                      {Body of main program Soggies.}
  Randomize;
  TotalBoxes := 0;
  For Trial := 1 To NumTrials Do
    Begin
      OneExperiment(NumBoxes);
      TotalBoxes := TotalBoxes + NumBoxes;
     Writeln('Trial ', Trial:2, ' took ', NumBoxes:2, ' boxes.')
    End; {For}
  Average := TotalBoxes / NumTrials;
  Writeln;
  Writeln('The average of all the trials was ', Average:7:3)
End.
```

Listing 11.4 (continued)

body. Note that this procedure uses two functions that are defined within it. Also, note that the `Type` definitions are included in the procedure, but not in the main program. They could be moved out into the main program, but there is no reason to do so. We will investigate `Soggies` further in the exercises, where we suggest a more efficient way of answering the question of `MoreNeeded?`.

PROBLEM-SOLVING EXAMPLE: THE TWELVE DAYS OF CHRISTMAS

How many golden rings did the young lady receive from her true love in the song "The Twelve Days of Christmas"? Five is *not* the correct answer! She received five golden rings on several consecutive days; hence, she had a whole pile of golden rings after the 12th day. In fact, how many gifts did she receive in all and how many of each of the different gifts did she receive? Since we are counting lots of things, you should smell an array. Let us suppose that `NumGifts` is an array of 12 integers. Note that, on any given day, the young lady receives gifts of all lower indices than the current day index. That is, on day 7 she receives 7 of gift 7, 6 of gift 6, 5 of gift 5, etc.

Here, then, is the pseudo-code outline of the program:

Initialize an array, GiftDesc, to the 12 gift descriptions
Initialize an array, NumGifts, to zeros
For Day from 1 to 12
    For Gift from Day backwards to 1
        Increment NumGifts[Gift] by Gift
Sum the entries of the array NumGift
Output the sum of each gift as well as the total of all gifts

You should trace the above outline to see that, on day 1, it gives 1 of gift 1, on day 2, it gives 2 of gift 2 and 1 of gift 1, etc. Observe that the order in which the gifts are given corresponds to the way the song is sung. The program `Xmas` is shown in Listing 11.5. Run `Xmas` to see how many gifts in all are involved in the song. We are deeply grateful to Fred Koch for granting us permission to use his nonstandard lyrics to this traditional song.

```
Program Xmas;
{$R+}
{This silly program sums the gifts of each type received by the fair
maiden in "The Twelve Days of Christmas." Special lyrics by Fred
Koch.                                                                }

Const NumDays = 12;

Type    DescType    =   Array[1..NumDays] Of String[25];
        GiftCounts  =   Array[1..NumDays] Of Integer;

Var     NumGifts  : GiftCounts;
        GiftDesc  : DescType;
        Day       : 1..NumDays;
        Gift      : 1..NumDays;
        SumGifts  : Integer;

Procedure Initialize(Var NumGifts:GiftCounts; Var GiftDesc:DescType);
{This procedure initializes the counters and gift descriptions.
Pre:   None
Post:  Each entry of NumGifts is zero and each entry of GiftDesc
       describes the gift first given on that day.                  }

  Var Day : 1..NumDays;

  Begin
    For Day := 1 To NumDays Do
      NumGifts[Day] := 0;
    GiftDesc[1] := 'a pickle in a peach pie';
    GiftDesc[2] := 'two talking turtles';
    GiftDesc[3] := 'three French chefs';
    GiftDesc[4] := 'four silly sisters';
    GiftDesc[5] := 'five frozen frogs';
    GiftDesc[6] := 'six ducks on diets';
    GiftDesc[7] := 'seven Santas sleeping';
    GiftDesc[8] := 'eight eggs escaping';
    GiftDesc[9] := 'nine noisy neighbors';
    GiftDesc[10] := 'ten tons of termites';
    GiftDesc[11] := 'eleven lizards laughing';
    GiftDesc[12] := 'twelve tubas tooting'
  End;                        {Definition of procedure Initialize.}

Function Sum (NumGifts : GiftCounts) : Integer;
{This function sums the gifts on each of the days.
Pre:   For each Day, NumGifts[Day] already has the number of gifts
       for that Day.
Post:  Sum returns the total of all the entries in NumGifts.    }
```

Listing 11.5

```
Var TempSum : Integer;
    Day      : 1..NumDays;
Begin
  TempSum := 0;
  For Day := 1 To NumDays Do
    TempSum := TempSum + NumGifts[Day];
  Sum := TempSum
End;                                {Definition of function Sum.}


Procedure PrintResults (NumGifts : GiftCounts; GiftDesc :
                                    DescType; SumGifts : Integer);
{This procedure prints the results of the program.

Pre:  NumGifts, GiftDesc, and SumGifts all have values.
Post: The values of the above are all printed in a readable format.}

  Var Day : 1..NumDays;
  Begin
    Writeln('Gift':10, 'Quantity Received':30);
    Writeln;
    For Day := 1 To NumDays Do
      Writeln(GiftDesc[Day]:25, NumGifts[Day]:5);
    Writeln;
    Writeln('The total number of gifts received is ', SumGifts)
  End;                          {Definition of procedure PrintResults.}

Begin                                {Body of main program Xmas.}
  Initialize(NumGifts, GiftDesc);
  For Day := 1 To NumDays Do
    For Gift := Day Downto 1 Do
      NumGifts[Gift] := NumGifts[Gift] + Gift;
  SumGifts := Sum(NumGifts);
  PrintResults(NumGifts, GiftDesc, SumGifts)
End.
```

Listing 11.5 (continued)

SUMMARY

The concept of an array is indispensable for writing programs of any size or sophistication. It has been our experience that arrays are often the point in a beginning programming course where many students begin to "lose it." One reason is that those students have never really understood the concepts of variables and memory locations, so when they try to use variable subscripts with an array, there is nothing but confusion. We encourage the reader to read and reread the chapter, study all the sample programs carefully, and tackle many of the exercises in this chapter. This will ensure that you have a thorough understanding of arrays. Many of these exercises also give practice using functions and procedures, as part of a divide-and-conquer strategy.

KEYWORDS

Array	Index
List	Table
Component type	Index type
Null string	Parallel array

SELF-TEST QUESTIONS

11.1   What is the output of each of the following segments?

a)
```
Var  A    : Array[1..5] Of Integer;
     I, J : Integer

   Begin
     J := 5;
     For I := 1 To 5 Do
       Begin
         J := J - 1;
         A[I] := I + J;
         Writeln(I:5, J:5, A[I]:5)
       End
   End.
```

b)
```
Var  B  : Array['A'..'Z'} of Real;
     Ch : Char;
     X  : Real;
   Begin
     X := 1.0;
     For Ch := 'N' Downto 'J' Do
       Begin
         X := 2.0 * X;
         B[Ch] := X;
         Writeln(Ch:5, B[Ch]:5:1)
       End
   End.
```

11.2   Declare appropriate arrays for each of the following situations:

a) An array to store the selling prices of the 5000 items at Ida Hoe's Hardware and Emporium

b) An array to keep track of the ID numbers (four digits) of each of Ida's 50 employees

c) An array to keep track of the hours worked by each of Ida's 50 employees

d) An array to keep track of the one day each week that each employee has off

e) An array to keep track of the number of dependents claimed by each employee

f) An array to keep track of the sex of each employee

g) An array to keep track of the quantity of each product on hand

11.3   Why should array parameters be variable parameters in procedures and functions?

EXERCISES

11.4   Modify Snidely1 so that it prints a message to each salesperson. Salespersons with sales of less than $5000.00 should be warned that their jobs (health) are in jeopardy, while those who reach the sales quota should be commended. Also print out a count of those reaching the quota as well as a count of those failing to reach the quota. Note that the order of the output is *fixed* by the order of the salespersons in the text file WidgetSales.Txt. You are *not* to use arrays in this problem.

11.5   Modify Snidely2 so that it prints two lists. First, print a list of all the salespersons whose sales exceed the average sales, then print a list of all salespersons whose sales do not exceed the average. Be sure to include a title for each list.

11.6   Modify Snidely1 so that it prints two lists. First, print a list of all the salespersons whose sales exceed $5000.00, then print a list of all salespersons whose sales do not exceed $5000.00. Do you need arrays for this problem?

11.7   The function MoreNeeded in Soggies checks all 10 premiums to see if any are needed. Obviously, it could stop looping as soon as it finds one premium that is still needed. Write such a version of MoreNeeded and try it out in Soggies.

11.8   Try to eliminate the function MoreNeeded from Soggies by using a counter that is incremented by 1 each time a new premium is obtained.

11.9   Modify the program Xmas (Bah, Humbug!) so that it also computes the retail value of the gifts received. For this purpose, add an array, RetailValue, to the program. Allow the user to enter the retail value of each gift, then itemize the gifts, showing the number and total value of each, as well as the total number and the total dollar value of all of the gifts.

11.10 Guess the number of jelly beans in the jar! Everyone enrolled in Pascal has entered the contest, and the data are available in the text file Candy.Txt, which contains two lines for each person:

```
Debby Fulton
327 76
```

The first line contains the name and the second line contains the guesses for the total number of jelly beans in the jar and the number of yellow jelly beans in the jar. You may assume that there are at most 100 contestants. The grand-prize winner is the person who guesses closest to, *but does not exceed*, the actual number of candies in the jar. Anyone who guesses within 25 of the *winning guess* is a runner-up and receives one jelly bean of each color. Anyone who guesses within 100 of the winning guess is a consolation prize winner and receives a jelly bean of his or her choice. The grand-prize winner gets all the jelly beans, except those awarded as runner-up and consolation prizes (and those eaten by the judges, Drs. Carmony and Holliday).

The actual number of jelly beans in the jar and the number of yellow jelly beans are given in the first line of the text file Candy.Txt. This is followed by pairs of lines giving names and guesses for each of the contestants.

Note the perverse rules of this game. For example, if there are 789 jelly beans in the jar and we have three contestants with guesses of 650, 790, and 551, then 650 is the grand-prize-winning guess; there are no runners-up; 551 gets a consolation prize; and 790 gets nothing. On the other hand, if the three guesses are 750, 790, and 551, then 750 wins and 790 is a consolation-prize winner.

Important: For this exercise, you may assume that there are no ties for the grand prize. The next exercise asks you to handle ties using the yellow guesses. Both exercises use the text file Candy.Txt. In this exercise, read Candy.Txt only until you find the name 'George Pryjma'. That is, treat 'George Pryjma' as a sentinel value marking the end of the file. If you stop without reading George's guesses, there will be no tie for the grand prize. Nevertheless, in this exercise you must be sure you properly ignore the data concerning yellow jelly beans.

11.11 Consider the above problem, but, in case of a tie for the grand prize, the winner is the person whose yellow guess comes closest to, but does not exceed, the actual number of yellow jelly beans. In this exercise you should read Candy.Txt to the end of the file.

11.12 The table below contains the tonnage of Smurfberry wine consumed in the United States and in Smurf Village during the years 1976 through 1985. Write a program that reads the data and prints two lists in the following format:

```
In the following years, the Americans drank more Smurfberry
wine:
1977
1979
...
```

```
In the following years, the Smurfs drank more Smurfberry wine:
1976
...
```

Table 11.3: Smurfberry Wine Consumption

	United States	Smurf Village
1976	23,358	25,212
1977	22,398	22,150
1978	19,327	24,386
1979	20,752	19,642
1980	23,882	26,321
1981	21,472	24,661
1982	24,752	25,371
1983	23,153	22,165
1984	21,252	21,853
1985	20,941	22,341

The data from Table 11.3 are available as the text file Smurf.Txt. This file contains 10 lines, each with two values. Note that the years are not included with the data.

11.13 The procedure Easter, from the exercises of Chapter 6, determines the day and month of Easter in a given year. The procedure is valid for the years 1901 to 2099. What date during the 20th and 21st centuries is the most common for Easter?

11.14 Each bottle of Debug, the headache-relief medicine for programmers, contains a letter on the inside of the bottle cap. You win a free bottle of Debug if you collect letters to spell

Out of every 100 bottles, there are

30 As
25 Bs
20 Cs
15 Is
10 Ss

Write a procedure that simulates the collecting of bottle caps until you win the prize. Write a program that runs your simulation 20 times and computes an average number of bottles purchased to win a free bottle.

11.15 Do Exercise 11.14, except collect letters to spell

 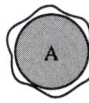 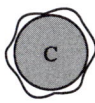 

where the distribution of the letters in 100 bottles is

10 As
10 Cs
20 Ls
25 Ps
35 Ss

Why is this program more difficult than the previous one?

11.16 Modify Xmas so that it "sings," using the nonstandard lyrics, "The Twelve Days of Christmas." By "sings," we mean to write the lyrics for all 12 verses in the correct order.

11.17 Suppose you and your friend are both collecting Soggies premiums and you will trade a Lowell Carmony (if you have an extra) for a Robert Holliday (if your friend has an extra). How many boxes on the average do you and your friend expect to buy to collect two complete sets of posters? Is it twice as many as it takes to collect one set?

ANSWERS TO SELF-TEST QUESTIONS

11.1 a)

1	4	5
2	3	5
3	2	5
4	1	5
5	0	5

b)

N	2.0
M	4.0
L	8.0
K	16.0
J	32.0

11.2 a) SellPrices   : Array[1..5000] Of Real;
     b) IDNums   : Array[1..50] Of Integer;
     c) Hours   : Array[1..50] Of Real;   {Real better than
                                                        Integer.}
     d) DayOff   : Array[1..50] Of Days;{Assumes user-defined}
                                                    {type Days.}
     e) NumDependents : Array[1..50] Of Integer;
     f) Sex   : Array[1..50] Of Char;
     g) OnHand   : Array[1..5000] Of Integer;

11.3 Because a value parameter is copied in the new procedure or function and copying all those values can be slow and waste memory as well.

12

SEARCHING AND SORTING

SEARCHING ARRAYS

It has been said that computers spend more time searching and sorting than doing any other activity. Whether this is true or not, these applications are certainly two of the most important to learn. Searching an array means, of course, that, given an array and a target, we are to find the location of the target in the array. The location is reported by giving the index of the target. Even with this simple notion, several problems can arise. For example, what if the target is in the array several times? What if the target is not in the array at all? We could, of course, ask that the search return all indices in the first case, but, since this is a beginning text, we will take the easy way out and assume that the search returns any of the indices involved. If the target is not in the array, we will assume that the search returns this information by returning some absurd value for the index. For example, if we are searching in an array whose indices run from 1 to some upper limit, we could have our search return the index of 0 to indicate an unsuccessful search.

LINEAR SEARCH

The simplest search, which we have already used in the widget problem in the previous chapter, is called a **linear search**. It begins at one end of the array and searches each element in order until the target is found or until we reach the other end of the array. Here is a pseudo-code outline of the linear search for a given `Target` in a `List` with indices from `Lo` to `Hi`. We assume that 0 is not a legal index and return it if the `Target` is not found in the array

Initialize Found to False
Initialize Index to Lo
While Index <= Hi and the Target hasn't been Found
    If List[Index] equals the Target then
        Found := True
    Else
        Index := Index + 1
If Target is still not Found then
        Index := 0

You should trace the above to see that if the Target is in the array, Found is set to True. We exit the While, and Index points to the place in the array occupied by the Target. On the other hand, if the Target is not in the array, we eventually exit the While after Index finally exceeds Hi and, at that point, we give Index the absurd value of 0. Of course, a program that uses this search also must test the value of the Index returned and, if it is 0, take appropriate action.

```
Function Linear1(Var List : SomeList; Target : ComponentType;
                              Lo, Hi : IndexType) : IndexType;
                                      {Not a complete program!}
{This function is our first implementation of the linear search.
It searches the array List from Lo to Hi for the given Target.

Pre:  List, Target, Lo, and Hi already have values stored in them.
Post: Linear1 returns the index of the first Target in List between
      Lo and Hi (if present) and it returns Absurd if Target is
      not found.                                                   }

  Var Found : Boolean;
      Index : IndexType;

  Begin
    Found := False;              {We haven't found the Target yet.}
    Index := Lo;                       {Begin at the beginning.}
    While (Index <= Hi) And Not Found Do     {Keep looking.}
      If List[Index] = Target Then
        Found := True                  {Eureka! Target is found.}
      Else
        Index := Index + 1;
    If Not Found Then
      Linear1 := Absurd                        {Return failure.}
    Else
      Linear1 := Index                         {Return success.}
  End;                          {Definition of function Linear1.}
```

Listing 12.1

Writing the pseudo-code for our linesr search as a Pascal function is extremely straightforward. We assume that List is of type SomeList, where SomeList is declared by

```
Type   SomeList = Array [Lo..Hi] Of ComponentType;
```

and that Lo and Hi are some constants of type IndexType and ComponentType is any type. We also assume that Absurd is a constant of the IndexType and that the function should return Absurd if the Target is not found in the List. The Pascal version of this function, Linear1, is found in Listing 12.1.

Again, the While in Linear1 has a compound condition and, thus, an If is needed after the While to decide whether the Target was Found or not. If you knew the Target was in the List, you could simplify the program. This suggests the following trick: Guarantee that the Target is found by putting it in the List! In fact, if the Target is put in a special zeroth cell of the array and the search proceeds down from Hi, our function is made much simpler, as in Listing 12.2:

```
Function Linear2(Var List : SomeList; Target : ComponentType;
                              Hi : IndexType) : IndexType;
                                  {Not a complete program!}
{This function is our second implementation of the linear search.
This version uses a special zeroth cell of the array (just for this
search) to make sure that the search will  succeed.  This version
assumes that elements are stored in the array from index 1 and begins
its search at the Hi end. As such, it returns the Index of the last
occurrence of the Target, if the Target is present in the array.
Otherwise, the search finds the Target at the zeroth cell and uses
this to report failure.
Pre:   List, Target, Lo, and Hi already have values stored in them.
Post:  Linear2 returns the index of the last Target in List between
       Hi and 1.  It returns 0 if the Target is not found in the
       List between Hi and 1.                                     }

  Var Index : IndexType;

  Begin
    List[0] := Target;    {Place Target so Search will  succeed.}
    Index := Hi;                      {Search backwards from Hi.}
    While List[Index] <> Target Do            {Keep looking.}
      Index := Index - 1;                     {Look backwards.}
    Linear2 := Index                   {Return Index where found.}
  End;                         {Definition of function Linear2.}
```

Listing 12.2

In Listing 12.2, we have assumed that List was declared with lower subscript 0, although the actual elements of the List are stored from index 1 up to Hi. The zeroth place in the List is for the Target. This means that the Target will be found. Hence, the While is very simple. Note that, since we search backwards, we return the index of the *last* Target in List. Of course, if the Target isn't in the original List, we find it at the zeroth place (since that is where we put it), our While terminates, and Linear2 returns the absurd index 0.

BINARY SEARCH

It is perhaps difficult to think of any other type of search to perform besides a linear search. What could we do that would be any better than starting at one end and looking through the array? Nothing, actually, unless the array is ordered. Consider the task of finding a book in the fiction section at the library. If the books are arranged by the colors of their jackets and all you know is the author's name, you would have no choice but to apply a linear search to the books in the fiction section. But, if the books are arranged alphabetically by the author's last name, you wouldn't start at one end of the fiction section and look at each book until you find the one you want! That is, you don't use a linear search at the library. Rather, you use your knowledge of the order of the alphabet to obtain useful information from a book, even if it is not the book you want. For example, if the first book you see is by Asimov and the book you are looking for is by Ludlum, you know that you are not really warm yet and you can shift over several aisles. If, however, you find yourself among the Vonneguts, you know you've gone too far. In fact, your Ludlum book should be about halfway between the Asimov books and the Vonnegut books. This method may seem very clear for actual use in a library, but difficult to give precisely to a computer. We will, therefore, refine and define the algorithm.

Another example, perhaps, makes it clear that we use ordered searches in many instances in everyday life. Finding a telephone number for a given Chicagoan is not difficult if you have the proper spelling of the name. Imagine the opposite problem: Given a Chicago telephone number, find the name of the person who has that telephone number. Unless you have a reverse directory, ordered by telephone number instead of name, you are forced to do a linear search through the directory.

The array must be ordered before we can apply our fancy search method. If the items in the array are not ordered, then the only information we can get from a cell is that it is—or is not—the cell we are looking for. However, if the array is arranged in order, then each cell gives us information. If it does not contain our target, it at least tells us on which side of that cell to concentrate our search, allowing us to zero in on the target much more quickly.

Assume that List is an ordered array. For definiteness, assume that the elements of List are in increasing order. Of course, only minor modifications are needed if the array is in decreasing order. The elements of List can be of any type, such as Integer, Real, Char, or user-defined. In what follows, assume that we are looking for Target in List between the indices Lo and Hi. The **binary search** algorithm proceeds as follows: Start the search in the middle of the array List. That is, let Mid be the middle index between Lo and Hi. Then consider List[Mid]. Of course, if List[Mid] is our

Target, our search stops with success. However, if our Target is less than List[Mid], it is clear that we should continue our search between the new limits, Lo and Mid - 1. On the other hand, if Target exceeds List[Mid], we should continue the search between the indices Mid + 1 and Hi. The easiest way to continue the search between Lo and Mid - 1 is to set Hi to Mid - 1 and repeat the entire process. Likewise, to continue between Mid + 1 and Hi, we simply give Lo the new value Mid + 1 and repeat the process. Let us illustrate this algorithm with an example.

Suppose we have a list consisting of the following numbers:

1	2	3	4	5	6	7	8	9	10	11	12	13	14	15
13	15	18	25	27	32	39	42	45	48	53	57	60	65	66

Assume that the Target is 48. Of course, we begin with Lo equal to 1 and Hi equal to 15. We set Mid equal to (Lo + Hi) Div 2, or 8 in this case. Since List[8] is 42, which is smaller than our Target, we know that 48, if in the List at all, must be in the half between List[9] and List[15]. Hence, we set Lo to 9 and continue. The midpoint between 9 and 15 is 12, so we consider List[12] next. Since List[12] is 57 and, therefore, too large, the search has narrowed to between the indices 9 and 11 for Lo and Hi, respectively. The Mid value of these is 10, so List[10] is the Target and the search ends with success.

Before we implement the binary search, consider how an unsuccessful search terminates. For example, suppose we search the above array for 26. We begin again with Lo equal to 1 and Hi equal to 15. The search begins at List[Mid] where Mid is 8. Since that value is too big, the search is narrowed to between the indices 1 and 7. The new Mid point is 4 and List[4] is too small, so the search continues between the indices 5 and 7. Since List[6] is too big, we continue between the indices 5 and 5. Aha! Since List[5] is not our Target, we must report a failure! Actually, there is no reason to consider the case where Lo equals Hi as a special case. First of all, we need to make one last check at that cell (List[5] in the above example) to see whether it is the Target or not. In our case the midpoint between 5 and 5 is, of course, 5. Hence, we compare Target and List[5]. Here, List[5] is too large. This means that we should set Hi to Mid - 1 and continue. Thus, Lo is 5 and Hi is now 4. The absurd condition that Lo is bigger than Hi is our signal that the Target is not in the array. What we have seen is that List[4] is too small and, hence, the Target, if in the List, must be at, or beyond, the 5th place in the List. Later, we learn that List[5] is too large. Hence, the Target is at, or before, the 4th place. These two conditions together are contradictory. Hence, we may safely conclude that our Target is not in the List.

The Pascal function for the binary search is given in Listing 12.3. It assumes the following Type declaration:

```
Type   SomeList = Array [IndexType] Of ComponentType;
```

where IndexType is any subrange of Integers and ComponentType is any type. It also assumes that List is ordered in an ascending sequence and that you wish the search to proceed between the indices Lo and Hi. Further, we assume that Absurd is a constant of IndexType and that its value is not in the range from Lo to Hi. Of course, the function returns the index of the Target, if the Target is found, and the ridiculous value Absurd, if the Target is not found.

It is worthwhile pointing out the difference in efficiency between the two kinds of searches. For example, if we are searching an array of size 1000, using a linear search, it will take, on the average, 500 comparisons to find the target, since we will need, on the average, to look at half of the elements before finding a target that is in the array. On the other hand, the binary search takes, in the *worst* case, only 10 comparisons, since we need only divide by two 10 times to reduce an interval of 1000 elements to a single element. To see that 10 halving operations are sufficient, start with 1000 and repeatedly halve it.

```
Function BinarySearch(List : SomeList; Target : ComponentType;
                                  Lo, Hi : IndexType) : IndexType;
                                          {Not a complete program!}
{This function implements binary search.
Pre:   List, Target, Lo, and Hi have values and List is in increasing
       order.
Post:  BinarySearch returns the index of the first Target found and
       Absurd if the Target is not found.                          }

  Var Mid    : IndexType;
      Found  : Boolean;
      Value  : ComponentType;

  Begin
    Found := False;                        {Target is not yet found.}
    While (Lo <= Hi) And Not Found Do           {Keep looking.}
      Begin
        Mid := (Lo + Hi) Div 2;
        Value := List[Mid];
        If Value = Target Then
          Found := True           {Eureka! Target has been found.}
        Else If Value > Target Then
          Hi := Mid - 1                     {Move Hi down below Mid.}
        Else
          Lo := Mid + 1                     {Move Lo up beyond Mid.}
      End; {If and While}
    If Found Then
      BinarySearch := Mid
    Else
      BinarySearch := Absurd
  End;                            {Definition of function BinarySearch.}
```

Listing 12.3

1. 1000   `Div` 2 is 500
2.   500   `Div` 2 is 250
3.   250   `Div` 2 is 125
4.   125   `Div` 2 is 62
5.   62   `Div` 2 is 31
6.   31   `Div` 2 is 15
7.   15   `Div` 2 is 7
8.   7   `Div` 2 is 3
9.   3   `Div` 2 is 1
10.   1   `Div` 2 is 0

At each stage, the number on the right is, in the worst case, the number of elements still to check. As we see, after 10 probes, the interval of uncertainty has been completely removed.

Note that doubling the size of the array *doubles* the number of comparisons needed with the linear search, while the number of comparisons needed in the binary search only increases by 1! For example, it will take, on the average, 1000 probes to find an element in an array of 2000 elements using linear search, but only 11 probes in the worst case with the binary search (because, after one probe in the middle, we will have reduced the search in the binary case to searching in an array of 1000 elements). The difference between these search methods becomes enormous as the array size gets large. For example, if the list is 1,000,000 elements long, the number of comparisons is 500,000 (on the average) for the linear search, compared with 20 for the binary search. We leave it to the reader to verify that 20 probes is sufficient. If the reader is surprised at this figure, think about how easy it is to find a book in a large library or a phone number in a large city telephone directory using an ordered search and how difficult these tasks would be if a linear search were used.

TIMING PROGRAM EXECUTION

Listing 12.4 shows a program, `Timer`, that introduces the Turbo Pascal specific built-in procedure `GetTime` that can be used to time program executions. All program `Timer` does is time your reaction speed in pressing the RETURN key. The program has nothing to do with searching or sorting, but the techniques introduced in `Timer` will be used in the next programs to illustrate the differences between various searches and various sorts. That is, although `GetTime` is nonstandard, we introduce it so that we can use it to do some rough comparisons of various searching and sorting algorithms.

`Timer` waits at the first `Readln` for you to press the RETURN key. It doesn't matter how slowly you do this, because the first `GetTime` is not executed until after the `Readln`. Actually, the program times the first call to `GetTime`, the prompts, and your response time to press the RETURN key again. Since the computer operates at speeds far in excess of human speeds, we attribute all of the wait time to you. To use `GetTime`, we need the phrase `Uses DOS`, as `GetTime`, in Turbo Pascal, is supplied in the DOS library. Also, note that `GetTime` needs four parameters that are of the special integer type `Word`. The user need not be concerned with these details, but should freely copy them into any program where timing is needed.

```
Program Timer; {$R+}
{This program illustrates the nonstandard procedure GetTime.
GetTime is a special Turbo Pascal procedure that reads the system
clock and is convenient for timing competing algorithms. See the
use of GetTime in the program Searches and the program Sorts. }

Uses DOS;                          {Loads necessary Turbo Pascal Libary.}

Var    StartHours, StopHours : Word;{Word is a Turbo Pascal type.}
       StartMins, StopMins   : Word;
       StartSecs, StopSecs   : Word;
       StartHuns, StopHuns   : Word;

Begin
  Writeln('Please press the RETURN key.');
  Readln;
  {First, read the clock to get the start time.}
  GetTime(StartHours, StartMins, StartSecs, StartHuns);
  Writeln('How fast can you press RETURN again?');
  Readln;
  {Now, read the clock again to get the stop time.}
  GetTime(StopHours, StopMins, StopSecs, StopHuns);
  Writeln('Start time was: ', StartHours:2, ':', StartMins:2,
                            ':', StartSecs:2, ':', StartHuns:2);
  Writeln;
  Writeln('Stop time was:  ', StopHours:2, ':', StopMins:2,
                            ':', StopSecs:2, ':', StopHuns:2)
End.
```

Listing 12.4

Figure 12.1 shows an execution of Timer. It leaves it to you to subtract and determine the delay between key presses. We leave it as an exercise for the reader to add embellishments to Timer.


```
Please press the RETURN key.

How fast can you press RETURN again?

Start time was: 10:15:03:22

Stop time was:  10:15:03:33
```

Figure 12.1

A MAJOR PROGRAM: SEARCHES

Listing 12.5 shows a major program, Searches, that dynamically illustrates linear and binary searches in an ordered array of 10,000 elements. The program is divided into three major subprograms:

GenArray   generates the ordered array to be searched
DoLinear   directs and times the linear searches
DoBinary   directs and times the binary searches

The main program calls GenArray *once* and then repeatedly gives the user a menu of the form:

L)inear Search
B)inary Search
Q)uit the program

Obviously, the first choice calls DoLinear, the second calls DoBinary, and the third lets the user out of the program.

GenArray, so that binary search can be applied, generates an array that is already ordered. To make the array interesting each element is randomly 1 or 2 more than the previous element. This is accomplished by the following pseudo-code:

Set A[1] to Random(2) + 1
For Index from 2 to upperlimit do
    A[Index] ← A[Index - 1] + Random(2) + 1

DoLinear controls the linear search and has our second version of Linear defined within it. Note that Linear is now a procedure, because it returns the index of the Target as well as the number of probes, NumProbes, needed by the search. DoBinary likewise controls the binary search and has the Binary procedure defined within it. The procedure Binary is so fast that we have found that it can do a search in no elapsed time! That is, GetTime measures fairly large, from the computer's point of view, ticks of the clock, and it is possible for Binary to have finished its work before GetTime can recognize any change in the clock. Also, GetTime often cannot distinguish between the time it takes Binary to search 1000 elements and the time it takes to search 10,000 elements. Therefore, to help alleviate these problems, DoBinary repeats each search 1000 times. This is done to help increase the timings so that differences in them will be seen as the array size changes. If you have a very fast processor, you may have to increase these constants to see the differences between linear and binary searches.

Program Searches; {$R+}
{This program illustrates the linear and the binary search in a
randomly generated array. So that the binary search will be
applicable, the array is generated in increasing order (i.e.,
already sorted).   }

Listing 12.5

```
Uses DOS;                    {Needed for GetTime. See Timer for details.}

Const    ArraySize = 10000;       {Change, run, and note timings.}
         NumRuns   = 1000;              {Number of binary searches.}

Type List = Array[0..ArraySize] of Integer;        {0th place for}
                                {second version of linear search.}

Var    Numbers   : List;
       Response  : Char;
       StartHrs  : Word;                      {All Word variables}
       StartMins : Word;                      {needed for timings.}
       StartSecs : Word;                      {All timing variables}
       StartHuns : Word;                      {are passed globally.}
       StopHrs   : Word;
       StopMins  : Word;
       StopSecs  : Word;
       StopHuns  : Word;

Procedure GenArray(Var Numbers : List);

{Pre:  None
 Post: Numbers is generated in increasing order with the first
       element 1 or 2 and each consecutive value 1 or 2 larger than
       the previous one.                                            }

  Var Index : Integer;

  Begin
    Writeln('Please wait - generating an ordered array of',
                              ArraySize, ' elements.');
    Numbers[1] := Random(2) + 1;        {Put 1 or 2 in 1st cell.}
    For Index := 2 to ArraySize do
      Numbers[Index] := Numbers[Index - 1] + Random(2) + 1
                        {Add 1 or 2 to previous array value.}
    End;                      {Definition of procedure GenArray.}

Procedure DoLinear(Var Numbers : List);

{This procedure prompts for the target and controls the invocation
of the actual linear search.

Pre:  Numbers has values stored in it.
Post: The time to do one linear search for a user-specified Target
      is printed.                                                  }

  Var Target    : Integer;
      Place     : Integer;
      NumProbes : Integer;
```

Listing 12.5 (continued)

```
Procedure Linear(Var Numbers : List; Target : Integer;
                 Var NumProbes : Integer; Var Place : Integer);
  {This nested procedure does the linear search. It counts the
  number of probes it needs to make into the array and returns the
  place of the Target in the array. It also uses the special 0th
  cell of the array to make the search simpler.

  Pre:   Numbers and Target have values.
  Post:  If Target is found, Place contains its index; otherwise,
         Place is zero. NumProbes contains a count of the number
         of cells tested.                                        }

  Var Index : Integer;

  Begin
    NumProbes := 0;
    Numbers[0] := Target;          {Place Target into the array.}
    Index := ArraySize;            {Begin search at the high end.}
    While Numbers[Index] <> Target Do
      Begin
        Index := Index - 1;
        NumProbes := NumProbes + 1
      End; {While}
    NumProbes := NumProbes + 1;     {Count probe to exit While.}
    Place := Index
  End;                              {Definition of procedure Linear.}
Begin                               {Body of procedure DoLinear.}
  Write('Please enter the target ');
  Readln(Target);
  Writeln('Press RETURN to begin the linear search.');
  Readln;
  GetTime(StartHrs, StartMins, StartSecs, StartHuns);
  Linear(Numbers, Target, NumProbes, Place);{Do linear search.}
  GetTime(StopHrs, StopMins, StopSecs, StopHuns);
  Writeln('D O N E !!');
  Writeln('Linear Search started at: ', StartHrs:2, ':',
           StartMins:2, ':', StartSecs:2, ':', StartHuns:2);
  Writeln('One Search completed at:  ', StopHrs:2, ':',
             StopMins:2, ':', StopSecs:2, ':', StopHuns:2);
  Writeln;
  If Place = 0 Then
    Writeln('Sorry, ', Target, ' was not in the array.')
  Else
    Writeln(Target, ' was in ', Place, 'th cell of the array.');
  Writeln(NumProbes, ' probes were needed to decide this.')
End;                                {Definition of procedure DoLinear.}
```

Listing 12.5 (continued)

```
Procedure DoBinary(Var Numbers : List);
{This procedure prompts for the Target and controls the invocation
of the actual binary search.

Pre: Numbers has values stored in it, in increasing order.
Post: The time to do 1000 binary searches for the Target is printed.}

  Var    Target     : Integer;
         Place      : Integer;
         NumProbes  : Integer;
         Run        : Integer;

    Procedure Binary(Var Numbers : List; Target : Integer;
                        Var NumProbes : Integer; Var Place : Integer;
                                          Lo, Hi : Integer);
    {This nested procedure does the binary search.
    Pre:    Numbers and Target have values and Numbers is in increasing
            order. Lo and Hi also have values.
    Post:   If Target is found, between Lo and Hi, Place contains its
            index; otherwise, Place is zero. NumProbes contains a
            count of the number of cells tested.                  }

  Var    Mid   : Integer;
         Found : Boolean;
         Value : Integer;

  Begin
    Found := False;
    NumProbes := 0;
    While (Lo <= Hi) And Not Found Do
      Begin
        Mid := (Lo + Hi) Div 2;
        Value := Numbers[Mid];
        NumProbes := NumProbes + 1;
        If Value = Target Then
          Found := True
        Else If Value > Target Then
          Hi := Mid - 1
        Else
          Lo := Mid + 1
      End; {If and While}
    If Found Then
      Place := Mid
    Else
      Place := 0
  End;                                    {Definition of procedure Binary.}
```

Listing 12.5 (continued)

```
Begin                                   {Body of procedure DoBinary.}
  Write('Please enter the target ');
  Readln(Target);
  Writeln('Press RETURN to begin the binary search.');
  Readln;
  GetTime(StartHrs, StartMins, StartSecs, StartHuns);
  For Run := 1 To NumRuns Do {Repeatedly do the binary search.}
    Binary(Numbers, Target, NumProbes, Place, 1, ArraySize);
  GetTime(StopHrs, StopMins, StopSecs, StopHuns);
  Writeln('D O N E !!');
  Writeln(Binary Search started at:          ', StartHrs:2, ':',
            StartMins:2, ':', StartSecs:2, ':', StartHuns:2);
  Writeln(NumRuns, ' searches completed at: ', StopHrs:2, ':',
              StopMins:2, ':', StopSecs:2, ':', StopHuns:2);
  Writeln;
  If Place = 0 Then
    Writeln('Sorry, ', Target, ' was not in the array.')
  Else
    Writeln(Target,' was in ', Place,'th cell of the array.');
  Writeln(NumProbes, ' probes were needed to decide this.')
End;                                {Definition of procedure DoBinary.}


Begin                                   {Body of main program Searches.}
  Randomize;
  GenArray(Numbers);                    {Generate the (sorted) array.}
  Repeat                                {Give user a menu of choices.}
    Writeln; Writeln;
    Writeln('  L)inear Search');
    Writeln;
    Writeln('  B)inary Search');
    Writeln;
    Writeln('  Q)uit this program');
    Writeln;
    Write('Please choose an option (L, B, Q) ');
    Readln(Response);
    Case Response of
      'L', 'l' : DoLinear(Numbers);
      'B', 'b' : DoBinary(Numbers);
      'Q', 'q' : {Do Nothing}
      Else Writeln('Pay Attention!')
    End {Case}
  Until (Response = 'Q') Or (Response = 'q')
End.
```

Listing 12.5 (continued)

```
. . .
D O N E ! !
Linear Search started at: 11:33:10:16
One search completed at:  11:33:10:82

Sorry, 1 was not in the array.
10001 probes were needed to decide this.

. . .
D O N E ! !
Binary Search started at:   11:33:20:88
1000 searches completed at: 11:33:23:16

Sorry, 1 was not in the array.
13 probes were needed to decide this.
```

Figure 12.2

Figure 12.2 shows some output from an execution of Searches looking for the Target 1. The program was run on a very slow processor, so the timing results that you get may be significantly different, but the relative differences between linear and binary search should still hold.

The linear search required 0.66 second to search the entire array, while binary search needed 2.36 seconds to determine the same result 1000 times. Thus, each binary search required approximately 0.00236 second and used only 13 probes on each search. In the exercises, we let the reader determine timings for other array sizes and graphically compare the two searches.

SORTING AN ARRAY

As we have seen, it is necessary that an array be in order before a binary search can be applied. Hence, sorting an array is obviously an important topic. Also, before a list is output for human consumption, it is often useful to sort the list first.

In this section, we present three different sorting methods and leave a fourth for the exercises. In Chapter 18, we will present a fifth sort method that is faster than any of the elementary sorts discussed here.

BUBBLE SORT

The bubble sort is best described by an example. Consider the unordered array A of Figure 12.3. Suppose our objective is to sort A in increasing order (smallest to largest). Note that the items in A are integers. We could just as well sort reals, or even strings, since the system knows the alphabetical ordering of strings. Also, we could just as well sort the list into descending order. Moreover, the given list has no duplicates (no 8 twice, for example), but duplicates do not cause any problems to the algorithm. We leave these cases to the reader as exercises.

Consider the bottom two elements of the array, as shown shaded in Figure 12.4a. Since 3 is smaller than 7, they are out of order, and we swap them to obtain Figure 12.4b.

Now, we use the next pair, 3 and 6, as shown shaded in Figure 12.4c. Since they are

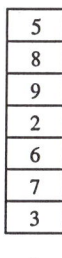

Figure 12.3

out of order, we swap them to obtain Figure 12.4d. The next pair, 2 and 3, of Figure 12.4e, are in order and, thus, are not swapped. Next, we consider the pairs of Figures 12.4f, 12.4h, and 12.4j, in turn, and swap to obtain the Figures 12.4g, 12.4i, and 12.4k, respectively. The array A is not yet in order, but it is more closely in order than it was. In particular, the 2 has bubbled to the top, explaining the name for this sort. The work depicted in Figure 12.4 is called the first pass of the bubble sort. What it did was bring the smallest element to the top (as well as bring other elements like 3 up a little). We now repeat the bubbling from the bottom. This will bring the second smallest element up. This second pass of the bubble sort is depicted, in less detail, in Figure 12.5.

In pass 2, Figure 12.5, there is no need to test the element bubbling up with the top element. Before we begin pass 2, we know that the smallest element is already at the top. Pass 2 will place the second smallest element at position 2 in the array. When pass 2 is complete, we will have the two smallest elements in the top two positions. It will be pass 3's job to bring the third smallest element to the third position. Thus, we see that each successive pass has less work to do. This is demonstrated in Figure 12.6, which shows the results of passes 3, 4, 5, and 6 with the bubble sort. The bar indicates elements that we know are already in their proper places and do not need to be compared on this pass. Figure 12.6 shows complete passes and not the atomic events of Figures 12.4 and 12.5. We leave it to the reader to take out scrap paper and check the results shown in Figure 12.6. Each pass does more than just bring the next lightest element to the top. Each pass starts at the bottom of the array and bubbles lighter elements up. For example, in pass 3, the 6 bubbles up until it it is stopped by the 5.

Observe that at most N - 1 passes are needed when sorting N elements, because when all but one element is in its proper place, the last element must also be in its proper place. Also, notice that the elements displayed in our example were actually sorted at the end of pass 4, but the algorithm didn't realize it. Below, we discuss a variant of bubble sort

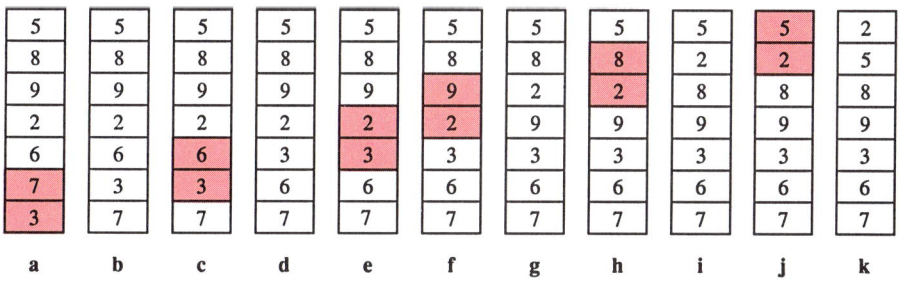

Figure 12.4

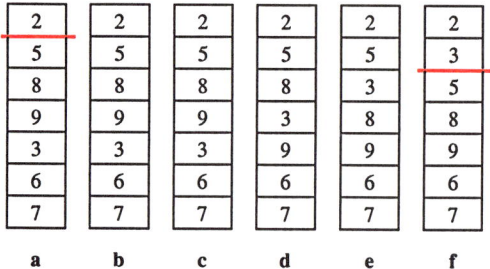

Figure 12.5

that tries to realize this and stop before all N - 1 passes are completed, if possible.

Here is the pseudo-code for the bubble sort on an array of N elements, indexed from 1. Notice how each successive pass is shorter than the previous one, since it only goes up to element number Pass + 1:

For Pass ← 1 to N - 1
    For Index ← N down to Pass + 1
        If A[Index] and A[Index -1] are out of order then
            Swap them

The Pascal for this pseudo-code is shown in Listing 12.6.

```
Procedure Bubble(Var A : ArrayType; SizeArray : Integer);
                              {WARNING: Not a complete program.}

Pre:   A is indexed from 1 to SizeArray and A already has values
       stored in it.

Post: A is sorted in increasing order.                        }

Var   Pass  : Integer;
      Index : Integer;

Procedure Swap(Var X,Y : Integer);
{Pre: X and Y have values.
Post: The values of X and Y are interchanged.                 }

  Var Temp : Integer;

  Begin
    Temp := X;
    X := Y;
    Y := Temp
  End;                                    {Definition of procedure Swap.}

Begin                                         {Body of procedure Bubble.}
  For Pass := 1 To SizeArray - 1 Do
    For Index := SizeArray Downto Pass + 1 Do
      If A[Index] < A[Index - 1] Then
        Swap(A[Index], A[Index - 1])
End;                                     {Definition of procedure Bubble.}
```

Listing 12.6

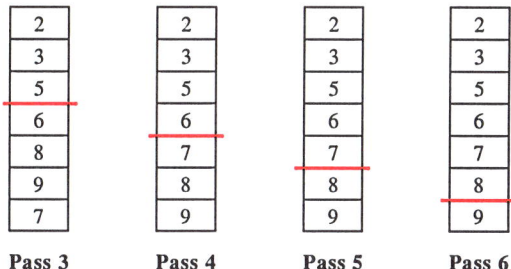

Figure 12.6

MODIFIED BUBBLE SORT

As we have seen, sometimes not all N - 1 passes are needed to sort N objects. Could we make the bubble sort more efficient by stopping early? How could we decide when it is safe to stop? Clearly, if we make no swaps during a pass, we can stop the whole process. Since we don't know how many passes will be needed, the outer loop will become a While instead of a For. We loop *while* we haven't completed N - 1 passes and *while* we still needed a swap on the last pass. These modifications to Bubble are shown using a Boolean SwapsNeeded in a ModifiedBubble sort shown in Listing 12.7.

```
Procedure ModifiedBubble(Var A : ArrayType; SizeArray : Integer);
                              {WARNING: Not a complete program.}
{This procedure does a modified bubble sort of the array A. It stops
when it discovers a pass on which no swaps were needed.

Pre:   A is indexed from 1 to SizeArray and A already has values
       stored in it.
Post:  A is sorted into increasing order.                         }

Var    Pass          : Integer;
       Index         : Integer;
       SwapsNeeded   : Boolean;

Procedure Swap(Var X,Y : Integer);
{Pre:  X and Y have values already.
Post:  The values of X and Y are interchanged.                    }

  Var Temp : Integer;
  Begin
    Temp := X;
    X := Y;
    Y := Temp
  End;                              {Definition of procedure Swap.}
```

```
Begin                          {Body of procedure ModifiedBubble.}
  Pass := 1;
  SwapsNeeded := True;         {Initialize SwapsNeeded for While.}
  While (Pass < SizeArray) And SwapsNeeded Do
    Begin
      SwapsNeeded := False;          {Assume no more swaps needed.}
      For Index := SizeArray Downto Pass + 1 Do
        If A[Index] < A[Index - 1] Then
          Begin
            Swap(A[Index], A[Index - 1]);
            SwapsNeeded := True     {Swap was needed after all.}
          End; {If and For}
      Pass := Pass + 1
    End {While}
End;                          {Definition of procedure ModifiedBubble.}
```

Listing 12.7

Later, we consider a program, Sorts, that compares our two versions of the bubble sort and lets us see how much (if any) our modified algorthim is better than our original version.

INSERTION SORT

We now consider a different sort, a simple and fairly efficient sort known as the **insertion sort**. Before we look at the implementation in Pascal, let's try to understand how insertion sort works. Insertion sort begins with the totally obvious idea that any list of one item is properly sorted. If we have a list of two items, we simply decide whether the second item should be inserted before or after the first item. If we have a list of three items, we ignore the third item for a moment and insert the second in the correct spot relative to the first. Then, we insert the third, either before the first, between the first and second, or after the second. In general, if we have N items, we insert the second, third, . . . , Nth items into their proper place, with regard to those already present. You have probably used the insertion sort, as it is the common sort that people use when dealt a hand of cards. That is, card players normally order their hand as they pick it up, inserting each new card in its proper place with respect to the cards already held.

We illustrate the idea of the insertion sort with an example. Let us sort the list

1	2	3	4	5	6
86	39	42	12	24	53

Since a one-element list is in order, we need insert only elements 2 through 6 into their proper places. The key to inserting an element is to ignore all elements with higher indices. That is, when inserting the Index th element, we need look only at elements 1 to Index - 1.

Index = 2, insert 39 with respect to the first element:

	1	2	3	4	5	6
Before:	86	39	42	12	24	53

	1	2	3	4	5	6
After	39	86	42	12	24	53

Index = 3, insert 42 with respect to the first two elements:

	1	2	3	4	5	6
Before:	39	86	42	12	24	53

	1	2	3	4	5	6
After	39	42	86	12	24	53

Index = 4, insert 12 with respect to the first three elements:

	1	2	3	4	5	6
Before:	39	42	86	12	24	53

	1	2	3	4	5	6
After	12	39	42	86	24	53

Index = 5, insert 24 with respect to the first four elements:

	1	2	3	4	5	6
Before:	12	39	42	86	24	53

	1	2	3	4	5	6
After	12	24	39	42	86	53

Index = 6, insert 53 with respect to the first five elements:

	1	2	3	4	5	6
Before:	12	24	39	42	86	53

	1	2	3	4	5	6
After	12	24	39	42	53	86

Presto, the list is sorted. Notice that all numbers to the left of the vertical bar are sorted and, on each pass, the number to the immediate right of the bar is inserted into its proper place with respect to those to the left.

Now that we understand how insertion sort works, our concern becomes implementing it in a fairly efficient manner in Pascal. To be specific, let us suppose that the array is A and that there are SizeArray elements in A. Here, in general pseudo-code, is the idea of the insertion sort:

For Index := 2 to SizeArray do
    Find the Place where A[Index] should follow A[Place]
    Slide elements from A[Place + 1] to A[Index - 1] up one cell
    Insert A[Index] into A[Place + 1]

Let's consider in more detail what is involved in finding the Place, sliding elements, and inserting a new element. In particular, consider the situation when the list is

	1	2	3	4	5	6
A:	12	39	42	86	24	53

and Index is 5; i.e., it is time to insert 24 into the list. We see that 39, 42, and 86 must slide over to make room for 24, but how do we instruct the computer to do this? First, we know that whenever we swap elements around, we need a temporary storage location so that we don't lose any values. Hence, let us first store 24 in Temp:

Temp: | 24 |

	1	2	3	4	5	6
A:	12	39	42	86	24	53

Now, cell A[5] is really not being used, so we can slide A[4] into A[5]:

Temp: | 24 |

	1	2	3	4	5	6
A:	12	39	42	86	86	53

Now, cell A[5] is free and we slide again:

Temp: | 24 |

	1	2	3	4	5	6
A:	12	39	42	42	86	53

And again:

Temp: | 24 |

	1	2	3	4	5	6
A:	12	39	39	42	86	53

Finally, A[1] is not larger than Temp, so the sliding stops and we insert Temp into A[2]:

Temp: | 24 |

	1	2	3	4	5	6
A:	12	24	39	42	86	53

Now the first five elements are sorted and the procedure continues by saving 53 in Temp, sliding 86 over, and then inserting 53 into its proper place. Observe that we have combined two lines of our pseudo-code, for now we are finding the *place* for the new element to be inserted as we *slide* the larger elements. Doing these steps together is much more efficient than doing them separately.

There is, however, one problem with our algorithm. What if the element to be inserted is smaller than all the others? Obviously, then, everybody should slide and the new element should be inserted into A[1]. However, we indicated above that the sliding should continue while the Temp element is smaller than the current element in the list. If we are not careful, we will get a subscript-out-of-bounds error. Namely, after we slide A[1] into A[2], our program is likely to check to see if the nonexistent element A[0] needs to slide.

One can handle this problem by special checks, but the most elegant method, since we need a temporary location anyway, is to declare zero to be a legal subscript for the

```
Procedure InsertionSort(Var A : List; SizeArray : Integer);
{This procedure sorts the array A using insertion sort. We assume
A has a zeroth element where temporary elements can be stored.

Pre:   A is indexed from 0 to SizeArray with values stored beginning
       at index 1.
Post: A is sorted in increasing order.                              }

Var    Index : Integer;
       Spot  : Integer;

Begin
  For Index := 2 To SizeArray Do
    Begin
      A[0] := A[Index];                    {Save A[Index] temporarily.}
      Spot := Index - 1;
      While A[Spot] > A[0] Do              {Slide bigger elements up.}
        Begin
          A[Spot + 1] := A[Spot];
          Spot := Spot - 1
        End; {While}
      A[Spot + 1] := A[0]                       {Insert new element.}
    End {For}
End;                        {Definition of procedure InsertionSort.}
```

Listing 12.8

array A and then use A[0] for Temp. Since we slide elements until we find one not smaller than A[0], A[0] itself, if necessary, stops the sliding! We have again, as in our elegant version of the linear search, found a clever use for a special zeroth element of an array. The procedure InsertionSort, given in Listing 12.8, sorts the list A of length SizeArray in ascending order using this technique.

A MAJOR PROGRAM: SORTS

A major program, Sorts, that allows us to compare our various sorting algorithms is given in Listing 12.9. Note that the main program is only five lines long. It calls Randomize and then GenArray to generate a random List of elements. The main program then calls the three control procedures DoBubble, DoModifiedBubble, and DoInsertion that manage the three sorting methods that we have described. Each control procedure prints the original array (to prove that each sort is starting with the same array), times the sort, and finally displays the sorted array. We leave it to the reader to determine (by inspecting the parameter-passing techniques) how the second and third sorts get the original array, and not the sorted array. In the exercises, we suggest another sort, known as selection sort, for you to add to the program Sorts.

```
Program Sorts; {$R+}
{This program illustrates the insertion sort and two versions of
the bubble sort. In the exercises, you are asked to add to this
program.                                                          }

Uses DOS;    {Special Turbo Pascal Library, needed for GetTime.}

Const ArrayLimit = 250;{Change, rerun, and observe the timings.}

Type ArrayType = Array[0..ArrayLimit] Of Integer;    {0th place}
                    {is for the trick in the insertion sort.}

Var    List      : ArrayType;
       StartHrs  : Word;              {Special Turbo Pascal type,}
       StartMins : Word;                         {for GetTime.}
       StartSecs : Word;                  {All the timing variables}
       StartHuns : Word;                      {are passed globally.}
       StopHrs   : Word;
       StopMins  : Word;
       StopSecs  : Word;
       StopHuns  : Word;

Procedure GenArray(Var A: ArrayType);
{Pre: None
Post: Random elements (0-999) are assigned to all ArrayLimit
      entries of A.                                              }

  Var Index : Integer;

  Begin
    For Index := 1 To ArrayLimit Do
      A[Index] := Random(1000)
  End;                            {Definition of procedure GenArray.}

Procedure PrintArray(Var A : ArrayType);
{Pre: A has values stored in it.
Post: All the values in A are printed, 10 to a line.             }

  Var Index : Integer;

  Begin
    For Index := 1 to ArrayLimit Do
      Begin
        If Index Mod 10 = 1 Then
          Writeln;
        Write(A[Index]:7)
      End
  End;                           {Definition of procedure PrintArray.}
```

Listing 12.9

```
Procedure Swap(Var X, Y : Integer);
{This procedure is placed so that any sort that needs it can call
it.
Pre:   X and Y have values.
Post:  The values of X and Y are interchanged.                    }

  Var Temp : Integer;

  Begin
    Temp := X;
    X := Y;
    Y := Temp
  End;                                {Definition of procedure Swap.}

Procedure DoBubble(List : ArrayType);
{This procedure controls the invocation of the bubble sort.
Pre:   List has values (but is unordered).
Post:  The values in List are displayed, then List is sorted. Timings
       for the sort are displayed, and then the sorted list is
       displayed.                                                 }

  Procedure Bubble(Var A : ArrayType);
  {This nested procedure does a bubble sort of the array A.
  Pre:   A has values stored in it.
  Post:  A is in increasing order.                               }

    Var    Pass  : Integer;
           Index : Integer;

    Begin
      For Pass := 1 To ArrayLimit - 1 Do
        For Index := ArrayLimit Downto Pass + 1 Do
          If A[Index] < A[Index - 1] Then
            Swap(A[Index], A[Index - 1])
    End;                              {Definition of procedure Bubble.}

  Begin                               {Body of procedure DoBubble.}
    Writeln; Writeln; Writeln;
    Writeln('Here is the original array:');
    Writeln;
    PrintArray(List);
    Writeln; Writeln;
    Writeln('Press RETURN to begin the bubble sort:');
    Readln;
    GetTime(StartHrs, StartMins, StartSecs, StartHuns);
    Bubble(List);
    GetTime(StopHrs, StopMins, StopSecs, StopHuns);
```

Listing 12.9 (continued)

```
        Writeln('Bubble Sort started at:  ', StartHrs:2, ':',
                StartMins:2, ':', StartSecs:2, ':', StartHuns:2);
        Writeln('Sort completed at:       ', StopHrs:2, ':',
                StopMins:2, ':', StopSecs:2, ':', StopHuns:2);
        Writeln;
        Writeln('Press RETURN to see the sorted array.');
        Readln;
        PrintArray(List);
        Writeln; Writeln;
        Writeln('Hit RETURN to continue.');
        Readln
    End;                             {Definition of procedure DoBubble.}
Procedure DoModifiedBubble(List : ArrayType);
{This procedure controls the invocation of the modified bubble
sort.
Pre:  List has values (but is unordered).
Post: The values in List are displayed, then List is sorted. Timings
      for the sort are displayed, and then the sorted list is
      displayed.                                                      }

    Procedure ModifiedBubble(Var A : ArrayType);
    {This nested procedure does a modified bubble sort of the array
    A. It stops when it discovers a pass where no swaps are needed.

    Pre:  A has values stored in it.
    Post: A is in increasing order.                                  }

    Var    Pass        : Integer;
           Index       : Integer;
           SwapsNeeded : Boolean;

    Begin
      Pass := 1;
      SwapsNeeded := True;
      While (Pass < ArrayLimit) And SwapsNeeded Do
        Begin
          SwapsNeeded := False;
          For Index := ArrayLimit Downto Pass + 1 Do
            If A[Index] < A[Index - 1] Then
              Begin
                Swap(A[Index], A[Index - 1]);
                SwapsNeeded := True
              End; {If and For}
          Pass := Pass + 1
        End {While}
    End;                      {Definition of procedure ModifiedBubble.}
```

Listing 12.9 (continued)

```
  Begin                         {Body of procedure DoModifiedBubble.}
    Writeln; Writeln; Writeln;
    Writeln('Here is the original array:');
    Writeln;
    PrintArray(List);
    Writeln; Writeln;
    Writeln('Press RETURN to begin the modified bubble sort:');
    Readln;
    GetTime(StartHrs, StartMins, StartSecs, StartHuns);
    ModifiedBubble(List);
    GetTime(StopHrs, StopMins, StopSecs, StopHuns);
    Writeln('Modified Bubble Sort started at: ',StartHrs:2,
          ':', StartMins:2, ':', StartSecs:2, ':', StartHuns:2);
    Writeln('Sort completed at:                  ',StopHrs:2, ':',
                StopMins:2, ':', StopSecs:2, ':', StopHuns:2);
    Writeln;
    Writeln('Press RETURN to see the sorted array.');
    Readln;
    PrintArray(List);
    Writeln; Writeln;
    Writeln('Hit RETURN to continue.');
    Readln
  End;                      {Definition of procedure DoModifiedBubble.}

Procedure DoInsertion(List : ArrayType);

{This procedure controls the invocation of the insertion sort.
Pre:  List has values (but is unordered).
Post:  The values in List are displayed, then List is sorted. Timings
      for the sort are displayed, and then the sorted list is
      displayed.                                                    }

  Procedure Insertion(Var A : ArrayType);

  {This nested procedure does the actual insertion sort of the array
  A.
  Pre:  A has values stored in it.
  Post: A is in increasing order.                                 }

    Var   Spot  : Integer;
          Index : Integer;

    Begin
      For Spot := 2 To ArrayLimit Do          {Insert the Spot-th}
                                                       {element.}
        Begin
          A[0] := A[Spot];        {Hold element to be inserted.}
          Index := Spot - 1;    {Try sliding previous elements.}
```

Listing 12.9 (continued)

```
        While A[Index] > A[0] Do                    {Slide and try}
          Begin                                     {previous element.}
            A[Index + 1] := A[Index];
            Index := Index - 1
          End; {While}
        A[Index + 1] := A[0]              {Insert the new element.}
      End {For}
  End;                                  {Definition of procedure Insertion.}

Begin                                  {Body of procedure DoInsertion.}
  Writeln; Writeln; Writeln;
  Writeln('Here is the original array:');
  Writeln;
  PrintArray(List);
  Writeln; Writeln;
  Writeln('Press RETURN to begin the insertion sort:');
  Readln;
  GetTime(StartHrs, StartMins, StartSecs, StartHuns);
  Insertion(List);
  GetTime(StopHrs, StopMins, StopSecs, StopHuns);
  Writeln(Insertion Sort started at: ', StartHrs:2, ':',
          StartMins:2, ':', StartSecs:2, ':', StartHuns:2);
  Writeln('Sort completed at:        ', StopHrs:2, ':',
            StopMins:2, ':', StopSecs:2, ':', StopHuns:2);
  Writeln;
  Writeln('Press RETURN to see the sorted array.');
  Readln;
  PrintArray(List);
  Writeln; Writeln
End;                                  {Definition of procedure DoInsertion.}

Begin                                  {Body of main program sorts.}
  Randomize;
  GenArray(List);
  DoBubble(List);
  DoModifiedBubble(List);
  DoInsertion(List)
End.
```

Listing 12.9 (continued)

In the exercises, you are invited to run Sorts with several different values for the constant ArrayLimit. We strongly suggest that you do this exercise, since it will show you how our three sorts compare with each other on random data. It will also give you some idea of how the complexity of sorting grows as the size of the array grows.

SUMMARY

The concepts of searching and sorting are of obvious importance. We have seen that sorting is necessary before the elegant binary search can be applied. Also, almost all output that is meant for humans is sorted in some way before being displayed. You should, therefore, become familiar with searching and sorting techniques. In the exercises, we suggest a fourth simple sort known as **selection sort**. We strongly suggest that you write this sort and add it to the `Sorts` program. This will permit you to see how selection sort compares, with random data, to our other sorts. In Chapter 18, we'll introduce another sort, **quick sort**, that is faster than any of the sorts described here.

KEY ALGORITHMS

In reviewing the material of this chapter, be sure that you can describe the ideas behind each of the following algorithms:

Linear search   Binary search
Bubble sort   Modified bubble sort
Insertion sort

SELF-TEST QUESTIONS

12.1 What change is necessary to the bubble sort to make it sort in descending order? Likewise, what change is necessary to the insertion sort to make it sort in descending order?

12.2 Show each pass on the following array as it is sorted by

a) Bubble sort

b) Modified bubble sort

c) Insertion sort

1	2	3	4	5	6	7	8	9	10
22	47	72	34	15	66	98	7	53	38

Remember that a pass—for bubble sort, for example—is one complete set of swaps, not just the swapping of 53 and 38. In general, a pass is one complete execution of the outside loop.

EXERCISES

12.3 (Selection sort) Another simple sort is known as selection sort. It works as follows: On the first pass, find the largest element in the array and swap this element with the last element in the array. For example, if the array is

1	2	3	4	5	6	7	8
12	6	18	24	15	9	2	11

then, on pass 1, it finds 24 in the fourth place and swaps 24 and 11, putting 24 at the end:

1	2	3	4	5	6	7	8
12	6	18	11	15	9	2	24

On the second pass, it finds the largest element among the first N - 1 elements (N is the number of elements in the array) and swaps it with the (N - 1)st element. In our example, 18 is found, in the third place, and swapped with 2 to give

1	2	3	4	5	6	7	8
12	6	2	11	15	9	18	24

On successive passes, the next biggest element is found and moved to the end of the array. After N - 1 passes, the array is sorted.

Write out the successive passes of selection sort on the array from problem 12.1.

Write a Pascal procedure `Selection` that implements this sort. Implement `Selection` with a `MaxPos` function that finds the position of the maximum element in the array up to some designated element. Verify that your `Selection` procedure works by having it sort 25 randomly generated numbers into ascending order.

12.4 Add your procedure `Selection` to the program `Sorts` by adding a new procedure `DoSelection`. Run `Sorts` with `ArrayLimit` having the values 62, 125, 250, 500, 707, and 1000 and time each of the four sorts on each of the array sizes. Graph your results. What is the order of finish of the four sorts and what happens, with any of these algorithms, to the time needed to sort an array when the array size is doubled? What relationship do you find between the timings for 500, 707, and 1000 elements? For your information, $707 \approx 500 \sqrt{2}$ and $1000 \approx 707 \sqrt{2}$. Also, from these timings, what conclusions do you make about modified bubble sort as compared to bubble sort with randomly selected data?

12.5 Suppose you gave each of our sorts an array A that is already sorted. Are any of the sorts smart enough to realized this? Describe the amount of work that each sorting algorithm needs to perform to sort an already ordered array. Predict an order of finish for the sorts and check your results by modifying the program Sorts so that each sort begins with an ordered array.

12.6 Run the program Searches varying the array size. Graph the results of the timings for both the linear and the binary searches as a function of the array size. Don't forget to divide the binary times by 1000, since DoBinary does 1000 searches to make the time of a binary search measurable. What are the shapes of these two curves? With a very fast processor, you may have to increase the constants (ArraySize and NumRuns) of the program to be able to measure the time needed for the sorts.

12.7 Refer back to the Snidely programs of the previous chapter and write a program that ranks the salespersons for Snidely by their total values of goods sold.

12.8 The Lake Forest College Running Club needs a program to sort out the winner in its Strawman Triathlon. The competition consists of a 1/4-mile swim, a 5-mile bicycle ride, and a 2-mile run. The data for each competitor are available on the text file Triath.Txt on the diskette accompanying this book. There are two lines for each person. The first line is the name, of type String[30]. The second line contains a category (the character 'S', 'F', or 'A' for student, faculty, or administration, respectively) followed by three real numbers representing, in hours, the swim time, bike time, and run time, respectively.
Write a program that prints out the following:

```
The winner of the Swim Competition was... with a time of...
The winner of the Bicycle Competition was... with a time of...
The winner of the Running Competition was... with a time of...
The winner of the Overall Competition was... with a time of...
```

(Of course, the winner of each individual competition is the individual with the fastest time for that event, while the winner of the overall triathlon is the individual with the fastest combined time. You do not need to worry about ties.)

The above four statements should be followed by a table that prints all the entrants in increasing order of total time; e.g., the winner is listed first and the loser is listed last. Each line in the table should contain the participant's name and category, followed by the three individual times and the total combined time. When you swap total times, be sure to swap the individual event times and the names so that each individual's data are kept together.
(Note: The category is not really used in this exercise. It is included for use with an exercise in Chapter 19.)

ANSWERS TO SELF-TEST QUESTIONS

12.1 In each case, we need only replace the $>$ of Listings 12.6 and 12.8 with $<$.

12.2 a) Bubble sort:

```
Pass 1:    7  22  47  72  34  15  66  98  38  53
Pass 2:    7  15  22  47  72  34  38  66  98  53
Pass 3:    7  15  22  34  47  72  38  53  66  98
Pass 4:    7  15  22  34  38  47  72  53  66  98
Pass 5:    7  15  22  34  38  47  53  72  66  98
Pass 6:    7  15  22  34  38  47  53  66  72  98
```
Passes 7, 8, and 9 are the same as Pass 6

b) Modified bubble sort is the same as bubble sort, except that the modified bubble sort stops after pass 7 (not pass 6), since no swaps were needed on pass 7.

c) Insertion sort:

```
Pass 1:    22  47  72  34  15  66  98   7  53  38    47 is inserted
Pass 2:    22  47  72  34  15  66  98   7  53  38    72 is inserted
Pass 3:    22  34  47  72  15  66  98   7  53  38    34 is inserted
Pass 4:    15  22  34  47  72  66  98   7  53  38    15 is inserted
Pass 5:    15  22  34  47  66  72  98   7  53  38    66 is inserted
Pass 6:    15  22  34  47  66  72  98   7  53  38    98 is inserted
Pass 7:     7  15  22  34  47  66  72  98  53  38     7 is inserted
Pass 8:     7  15  22  34  47  53  66  72  98  38    53 is inserted
Pass 9:     7  15  22  34  38  47  53  66  72  98    38 is inserted
```

13

ARRAYS: TABLES

MULTIDIMENSIONAL ARRAYS

The fact that you are reading this chapter labels you as a survivor of the one-dimensional arrays studied in Chapter 11. This chapter should seem natural to those who have learned the previous material well (but may well push others over the edge). The main subject of this chapter is the care and feeding of two-dimensional arrays. Arrays in Pascal can come in any dimension, but two-dimensional arrays are very common, and anyone who can handle them well understands the general principles and can implement 17-dimensional arrays without us.

A secret, well-kept from students, is that a two-dimensional array is nothing other than a table of information. For instance, the table of marshmallow production in the United States and in the Grand Duchy of Fenwick (Table 11.2 repeated below as Table 13.1) is an example of a two-dimensional array. It is two-dimensional since it has rows and columns. In this case, each row is a one-dimensional array of 2 elements (don't count the index) representing marshmallow production in a given year. In contrast, each column is a one dimensional array of 10 elements representing marshmallow production over the 10 years in a given country. That is, the rows are indexed by years and the columns are indexed by countries. A particular entry in the table is determined if we fix a year and a country. For example, the marshmallow production in the Grand Duchy in 1980 is easily determined to be 6392.5 tons.

We recommend that the reader view a one-dimensional array as a list of items and, likewise, view a two-dimensional array as a table of items. The word array has frightened many a beginning student of programming. Realizing that an array is really not some strange object, created by your professors to paralyze you, is very important. Arrays, as we will see throughout the remainder of this book, are critical to programming.

Table 13.1: Tonnage of U.S. and GDF Marshmallows

	U.S. Tonnage	GDF Tonnage
1975	44,573.5	583.4
1976	46,734.9	692.5
1977	46,934.6	1,745.2
1978	48,324.3	2,482.4
1979	48,056.2	3,264.1
1980	47,298.4	6,392.5
1981	45,238.4	9,883.4
1982	44,573.2	12,389.0
1983	42,745.1	15,399.3
1984	39,298.0	19,343.2

It may become difficult to picture, but, if we add other products to our example, we obtain a three-dimensional array. If we were to keep track of the production of marshmallows, bicycles, paper clips, and moustache wax over a period of several years in the U.S. and the GDF, we would have a table with three indices. To determine a specific entry, we would need to give a product, a year, and a country. If we add a further complication, such as the color of the product, then we have a four-dimensional array. Again, Pascal has no limit to the number of dimensions that a given table may have. However, the reader should be aware that seemingly innocent tables can be giant memory hogs. For example, if the table suggested above stores information for 20 products over a 10-year span for 15 countries and lists 12 colors for each product, then that table occupies 36,000 cells in memory (why?). If each cell is a Turbo Pascal Real occupying 6 bytes, our array occupies 216,000 bytes of memory!

As with one-dimensional arrays, we have two major questions that we must answer. How does one declare and how does one use multidimensional arrays? The following declarations should seem natural:

```
Type   Countries   =  (US, GDF);
       Colors      =  (Red, Green, Orange, Yellow, Blue);
       Categories  =  (Faculty, Student, Alumnus, Guest);
       Students    =  (Amy, Bill, Carol, David, Edith, Fred);
       Grades      =  (A, B, C, D, F, INC, W, WP, WF);

Var    Marshmallows : Array [1975..1984, US..GDF] Of Real;
       Gradebook    : Array [Amy..Fred, 1..10] Of Grades;
       ParkingFees  : Array [1980..1990,Faculty..Guest,
                                        Red..Blue] Of Real;
       MultTable    : Array [0..9, 0..9] Of Integer;
```

Marshmallows is, as previously discussed, a table of 20 entries arranged into 10 rows and 2 columns. If Year and Country are identifiers of the obvious types, Marshmallows[Year,Country] is a real number representing the tonnage of marshmallows produced in that Country in the given Year. Gradebook, on the other hand, is a table of 60 entries arranged in 6 rows and 10 columns. The rows of Gradebook are indexed by students' names, and the columns are indexed by the subrange of integers from 1 to 10. Gradebook[Carol,7] is of type Grades and represents the grade Carol received from Professor Pedantics on project number 7.

ParkingFees is an example of a three-dimensional array. It is a table of the history of parking fees at Granola State University for the years 1980 to 1990 for the various categories of users (faculty to guests) and for the various lots on campus, which are identified by colors. That is, if Year, Class, and Hue are variables of the proper types, then ParkingFees[Year,Class,Hue] represents the fee needed to park in a lot of color Hue for a user of the given Class in the given Year. MultTable is a simple two-dimensional array—and we hope that MultTable[R,C] stores the product of R and C, the row and column indices, each of which we assume is between 0 and 9.

There is an alternative form of the array declaration for multidimensional arrays that we now discuss. Since any type can be placed after the Of in an array declaration, it is possible to define an array as follows:

```
AddTable : Array [0..9] Of Array [0..9] Of Integer;
```

For most purposes, this is equivalent to the array definition of MultTable given above. That is, AddTable[R,C] is an integer—we hope, the sum of R and C, the row and column indices.

MultTable must be used with zero or two indices. For example, if we assume that DivTable is another variable declared in the *same* declaration as MultTable, then both of the following are valid:

```
DivTable := MultTable;       {This is an entire array operation.}
            {It is valid only if both arrays are of the same type.}

MultTable[7,6] := 42;                      {This is an operation on}
                                           {a specific element.}
```

On the other hand, AddTable may be used with zero, one, or two indices. For example, if SubTable is another variable declared in the *same* declaration as AddTable, then all of the following are valid:

```
SubTable := AddTable;                      {Entire array operation.}

AddTable[3] := AddTable[7];                {This is a row operation.}
                                           {The 7th row of AddTable is}
                                   {assigned to the 3rd row of AddTable.}

AddTable[4,7] := 11;               {Operation on a specific element.}
```

AddTable[R] is itself an array of 10 integers and can be assigned any value of that same type. In the above example, the 3rd row of the table is replaced by the contents of the 7th row. In summary, the two forms are very close. If one would like to do entire row operations, the second form *must* be used. If there is no need in the given application for such operations, the first form is the preferable form to use. Also, since AddTable[R] is an array, we may write AddTable[R][C] to indicate the Cth item in the Rth row of AddTable. This is an alternative form to the more familiar expression AddTable[R,C].

TYPES AND ARRAYS

Finally, we need to make a remark about when two variables in Pascal have the same type. Although this may seem obvious, it isn't. First, if a type has a name, then all variables of that type, or that are subranges of that type, are naturally considered to be of the same type. Prior to Chapter 11, this was always the situation. However, if we declare a variable

```
List : Array [1..10] Of Integer;
```

then List is said to be declared **anonymously**; that is, without a type *name*. In the anonymous case, variables are of the same type only if they are declared in the *same* variable declaration. Consider the following example:

```
Var   List1 : Array [1..10] Of Integer;
      List2 : Array [1..10] Of Integer;
```

In the above case, the statement List1 := List2 is illegal, because the two variables are not of the same type. If we want them to be of the same type, we have two alternatives. The first one is to declare them together, *on the same line:*

```
Var   List1, List2 : Array [1..10] Of Integer;
```

The second alternative involves making up a type name and using it in the variable declarations:

```
Type  SomeList = Array [1..10] Of Integer;

Var   List1 : SomeList;
      List2 : SomeList;
```

In each of the previous two situations, List1 := List2 is now legal because both variables are of the same type.

This example points out a situation when the invention of a type name is desirable (or required). Although we can use the first alternative to declare things together within any one block, we must use the second alternative if we are to set up argument/ parameter correspondences with procedures and functions. This point is often a source of confusion (understandably) to beginners. Simply remember that to use arrays as arguments or parameters, the arrays must be declared with *named* types. They cannot be passed anonymously.

PARALLEL ARRAYS

A two-dimensional array often has several parallel one-dimensional arrays associated with it. For example, suppose `Marks` is an array declared by

```
Marks : Array [1..30, 1..10] Of Integer;
```

We assume that `Marks` is to be used to keep the scores of up to 30 students on up to 10 homework assignments. An obvious parallel array would be an array in which to keep the names of the students. Since strings are not compatible with integers, we must use different arrays for the names and for the marks. Therefore, we could declare `Names` by

```
Names : Array [1..30] Of String[25];
```

The reader should reflect upon why we chose `1..30` and not `1..10` in the above definition of `Names`. Two other arrays logically associated with `Marks` would be `StudentAverage` and `ClassAverage`. `StudentAverage`, of course, is designed to hold the average of each student, while `ClassAverage` is supposed to keep track of the class average on each homework assignment. Hence, we declare these two arrays (very differently) as follows:

```
StudentAverage : Array [1..30] Of Real;
ClassAverage   : Array [1..10] Of Real;
```

We hope that the picture of Figure 13.1 helps to explain these parallel arrays. Simply for human understanding, those that deal with rows of `Marks` are drawn in a vertical format, while those that deal with columns of `Marks` are drawn in a horizontal format.

SIMPLE OPERATIONS ON TWO-DIMENSIONAL ARRAYS

For each of the following segments, we assume that the arrays `Marks`, `Names`, `StudentAverage`, and `ClassAverage` have been declared as in the previous section. Further, we assume that the arrays `Marks` and `Names` already have values stored in them and that any index variables that we need have been so declared.

Example 1: Assign the score 0 to the element in the 3rd row and 2nd column.

Trivially, we write:

```
Marks[3,2] := 0;
```

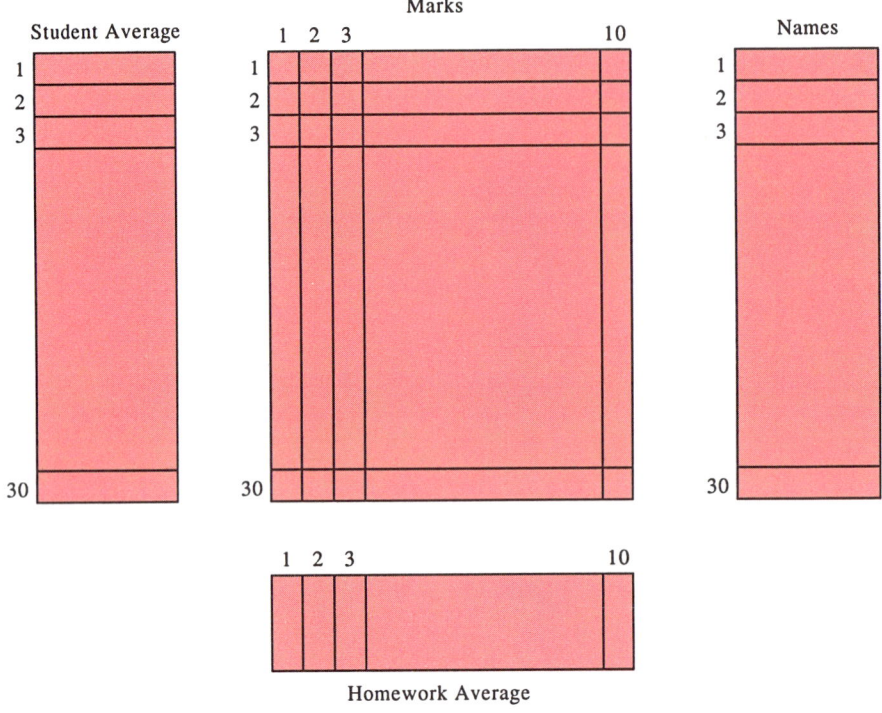

Figure 13.1

This assignment means that we have given the 3rd student the mark of 0 on the 2nd homework assignment. This is radically different from

```
Marks[2,3] := 0;
```

so be very careful with the order of the indices!

Example 2: Assign the score of 100 to each element in the 17th row.

Here, obviously, someone has purchased failure-insurance. The point is that a row operation corresponds to an individual, while a column operation corresponds to a particular homework assignment. We use a For loop:

```
For Paper := 1 To 10 Do
  Marks[17, Paper] := 100;
```

Example 3: Assign the score of 0 to each element in the 6th column.

This time, everyone got caught cheating on homework assignment number 6. We obviously use a loop, but note that we loop 30 times, not 10, and also notice carefully the placement of the constant 6 in this example and the constant 17 in the previous example.

```
For Person := 1 To 30 Do
  Marks[Person, 6] := 0;
```

Example 4: Count the number of 0s in the Rth row, where $1 \leq R \leq 30$.

This counts the number of homework assignments blown off by the Rth student. The segment is very straightforward, assuming that all the variables have been previously defined:

```
BlownOff := 0;
For Paper := 1 To 10 Do
  If Marks[R, Paper] = 0 Then
    BlownOff := BlownOff + 1;
```

Example 5: Count the number of 100s on the Hth homework assignment, where $1 \leq H \leq 10$.

This is clearly a column operation. The details are left to the reader.

Example 6: Count the number of 100s in the entire array Marks.

For this purpose, assume that NumAssignments is an integer (at most 10) that contains the number of assignments actually given and that NumStudents is also an integer (at most 30) that contains the actual number of students in the class. That is, only NumStudents rows and NumAssignments columns of the array Marks are in use. There are two obvious ways to proceed:

```
Count := 0;
For Row := 1 To NumStudents Do
  For Col := 1 To NumAssignments Do
    If Marks[Row, Col] = 100 Then
      Count := Count + 1;
```

or

```
Count := 0;
For Col := 1 To NumAssignments Do
  For Row := 1 To NumStudents Do
    If Marks[Row, Col] = 100 Then
      Count := Count + 1;
```

The reader should trace both of the above segments to discover the slightly different paths taken to achieve the same final counts. For simplicity in the exposition, let us assume for a moment that NumStudents is 30 and NumAssignments is 10. The first solution considers the elements of Marks in **row order**. That is, it looks at Marks[1,1], Marks[1,2], Marks[1,3],..., Marks[1,10], then looks in the second row at Marks[2,1], Marks[2,2], Marks[2,3],..., Marks[2,10] and proceeds in this manner through the rows of Marks. The second solution, on the other hand, has the column index in the outside loop and, hence, it changes more slowly than does the row index. The second method, therefore, is known as **column order**. Trace enough of it to see that the elements considered are Marks[1,1], Marks[2,1], Marks[3,1], ..., Marks[30,1], then the second column's Marks[1,2], Marks[2,2], Marks[3,2], ..., Marks[30,2], etc. In a situation where our object is simply to count the number of times that a particular value occurs in a given table, it obviously doesn't matter whether we proceed in row or column order. But, as we will see in Examples 7 and 8, sometimes one needs row order and sometimes one needs column order.

Example 7: Compute and store the entries of the array StudentAverage.

Recall the picture of Figure 13.1. For each student, we add his or her scores and divide by NumAssignments. Of course, we must repeat this operation NumStudents times, storing the results at each stage in the proper place in the array StudentAverage. Since the outside loop is on people, the solution uses row order:

```
For Person := 1 To NumStudents Do
  Begin
    Sum := 0;                                {Placement important!}
    For Paper := 1 To NumAssignments Do
      Sum := Sum + Marks[Person, Paper];
    StudentAverage[Person] := Sum / NumAssignments
  End;
```

Please observe very carefully the placement of the Sum := 0 statement. Why must it go between the Fors instead of before both or inside both?

Example 8: Compute and store the entries of ClassAverage.

This time we must process the array by papers, not people. Hence, a column order is appropriate. We leave the details to the reader and refer the reader, for reference, back to Figure 13.1.

Example 9: Assuming that Who is a String variable containing the name of one of our students, find the score of Who on paper number 5.

First, we must find Who in the parallel array of Names, then, remembering the index, look up Who's score on paper 5 in the table Marks. For this segment, let us assume a linear search function, called Find, that accepts an array of names and a target string and returns the index of the target in the array (or zero if the search is unsuccessful).

With this black box, the segment is easy:

```
Place := Find(Names, Who);
If Place = 0 Then
  Writeln('Sorry, ', Who, ' is not in the class.')
Else
  Writeln(Who, ' has a score of ', Marks[Place, 5]);
```

AN EXTENDED EXAMPLE

In Chapter 11, we considered an extended example involving The Widget Works. The astute reader realizes, no doubt, that the example was fictitious and was devised just to give an example of one-dimensional arrays. The truth, of course, is that The Widget Works has a whole line of products and, hence, needs a two-dimensional array to keep track of sales of individual products by individual salespersons. For simplicity, let us assume that The Widget Works has at most 100 salespersons and has 10 distinct products. We assume that each salesperson has an identification number between 1 and 100 and that each product has a product number between 1 and 10. Hence, we declare arrays Amounts and Names as follows:

```
Type    SalesArray  =   Array [1..100, 1..10] Of Integer;
        NamesArray  =   Array [1..100] Of String[30];

Var     Amounts  : SalesArray;
        Names    : NamesArray;
```

Figure 13.2 illustrates the relationship between Amounts and Names. Other parallel arrays are explained as they are used. We now write some segments that solve simple problems posed by Snidely Whiplash, the sales manager. In each segment, we assume that the arrays Amounts and Names already have values. We also assume that any indices needed have been declared.

Example 10: Snidely would like to see how salesperson number 15 is doing.

Listing the sales by product for salesperson number 15 is a row operation on the array Amounts. Here is the segment:

```
Writeln('Sales by ', Names[15], ': ');
For Col :=1 To 10 Do
  Writeln('Quantity of product # ', Col, ' was ', Amounts[15, Col]);
```

Example 11: Determine for Snidely the total number of product number 6 that has been sold by all salespersons.

We need to scan down the 6th column of the array Amounts totaling the entries. Here is the segment:

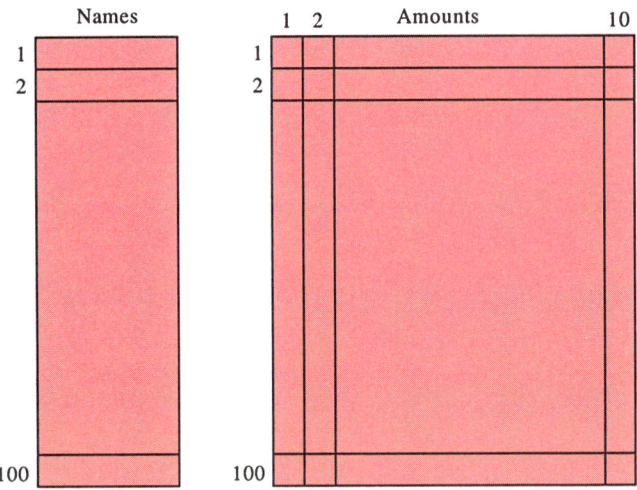

Figure 13.2

```
Total6 := 0;
For Row := 1 To 100 Do
  Total6 := Total6 + Amounts[Row, 6];
Writeln('The company total for product #6 is ',Total6);
```

In the above examples, we have used the index names `Row` and `Col` to suggest the type of operation we are performing on the array `Amounts`. Alternatively, it would be proper and acceptable to use index names that referred to the underlying application. For example, in the first case, an index such as `ProdNum` would clearly indicate that we were looping on products. In the second example, an index such as `ID` or `SalesPerson` would clearly indicate that we were looping on people. Either way is correct and infinitely better than totally meaningless indices such as `X` and `Y`.

Example 12: Let `PersonTotals` be an array in which `PersonTotals[ID]` will hold the total number of products sold by salesperson number `ID`.

Since `PersonTotals` has an entry for each salesperson, it is declared by

```
Var PersonTotals : Array [1..100] Of Integer;
```

To compute the entries of `PersonTotals`, we need to sum the entries of row 1, then sum the entries of row 2, etc. Here is the segment:

```
For ID := 1 To 100 Do
  Begin
    PersonTotals[ID] := 0;
    For Prod := 1 To 10 Do
      PersonTotals[ID] := PersonTotals[ID] + Amounts[ID, Prod]
  End;
```

Example 13: Write a segment to compute and fill the array ProdTotals, so that ProdTotals[ProdNum] contains the total number of that product sold by all the salespersons.

This is left as an exercise. Do not forget to declare ProdTotals properly.

Example 14: The array PersonTotals is not a very meaningful array. Since The Widget Works sells paper clips as well as tanks, it doesn't make much sense simply to total up the number of products sold by each individual. Total value of goods sold would be more meaningful to The Widget Works management. Therefore, we need two more arrays, Price and SalesTotals. Price is to contain the selling prices of the products, and SalesTotals is to contain the total dollar amount of sales by each salesperson.

Price and SalesTotals are declared by

```
Var Price        : Array [1..10] Of Real;
    SalesTotals  : Array [1..100] Of Real;
```

In the following segment, we assume that Price already has values and use these to compute the entries of SalesTotals:

```
For ID := 1 To 100 Do
  Begin
    SalesTotals[ID] := 0.0;
    For ProdNum := 1 To 10 Do
      SalesTotals[ID] := SalesTotals[ID] + Amounts[ID, ProdNum]
                                            * Price[ProdNum]
  End;
```

Example 15: Now, let us consider how the array Amounts could obtain values in the first place. We assume that each salesperson, on completing a sale, fills out a sales transaction form. The information needed on that form is the salesperson's ID, the product number (ProdNum) of the product, and the quantity (Qty) of the product sold. For example, the transaction 17 6 12 indicates that salesperson number 17 has sold 12 more of product number 6. We save (batch) the transactions for a two-week period, then create a text file, Widgets2.Txt, containing them. We expect (Snidely demands it) that there will be many transactions for each salesperson. Thus, the array Amounts is really 1000 accumulators for running sums. For example, all the above transaction does is add 12 to the current value in the 17th row and 6th column of Amounts. Of course, before we process the transactions, we should initialize every entry of the table to zero. This is left as an exercise for the reader. Here is the segment that processes the transactions:

```
Assign(Input, 'A:\Ch13\Widgets2.Txt');
Reset(Input);
While Not Eof Do
  Begin
    Readln(ID, ProdNum, Qty);
    Amounts[ID, ProdNum] := Amounts[ID, ProdNum] + Qty
  End;
```

The exercises at the end of this chapter indicate many other segments that you may write for Snidely.

AN EXAMPLE: PROCESSING SAT SCORES

As another example of parallel array processing, let us suppose we have data on approximately 150 students who have taken the SAT exams. We would like to read in these data and store them in appropriate arrays. Since part of the information is numeric and part of the information is alphabetic (String), we need to use two arrays. One of the weaknesses of arrays is that they may store information of only one fixed type. When we have several types of data, we are forced to use several parallel arrays. Let us assume that each student, has taken the verbal and the mathematics portions of the SAT examinations. Hence, for each student, we store three scores: verbal, mathematics, and composite (the sum of the verbal and mathematics scores). Computers can add more quickly and accurately than can people, so there is no reason for us to enter the composite score; the computer can compute it by itself. Thus, for each individual, we have a name (30 characters) and two scores to enter. Logically, the data might appear as follows:

```
Lowell Carmony
750 790
Robert Holliday
260 310
Jacque Strappe
130  40
Hi Ique
800 740
...
...
```

Notice that the names are not listed separately from the scores. We cannot read in the 150 names followed by the 300 scores. We must read a name, then two scores for that person, and then repeat the process. Often, the data are prepared by someone other than the programmer and the programmer must adjust to the given data. The program of Listing 13.1 reads the data from the text file SATScores.Txt and computes and prints the composite scores.

PROBLEM SOLVING EXAMPLE: THE GAME OF LIFE

As a more complex example of two-dimensional arrays, consider John Conway's simple rules for the birth and death of cells in an organism, known as the **Game of Life**. This game is played on a two-dimensional grid, where each cell is either occupied (marked with an X) or empty (marked with a blank). Each cell has eight neighboring cells, corresponding to the cells that surround the given cell. Figure 13.3 illustrates the eight neighboring cells for a given cell that is marked with an X, while the neighboring cells are marked with *s, which can indicate an X or a blank. The number of neighbors of a cell is the number of Xs in these surrounding eight cells.

```
Program SATExams; {$R+}
{This program illustrates the use of two-dimensional arrays as well
as parallel arrays. The program reads from the text file
SatScore.Txt which contains, for each individual, two lines. The
first contains the name of the individual and the second contains
the individual's verbal and math SAT scores. The individual's
composite score is not in the file, but is computed by the program.
We assume that at most 150 people are in the text file. See the
exercises for an extension of this program that makes use of the
arrays.                                                           }

Const Max = 150;                          {Maximum number of people.}

Type   ScoreType  =  (Verb, Math, Comp);
       NameList   =  Array[1..Max] of String[25];
       SATList    =  Array[1..Max, Verb..Comp] of Integer;

Var    Names   :  NameList;
       SAT     :  SATList;
       Person  :  0..Max;

Begin
  Assign(Input, 'A:\Ch13\SATScores.Txt');
  Reset(Input);
  Writeln('Name':25, 'Verbal':10, 'Math':10, 'Composite':15);
  Writeln;
  Person := 0;
  While Not Eof Do
    Begin
      Person := Person + 1;
      Readln(Names[Person]);
      Readln(SAT[Person, Verb], SAT[Person, Math]);
      SAT[Person, Comp] := SAT[Person, Verb] +
                                            SAT[Person, Math];
      Writeln(Names[Person]:25, SAT[Person, Verb]:10,
                  SAT[Person, Math]:10, SAT Person, Comp]:15)
    End {While}
End.
```

Listing 13.1

```
          *   *   *
          *   X   *
          *   *   *
```

Figure 13.3

Figure 13.4

Conway describes two ways that an organism can die. The X in Figure 13.3 will die of **loneliness** if it doesn't have at least two neighbors. That is, if only one or zero of the *s are Xs, the central X dies of loneliness and is replaced in the next generation by a blank. Organisms can die of overcrowding, too. If an X has more than three neighbors, it dies of **overcrowding**. That is, if four or more of the *s are Xs, the central X dies and is replaced by a blank in the next generation.

There is one method for new organisms to be born. A *blank* cell that has exactly three neighbors has a **birth** in it in the next generation. A birth is recorded, of course, by changing the blank to an X.

A final rule is that all births and deaths occur *simultaneously*. This means that a cell can contribute a third neighbor to a blank cell, causing a birth, and then, because the cell has only one neighbor, it expires of loneliness. For example, consider the situation of Figure 13.4a. In that figure, the leftmost X has only one neighbor and is about to die of loneliness. But note that the cell marked with a period (this cell is assumed blank, but marked so you can see it) has, counting the dying cell, exactly three neighbors. Therefore, there is a birth in the cell marked with a period and a death in the leftmost X. Likewise, the rightmost X dies and, likewise, in Figure 13.4a, a birth occurs in the cell below the center X. The center X has two neighbors and, thus, survives. No other blank cell has three neighbors, so the next generation is as shown in Figure 13.4b.

Conway's Game of Life, then, is to start with some configuration of cells and to compute new generations. As soon as we have done some examples by hand, we will turn to writing a program that will produce new generations for us. We urge you to take scrap paper and check our work as a check on your understanding of the Game of Life. Let us begin with the simple organism of Figure 13.5a. The reader should check that there are two deaths (by loneliness) and four births, giving the generation of Figure 13.5b.

In Figure 13.5b, the two central Xs die of overcrowding, there are no deaths by loneliness, and two births occur adjacent to the deaths. Thus, the next generation is as

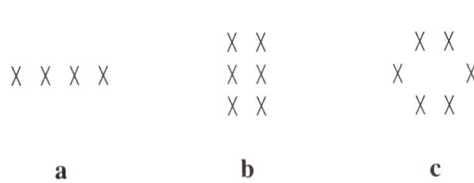

Figure 13.5

```
X . . . X
. . . . .
. . X . .
. . . . .
X . . . X
```

Figure 13.6

shown in Figure 13.5c. In Figure 13.5c, every X has two neighbors and, hence, survives. Furthermore, no blank cell has exactly three neighbors, so there are no births. The organism of Figure 13.5c is **stable**, meaning that all of its future generations are the same. An organism is stable when no births or deaths occur. One of the interesting things about the Game of Life is that many initial organisms do, eventually, reach a stable state.

It is possible for an organism to die out. For example, consider the organism of Figure 13.6, where the blank cells are marked with a period so that the spacing is clear. The Xs are separated and they all die of loneliness. No blank cells with three neighbors exist, so there are no births. This organism goes **extinct** in the next generation.

It is possible for an organism to **oscillate**. We already have an example of this in Figure 13.4. We previously argued that Figure 13.4b is the next generation after Figure 13.4a. Now, observe that Figure 13.4a is the next generation after Figure 13.4b. That is, the organism flashes back and forth between three horizontal and three vertical Xs.

The most interesting organisms are the **spaceships**. These are organisms that move across the plane and then rearrange themselves in a new location to look exactly as they did in a previous generation. We leave it to the reader to verify that, in four generations, the organism of Figure 13.7 will have the same shape and orientation as it currently does, except that it will have picked itself up and moved east one column!

Because the production of generations is tedious and error-prone for humans, let's write a program to automate the process. Obviously, the game is played on a two-dimensional grid and, hence, the program will be a good example of a complex program involving two-dimensional arrays. Also, the situation is complex enough that it provides a good example of the problem-solving process. We strongly urge the reader to check the generations of the previous figures by hand, as a means of understanding the problem.

We begin the design process by considering a divide-and-conquer strategy for the problem. What are the big modules that we need to solve this problem? In no particular order, we clearly need a `NextGeneration` procedure that computes the generations for us. A `Generation` counter to keep track of the generations is useful, as is a `Display` procedure to show the generations. Of course, we need a procedure that will

```
X X X
    X
  X
```

Figure 13.7

generate the initial organism. We could generate the initial organism randomly, but it would be better to let the user choose the initial organism by entering coordinates (row and column) for the initial Xs. This means that we need to initialize the board to blanks before we begin. Also, we need some means of deciding how many generations to display. We could arbitrarily display five generations, but perhaps it would be better to let the user decide when enough generations have been produced. Putting all these ideas in order leads us to the following pseudo-code:

Initialize the Board to blanks and the Generation counter to zero
Let the user enter the coordinates of the organism
Display the initial Board
Repeat
   Produce the NextGeneration of the Board
   Increment the Generation counter
   Display the Board and the Generation counter
Until the User is Tired of seeing generations

Now, we must refine each piece of the pseudo-code until it is reduced to elements that are easily expressed in Pascal. Let us take the lines of the pseudo-code in order.

Initialize the Board to blanks and the Generation counter to zero

One fact that must be recognized is that the computer will play on a finite board, while Conway's original game was to be played on an infinite grid. As long as our board is big enough and we place our initial organisms near the center, then, for many generations, our generations will be Conway's true generations. To display a board conveniently on the screen, we have arbitrarily decided to play the game on a 15 x 15 grid. Thus, it takes 15 lines to display a board, leaving a few lines for instructions and responses from the user.

Thinking ahead, we will have to count the neighbors of a given cell on the board. A cell along an edge, or a cell in a corner, causes special problems, because we are likely to get an out-of-bounds error in trying to count the eight neighbors of such a cell. A simple solution is to declare the board `0..16` by `0..16` instead of `1..15` by `1..15`. We use only the interior rows (`1..15`) and columns (`1..15`) to store the organism and use the `0`th and `16`th rows and columns to provide a border so that every playable cell has eight neighbors. This makes the counting of neighbors much simpler, since there are no longer any special edge and corner cases to consider.

Here is the pseudo-code for the `Initialize` procedure:

Set Generation to 0
For Row from 0 to 16
   For Col from 0 to 16
      Set Board[Row, Col] to Blank

Let the user enter the coordinates of the organism

This procedure prompts the user to enter a row and column and then places an X in that position on the board. How many Xs should the user enter? Rather than selecting a fixed number, let's give the user the freedom to enter any number of Xs. Therefore, we can use a `Repeat...Until` and the user can indicate, via a sentinel, that data entry is complete. Since 0 0 is not a legal pair of coordinates, we will use this pair as the sentinel. Here then is the pseudo-code for the `EnterCoord` procedure:

Repeat
    Prompt user for a pair of coordinates (0 0 to terminate data entry)
    Read in the Row and Col values
    If Row and Col are legal and not the pair 0 0 then
        Set Board[Row, Col] to an X
Until Row = 0 and Col = 0

Display a board and the Generation counter

Obviously, we need only one `Display` procedure to display the initial `Board` or any of the other `Boards`. This procedure simply uses nested `Fors` to print out the contents of the `Board`. Although some attention to detail is necessary to make the `Board` easily understood, a detailed pseudo-code is not necessary for this procedure. The details will eventually be given in Listing 13.2 below. Figure 13.8 shows sample output from our `Display` procedure, assuming that the data entered were 5 5, 5 6, 5 7, and 0 0. Each character on the board is displayed in Figure 13.8 in three columns, so that the image is nearly square and so that column headings can be written to aid the user in understanding the figure.

Produce the NextGeneration of the Board

This procedure is clearly the heart of the game. We must remember that births and deaths are to occur simultaneously. This creates a small problem. Consider, again, the example of Figure 13.4a, reproduced for your convenience as Figure 13.9.

```
Here is generation #0
         1  2  3  4  5  6  7  8  9 10 11 12 13 14 15
    1
    2
    3
    4
    5                X  X  X
    6
    7
    8
    9
   10
   11
   12
   13
   14
   15
```

Figure 13.8

$$\overset{\textstyle .}{X}\ X\ X$$

Figure 13.9

We know that the leftmost X dies of loneliness and that, simultaneously, there is a birth in the cell marked with a dot. However, if we delete the leftmost X before we consider the marked cell for a birth, there will be no birth, since the given cell no longer has three neighbors. On the other hand, if we first add an X to indicate a birth at the marked cell, the leftmost X will not die, since it now has two neighbors. How do we get the computer to consider these two events simultaneously? The simple solution is to make a copy, TempBoard, of the Board and then make changes only to TempBoard *based on* the contents of Board. That is, since the leftmost X has only one neighbor on the Board, it is replaced on the TempBoard by a blank. Then, since the marked cell still has three neighbors on the Board, it is replaced on the TempBoard by an X. In this manner, we can construct, cell by cell, the new generation without making any changes to the old generation. Only when we are all finished do we copy the new TempBoard into Board. Here is the pseudo-code for NextGen. Note carefully the use of TempBoard and Board.

```
Set TempBoard to Board
For Row from 1 to 15
    For Col from 1 to 15
        If TempBoard[Row, Col] is a blank then              --Consider a birth
            If cell Row, Col has three neighbors on the Board then
                Set TempBoard[Row, Col] to an X             --We have a birth
            Else              --Do nothing to the blank cell as there is no birth here
        Else                           --The board was not blank; consider a death
            If cell Row, Col has less than two neighbors on the Board then
                Set TempBoard[Row, Col] to a blank          --Death by loneliness
            Else If cell Row, Col has more than three neighbors on the Board then
                Set TempBoard[Row, Col] to a blank       --Death by overcrowding
            Else       --Do nothing to the survivor who has two or three neighbors
Set Board to TempBoard
```

All of this pseudo-code is elementary, except for the counting of the neighbors of a cell. We need a function that checks the eight neighboring cells and returns a count of the number of Xs found. Note that the eight surrounding cells are in the rows and columns with values from 1 less to 1 more than the given row and column. For example, the neighbors of row 3 and column 8 are the elements of rows 2, 3, and 4 in columns 7, 8, and 9. Whoa, except that this also counts the cell 3, 8 as a neighbor of itself. Therefore, we can count these 9 cells and then subtract 1 if the given cell itself contains an X.

Set Count to zero
For R from Row - 1 To Row + 1
    For C from Col - 1 To Col + 1
        If Board[R, C] is an X then
            Increment Count by one
If Board[Row, Col] is an X then   --We counted it as a neighbor of itself
    Decrement Count by one
Set the function NumNeighbors to Count

The User is Tired of seeing generations

This last module of the main pseudo-code can easily be implemented as a Boolean function, UserTired, which returns True if the user wants to quit and False, otherwise. The pseudo-code is

Ask user if another generation is desired (Y/N)
Read the user's Response
Make sure Response is uppercase
Set UserTired to the equality of Response and 'N'

Finally, we have refined each portion of the pseudo-code to a point where we can proceed to the implementation. This is shown in the lengthy Listing 13.2. Yet, the reader who has carefully followed us to this point should have no trouble understanding this program consisting of a main program and six procedures and functions (some nested within others). Note that the magic number 15 has been replaced by a constant in case you would like to change the board size. Also, note how the main program resembles the initial pseudo-code with only the addition of small details such as the use of a Readln to freeze the screen so that the output does not scroll off the screen before the user has a chance to see it. Several improvements to the design are suggested in the exercises.

```
Program Life; {$R+}
{This program displays generations of Conway's Game of Life. See
the text for an explanation of the rules.                          }

Const  Size  =      15;
       Blank =      ' ';

Type BoardType = Array[0..Size + 1, 0..Size + 1] Of Char;

Var    Board     : BoardType;
       Generation : Integer;

Procedure Initialize(Var Board : BoardType; Var Generation :
                                                      Integer);
{Pre:  None                                                       }
Post:  This procedure initializes Generation to zero and Board to
       all blanks.                                                }

   Var Row : 0..Size + 1;
       Col : 0..Size + 1;
```

Listing 13.2

```
Begin
  Generation := 0;
  For Row := 0 To Size + 1 Do            {Blank playing surface}
    For Col := 0 To Size + 1 Do                    {of the Board.}
      Board[Row, Col] := Blank
End;                                {Definition of procedure Initialize.}

Procedure EnterCoord(Var Board : BoardType);
{Pre:  The Board has its initial value (Blanks in the playing area).
Post:  At any legal coordinate entered by the user, an X is placed.}

  Var Row : Integer;
      Col : Integer;

  Begin
    Repeat
      Writeln('Enter the row and column of the organism.');
      Writeln('Coordinates must be between 1 and ', Size, '.');
      Write('Enter 0 0 to terminate data entry. ');
      Readln(Row, Col);
      If (Row > 0) And (Col > 0) And (Row <= Size) And
                                          (Col <= Size) Then
        Board[Row, Col] := 'X'
    Until (Row = 0) And (Col = 0)
  End;                              {Definition of procedure EnterCoord.}

Procedure Display(Var Board : BoardType; Generation : Integer);
{Board is a Var parameter to avoid making a copy of it on each call.
Pre:   Board and Generation have values.
Post:  The values of Board and Generation are displayed.          }

  Var Row : 1..Size;
      Col : 1..Size;

  Begin
    Writeln; Writeln;
    Writeln('Here is generation #', Generation);
    Writeln;                              {Next write the column numbers.}
    Write('     1  2  3  4  5  6  7  8  9 10 11 12 13 14 15');
    Writeln;
    For Row := 1 To Size Do
      Begin
        Write(Row:2, '  ');                     {Write the row numbers.}
        For Col := 1 To Size Do
          Write(Board[Row, Col]:3);
        Writeln                              {Print one row per line.}
      End {For on Row}
  End;                                {Definition of procedure Display.}
```

Listing 13.2 (continued)

```
Procedure NextGen(Var Board : BoardType);
{This procedure produces the next generation of the Board. Any blank
cell with exactly three neighbors has a birth in it. Any occupied
cell with less than two or more than three neighbors has a death
in it. All births and deaths occur simultaneously.
Pre:   Board has values.
Post:  All the births and deaths have been recorded on the Board.}
  Var Row, Col  : 1..Size;
      TempBoard : BoardType;

  Function NumNeighbors(Var Board:BoardType; Row,Col:Integer):Integer;
  {This function counts the number of neighbors of the given cell.
  Pre:    Board, Row, and Col all have values.
  Post:   The eight cells around the given cell are tested and a count
          of the number of Xs found in these cells is returned. }

    Var R     : 0..Size + 1;
        C     : 0..Size + 1;
        Count : Integer;

    Begin
      Count := 0;
      For R := Row - 1 to Row + 1 Do       {Count Xs in block of}
        For C := Col - 1 To Col + 1 Do     {nine cells including}
          If Board[R, C] = 'X' Then             {the given cell.}
            Count := Count + 1;
      If Board[Row, Col] = 'X' Then             {Subtract 1 if the}
        Count := Count - 1;                      {given cell is an X.}
      NumNeighbors := Count
    End;                       {Definition of function NumNeighbors.}
  Begin                              {Body of procedure NextGen}
    TempBoard := Board;          {Copy the Board into TempBoard.}
            {Now, add births and delete deaths from TempBoard.}
    For Row := 1 To Size Do
      For Col := 1 To Size Do
        If TempBoard[Row, Col] = Blank Then
          If NumNeighbors(Board, Row, Col) = 3 Then
            TempBoard[Row, Col] := 'X'{Record birth on TempBoard.}
          Else                       {Do nothing to the blank cell.}
        Else                        {An organism occupies the cell.}
          If NumNeighbors(Board, Row, Col) < 2 Then
            TempBoard[Row, Col] := Blank    {Death--loneliness.}
          Else If NumNeighbors(Board, Row, Col) > 3 Then
            TempBoard[Row, Col] := Blank {Death--overcrowding.}
          Else  {Do nothing to survivor with 2 or 3 neighbors.}
    Board := TempBoard           {Copy new generation into Board.}
  End;                            {Definition of procedure NextGen.}
```

Listing 13.2 (continued)

```
Function UserTired : Boolean;

{Pre: None

Post: UserTired is True if the user says he or she doesn't want
      any more generations. Otherwise, UserTired is False.    }

  Var Response : Char;

  Begin
    Writeln;
    Write('Do you want another generation? (Y/N) ');
    Readln(Response);
    Response := UpCase(Response);
    UserTired := (Response = 'N')
  End;                            {Definition of function UserTired.}
Begin                                      {Body of program Life.}
  Initialize(Board, Generation);
  EnterCoord(Board);
  Display(Board, Generation);
  Writeln; Writeln('Press RETURN to continue');
  Readln;
  Repeat
    NextGen(Board);
    Generation := Generation + 1;
    Display(Board, Generation)
  Until UserTired
End.
```

Listing 13.2 (continued)

SUMMARY

The concept of arrays was introduced in Chapter 11, but only to represent simple lists. In this chapter, we have extended that useful concept to include tables of two or more dimensions. It should be obvious that lists and tables are fundamental ways of structuring data and, hence, taking the time to understand them is important to the student. We urge you to consider some of the quick Snidely exercises given below, as well as a couple of the more substantial problems.

KEYWORDS

Arrays	Tables
Lists	Parallel arrays
Row operations	Column operations
Anonymous types	Named types

SELF-TEST QUESTIONS

13.1 a) Declare an array `Inventory` to keep track of the quantities of 500 products stored at 25 warehouses.

b) Declare `Descriptions` to be an array of English descriptions, such as "Widget Main Bearing," for the products.

c) Declare `Locations` to be an array of the cities in which the warehouses are located.

13.2 How much memory does the following array use? (Assume that Reals occupy 6 bytes each and assume that the user-defined type `Days` has already been defined.)

```
Var A : Array['A'..'Z', Mon..Sun, 1975..1995] Of Real;
```

13.3 Assume that `Marks` is the array of the text. What is the difference between `Marks[3,2]` and `Marks[2,3]`?

EXERCISES

13.4 Distinguish row and column order for processing a table. Consider Figure 13.1 and assume that the table `Marks` has values stored in it. Which method, row or column order, do you use to compute the entries of the array `StudentAverage`? Which method do you use to compute the entries of `ClassAverage`? Explain your answers.

13.5 Write the segment for Example 5 of the text.

13.6 Write the segment for Example 8 of the text.

13.7 Write the segment for Example 13 of the text.

13.8 Write a segment for `Snidely` that finds the winner of the sales contest. That is, find the person whose total value of sales is the greatest.

13.9 The text file `SATScores.Txt` contains names and two scores (verbal and math) for at most 150 students. The names and scores are on separate lines. Modify the program `SATExams`, of the text, which reads the data into two arrays so that it also sorts the scores. The output should be three lists, in descending order by each type of score, giving the name and scores of each student. That is, rank the students by verbal, math, and composite scores. Caution: Be sure you keep the scores associated with the correct people.

13.10 Generate enough generations of the following organisms (by hand) to classify the following organisms as oscillating, (about to be) stable, spaceship, or (about to be) extinct. Check your work by running the program `Life`.

a) `XXXXX`

b) `XX XX`
   `  XX`

c) `X`
   ` X`
   `  X`
   `   X`
   `    X`

d) `    XX`
   `   X X`
   `    X`

13.11 Make the following improvements to the appropriate procedure or function in `Life`.

a) If the user enters a coordinate of a cell that already has an X in it, then that X is erased. For example, if the user enters 4 4 by mistake, then he or she can erase that X by entering 4 4 again (before entering 0 0).

b) Display the initial board after the user enters 0 0, and if the user doesn't like the initial configuration, return to the data-entry procedure to add and delete to the present configuration.

c) If the organism dies out, exit the program with an appropriate message.

d) If the organism reaches stability, exit the program with an appropriate message.

e) If the organism oscillates between two positions, exit the program with an appropriate message.

ANSWERS TO SELF-TEST QUESTIONS

13.1
```
Var   Inventory     : Array[1..500, 1..25] Of Integer;
      Descriptions  : Array[1..500] Of String[30];
      Locations     : Array[1..25] Of String[20];
```

13.2   26 * 7 * 21 * 6 = 22932 bytes.

13.3 Marks[3,2] is the element in the third row and second column, while Marks[2,3] is the element in the second row and third column. In the given example, Marks[3,2] is the third student's score on the second quiz, while Marks[2,3] is the second student's score on the third quiz. To the second and third students, this difference is a big deal!

14

RECORDS

When we open a standard manila file folder, we usually find many forms, one for each person or product involved. These forms are called **records**. For example, the Social Security Administration (the FBI, too) almost certainly has a record on you. That record collects all the information that is kept about you, such as name, social-security number, birthdate, address, and a list of contributions by you and your employers to your retirement. Likewise, The Widget Works has an inventory record for each product kept in the warehouse. That record contains the product number, the cost, the supplier, the quantity, etc., of the given product.

The individual data items that make up the record are called the **fields** of the record. In our examples above, the name, the address, the social-security number, the supplier, the cost, etc., are all fields of their respective records. Records and fields are easy to distinguish. The record is the aggregate information about one person or product. The fields are the individual data items of which the record is composed.

In this chapter, we will consider only records, or arrays of records, that are stored in the volatile memory of the computer. In the next chapter, we take up the more interesting and valuable study of external disk files, which are collections of records stored on the disk. Arrays of records allow us to introduce and study the material of this chapter without worrying about disk input and output. However, arrays of records have some serious limitations: They must be small enough to fit in memory, and they are lost when the computer is turned off. Therefore, this chapter should be considered as preliminary to the next chapter, where we learn how to deal with very large, permanent collections of records (files).

As an example to develop, let us create a means to keep track of a group of students; say, those enrolled in a first Pascal class. Each person will have a record, and we must first decide upon the fields that will compose that record. Let's say that we will keep the name, year in school, identification number, grade point average, fee status (paid or unpaid), and sex of each member of the class. Since Pascal is a strongly typed

```
Type  ClassType      =   (Frosh, Soph, Jr, Sr);
      StudentRecord  =   Record
                            Name  : String[25];
                            Year  : ClassType;
                            ID    : String[11];
                            GPA   : Real;
                            Fees  : Boolean;
                            Sex   : Char
                         End;


Var   Students   : Array[1..30] Of StudentRecord;
      OneStudent : StudentRecord;
```

Listing 14.1

language, we must also decide the type of each of these fields. Clearly, name should be a String; say, of maximum length 25. Let us also suppose that the identification numbers have the form XXX-XX-XXXX and, thus, are strings of length 11. For the year in school, we will use the abbreviations Frosh, Soph, Jr, and Sr and will define an enumerated type for this purpose. Fee status can be chosen to be of type Boolean, while sex can be chosen to be of type Char. We see one fundamental difference between records and arrays—the types do not all need to be the same in a record. Indeed, our example is fairly typical in that records are often composed of many very different kinds of fields. Both records and arrays are sequences of information, but there is a fundamental distinction between arrays and records. Records are used to gather various nonhomogeneous information about an individual, while arrays are used to gather homogeneous information from a group of individuals. An array of names or an array of grade point averages has one cell for each individual. The array provides a cross section of information of one kind. The record provides an aggregate of all the different kinds of information about the individual or object. Using arrays, the information is grouped by kind; using records, the information is grouped by the individual or object to whom the information refers.

To continue our example, a record type, StudentRecord, and an array of those records, Students, in which we can store information about many students, are declared as shown in Listing 14.1.

The variable OneStudent is a record variable. That is, it is an aggregate name for the six fields we have listed. In a moment, we'll see how to access those individual fields. Students, on the other hand, is an array of 30 records. Students[17] is, of course, the record of the 17th student. Since Students[17] and OneStudent are both of type StudentRecord, they may be assigned, one to another, as in

```
Students[17] := OneStudent;
```

That is, Pascal allows whole record operations.

```
Var Students : Array[1..30] Of Record
                              Name : String[25];
                              Year : ClassType;
                              ID   : String[11];
                              GPA  : Real;
                              Fees : Boolean;
                              Sex  : Char
                            End;
```

Listing 14.2

A record is declared by using the Record and End keywords and by placing the field names along with their types between the Record and End. Note that there is no Begin to match the End. In the example above, this record is declared and given a name in the type section. It is also possible to use anonymous record types. Thus, the declaration of Students in Listing 14.1 is equivalent to the segment shown in Listing 14.2.

The first method of Listing 14.1, with the named type, is preferable on several grounds. First, it is less intense and, hence, clearer. Second, and most important, once the record type StudentRecord is defined, it may be used throughout the program. Variables such as OneStudent can be defined without repeating the record definition. Also, with the named record type, procedures and functions can be written that accept arguments of type StudentType. Hence, in the examples to follow, we will always choose names for our record types.

FIELD SELECTION

The individual fields of a record are chosen by a mechanism known as **selection**, which simply adds the field name to the record name, separating them by a period. For example, OneStudent.Name is the name field of the record OneStudent. Also, OneStudent.Year, OneStudent.ID, OneStudent.GPA, OneStudent.Fees, and OneStudent.Sex denote the other fields of OneStudent. Hence, the statements shown in Listing 14.3 are all legal statements.

```
Writeln(OneStudent.Name);
If OneStudent.Fees Then                                      {Fees paid?}
  If (OneStudent.Class = Sr) And (OneStudent.GPA >= 3.75) Then
    Honor(OneStudent)                          {Invoke Honor procedure.}
  Else                                                   {Do nothing.}
Else
  SendBill(OneStudent);                  {Invoke SendBill procedure.}
```

Listing 14.3

PROBLEM-SOLVING EXAMPLE: THE NOTEL HOTEL

Let us set up an array of records to keep track of the employees for a small hotel, the NoTel Hotel. We'll need a record for each employee and we will suppose that the hotel has at most 50 employees. Therefore, we will need an array of 50 records to hold the information on all the employees. The format of each record will be decided by the administration of the hotel. Let us suppose that they have agreed to store the identification number, name, address, department, birthdate, date of employment, marital status, and salary of the employee. Thus, we see that each record consists of eight fields. For each of these fields, we must determine an appropriate type.

The name is, of course, a String, or it could be three separate Strings (first name, middle initial, and last name). In Chapter 17, we'll learn how to manipulate strings so that we can put together and take apart names and, thus, change from one form to the other. Here, we will assume that it has been decreed that we store three separate names. To keep the number of fields in the employee's record from increasing (and to make the example more interesting), we will use a name field that is itself a record consisting of the three parts of the name. That is, we will have a record, one of whose fields is itself a record. This nesting of records is very common in complex data structures. In fact, the birthdate field and the date of employment field are clearly of the same type. Let us call this type `DateType`. To implement `DateType`, we could use a string such as '1/1/1991', but it would be more convenient to think of a `DateType` as the aggregate of three things: a day, a month, and a year. Hence, `DateType` itself can be implemented as a record containing three fields.

Likewise, the address can be broken down into its components: street address, city, state, and zip. Hence, we will make the address field of type `AddressType`, which is itself a record with four fields. Marital status and department are simple, user-defined types. The possibilities for marital status are `Single`, `Married`, `Separated`, and `Divorced`, while the various possibilities for department are `Administrative`, `FoodServices`, and `Housekeeping`. We will declare the `Salary` to be Real. Actually, to ensure accuracy, `Salary` might better be declared to be of type Longint or Comp (see Chapter 10 for details). Here we will not be concerned with the need for such precision. Finally, let the `IDNumber` be a three-digit integer in the range 100 to 999. Listing 14.4 contains the complete declaration of the record type and an array of 50 of those records.

Assuming that the array `Employees` has values stored in it, and that `Index` is some integer in the range 1 to 50, then `Employees[Index]` is the complete record of the Indexth employee of the hotel. As in the previous example, the IDNumber of this employee is `Employees[Index].IDNumber`, while the birthdate of this person is `Employees[Index].BirthDate`. Since the birthdate is itself a record, we can obtain the month of birth with the expression

```
Employees[Index].BirthDate.Month
```

Likewise, since we can access the characters in a string as though the string were an array, the expression

```
Employees[Index].Name.Last[1]
```

```
Type   Months      = 1..12;
       Days        = 1..31;
       Years       = 1860..2050;
       Departments = (Administrative, Housekeeping,
                                            FoodServices);
       Stats       = (Single, Married, Divorced, Separated);
       InfoString  = String[20];

       NameType = Record
                      First  : InfoString;
                      Middle : Char;
                      Last   : InfoString
                  End;

       DateType = Record
                      Month : Months;
                      Day   : Days;
                      Year  : Years
                  End;

       AddressType = Record
                         Street : InfoString;
                         City   : InfoString;
                         State  : InfoString;
                         Zip    : String[5]
                     End;

       OneEmployee = Record
                         IDNumber   : 100..999;
                         Name       : NameType;
                         Address    : AddressType;
                         BirthDate  : DateType;
                         EmployDate : DateType;
                         Department : Departments;
                         MStatus    : Stats;
                         Salary     : Real
                     End;

       EmployeeRecords = Array[1..50] Of OneEmployee;


Var Employees : EmployeeRecords;
    Index     : 1..50;
```

Listing 14.4

finds the first character in the Last field of the Name field of the Indexth employee's record. In other words, it is the first initial of the last name of the Indexth employee.

As a perk to its employees, the hotel administration hosts a birthday dinner during the birth month of all employees who have been employed for at least 10 years. That is, the June party is for all those employees with birthdays in June, who have been with the hotel for 10 years or more. We are to write a program that prompts the user to enter the current month and year and then searches the records and prints the names of all employees that should be honored that month. Here is our solution in pseudo-code:

Enter the data into the array Employees
Prompt user for desired Month
Prompt user for the CurrentYear
Examine the Employees records and invite those who have the given birth month
    and have been employed since CurrentYear - 10

The last line of pseudo-code becomes a very straightforward procedure. We simply examine the records, in turn, of the Employees and print the name fields, whenever we find someone who satisfies the given conditions. To illustrate record notation, the program is shown in Listing 14.5. To avoid extensive interactive data entry, the procedure EnterData reads from a text file, Hotel.Txt, the contents of which are shown in Figure 14.1. Also, since they are not relevant to the party problem, the address, marital status, and department have been dropped from the example. Furthermore, the name has been simplified to one string of 30 characters. The second line for each person contains the IDNumber, the BirthDate, the EmployDate (each date is three integers representing month, day, and year), and, finally, the Salary.

```
Glen Coe
444 6 8 1943 12 1 1980 1250
Win N. Etka
123 6 14 1937 3 11 1975 1580
Hi Wood
589 11 1 1925 6 30 1985 975
Wil Met
975 6 16 1958 9 1 1984 850
Morton Grove
345 6 23 1950 6 24 1980 1000
Wall Kegan
888 6 1 1935 12 1 1975 1435
Ken L. Worth
777 5 21 1940 2 10 1977 1225
Evan S. Ton
111 12 6 1945 10 22 1970 1450
```

Figure 14.1

```
Program Party; {$R+}

{This program invites employees to this month's birthday party.
Those who have been employed for 10 years are to be invited during
their birth month to the special dinner party.                    }

Const NumEmployees = 50;

Type Months    = 1..12;
     Days      = 1..31;
     Years     = 1860..2050;
     NameType = String[30];

     DateType = Record
                    Month  : Months;
                    Day    : Days;
                    Year   : Years
                End;

     OneEmployee = Record
                       IDNumber   : 100..999;
                       Name       : NameType;
                       BirthDate  : DateType;
                       EmployDate : DateType;
                       Salary     : Real
                   End;

     EmployeeRecords = Array[1..NumEmployees] Of OneEmployee;

Var Employees   : EmployeeRecords;
    BirthMonth  : Months;
    CurrentYear : Years;
    Count       : Integer;

Procedure EnterData(Var Employees:EmployeeRecords; Var Count:Integer);
{This procedure reads the data from the text file Hotel.Txt into
the array Employees and counts the number of employees.
Pre:  None
Post: At most 50 records are read into the array Employees, and
      Count contains a count of the number so filled.              }

  Begin
    Assign(Input, 'A:\Ch14\Hotel.Txt');
    Reset(Input);
    Count := 0;
```

Listing 14.5

```
      While Not Eof Do
        Begin
          Count := Count + 1;
          Readln(Employees[Count].Name);
          Read(Employees[Count].IDNumber);
          Read(Employees[Count].BirthDate.Month,
                              Employees[Count].BirthDate.Day,
                            Employees[Count].BirthDate.Year);
          Read(Employees[Count].EmployDate.Month,
                              Employees[Count].EmployDate.Day,
                          Employees[Count].EmployDate.Year);
          Readln(Employees[Count].Salary{This is the 2nd Readln.}
        End {While}
    End;                            {Definition of procedure EnterData.}
Procedure Invite (Var Employees : EmployeeRecords; Count : Integer;
                        BirthMonth : Months; ThisYear : Years);
{This procedure finds and invites the employees whose birthdays
fall in the given month and who have been employed 10 years.
Employees is passed as a variable parameter to avoid copying the
array.
Pre:   All four parameters have values stored in them.
Post:  Those whose birthdays fall in the given month, and who have
       been employed 10 years, have their names printed.        }
  Var Index : Integer;
  Begin
    Writeln;
    Writeln('Employees invited to this month''s party are:');
    For Index := 1 To Count Do
      If Employees[Index].EmployDate.Year <= ThisYear - 10 Then
        If Employees[Index].BirthDate.Month = BirthMonth Then
          Writeln(Employees[Index].Name)
  End;                              {Definition of procedure Invite.}
Procedure Prompt (Var BirthMonth : Months;
                                        Var CurrentYear : Years);
{This procedure prompts the user for the month and year of the party.
Pre:   None
Post:  BirthMonth and CurrentYear obtain values chosen by the user.}
  Begin
    Write('Enter the birth month of the party (1..12): ');
    Readln(BirthMonth);
    Write('Enter the current year: ');
    Readln(CurrentYear)
  End;                              {Definition of procedure Prompt.}
```

Listing 14.5 (continued)

```
Begin                                          {Body of main program Party.}
  Prompt(BirthMonth, CurrentYear);
  EnterData(Employees, Count);
  Invite(Employees, Count, BirthMonth, CurrentYear)
End.
```

Listing 14.5 (continued)

We also note, for the careful reader, that our Party program may not work quite the way intended by the hotel management. Very often, we find that the problem that we thought was so clear turns out, in fact, to be somewhat ambiguous. Take the case of the June, 1990 party. Should an employee, such as Glen Coe of Figure 14.1, born in June, 1943, who began employment in December, 1980, be honored or not? The employee is in his 10th year of employment, but has not yet completed 10 full years with the company. The procedure Invite invites such employees. We leave it as an exercise to modify the program so that it doesn't invite anyone who has not yet *completed* 10 full years of employment.

This example shows that processing an array of records is really no different from processing an array of integers. One can search such an array of records for a certain target field. Of course, if the array of records is first sorted on some field, it is possible to conduct a binary search of the records using that field. Since these are straightforward extensions of the binary search and sorts from a previous chapter, we leave these topics as exercises.

THE WITH STATEMENT

Even the simple procedures Invite and EnterData show how awkward record variables can become, because of the repetition of the record variable name. Fortunately, there is a construct, the With, that permits an abbreviation of some record names. The With is probably best illustrated with an example. Listing 14.6 gives an equivalent form for the messy While in the body of procedure EnterData.

```
With Employees[Count] Do
  While Not Eof Do
    Begin
      Count:= Count + 1;
      Readln(Name);
      Read(IDNumber);
      Read(BirthDate.Month, BirthDate.Day, BirthDate.Year);
      Read(EmployDate.Month, EmployDate.Day, EmployDate.Year);
      Readln(Salary)
    End;  {With and While}
```

Listing 14.6

The format of the `With` statement is

```
With RecordVariable Do
  Statement
```

where the statement may be compound, if necessary. Any variable used in the body of the `With` is first considered to be a reference to a field in the record variable that follows the keyword `With`. Thus, we do not have to keep repeating the name of the record variable. Consider the following example:

```
With ThisRecord Do
  Begin
    X := X + 1;
    Y := Y + 1;
    Z := Z + 1
  End;
```

Suppose that there is a variable `X` declared in some block containing this statement and that `X` is also a field of `ThisRecord`. Then `X`, within the `With`, refers to the `X` field of `ThisRecord`, and not the variable `X` of the surrounding block. Suppose that there is no `Y` field of `ThisRecord`, but there is a `Y` variable in some block containing the `With` statement. Then, the reference is really to the first such `Y`. Suppose that there is no variable `Z` declared and there is no `Z` field to `ThisRecord`. Then, the reference to `Z` is an undeclared-identifier error.

VARIANT FIELDS

Suppose we are in charge of maintaining records of motorized vehicles for a given state. All records would likely have certain common fields—for example, name of owner, serial number, and year. However, other fields may be common only to certain types of records. For example, if motorcycles are taxed based on engine size, cars based on number of cylinders, and trucks based on weight or number of axles, we can see how a motorcycle record might look different from an automobile or truck record. Pascal has a capability, called **variant records**, that allows precisely this kind of flexibility. A variant record contains a field called a **tag field**. It is the value of this field that determines the structure of the record. Again, we give an example and then discuss the construct. Listing 14.7 shows a variant record declaration.

In the example, we assume that the types `NameType` and `AddressType` have been defined as record types. The tag field in the above definition is `VehType`. Its value determines the structure of the remainder of the record. Note that the variant declaration is much like the `Case` statement. However, note that the tag variable has its type given. Also, note that there is no `End` for the `Case`, only an `End` for the `Record`. Finally, note the parentheses that are required to enclose the variant fields for each case.

If `Veh1` is a variable of type `VehicleReg`, and if `Veh1.VehType` currently contains the value `Truck`, then the *structure* of the record `Veh1` is as shown in Listing 14.8. Likewise, if `Veh1.VehType` is `Automobile`, the *structure* of the record is as shown in Listing 14.9.

```
Type VehicleType = (Automobile, Truck, Motorcycle);
     VehicleReg  = Record
                        Owner         : NameType;
                        Address       : AddressType;
                        Year          : 1920..2000;
                        SerialNo      : String[15];
                        Make          : String[15];
                        Model         : String[15];
                        Case VehType : VehicleType Of
                          Automobile : (Cylinders  : 1..12);
                          Truck       : (Axle       : 2..6;
                                         Weight     : Real);
                        Motorcycle : (EngineSize : 100..500)
                    End; {Record}
```

Listing 14.7

```
Record
  Owner    : NameType;
  Address  : AddressType;
  Year     : 1920..2000;
  SerialNo : String[15];
  Make     : String[15];
  Model    : String[15];
  VehType  : VehicleType;
  Axle     : 2..6;
  Weight   : Real
End; {Record}
```

Listing 14.8

```
Record
  Owner    : NameType;
  Address  : AddressType;
  Year     : 1920..2000;
  SerialNo : String[15];
  Make     : String[15];
  Model    : String[15];
  VehType  : VehicleType;
  Cylinders : 1..12
End; {Record}
```

Listing 14.9

```
Record
  Owner       : NameType;
  Address     : AddressType;
  Year        : 1920..2000;
  SerialNo    : String[15];
  Make        : String[15];
  Model       : String[15];
  VehType     : VehicleType;
  EngineSize  : 100 .. 1500
End; {Record}
```

Listing 14.10

```
Case Veh1.VehType Of
  Automobile : Writeln('Number of cylinders: ',Veh1.Cylinders);
  Truck      : Begin
                  Writeln('Weight ', Veh1.Weight:8:2);
                  Writeln('Number of axles: ', Veh1.Axle)
               End;
  Motorcycle : Writeln('Engine size: ', Veh1.EngineSize)
End; {Case}
```

Listing 14.11

and, if Veh1.VehType is Motorcycle, then the *structure* of the record is as shown in Listing 14.10.

Not surprisingly, a variant record is most often manipulated with a Case statement. For example, the segment of Listing 14.11 prints the appropriate variant fields of a given record Veh1.

Variant records allow the compiler to use memory efficiently. That is, instead of requiring the compiler to reserve storage for all possible fields—i.e., Weight, Axles, Cylinders, and EngineSize—and then using only those applicable, with variant records the compiler reserves just enough space to handle any one of the three kinds of records. The amount of storage reserved for a motorcycle will be the same as that for a truck, even though a truck's record appears to be larger. The compiler does this because, during the course of execution, the value of the tag field can be changed from Motorcycle to Truck, in which case the structure of the record would have to reflect this change.

In fact, it is this changing of the tag field that makes variant records, in our opinion, more appropriate for advanced programmers than for beginning programmers. For example, suppose we have a variable Veh1 with current values:

```
Veh1.Name--A.J. Foyt
Veh1.Address--Motor Speedway, Indianapolis, IN
Veh1.SerialNo--123456789A
```

```
Veh1.Year--1983
Veh1.Make--Ford
Veh1.Model--Escort
Veh1.VehType--Automobile
Veh1.Cylinders--4
```

Now, consider the effect of the following statement:

```
Veh1.VehType := Truck;
```

Such a statement is legal, but if this statement is not accompanied by statements that give values to `Veh1.Axle` and `Veh1.Weight`, then we have the following picture:

```
Veh1.Name--A.J. Foyt
Veh1.Address--Motor Speedway, Indianapolis, IN
Veh1.SerialNo--123456789A
Veh1.Year--1983
Veh1.Make--Ford
Veh1.Model--Escort
Veh1.VehType--Truck
Veh1.Cylinders--4
```

Of course, the above picture does not make sense. Trucks do not have a `Cylinders` field. They have `Weight` and `Axle` fields. The problem with variant records in Pascal is that it is the programmer's responsibility, not the compiler's, to make sure that things make sense. If the programmer doesn't carefully manage variant records, Pascal allows the above picture of a `Truck` with a `Cylinders` field. Furthermore, there is then much confusion about what the values of `Veh1.Weight` and `Veh1.Axle` are, and whether a reference to `Veh1.Cylinders` is legal. We feel that the burden of managing the structure of a variant record should be on the compiler, not the beginning programmer. The compiler, for example, should not allow a change to the tag field unless the entire record is being updated. Because the compiler doesn't worry about such details, we feel that variant records are best left to advanced programmers.

We close this discussion by mentioning that many computer scientists believe that variant records, as implemented in Pascal, should be outlawed altogether. Because a compiler is likely to allow an incorrect structure of a variant record, advanced programmers can use variant records to trick the compiler into allowing them to do things that would otherwise be illegal. That is, variant records help devious programmers work around many of the safety features that are incorporated into a language like Pascal.

AVOIDING STRINGS

Standard Pascal doesn't contain a String type and, in this section, we demonstrate how one could survive in a Pascal without strings. Niklaus Wirth wanted his original Pascal to be small and simple. Therefore, he chose to omit a built-in String type, leaving the creation of this data type to the user. The Char type is, of course, a part of standard Pascal and, as we will see, the String type can be based on the Char type. Writing one's own string package is not very difficult now that you know about arrays and records. However, for the beginning programmer, Strings are certainly a convenient data type and, hence, in this book, we have permitted, from the beginning, the use of Turbo Pascal's String type. Now, we come clean and show you how you could function in a Pascal without a built-in String.

A String is very much like an array of characters. The problem with defining a String to be an array of characters is that arrays in Pascal always have to be of some fixed length. That is, if we view 'John' and 'Marsha' as arrays of characters, then 'John' is an array of four characters and 'Marsha' is an array of six characters. Since Pascal is so strongly typed, arrays of four characters and arrays of six characters are considered to be distinct types and, hence, are not compatible. That is, in standard Pascal, the expression

```
'John' < 'Marsha'
```

is not True (or even False), but a type-compatibility error, since 'John' and 'Marsha' are of differing types. (Of course, in Turbo Pascal, the expression is True.) In standard Pascal, the comparison is as silly as 3.14 < 'X', which mixes reals and characters. It is possible to agree that Strings are arrays of, say, 20 characters and to pad 'John' with 16 blanks and 'Marsha' with 14 blanks, but typing

```
If 'John            ' < 'Marsha          ' Then ...
```

is pretty awkward.

One solution is to agree that a String is an array of characters that also has a length attribute. The array must be of fixed size, but the length attribute tells how many of the characters are currently being used. Thus, a String can be defined to be a record (surprise!) with two fields, Arr, an array of characters, and Len, an Integer. Since Arr has to be declared of some fixed size, we choose a constant StringMax for this length. The value of StringMax is arbitrary, but 80 and 255 are common, reasonable choices:

```
Const StringMax = 80;
Type StringType = Record
                    Arr : Array [1..StringMax] Of Char;
                    Len : 0..StringMax
                  End;
Var Name    : StringType;
    Address : StringType;
```

Name.Arr[1] holds the first initial of the name, and Address.Len holds the number of characters *actually* in the address. Notice that Len was declared to be in the subrange from zero to StringMax. If X is of StringType and X.Len is zero, then X is the **null** string consisting of no characters. In Chapter 17, we'll see that the null string plays a role similar to that of zero in arithmetic.

```
Function Length(X : StringType) : Integer;
{Pre: X has values already stored in it.
Post: The length of the string X is returned.                    }
  Begin
    Length := X.Len
 End;                                    {Definition of function Length.}
```

Listing 14.12


```
Procedure WriteString(X : StringType);
{Pre: X has some values stored in it.
Post: The characters in X.Arr up to X's length are printed.     }
  Var Index : Integer;
  Begin
    For Index := 1 To Length(X) Do
      Write(X.Arr[Index])
    End;                        {Definition of procedure WriteString.}
```

Listing 14.13

A string package is more than just a declaration of a StringType. The package should also contain useful functions and procedures for dealing with strings. In Chapter 17, we present the built-in procedures and functions for dealing with strings. This section is meant as a survival course in how to function in a Pascal without strings. It is also an interesting application of records and a review of functions and procedures.

Our first function, Length, returns the length of a string. If X is declared to be a StringType, then X.Len is the length of X. Why do we need a function for this? We don't absolutely need the function, but we might like to have it to help make our string package more natural. That is, the function Length hides the implementation and allows us to write Length(X) rather than X.Len. With the implementation hidden, our programs are clearer, and a beginner who has never even heard of records can use our string package. Listing 14.12 shows the simple function Length.

One disadvantage of our StringType is that we cannot write a string because we cannot write (directly) arrays and records. Therefore, we need a procedure WriteString that will output a string for us. Such a procedure is shown in Listing 14.13.

Notice that WriteString writes only Length(X) characters of X. Of course, WriteString is not as convenient to use as Turbo Pascal's built-in String type (which can be written with an ordinary Write statement). Using WriteString to output

```
Congratulations, John, you are the winner!
```

where 'John' is filled in from the value of Name, uses the statements

```
Procedure Concat (X, Y : StringType; Var Z : StringType);
{Pre: X and Y already have string values.
Post: Z is X followed by Y--if it fits. Otherwise, the part that
      fits is put in Z and a truncation message is issued.    }

Var  Index    : Integer;
     TempLen  : Integer;

Begin                          {Determine the length of the result.}
  TempLen := X.Len + Y.Len;
  If TempLen > StringMax Then
    Begin
      Writeln('Concatenation overflow, result is truncated.');
      TempLen := StringMax
    End; {If}
  Z.Len := TempLen;

  {Place the characters from X into the result.}
  For Index := 1 To X.Len Do
    Z.Arr[Index] := X.Arr[Index];

  {Place as many characters from Y into the result as will fit.}
  For Index := X.Len + 1 To Z.Len Do
    Z.Arr[Index] := Y.Arr[Index - X.Len]
End;                           {Definition of procedure Concat.}
```

Listing 14.14

```
Write('Congratulations, ');
WriteString(Name);
Writeln(', you are the winner!');
```

As a more complex example of a string procedure, let us consider **concatenation**. Concatenation certainly sounds complex, but it is really one of the simplest ideas possible. The roots of the word mean to "chain together" and every preschool youngster practices concatenation when pushing alphabet blocks together to form words. For example, the concatenation of the two strings 'Turbo' and 'Pascal' is 'TurboPascal'. The concatenation of two strings produces the new string obtained by joining the two strings together. Any procedure that defines a string must give that string a length, as well as place values in the Arr field of the string. The length seems obvious: The length of the new string is the sum of the lengths of the old strings. But wait, what if both of the old strings are pretty long? The new string could be too long to fit into StringMax characters. We do the following: We store all the characters of the first string and as many as fit of the second string. If necessary, we also announce that the result was too long and truncation of the result occurred. The procedure Concat is given in Listing 14.14. The alert reader will want to know why we haven't written Concat as a function, since it is returning a single result. The answer is that standard Pascal permits functions to return only simple results (not compound ones like arrays and records). That is, standard Pascal allows functions to compute only reals, integers, characters, Booleans, and enumerated user-defined types. We have followed that convention here.

You should verify that the first section defines Z.Len to be the smaller of StringMax and the sum of X.Len and Y.Len. The second section copies the characters of X into the first X.Len locations of the Arr field of Z. The third section copies characters, up to the length of the concatenation, from Y and places them after the characters from X. Note that the expression Index - X.Len runs up from 1 as Index runs up from X.Len + 1. Also, note in section one that we did not write

```
Z.Len := X.Len + Y.Len;
If Z.Len > StringMax Then ...
```

because the assignment may well generate an out-of-range error. That is, if X.Len + Y.Len is greater than StringMax, it cannot, even temporarily, be assigned to the Len field of the result. If you wish to avoid the need for the temporary variable, you should write

```
If X.Len + Y.Len > StringMax Then
  Begin
    Writeln('Concatenation overflow, result is truncated.');
    Z.Len := StringMax
  End
Else
  Z.Len := X.Len + Y.Len;
```

With these examples, we leave other string-handling functions and procedures, such as ReadString, Left, Right, and Mid (described below), to the exercises.

KEYWORDS

Record	Field
Selection	With
External files	Arrays of records
Variant record	Tag field
StringType (user-defined)	

SELF-TEST QUESTIONS

14.1   What are the limitations of storing information about a group of people in an array of records?

14.2 What are the differences between records and arrays?

14.3 Declare an array of 100 records to keep track of the inventory for The Widget Works. Be sure to include part number, description, number on hand, number on order, and price in your record.

14.4 Why would one array of records be more convenient for storing the Widget Works inventory than five parallel arrays? Hint: Consider sorting the inventory on part numbers.

EXERCISES

14.5 Write a `ReadString(S)` procedure for our string package. That is, since the standard `Read/Readln` statements cannot be used to read arrays or records, write a procedure that reads a line of characters (one at a time) into a variable S of type `StringType`. Use `Eoln` to control the input.

14.6 Write a `Left(S, N, T)` procedure that sets T to the `StringType` consisting of the first N characters of S. For example, if S is a `StringType` with current value `'Programmer'`, then `Left(S, 3, T)` assigns T the value `'Pro'`. Generate an error message if N > `Length(S)`.

14.7 Write a procedure `Mid(S, N, M, T)` that assigns to T the M characters of S starting at the Nth character of S. For example, if S has current value `'Programmer'`, `Mid(S, 4, 4, T)` assigns T the value `'gram'`. Generate an error message, if appropriate.

14.8 Modify the `Party` program of the text so that employees in their 10th year of service are not honored unless they have actually completed 10 full years of service.

14.9 Modify the `Party` program so that the employees are sorted and output in order by `IDNumber`.

14.10 Modify the program of the previous exercise to do a binary search (by `IDNumber`) for a given employee.

14.11 Discuss why, as organized, it is not possible to sort the employees of the program `Party` into alphabetical order. What changes to the record design are needed to allow such sorting? Discuss the changes needed to the `EnterData` procedure to accommodate your changes in the record design.

ANSWERS TO SELF-TEST QUESTIONS

14.1 Arrays of records are stored in the main memory of the computer. Therefore, they are limited in number to what will fit in memory, and they are lost when the power is turned off. In the next chapter, we will solve these problems.

14.2 Arrays are homogeneous data structures in which the components are all of some fixed type. Records are heterogeneous data structures in which the components are of many types. The array groups like information, such as names or addresses, across individuals, while records group all of the information about an individual.

14.3

```
Type OneRec = Record
                    PartNumber  : Integer; {or String[10]}
                    Description : String[50];
                    NumOnHand   : Integer;
                    NumOnOrder  : Integer;
                    Price       : Real
                End;

      InventoryRecs = Array[1..100] Of OneRec;

Var Inventory : InventoryRecs;
```

14.4 The array of records gathers the information in a more logical manner by grouping all of the information by object, instead of by kind. Furthermore, if we wish to sort the inventory on part numbers, then, with arrays, we must remember to swap all of the parallel arrays whenever we swap part numbers (to keep the information associated with the proper part numbers). With records, we just swap the records according to their part numbers, and all of the associated information is taken care of automatically.

15

FILES

In this chapter, we discuss both sequential and random-access files. Because sequential files are included in standard Pascal, we begin with them. A **sequential file**, as the name suggests, is simply a sequence of records. We view a sequential file as in Figure 15.1.

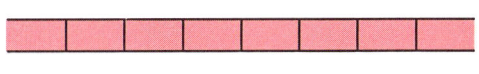

Figure 15.1

Thus, a sequential file is very much like an array. There are, however, some critically important differences. One difference is the manner in which elements are accessed. In an array, you may access the elements in any order, simply by giving the appropriate subscript. That is, you may first consider A[17], then jump to A[45], and then go back to A[3]. This method of access is called **direct** or **random access**. In a sequential file, access always begins with the first element and proceeds element by element (1st, 2nd, 3rd, …) through the file. Therefore, this method of access is called **sequential access**. If you think of a book as a file of words, then you normally access a novel in sequential order, from first to last (except when you jump ahead to the last page to find out who did it). The array is a random-access data structure, and the sequential file of standard Pascal is, of course, a sequential data structure. As mentioned, Turbo Pascal provides random access for files, but, because this is not standard, and because sequential files are of importance on their own, we temporarily restrict the term files to mean sequential files. Remember that sequential access of a file means that, to read the 7th record, you must first read the first six records and there is no going back. Once you have read the 19th record, you can't back up and read the 18th record—all you can do is get the next (20th) record.

Another major difference between files and arrays is the physical location of the information. An array is always in the volatile memory of the computer. A file is usually stored on some kind of disk. As a consequence, the information is not volatile—that is, is not lost—when the computer is turned off. Since disk space is usually far larger than RAM memory in the computer, files can be far larger than arrays. Indeed, many files are so large that they cannot fit into memory. We access the file—sequentially— a record at a time, and only the current record is actually in memory. A disadvantage of disk files, as compared to arrays, is that disk access time is much greater than is memory access time. Hence, it is slower to read or write to a file than it is to read or write an element of an array.

In summary, sequential files are in many ways very limited, but their major advantages are that they can be very large and they can store information that is not lost when the current program is finished. Imagine how worthless a payroll program would be, if, before each pay period, we had to type in all the data! With a file, we can store the name, address, number of dependents, total tax withheld, etc., on disk. Then, each pay period, we read the file sequentially from the beginning, compute and print the paychecks, and write the new information back to the disk to be used next time. Because of this ability to store information permanently, it is difficult to think of a business example where files are not important.

A file is declared much as an array is. The actual syntax is

```
Var    F : File Of SomeType;
```

where SomeType is any nonfile type. SomeType is normally a record, but you may have a file of integers or even a file of Boolean values. Note that the declaration is like the array declaration

```
Var    A : Array[1..1000] Of SomeType;
```

except for the keywords File and Array and the important fact that no size declaration is given for a file. The file F can grow to fill all available disk space. The array A, on the other hand, is fixed at 1000 elements.

To continue our example from the previous chapter, if we wanted to create a permanent file on a group of students, we might well declare

```
Type ClassType = (Frosh, Soph, Jr, Sr);

     StudentRecord = Record
                   Name       : String[30];
                   Class      : ClassType;
                   ID         : String[11];
                   GPA        : Real;
                   FeeStatus  : Boolean;
                   Sex        : Char
                 End;

     StudentFile = File Of StudentRecord;
```

```
Var Students   : StudentFile;
    OneStudent : StudentRecord;
```

Here, we have named the file type StudentFile, so that variables of this type can easily be passed as parameters in functions and procedures. We could also have used the anonymous declaration

```
Students : File Of StudentRecord;
```

but, as mentioned in Chapter 10, named types are generally preferred over anonymous types. Also, whenever a file is passed as a parameter, it *must* be passed as a variable parameter. Upon reflection, this requirement is clear, as we certainly do not want the procedure or function to try to make a copy of the entire file! Thus, always remember that file parameters must be variable parameters.

RESET, REWRITE, AND CLOSE

Now that we have seen how to declare a file, the only thing left to do is to see how to manipulate files. Perhaps because files are so important in real applications, students think that files must be very difficult. Some older languages did make file handling a particularly tricky topic, but in Pascal, sequential files are very easy to use. We may either read from or write to a sequential file. In a read, we take information from the file and bring it into the computer's memory. In a write, we place information from memory into the file.

To create a file, you use the Rewrite statement. This creates the file and prepares it for use. If the file already exists, then Rewrite *deletes* the old version of the file and begins a new version. The syntax of the Rewrite statement is

```
Rewrite(F);
```

where F is the name of the file *in the program*. Because our programs run under the DOS operating system, Turbo Pascal provides a means of assigning F a SystemName, which is the DOS system name of the file. This is done via the Assign statement that we are familiar with from text files. Here are two examples of Rewrites and Assigns:

```
Assign(Students, 'A:\Student.Dat');
Rewrite(Students);

Assign(Faculty, 'B:\Ch15\Faculty.Dat');
Rewrite(Faculty);
```

The first pair indicates that the file identifier Students, which must have been declared in the program, is attached to a file with the DOS name, Student.Dat, on the disk in drive A:. The second Assign and Rewrite pair attaches Faculty to the file Faculty.Dat in the subdirectory \Ch15\ on the disk in drive B:.

The Rewrite is the standard Pascal statement for opening a file in preparation for writing to (creating) that file. Standard Pascal is not concerned with any particular operating system and, therefore, need not be concerned with any such details. Assign, therefore, is a special Turbo Pascal statement that tells the program how to name your file under DOS. After the Assign and Rewrite pair creates your file, you will see entries for Student.Dat or Faculty.Dat on your disk when you use the Dir A: or Dir B:\Ch15\ directory commands.

The SystemName can be given as a string variable, so that the user can select the name of the file at execution time:

```
Writeln('Enter the name of the file to be created.');
Readln(FileName);
Assign(F, FileName);
Rewrite(F);
```

The above segment assumes that F has been declared in the Var section as a File variable of some sort and that FileName is a String variable. The segment creates a new file whose DOS name is whatever name the user enters (and this must, of course, be a legal DOS name).

To write information to a file created by Rewrite, we use our friend Write. The syntax is

```
Write(F, RecordName)
```

where F, of course, is the file variable and RecordName is the record that you would like written to the file. We see that whole records are written to the file. You do not write the individual fields of the record. In our example from above, we would first assign values to the fields of OneStudent and then write all that information to the file Students with the single statement

```
Write(Students, OneStudent);
```

Notice that the above Write does not cause any output to occur on the screen; rather, it writes all the information contained in the record OneStudent to the file Student.Dat, associated via the Assign with the file Students. The general form of the Write statement has a file name after the opening parenthesis. If that file name is missing, the system assumes that you want to use the normal output file that sends information to your screen. But if a file name is present, the information is written to the given file. If X, Y, and Z are integer variables, then

```
Write(X, Y, Z);
```

and

```
Write(Output, X, Y, Z);    {Output is name of standard output file.}
```

are equivalent and cause output to the screen, but the latter, because it is longer, is not often used.

Notice that we used Write, not Writeln, with the file. A general file is not composed of separate lines, but is organized as one long sequence of records. Hence, never use Writeln with general files (one exception to this, the text file, is discussed later).

If a file already exists, you can prepare it for use with the Reset statement. The format of the Reset is

```
Reset(F);
```

where F is the File variable. Of course, in Turbo Pascal, Resets will normally be preceded by an Assign, so that DOS can find the actual disk file that you want to open. Thus, a typical Assign and Reset pair would be

```
Assign(Faculty, 'B:\Ch15\Faculty.Dat');
Reset(Faculty);
```

where Faculty is a File variable of the appropriate type (the same type as that used to create the file).

Generally, every Reset or Rewrite will be preceded by an Assign. Since the Reset expects to find the named file, it is an error in a Reset statement if there is no file with the given DOS file name. Rewrite doesn't care whether the file already exists or not, but Rewrite will destroy any previous version of the file, so be careful with Rewrite! In our simple file introductory programs, it will also be our rule of thumb that each file be opened (via Reset or Rewrite) a very small number of times (often exactly once) and, therefore, the Reset and Rewrite almost certainly do not belong in processing loops. In any case, there is only one Assign statement per actual file.

The statement

```
Reset(F);
```

by itself, without an Assign, on a file that was previously opened with an Assign and Reset or Rewrite pair, rewinds the file and prepares it to be read from the beginning. Reset(F) is, therefore, useful if one part of your program creates a file with a Rewrite and, later, another part of that same program needs to read from the file.

As you may have guessed, we use Read to get information from a file. The format of the Read is

```
Read(F, RecordName)
```

which, of course, obtains the next record from the file F and places the information into RecordName. For example,

```
Read(Students, OneStudent);
```

obtains the next student's record and places the information in OneStudent's fields. There should be no confusion between reading the file F and reading the keyboard. If no file is given, the system expects the input to be from the keyboard. The name of the standard input file is Input, so the following are equivalent:

```
Read(X, Y, Z);
```

and

```
Read(Input, X, Y, Z);
```

Notice that `Read`, not `Readln`, is used to obtain information from a general file. This is because a general file is not organized into lines, but is just one long sequence of records.

What is opened by a `Reset` or `Rewrite` should eventually be closed, and that is the purpose of the `Close` statement, whose format is

```
Close(F);
```

`Close` breaks the association between `F` and any external file and marks that file as closed. The Turbo Pascal system automatically closes any files that we forget to close, but it is good programming practice to be responsible for our own files. Hence, we should explicitly close files when we no longer need them. Note that, to keep the discussion concerning redirecting input in Chapter 4 as simple as possible, we did not close the files in those examples.

A few words on the placement of the `Reset`, `Rewrite`, and `Close` statements may be in order. In a simple program, the `Reset`s and `Rewrite`s are at the beginning of the program, while the `Close`s are at the end. As mentioned, almost certainly, none of these statements belong within a processing loop. If your `Rewrite`, for example, is in a processing loop, you are continually deleting your file and beginning over. All you have at the end is the last record written to the file. In a more complex program, you may use `Reset`, `Rewrite`, and `Close` in the middle of the program, but these statements are almost certainly placed between processing loops. Any one file is opened and closed only a very small number of times.

Listings 15.1 and 15.2 show two simple but important programs that the reader should consider carefully. The first creates a file of five student records, and the second fetches those records. We choose to create a file with only five records, because you are asked to enter the data interactively, but the principle is the same for 500 or 5000 records. You should run `Create` and then `Fetch` to verify the programs and your files. When you quit, notice that there is a new file on your disk. Remember that `Fetch` will still work when you come back next week, as long as the file you have created is not discarded.

In `Fetch`, of Listing 15.2, the processing loop of the `WriteData` procedure is controlled by an end-of-file condition. The expression `Eof(Students)` is, of course, `False` unless the last record has been read from the `Students` file. Thus, `Eof(F)` works just like our friend `Eof`, except that `Eof(F)` tells us whether file `F` is at the end or not. `Eof` is equivalent to `Eof(Input)`, but, as usual, the system infers `Input` if no file is mentioned. `Eof(F)` is a very useful way to control the processing of the reading of the file `F`, and the reader should expect to use it often.

```
Program Create; {$R+}
{This program creates a sequential disk file of five student
records. Use Fetch to recover the records.                    }

Const NumStudents = 5;
Type NameString  = String[30];
     ClassString = String[5];
     IDString    = String[11];

     StudentRecord = Record
                        Name      : NameString;
                        Class     : ClassString;
                        ID        : IDString;
                        GPA       : Real;
                        FeeStatus : Boolean;
                        Sex       : Char
                     End; {Record}

     StudentFile = File of StudentRecord;

Var Students   : StudentFile;
    OneStudent : StudentRecord;
    FileName   : NameString;

Procedure Purpose;

{Pre: None
Post: The purpose of this program is written to the screen.   }

  Begin
    Writeln('This program creates a sequential file of ',
                                        NumStudents);
    Writeln('student records, and names the file according ');
    Writeln('to your wishes. Use Fetch to recover the file.');
    Writeln
  End;                      {Definition of procedure Purpose.}

Procedure ObtainFileName (Var FileName : NameString);

{Pre: None
Post: The user chooses the FileName for the file.            }

  Begin
    Writeln('Enter the name of file to be created. Enter a');
    Writeln('legal DOS name such as "A:\Ch15\Students.Dat".');
    Readln(FileName)
  End;                 {Definition of procedure ObtainFileName.}
```

Listing 15.1

```
Procedure ObtainData (Var Students : StudentFile);
{Pre: None
Post: NumStudents records are obtained from the user and are
      written to the file Students.                              }

  Var Index      : Integer;
      OneStudent : StudentRecord;
      Fees       : String[5];

  Begin
    For Index := 1 To NumStudents Do{Create records for the file.}
      With OneStudent Do                        {Note use of With}
        Begin                        {to avoid long record names.}
          Write('Enter the name of next student: ');
          Readln(Name);
          Write('Enter class (Frosh, Soph, Jr, or Sr): ');
          Readln(Class);
          Write('Enter ID (XXX-XX-XXXX): ');
          Readln(ID);
          Write('Enter GPA for ', Name, ': ');
          Readln(GPA);
          Write('Enter fee status (True for paid): ');
          Readln(Fees);
          FeeStatus := (Fees = 'True');
          Write('Enter sex (M or F): ');
          Readln(Sex);
          Write(Students, OneStudent)        {Write to the file.}
        End {With and For}
  End;                              {Definition of procedure ObtainData.}

Begin                                         {Body of program Create.}
  Purpose;
  ObtainFileName(FileName);
  Assign(Students, FileName);
  Rewrite(Students);
  ObtainData(Students);
  Close(Students)
End.
```

Listing 15.1 (continued)

```
Program Fetch; {$R+}
{This program reads a sequential disk file of student records.
Use Create to construct the records.                              }

Type NameString  = String[30];
     ClassString = String[5];
     IDString    = String[11];
```

Listing 15.2

```
       StudentRecord = Record
                          Name      : NameString;
                          Class     : ClassString;
                          ID        : IDString;
                          GPA       : Real;
                          FeeStatus : Boolean;
                          Sex       : Char
                       End; {Record}

      StudentFile = File Of StudentRecord;

Var Students : StudentFile;
    FileName : NameString;

Procedure ObtainFileName (Var FileName : NameString);
{Pre: None
Post: The user chooses the FileName for the file.                     }
  Begin
    Write('Enter the name of the file you wish to read: ');
    Readln(FileName)
  End;                      {Definition of procedure ObtainFileName.}

Procedure WriteData (Var Students : StudentFile);
{Pre: Data are stored in the file Students.
Post: The data from Students are displayed.                          }
  Var OneStudent : StudentRecord;
      Fees       : String[5];

  Begin
    While Not Eof(Students) Do
    With OneStudent Do    {Notice With to avoid long record names.}
      Begin
        Read(Students, OneStudent);
        Writeln(Name);
        Write(Class:6, ID:12, GPA:8:2);
        If FeeStatus Then Fees := 'True' Else Fees := 'False';
        Writeln(Fees:6, Sex:2);
        Writeln
      End {While and With}
  End;                              {Definition of procedure WriteData.}

Begin                                     {Body of main program Fetch.}
  ObtainFileName(FileName);
  Assign(Students, FileName);
  Reset(Students);
  WriteData(Students);
  Close(Students)
End.
```

Listing 15.2 (continued)

The file `Students` was passed as a variable parameter to the procedure `WriteData`. Since `WriteData`'s job is to print out the contents of the file, and not to change the file, you might have expected `Students` to be a value parameter to `WriteData`. However, as mentioned previously, since a value parameter makes a copy (in memory) of the actual argument, a file parameter can *never* be a value parameter. Pascal requires that file parameters always be variable parameters, even if the procedure intends no changes to the file.

The program `Fetch` is needed to view the file `Student.Dat`. If you load `Student.Dat` into the editor or use the `Lister` program to send `Student.Dat` to the printer, you will get gibberish. The reason for this is that the data in `Student.Dat` are stored in computer-readable form, not human-readable form. There is a human-readable form of files, called text files. We have used text files since Chapter 4, and they are discussed in more detail later in this chapter. The advantage of a text file, from the human point of view, is that it is understandable. However, from the computer's point of view, a text file must first be converted from the human format to the computer's format for processing. That is, the integer 30000 in a text file is represented by the string of five characters `'30000'` and must be converted to the computer's representation of an integer as it is read into memory. General files of records, such as `Student.Dat`, are stored with the computer's representations and, hence, processing is faster and storage requirements are often less. For example, the integer 30000 is stored in just 2 bytes. Remember that general files are not human readable and that some procedure such as `Fetch` is needed to see the contents of a general file.

FILE APPLICATIONS: MERGING AND UPDATING

We consider two traditional, important uses of sequential files. The first is the **merging** of two files into one new file. This is a frequent business problem when, for example, two mailing lists need to be combined into one new list. We assume that the two lists are ordered in some way, and the object of the merge is to form a new ordered list containing all of the items from the two lists. The second problem deals with the **updating** of a file of accounts. This is a very standard billing problem, where we need to reflect both charges and payments made by the customers. Actually, the second problem is also a kind of merge. We are merging old balances with current transactions to yield new balances. In the true merge, we are merging files with the same structure to yield a new file of that same structure. In the update problem, the balances and transactions are different kinds of records, but the end result is still the merging of this information into new balance records. For this reason, we consider the merge problem in considerable detail and leave the update problem as an exercise.

PROBLEM-SOLVING EXAMPLE: THE MERGING OF ADAM AND EVE

To be specific, let us suppose that Adam Firstperson and Eve Applesnake have decided to get married. Being a modern couple, they both keep track of their friends with the computer. The problem is to merge the file `Adam.Frn` with the file `Eve.Frn` to produce a new file `Adam&Eve.Frn`. We suppose that both `Adam.Frn` and `Eve.Frn` are ordered alphabetically, and we suppose that no one is on both lists. The assumption that there are no duplicates is simply for convenience. In the exercises, we let the reader extend the program to handle duplicates. We also make the unwarranted assumption that the two files Adam.Frn and Eve.Frn have the same structure. That is, they both contain the same kinds of records. Again, we leave it to the reader to consider what to do if this is not the case. For simplicity, let us assume that both files contain records with last name, first name, and telephone number. Of course, the merged file is also to be in alphabetical order.

Consider for a moment how you would merge two lists manually (See Figure 15.2). You look at the top item of each list and move the smallest to the new list. Then, consider the new top items and continue this process until one list is exhausted. At that point, move all the remaining items to the new list. Here is the pseudo-code:

Open the input files and obtain the first record from each
Open the output file
While the merge is not complete
    Compare the current records of each file
    Write the smallest record to the output file
    Read the next record of the file whose record was written

The first two lines of the pseudo-code are easy to implement, but, since we need to open and read a record from both input files, we'll write a procedure OpenRead and invoke it on both input files. We will have to watch for the end of file on both of the input files. For this purpose, it is convenient to have Boolean variables, AdamLast and EveLast, that are False unless we are processing the last record of the given file. OpenRead can also initialize these Booleans for us. Here is the detailed pseudo-code for OpenRead:

Assign F to the proper DOS name
Reset F
Read the first record from F into a record variable, Friend
If F is now at Eof then set Last to True, otherwise set Last to False

The difficult part of this problem is deciding when the merge is complete. It is not complete when we find the end of one of the files, because the other file might still have

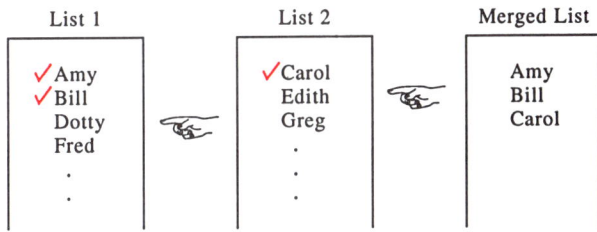

Figure 15.2

records in it that need to be transferred to the new file. To force the merge to continue, we can use the following trick: When either of the files reaches Eof, we can put a string of zs in the corresponding last name field of the record for that file. The point is that any real data in the other file will come before the string of zs and, thus, will be written to the merged file. We see that the merge will be complete only when both last-name fields are strings of zs. This can be expressed (using a While-like construct) in the following pseudo-code:

While Adam's Friend's Last Name <'zzzzz' or Eve's Friend's Last Name <'zzzzz'
   If Adam's Friend comes before Eve's Friend then
      Write Adam's Friend to the output file
        If AdamLast is True then
          Set Adam's Friend's Last Name to 'zzzzz'
        Else
          Read the next record from Adam's file
          If Adam's file is at Eof then set AdamLast to True
   Else
      Do the same for Eve's file

Since we need to do essentially the same thing to Adam's file as to Eve's file, we will write a procedure WriteReadNext that writes the current record and gets the next record of a given file. Finally, all this is put together in the Pascal program Merge shown in Listing 15.3.

```
Program Merge; {$R+}
{This program merges the files Adam.Frn and Eve.Frn into
Adam&Eve.Frn. The two files Adam.Frn and Eve.Frn are on the disk
of sample programs that accompany this book. They are in the Ch15
subdirectory and the disk is assumed to be in drive A:. Also note
that both input files are assumed to be in order by last name. The
program MakeFrnd is also on the disk in case you would like to
construct your own files to merge.                             }

Type FriendsRecord = Record
                            Last      : String[15];
                            First     : String[15];
                            Telephone : String[12];
                         End; {Record}

     FriendsFile = File Of FriendsRecord;

     FileType    = String[25];
```

Listing 15.3

```
Var Adam         : FriendsFile;
    Eve          : FriendsFile;
    Friends      : FriendsFile;
    AdamsFriend  : FriendsRecord;
    EvesFriend   : FriendsRecord;
    AdamLast     : Boolean;
    EveLast      : Boolean;

Procedure OpenRead(Var F : FriendsFile; Var Last : Boolean;
               Var Friend : FriendsRecord; FileName : FileType);

{Pre:  FileName has a legal DOS file name of a nonempty file.
 Post:  The file F is opened and the first record is read into Friend.
        Last is set to True if the last record was read and to False
        otherwise.                                                  }

  Begin
    Assign(F, FileName);
    Reset(F);
    Read(F, Friend);
    If Eof(F) Then
      Last := True
    Else
      Last := False
  End;                         {Definition of procedure OpenRead.}

Procedure WriteReadNext(Var F1, F2 : FriendsFile; Var Friend :
                        FriendsRecord; Var Last : Boolean);

{Pre:  Last has a value (True or False) and Friend has values in
        it.
 Post:  The record Friend is first written to the file F2. Then, if
        Last is True, Friend.Last is set to 'zzzzz'. Otherwise, the
        next record from F1 is read into Friend. If F1 is now at Eof,
        then Last is set to True.                                   }

  Begin
    Write(F2, Friend);
    If Last Then
      Friend.Last := 'zzzzz'
    Else
      Begin
        Read(F1, Friend);
        If Eof(F1) Then
          Last := True
      End
  End;                      {Definition of procedure WriteReadNext.}
```

Listing 15.3 (continued)

```
Begin                                    {Body of main program Merge.}
  OpenRead(Adam, AdamLast, AdamsFriend, 'A:\Ch15\Adam.Frn');
  OpenRead(Eve, EveLast, EvesFriend, 'A:\Ch15\Eve.Frn');
  Assign(Friends, 'A:\Ch15\Adam&Eve.Frn');
  Rewrite(Friends);
  While(AdamsFriend.Last < 'zzzzz') Or
                               (EvesFriend.Last < 'zzzzz') Do
    If AdamsFriend.Last < EvesFriend.Last Then
      WriteReadNext(Adam, Friends, AdamsFriend, AdamLast)
    Else
      WriteReadNext(Eve, Friends, EvesFriend, EveLast)
  Writeln('Merge completed. Use ViewFrnd to see the result.');
  Close(Adam); Close(Eve); Close(Friends)
End.
```

Listing 15.3 (continued)

The files Adam.Frn and Eve.Frn, as well as the program Merge, are on the disk accompanying this book, so that you can try out the program. You may also want to use the program ViewFrnd to see the contents of Adam.Frn, Eve.Frn, and Adam&Eve.Frn. To create your own lists to merge, use the program MakeFrnd. MakeFrnd and ViewFrnd are included on the disk, but are not listed here since they are easy modifications of the programs Create and Fetch discussed earlier. A modification of ViewFrnd, called ViewFrn2, is listed in the last section of this chapter. When using MakeFrnd, be sure to enter the names in alphabetical order. (Why?)

UPDATING FILES: EZ COME—EZ GO

The EZ COME—EZ GO credit card company keeps a master file on everyone who carries one of its credit cards. Each record in the file contains information about a customer, including name, address, employer, annual salary, years employed by present company, name of bank, account number at the bank, EZ COME—EZ GO account number, mother's maiden name, etc. To keep it simple, we suppose, in our example, that only the name, the EZ COME—EZ GO account number, the current balance, and the credit limit are kept for each individual. The credit limit is, of course, the maximum amount that you are allowed to charge to your account. The problem is that people are always using their cards, running around charging things, and, occasionally, paying their bills. We must write a program to update the accounts for EZ COME—EZ GO.

Every time someone uses a credit card, a transaction slip is prepared. For simplicity, we assume that there are only three kinds of transactions: payments, charges, and changes of credit limits. Of course, a more realistic example would also need to be able to handle changes of address, changes of name, interest charges, etc. Let us assume that the three transactions we are considering are coded by the letters P, C, and L. The transaction does not need to contain the complete credit history of the individual involved. The purpose of the transactions is to report that some action has taken place in a given account. Hence, all that is required on a transaction is an account number, a transaction code, and an amount. For example, these three transactions

```
25385P9.98
14676L3500.00
20032C49.98
```

indicate that the person whose account number is 25385 has paid $9.98 on his or her bill, the person with account 14676 has had the credit limit on his or her account changed to $3500.00, and someone has charged $49.98 to account 20032. It would be better to include the name of the customer on transactions and, then, not update an account unless both the name and the account number match. That way, a simple typing error, such as typing 25835 for 25385, could be caught by the program. In our simple case, we will initially make the totally ridiculous assumption that the data are correct. Since EZ COME—EZ GO has millions of customers using its cards daily, you see how unwarranted this assumption is.

At first glance, this update problem does not appear to be a good one for a sequential file. An external file is needed simply because of the volume of data involved. There is no way that all of the millions of accounts can be read into an array. But, with a sequential file, processing would appear to be very slow.

For example, to process the above transactions, we could proceed as follows: Hunt for account number 25385 and update that account. Then, reset the file and hunt for account number 14676, etc. Each time, we would need to reset the file and sequentially search from the beginning for one particular account. Sometimes we would get lucky, sometimes unlucky. On the average, we would need to look through half the accounts just to update one. That is too slow.

What we seem to need is some kind of random access for the records of the file, so that we can quickly jump from account 25835 to account 14676, etc. As mentioned, random-access files are supported in Turbo Pascal—and they are discussed below. However, sequential access is sufficient for the current problem if we make the observation that the update does not have to take place immediately upon receipt of the transaction. EZ COME—EZ GO bills its customers once a month, so it is necessary to update accounts only once a month. Hence, the transactions can be saved, or batched, and processed all at once instead of individually. The final ingredient to the solution is to require that the file of master accounts and the file of transactions be sorted on ascending account numbers.

Thereforc, if account 10012 is the first account, all transactions for that account are at the front of the transaction file. After account 10012 is updated, processing can proceed to the second record of the file. Of course, it is possible that someone has not used his or her EZ COME—EZ GO credit card at all this month and, hence, some of the records do not need to be updated. Since EZ COME—EZ GO knows by experience that most customers use their cards very frequently, there are few records that do not require updating and this is, therefore, a very efficient algorithm to use on the update problem. With one pass over the file of master accounts and one pass over the file of transactions, we can create the updated file of new master accounts.

We leave the update problem to the exercises with the following cautions: Be aware that there are, in general, many transactions that match any one master account. A person is certainly allowed to use his or her credit card more than once a month. Each use of the card, as well as any payments made, create transactions. The point is that the newly updated record should not be written to the file until all transactions for that account have been processed. If we assume that OldMaster and Transactions are the input files to your program, your program should create a new file called NewMaster. You need to create a new file NewMaster because it would be dangerous to try to update OldMaster as you go, for suppose your program blows up during execution. You may then have a mixed file with some updated accounts and some nonupdated accounts. How do you proceed? It is better to preserve your input data, so that if the program dies, you can try again. Of course, next month we rename NewMaster as OldMaster and create a new NewMaster.

TEXT FILES

A **text file** is a special file of characters that is organized into lines. A text file is in a human-readable format. The standard input and output files, Input and Output, are such files. Ever since Chapter 4, we have been redirecting Input to come from a text file on disk. All the file operations described previously apply to text files and, in addition, other procedures and functions, such as Readln, Writeln, and Eoln, apply to text files (because text files really are organized into lines). Besides redirecting Input or Output to a text file, a text file F may be declared using the keyword Text as follows:

```
Var F : Text;
```

Turbo Pascal allows the user to read or write Integers, Reals, Characters, or Strings with text files. That is,

```
Read(F, X);
```

reads, depending on X's type, the next Character, Integer, Real, or String from the file associated with F. If X is a String variable with a maximum length of MaxChars, the read will assign the next MaxChars characters on that line to X. If there are fewer than MaxChars characters on the line, all of the characters to the next end-of-line (or end-of-file) marker are assigned to X. However, a Read of a String variable does *not* advance the file pointer beyond the current end-of-line marker and, thus, subsequent reads to X assign X the null string. For this reason, one normally uses

```
Readln(F, X);
```

with a String variable.

Eoln(F) is set to True if the last character read was the last character of the current line. Likewise, Eof(F) is True if the last character read was in fact the last character of the file.

Write may be used with variables or expressions of Character, Integer, Real, or String types. In addition, the Writes may be formatted, exactly as with the standard output file Output. That is, you may give a width factor (and optionally, with reals, the number of places to the right of the decimal point) and your values will be right justified in a field of that width. If the width you specify is too small, then the system elbows enough room so that your value can be printed.

PROBLEM-SOLVING EXAMPLE: QWERTY

To illustrate text files, consider a program that compares two typewriter keyboards. Many people have suggested alternative keyboards to the standard QWERTY keyboard. The QWERTY keyboard is so named because of the placement of the first six keys on the upper row of keys. The particular arrangement of letters in the QWERTY keyboard was chosen in the late 19th century. At that time, human typists could push the new typewriter technology to its limits and jam keys by typing too fast. Hence, the QWERTY keyboard was chosen, partially, to slow humans down. Today, of course, microcomputers can respond to key presses in microseconds, so there is little danger of humans typing faster than machines can respond. One of the many keyboards that has been proposed to supplant the QWERTY keyboard is the Dvorak keyboard, whose layout is depicted in Figure 15.3.

Perhaps there will come a day when systems such as Dvorak's will be in widespread use. If Dvorak's system can be demonstrated to be much better, perhaps new typists will learn this system while old QWERTY typists die out. Let us consider a simple test of the two systems. We take a text file, read the file, and count the number of times our fingers leave the home row, both for the QWERTY system and for the Dvorak system. Of course, the number of times we leave the home row is not the only factor that makes for a good keyboard, but it illustrates our point sufficiently. The pseudo-code for the program is quite simple:

Open the text file for reading
Set QWERTY and Dvorak Hops counters to zero
While Not Eof on the text file
    Read a character Ch
    If Ch is on the QWERTY home row then
        Do nothing
    Elsc
        Increment QWERTYHops
    If Ch is on the Dvorak home row then
        Do nothing
    Else
        Increment DvorakHops
Announce the results

The program Keys that makes this comparison is shown in Listing 15.4. Note that the Case construct is useful not because of the large number of cases, but because of the multiple labels that define the first case in each instance. The text file Typing.Txt

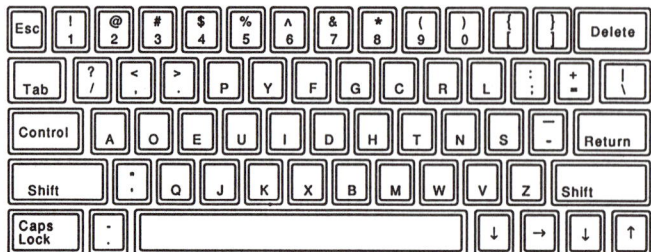

Figure 15.3

basically contains the text of the previous two paragraphs. The output of the program Keys is

```
The QWERTY keyboard needed 1032 jumps.
The Dvorak keyboard needed 650 jumps.
```

You can also create your own text file if you wish. Be sure to use only uppercase letters, since these are all that the program Keys looks for. Also, note that in the program we have declared a file variable, F, of type Text, rather than redirect the Input file, as we have done since Chapter 4.

RANDOM-ACCESS FILES

Standard Pascal does not support random-access files, so the reader should be forewarned that programs using this method of file access may not be portable to other Pascals. Even other Pascals that support random-access files do not use quite the same procedures as described here. Nonetheless, because of their power, random-access files are very useful tools.

Random access, again, simply means that we have the right to access the records of a file in any order. We may read record number 45 first, then back up to examine record number 2, then advance to record number 89. We are not limited, as with sequential files, to processing the records in their natural order.

Random-access files are very powerful and flexible. Fortunately, we now learn that manipulating random-access files in Turbo Pascal is really as easy as manipulating sequential files. In fact, in Turbo Pascal, the sequential files that we have been dealing with are really random-access files! We have concealed this fact only because sequential files can be useful and they are all that standard Pascal has.

Obviously, with random-access files, there must be some mechanism for us to select the particular record that we wish. This we do through the Seek procedure,

```
Seek(F, N);
```

which advances (or retreats) the file pointer associated with F so that the next read or write is to the Nth record of the file. N, of course, must be an integer constant, variable,

```
Program Keys; {$R+}
{This program compares the Dvorak and QWERTY keyboards. It reads
a text file, Typing.Txt, and counts how many times your fingers
would have to leave the home row on each keyboard.          }



Var DvorakHops  : Integer;
    QWERTYHops  : Integer;
    Ch          : Char;
    F           : Text;



Begin
  Assign(F, 'A:\Ch15\Typing.Txt');
  Reset(F);
  DvorakHops := 0;
  QWERTYHops := 0;
  Writeln('Here is the text file:');
  Writeln;
  While Not Eof(F) Do
    Begin
      Read(F, Ch);
      Write(Ch);                      {Echo the input to the screen.}
      Case Ch Of
        'A', 'S', 'D', 'F', 'G', 'H', 'J', 'K', 'L', ';', '''' :
                                      {QWERTY home row--Do nothing.}
        Else
          QWERTYHops := QWERTYHops + 1
      End; {Case for QWERTY keyboard}
      Case Ch Of
        'A', 'O', 'E', 'U', 'I', 'D', 'H', 'T', 'N', 'S', '-' :
                                      {Dvorak home row--Do nothing.}
        Else
          DvorakHops := DvorakHops + 1
      End {Case for Dvorak keyboard}
    End; {While}

  Writeln;
  Writeln;
  Writeln('The QWERTY keyboard needed ', QWERTYHops,' jumps.');
  Writeln('The Dvorak keyboard needed ', DvorakHops,' jumps.');
  Close(F)
End.
```

Listing 15.4

or expression. Also, to make life as difficult as possible, records are numbered from zero. That is, the first record is record number zero. Hence, to get the tenth record in the file, you should seek the ninth record from the system. Also, if N is larger than the number of records in the file, the file is advanced to the end and Eof(F) becomes true, but no error message is issued. This is so that you may append records to the end of a random-access file, even without knowing how many records are in the file.

In summary, we open random access files with Assign and Reset just as we open a sequential file for reading, and then we precede every Read or Write with a Seek to the record we wish to access. In fact, Turbo Pascal allows us to mix sequential and random-access modes. Thus, a file created sequentially with Rewrite can later be opened for random access with the Reset statement.

Here is a segment that outlines how to update the Nth record of our file Students:

```
Assign(Students, 'A:Students.Dat');
Reset(Students);
...
...
Seek(Students, N);      {We assume N already has a proper value.}
Read(Students, OneStudent);
...
...
                        {Update the record OneStudent as needed.}
...
...
Seek(Students, N);
Write(Students, OneStudent);{Write updated record to the file.}
```

Note that both the Read and the Write are preceded by Seeks. Forgetting to precede each Read or Write with a Seek is a common error, but you are less likely to make this error if you understand why the Seeks are necessary: After the Read obtains the Nth record, the file is automatically advanced to the $(N+1)$st record. If you forget to Seek back to the Nth record, your Write actually overwrites the $(N+1)$st record, wiping it out and leaving your file with two versions of the Nth record. The reason that the system operates in such a perverse way is that this permits you to mix random and sequential access. If you Seek the Nth record and then do five consecutive Reads (without Seeks), you obtain records N, $N+1$, $N+2$, $N+3$, and $N+4$. Since the manipulation of random-access files is so much like the manipulation of sequential files, we leave the remainder of this discussion to the exercises.

GET AND PUT

Standard Pascal provides an alternative method of I/O (input and output) in addition to Read and Write. Get and Put are more primitive routines than Read and Write, and understanding Get and Put helps you understand more clearly how I/O really operates.

For some reason, Get and Put have never been implemented in Turbo Pascal. Generally, Turbo Pascal is an extension of standard Pascal, but this is the one major instance where Turbo Pascal fails to implement a feature of standard Pascal. Fortunately, Get and Put add no new power to the language and anything that you can do with Get and Put you can do with Read and Write. Therefore, the remainder of this section cannot be implemented in Turbo Pascal, but it is, nonetheless, important to help the reader understand how input and output actually take place.

Every time we declare a file F of SomeType, the system allocates a buffer or window in memory for the file F. We depict the file F and its buffer in Figure 15.4. It is important to realize that the file F resides on a disk external to main memory, while the buffer is in main memory. The buffer has the same type as the record type of the file F. If we think of the buffer as containing the current record of the file, we see where the terminology "window to the file" comes from. All input from the file, and all output to the file, must go through the buffer. The system name for the buffer to the file is F^, which should be read as "the buffer to file F." On many keyboards, the buffer character (^) is typed by holding down the SHIFT key and pressing the 6 key.

Get(F) simply transfers information from the next record of F to the buffer F^. Of course, it also advances the file so that the next Get obtains the next record. After a Get(F), *not* Get(F^), the fields of F^ have values (unless there was no record to get, in which case Eof(F) is set to True). A Put(F), *not* Put(F^), transfers the information in the buffer F^ out to the next record of the file F. Hence, before we execute a Put(F), we should place values in the fields of F^.

It is very important to note *and remember* that a Reset *always* does an automatic Get. Hence, a Reset prepares the file F and brings the first record into the buffer F^. Students often forget that Reset includes the first Get and do their own Get. Then, they wonder where the first record of their file went!

Before we demonstrate, with a complete example, the correct placement of Gets in a program, we indicate how Read and Write can be implemented with Gets and Puts. Let us suppose that F is a file of SomeType and that R is a record of SomeType. We know that Read(F,R) reads the next record of the file F into the record R. Since Reset did an automatic Get, the first record is already in the buffer F^. Noting that F^ and R are both records of SomeType, we see that Read(F,R) is equivalent to

```
R := F^;                        {Transfer buffer to R.}
Get(F);                         {Prepare buffer for next Read.}
```

The order of these two statements is critical. The order is not what the beginner would

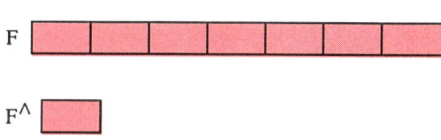

F

F^

Figure 15.4

```
{Using Gets}
Reset(F);
While Not Eof(F) Do
  Begin
    ... {Process F^}
    Get(F)
  End;
```

a)

```
{Using Reads}
Reset(F);
While Not Eof(F) Do
  Begin
    Read(F,R);
    ... {Process R}
  End;
```

b)

Figure 15.5

```
Program ViewFrn2;
{This program views the files Adam.Frn, Eve.Frn, or Adam&Eve.Frn
and illustrates the use of Get instead of Read. These are not
available in Turbo Pascal, so this program will not compile or run
in Turbo Pascal.                                                    }

Type FriendsRecord = Record
                       Last      : String[15];
                       First     : String[15];
                       Telephone : String[12]
                     End; {Record}

Var Generic : File Of FriendsRecord;
    Ans     : Char;

Begin
  Repeat
    Write('View Adam''s, Eve''s, or Adam&Eve''s file?" (1/2/3) ');
    Readln(Ans);
    Case Ans Of
      '1' : Reset(Generic, 'A:\Ch15\Adam.Frn');
      '2' : Reset(Generic, 'A:\Ch15\Eve.Frn');
      '3' : Reset(Generic, 'A:\Ch15\Adam&Eve.Frn');
      Else Writeln('Pay Attention!!!')
    End {Case}
  Until (Ans = '1') Or (Ans = '2') Or (Ans = '3');

  While Not Eof(Generic) Do
    Begin
      Writeln(Generic^.First, ' ', Generic^.Last);
      Writeln(Generic^.Telephone);
      Writeln;
      Get(Generic)
    End; {While}
  Close(Generic)
End.
```

Listing 15.5

expect, but the explanation is that the buffer is always one record ahead of the `Read`, because of the original `Get` done by the `Reset`.

Likewise, `Put` can be used instead of `Write(F,R)`. `Write(F,R)` writes the information in `R` out to the file `F`. Hence, `Write(F,R)` is equivalent to

```
F^ := R;                    {Transfer information to the buffer.}
Put(F);                     {Put the information out to the file.}
```

The fact that `Reset` does the first `Get` also means that a control loop using `Get`s is structured differently than it would be with `Read`s. Figure 15.5 shows the differences. Note that the `Get` is at the bottom of its loop and that the corresponding `Read` is at the top of its loop. The loop with the `Get` seems unusual, since we use `F^` before we do a `Get`. We leave the explanation for the reader.

The simple program `ViewFrn2`, of Listing 15.5, would allow you to see the contents of any of the files `Adam.Frn`, `Eve.Frn`, or `Adam&Eve.Frn` used in the `Merge` problem earlier in this chapter. Study the listing to see that the main `While` loop is controlled exactly as described above.

SUMMARY

Arrays, records, and files are the three most fundamental data structures in computer programming. Almost any sophisticated applications program uses at least one, if not all three, of these structures. Arrays of records and files of records are the most natural ways to structure most kinds of data, so it is crucial that the beginning programmer establish a strong understanding of each of these concepts. In fact, as programs become more complicated, the programmer soon learns that understanding the data is as important as writing the algorithms to process the data.

KEYWORDS

Random access	Sequential access
`Reset`	`Rewrite`
`Close`	Text files
`Get`	`Put`

SELF-TEST QUESTIONS

15.1 What are the differences between arrays and sequential files? What are the advantages of each over the other?

15.2 What are the differences between a text file and a general file? What are the advantages of each over the other?

15.3 Why are file parameters required to be variable parameters?

15.4 Repeat Exercise 14.3, except declare a file to keep track of The Widget Works inventory.

15.5 Discuss the similarities and differences between arrays and random-access files.

EXERCISES

15.6 The file `Years.Dat`, on the disk accompanying this book, contains records with two fields, a name (25 characters) and an integer representing the number of years that the person has been working at The Widget Works. For example, the record

```
Coffy Breaks
27
```

indicates that Coffy has been with the firm for 27 years. Snidely has decided to give year-end bonuses to those employees who have been with the company for at least 25 years. The bonus is to be $100 for every year beyond the 24th year of service. Thus, Coffy's bonus is $300. Write a program that reads `Years.Dat` and creates a file `Bonus.Dat` that contains the names of the employees earning a bonus, as well as the amount of that bonus. Also include a procedure to allow you to view `Bonus.Dat` and thereby verify that it is correct.

15.7 Write the update program described in the text for the EZ COME—EZ GO Company. The disk accompanying this book contains the files `Old.Dat` and `Trans.Dat`. Each record of `Old.Dat` contains four fields: a name (25 characters), an account number (integer), the current balance (real), and the credit limit (real). As described in the text, each record of `Trans.Dat` contains three fields: an account number (integer), a transaction code (1 character), and an amount (real). You may assume that both `Old.Dat` and `Trans.Dat` are in order by account number.

Your program should create `New.Dat` and `Trouble.Dat`. `New.Dat` contains the updated records for all customers. `Trouble.Dat` contains the record of any individual whose current balance exceeds his or her current credit limit. Include procedures so that you can view the contents of `Old.Dat` and `Trans.Dat`, as well as `New.Dat` and `Trouble.Dat`.

15.8 Use `MakeFrnd`, from the disk accompanying this book, to create new versions of `Adam.Frn` and `Eve.Frn`. Include two or three individuals on both files. Modify `Merge` so that it handles these duplicates properly.

15.9 What could we do if the files `Adam.Frn` and `Eve.Frn` do not have exactly the same structure? Suppose the fields are similar, but not exactly the same. For example, maybe Adam keeps phone numbers as strings of 8 characters (555-1212) while Eve keeps phone numbers as strings of 12 characters (708-555-1212). Neither wants to recreate his or her file from scratch. How can they most easily merge the two different files?

15.10 Write a small inventory-control program for The Widget Works. Since there are 10 products, write a procedure that creates an `Invent.Dat` file of 10 records containing

Description (25 characters)
PartNo (1--10)
QuantityOnHand (integer)
QuantityOnOrder (integer)
Cost (real)

Write a procedure `LookUp` that uses the part number to find the corresponding record in the random-access file `Invent.Dat`. Remember that part number 7 is stored in record 6 of the file. Allow the user to change the quantity on hand or the cost to reflect sales, receipt of goods, or price gouging.

15.11 Consider the following segment and suppose that `F` has been declared to be a file of `SomeType`, where `SomeType` is a record with a `Name` field. Explain how `F^.Name` can have a value before the first `Get` from the file! What does the segment do?

```
Assign(F, 'A:\Ch15\SomeFile.Dat');
Reset(F);
While Not Eof(F) Do
  Begin
    Writeln(F^.Name);
    Get(F)
  End;
```

15.12 The following program is a buggy version of program `Fetch` of the text. Debug it.

```
Program BugFetch;
{This is a buggy version of program Fetch. You will first need
to run Create to construct the records that this program tries
to Fetch.                                                       }

Type NameString  = String[25];
     ClassString = String[5];
     IDString     = String[11];

     StudentRecord = Record
                       GPA       : Real;
                       Name      : ShortString;
                       Class     : ClassString;
                       ID        : IDString;
                       FeeStatus : Boolean;
                       Sex       : Char;
                     End; {Record}

     StudentFile = File Of StudentRecord;
```

```
Var Students : StudentFile;
    FileName : NameString;

Procedure ObtainFileName (Var FileName : NameString);
{Pre:  None
Post:  The user chooses the FileName for the file.          }

  Begin
    Write('Enter the name of the file to be read: ');
    Readln(FileName)
  End;            {Definition of procedure ObtainFileName.}

Procedure WriteData (Students : StudentFile);
{Pre:  Data are stored in the file Students.
Post:  The data from Students are displayed.               }

  Var OneStudent : StudentRecord;
      Fees       : String[5];

  Begin
    While Not Eof Do
    With OneStudent Do               {Notice With to avoid}
      Begin                          {long record names.}
        Read(Students, OneStudent);
        Writeln(Name);
        Write(Class:6, ID:12, GPA:8:2);
        If FeeStatus Then Fees := 'True'
        Else Fees := 'False';
        Writeln(Fees:6, Sex:2);
        Writeln
      End {While and With}
  End;                    {Definition of procedure WriteData.}

Begin                               {Body of main program Fetch.}
  ObtainFileName(FileName);
  Assign(Students, FileName);
  Rewrite(Students);
  WriteData(Students);
  Close(Students)
End.
```

ANSWERS TO SELF-TEST QUESTIONS

15.1 Arrays are stored in main memory, while files are stored on a disk. Array access is, therefore, faster than file access (since the file access involves a mechanical drive). Arrays also support random access, while sequential files allow only sequential access. Files, however, can be much larger than arrays (because disk space is greater than main memory), and files are stored permanently, while arrays are in volatile memory.

15.2 A text file is essentially a file of characters and is, therefore, human readable. A general file is stored in computer formats and is, therefore, not human readable. The advantage of text files is that the data are easily understood and modified by humans. The advantages of general files is that they are faster to process (as no conversion of the data is required by the computer) and they are more compact in their storage requirements.

15.3 The file does not reside in memory and cannot be copied (as it would be if it were a value parameter).

15.4
```
Type InventoryRec = Record
                        PartNumber  : Integer;
                        Description : String[50];
                        NumOnHand   : Integer;
                        NumOnOrder  : Integer;
                        Price       : Real
                     End;

    InventoryFile = File Of InventoryRec;
          {Only change is File instead of Array[1..100].}

Var Inventory : InventoryFile;
```

15.5 Both are random-access data structures. Array access is faster because the array is in memory. File access is slower because of the mechanical disk drive. The file can grow to fill all available disk space, while the array is constrained both by its declared size and the fact that it must fit into the relatively smaller memory of the computer. The file is also permanent, while the array is in volatile memory.

16

SETS

The final structured type available in Pascal is the Set type. While nearly all modern, structured languages have arrays and records, very few of them have a set capability. This is unfortunate, because sets are easy to use and easy to understand.

The word *set* has many different meanings. In fact, the dictionary listing for set is typically one of the longest. In mathematics, a set is just a collection of objects. However, in a programming language, it is necessary to place some restrictions on sets. Sets in Pascal are not quite as general as sets in elementary mathematics. The major restrictions are

1. The elements of a set must all be of the same *ordinal* type. This means that sets cannot contain real numbers, strings, records, or arrays, nor can a set contain both integers and characters.
2. Sets must be finite.

The second restriction makes sense, since the computer is a finite machine. In fact, each Pascal implementation imposes an upper limit on the size of any set. Many implementations impose a fairly severe size limitation of 64, 128, or 256 elements in a set. (Turbo Pascal restricts the size of a set to 256 elements.) The allowable types for set elements are Char (or a subrange of Char), a user-defined, enumerated type (or a subrange), and a subrange of the Integer type between 0 and 255. We suggest defining subranges, particularly for sets of integers, and then using these subranges in set declarations. Specifically, do *not* use Integer as the type of a set element. Examples of set declarations are given after a discussion of the operations on sets.

Sets in Pascal are enclosed in square brackets. So,

```
['a', 'e', 'i', 'o', 'u']
```

is the set of lowercase vowels. Although square brackets are also used for array subscripts, we can always tell from the context of a statement what the square brackets mean.

SET OPERATIONS

There are three basic operations performed on sets. These operations are binary operations because they take two sets as input and produce a third set as output. These operations are **union**, **intersection**, and **difference**.

Union (denoted in Pascal by +): The union of two sets A and B consists of all the elements that belong to either A or B. With sets, we are concerned only with whether an element belongs to a set or not. There is no concept of belonging to a set twice. So, if an element belongs to both A and B, it appears in the union of A and B once. Thus, if A is [1, 2, 3] and B is [2, 3, 4], then A + B is [1, 2, 3, 4].

Intersection (denoted in Pascal by *): The intersection of two sets A and B consists of the elements that belong to both A and B. So, if A is [1, 2, 3] and B is [2, 3, 4], then A * B is [2, 3]. There is the possibility that two sets have no elements in common. For example, let C be [1, 2] and D be [3, 4]. Since the intersection of two sets results in a set, what set is C * D? This is the set that contains no elements, called the **empty** or **null set**. In Pascal, the empty set is denoted by [ ]. So, C * D is [ ].

Difference (denoted in Pascal by -): The difference of two sets, written A - B, is the set that contains the elements of A that do not belong to B. In other words, to form A - B, simply remove from A any elements that also belong to B. So, if A is [1, 2, 3, 4, 5] and B is [3, 4, 5, 6, 7], then A - B is [1, 2].

In addition to the three binary operations on sets, Pascal also provides for some Boolean tests on sets. The first of these is the **equality** test between sets. That is, one may test whether two sets are equal or not. Two sets are equal if they contain exactly the same elements. We mention here that sets are unordered structures. That is, the order in which the elements of a set are listed is irrelevant. So, [1, 2, 3] = [3, 1, 2] is True. Additionally, there are two other Boolean tests that apply to sets. These are **subset** and **membership**.

Subset (denoted in Pascal by <=): This test involves two sets. A set A is a subset of a set B if every element of A is also an element of B. So, if A is [1, 2, 3], B is [2, 3, 4], and C is [2,3,1,6], then A <= B is False while A <= C is True.

Membership (denoted in Pascal by In): This test involves an element and a set. The result of the test is True if the element belongs to the set, and False if the element is not a member of the set. For example, if A is a set of integers with current value [1, 2, 3] and if X and Y are integer variables with current values 2 and 5, respectively, then X In A is True, Y In A is False, and (Y - X) In A is True. This last example shows that the element in question does not have to be a variable, but can be any expression whose type is the same as that of the members of the set in question.

COMMON SYNTAX ERRORS WITH SETS

There are two common sources of syntax errors among beginning Pascal programmers when working with sets. The first of these deals with confusion between the In and the <= relations. Remember that <= stands between two sets, while In stands between an element and a set. Thus, with X an integer and A a set (of small integers), the statements on the left below are valid Boolean expressions, while those on the right are invalid:

Valid Boolean Expressions	Invalid Constructs
X In A	X <= A
[X] <= A	[X] In A

The second difficulty is in testing if an element X is *not* a member of a set A. Many beginners write an *incorrect* test like this:

If X Not In A Then ...

This is, of course, wrong because Not is an operator that takes a single Boolean input (a value that is either True or False) and reverses it. In the above formulation, an attempt is made to apply the Not operator to In A, which is certainly not a Boolean value (since it isn't even a complete expression). What is needed is the membership test applied first, giving a True or False value, and then the Not applied to this. But there is still a chance for error, as many beginners then write a second *incorrect* version:

If Not X In A Then ...

The reason that this is still wrong is that the Not operator has the highest precedence of all Pascal operators. This means that the Not operator is always applied as soon as possible. So, the system tries to perform Not X, which, again, is nonsense (unless X happens to be a Boolean type, which is unlikely). So, parentheses are necessary, and the correct syntax is

If Not (X In A) Then ...

SET DECLARATIONS

Set types are defined and set variables are declared using the keywords Set and Of. We give several examples below, but first we point out that the subrange notation, such as 1..10, introduced in Chapter 10, can also be used with sets. Therefore, the two sets

[1, 4, 5, 6, 7, 9, 10] and [1, 4..7, 9, 10] are the same sets. With this introduction, consider the following declarations:

```
Type Digits    = Set Of '0'..'9';
     Uppercase = Set Of 'A'..'Z';
     Colors    = (Red, Violet, Blue, Green, Yellow, Orange);

Var Nums      : Digits;
    Numbers  : Set Of 0..9;
    Small    : Set Of 1..5;
    Rainbow  : Set Of Colors;
    Letters  : Uppercase;
```

Some remarks are in order. Nums and Numbers are two sets with different types of objects. The elements of Nums are characters, while the elements of Numbers are integers. It is important to realize that the variable declaration for Small is like any other variable declaration in its effect, that of simply naming a variable and telling what its type is. Small is *not* initialized as a set containing the integers from 1 to 5, as many beginners seem to think it is. Small is a set identifier that is *permitted* to contain only the integers from 1 to 5, but the variable declaration does not assign any values to Small. This must be done with an assignment statement. So, if the first statement in the body of the program were

```
Small := [1, 3, 5];
```

then Small would, in fact, contain the odd integers from 1 to 5.

We mention, again, the difference between defining type names and then declaring variables using the type names (as is done with Letters above) and declaring variables anonymously; i.e., without using a type name (as is done with Numbers). The difference is that anonymous variables may not be used as the arguments to procedures and functions, since arguments and parameters must have type names. So, if we wanted Numbers to be the input to some function, we would need to define a type name, like

```
Type  Values = Set Of 0..100;
```

and then declare

```
Var  Numbers : Values;
```

SETS AS FILTERS

A very common problem in programming is examining data to make sure they are of the proper form. An example from Chapter 10 involved reading in exam scores from the keyboard and computing a grade point average. Since typing errors are very likely, a thorough program needs to test each input to make sure it is a legal one; i.e., one of the characters 'A', 'B', 'C', 'D', or 'F'. In most languages, this test would be made as follows:

```
Repeat
  Writeln('Enter the next exam score.');
  Readln(Score);
  If (Score < 'A') Or (Score > 'F') Or (Score = 'E') Then
    Writeln('Illegal input. Try again.')
Until (Score >= 'A') And (Score <= 'F') And (Score <> 'E');
```

However, in Pascal, such a filtering out of bad data is most naturally accomplished by using a set, because all we are doing is making sure that the input belongs to a certain set of values. So, with the variable declaration

```
Var  ValidGrades : Set Of Char;
```

and the assignment statement

```
ValidGrades := ['A'..'D', 'F'];
```

the above loop can be written as

```
Repeat
  Writeln('Enter the next score.');
  Readln(Score);
  If Not (Score In ValidGrades) Then
    Writeln('Illegal input. Try again.')
Until Score In ValidGrades;
```

As another example, suppose we wanted to read some text from a file and count the number of words. We assume that the text contains only letters, digits, blanks, and the following punctuation symbols: , ! . ? " ;

In fact, let us write a program to count the words in the text file Ch15\Typing.Txt, previously used by another program in Chapter 15. For simplicity, we assume that the file begins with a word and ends with a single punctuation mark. The program assumes that words are composed of alphabetical and numeric characters (an AlphaNumeric set) and that words are separated by blanks and/or punctuation (a Separator set). Our program is general, of course, in the sense that it counts the number of words in any text file that begins with a word, ends with punctuation, and consists only of the given characters.

The program reads one character at a time. Every time a separator is read, word scanning stops and WordScanning is set to False. Every time word scanning is off and we find an AlphaNumeric character, then we have found a new word and word scanning is turned back on. Hence, our pseudo-code is

Open the file Ch15\Typing.Txt for reading
Set AlphaNumeric to the set of letters and digits
Set Separators to the set of punctuation
Initialize Count to 1 and ScanningWord to True   --The file begins with a word
While there are more characters in the file
   Read a character Ch and write it to the screen
   If Ch is in the set of separators then
     Set ScanningWord to False
   If Ch is in AlphaNumeric and ScanningWord is False then
     Set ScanningWord to True   --The start of a new word has been found
     Increment Count
Output the Count of the number of words found

Listing 16.1 shows the complete program `WordCntr` that implements our design.

```
Program WordCntr; {Word Counter} {$R+}
{This program counts the words in the text file Ch15\Typing.Txt.}

Var  AlphaNumeric : Set Of Char;
     Separators   : Set Of Char;
     Ch           : Char;
     ScanningWord : Boolean;
     Count        : Integer;
     WordFile     : Text;
Begin
  Assign(WordFile, 'A:\Ch15\Typing.Txt'); Reset(WordFile);
  AlphaNumeric := ['A'..'Z', 'a'..'z', '0'..'9'];
  Separators := [' ', '.', ',', '?', '!', ';', Chr(10)];
  Count := 1;          {Chr(10) in the above set detects RETURNs.}
  ScanningWord := True;
  While Not Eof(WordFile) Do
    Begin
      Read(WordFile, Ch);
      Write(Ch);                   {Echo the input file to the screen.}
      If Ch In Separators Then
        ScanningWord := False;
      If (Ch In AlphaNumeric) And Not ScanningWord Then
        Begin                      {Start of a new word has been found.}
          ScanningWord := True;
          Count := Count + 1
        End
    End; {While}
  Writeln; Writeln;
  Writeln('There are ', Count , ' words in the text file.')
End.
```

Listing 16.1

The result of running `WordCntr` with the `Typing.Txt` file of the previous chapter is

```
There are 216 words in the text file.
```

Some modifications to this program are suggested in the exercises.

SETS AS DATA STRUCTURES

We now turn our attention to a different use of sets. In these next examples, sets are not used as filters, but as the natural data structure for solving the given problem. In each case, there is an alternative solution that does not employ sets--typically, an array solution. However, it should be clear that the set solution is somehow better. By this, we mean that the set solution provides a clearer, less complicated algorithm for solving the problem than does the array solution. We repeat our earlier advice: "The sooner you start coding, the longer the job will take." In other words, the more time spent planning a solution, the better the solution will probably be. This does not mean just planning the algorithm, but also analyzing the best way to represent the data. Often, the proper choice of data structures can make a significant difference in the overall solution to a problem. This is an important lesson for programmers to learn and can be summarized by the following famous equation:

Programs = Data Structures + Algorithms

What we hope to illustrate with the following examples is that using sets to structure the data often makes the algorithm much simpler and, thus, makes programs much easier to write.

PROBLEM-SOLVING EXAMPLE: SOGGIES, AGAIN

Each box of Soggies breakfast cereal contains one of 10 different prizes. If the prizes are distributed at random, how many boxes of cereal must you purchase, on the average, to acquire all 10 different prizes?

We solved this problem in Chapter 11, using arrays. Again, we generate a random integer between 1 and 10 to simulate winning one of the 10 prizes. We stop when we have won all 10 prizes. Using sets, we start with the empty set `[]` (the set of prizes won so far); each time we win a prize, we add the number of that prize to the set (using set union); and we quit purchasing boxes of cereal when the set equals `[1..10]`. Note that sets are a natural structure for this problem because of the nature of set union. If we win a prize for the second or third or subsequent time, it does not hurt anything to add (via union) that prize number to the set again. The solution to the problem, which simulates 20 different people purchasing boxes of Soggies until each has obtained all 10 prizes, is given in Listing 16.2.

```
Program SetSoggs; {Set Soggies} {$R+}
{This program uses sets to solve the Soggies problem.        }

Const  Experiment = 20;

Type  Numbers = 1..10;

Var    Prizes  : Set Of Numbers;
       Premium : Numbers;
       Count   : Integer;
       Trials  : Integer;
       Total   : Integer;
       Average : Real;

Begin
  Randomize;
  Total := 0;
  For Trials := 1 To Experiment Do
    Begin
      Prizes := [];          {Initialize Prizes to the empty set.}
      Count := 0;
      Repeat
        Premium := Random(10) + 1;
        Prizes := Prizes + [Premium];
        Count := Count + 1
      Until Prizes = [1..10];
      Writeln('It took ', Count , ' boxes to get them all.');
      Total := Total + Count
    End; {For}
  Average := Total / Experiment;
  Writeln;
  Write('The average was ', Average:5:2);
  Writeln(' boxes to get all 10 prizes.')
End.
```

Listing 16.2

The above solution is quite straightforward, but there are some important comments to make. The variable Premium takes on random values between 1 and 10, representing the prize won. It is this value that needs to be added to the set of Prizes. This is accomplished using set union, but set union is an operation applied to two *sets*. Therefore, the brackets around Premium are absolutely necessary. If Premium is a Number, then [Premium] is a set consisting of one Number. Beginners often write the syntactically *incorrect* statement

```
Prizes := Prizes + Premium;          {Error: Type mismatch.}
                                     {Addition or union?}
```

which generates a type-incompatibility error. Also, note that the use of the empty set as the initial value of the set of prizes is similar to the use of 0 to initialize running summations and counters.

PROBLEM-SOLVING EXAMPLE: THE GAME OF TAXMAN

The next example is one of our favorites. It demonstrates very clearly the importance of using the appropriate data structure. It is also complex enough that a divide-and-conquer approach using procedures and functions is helpful in solving the overall problem. Finally, the finished product is an entertaining and challenging number game for one player to play against the computer.

Taxman is a one-player number game designed by Diane Resek of San Francisco State University. The player chooses how many numbers (positive integers) are in the game, from 1 up to some upper limit. During the course of the game, the player and the computer each accumulate a total. The object of the game is for the player to accumulate a larger total than the computer, hereafter referred to as the Taxman.

The player's total accumulates simply by selecting one of the numbers left in the game. The Taxman then gets all the numbers left in the game that divide evenly into the player's chosen number. Once numbers are used (by either the player or the Taxman), they are removed from the game.

There is one major restriction on the numbers that the player may select. As in real life, the Taxman must always get something, so the player can never select a number unless at least one proper divisor of that number remains in the game. Once no numbers with divisors remain (at the end of the game), the Taxman gets all the numbers left and the game is over.

For example, suppose the game is played with the numbers 1, 2, 3, 4, 5, and 6. If the greedy player chooses 6, the Taxman gets all the divisors of 6; namely, 1, 2, and 3. But now, the only numbers left in the game are 4 and 5. Neither has a divisor left in the game, so the Taxman gets those, too, and wins 15 ($1 + 2 + 3 + 4 + 5$) to 6. However, if the player is a bit smarter and chooses 5 first, the player gets 5 and the Taxman gets 1. Now the numbers remaining are 2, 3, 4, and 6, and the smart player chooses the 4 (before the 6), giving the Taxman 2. Finally, the player chooses 6 and wins 15 ($5 + 4 + 6$) to 6 ($1 + 2 + 3$). When played with more than 50 numbers, the game can be quite challenging. Beginners are often surprised at the treasures they give the Taxman after a seemingly innocent choice (like 48).

An array solution to the game of Taxman is certainly possible and is usually required in a language without sets. However, with arrays, there is a bothersome detail in the algorithm; namely, testing if the game should be terminated--i.e., discovering when there are no numbers with divisors left in the game. Array solutions typically use a Boolean component of `True` to denote that a number is still left in the game and a `False` to denote that a number has been removed from the game. How, then, is the `EndofGame` condition noted? The array must be scanned looking for a number left in the game, and then the divisors of that number must be examined to see if any of them are left. If none remain, then another number remaining in the game must be located and a similar test applied to its divisors. This looping and testing can become quite tedious, and the algorithms often become unnecessarily complicated.

However, when one considers using sets, some new ideas spring forth. Although these ideas can be implemented in the array solution, it is interesting that the ideas seem to come to programmers who are thinking about sets in the first place. The point to be made here is that it is important to be thinking about solving the problem in its most natural setting and not about how to manipulate arrays.

Suppose the game consists of the numbers from 1 to N. Then the only integers that can ever qualify as divisors are 1 to (N Div 2) and, in fact, each of these numbers will be the divisor of some number in the game. When the set of possible divisors is empty, the game is over.

Another detail handled nicely with sets is determining whether a choice made by the player is illegal, because it has no divisors left in the game. The set of divisors of the chosen number is formed, and if the intersection of this set with the numbers remaining in the game is empty, the choice is illegal. For example, if the player chooses 12, the set of divisors of 12, [1, 2, 3, 4, 6], is formed and the choice is illegal if and only if this set has an empty intersection with the set of possible divisors.

Since this problem is rather complex, we present an outline of its solution in pseudo-code. This solution provides another example of structured, top-down programming, where a sequence of small procedures is used to divide and conquer the original problem. Observe how closely the pseudo-code resembles the main program in the Pascal solution.

Set up the original list of numbers
Repeat
    Repeat
        Display the scores and the remaining list of numbers
        Obtain a choice from the player
        Form the divisors of that choice
        If no divisors of the choice remain, threaten the player with an audit
    Until the player makes a legal choice
    Update the scores
Until the player has no legal choices
Give the rest of the numbers to the Taxman
Determine the winner

Listing 16.3 shows the implementation of our algorithm in Pascal. The reader should study the details of the implementation as well as run the program to play the game of Taxman.

The Pascal solution given in Listing 16.3 should be read from the bottom up. That is, the reader should first read the main program at the bottom of the listing to see the overall strategy of the solution. Then, as each procedure or function is invoked, the details of that particular procedure or function can be examined. Run the program and see if you can beat the Taxman with 50 or more numbers in the game.

```pascal
Program Taxman; {$R+}
{This program plays the game of Taxman, a number game created by
Diane Resek. See the text for the rules of the game.            }

Type  NumberSet = Set Of 1..100;

Var   Limit        : Integer;
      Choice       : Integer;
      PlayerScore  : Integer;
      TaxmanScore  : Integer;
      NumberPool   : NumberSet;
      Divisors     : NumberSet;

Procedure SetUp;
{Pre:  None
Post:  Via global variables, TaxmanScore, PlayerScore, Limit, and
       NumberPool all receive values.                           }

  Begin
    TaxmanScore := 0;
    PlayerScore := 0;
    Repeat
      Writeln('How many numbers do you want to play with?');
      Write('The maximum number allowed is 100: ');
      Readln(Limit)
    Until Limit In [1..100];
    NumberPool := [1..Limit]
  End;                                {Definition of procedure SetUp.}

Procedure DisplayScores;
{This procedure uses global variables to display both scores and
the remaining list of numbers.

Pre:   TaxmanScore, PlayerScore, Limit, and NumberPool all have
       values.
Post:  The values of TaxmanScore, PlayerScore, and the elements of
       NumberPool are displayed on the screen.                  }

  Var  Index : Integer;

  Begin
    Writeln;
    Writeln('Your score: ', PlayerScore);
    Writeln('Taxman:     ', TaxmanScore);
```

Listing 16.3

```
      Writeln;
      For Index := 1 To Limit Do
        If Index In NumberPool Then
          Write(Index:4);
      Writeln
    End;                        {Definition of procedure DisplayScores.}


Procedure Obtain (Var Choice : Integer);
{This procedure loops until the player makes a legal choice.
Pre:   None
Post:  Choice has a legal value chosen by the user.                  }

    Begin
      Repeat
        Writeln;
        Write('What is your choice? ');
        Readln(Choice);
        If Not (Choice In NumberPool) Then
          Writeln('Try that again and I will have you audited!')
      Until Choice In NumberPool
    End;                            {Definition of procedure Obtain.}



Procedure FormDivisors (Choice : Integer; Var Divisors :
                                                NumberSet);
{This procedure builds the set of divisors of the player's number.
Pre:   Choice has a value stored in it.
Post:  The set of Divisors of Choice is created and returned.  }

    Var  Index : Integer;

    Begin
      Divisors := [];
      For Index := 1 To Choice Div 2 Do
        If Choice Mod Index = 0 Then
          Divisors := Divisors + [Index]              {Set union with}
                                                      {singleton set.}
    End;                    {Definition of procedure FormDivisors.}

Function Sum (Nums : NumberSet; Limit : Integer) : Integer;
{Pre:  Nums is a set of integers with largest possible element Limit.
Post:  Sum returns the sum of the elements of Nums.                  }

    Var    Index : Integer;
           Total : Integer;
```

Listing 16.3 (continued)

```
Begin
  Total := 0;
  For Index := 1 To Limit Do
    If Index In Nums Then
      Total := Total + Index;
  Sum := Total
End;                               {Definition of function Sum.}


Procedure UpdateScores (Choice : Integer; Divisors : NumberSet;
                        Var TaxmanScore, PlayerScore : Integer;
                             Var NumberPool : NumberSet);
{Pre:  Choice is an integer value and Divisors is a set of Numbers.
       PlayerScore and TaxmanScore are integers, and NumberPool is
       the numbers left in the game.
Post:  The value of Choice is added to PlayerScore, and the sum of
       the elements of Divisors is added to TaxmanScore. Choice and
       Divisors are removed from NumberPool.                      }


  Var  Index : Integer;


  Begin
    PlayerScore := PlayerScore + Choice;
    TaxmanScore := TaxmanScore + Sum(Divisors);
    NumberPool := NumberPool - [Choice]; {Remove Choice and its}
    NumberPool := NumberPool - Divisors;   {Divisors from game.}
    Writeln;
    Write('The Taxman gets: ');
    For Index := 1 To Choice Div 2 Do
      If Index In Divisors Then
        Write(Index:4);
    Writeln
  End;                      {Definition of procedure UpdateScores.}

Procedure DetermineWinner(TaxmanScore, PlayerScore : Integer);
{Pre: Both scores have values stored in them.
Post: A win, lose, or tie message is printed depending on the
      scores.                                                      }


  Begin
    Writeln; Writeln;
    If TaxmanScore > PlayerScore Then
      Writeln('The Taxman won--as usual.')
    Else If PlayerScore > TaxmanScore Then
      Writeln('You won--expect an audit soon.')
```

Listing 16.3 (continued)

```
    Else
      Writeln('The game ended in a tie.')
  End;                    {Definition of procedure DetermineWinner.}


Begin                                   {Body of main program Taxman.}
  SetUp;                             {Globally initialize everything}
                                      {and obtain Limit from user.}
  Repeat
    Repeat
      DisplayScores;{Globally display scores and numbers left.}
      Obtain(Choice);
      FormDivisors(Choice, Divisors);
      Divisors := Divisors * NumberPool;          {Restrict to}
                                                {divisors left.}
      If Divisors = [] Then
        Writeln('Don''t try to cheat the Taxman!')
    Until Divisors <> [];
    UpdateScores(Choice, Divisors, TaxmanScore, PlayerScore,
                                                  NumberPool)
  Until NumberPool * [1..(Limit Div 2)] = [];   {Until the set}
                            {of possible divisors is empty.}
  Writeln('No factors remain--the Taxman takes all.');
  TaxmanScore := TaxmanScore + Sum(NumberPool);
  NumberPool := [];
  DisplayScores;                          {Display the final scores.}
  DetermineWinner(TaxmanScore, PlayerScore)
End.
```

Listing 16.3 (continued)

PROBLEM-SOLVING EXAMPLE: THE HIERARCHICAL COMPANY

The last example of the chapter points out that, although the elements of a set must be of some simple, ordinal type, the components of other structured types can, in fact, be sets. For example, we can declare arrays of sets or records with set components. Such a scheme can be very useful, particularly in applications related to graph theory. Graph theory is an area of discrete mathematics that is becoming increasingly important. A **graph** is simply a set of points with some pairs of the points joined by edges. Graphs are very useful in representing various kinds of data. Examples include communications networks, transportation networks, relationships between pairs of people in a psychological study, and relationships between resources and users of a multiuser computer system.

The example we wish to consider is the following: The employee records of the Hierarchical Company contain an employee identification number and the identification number of the employee's immediate supervisor. The president of the company

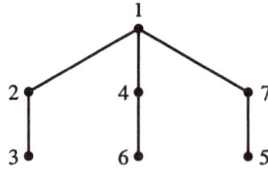

Figure 16.1

has employee number 1 and, of course, no supervisor. We present a program that reads in each employee's number, except for the president, followed by the number of the immediate supervisor of that employee. The program then prints out a summary listing all the subordinates of each employee.

   For example, suppose the graph in Figure 16.1 represents the supervisor/subordinate relationships among the company's employees.

The input, corresponding to the graph of Figure 16.1, might be as follows:

```
5 7
7 1
2 1
6 4
3 2
4 1
```

The pertinent output in this case would be

```
The subordinates of Employee 1 are: 2 3 4 5 6 7
The subordinates of Employee 2 are: 3
The subordinates of Employee 3 are: None
The subordinates of Employee 4 are: 6
The subordinates of Employee 5 are: None
The subordinates of Employee 6 are: None
The subordinates of Employee 7 are: 5
```

Now, suppose the relationships are given by the graph in Figure 16.2. Then, the input might look like this:

```
2 1
4 3
5 3
6 5
7 1
3 2
```

The pertinent output would be

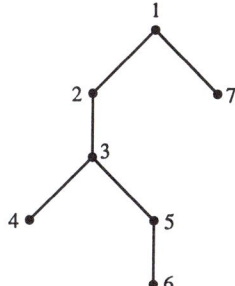

Figure 16.2

```
The subordinates of Employee  1 are: 2 3 4 5 6 7
The subordinates of Employee  2 are: 3 4 5 6
The subordinates of Employee  3 are: 4 5 6
The subordinates of Employee  4 are: None
The subordinates of Employee  5 are: 6
The subordinates of Employee  6 are: None
The subordinates of Employee  7 are: None
```

To solve this problem, we use an array of sets. The array contains a component for each employee. Each of these components is a set that represents the subordinates of that employee. Whenever we read an employee's number, followed by the supervisor's number, we do the following:

1. Place the subordinate's number into the supervisor's set.
2. Add the subordinate's set into the supervisor's set.
3. Add the supervisor's set (since it has now possibly changed) into any set that contains the supervisor's number.

The solution, shown in Listing 16.4, obtains the structure of the company from the user at the keyboard, who enters `Worker, Boss` pairs for the graph in question. The user enters `0 0` to terminate the input. Run the program and enter either of the graphs given in Figures 16.1 and 16.2, or any other graph of your choosing (with at most 10 employees). Note that the pairs may be entered in any order.

```
Program Hierarch; {Hierarchy} {$R+}
{This program prompts the user for pairs of integers representing
ID numbers of worker and boss pairs. For example, 6 4 indicates that
6's boss is 4. The program then lists the subordinates of each
employee. We assume that worker #1 is the boss and has no boss above
him or her.                                                          }
```

Listing 16.4

```
Const  CompanySize = 10;


Type  Subordinates = Set Of 2..CompanySize;


Var    Inferiors  : Array [1..CompanySize] Of Subordinates;
       Worker     : Integer;
       Boss       : Integer;
       Person     : Integer;
       Individual : Integer;

Begin
  For Person := 1 To CompanySize Do
    Inferiors[Person] := [];        {Initialize all sets to null.}
  Writeln('For this program we assume at most 10 employees');
  Writeln('numbered from 1 to 10.');
  Write('Please enter two numbers--a worker and boss pair. ');
  Readln(Worker, Boss);
  While Worker <> 0 Do
    Begin
  {Add Worker and all his or her subordinates to the Boss' set}
      Inferiors[Boss] := Inferiors[Boss] + [Worker] +
                                          Inferiors[Worker];
      For Person := 1 To CompanySize Do
            {Add the Boss's set to the set of anyone superior.}
        If Boss In Inferiors[Person] Then
          Inferiors[Person] := Inferiors[Person] +
                                          Inferiors[Boss];
      Writeln('Please enter two numbers, a worker and a boss.');
      Write('Enter 0 0 to terminate the input. ');
      Readln(Worker, Boss)
    End; {While}
  For Person := 1 To CompanySize Do            {Output the sets.}
    Begin
      Write('The subordinates of Employee', Person:2,'are:');
      If Inferiors[Person] = [] Then
        Write('None')
      Else
        For Individual := 1 To CompanySize Do
          If Individual In Inferiors[Person] Then
            Write(Individual:4);
      Writeln
    End {For}
End.
```

Listing 16.4 (continued)

SUMMARY

Although sets are rare among programming languages, they are an important part of the Pascal language. The filter example certainly makes a strong case for using sets to validate input. But not only are sets convenient to use, they are easy to understand. Beginning programmers tend to have more success (at least, less trouble) understanding sets than they do understanding arrays or records. Sets also give the programmer more options for structuring data, and the more options available, the more natural the algorithm for solving a problem is likely to be. We invite those readers who are not convinced of this to write their own array version of Taxman and compare the readability of the array version with that of the set version.

KEYWORDS

Set	Null set
Union	Intersection
Difference	In
Subset	Filter

SELF-TEST QUESTIONS

16.1 If R, S, and T are sets of characters and S is `['A','E','I','O','U']`, while T is `['Z','E','B','R','A']`, find the value of R after each of the following assignments:

a) `R := S * T;`   b) `R := S + T;`

c) `R := S + S;`   d) `R := T * T;`

e) `R := S - T;`   f) `R := T - S;`

g) `R := S - S;`   h) `R := S + [];`

i) `R := S * [];`   j) `R := S - [];`

16.2 Suppose S and T are as above. Which of the following are legal Pascal expressions? For those that are legal, indicate their value.

a) `S <= T`   b) `S In T`

c) `[ ] <= T`   d) `'A' In S`

e) `['A'] In T`   f) `'B' <= T`

g) `['B'] <= S`   h) `'B' Not In 'T'`

i) `Not 'B' In S`   j) `Not ('B' In S)`

16.3 Assume that S and T are as above and indicate the output of each of the following segments:

a)
```
For Ch := 'A' To 'Z' Do
   If Ch In S Then
      Write(Ch:2);
 Writeln;
```

b)
```
For Ch := 'Z' Downto 'A' Do
   If Ch In S Then
      Write(Ch:2);
 Writeln;
```

c)
```
Ch := 'A';
 While Ch <= 'Z' Do
   Begin
      If Ch In (S + T) Then
        Write(Ch:2);
      Ch := Succ(Succ(Ch))
   End;
 Writeln;
```

d)
```
For Ch := 'A' To 'Z' Do
   If Not (Ch In S) Then
      Write(Ch:2);
 Writeln;
```

EXERCISES

16.4 Write a set version of the program Keys (Chapter 15) that reads the text file Ch15\Typing.Txt and compares the QWERTY and Dvorak keyboards.

16.5 Our program Hierarch outputs information for 10 employees even if there are only seven employees in the data. Modify Hierarch so that it reports the subordinates of an employee only if that employee's number was entered.

16.6 (Primes Revisited) If a whole number is not prime, it must have a prime divisor less than or equal to its square root. Since Maxint is 32767 and its square root is 181.01657, any odd integer represented in Turbo Pascal's Integer type must be either prime or divisible by some prime between 3 and the largest prime less than or equal to 181.

Write a procedure GenPrimes that generates the set of odd primes through 181. Notice that since the square root of 181 is 13.45362, you need use only the divisors 3, 5, 7, 11, and 13 to generate the primes less than or equal to 181.

Write a function Prime, that uses the set generated above, to test for primehood any large (up to Maxint) odd integers entered by the user.

16.7 Write a program that reads a sentence from the keyboard and provides three lists:

1. All the letters included in the sentence
2. All the letters excluded from the sentence
3. All the letters included exactly once in the sentence

Remember that 'A' and 'a' are distinct letters.

16.8 (Artificial Intelligence) Modify Taxman so that the computer plays for you. Try devising your own strategy, but a simple plan is to have the computer make the play that maximizes its score on the current round. That is, the computer takes `Choice` where

`Choice` minus the sum of the divisors of `Choice` (still in the game)

is as large as possible.

16.9 Modify the `WordCntr` program so that it computes the average word length as well as finds the maximum word length in the text file.

ANSWERS TO SELF-TEST QUESTIONS

16.1 The characters in the sets may be listed in any order.
a) `['A','E']`   b) `['A','B','E','I','O','R','U','Z']`
c) `S`   d) `T`
e) `['I','O','U']`   f) `['B','R','Z']`
g) `[]`   h) `S`
i) `[]`   j) `S`

16.2 a) Legal, `False`.   b) Illegal.
c) Legal, `True`.   d) Legal, `True`.
e) Illegal.   f) Illegal.
g) Legal, `False`.   h) Illegal.
i) Illegal.   j) Legal, `True`.

16.3 a) A E I O U   b) U O I E A
c) A E I O U   d) B C D F G H J K L M N P Q R S T V W X Y Z

17

STRING MANIPULATION

Computers probably spend more time dealing with nonnumeric data than they do performing numeric calculations. Computers maintain lists of names, addresses, account numbers, and part numbers. Authors write books and articles using word-processing programs and then store their works on magnetic disks. Thus, the programmer must have the ability to manipulate character information in a computer. Turbo Pascal has a powerful String package for manipulating characters. Before we investigate this, however, we will review the facilities available in standard Pascal.

The fundamental built-in type in Pascal for handling characters is the Char type. Recall that variables of type Char consist of only one character. That is, character variables in Pascal are not used to store words, names, or addresses. We looked at a few simple examples in Chapter 10 that used the character type. The reader should recall that such simple tasks as changing a name from Last, First Middle to F. M. L. involved setting up `Repeat...Until` loops to process the information character by character.

Not every version of Pascal has a built-in string package, and there are certainly occasions where a program must process names, or some other kind of data, that are more than just a single character. In standard Pascal, this processing is done using arrays of characters, as discussed in Chapter 14. For example, if we wanted to read the name `'Smokey The Bear'` (RETURN) from the keyboard and store it in the array `Name`, we could do it as follows:

```
Index := 0;
While Not Eoln Do
  Begin
    Index := Index + 1;
    Read(Name[Index])
  End;
Readln;
```

Here, we assume that Name is declared as an Array [1..15] Of Char. The difficulty of doing this is that the length of Name is a **static** attribute (or characteristic). The adjective *static* is a common one in computer science. It is usually used in contrast to **dynamic**. Static means unchanging, while dynamic means varying. So we would be unable to store a value in Name that was longer than 15 characters.

STRINGS IN TURBO PASCAL

As we know, strings are declared using the word String. When a string is declared, a **size** attribute, ranging from 1 to 255 and enclosed in brackets, can be given for the string. When there is no size given, the default value of 255 is assumed. An example of each declaration is given below:

```
Var    Name     : String;
       Address  : String[30];
```

We point out that the *size* of a string is a static attribute indicating the maximum allowable length of any value of that string. However, the *length* of the string is in fact dynamic. So, a string variable can store values of any length up to its maximum.

There is a special string called the **null string**. This string has length 0 and is denoted by ' ' (two single quotes with nothing between them). Beginners often confuse the null string with a blank. Although we can't see either one of them well, they are different. A blank is just another character (entered by typing the space bar) and, treated as a string, has length 1. There are blanks between the words of this sentence (and we can see them). The null string, however, has length 0 and, therefore, consists of no characters at all. We could place 100 or 1000 null strings within the string 'Null' and, when we printed the string, it would still look like 'Null'. Believe it or not, the null string is very useful. It is often the initial value of strings, just as 0 is often the initial value of integer counters or running summations or the empty set is often the initial value of sets.

If one wants to think of strings as arrays of characters, Turbo Pascal gives that flexibility. If St is a String with current value 'Smokey The Bear', then St[4] is 'k', and the assignment statement

```
St[12] := 'P';
```

changes the value of St to 'Smokey The Pear'. If a reference is made to a component of a string that is undefined (in this case, for example, St[200]), this is a range-check error (which again shows why it is important to have {$R+} in all our programs).

Occasionally, treating a string as an array of characters is useful, but for the most part, the programmer is better off using the built-in string functions of Turbo Pascal. Before we present these, we describe the simple operations on strings that are available for most Pascal types.

First of all, assignments can be made freely among String types. Because of the dynamic property of string length, we do not have to worry about length compatibility. However, we do need to make sure that we do not violate any size restriction. For example, if `St1` is declared to have maximum size 2, then the assignment statement

`St1 := 'ABC';`

will give `St1` the value `'AB'`. There is no error message (we would like to see one) and the `'C'` is just lost.

We can also test the standard relations between two strings; namely, =, <>, <, <=, >, and >=. The less than and greater than relations with strings are **lexicographic** (or alphabetic) relations. So, to say that string `St1` is less than string `St2` means that the value of `St1` comes before the value of `St2` in the dictionary. Actually, since strings can contain any valid character, it is the ASCII code that really determines the lexicographic ordering. There are several points that need to be made concerning this ordering. The uppercase letters precede the lowercase letters, so `'Banana'` is less than `'apple'` (since `'B' < 'a'`). The blank (or space) precedes all letters, so `'Cat ' <` `'Cats'`. Finally, `'Cat '` is not equal to `'Cat'`, since they are of different lengths. In fact, `'Cat' < 'Cat '` and, in general, an initial substring of a string is less than the string itself.

TURBO PASCAL'S STRING FUNCTIONS AND PROCEDURES

First we introduce several built-in string functions and procedures of Turbo Pascal. We follow the descriptions of these with several examples.

The Length Function

Format: `Length(Str)`, where `Str` is any String value.
Result: Returns the current length of `Str`.
Example: If `Str` is `'Smokey The Bear'`, then `Length(Str)` is 15.

The Position Function

Format: `Pos(Substr, Str)`, where `Substr` and `Str` are any String values.
Result: A search for an occurrence of the value of `Substr` within `Str` is made. The function returns the position of the first character of `Substr` within `Str`. If `Substr` is not found, the function returns zero.
Example: If `Str` is `'Smokey The Bear'`, `Sub1` is `'The'`, and `Sub2` is `'the'`, then `Pos(Sub1, Str)` is 8 and `Pos(Sub2, Str)` is 0. Also, `Pos('e', Str)` is 5, since that is the position of the first `'e'` in `Str`.

The Concatenation Function

Format: `Concat(Str1, Str2, Str3, ..., StrN)`, where each parameter is a String value. The number of parameters to this function is not fixed. There is no apparent maximum to the number of parameters allowed, as we have tried an example with 300 parameters. Of course, the result is truncated to 255 characters, since that is the maximum string length in Turbo Pascal.
Result: The parameters are concatenated in the order listed.

Example: If `Str1` is `'dog'` and `Str2` is `'house'`, `Concat(Str1,Str2)` equals `'doghouse'`, while `Concat(Str2, Str1)` equals `'housedog'`.

The Copy Function

Format: `Copy(Source, Index, Count)`, where `Source` is a String value and `Index` and `Count` are Integer values.

Result: This function returns the String value that is `Count` characters long and begins at position `Index` of `Source` (i.e., at position `Source[Index]`).

Example: If `Str` is `'Example'`, `Place` is 3, and `Len` is 2, then `Copy(Str, Place, Len)` is `'am'`. Note that if the `Copy` function attempts to access characters outside the range of the `Source` string, this is *not* considered an error. Only those characters within the range of `Source` are actually copied. So, if `Str` is as above, then `Copy(Str, 3, 9)` is `'ample'`.

The Delete Procedure

Format: `Delete(Source, Index, Count)`, where `Source` is a String variable and `Index` and `Count` are `Integer` values.

Result: The substring of `Source` of length `Count`, beginning at position `Index`, is deleted from `Source`. Note that the value of `Source` is actually changed by the `Delete` procedure.

Example: If `Source` is `'Through'`, then `Delete(Source, 2, 2)` causes the value of `Source` to be changed to `'Tough'`. As with `Copy`, if characters are referenced outside the range of `Source`, there is no error, but only characters within the range are deleted.

The Insert Procedure

Format: `Insert(Source, Destination, Index)`, where `Source` is a String value, `Destination` is a String variable, and `Index` is an Integer value.

Result: The String value given by `Source` is inserted into the String value of `Destination`, beginning at position `Index`. The value of `Destination` is changed by the `Insert` procedure.

Example: If `Source` is `'re'` and `Destination` is `'Bad'`, `Insert(Source, Destination, 2)` changes `Destination`'s value to `'Bread'` and `Insert(Source, Destination, 3)` is `'Bared'`. If `Index` is greater than `Destination`'s length, the insertion is at the right end of `Destination`.

STRING EXAMPLES

Now, we use these procedures and functions to do some string processing. Some of the following examples have no apparent realistic applications, but are included just for practice.

Example 1: Suppose `Word` is a String variable. Write a segment to interchange the first and last letters of `Word`. That is, if `Word` is `'Something'`, the segment should change the value of `Word` to `'gomethinS'`. While this may sound easy, the reader is encouraged to try to accomplish this, before looking at the solution below. The solution should be a general one, not one that works just for the particular string `'Something'`.

This can actually be performed with one very busy statement, but for readability purposes, we write this as four statements:

```
First := Copy(Word, 1, 1);          {First := Word[1] also works.}
Last := Copy(Word, Length(Word), 1);
Middle := Copy(Word, 2, Length(Word) - 2);
Word := Concat(Last, Middle, First);
```

It is worthwhile to explain the above process in detail. We are assigning a new value to `Word`, the concatenation of three strings—`'g'` + `'omethin'` + `'S'`. Clearly, the first statement assigns the first letter of `Word` to `First`. Also, the second statement assigns the last letter of `Word` to `Last`. Notice that the use of the `Length` function, within the `Copy` function, is one way to make the solution a general one. Since we don't know how long the word is, we use `Length` to find the end of the word for us. To obtain the middle part of the word, we start at position 2 and extract all of `Word` except for the first and last letters. Thus, we want all but two characters, or `Length(Word) - 2` characters. A common mistake of beginners is to write `Length(Word - 2)`. This is nonsense, because `Word - 2` is a meaningless expression involving strings and integers. If the reader tests the above segment with several cases, it might be easy to be convinced that the solution is a completely general one. This demonstrates the danger of jumping to conclusions. There is, in fact, one case where the above segment does not perform as it should; namely, when the length of `Word` is exactly one. What happens? We leave the details to the reader.

Example 2: Write a program to change the form of `Name` (a String variable) from `First Middle Last` to `Last, F. M.`

We will use the `Pos` function to find the blanks between names, the `Copy` function to extract the first and middle initials, and then the `Delete` procedure to remove the first and middle names from `Name`. The solution is given in Listing 17.1.

Example 3: Enter a sentence, of less than 256 characters, from the keyboard, and count the number of occurrences of `'e'`. For simplicity, we will not search for uppercase `'E'`s, but we mention that in many text-processing situations, care must be taken to handle both uppercase and lowercase letters.

The solution is shown in Listing 17.2. Since the `Pos` function always searches from the beginning of the string, whenever we find an `'e'`, we chop off the first part of `Sentence` up through that `'e'`. While this makes the searching more efficient, we are able to do this only because we don't need to save the value of `Sentence`.

```
Program Reverse; {$R+}
{This program reverses a name. Given First Middle Last, it changes
the name to the form Last, F. M.                                        }

Const  Period = '.';
       Comma  = ',';
       Blank  = ' ';

Var    First, Middle : Char;
       Name           : String[40];
       Place          : Integer;

Begin
  Writeln('Enter a name in the form: First Middle Last');
  Readln(Name);
  First := Name[1];                      {Find the first initial.}
  Place := Pos(Blank, Name);              {Find the first blank.}
  Middle := Name[Place + 1];             {Find the middle initial.}
  Delete(Name, 1, Place);             {Remove first name and blank.}
  Place := Pos(Blank, Name);               {Find second blank.}
  Name := Copy(Name, Place + 1, Length(Name) - Place);
                                       {Name now equals last name.}
  Name := Concat(Name, Comma, Blank, First, Period, Blank,
                                            Middle, Period);
  Writeln('The reversed name is: ', Name)
End.
```

Listing 17.1

```
Program Ease; {$R+}
{This program counts the number of 'e's in a sentence. Notice that
it does not count 'E's.                                            }

Var    Count, Place : Integer;
       Sentence     : String;

Begin
  Writeln('Enter a sentence.');
  Readln(Sentence);
  Count := 0;
  Place := Pos('e', Sentence);
  While Place <> 0 Do {While more 'e's are found, delete them.}
    Begin
      Count := Count + 1;
      Delete(Sentence, 1, Place);
      Place := Pos('e', Sentence)
    End;
  Writeln('The number of "e"s in the sentence is: ', Count)
End.
```

Listing 17.2

Example 4: Remove all occurrences of the letter 'e' from a given sentence, entered from the keyboard, and print the sentence without the 'e's.

We present two strategies for removing 'e's. The first strategy treats the string as an array of characters. The second makes use of the string functions and procedures. In the first, we copy Sentence into another string variable called Alternate. We do this by concatenating letters of Sentence one at a time to Alternate. Of course, we copy everything but the letter 'e'. This program, EChop1, is given in Listing 17.3.

The second program uses the Delete procedure to remove the occurrences of 'e' and doesn't require the additional storage of Alternate, because the occurrences of 'e' are removed directly from Sentence. Notice that the value of Sentence is changed by EChop2, shown in Listing 17.4.

One of the exercises at the end of the chapter is to test character strings to see if they are palindromes. Palindromes are words, phrases, or sentences that read the same forward and backward, like 'Madam, in Eden I'm Adam'. A good first step in that problem would be to follow the idea of this example and remove all blanks and punctuation marks to obtain 'MadaminEdenImAdam'.

Example 5: Examine a piece of text and change all occurrences of 'cie' to 'cei'.

Before providing the solution, we discuss the application behind such a process. Many word-processing programs can help find and correct spelling errors. Although most do so by looking words up in a dictionary stored on the disk, it may be possible, with certain rules, to program various error-detecting capabilities. This example is taking care of the rule:

I before E except after C

There are, of course, some exceptions to this rule (like "science" and its derivatives), but in many cases, the number of exceptions is small, and before a spelling change is

```
Program EChop1; {$R+}
{This program removes 'e's from a sentence.                              }
Var    Sentence  : String;
       Alternate : String;
       Place     : Integer;
Begin
  Writeln('Please enter a sentence.');
  Readln(Sentence);
  Alternate := '';      {Initialize Alternate to null string.}
  For Place := 1 To Length(Sentence) Do
    If Sentence[Place] <> 'e' Then
      Alternate := Concat(Alternate, Sentence[Place]);
  Writeln('The sentence without any "e"s is:');
  Writeln(Alternate)
End.
```

Listing 17.3

```
Program EChop2; {$R+}

{This program also removes 'e's from sentences.                    }

Var    Sentence : String;
       Place    : Integer;
Begin
  Writeln('Please enter a sentence.');
  Readln(Sentence);
  Place := Pos('e', Sentence);

  While Place <> 0 Do              {While there are 'e's left do ...}
    Begin
      Delete(Sentence, Place, 1);
      Place := Pos('e', Sentence)
    End;

  Writeln('The sentence without any "e"s is:');
  Writeln(Sentence)
End.
```

Listing 17.4

made, the program could make sure it is not changing one of the exceptional cases. Natural languages are so complex, compared to formal languages such as Pascal, that we are a long way from having computerized proofreaders. For example, imagine trying to teach a computer how to recognize when to use "there" as opposed to "their." Will computers ever understand the intended meaning of everyday phrases such as

This ticket good for one fare from **Chicago** to **Lake Forest** or **Vice Versa**.

or will computers expect people to travel from **Chicago** to **Vice Versa**? Despite such difficulties, natural language understanding remains one of the most researched areas of **artificial intelligence**.

The solution to the spelling checker is given in Listing 17.5. The program reads a list of words (all entered on one line) from the keyboard. One of its executions is shown in Figure 17.1.

```
Enter spelling list:
recieve deceive science believe percieve

The "corrected" list is:
receive deceive sceince believe perceive
```

Figure 17.1

```
Program Speller; {$R+}

{This program uses the "I before E except after C" rule to "correct"
some spelling errors in a line of input.                              }

Const Pattern = 'cie';

Var    Spelling : String;
       Place    : Integer;

Begin
  Writeln('Enter the spelling list:');
  Readln(Spelling);

  Writeln;
  Place := Pos(Pattern, Spelling);
  While Place <> 0 Do          {While the 'cie' pattern is found}
    Begin
      Spelling[Place + 1] := 'e';   {Do the surgery to replace}
      Spelling[Place + 2] := 'i';            {the 'ie' by 'ei'.}
      Place := Pos(Pattern, Spelling)
    End; {While}

  Writeln('The "corrected" list is:');
  Writeln(Spelling)
End.
```

Listing 17.5

In the program Speller, we have used both the string capability and the array of characters representation. The reason for mixing is one of efficiency. To find the pattern 'cie', it is easier to let the Pos function search, as opposed to doing a character-by-character search. Such a character search would involve stopping at each 'c', checking the next letter to see if it is an 'i', and, if so, checking to see if the next letter is an 'e'. However, once we have found such a pattern, it is more efficient to directly insert the two letters after the 'c', using the character components rather than employing the Delete/Insert procedures or the Concat/Copy functions. It is up to the programmer to choose those operations that are most efficient for the particular situation. In fact, we remark that using Pos, as we have here, is efficient in terms of the actual writing of the Pascal program, but is less efficient in terms of execution. The reason Pos is not very efficient in this case is that it returns to the beginning of the string each time to resume its search for the pattern 'cie' and, so, is searching over text that has already been processed. Other string packages often provide a function similar to Pos, but with the capability of specifying a starting position for the search, other than the first position of the string. Such implementations tend to increase searching efficiency. We leave the writing of such a search capability to the exercises.

SUMMARY

The beginner may be surprised at how often the need for character manipulation arises. It may seem that reversing strings is simply an exercise in using the string-manipulation functions. But consider a business that keeps all its customer records on disk. It is likely that these records are indexed by last names so that given records can be easily found. However, if the business wishes to pull the names from the disk to use in a letter, the names need to be in normal order. There are two options: Store the names twice, once as `Last, First` and another time as `First Last`. This uses twice as much storage and, although computer storage is becoming less and less expensive, it still isn't free. The other alternative is to store the names only in the form `Last, First` and make the software that processes the names and writes the letter manipulate the names into the form needed.

Systems programming is another area where manipulation of string information is crucial. A Pascal program is treated by the system translator as a string of characters. The translator's first job is to **parse** the program; that is, to break it up into its component parts, like keywords and operators, so that the program can be checked for syntax errors.

With so many different kinds of data being stored in computer systems, it is up to the programmer to find the way through the data, extracting the information needed for a given application. In many situations, the string-manipulation functions, like `Pos` and `Copy`, provide the easiest way to find the desired information.

KEYWORDS

Dynamic	Static
Null string	`Length`
`Pos`	`Concat`
`Copy`	`Delete`
`Insert`	Parse

SELF-TEST QUESTIONS

17.1 If S is the string `'This is an example of a string'`, find the value of each of the following expressions. Assume that the maximum length of S is 255.

a) `Length(S)` b) `Pos('e', S)`

c) `Pos('is', S);` d) `Pos(' is', S)`

e) `Pos('Is', S);` f) `Concat(S, S)`

g) `Concat('S', S)` h) `Concat('S', 'S')`

i) `Copy(S, 12, 7)` j) `Copy(S, Length(S) - 5, 6)`

17.2 Assume that S is as above and determine the value of S after each of the following statements.

a) `Delete(S, 5, 6);` **b)** `Delete(S, Length(S) - 11, 12);`

c) `Insert('NOT ', S, 9);` **d)** `Insert(S, S, Length(S) Div 2)`

17.3 What is the output of the following segment? What does it do?

```
S := 'The quick brown fox jumps over the lazy dog';
For Letter := 'a' To 'z' Do
  Begin
    Place := Pos(Letter, S);
    If Place > 0 Then
       Delete(S, Place, 1)
  End;
Writeln(S);
```

EXERCISES

17.4 Write a function, `CountZz`, that accepts a String and counts the number of Zs (both `'z'` and `'Z'`) in the string.

17.5 Write a function `Distinct` that accepts a String and outputs `True` only if all the characters of the String are distinct. For example, `Distinct('BASIC')` is `True`, while `Distinct('Pascal')` is `False` since Pascal contains two `'a'`s. Notice that `Distinct('Bob')` is True.

17.6 As chief censor of Sikinia, it is your duty to implement the latest royal decree, which states:

Henceforth, Red shall be called White and White shall be called Red.

Write a program that reads a sentence, such as the above royal decree, and outputs the censored version. Be careful that you do not keep changing the same word over and over.

17.7 riteWay ayay rogrampay hattay ranslatestay entencessay intoyay igPay atin-Lay. The rules for Pig Latin are:

If a word begins with a vowel, "yay" is added to the end of the word. Thus, "Apple" becomes "Appleyay." On the other hand, if a word begins with a consonant, that consonant is moved to the end and "ay" is added. Thus, "Zenith" becomes "enithZay."

17.8 Write a program that translates Pig Latin back into English. Are there any problems with this translation? Can you think of a word or sentence that can't be translated back without ambiguity?

17.9 Write the function `Place(Str, Pattern, Start)`, which is a smart version of `Pos(Str, Pattern)`. `Place` returns the position of the first occurrence of the string `Pattern` in the target string `Str`, starting its search at the `Start`th place. For example, `Place('Pascal', 'a', 3)` returns 5, the location of the first `'a'` at, or after, the third character in `'Pascal'`.

17.10 A palindrome is a phrase that reads the same backward as forward. For example,

`Able was I ere I saw Elba`

is a palindrome. The notion of a palindrome can be extended to include phrases such as

`Madam, in Eden I'm Adam`

that, except for blanks and punctuation, read the same backward as forward. We include such phrases in our definition of a palindrome.

Write a procedure `Strip` that removes all the blanks and punctuation from a String. `Strip` may assume that commas, apostrophes, and hyphens are the only punctuation in the given String. Thus, `Strip` would turn the above String into `'MadaminEdenImAdam'`.

Write a procedure `Flip` that reverses a given String. For example, `Flip` would turn `'Pascal'` into `'lacsaP'`.

Write a procedure `LowerCase` that converts all the letters of a given String to lowercase. Thus, `LowerCase` would convert `'Pascal'` into `'pascal'`. Note that `LowerCase` leaves the blanks and punctuation, if any, alone. Hint: `LowerCase` should make use of the built-in functions `Ord` and `Chr`.

Write a program that finds the winner in a palindrome contest. The rather strange rules of the contest are

1. If an entry is not a palindrome, it scores 0 points.
2. If an entry is a palindrome, it scores 1 point for each character, not counting blanks or punctuation. Thus, 'Madam, in Eden Im Adam' scores 17 points.
3. If an entry is a palindrome with respect to blanks and punctuation, then it scores a bonus of 30 points. Thus, 'Able was I ere I saw Elba' scores 19 + 30 = 49 points. Note that case changes are allowed in entries.

The contestants and their entries are shown below. These data (two lines per contestant) are also available as `Pals.Txt` on the sample disk that accompanies this book.

Name	Entry
Eve Firstperson	Eve
Adam Firstperson	Madam, in Eden I'm Adam
Abel Firstperson	Abel was I ere I saw Cain
Napoleon Bonaparte	Able was I ere I saw Elba
Minnesota Fats	Doc, note, I dissent--a fast never prevents a fatness--I diet on cod
Theodore Roosevelt	A man, a plan, a canal, Panama
Marquis de Sade	Evil I did dwel--lewd did I live

Your program should output each person's score, whether the bonus was earned, and, finally, the name of the winner followed by the winning entry.

17.11 Write a program that plays a game of hangman. In the game of hangman, the computer selects a secret word, at random, from a text file of words. The computer displays a star (*) for each letter in the word, thereby giving the player the length of the word. The player then tries to guess the word letter by letter. If the letter guessed is in the word, the computer shows all instances of that letter in the given word. For example, if the secret word is 'hangman' and the guess is 'a', the display changes from '*******' to '*a***a*'. If the player guesses the letters of the word without guessing five wrong letters, the player wins; otherwise, the player hangs.

ANSWERS TO SELF-TEST QUESTIONS

17.1   a) 30   b) 12
       c) 3   d) 5
       e) 0
       f) 'This is an example of a stringThis is an example of a string'
       g) 'SThis is an example of a string'
       h) 'SS'
       i) 'example'
       j) 'string'

17.2   a) 'This example of a string'
       b) 'This is an example'
       c) 'This is NOT an example of a string'
       d) 'This is an exaThis is an example of a stringmple of a string'

17.3   The segment removes the first instance of each letter from 'a' to 'z' from S. The output is T o u oer he o

18

RECURSION

In Pascal, it is possible for a procedure or function to invoke itself. This is known as **recursion**, because the function or procedure *reoccurs* within itself. This chapter illustrates several instances in which recursion leads to elegant solutions of seemingly complex problems. We provide several examples, so that you may begin to recognize situations where recursion is an appropriate instrument to apply.

To avoid an infinite sequence of calls, there must, of course, be some means whereby the given procedure or function stops invoking instances of itself. Thus, for recursion to apply, both of the following must be true:

1. There must be at least one trivial case that ends the sequence of recursive calls.
2. There must be some way to put together solutions to *easy* instances to solve *hard* instances of the problem.

Let us consider an example to see how these principles apply. The factorial function is the first, standard example of recursion. For example, 5! (read "five factorial") is 5 * 4 * 3 * 2 * 1 or 120. In general, N! (read "N factorial") is N * (N - 1) * (N - 2) *… * 3 * 2 * 1. This expression, written equivalently as N! = N * (N - 1)!, is the approach needed if we wish to write a recursive factorial function. This last equation says that the *hard* problem of finding N! can be solved by simply multiplying N and (N - 1)!. Likewise, (N - 1)! is simply the product of N - 1 and (N - 2)!. To prevent infinite descent, we need a trivial, nonrecursive case that ends the process. Since 0! is traditionally defined to be 1, we use this case to end the recursion.

Here, then, is the simple, recursive pseudo-code to compute `Factorial(N)`:

If N is 0 then
   Factorial is 1
Else
   Factorial is N * Factorial(N - 1)

```
Function Factorial(N : Integer) : Integer;
                                        {Not a complete program.}
{Pre: N has a value such that N! does not cause overflow.
Post: The function returns the value of N factorial.           }
  Begin
    If N = 0 Then
      Factorial := 1
    Else
      Factorial := N * Factorial(N - 1)
  End;                {Recursive definition of function Factorial.}
```

Listing 18.1

For example, trace how the computer could use the above pseudo-code to compute 3!. First, 3! = 3 * 2!, and 2! = 2 * 1!; and 1! = 1 * 0!. Since 0! is defined to be 1, the computer traces backward that 1! is also 1, 2! is 2, and, thus, 3! is 6. Listing 18.1 shows the recursive, Pascal version of Factorial.

Notice that the Then clause contains the trivial case, in which Factorial is simply assigned a value. The Else clause contains the general case, in which the factorial of N is computed using the factorial of N - 1. Also, observe that, unlike nonrecursive functions, recursive functions are allowed to use the function name on the right-hand side of an assignment statement within the body of the function. As an exercise to aid in your understanding of recursion, carefully trace, in the code of Listing 18.1, the evaluation of Factorial(5). If you see how Factorial(5) is evaluated, you are well on your way to understanding recursion.

Factorial quickly overflows the Integer type. Actually, 8! already overflows Integers and 13! overflows even LongInts, so LongInts postpone the overflow problem only a little bit. Furthermore, note that recursion is not needed to compute the factorial function. Indeed, we leave it as an exercise to implement Factorial as a simple, iterative (looping) function. This illustrates a fact about recursion: Any problem that can be solved with recursion can also be solved without recursion. Why then should students waste their time studying recursion? The answer, illustrated in the examples that follow, is that, in many instances, recursion provides a short and elegant solution to what appear to be very complicated problems. Recursion is simply a tool that can make problem solving easier. The trick is to learn to recognize when recursion applies. Let us consider several situations, some old, some new, in which recursion can be used.

First, observe that, while Factorial provides a simple example of recursion, the iterative solution is just as simple and is, in fact, more efficient, since recursive functions always involve some overhead to keep track of the environments that are required each time a procedure or function calls itself (or another procedure or function). Factorial is not a good example of a situation in which recursion should be used (but it does provide a simple first example). We now turn to some problems where recursion provides an elegant solution. We leave the reader to consider how difficult the nonrecursive solutions, in each case, would be.

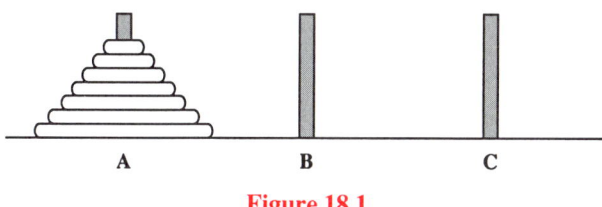

Figure 18.1

THE TOWERS OF HANOI

An excellent example of the power of recursion is provided by the puzzle known as the Towers of Hanoi. Figure 18.1 illustrates the puzzle, in which one must move the tower of disks from peg A to peg C. The simple rules are

1. You can move only one disk at a time.
2. You can never place a large disk on a small disk.

If you have never played with this puzzle, make some disks from paper and solve the puzzle with three or four disks before reading the next section.

We will write a procedure `Towers(N,'A','B','C')` that will solve general Towers of Hanoi problems. That is, given a positive integer N, and three pegs labeled `'A'`, `'B'`, and `'C'`, the procedure should give us explicit, move-by-move intructions for getting the N disks from peg `'A'` to peg `'C'`, using peg `'B'` as the auxiliary peg. For example, the output from `Towers(2,'A','B','C')` should solve the two-disk problem with the following instructions:

```
Move disk 1 from peg A to peg B.
Move disk 2 from peg A to peg C.
Move disk 1 from peg B to peg C.
```

Throughout this discussion, disk 1 is the smallest disk, disk 2 is the next smallest, etc.

It is far from obvious how to write the procedure `Towers`. Let us look for a recursive solution. We need a trivial case of the puzzle to end the recursion. If there were going to be a Towers of Hanoi puzzle on your final exam, how many disks would you like to see on the first peg? Most of us would agree that the puzzle with only one disk is, indeed, trivial. Secondly, how can we use solutions to smaller puzzles to help us solve the N disk puzzle? Figure 18.2 shows how to patch solutions to easier puzzles together to solve bigger puzzles. We solve the N disk puzzle in three stages:

Move the N - 1 top disks from peg A to peg B
Move disk N from peg A to peg C
Move the N - 1 top disks from peg B to peg C

Moving the N - 1 top disks is simply an instance of solving the N - 1 disk problem. Thus, we have an algorithm, much as in the factorial problem, for solving N disk puzzles from N - 1 disk puzzles. Listing 18.2 shows the Pascal for our pseudo-code.

```
Procedure Towers (N : Integer; From, Aux, Dest : Char);
                                        {Not a complete program.}
{This recursive procedure solve Towers of Hanoi puzzles.
Pre:   All 4 parameters have distinct values.
Post:  Instructions for moving N disks from the From peg to
       the Dest peg, using Aux as the auxiliary peg, are written.}
Begin
  If N = 1 Then                                        {Trivial case.}
    Writeln('Move disk 1 from peg ', From, ' to peg ', Dest)
  Else                                                 {Recursive case.}
    Begin
      Towers(N - 1, From, Dest, Aux);
      Writeln('Move disk ', N , ' from peg ', From, ' to peg ',
                                                         Dest);
      Towers(N - 1, Aux, From, Dest)
    End {If}
End;                      {Recursive definition of procedure Towers.}
```

Listing 18.2

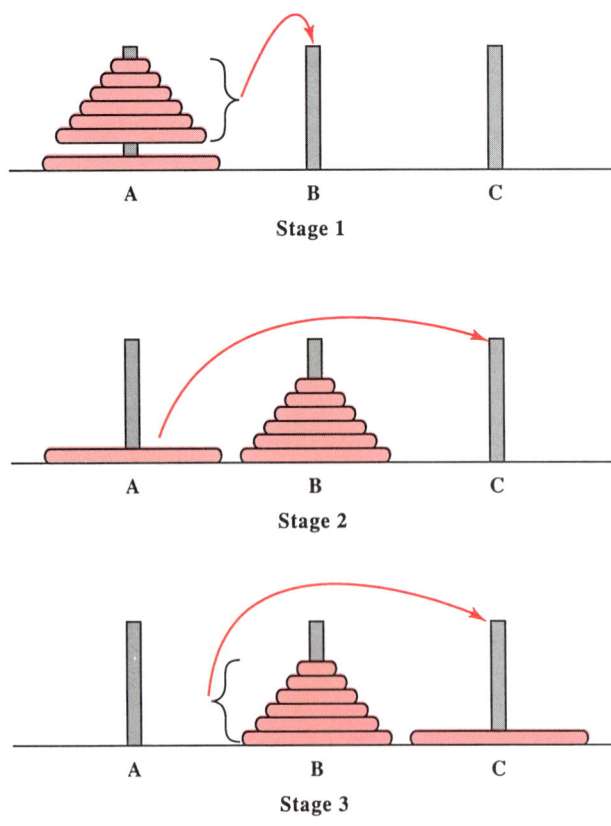

Figure 18.2 Recursive Solution

You should work through the procedure `Tower`, for N equal to 2 or 3, to see how it works. In particular, note how the `From`, `Dest`, and `Aux` pegs are used. That is, to move N disks from the `From` peg to the `Dest` peg, the `Tower` procedure first moves N - 1 disks from the `From` peg to the `Aux` peg, using the `Dest` peg as the auxiliary peg. Then, it moves the Nth disk to the `Dest` peg and then moves the N - 1 disks from the `Aux` peg to the `Dest` peg, using the `From` peg as the auxiliary.

Listing 18.3 shows the complete program `Hanoi` that prompts the user to enter N, the number of disks, then invokes the recursive procedure `Towers` to print the explicit instructions for moving the N disks from peg `'A'` to peg `'C'`. If you are not impressed with the brevity and elegance of this solution, consider writing your own *nonrecursive* solution. We think you will quickly learn to appreciate recursion.

```
Program Hanoi; {$R+}

{This program recursively solves Towers of Hanoi puzzles.}

Var  N : Integer;

Procedure Towers (N : Integer; From, Aux, Dest : Char);

{This recursive procedure solves Towers of Hanoi puzzles.
Pre:   All 4 parameters have distinct values.

Post:  Instructions for moving N disks from the From peg to the Dest
       peg, using Aux as the auxiliary peg, are written.         }

  Begin
    If N = 1 Then                                {Trivial case.}
      Writeln('Move disk 1 from peg ', From, ' to peg ', Dest)
    Else
      Begin                                    {Recursive case.}
        Towers(N - 1, From, Dest, Aux);    {Take top disks off}
        Writeln('Move disk ', N:1,' from peg ', From,
                                          ' to peg ', Dest);
        Towers(N - 1, Aux, From, Dest) {Move top disks back.}
      End {If}
  End;              {Recursive definition of procedure Towers.}


Begin                              {Body of main program Hanoi.}
  Writeln('Please enter the number of disks in the puzzle.');
  Readln(N);
  Towers(N, 'A', 'B', 'C')
End.
```

Listing 18.3

RECURSIVE PALINDROMES

In Chapter 17, we presented an exercise to test strings to see if they were palindromes. A palindrome, of course, is a phrase that reads the same backward as forward. Let us write a recursive function to test for palindromes. In general, we need check only the first and last letters of a string. If they are different, the string cannot be a palindrome. If they are the same, throw them away and repeat the process on the remaining string. Eventually, we must come down to a string of zero or one character. These are our trivial cases because any such string is a palindrome. Here, then, is our pseudo-code:

If the length is zero or one, then the string is a palindrome
Else if the first and last characters don't match then it isn't
Otherwise, throw away the first and last characters and repeat

The resulting recursive function, Palindrome, is contained, along with a main program to show it off, in Listing 18.4.

```
Program RecPals; {Recursive Palindromes} {$R+}
{This program uses the recursive function Palindrome to test given
strings to see if they are palindromes.                          }

Var  Sentence : String;

Function Palindrome (S : String) : Boolean;
{Pre: S has a value.
Post: Palindrome returns True if and only if S is a palindrome.}
  Begin
    If (Length(S) = 0) Or (Length(S) = 1) Then
      Palindrome := True        {Trivial case of a palindrome.}
    Else If S[1] <> S[Length(S)] Then
      Palindrome := False     {Trivial case of a nonpalindrome.}
    Else
      Begin{Remove the first and last characters and try again.}
        Delete(S, 1, 1);
        Delete(S, Length(S), 1);
        Palindrome := Palindrome(S)
      End {If}
  End;              {Recursive definition of function Palindrome.}
Begin                            {Body of main program RecPals.}
  Writeln('Please enter your candidate sentence:');
  Readln(Sentence);
  If Palindrome(Sentence) Then
    Writeln('It is a palindrome.')
  Else
    Writeln('Sorry, not a palindrome.')
End.
```

Listing 18.4

Table 18.1: Recursive Counting

Length	Number of Strings
1	2
2	3
3	5
4	8
5	13

RECURSIVE COUNTING

The next example is a counting problem. Suppose you would like to know how many strings, of a certain length, of 0s and 1s you can form that do not contain two consecutive 1s. For example, there are three such strings of length 2. They are 00, 01, and 10. Likewise, there are five of length 3. They are 000, 001, 010, 100, and 101. Can you find the eight of length 4 and the 13 of length 5? (How about the 17,711 of length 20?) More importantly, do you see a pattern that will help you compute these numbers? Table 18.1 shows the values for lengths up to 5.

We hope a pattern becomes clear. The next value is always the sum of the last two values. In general, if Count(N) counts the number of such strings of length N, then Count(N) is Count(N - 1) + Count(N - 2). This is clearly a recursive relationship! Since the recursive expression involves two previous values, we need two trivial cases to get us started. We take Count(1) as 2 (since 0 and 1 are the two strings of length 1) and Count(2) as 3 as the trivial cases and use the recursive formula for any N larger than 3.

You may recognize this sequence of numbers as the **Fibonacci** sequence. This sequence has been of interest for many centuries and, as this problem illustrates, the Fibonacci sequence appears, most unexpectedly, in many counting problems.

Before we write the program, let's see if we can understand where the recursive relationship comes from. Consider constructing a string of length N that does not contain two consecutive 1s. It starts with either a 0 or a 1. If it starts with a 1, it must have a 0 next (why?), and then there are N - 2 places left to consider. Any legal string of N - 2 characters can occupy these spots. Hence, there are Count(N - 2) legal strings of length N that begin with a 1. We ask the reader to argue that there are Count(N - 1) legal strings of length N that begin with a 0. Thus, there are Count(N - 1) + Count(N - 2) legal strings of length N altogether, and the recursive relationship is established. If you are still confused, try to see how the eight legal strings of length 4 come from the five strings of length 3 and the three of length 2.

Notice that we do not need two separate cases for the two trivial cases. Because of the simplicity of the situation, we have Count(N) = N + 1 for both values of N. The simple program, ZeroAndOne, which invokes the recursive procedure Count, is given in Listing 18.5. We have used the type LongInt instead of Integer for Count (to postpone overflow problems).

```
Program ZeroAndOne; {Zero&One is DOS name.} {$R+}
{This program uses the recursive function Count(N) to count the
number of strings of 0s and 1s of length N that do not contain two
1s in a row.                                                      }

Const NumTerms = 25;

Var  N : Integer;

Function Count (N : Integer) : LongInt;
{Pre:  N is an integer with a value that will not cause overflow.
Post:  Count returns the number of strings of 0s and 1s of length
       N that do not contain two 1s in a row.                     }

  Begin
    If N < 3 Then
      Count := N + 1
    Else
      Count := Count(N - 1) + Count(N - 2)
  End;                    {Recursive definition of function Count.}

Begin                                {Body of main program ZeroAndOne.}
  Writeln('N' : 3, 'Number of strings' : 20);
  For N := 1 To NumTerms Do
    Writeln(N:3, Count(N):10)
End.
```

Listing 18.5

Run the program ZeroAndOne and watch it slow down as N grows. Why does the program get so slow? Computers are supposed to be fast, but when the output reaches the 20s, it gets much slower than humans. For example, suppose the output is as follows:

```
...      ...
19      10946
20      17711
21      28657
22      46368
23      75025
24     121393
```

All the computer has to do to get the 25th term is to add 75,025 and 121,393. Why does it take so long? The answer is that, even though the computer has only to add Count(24) and Count(23) to find Count(25), the computer didn't remember Count(24) or Count(23) and has to compute them both again. Of course, Count(24) involves Count(23) and Count(22), etc. And then, when it finally computes Count(24), it discovers that it needs Count(23) and starts all over on that calculation. Remember that computers are dumb and that recursion can be very inefficient!

Recursion is not really appropriate for this situation, and we leave the details of a more efficient, nonrecursive solution of this problem to the exercises.

QUICK SORT

We close the chapter by providing a sort routine that uses recursion and executes much more quickly than any of the sort routines we considered in Chapter 12. The sort is called **quick sort** (developed by Anthony Hoare) and, on random data, it is generally the fastest of all known sorts. To see how much faster quick sort is, we invite the reader to include quick sort in the `Sorts` program of Chapter 12 and race it against those sorts on an array of size 1000.

The basic idea behind quick sort is a **pivot**. To perform a pivot, we select a pivot element and then adjust the data so that the following conditions are satisfied:

1. The pivot element is in its proper place in the array.
2. All items smaller than the pivot element occur in the array before the pivot element, and all items larger than the pivot element occur in the array after the pivot element.

In other words, the pivot element is in its correct position and all other items are correct *relative* to the pivot element. For example, suppose we have an array with values

```
33   57   48   37   12   92   86   25
```

If we choose 33 as the pivot element and perform a pivot, the array might look like this:

```
25   12   33   37   48   92   86   57
```

We say *might* look like this, because there is no requirement as to how the elements larger (or smaller) than 33 must be arranged. We have ensured only that the elements larger (smaller) come after (before) 33. So another legal picture of the array is

```
12   25   33   57   92   37   48   86
```

Where does recursion fit in? Well, now that 33 is in its proper place, it naturally divides the array (let's use our second picture) into two halves, the subarray 12 25 and the subarray 57 92 37 48 86. Since these are correct, relative to 33, if we could sort these individually, the entire array would be sorted. How do we sort these small arrays? Let's try the same approach. Let's choose the first element in each of those as pivot elements, perform a pivot, and obtain

```
12   25   33   48   37   57   92   86
```

Now, 33 originally divided the array into two pieces, a left half and a right half. Likewise, we can think of 12 as dividing the left half into two pieces. The first fourth of the array is empty and the second fourth contains 25. Similarly, 57 has divided the right half of the orginal array into two pieces, 48 37, and 92 86. Both the first fourth and the second fourth of the array are now easy to sort—they contain zero and one element, respectively. We have arrived at the trivial case for those pieces. We could next perform a pivot on 48 37, using 48 as the pivot element, and on 92 86, using 92 as the pivot element. After these pivots, which conceptually divide each fourth of the array into two pieces (eighths), all the pieces are so small that sorting becomes trivial (in fact, the array would now be sorted). This is the idea behind quick sort.

To repeat the basic approach: We perform a pivot. With each pivot, we get an element in its correct position, with everything else positioned correctly relative to the pivot element. The pivot element splits the array into two smaller pieces, and we attack those pieces with the same strategy. If we really wanted to fine-tune our quick-sort approach, we could get sophisticated about how we choose the pivot element. However, for our purposes, quick sort works just fine if we choose the first element of the array as the pivot element.

Our first task will be to write a Pivot procedure. This procedure needs to move the pivot element to its correct position and also move the other elements of the array, if necessary, to the correct side of the pivot element. Consider the following array:

35   27   88   13   65   72   54   19   6   95

Our pivot element will be 35. Where should 35 go? By looking at all the elements and counting, we can see that it belongs in the fifth position. We could swap the 35 and the 65. Then, we would need to pass back through the array adjusting anything that is out of place relative to 35. The first item we would see would be 65 (since it traded places with 35). It needs to move to the right of 35, but where? Actually, anywhere to the right is fine. But we need to make a place for it. Obviously, we don't want to trade 65 with something else bigger than 35, or we won't have made much progress. So, it seems as if we should find something to the right of 35 that is smaller, and trade that with 65. This is the essential idea behind a pivot, but one of the tricks of quick sort is to do all this data movement efficiently. So, we improve on the idea and suggest the following strategy:

1. Move 35 to a temporary location. (This effectively frees the first position in the array.)

                                                                                    Temp

35   27   88   13   65   72   54   19   6   95   35

2. Since the first position should hold a small element (relative to 35), let's scan downward from the top of the array until we find something smaller than 35 (in our example, the 6). Let's move that element to the position 35 held, and remember, with an arrow, where we stopped.

                                                    ←———   Temp

6   27   88   13   65   72   54   19   **6**   95   35

3. Now, the ninth position in the array is effectively free and is ready to hold something larger than 35. So let's scan from the bottom this time, until we find something (88) bigger than 35, and move it to position 9. Again, we remember where we stopped with an arrow.

```
                                                                    Temp
 ⟶                                            ⟵
 6   27   88   13   65   72   54   19   88   95            35
```

4. Now, position 3 is free (even though the 88 is still there), so let's do what we did in step 2, but starting from where we stopped. So, we find the 19, which is less than 35, and move it left (to position 3).

```
                                                                    Temp
 ⟶                                   ⟵
 6   27   19   13   65   72   54   19   88   95            35
```

5. We repeat step 3, working our way up through the array (again, from where we stopped), looking for an element larger than 35 to place where the 19 (upper 19) was. Thus, we find and move 65.

```
                                                                    Temp
 ⟶                              ⟵
 6   27   19   13   65  72  54  65  88  95                 35
```

6. Now, we try to repeat step 2, but as we work down, we get to where we stopped on our upward swing, before we find anything smaller than 35. This place, where our two arrows meet, marks the spot where 35 should be placed. So, we store the value of Temp there.

```
                                                                    Temp
 ⟶⟵
 6   27   19   13   35   72   54   65   88   95            35
```

Our pivot is complete, as 35 is in the fifth place, with everything smaller to the left and everything larger to the right. If we wish to attack the smaller arrays with the same Pivot procedure, the procedure essentially needs to know where the two smaller pieces of the array are. In our example, the left half of the array ranges from position 1 to position 4, while the right half ranges from position 6 to position 10. Observe that these bounds can be determined if we know the position of the pivot element (in this case, position 5). Thus, the Pivot procedure, in addition to doing the data movement, will also return the final resting place of the pivot element. With that lengthy explanation, we present in Listing 18.6 the procedure Pivot.

```
Procedure Pivot(Var A:ArrayType; Low, High:Integer; Var Pos:Integer);

{This procedure performs a pivot on a portion of the array A,
beginning at position Low and ending at position High. The pivot
element is the first element of the array; i.e., the element at
position Low.

Pre:   A, Low, and High all have values.
Post:  The pivot element, originally at position Low, is moved to
       its correct position in the array, and all other elements
       in the subarray from position Low to High are placed correctly
       relative to the pivot element. Pos is given the value
       corresponding to the new position of the pivot element. }

Var  Temp : Integer;

Begin
  Temp := A[Low];                          {Store the pivot element.}
  While Low < High Do            {Low works up, High works down.}
    Begin                     {When they meet, the pivot is complete.}
      While (Temp <= A[High]) And (Low < High) Do
        High := High - 1;{Move High down until we find a small}
                            {element or until High meets Low.}
      If Low < High Then   {Did we find a small element? If so,}
        Begin              {move it down and start an upward scan.}
          A[Low] := A[High];
          Low := Low + 1;
          While (Temp >= A[Low]) And (Low < High) Do
            Low := Low + 1;     {Move Low up until we find a big}
                            {element or until Low meets High.}
          If Low < High Then{Did we find a big element? If so,}
            Begin             {move it up and start another down}
              A[High] := A[Low];   {scan, from the point where}
              High := High - 1     {the previous one stopped.}}
            End {Inner If}
        End {Outer If}
    End; {Outer While}
  A[Low] := Temp;                          {Low and High have met.}
  Pos := Low               {Pos carries that value back to the main}
                            {program for subsequent calls to Pivot.}
End;                                    {Definition of procedure Pivot.}
```

Listing 18.6

   The above procedure is probably the most complex one, logically speaking, of this entire text. The nested structure (of a While inside an If inside another While) is necessary, because we alternate downward swings and upward swings, but we don't know which kind of scan will be our last. So, we can't simply have one While loop (say,

```
Procedure QuickSort(Var A : ArrayType; Low, High : Integer);
                                        {Not a complete program.}
{This procedure calls Pivot, then uses the position of the pivot
element to sort recursively the array A.
Pre:  All the parameters have values.
Post: The array A is sorted in increasing order.                }

Var  Place : Integer;

Begin                   {Trivial case--Low >= High--means we have an}
  If Low < High Then   {array of size 0 or 1, so we do nothing.}
    Begin
      Pivot(A, Low, High, Place);        {Perform the pivot.}
      QuickSort(A, Low, Place - 1);            {Left half.}
      QuickSort(A, Place + 1, High)           {Right half.}
    End {If}
End;              {Recursive definition of procedure QuickSort.}
```

Listing 18.7

the upward scan) follow the other (the downward scan). This procedure does perform the pivot rather efficiently, and the reader who can trace through this procedure can certainly lay claim to understanding the control structures of Pascal.

We still aren't finished with quick sort. We need a recursive procedure that invokes the Pivot procedure. In our example, after the pivot, the array looks like this:

```
6   27   19   13   35   72   54   65   88   95
```

Next, we can perform a pivot on the subarray 6 27 19 13 and the subarray 72 54 56 88 95. In general, knowing where the pivot element ended up (this is the purpose of Pos in the Pivot procedure) tells us where the next two pieces of the array can be found. Listing 18.7 demonstrates this idea with the recursive procedure QuickSort.

A main program containing QuickSort and Pivot would make an intital call of

```
QuickSort(A, 1, MaxSize);
```

where MaxSize is the upper bound on the size of the array A. Note that, in our example, the QuickSort procedure, after performing the first pivot, calls QuickSort(A,1,4) and QuickSort(A,6,10). Let's consider the second of these calls to QuickSort. It would perform a pivot on positions 6 through 10 of A:

Before Pivot: 72   54   65   88   95

After Pivot :   65   54   **72**   88   95   (Pos is 8)

After this pivot is complete, QuickSort would call QuickSort(A,6,7) and

`QuickSort(A,9,10)`, using *its values* for `Low` (6), `High` (10), and `Pos` (8). By tracing a small, but complete, example, the reader should be able to see the magic of recursion taking over, sorting the entire array. So that you will not have to type in `Pivot` and `QuickSort`, the disk that accompanies this book has a brief program, `TryQuick`, that contains both the `Pivot` and `QuickSort` procedures.

SUMMARY

We conclude the chapter with some comments on the efficiency of quick sort. If our pivot element ends up about in the middle of the array, then, when we split the array into two pieces, each of those pieces is about half the size of the original. If we continue to get lucky (where the pivot element ends up near the middle), the entire sort process is controlled by how many times we can split an array in half. For example, an array with 1,000,000 elements can be split in half only 20 times before each piece is of size 1. So, we can see that quick sort can work very quickly on large arrays, if the data are random (because with random data, we should expect to get reasonably lucky—i.e., the pivot element is likely to be about in the middle of the data). However, there is a drawback to quick sort if the data that we are trying to sort are nearly sorted. Then, our pivots split the array into two unbalanced pieces, a very small piece and a very large one. The subsequent pivot on the large piece is likely to produce the same kind of splitting, so that for an array of 1,000,000 elements, we might need to perform nearly 1,000,000 pivots. In this situation, quick sort becomes one of the slowest sorts. But, as mentioned before, when sorting random data, quick sort tends to outperform all other known sorting algorithms. We invite the reader to experiment with these kinds of questions in the exercises.

KEYWORDS

Recursion	Factorial
Towers of Hanoi	Fibonacci
Quick sort	Pivot

SELF-TEST QUESTIONS

18.1 Why is the body of a recursive procedure nearly always implemented as an `If...Then...Else`?

18.2 Why is the body of `QuickSort` just a simple `If...Then`?

18.3 Why is recursion sometimes very inefficient? Explain why the `Count` function of the text is so slow.

18.4 Carefully trace the execution of `QuickSort` on the following array:

```
48  12  62  24  98  31  53
```

EXERCISES

18.5 Write a nonrecursive version of the program `ZeroAndOne` from the text.

18.6 Write a recursive function `Exponent(X,K)` that computes X^K. Is this an appropriate use of recursion?

18.7 The greatest common divisor (`GCD`) of two positive integers X and Y is defined to be the largest positive integer that divides evenly into both X and Y. For example, `GCD(21,15)` is 3, `GCD(22,15)` is 1, and `GCD(30,15)` is 15. The Euclidean algorithm is a standard way of finding the `GCD` of two integers. The Euclidean algorithm essentially says: Divide Y into X, where Y is the second of the two numbers. (Usually, Y is the smaller of the two numbers, but this is not necessary.) If Y divides evenly into X, then the `GCD(X,Y)` is Y. If Y does not divide evenly into X, take the remainder and divide it into Y. If that division is not even, divide the second remainder into the first remainder. Continue this process until a division operation has no remainder. The divisor for the last division is the `GCD` of X and Y.

The two statements below give a nice recursive formulation for the Euclidean algorithm. Use these to write a recursive function to compute the `GCD` of two integers. Test your function on several pairs of integers by writing a main program that asks for two integers, from the keyboard, and computes their `GCD`.

$$\text{GCD(X, Y)} = \text{Y if X Mod Y} = 0$$
$$\text{GCD(X, Y)} = \text{GCD(Y, X Mod Y) if X Mod Y} \neq 0$$

18.8 Wallalumps breed according to the following strange rules: One- and two-year-old Wallalumps produce one child each. Three-year-old Wallalumps produce two children each. Older Wallalumps do not bear children. Assuming that you begin with 10 one-year-old Wallalumps and 10 two-year-old Wallalumps and that no Wallalumps die, write recursive and nonrecursive versions of a program to count the Wallalump population for each of the next 10 years.

18.9 Add the `QuickSort` procedure to the program `Sorts` of Chapter 12. Time and graph the results of `QuickSort` and the other sorts on variously sized arrays of random data. What is the order of finish of the sorts?

18.10 Repeat the above exercise, except use arrays that are already in order. Why is the order of finish so different in this case?

18.11 Write a nonrecursive version of the `Factorial` function.

18.12 There is an ancient legend that says that, in a temple somewhere in the Far East, high priests are solving a Towers of Hanoi puzzle with 64 golden disks. The legend says that when they complete the puzzle, the world will end! Find out whether you should bother studying for next week's exams. That is, assuming that the priests can move one disk every second, and that they work in shifts so that the work progresses 24 hours a day, seven days a week, how long will it take them to solve the puzzle? Hint: Begin with puzzles of 1, 2, or 3 disks and determine the number of moves needed to solve these puzzles. Look at the nature of the recursive solution and generalize your formula to a formula that tells you how many moves are needed to solve any N disk puzzle.

18.13 Consider the example from the text concerning strings of 0s and 1s without consecutive 0s, and argue that there are `Count(N - 1)` legal strings of 0s and 1s that begin with a 1.

18.14 Without using arrays or strings, read a line of characters and print them backward.

18.15 Write a procedure `PrintLongInt(N)` that will print the value of its parameter N with appropriate commas. That is, `1234567890` prints as `1,234,567,890`.

ANSWERS TO SELF-TEST QUESTIONS

18.1 The `Then` clause catches the trivial nonrecursive case(s), while the `Else` clause is for the recursive case where big problems are solved in terms of smaller problems.

18.2 There is nothing to do in the trivial case of zero or one element, so that part of the body can be omitted. To make the body an `If...Then...Else`, as in all the other recursive procedures, we could write

```
If Low >= High Then
  {Do nothing with an array of size 0 or 1.}
Else
  Begin
    Pivot(A, Low, High, Place);        {Perform the pivot.}
    QuickSort(A, Low, Place - 1);             {Left half.}
    QuickSort(A, Place + 1, High)            {Right half.}
  End; {If}
```

18.3 Each call of a function or a procedure requires a new environment, as described in Chapter 9. When a function or procedure calls itself extensively, this can lead to inefficiencies in speed and in memory management. The function `Count` is a good example of this. All it has to do to compute `Count(N)` is add `Count(N - 1)` and `Count(N - 2)`. But first, it has to compute these. In computing `Count(N - 1)`, it has to compute `Count(K)` for all smaller values of K. Then it needs to compute `Count(N - 2)` and repeats almost all of this work over again!

18.4 The first pivot element is 48. After the first pivot, we have `Pos` equal to 4 and the array has become

```
31  12  24  48  98  62  53
```

Now, QuickSort calls itself on indices 1 to 3 and then on indices 5 to 7. The second call, of course, will not be executed until the first is completed. The first call uses 31 as the pivot to produce

```
24  12  31  48  98  62  53
```

and two more calls to QuickSort, one on indices 1 to 2 and then one on indices 4 to 3. The first of these calls pivots on 24 to give

```
12  24  31  48  98  62  53
```

and two calls to QuickSort, with indices 1 to 1 and 3 to 2, respectively. Both of these calls are trivial, so the recursion does not proceed deeper. Rather, the system returns to the next active call, which is the second call with 31 as the pivot. This is a trivial call with indices 4 and 3. Hence, the recursion unwinds to the top level and the left half of the array is sorted. We can now trace the second call to QuickSort produced by the pivot 48 with indices 5 to 7. This pivots on 98, produces

```
12  24  31  48  53  62  98
```

and creates two more calls to QuickSort. The first of these, with indices of 5 and 6, pivots on 53 to produce

```
12  24  31  48  53  62  98
```

and two trivial calls (with indices 5 to 4 and 6 to 6). Thus, the system returns to the other call produced by the pivot element 98. This is also trivial, since the indices are 8 and 7. Thus, the sort is complete and the final array is

```
12  24  31  48  53  62  98
```

19

POINTERS AND LINKED LISTS

The array is an example of a **static** data structure. It is called static because its size must be fixed when the program is written. For example, suppose you have an array of 100 elements, but suddenly you find that you need to store a 101st element in the array. It can't be done without halting the program, changing the declaration of the array, and running the program again. In this chapter, we are going to introduce linked lists as an example of a **dynamic** data structure. As we'll see, linked lists can grow to any arbitrary size (that fits into the RAM memory of the computer) and are not limited to some fixed, predeclared size.

In the general situation, you may need many arrays. Being static data structures, this probably leads to a poor utilization of memory. Figure 19.1 illustrates a frustrating problem that can occur with separate arrays.

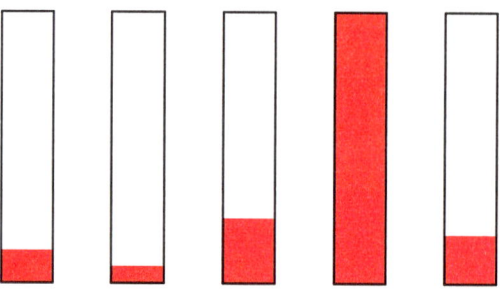

Figure 19.1

506

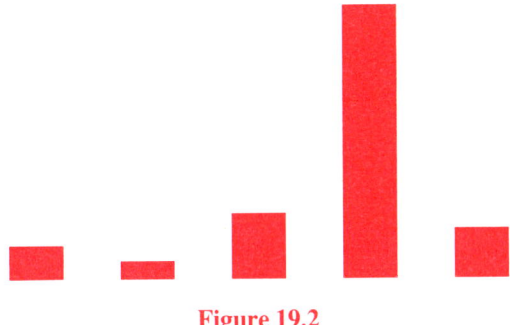

Figure 19.2

As illustrated, four of the arrays are nearly empty and, hence, great amounts of memory are being wasted. But unfortunately, one of the arrays has overflowed, and the program abends (abnormally ends), because there is no more room in the indicated array. We call this poor memory management because we have simultaneously wasted memory in four of the arrays, yet have no available memory in the other array.

With linked lists, memory utilization is as depicted in Figure 19.2. Each dynamic list uses just the amount of memory that it needs. Overflow occurs only when all available memory in the computer is in use.

In the dynamic situation, the system keeps track of memory utilization and gives and takes back memory from our linked lists. For now, let us suppose we have two black boxes, New and Dispose, that magically fetch and dispose of memory for us. We will have more to say about New and Dispose later.

The array is, of course, an ordered sequence of elements. The elements of an array are even stored physically in order in the computer's memory. We will want our linked lists to be ordered sequences of elements, but we will not insist that the elements of the linked list be stored physically in order. That is, we will distinguish between the logical order and the actual physical order of the elements. As long as we can easily recover the logical order, it is not essential that the elements actually be kept in physical order. The mechanism that we use to recover the logical order is simple: Each element contains a pointer to the next logical element. Thus, a linked list is usually drawn as in Figure 19.3.

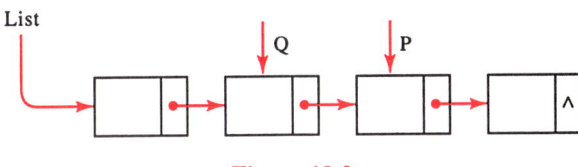

Figure 19.3

Figure 19.4

It is important to realize that the cells depicted above may be anywhere in memory. For example, the element that P points to is logically the element after the element that Q points to. However, the cell that P points to may come before, or even be on the other side of memory from, the cell that Q points to. As long as we have a pointer, List, to the first cell, we can use the pointers to recover the logical order of the linked list. The components of a linked list are called **nodes**. As shown in Figure 19.3, we implement the nodes of a linked list as records with two fields. The first field is an information field and the second field is a link field to the next node in the list. The information field is determined by the given application. If much information is being stored, then the information field can be organized as a record. In the example that follows, suppose that the information field consists of just a name (30 characters) and an identification number (integer).

We first turn to the question of how the link field is implemented. This situation is so important that Pascal provides a pointer type just to implement such dynamic data structures. A pointer is declared as follows:

```
Var   P : ^Integer;              {P is a pointer to an integer.}
      X : Integer;                         {X is an integer.}
```

Notice the little ^ in the declaration. This means that P is not an integer, but a **pointer** to an integer. That is, P contains the address of a cell that can contain an integer. Contrast the difference between P and X, as shown in Figure 19.4.

Since P is a pointer (and not an integer), the assignment P := 6 is an illegal mixing of types and does *not* assign 6 to the integer that P points to. The correct statement is

```
P^ := 6;
```

and this is read as "The integer that P points to is assigned the value 6."

Notice that the ^ symbol is used in two distinct ways that the beginner must carefully distinguish:

1. The symbol ^ is used on the *left* of type names in Var and Type sections to declare pointer variables.
2. The symbol ^ is used on the *right* of pointer variables in the body of the program to reference the actual element that the pointer is pointing to.

The beauty (and confusion) of pointers is that we can use both the pointer (address) as well as the value (contents) of the cell being pointed to. That is, if P and Q are pointers to the same type, then both of the following are valid:

```
Q := P;                                    {Pointer assignment.}
Q^ := P^;                                  {Contents assignment.}
```

The first statement assigns P's value to Q, so that Q now points to the same cell that P does. The second assigns the value pointed to by P to the cell that Q points to. Both operations are needed in what follows. The first moves pointers, the second moves information accessed through the pointers. For example, suppose that P initially points to an integer with the value 7 , while Q initially points to an integer with the value 4. Then the effect of each of the above assignments is illustrated in Figure 19.5.

Let's use pointers to declare a linked list. The complete declaration is given in Listing 19.1.

```
Type InfoField = Record
                      Name : String[30];
                      IDNo : Integer
                   End;

     ListPtr = ^Node;

     Node = Record
               Info : InfoField;
               Link : ListPtr
            End;

Var   List    : ListPtr;
      NewInfo : InfoField;
      Index   : Integer;
```

Listing 19.1

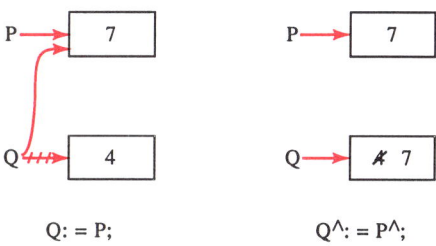

Q: = P;   Q^: = P^;

Figure 19.5

Observe that the Node is a record with two fields, as promised. The information field is very straightforward. The link field is of type ListPtr, which is simply a pointer to another Node. Note the chicken-and-egg problem with this declaration. That is, a Node references a ListPtr and a ListPtr references a Node. This is the one case in Pascal in which something may be referenced before it is declared. That is, it is legal to declare a pointer to an object even before that object is itself declared. Also, notice that we keep track of a linked list with just one pointer, List, to the first element of the list.

OPERATIONS ON LINKED LISTS

Suppose that List has been declared, as above, as a ListPtr. Recall that declaring List does not give it any initial value. How should we initialize List? We will suppose that every list has a special first element, called a **listhead**. The purpose of the listhead is twofold: It makes every list, even the empty list, visible and it makes many routines that follow easier to write. Figure 19.6 depicts two linked lists with listheads.

List1, in Figure 19.6, contains three elements (in addition to the listhead). List2 is the empty list that contains no elements (other than the listhead). The last element of a list needs a special **null pointer** to indicate that there is no next element. In List2, we see that the pointer field of the listhead contains this special value. Again, because of this need, Pascal contains a special pointer constant, Nil, for precisely this situation. The Nil pointer is used to mark the end of a linked list. It is important that the last link be set to Nil, for if some old pointer value is left in the last link field, then we might, mistakenly, think that the list goes on beyond the last element and we would likely end up accessing invalid data.

Thus, to initialize List, we need to get a new node (the listhead) and make List point to this node. We also need to put Nil in the link field of this node. Note that we do not need to place any information in the information field of the listhead. Listing 19.2 shows the Initialize procedure in Pascal.

The built-in procedure New is very useful. If P is a pointer to some type T, New(P) causes the system to allocate a new cell in memory of type T and to place the address of this cell in P. One should always draw pictures with linked lists to help visualize what is happening in the computer's memory. Figure 19.7 depicts the action of New(List).

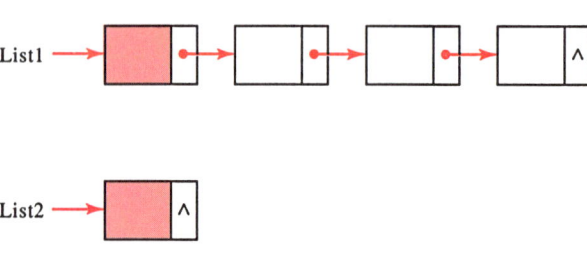

Figure 19.6

```
Procedure Initialize (Var List : ListPtr);
                                      {Not a complete program.}
{This procedure initializes List to the null or empty list.

Pre:  None
Post: List points to a new listhead that has a null pointer.  }

  Begin
    New(List);
    List^.Link := Nil
  End;                           {Definition of procedure Initialize.}
```

Listing 19.2

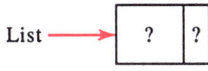

Figure 19.7

Another simple, useful procedure is one that prints the contents of a linked list. Clearly, the only way to print the contents of the nodes is to trace through the pointers, going from node to node until we encounter the Nil pointer. We must also remember to skip the listhead and begin with the first node. Here is the pseudo-code for our plan:

Set P to the link field of List   --P now points to first element
While P isn't Nil do
   Print the contents of the node P points to
   Advance P to the next node   --P becomes link of P

Listing 19.3 gives the Pascal equivalent of the above. The reader should draw a picture, such as Figure 19.6, and carefully trace the code.

A routine to print a list is not of much value unless we also have routines that allow us to construct lists. As we'll see, inserting and deleting elements from lists is not difficult. Indeed, as Figure 19.8 shows, to insert an element after the element that Q points to involves only getting a new node, putting the new information into it, and then adjusting a couple of links.

For ease in discussion in the remainder of the chapter, we will use some imprecise, but shorter, terminology. Namely, we will refer to "node P," although P is a pointer to a node and not a node itself. When we make such a reference, we are, of course, referring to the node pointed to by P. With this convention, we do not have to keep repeating phrases like "the node pointed to by P." With this in mind, we present the pseudo-code for the insertion operation that places a new node after node Q:

```
Procedure PrintList (List : ListPtr); {Not a complete program.}
{This procedure traverses the linked List and prints the info
fields.
Pre:  List points to a linked list, possibly null.
Post: The contents of each node of the list are printed in turn.}

  Var  P : ListPtr;

  Begin
    P := List^.Link;
    While P <> Nil Do
      Begin
        Writeln(P^.Info.Name:30, P^.Info.IDNo:10);
        P := P^.Link
      End
  End;                              {Definition of procedure PrintList.}
```

Listing 19.3

Get a new node and let P point to it
Place the new information in the info field of node P
Set the link field of node P equal to the link field of node Q
Set the link field of node Q equal to P

The reader should verify that these instructions produce the drawing of Figure 19.8.
To test your understanding, you should also draw a picture and see what is wrong with
the above pseudo-code if we reverse the order of the last two statements. When
changing link fields, you should always be careful to consider the order in which you
make your changes.

We include our insertion routine in a procedure Build that constructs an ordered,
linked list. That is, we choose to insert new elements into the list so that the list remains
ordered. Notice that PrintList then prints the list in order! How do we find the correct

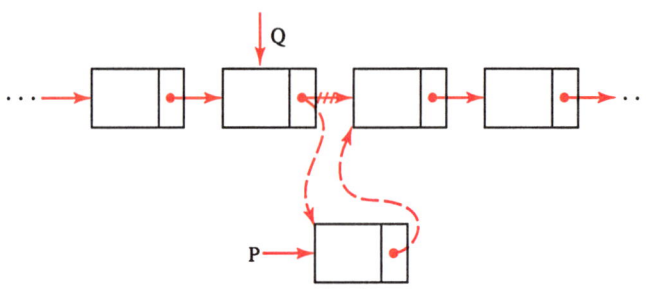

Figure 19.8

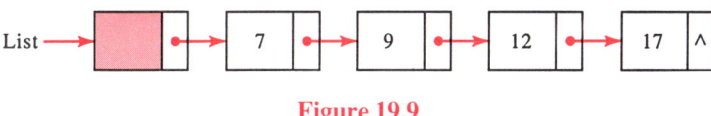

Figure 19.9

place for a new element? We use two pointers, P and Q, with Q following behind P. We want to find the place where Q's info is smaller than the new info and P's info is larger than the new info. Then, clearly, the new node belongs between P and Q, so we use the above routine to insert it after Q. What if the new info belongs at the end of the list? Then P eventually becomes Nil and we insert after Q anyway. Hence, *since we are only interested in* Q, we can set P to Nil as a signal that the proper place has been found. Our Build routine in pseudo-code is

Set Q to List
Set P to link of List   --Q will follow behind P
While P is not Nil do
    If P's info is bigger than the new info then
        Set P to Nil   --Exit the loop with place found
    Else   --Advance Q and P and keep looking
        Set Q to P
        Set P to link of P
Insert the new element after the node that Q points to

Trace the above pseudo-code, inserting 13 into the linked list shown in Figure 19.9.

The Pascal equivalent of our pseudo-code is given in Listing 19.4. It orders the nodes by the IDNo field of the information record. In our pseudo-code, we did not worry about such details. Of course, in the actual implementation, we have to choose one of the fields as the **key** field on which all of the nodes are ordered. It is just a minor modification to order the nodes alphabetically by name.

Note that Build works even if the linked list is initially empty. In that case, Q points to the listhead and P is already Nil; hence, the While executes zero times and the new element is inserted after the listhead. Thus, Build can be used, after Initialize, to construct an ordered, linked list.

We have gathered the procedures Initialize, Build, and PrintList into a main program, LinkList, that uses these procedures to build an ordered, linked list of 10 elements. The program is shown in Listing 19.5. You should run the program with data of your own design.

Deleting from a linked list is also easy. As shown in Figure 19.10, we have only to adjust a pointer to delete the node that P points to. However, note that since the link field of the node before P must be changed, it is a good idea to have a pointer Q to the node that precedes P.

Also, what will we do with the newly freed node P? It would be wasteful to simply abandon it. We should return it to the system for recycling. Since this is a common and important need with dynamic memory allocation, Turbo Pascal provides a built-in

```
Procedure Build (List : ListPtr; NewInfo : InfoField);
                                      {Not a complete program.}
{This procedure adds a new node with NewInfo in it and preserves
the order of the linked List.

Pre:   List is pointing to an ordered linked list (possibly null).

Post: An element with NewInfo as its information field has been
       inserted into the list, preserving the order, which is based
       upon the IDNo field of the record.                        }

  Var  P, Q : ListPtr;

  Begin
    Q := List;                             {Q will follow behind P.}
    P := List^.Link;      {New element will go between Q and P.}

    While P <> Nil Do
      Begin
        If P^.Info.IDNo >= NewInfo.IDNo Then
          P := Nil    {Exit loop, we have found place for node.}
        Else
          Begin                               {Keep looking.}
            Q := P;                  {Move Q and P forward one link.}
            P := P^.Link
          End {If}
      End; {While}

    New(P);                          {Get new node, put info into it,}
    P^.Info := NewInfo;                         {link it in after Q.}
    P^.Link := Q^.Link;
    Q^.Link := P
  End;                                 {Definition of procedure Build.}
```

Listing 19.4

recovery procedure, Dispose(P). We should think of Dispose(P) as the opposite of New(P). New(P) allocates a unit of memory from the system for our use, while Dispose(P) returns that unit of memory to the system. We leave the details of the deletion routine to the exercises, but do not forget to invoke Dispose in your deletion routine.

SUMMARY

This brief introduction to pointers and linked lists has hopefully convinced you of their utility. In a second course, you will make a more detailed study of linked lists and other

```
Program LinkList; {$R+}
{This program illustrates the use of linked lists.}

Const  NumNodes = 10;

Type  InfoField = Record
                    Name : String[30];
                    IDNo : Integer
                  End;

      ListPtr   = ^Node;

      Node      = Record
                    Info : InfoField;
                    Link : ListPtr
                  End;

Var   List    : ListPtr;
      NewInfo : InfoField;
      Index   : Integer;

{Procedures Initialize, PrintList, and Build go here.          }

Begin                             {Body of main program LinkList.}
  Initialize(List);
  For Index := 1 To NumNodes Do
    Begin
      Writeln('Please enter name number ', Index );
      Readln(NewInfo.Name);
      Writeln('Please enter the ID number for ', NewInfo.Name);
      Readln(NewInfo.IDNo);
      Build(List, NewInfo)
    End; {For}
  Writeln;
  Writeln('Here is your list in order by ID number:');
  PrintList(List)
End.
```

Listing 19.5

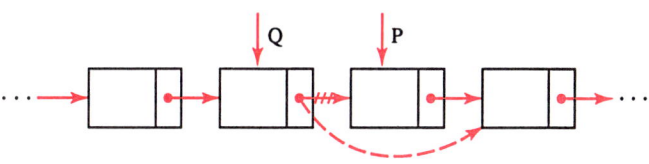

Figure 19.10

dynamic data structures (such as trees) that are implemented with pointers. We have included this brief discussion of these topics so that you can appreciate the power of pointers and linked lists and can see that there is much more to learn, particularly about the way in which data are structured in the computer. As we have tried to point out in our discussions of arrays, records, and sets (the built-in data-structuring tools of Pascal), how you structure the data is as important as, and can influence, the algorithm needed to solve a given problem. A second course builds on the ideas presented here to create new data-structuring tools that are not built into Pascal.

KEYWORDS

Pointers	Nodes
Linked lists	Arrays
Physical order	Logical order
Static	Dynamic
New	Dispose
Nil	Listhead

SELF-TEST QUESTIONS

19.1 What is wrong with the following pseudo-code to insert a new node into a linked list after the node that Q is pointing to? Start with the before picture of Figure 19.8 and draw a new picture to help explain your answer.

    Get a new node and let P point to it
    Place the new information in the info field of node P
    Set the link field of node Q equal to P
    Set the link field of node P equal to the link field of node Q

19.2 What are the advantages of a linked list over an array? Can you think of any disadvantages of linked lists?

19.3 Assuming the following declarations and initializations, which of the following assignments are valid? For those that are invalid, indicate why. For those that are valid, indicate what the assignment does.

```
Var    P : ^Integer;
       Q : ^Integer;
       N : Integer;

Begin
  New(P);
  P^ := 5;
  N := 17;
  ...
```

a) `N := P;`   b) `P := N;`

c) `P^ := N;`   d) `N := ^P;`

e) `^P := N;`   f) `N := P^;`

g) `Q := P;`   h) `P := P^;`

i) `Q^ := 7;`   j) `P^ := 0;`

EXERCISES

19.4 Write a function `CountNodes` that accepts a pointer to a list and returns a count of the number of nodes in the list. Do not count the listhead.

19.5 Write a procedure `Delete(List, IDNum)` that deletes the node from the linked `List` whose `IDNo` is the given `IDNum`. If there is no such node, `Delete` prints a "Sorry, not found" message. Remember to invoke `Dispose` to actually free the given node.

19.6 Write a procedure `Flip(List)` that inverts the order of `List`. That is, the last element is now the first element, the next-to-last element is now the second element, etc.

19.7 Write a procedure `ReversePrint(List)` that prints the elements of a linked list in reverse order.

19.8 The Lake Forest College Running Club needs a program to sort out the winner in its Strawman Triathlon. The competition consists of a 1/4-mile swim, a 5-mile bicycle ride, and a 2-mile run. The data for each competitor are available on the text file `Ch19\Triath.Txt` on the disk accompanying this book. There are two lines for each person. The first line is the name, of type `String[30]`. The second line contains a category (either the character `'S'`, `'F'`, or `'A'` for Student, Faculty, or Administration, respectively) followed by three real numbers representing, in hours, the swim time, bike time, and run time, respectively.
Using linked lists with pointers, identify the following individuals:

1. The overall grand champion (best sum of times)
2. The grand champion and runner-up in each category
3. The overall best swimmer and runner-up
4. The overall best biker and runner-up
5. The overall best runner and runner-up
6. Best-Sport Award (worst sum of times)

In case of a tie for a first prize, award duplicate prizes and no runners-up prizes in that competition. In case of ties only among the runners-up, award duplicate runners-up prizes.

Hint: Use several ordered, linked lists. Insert each person into the appropriate lists. Take advantage of modular programming—do *not* write an insertion routine for each list!

Warning: Remember, do not test real numbers for true equality.

ANSWERS TO SELF-TEST QUESTIONS

19.1 The order of the last two statements is incorrect. This causes node P to point to itself. This loses the rest of the linked list and makes the linked list infinitely long, since we never come to a Nil pointer by following pointers. The picture is as follows:

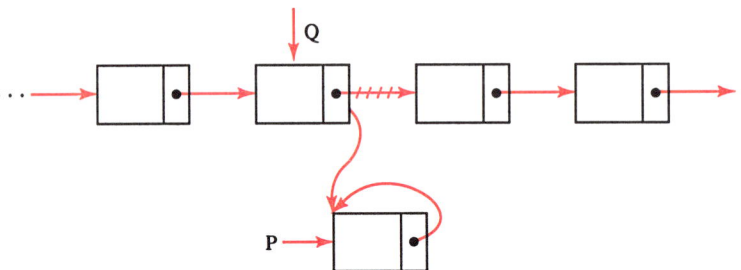

19.2 The linked list makes better use of memory, using only what it needs. The linked list can grow, at run time, to any size that will fit in computer memory, while the array is of a fixed size declared at compile time. Insertions and deletions are easy in the linked list, but are not easy in an ordered array. On the other hand, the array is a random-access data structure and the linked list is a sequential data structure. Also, linked lists contain a certain amount of overhead for storage of the pointers. (In Turbo Pascal, a pointer is implemented as a 2-byte address. Thus, a linked list of integers will be twice as big as an array of integers of equal size.) With large records, however, this extra overhead is negligible. Finally, because they are built in, arrays are perceived as easier to use than linked lists. However, as this chapter has shown, linked lists are really a very simple idea and their implementation is also quite elementary.

19.3 a) Invalid. Type mismatch.
   b) Invalid. Type mismatch.
   c) Valid. The value 17 is placed in the cell that P points to.
   d) Invalid. The ^ is used on the left only in a pointer declaration.
   e) Invalid. The ^ is used on the left only in a pointer declaration.
   f) Valid. The value 5 is stored in N.
   g) Valid. Q points to the same cell that P points to.
   h) Invalid. Type mismatch.
   i) Invalid. Before Q^ is used, Q must point to a cell (via New(Q) or Q := P).
   j) Valid. The cell that P points to is set to 0.

20

SEPARATE COMPILATION

Separate compilation is a simple and powerful idea. Do not let its place at the end of this book fool you into thinking that it is esoteric or a difficult topic to master. Separate compilation is placed last only because it is not part of standard Pascal and is not yet generally included in a first programming course. We hope to argue that it is, however, an exceedingly important topic and one that the developing programmer should learn to use.

Separate compilation means that we have the capability to compile our program in parts and the necessity to recompile only the portions of a program that change. Separate compilation simplifies the task of writing and maintaining large programs. Consider a large payroll program. Such a program contains many constants, such as the amount to withhold for social security, for health insurance, for union dues, etc. Naturally, these constants change from time to time. It seems wasteful to recompile an entire program that may run to tens of thousands of lines just to change the social-security rate from 7.35 percent to 7.55 percent. Many of the routines that are recompiled have nothing to do with the constant that has changed. With separate compilation, we subdivide the program into logical units and compile them separately. For example, one of these units might define all the constants needed by the payroll program. Others contain the many procedures and functions needed to obtain, update, and process the data, as well as procedures to print the checks. The point is that if the social-security withholding rate changes, then only the unit that defined this rate would need to be recompiled. The other units are independent of this change and do not need to be recompiled.

Another, and more important, consequence of separate compilation is that the programmer can begin to build up his or her own library of types, procedures, and functions. That is, the objects that you create for one situation can be used, if appropriate, without change, or even recompilation, in another situation. For example, routines that sort arrays of names can be written and compiled once and then used in subsequent programs almost as built-ins. The details of how this is accomplished are amazingly simple, and we urge the reader to learn to use the technique of separate compilation.

THE SYNTAX OF SEPARATE COMPILATION

Turbo Pascal calls a separately compilable portion of a program a **unit**. A unit has the following structure:

```
Unit NameOfUnit;

Interface
  A list of the variables, types, and headings for the procedures
  and functions that will be defined in this unit.

Implementation
  The actual bodies of the procedures and functions listed in the
  Interface section.
```

That is, a `Unit` contains three new keywords. The first of these is `Unit` itself, which is used in much the same way as the keyword `Program`. Each `Unit` consists of two portions. The `Interface` part of a unit is the public part of the unit. This small section lists the objects that are defined by the unit. For example, only the headings of procedures and functions are given in this portion. We call the `Interface` section the public section, because the user needs to be able to read this portion of the unit to find the name of the objects and, for procedures and functions, how many parameters they have, in what order they must be written, and what kind of results, if any, they return. Any variables or types declared in the `Interface` section are also available for any program that uses the unit. Thus, the `Interface` section should be clearly commented so that the user can understand the objects that it provides. The `Implementation` section, on the other hand, is where all the details are actually provided. The casual user of the `Unit` has no need to pry into these details. They need to be investigated only if the `Unit` is not working as promised, or if a new, improved implementation for one of the procedures or functions is planned.

AN EXAMPLE OF A UNIT

Let us make all this concrete with an example. Because we want to illustrate the idea of separate compilation, we pick a small, simple example. Suppose we often have need for a `DaysType` that contains the days of the week. Many times, we have mentioned that you can't read or write user-defined types. Therefore, we will write a unit to create such a type, along with procedures and functions to manipulate it. Finally, we will illustrate how easy it is to use these objects in *any* subsequent program.

First, we must decide what will be in our unit. Obviously, our unit will define the new type `DaysType`. We also promised the procedures `WriteDay` and `ReadDay`. To illustrate a function, we include Tomorrow, whose purpose is obvious. At this point, we can write the interface portion of the unit. This is shown in Listing 20.1.

```
Unit DayStuff; {$R+} {Notice the word Unit instead of Program.}

Interface {Note new word Interface. This marks the public part}
          {of the unit, where we list the types, procedures,}
              {and functions that are defined in this unit.}

Type DaysType = (Mon, Tues, Wed, Thurs, Fri, Sat, Sun);

Procedure WriteDay(Day : DaysType);

Procedure ReadDay(Var Day : DaysType); {This procedure doesn't}
                        {do any error checking, so type carefully!}

Function Tomorrow(Day : DaysType): DaysType;{Returns next Day.}

Implementation
   ...
```

Listing 20.1

The only thing that remains is the Implementation section of the unit. This is where the actual details of our procedures and functions are placed. Therefore, there is little new in this part of the unit, but for completeness, we give the details.

First, we consider how to implement WriteDay. A Case based upon the parameter Day seems like a good way to convert the user-defined DaysType into a string that can be written. Thus, the heart of WriteDay is

```
Case Day Of                        {Outline of body of WriteDay.}
   Mon : Write('Monday');
   Tues: Write('Tuesday');
      ...
End {Case}
```

Why can't ReadDay be written with a similar Case?

```
Case DayString Of          {Incorrect outline of body of ReadDay.}
   'Monday' : Day := Mon;
   'Tuesday': Day := Tues;
      ...
End {Case}
```

The reason the `ReadDay` outline does not work is that Strings are not allowed as case labels. Therefore, we must try something else. One idea is to put the strings `'Monday'`, `'Tuesday'`, etc., into an array indexed from 1 to 7. Then we read, as a String, the input from the user and search the array for the given String. For example, if the user types `'Friday'`, then we find it at the fifth spot in the array. Therefore, if we initialize `Day` to `Mon` and use `Succ` four times, `Day` receives the correct final value. In pseudo-code, here is the body of `ReadDay`:

Declare an array DayNames of seven strings
Initialize DayNames to the values 'Monday' through 'Sunday'
Read a DayString from the user
Set Day to Mon
Set Index to 1
While DayNames[Index] ≠ DayString
   Increment Day and Index

Note that we are expecting the user to type one of the seven strings stored in the array `DayNames`. Since human input is involved, this is a likely source of errors. However, to keep the example simple, we will not worry about this problem. Also, `ReadDay` initializes the array of `DayNames` each time it is called. It would be more efficient to have an `InitDays` procedure that we could call once, before any calls to `ReadDay`. We leave this and other improvements of the unit to the reader.

Finally, we have the function `Tomorrow` to implement. This function is trivial and is given by

```
If Day = Sun Then
   Tomorrow := Mon
Else
   Tomorrow := Succ(Day)
```

There are several reasons, however, that we might include such a function in our unit. One is that `Tomorrow`'s mnemonic value is much better than `Succ`'s. That is, it is hard to forget what `Tomorrow` does. Also, a beginner, who has not heard of `Succ`, can use `Tomorrow` with confidence. With `Tomorrow`, you do not even have to remember where the special case occurs. Is it the `Succ` of `Sat` or the `Succ` of `Sun` that gives trouble? It depends upon how the type was defined. With `Tomorrow`, there are no such worries, because it has the special case built into its definition. We can use `Tomorrow` in a natural manner on any value of `DaysType`.

The complete details of the unit `DayStuff` are given in Listing 20.2. Study the listing carefully, considering the placement of the various parts. There should be three small surprises in the `Implementation` section of the listing. First, notice the short form of the headings of the procedures and functions. Observe that in the `Implementation` section, no parameters or types need be given. These short forms are permitted because the full forms have already been given in the `Interface` section. It is clear that, since several bodies are included, some minimal sort of heading is required so that the system can match bodies with headings. Although the headings in the `Implementation` section are truncated, the parameters as listed in the `Interface` section are used in the actual implementations. To illustrate the possibilities, we have shown the shortened headings in the Implementation section. However, we think that the abbreviated headings make the implementations mysterious, and we strongly suggest that the user supply the full procedure and function headings in the Implementation section of the unit.

```
Unit DayStuff; {$R+} {Notice the word Unit instead of Program.}

Interface {Note new word Interface. This marks the public part}
         {of the unit where we list the types, procedures,}
            {and functions that are defined in this unit.}

Type DaysType = (Mon, Tues, Wed, Thurs, Fri, Sat, Sun);

Procedure WriteDay(Day : DaysType);

Procedure ReadDay(Var Day : DaysType); {This procedure doesn't}
                    {do any error checking, so type carefully!}

Function Tomorrow(Day : DaysType): DaysType;{Returns next Day.}

Implementation                  {Note the new word Implementation.}
             {This marks the private section where the actual}
{implementations of the things defined in the interface are given.}

Procedure WriteDay;      {Note that it is not necessary to list}
                         {the parameters again--but it may well}
                            {be a good idea to list them, anyway.}
  Begin
    Case Day Of
      Mon   : Write('Monday');
      Tues  : Write('Tuesday');
      Wed   : Write('Wednesday');
      Thurs : Write('Thursday');
      Fri   : Write('Friday');
      Sat   : Write('Saturday');
      Sun   : Write('Sunday')
    End {Case}
  End;                        {Definition of Procedure WriteDay.}

Procedure ReadDay;
  Var DayString  : String[9];     {These are private to this}
      DayNames   : Array[1..7] of String[9];  {procedure and}
      Index      : Integer;       {cannot be exported with the}
      Count      : Integer;          {unit to other programs.}
```

Listing 20.2

```
Begin
  DayNames[1] := 'Monday';
  DayNames[2] := 'Tuesday';
  DayNames[3] := 'Wednesday';
  DayNames[4] := 'Thursday';
  DayNames[5] := 'Friday';
  DayNames[6] := 'Saturday';
  DayNames[7] := 'Sunday';
  Readln(DayString);                 {Get string value from user.}
  Index := 1;                        {Search array for DayString.}
  Day := Mon;
  While DayNames[Index] <> DayString Do     {User input error}
    Begin                            {will cause range-check error.}
      Index := Index + 1;               {Increment Day and Index.}
      Day := Succ(Day)
    End {While}
End;                                 {Definition of Procedure ReadDay.}
Function Tomorrow;
  Begin
    If Day = Sun Then
      Tomorrow := Mon
    Else
      Tomorrow := Succ(Day)
  End;                               {This semicolon is required!}
End.                                 {End of Unit, just like Program.}
```

Listing 20.2 (continued)

The other two surprises come at the end of the unit's listing. Notice that the last line is End. just like in a program. The really odd part is that there is no Begin to match this End. Actually, a unit can have a body of its own, and an example of this is given later in the chapter. When a unit has no body, it must still have the End. The last surprise is that the compiler insists upon a semicolon on the next-to-last line in Listing 20.2. Normally, no semicolon is required between Ends. However, in this case, it seems that Turbo Pascal is supplying an implicit Begin for the (empty) body of the unit and, therefore, wants, as usual, a semicolon before this Begin. That is, this is just like in a Program, where a semicolon is required after the last procedure or function definition and before the Begin of the body of the Program.

THE COMPILATION OF A UNIT

A unit is not a program and, therefore, a unit cannot be run by itself. A unit must be compiled before it can be used by a main program. In addition, the compilation must be saved to disk, so that it is available when the main program is loaded into memory and run. We compile a unit to disk as follows:

Press ALT-C to bring down the compile menu. Press D to change the Destination to Disk. Press ESC to remove the compiler window. Finally, press ALT-F9 to compile your unit. If you have any errors, you will have to debug your unit.

We recommend that you try the above sequence of steps on the unit DayStuff. For your convenience, DayStuff is available on the disk that accompanies this book. Our next step is to illustrate how easy it is to use the objects defined in our unit.

A MAIN PROGRAM THAT USES OUR UNIT

Listing 20.3 illustrates a short program that shows off our unit. Notice that the program contains the line

```
Uses DayStuff, CRT;
```

This is all that is necessary to import the types, procedures, and functions defined in DayStuff and CRT into our program. CRT is, of course, a library of routines, including ClrScr, supplied by Turbo Pascal. DayStuff, on the other hand, is our own unit. The point is that DayStuff, once compiled, is used exactly as is the supplied library CRT. Any program, in the future, that needs the user-defined DaysType or the procedures and functions WriteDay, ReadDay, or Tomorrow can use them as easily as this short program does.

```
Program TryDays; {$R+}
{This program trys out the DayStuff unit.}

Uses DayStuff, CRT;

Var  Day : DaysType;

Begin
  ClrScr;
  Repeat
    Write('Enter a day of the week (Friday to Quit): ');
    ReadDay(Day);
    Day := Tomorrow(Day);
    Write('The day after that is ');
    WriteDay(Day);
    Writeln
  Until Day = Sat        {Because Friday has been "tomorrowed."}
End.
```

Listing 20.3

SCOPE WITHIN UNITS

A unit can declare variables in several ways. Those that are declared within the bodies of procedures and functions are, of course, local to those procedures and functions. Variables that are declared in the Implementation section, but not within any procedure or function, are called **static** variables and are discussed in the next section. Here, we mention that variables declared in the Interface section are available as global variables to any program that uses the unit. For example, suppose a unit declares an X and a Y in the Interface section. Further, suppose that a program using that unit declares its own X but no Y. Then, as you would expect, that program has access to its own X, which masks the X of the unit. Since there is no local Y, the program has access to the Y of the unit. That is, any identifier, whether it be a variable, a type name, or a procedure or function name, is always the local instance (when it is defined locally). When no local instance is given, the system searches the units listed in the Uses clause in *reverse* order for the object. That is, if there is no local Y, then the last unit is searched and, if no Y is found there, the previous units are searched until Y is found. Of course, if Y is never found, then it is an undeclared-identifier error. This subject, the scoping of names within units, is considered further in the exercises.

STATIC VARIABLES

Variables in standard Pascal are either global or local. Units in Turbo Pascal provide a third kind of variable, a **static** variable. A static variable, like a local variable, cannot be seen or modified outside the unit in which it is defined. A static variable, like a global variable, does not lose its value between calls to the unit. Thus, a static variable provides a way for a unit to squirrel away information between calls to that unit. To be static, a variable must be declared in the Implementation section, but not within any procedure or function.

Since presidents of the United States follow the advice of astrologers, let us illustrate static variables by writing an Advice unit, whose only export is a procedure Astrologer, which gives different advice each of the first five times it is called (and from then on says "don't bother me anymore"). Obviously, Astrologer needs the services of a counter. But where should this counter be stored? If it is local to the procedure Astrologer, it will not be able to preserve its values between calls to Astrologer. Clearly, the main program can use a (global) variable for the counter. But then the user might inadvertently (or advertently) forget to increment the counter or might reset the counter to zero. Clearly, users cannot be trusted, and the counter should be kept somewhere else. A static variable provides the convenient solution.

Study Listing 20.4, which illustrates a static variable Count. Note that Count is declared in the Implementation portion of the unit, but not within the body of any procedure or function. This is what makes Count static. If Count were declared in the Interface section, then it would be available for inspection and change in the main program. If Count were declared in the body of Astrologer, then it would be local to that procedure.

```
Unit Advice; {$R+}
{This unit illustrates the use of a static variable, Count, that
keeps track of the total number of calls to this unit.          }

Interface

Procedure Astrologer;
{This procedure uses the value of the static variable Count to give
the user different advice on each of the first five calls.      }

Implementation

Var  Count : Integer;                   {Count is a static variable,}
                                            {private to the unit.}


Procedure Astrologer;
  Begin
    Count := Count + 1       {Count the call to this procedure.}
    Writeln;
    If Count > 5 Then
      Writeln('You are too dependent. Make your own decisions!')
    Else
      Case Count Of
        1: Writeln('1. Today you will meet an alien.');
        2: Writeln('2. Today is a good day for new projects.');
        3: Writeln('3. Danger!! Avoid lunch today.');
        4: Writeln('4. Today is a bad day for old projects.');
        5: Writeln('5. Watch out for falling bricks.')
      End; {Case and If}
    Writeln
  End;{Definition of procedure Astrologer. Note needed semicolon.}

Begin                                        {Body of unit Advice.}
  Count := 0;{This initialization occurs before the program runs.}
End.
```

Listing 20.4

Another difference, seen in Listing 20.4, between this example and the previous one is that the unit has a body, albeit trivial, at the bottom of the listing. This body is executed once, before the main program begins execution. Its purpose, of course, is to initialize the static variable Count to zero. If several units are loaded into your program, then their bodies, if any, are executed before the main program and in the order in which they are listed in the Uses statement. Thus, the sole purpose of unit bodies is to initialize conditions for later calls to the unit.

Listing 20.5 shows a program that imports the Astrologer procedure from the Advice unit. The program repeatedly calls Astrologer until the user tires of its

```
Program Advisor; {$R+}

{This program illustrates static variables in the unit Advice.}

Uses CRT, Advice;

Var Response : Char;

Begin
  ClrScr;
  Repeat
    Writeln('Press RETURN to get my personalized advice:');
    Readln;
    Astrologer;
    Write('Do you want more advice? (Y/N) ');
    Readln(Response);
    Response := UpCase(Response)
  Until Response = 'N'
End.
```

Listing 20.5

advice. We strongly recommend that you trace the program Advisor and then run it to check that it does maintain a Count of how many times it has been called and does offer the expected advice on each call.

Finally, we suggest that you try to increment Count from within the program. Your inability to do so shows that Count is private to its unit.

In an advanced course on data structures, static variables are very important, as they provide a means for units to implement data hiding. This means that details that the user does not need to know can be kept from the user. Thus, the user cannot modify one of the key components of the unit, even accidentally.

SUMMARY

We hope you see the utility in Turbo Pascal of separate compilation through units. We have given two very simple examples, but the potential in complex situations should be clear. Sorts, character-manipulation routines, user-defined types, and linked lists all provide a vast collection of useful units. Once we have solved these problems and put them into a unit, we have a library that we can use at will in future programs.

KEYWORDS

Separate compilation   Unit
Interface   Implementation
Static variable

SELF-TEST QUESTIONS

20.1 Give two advantages of separate compilation.

20.2 What goes into the `Interface` portion of a unit?

20.3 What goes into the `Implementation` portion of a unit?

EXERCISES

20.4 Modify procedure `ReadDay` in unit `DayStuff` so that it allows the user to type either the short or long form for the day of the week (`Mon` or `Monday`) and traps errors so that input such as `Donnerstag` does not cause a range error.

20.5 Consider the unit `OddStuff` and the program `Ex20_5` shown below. Two lines in the program cause compile-time errors. Which lines are they and what is the nature of the errors? What is the output from the program if the two lines are removed? Explain the output.

```
Unit OddStuff; {$R+}

Interface

Var   A : Integer;
      B : Integer;

Procedure Show;

Implementation

Var   C : Integer;

Procedure Show;
  Begin
    Writeln('In the unit A = ', A, ' B = ', B, ' C = ', C)
  End;

Begin
  A := 10;
  B := 20;
  C := 30
End.                          {Compile this unit by itself.}


Program Ex20_5; {Exercise 20.5} {$R+}
Uses CRT, OddStuff;

Var   A : Integer;
```

```
Begin
  A := 100;
  B := 200;
  C := 300;
  Writeln('A = ', A);
  Writeln('B = ', B);
  Writeln('C = ', C);
  Show
End.
```

20.6 Trace the output of the program `ShowTell`, which uses the units `One` and `Two`. Run the program and check your work. Explain where each output comes from and why this `X` or that `Show` is used instead of one of the others.

```
Unit One; {$R+}
Interface
Var X, Y : Integer;
Procedure Show;

Implementation
Var Z : Integer;
Procedure Show;
  Begin
    Writeln('Show from Unit One: ', X:5, Y:5, Z:5)
  End;
Procedure Tell;
  Begin
    Writeln('Tell from Unit One: ', X:5, Y:5, Z:5)
  End;
Begin
  X := 10;
  Y := 20;
  Z := 30
End.                                      {Compile this unit by itself.}

Unit Two; {$R+}
Interface
Var X, Z : Integer;
Procedure Show;
Procedure Tell;

Implementation
Var Y : Integer;
Procedure Show;
  Begin
    Writeln('Show from Unit Two: ', X:5, Y:5, Z:5)
  End;
```

```
Procedure Tell;
  Begin
    Writeln('Tell from Unit Two: ', X:5, Y:5, Z:5)
  End;
Begin
  X := 100;
  Y := 200;
  Z := 300
End.                              {Compile this unit by itself.}

Program ShowTell; {$R+}
Uses Two, One, CRT;
Var Y : Integer;

Begin
  ClrScr;
  X := 1;
  Y := 2;
  Z := 3;
  Writeln('Main program:  ', X:5, Y:5, Z:5);
  Show;
  Tell
End.
```

20.7 Pick your favorite sorting routine and write a unit that exports a sort on arrays of 100 strings. Suppose each string consists of up to 30 characters each. In your unit, make the 100 and 30 constants so that they can easily be changed.

ANSWERS TO SELF-TEST QUESTIONS

20.1 Separate compilation allows programs to be compiled in pieces. Only the pieces that change need to be recompiled. Separate compilation allows us to create our own libraries of types, procedures, and functions that we use all the time.

20.2 The Interface portion of the unit is the public portion of the unit. Here the objects that are available for export from this unit are listed and described with many comments.

20.3 The Implementation portion of the unit is the private portion of the unit where the details of the actual implementations are given.

FORMATTING AND
BACKING UP DISKS

THE NEED FOR BACKING UP AND FORMATTING

Before a disk can be used to store programs, it must be formatted, which can be thought of as the process of "combing" the magnetic particles on the disk so that information can later be placed on the tracks of the disk. Backup copies of disks are made so that if one disk should ever fail, you still have a working copy of that disk. You should make backup copies of all of your Turbo disks and then put the originals away in a safe place. The program Diskcopy, described below, formats a new disk and then copies information from an old disk to the new one. As such, Diskcopy is ideal for making backup copies of disks. The program Format, also described below, formats a new disk. Blank, formatted disks are handy for storing your own programs.

DISKCOPY — MAKING BACKUPS

To back up your Turbo Pascal diskettes you will need blank diskettes and your DOS disk (DOS is the Disk Operating System) that came with your computer. Since there are several versions of DOS, the messages that you receive from your PC may differ slightly from those given here, but the meanings should clearly be equivalent. For the moment, to keep things simple, we shall assume that you have two floppy drives. If you have only one floppy drive, see the remarks at the end of this section.

1. Turn on the computer with the DOS disk in drive A. (Drive A is the disk whose light comes on when you turn on the computer.) You will probably need to enter the date (in the form 5-31-91) and the time (11:30), but you will eventually receive the system prompt:

A>

2. With the DOS disk still in drive A, type

```
Diskcopy A: B:
```

and then press RETURN. Note carefully the spaces before the A: and the B: and note the two colons.

3. You will receive a message similar to the following:

```
Place the source disk in A and the destination disk in B.
Press RETURN when ready.
```

  Before you proceed, pause to understand that the source is the disk that you want to copy and that "destination" refers to one of the new, blank disks. Therefore, place the disk to be copied in drive A and one of the blank disks in drive B. Press RETURN as instructed.

4. The process of backing up your disk will take a couple of minutes. Your new disk will first be formatted, and then the information from the source disk will be copied to the destination disk.

5. When the process is complete, immediately place a label on the new disk so that you will be able to identify the disk when it is needed.

  If you want to copy other disks and, if you are at the A> prompt, repeat the process beginning at step 2. Some versions of DOS will ask you if you want to copy another disk. If so, type Y and repeat the process beginning at step 3.

Single Floppy Drive Users

If you have only one disk drive, then almost nothing changes! You can type exactly the commands shown above as your computer is smart enough to use your one drive as both the A and the B drive. You will, however, need to swap disks as instructed by the computer. Be careful to keep source and destination straight in your mind.

FORMATTING SYSTEM AND DATA DISKS

Before we show you how to format disks, some brief introductory remarks about the various kinds of disks will be helpful. A **data disk** is just a formatted disk on which programs (data) can be stored. However, a data disk can not be used to start up the computer. A **system disk** is a formatted disk with enough of the DOS system to enable the computer to start up (boot up). Data can be saved on a system disk, but because the system takes up space on the disk, it is best to use data disks instead of system disks whenever possible.

Floppy Drive Users

Users with no hard drives will need to format two, and preferably three, disks, one system disk and two data disks. The System Disk will become, in Appendix B, your Turbo Pascal system disk. This disk is used to start up your computer and can also be used to store the programs that you write. One of the data disks will become (See Appendix B) the Turbo Pascal Work Disk. This disk will have the Turbo Pascal compiler and editor on it. The other data disk (optional) will be used to back up the programs that you write. Because disks do occasionally go bad, it is wise always to back up your programs. This simply means saving your programs in two locations, so that if one disk is lost or becomes damaged, your work is not lost. Many students have learned the importance of backing up their work the hard way!

Hard Drive Users

Hard drive users will need to format only one or two data disks on which to store their programs, because their hard drive, usually `C:`, acts as their system disk. Hard drive users should read the above remarks about the importance of backing-up programs. Never store your programs only on the hard drive. Always back them up to at least one floppy.

Formatting Disks

In summary, floppy drive users will need to format one system disk and one or two data disks. Hard drive users will only need to format one or two data disks. First, here are instructions for formatting a data disk:

1. Turn on the computer with your DOS disk in drive A. Answer date and time questions until you get the system prompt:

```
A>
```

If you already have this prompt, then you do not need to turn the computer off and on again.

2. With the DOS disk still in drive A type

```
Format B:
```

(note the space before the `B:` and note the colon) and then press RETURN.

3. You will receive instructions such as

```
Insert new disk in drive B
and press RETURN when ready.
```

Do as instructed.

4. After a minute or so your disk will be formatted and you will be asked to enter a desired volume label of up to 11 characters. Type `TurboPascal` or `Lowellsdisk` or some such name and press RETURN.

5. You will then be asked if you want to format another disk. Answering `Y` will start the process over, answering `N` will return you to the system prompt.

6. Place a paper label on the disk and write the volume name that you entered at step 4. Floppy-drive users should label one of the data disks "Turbo Pascal Work Disk." In Appendix B we will learn how to install the Turbo Pascal software on this disk.

   If you have only one drive, follow the above process exactly. Your system will use its one drive as both the `A` and `B` drives.

   As discussed above, if you have only floppy drives, you will also need to format a system disk. To do so, follow the above instructions, except that in step 2 type

`Format B:/S`

Note the space before the B and then type the 4 characters B:/S with no spaces at all. Floppy drive users should label this disk "Turbo Pascal System Disk." After the Work Disk is installed in Appendix B, the Turbo Pascal System and Work Disk will be ready for use as described in Chapter 2.

B

INSTALLING TURBO PASCAL

INSTALLATION ON FLOPPY DRIVE SYSTEMS

To install Turbo Pascal, you will need a formatted data disk and a formatted system disk. See Appendix A for instructions on making such disks. You should also be using copies, not the originals, of your Turbo Pascal disks.

Installing Turbo Pascal means placing the software that you will need onto your disk. Programs are copied from one disk to another by using the DOS Copy program. For simplicity, we assume that you have two floppy drives. If you only have one drive, see the remarks at the end of this section. If you have a hard drive, then see the final section of this appendix.

The installation procedure is similar, ending up with the same four files on your data disk, but slightly different procedures are needed depending on the version of Turbo Pascal that you have. We, therefore, describe the process for each version. If you are not sure which version of Turbo Pascal you have, find the description that matches your disk names. Also, note that some of the programs are copied to a data disk and some of the programs are copied to a system disk. Please read the instructions carefully!

Turbo Pascal 4.0 Users

1. We assume that your system is at the system prompt:

```
A>
```

Place your newly formatted, blank *data* disk in drive B.

2. Place the Turbo Pascal Compiler disk in drive A and type

```
Copy A:Turbo.* B:
```

Be careful to include only two spaces in this line (before the A and the B). Don't forget the one period (not at the end) and the two colons. The * is a wildcard that will match anything, and this command will copy three Turbo files to your new disk. These files are Turbo.Exe (the compiler), Turbo.Tpl (the Turbo Pascal Libary), and Turbo.Hlp (the help file).

3. Place the Turbo Pascal Utilities/Examples disk in drive A and your *system* disk (note change) in drive B and type

```
Copy A:Lister.Pas B:
```

(Note the two spaces, two colons, and one period.) This command will copy a utility program to your disk that will allow you to print listings of your programs (if you have a printer). Label your data disk as your Turbo Pascal Work Disk and label your system disk as your Turbo Pascal System Disk. These are the names used in Chapter 2 to refer to these disks.

  If you have only one drive, then follow the above instructions, and follow the prompts of your system, swapping disks in and out of your drive as requested by your system.

  The Graphics/MicroCalc disk contains sample programs and graphics utilities that are not needed by the beginner. If you wish to investigate these facilities of Turbo Pascal, check your Turbo Pascal manuals. Please note that there are many more programs on each of the Turbo Pascal disks. We have instructed you to load a minimal system that contains all you will need to write your own programs. When you know a little more Pascal we suggest you read your manuals and investigate the disks more completely.

Turbo Pascal 5.0 Users

Follow the process given above for 4.0 users, except execute step 2 twice, once with the Install/Compiler disk in drive A and once with the Help/Utilities disk in drive A. This will copy Turbo.Exe, Turbo.Tpl and Turbo.Hlp onto your disk in drive B. Also, in step 3, the Lister.Pas file will be found on the BGI/Demos/Doc/Turbo3 disk.

Turbo Pascal 5.5 Users

Follow the instructions in step 2 above with the Install/Compiler disk in drive A to copy Turbo.Exe and Turbo.Tpl to drive B. Unfortunately, Turbo.Hlp and Lister.Pas are in an archived (packed) form to save space and they must be unpacked. Also, Turbo.Hlp is so large that it will not fit on the same disk as Turbo.Exe and Turbo.Tpl. We therefore recommend that you place Turbo.Hlp on your system disk. To unpack these files and copy them to the correct disks, proceed as follows:

3. Place the Tour/Online Help disk in drive A and your *system* disk in drive B. Then type

A:Unpack Help B:

Please note that the above command contains exactly two blanks.

4. Next you must copy the unpack utility to the OOP/Demos/BGI/Doc disk. To do this, place the Tour/Online disk in drive A and the OOP/Demos/BGI/Doc disk in drive B and type

Copy A:Unpack.Com B:

Again, be sure this command contains only the two blanks shown.

5. Finally, we can unpack Lister.Pas as follows: Place the OOP/Demos/BGI/Doc disk in drive A and your *system* disk in drive B and type

A:Unpack Demos B: Lister.Pas

(This time make sure that your command contains the three blanks shown.)

Hard Disk Users

If you have a hard disk, then you will probably want to place Turbo Pascal on your hard disk. We suggest that you make a subdirectory, Turbo, where you keep all of your Turbo Pascal programs.

1. Begin from the system prompt

C>

2. To make a Turbo subdirectory, type

Md Turbo

and then press RETURN. The command Md stands for make directory.

3. To enter your new directory, type

Cd Turbo

and then press RETURN. The command Cd stands for change directory.

4. Now proceed as in steps 2 and 3 above for floppy disk users (and for your version of Turbo Pascal), except that you substitute C: for B: in all statements. Alternately, if you have lots of room on your hard drive, you can copy all of the Turbo Pascal files to your hard drive by placing each Turbo Pascal disk, in turn, in drive A and typing

Copy A:*.* C:

APPENDIX
C

TURBO PASCAL SYNTAX DIAGRAMS

For purposes of quick reference, an alphabetical listing of the syntax diagrams for Turbo Pascal is given here. These are as specified by Borland International Inc.

Absolute Clause

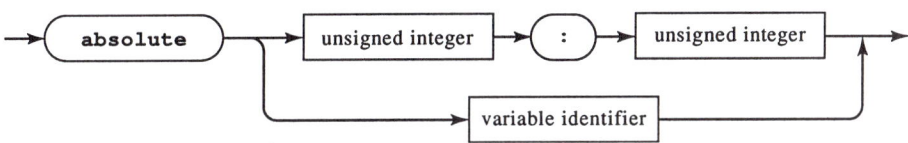

Actual Parameter

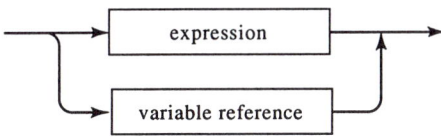

Actual Parameter List

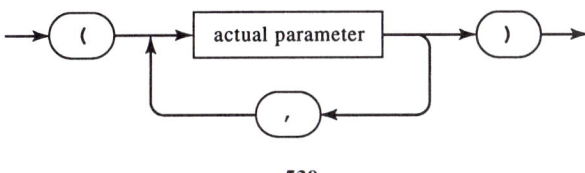

Array Constant

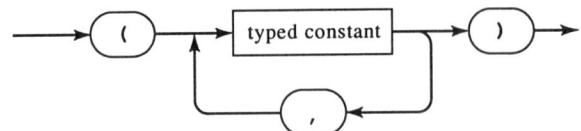

Array Type

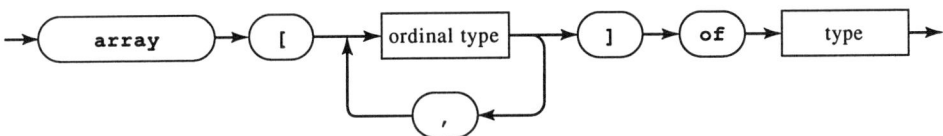

Assignment Statement

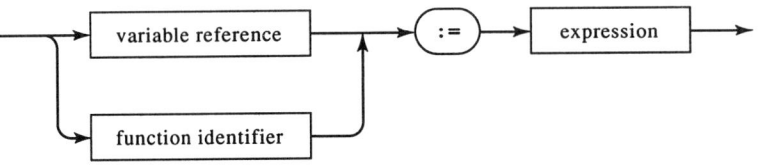

Block

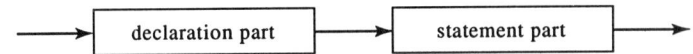

Case

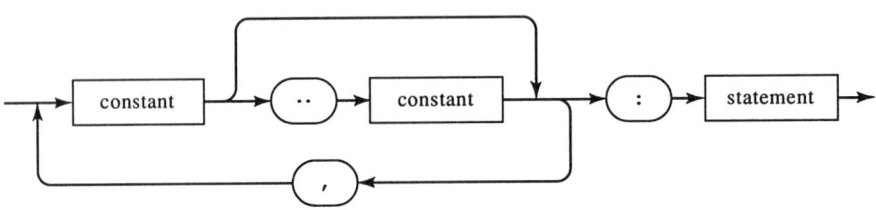

Case Statement

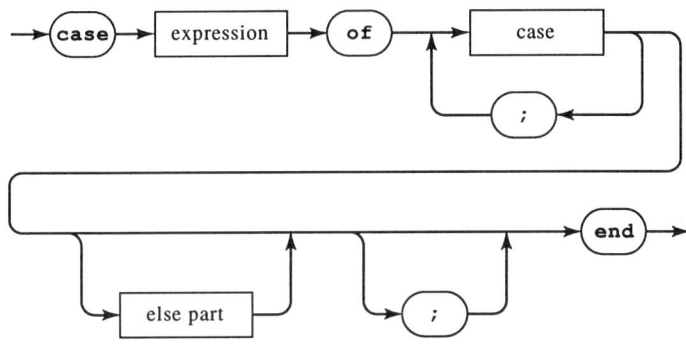

Character String

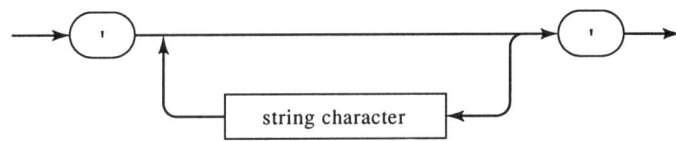

Compound Statement

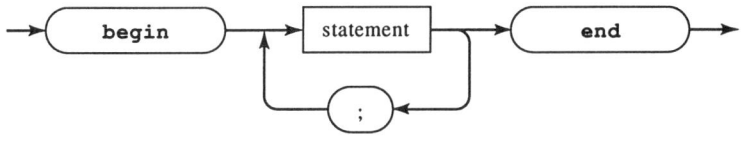

Conditional Statement

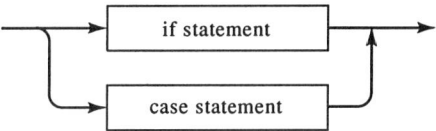

Constant

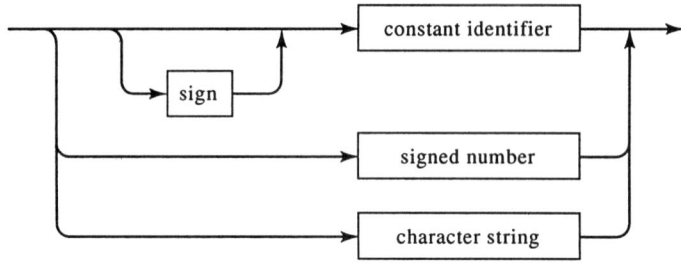

Constant Declaration

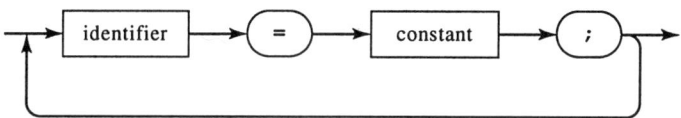

Constant Declaration Part

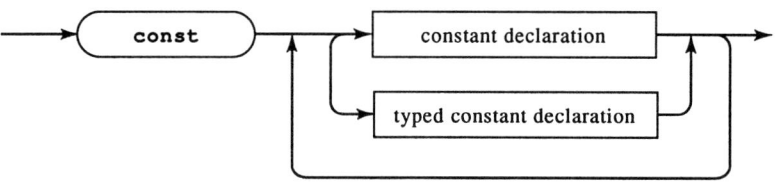

Declaration Part

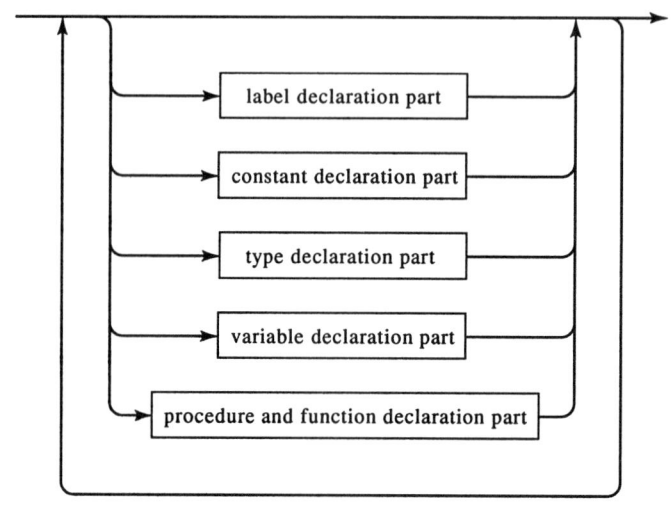

Digit

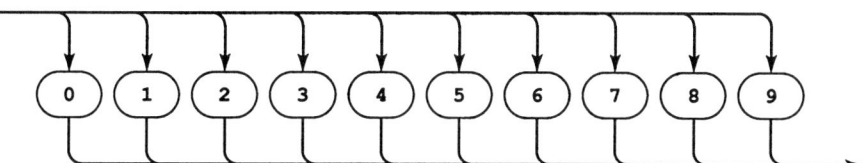

Digit Sequence

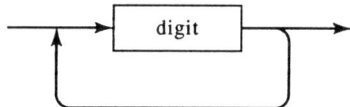

Else Part

Enumerated Type

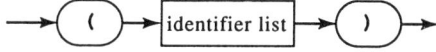

Expression

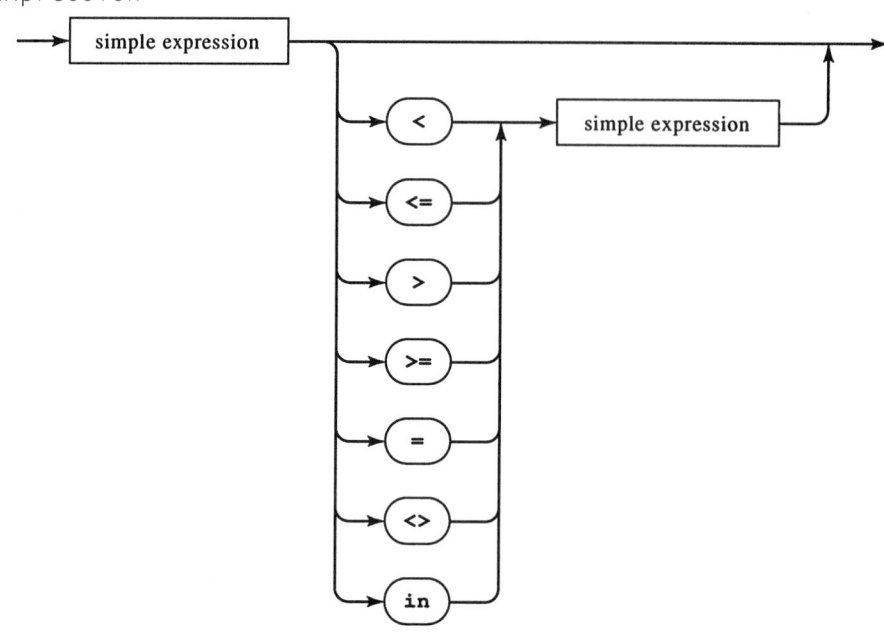

Factor

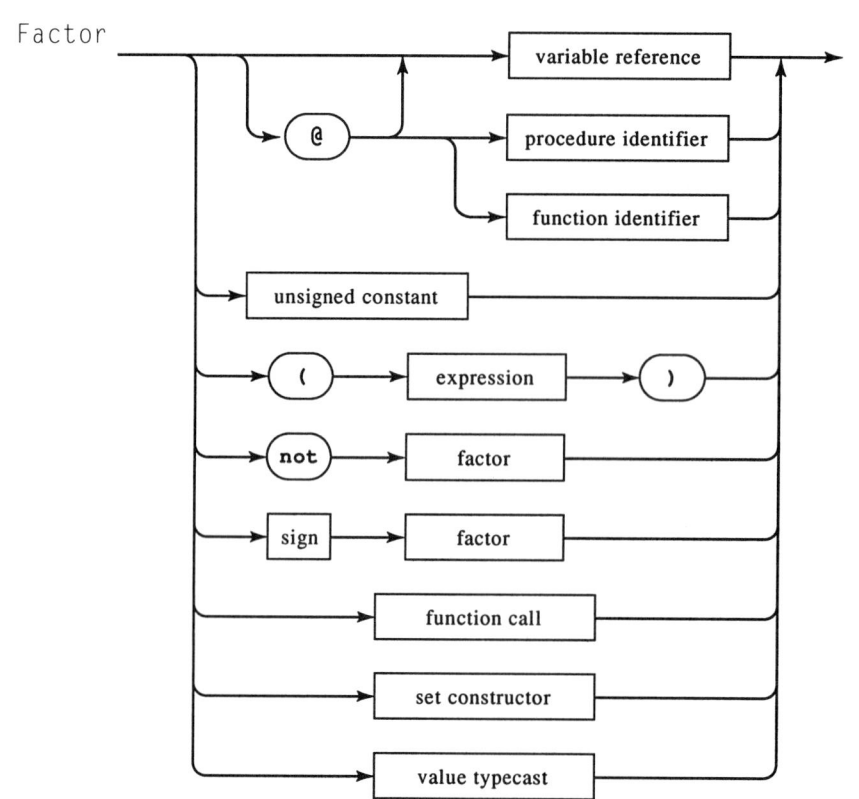

Field List

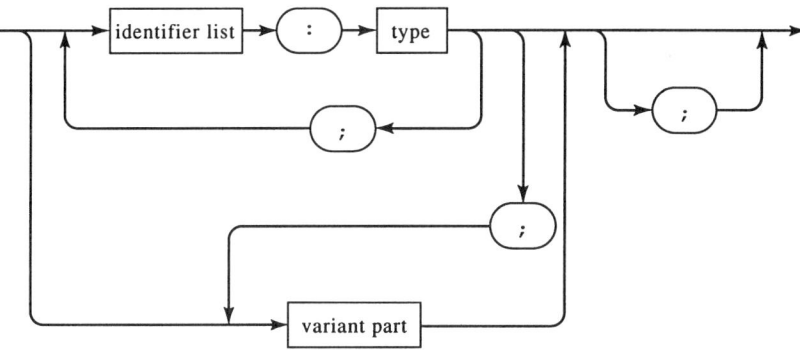

File Type

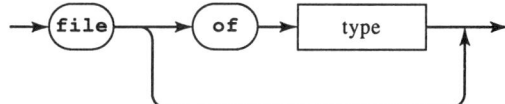

For Statement

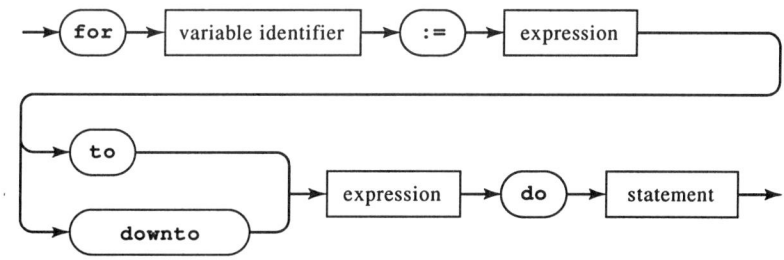

Formal Parameter List

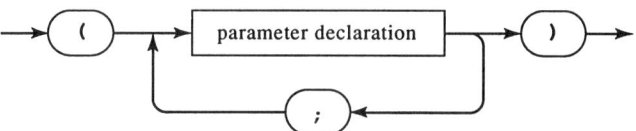

Function Body

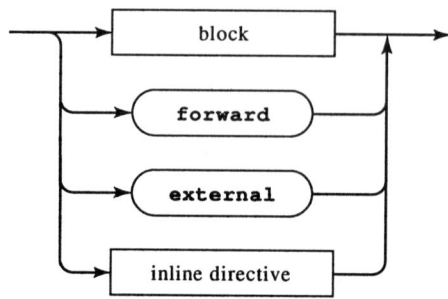

Function Call

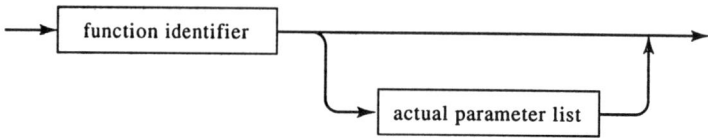

Function Declaration

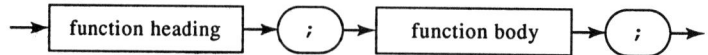

Function Heading

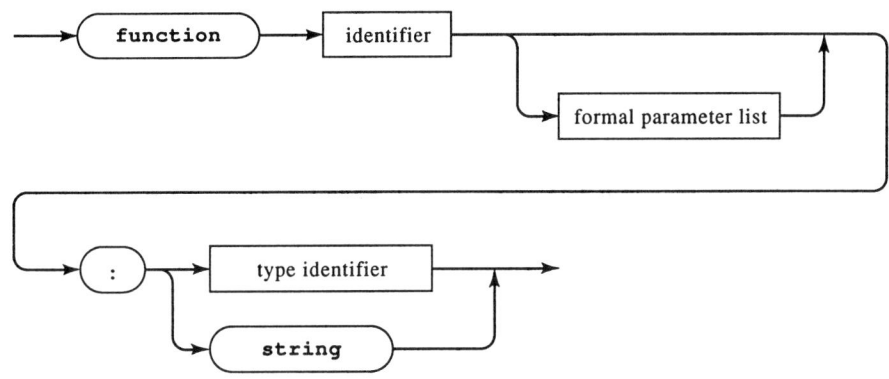

GoTo Statement

Hex Digit

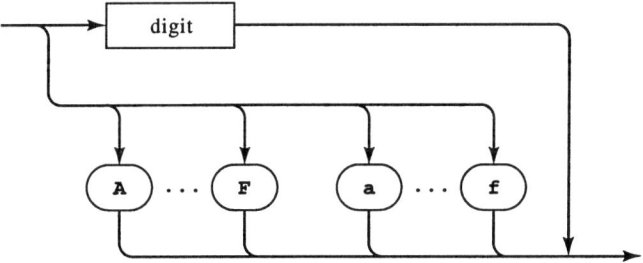

Hex Digit Sequence

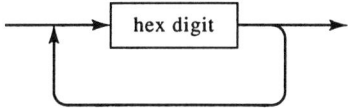

Identifier

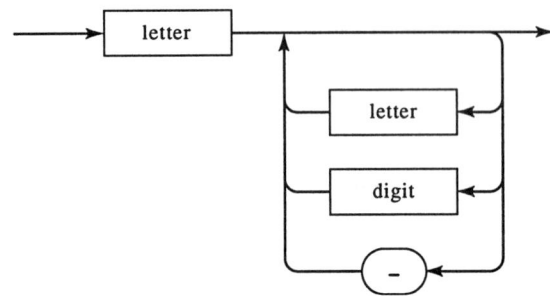

Identifier List

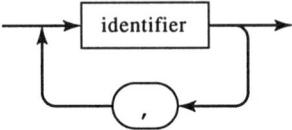

If Statement

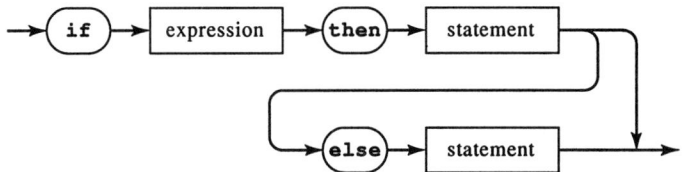

Implementation Part

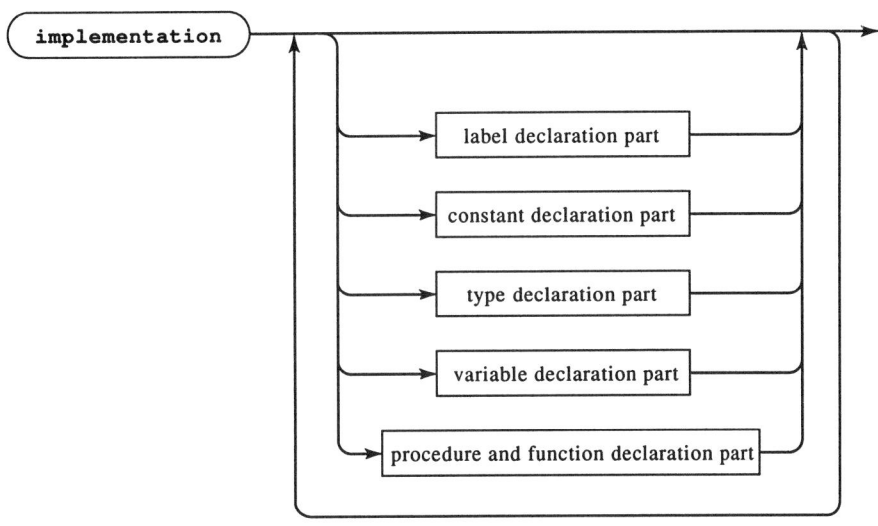

Initialization Part

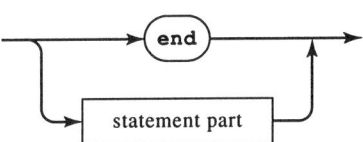

Interface Part

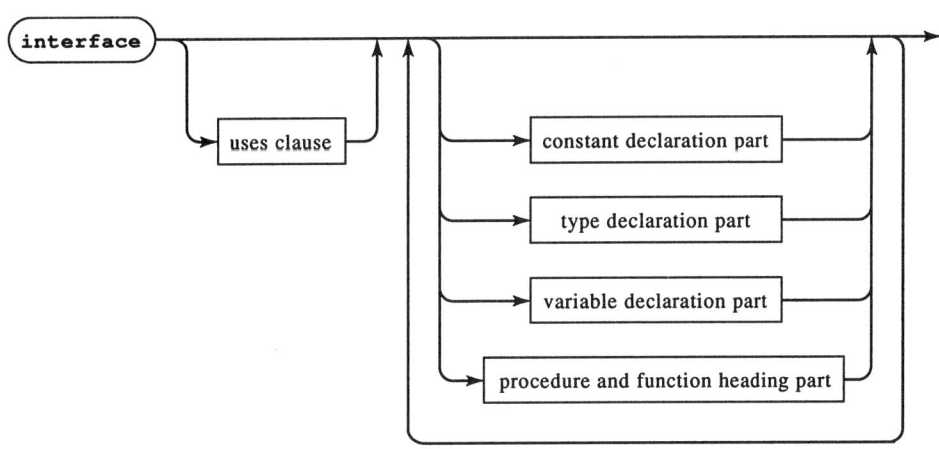

Label

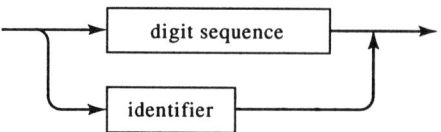

Label Declaration Part

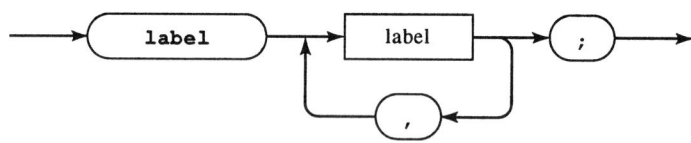

Letter

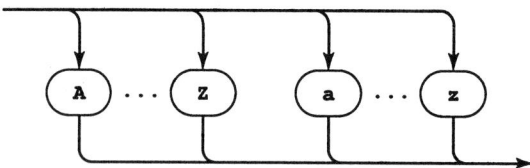

Ordinal Type

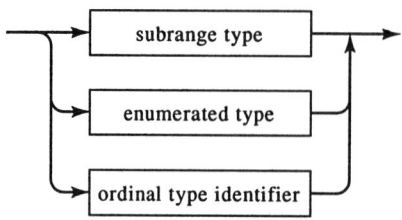

Ordinal Type Identifier

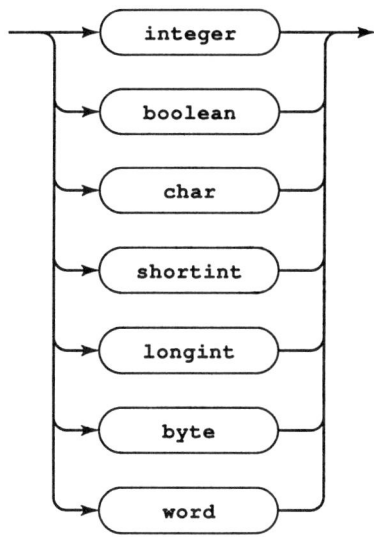

Parameter Declaration

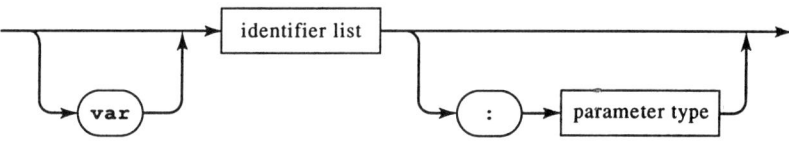

Parameter Type

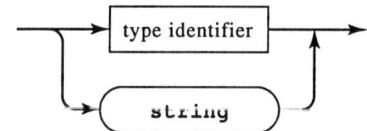

Pointer Type

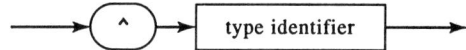

Procedure and Function Declaration Part

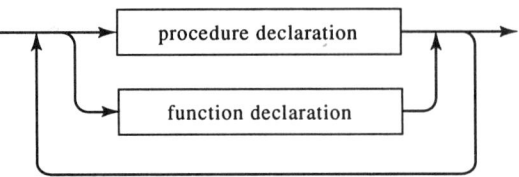

Procedure and Function Heading Part

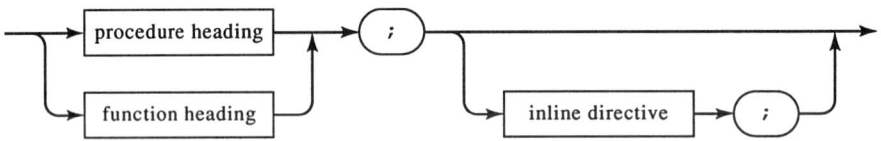

Procedure Body

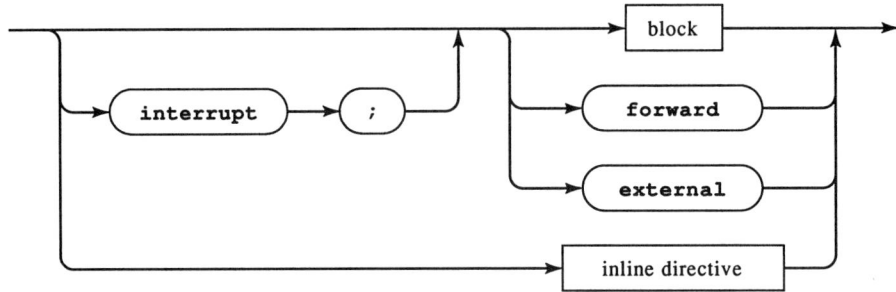

Procedure Declaration

Procedure Heading

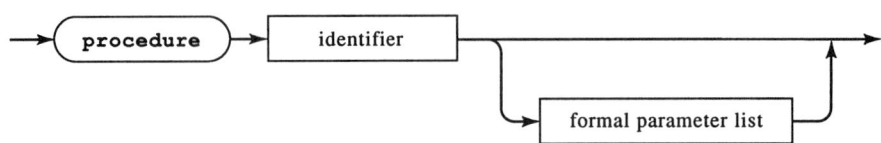

Procedure Statement

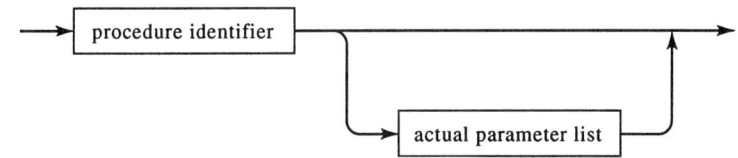

Program

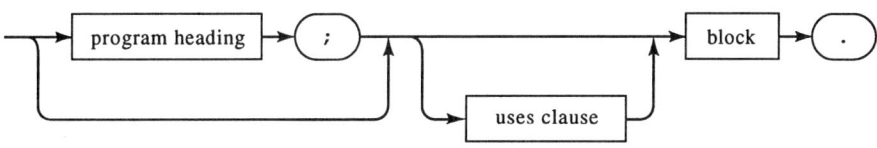

Program Heading

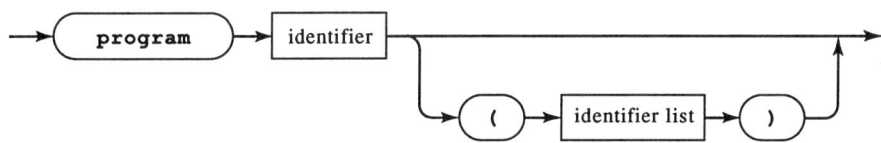

Real Type

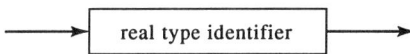

Real Type Identifier

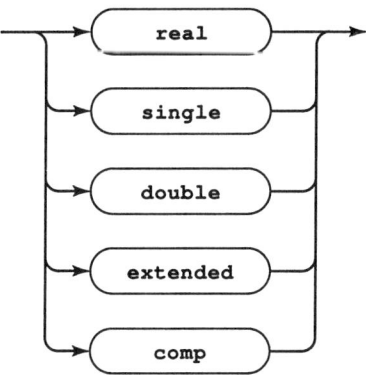

Record Constant

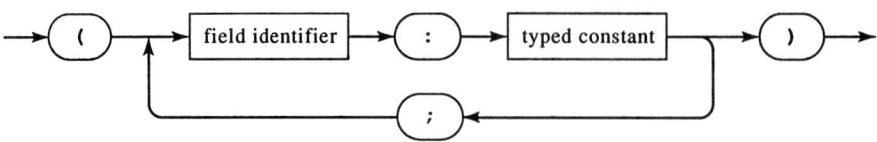

Record Type

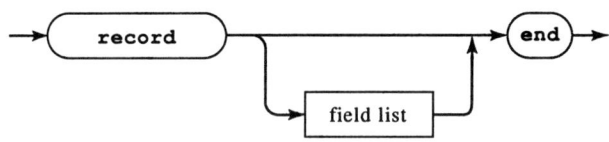

Repeat Statement

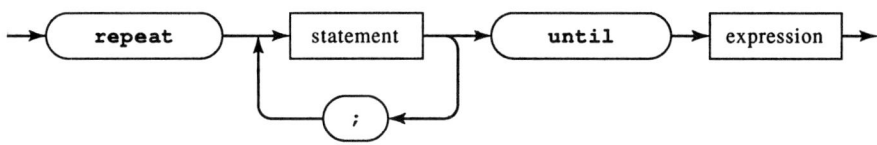

Repetitive Statement

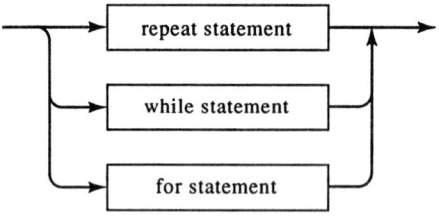

Scale Factor

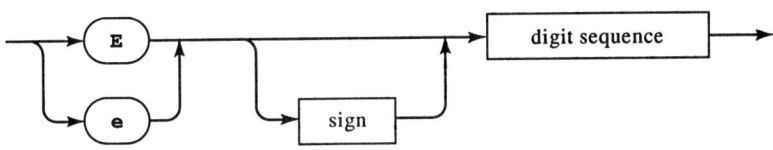

Set Constant

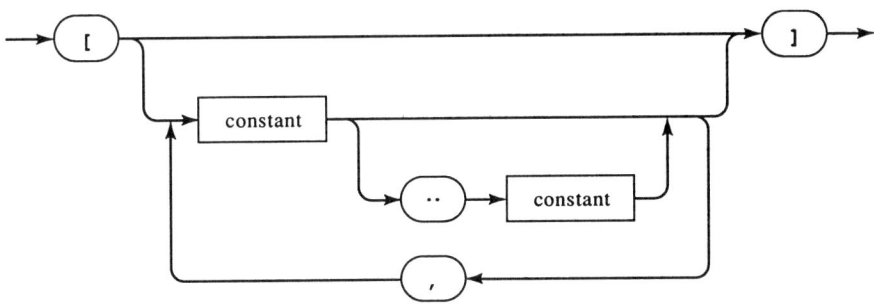

Set Constructor

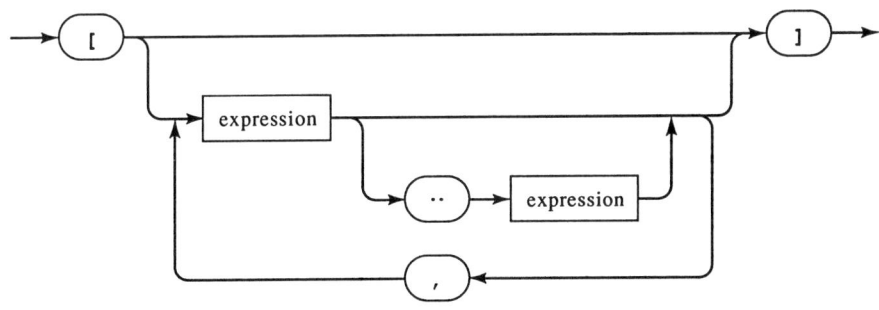

Set Type

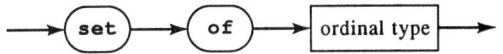

Sign

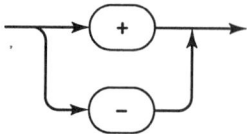

Signed Number

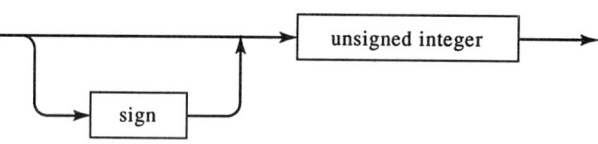

Simple Expression

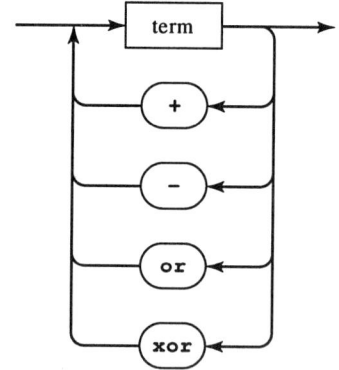

Simple Statement

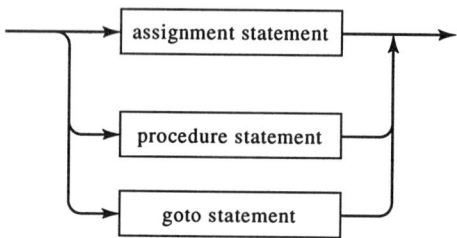

Simple Type

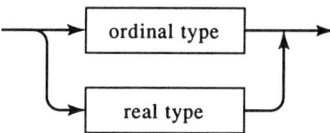

Statement

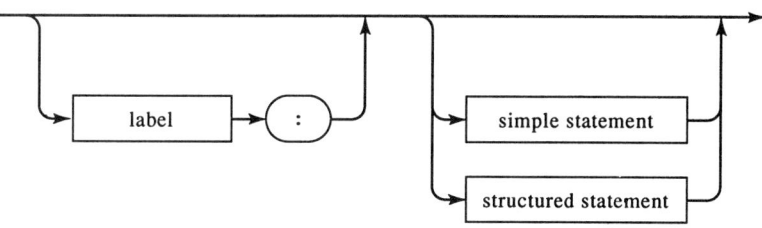

Statement Part

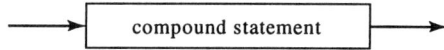

String Character

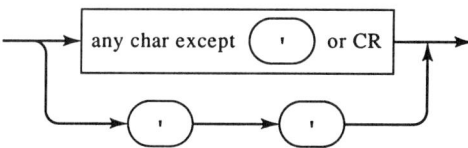

String Type

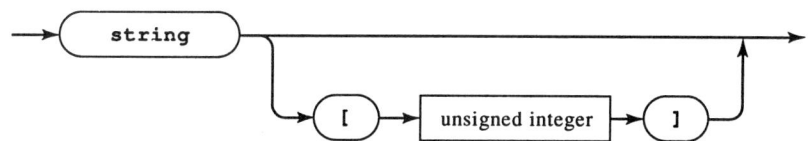

Structured Statement

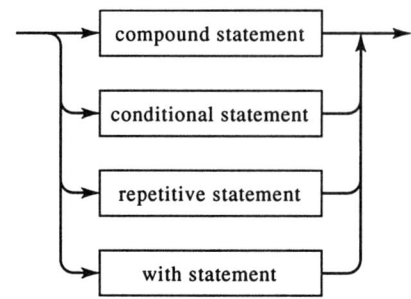

Structured Type

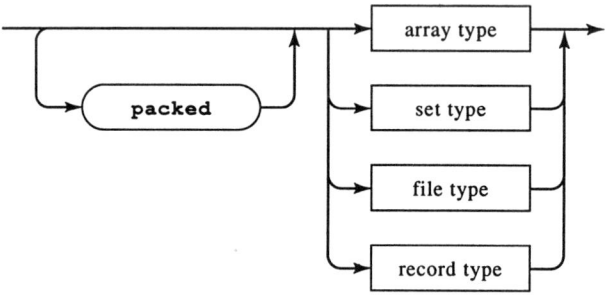

Subrange Type

Term

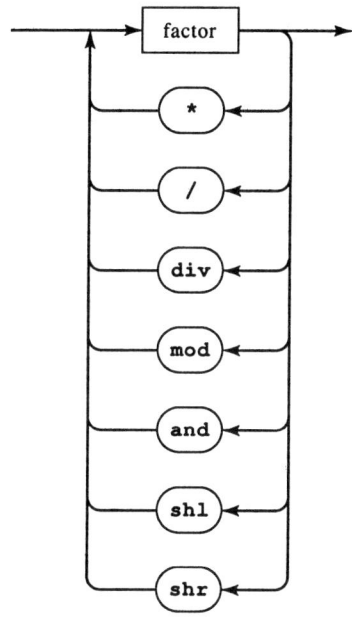

Type

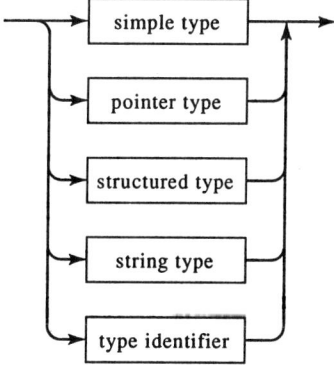

Type Declaration

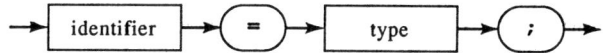

Type Declaration Part

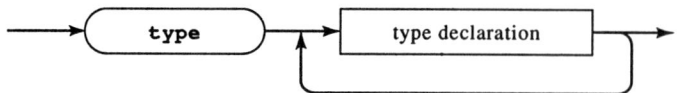

Typed Constant

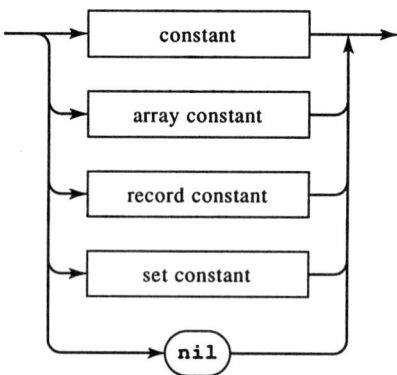

Type Constant Declaration

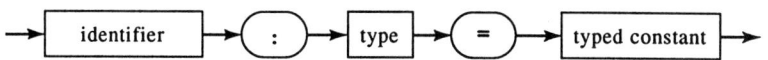

Unit

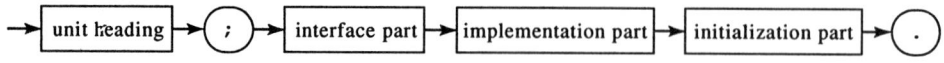

Unit Heading

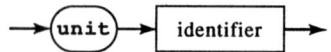

Unsigned Constant

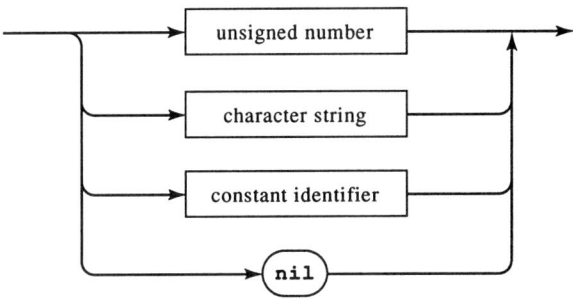

Unsigned Integer

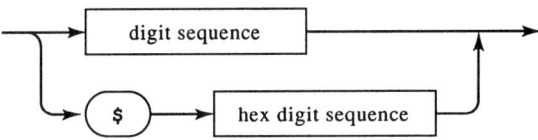

Unsigned Number

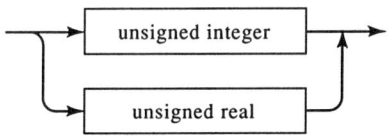

Unsigned Real

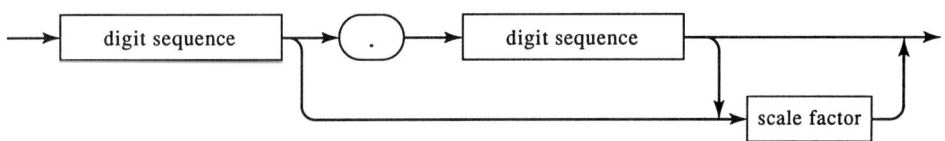

Uses Clause

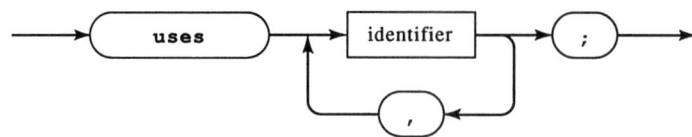

Value Typecast

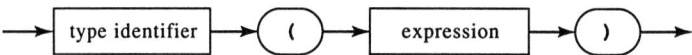

Variable Declaration

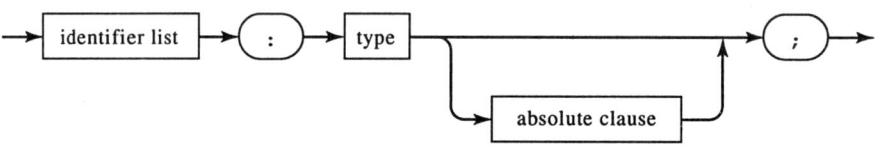

Variable Declaration Part

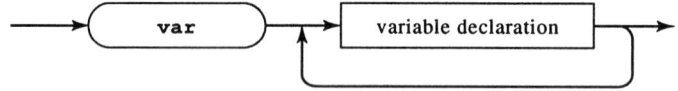

Variable Reference

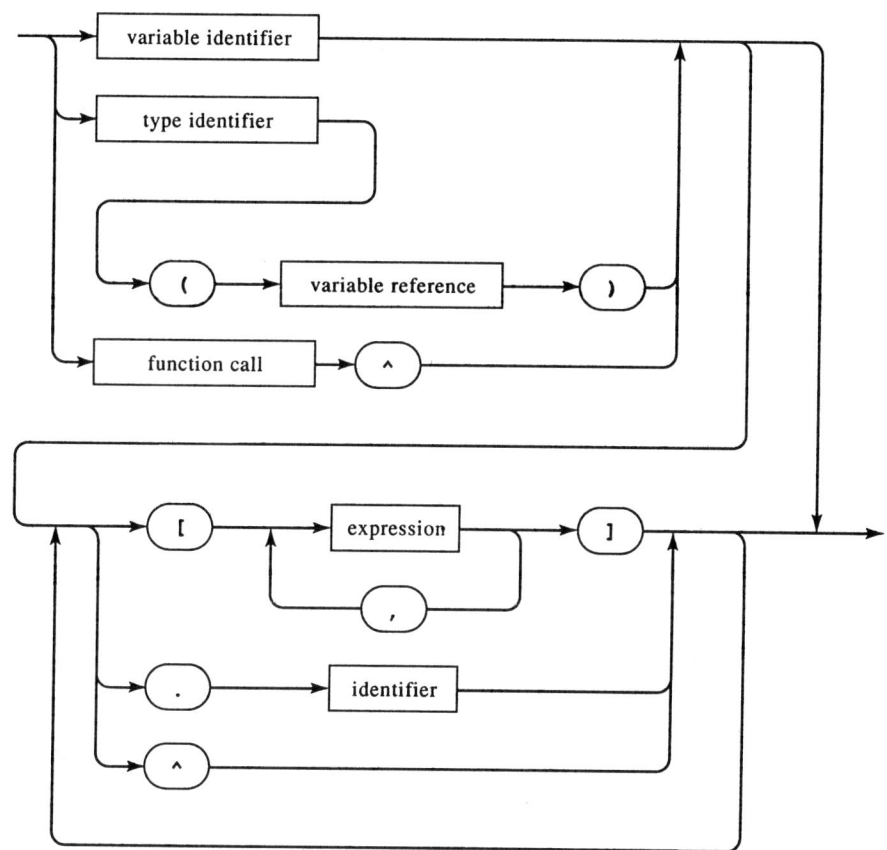

Variant Part

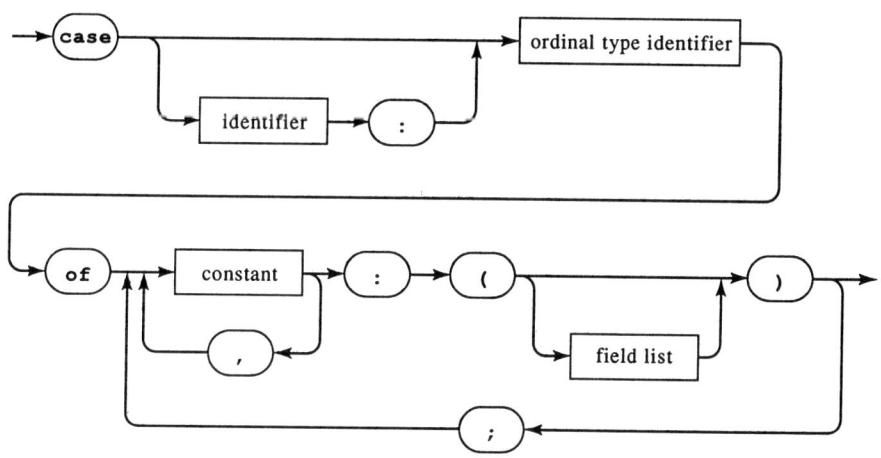

While Statement

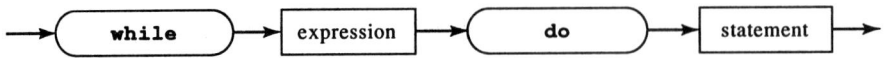

With Statement

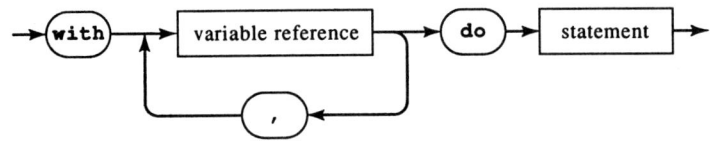

APPENDIX
D

TURBO PASCAL RESERVED WORDS

The following are keywords in Turbo Pascal and, as such, are reserved by the compiler. Do not use these terms as identifiers in programs.

Absolute	Nil
And	Not
Array	Of
Begin	Or
Case	Packed
Const	Procedure
Div	Program
Do	Record
Downto	Repeat
Else	Set
End	Shl
External	Shr
File	String
For	Text
Forward	Then
Function	To
Goto	Type
If	Unit
Implementation	Until
In	Uses
Inline	Var
Interface	While
Interrupt	With
Label	Xor
Mod	

INDEX

Ordering Information for
DISK OF SAMPLE PROGRAMS

For your convenience, a disk is available to accompany this book. The disk contains all the sample programs from the book as well as text files for the sample programs and the exercises. It also contains the many buggy programs described in the exercises. The disk does *not* contain the Turbo Pascal software.

To order the disk, please return the order form below with your check, money order, or school purchase order.

ORDER FORM

Write to: Dr. Lowell A. Carmony, Computer Science Dept.,
             Lake Forest College, Lake Forest, IL 60045

Prices subject to change without notice.
ALL ORDERS FROM INDIVIDUALS MUST BE PREPAID.

Sample Disk

Quantity_____ @ $20.00   Amount Enclosed $ _____

Select desired disk size. (5.25-inch disk sent if no choice is indicated).

☐ 5.25-inch disk

☐ 3.5-inch disk

Name _____

Address _____

_____

City _____ State _____ Zip _____